Truth on Trial in Thailand

Since 2005, Thailand has been in crisis, with unprecedented political instability and the worst political violence seen in the country in decades. In the aftermath of a military coup in 2006, Thailand's press freedom ranking plunged, while arrests for lèse-majesté have skyrocketed to levels unknown in the modern world. *Truth on Trial in Thailand* traces the 110-year trajectory of defamation-based laws in Thailand. The most prominent of these is lèse-majesté, but defamation aspects also appear in laws on sedition and treason, the press and cinema, anti-communism, contempt of court, insulting of religion, as well as libel. This book makes the case that despite the appearance of growing democratization, authoritarian structures and urges still drive politics in Thailand; the long-term effects of defamation law adjudication has skewed the way that Thai society approaches and perceives "truth."

Employing the work of Habermas, Foucault, Agamben, and Schmitt to construct an alternative framework to understand Thai history, Streckfuss contends that Thai history has become "suspended" since 1958, and repeatedly declining to face the truth of history has set the stage for an endless state of crisis.

This book will be of interest to students and scholars of South East Asian politics, Asian history, and media and communication.

David Streckfuss is an independent scholar who has lived in Thailand for more than 20 years. His work primarily concerns human rights, and political and cultural history.

Rethinking Southeast Asia

Edited by Duncan McCargo, University of Leeds, UK

Southeast Asia is a dynamic and rapidly-changing region which continues to defy predictions and challenge formulaic understandings. This series publishes cutting-edge work on the region, providing a venue for books that are readable, topical, interdisciplinary and critical of conventional views. It aims to communicate the energy, contestations and ambiguities that make Southeast Asia both consistently fascinating and sometimes potentially disturbing.

This series comprises two strands:

Titles which address the needs of students and teachers, published in both hardback and paperback. Titles include:

Rethinking Vietnam
Duncan McCargo

Rethinking Southeast Asia is also a forum for innovative new research intended for a more specialist readership, published in hardback only. Titles include:

1. **Politics and the Press in Thailand**
   Media machinations
   Duncan McCargo

2. **Democracy and National Identity in Thailand**
   Michael Kelly Connors

3. **The Politics of NGOs in Indonesia**
   Developing democracy and managing a movement
   Bob S. Hadiwinata

4. **Military Politics and Democratization in Indonesia***
   Jun Honna

* Now available in paperback

5. **Changing Political Economy of Vietnam**
   The case of Ho Chi Minh City
   Martin Gainsborough

6. **Living at the Edge of Thai Society**
   The Karen in the Highlands of Northern Thailand
   Claudio O. Delang

7. **Thailand Beyond the Crisis**
   Peter Warr

8. **Virtual Thailand**
   Media and culture politics in Thailand, Malaysia and Singapore
   Glen Lewis

9. **Decentralization and *Adat* Revivalism in Indonesia**
The politics of becoming indigenous
Adam D. Tyson

10. **Truth on Trial in Thailand**
Defamation, treason, and lèse-majesté
David Streckfuss

Truth on Trial in Thailand

Defamation, treason, and lèse-majesté

David Streckfuss

Routledge
Taylor & Francis Group
LONDON AND NEW YORK

First published 2011
by Routledge
2 Park Square, Milton Park, Abingdon, Oxon OX14 4RN

Simultaneously published in the USA and Canada
by Routledge
270 Madison Avenue, New York, NY 10016

Routledge is an imprint of the Taylor & Francis Group, an informa business

Typeset in Times New Roman by
RefineCatch Limited, Bungay, Suffolk
Printed and bound in Great Britain by
MPG Books Group, UK

British Library Cataloguing in Publication Data
A catalogue record for this book is available from the British Library

Library of Congress Cataloging-in-Publication Data
Streckfuss, David.
Truth on trial in Thailand : defamation, treason, and lèse-majesté / David Streckfuss.
p. cm.—(Rethinking Southeast Asia)
Includes bibliographical references and index.
1. Libel and slander—Thailand. 2. Lèsé-majesty—Thailand. 3. Political crimes and offenses—Thailand. I. Title.
KPT4147.S77 2010
345.593′0256—dc22 2010002029

ISBN: 978-0-415-41425-8 (hbk)
ISBN: 978-0-203-84754-1 (ebk)

To my teachers
Thongchai, Al, Katherine, and John Smail

To my American family
To my father Richard Streckfuss, for his steadfast belief in truth and a free press
To my mother, Mary Jane, for her quiet perseverance
To my sister, Amy Smith, for being a mainstay in my life

To my Thai family
To my wife and friend, Patcharin Wisetdee, for all things
To my children of mixed nationalities, Mitrianna, Henrick, and Sasithorn

And to all in the Northeast and throughout the land
For hope of a freer and more just Siam

The process [of mass-media deception] has to be conscious, or it would not be carried out with sufficient precision, but it also has to be unconscious, or it would bring with it a feeling of falsity and hence of guilt {. . .} To tell deliberate lies while genuinely believing in them, to forget any fact that has become inconvenient, and then, when it becomes necessary again, to draw it back from oblivion for just so long as it is needed, to deny the existence of objective reality and all the while to take account of the reality which one denies – all this is indispensably necessary.

(George Orwell, *1984*)

Contents

Figures

Tables

Acknowledgments

Woe to the historian whose subject matter refuses to march politely into the past and stay there. It has been the fortune and misfortune of this book that its subject matter—defamation, treason, and *lèse-majesté*—is very much alive and shaking the Thai political landscape now more than ever before. Present events cannot be fully appreciated without a sustained historical treatment of defamation-based laws: the sheer force of events compels us to tread into the twilight world of criminality, state of the exception, and the ever shifting terrain of discursive crimes.

This book was first conceived as part of a three-volume set. The first was to be an expedition into the world of nineteenth- and early twentieth-century Siam in an effort to capture more precisely the intellectual, religious, and cosmological roots of what I call in this book the "narrow Thai Theravada Buddhist tradition" and what Giorgio Agamben and Carl Schmitt call the "state of exception." This book, the second in the set, compresses provisional impressions into a few chapters and expands into what I have termed "defamation regimes"—a social and political formation that over time develops a kind of "defamation thinking" and "impulse" that focuses on the insult of the defamatory statement, often at the expense of the truth. Defamation thinking has become most prominent in the world of the Thai *lèse-majesté* law. The third volume was to be a global examination of *lèse-majesté*-like laws and their various trajectories within monarchical and monarchical-like countries.

This book, however, has been no great joy to write: the conclusions leading from its analysis do not provide much relief and give little direction about how this historical problem may be resolved. In the meantime, the hyperfocus on the mechanisms of the defamation regime has drawn Thai society's attention away from what might have been a harbinger of a more just and balanced society—for instance, the people's movement, represented by groups such as the Assembly of the Poor, who now languish from society's disinterest.

I consider most of the perspectives presented here derivative, composites, of others' works. I draw from a number of scholars outside the field of Thai or Southeast Asian studies, primarily Michel Foucault, Jürgen Habermas,

Giorgio Agamben, and Carl Schmitt. Within the fields of Thai history and politics, this work would not have even been conceivable without the prior work of Ben Anderson (whose article on Thai studies was presented to me on my first day in graduate school, an event from which I have yet to recover), Thongchai Winichakul (whose dissertation I read upon his coming to Wisconsin, another event that rocked my perspective), and Craig Reynolds, whose work spans the full scope of Thai intellectual history and who encouraged me to put my "quirky" ideas on paper. More recently, I have benefited from the perspectives of the provocative work of Duncan McCargo, the inexhaustible Michael K. Connors and his breathtaking (and rather depressing) *Democracy and National Identity in Thailand* (which really could be the endnote source of my entire Chapter 9), and the brutal pathos created by Katherine Bowie in her work on village scouts. I also should acknowledge my intellectual debt to Christine Gray and the extraordinary analysis in her still-unpublished dissertation. This project has also been influenced by the pioneering work of Tamara Loos, Nidhi Eoseewong, Peter A. Jackson, Michael Herzfeld, Kevin Hewison, Patrick Jory, and Annette Hamilton. This book is a quirky chronology of Thai history, and I have benefited much from the sober and sure-stepped *A History of Thailand* by Chris Baker and Pasuk Phongpaichit and the insights and perspectives by Maurizio Peleggi's *Lords of Things* and *Thailand: The Worldly Kingdom.*

This work has been so long in coming that it has become impossible for me to thank everyone who assisted me in one way or another since I began my dissertation research in 1989. Much of my original framework was created in conjunction with my advisor, Thongchai Winichakul. He has been teacher, friend, and comrade. Alfred W. McCoy helped me hone my skills as a historian. Katherine Bowie never allowed me to ignore class. To these three at the University of Wisconsin-Madison, I apologize for being a bit late with this and hope you recognize your contribution in the better parts of this book. Charles F. Keyes has been teacher and friend, with whom I share a love for the Northeast. I should also thank *Ajaan* Sulak Sivaraksa, who is always a gracious and challenging host when I've stayed at his home, even when we disagreed.

For getting me to revive this project, and providing guidance and encouragement entirely along the way, I have to thank Duncan McCargo, a demanding editor, to be sure, but also one who has, over these many years, been an enthusiastic supporter of this project. I must thank those who have commented on my various drafts. Chris Baker provided challenging comments that pushed me ever forward. Michael Connors gave me remarkable encouragement and detailed comments. I thank Kevin Acers for his timely and helpful criticisms. On the ground, I must give a special thanks to Philip Mangis, my friend and colleague who has seen me through this entire process, and to Eli Elinoff, whose suggestions have revolutionized the structure of this book, and who has seemed even more excited than I about this project. I must also thank Craig Reynolds, Thongchai Winichakul, Maurizio Pellegi, and

Tim Rackett for taking the time to review various parts of the manuscript and provide comment. A very, very special thanks goes to Leedom Lefferts for his painstaking editing and commentary. And finally I would be remiss to leave out thanks to my copy editor, Susan Dunsmore, and project manager, Mel Dyer.

It seems that each of those who helped read over the manuscript especially liked certain parts, while others advised cutting those very same parts. Always eager to please and not wanting to disappoint, I left any section a number of readers liked. The result, no doubt, is an overly long book that no one will like unreservedly, but at least hopefully one that all will find some part of to be of use.

Some of those in Thailand who have helped me in various ways along the way include, in no particular order: Somchai Preechasilpakul, Thanapol Eawsakul of *Fah Diew Kan* magazine, Pravit Rojanapruk, Supinya Klangnarong, Srirak Plipat, Frank Munger, Marwaan Macan-Markar of the Inter Press Service, Jonathan Head, Nic Dunlop, Andrew Marshall, Somkiat Ponpai, Decha Premrudelert, Bamrung Boonbanya, Suvit Kulapwong, Wattana Sugunnasil, Curtis Borden, Suban Kaewkanya, Jon and Giles Ungpakorn, Atiya Achakulwisut, Søren Ivarsson, Grant Evans, Kevin Hewison, Lotte Isager, Peter A. Jackson, Martin Platt, Nattapoll Chaiching, Ukrist Pathmanand, Johannes Dragsbæk Schmidt, Frank Anderson, Thanes Wongyannava, Andrew Walker, Anne Hansen, Justin McDaniel, Bandit Aneeya, Peter Koret, Allyn Steele, Arunee Sriruksa, John Mark Belardo, Jintana Rattanakhemakorn, Suree Wongsak, Suriyasai Katasila, Somchai Homla-or, Naruemon Thabchumpon, Nalinee Tantuvanit, Patcharin Lapanun, Gerald Frye, Buapun Promphakping, Nirmal Ghosh, and Simon Montlak of the *Christian Science Monitor*.

A special appreciation goes to all of those who were interviewed for this book: Samphan Satthaporn, Nikhom Intasen, Somchat Bangjaeng, Suttipong Jangariyawong, Kavi Chongkittavorn, Thakul Boonparn, Somchai Krusuansombat, Suchart Srisuwan, Kiatichai Pongpanich, Chotisak Onsoong, Jakrapob Penkair, Wattanasak Mungkandee, Stephen Frost, Harry Nicolaides, Chairat Saeng-arun, and a number of anonymous sources.

I also thank the Council on International Educational Exchange (CIEE) for its generous financial support for this project, and my colleagues there, Daniel Olds, Chris Bettera, Mick Vande Berg, Martin Hogan, and Steve Trooboff, for encouragement and for allowing me the time and space to work on this book. I would also like to thank Wofford College's History Department, and its head, Phil Racine, for offering me a wonderful time there as the Visiting Jones Professor. It was during my tenure there that this book really took shape.

Many of those who have helped me with this book do not share my views, which are mine alone.

David Streckfuss
24 September 2009

Introduction

The defamation dilemma of Thailand

Writing history on occasion can be a perilous undertaking. Historians writing about recent events are committing inherently public acts. Especially when touching upon the motivations and actions of living or recently deceased people whose reputations are protected by defamation laws, historians need to exercise discretion. In his essay, "Defamation Cases against Historians," Antoon de Baets points out that historians have become embroiled in defamation cases about important "contemporary events" such as "World War II (particularly war crimes, collaboration, and resistance) and colonial wars." The issues involved in defamation are those "central to the historical profession": "living versus deceased persons; facts versus opinions; legal versus historical truth; the relationship between human dignity, reputation, and privacy; the role of politicians, veterans, and Holocaust deniers as complainants; the problem of amnestied crimes."[1]

Historians have an obligation to speak to the truth as they see it, but as de Baets argues, historians must make "privacy-sensitive or potentially offending, statements only when the public interest is served."[2] Problems have arisen for historians tried for defamation:

> [I]f the judge disagrees with their position, and if that position can be shown to be plausible or probable, the lesson is bitter and will make historians muse on the differences between legal and historical judgment and the distance between legal and historical truth. They will devote sad reflections on the limits of the expression of historical truth. Knowing and expressing the historical truth are two different things indeed.[3]

In more extreme cases, De Baets cautions, "[D]efamation cases and threats to sue in defamation have a chilling effect on the historical debate; they are often but barely veiled attempts at censorship."[4]

The peculiar quandary of the historian in defamation cases is exacerbated in the Thai context.[5] In his recent piece on Thai historiography, Patrick Jory has pointed out that historians of Thailand have been in an acutely sensitive situation for more than half a century, as perceived criticism of the monarchy

> is effectively unconstitutional, may count as a criminal offence, and in theory could also be regarded as an act of treason. Not surprisingly, a long list of books deemed critical of the monarchy, including histories, are officially banned in Thailand. Controversial events of the last 60 years involving the king are dangerous territory for Thai historians to tread and are treated with a high degree of self-censorship.[6]

How does one write a history about the monarchy, a "sacred sphere" in Thailand, protected by laws akin to blasphemy and heresy?

More than other crimes, defamation is particularly sensitive to the political, cultural, and religious milieu in which it occurs. Defamation is designed to protect against false allegations. Therefore, the way that Thai society perceives reality and the truth provides the larger context of defamation-based crimes. Thai Theravada Buddhism is portrayed by its proponents as an eminently rational religion that complements and extends empirical science. Comparatively speaking, this may be so, given that the faith-based orientations of Christianity or Islam *as religions* have often put them in opposition to science. In contrast, Buddhism provides exquisitely detailed instructions for those willing to take The Path. It promises that with diligence one will discover the Truth of Reality. The famous Thai Buddhist thinker Buddhadasa Bhikkhu wrote:

> A more profound aspect is Buddhism as Truth, the deep hidden truth lying below the surface and invisible to the ordinary man. To see this truth is to know intellectually the emptiness of all things; the transience, unsatisfactoriness, and non-self of all things; to know intellectually the nature of suffering, of the complete elimination of suffering and of the way to attain the complete elimination of suffering; to perceive these in terms of absolute truth, the kind that never changes and which everyone ought to know. This is Buddhism as Truth.[7]

Buddhism provides, continued Buddhadasa, "an organized practical understanding of the true nature of things," or simply, "what is what."[8] Using "the Buddhist method," we will be able to "come to know things aright," which is to say,[9]

> All phenomena are merely products of causes. The world is just a perpetual flux of natural forces incessantly interacting and changing. Buddhism points out to us that all things are devoid of any self entity. They are just a perpetual flux of change, which is inherently unsatisfactory . . . because of the lack of freedom, the subjection to causality. This unsatisfactoriness will be brought to an end as soon as the process stops; and the process will stop as soon as the causes are eliminated so that there is no more interacting. This is a most profound account of "what is what" or the nature of things, such as only an enlightened

> individual could give. It is the heart of Buddhism. It tells us that all things are just appearances.[10]

It may well be indeed that on an individual level Buddhist practitioners in overwhelmingly Buddhist Thailand do have some profound spiritual access to the true state of things. Millions, both Thai and foreign, can attest to the transformative power of Buddhism in their personal lives.

But this same Thai Theravada Buddhism, with its view of "Truth" and impermanence, when extended beyond individual, spiritual lives to political, social, and cultural realms, may have less salubrious effects. While Buddhism seems to caution against clinging, "Thainess" (the quality of being Thai) is seen as immortal and never changing. At a time when the ideological edifice of Thainess begins to crumble, supporters of Thainess cling ever more jealously.

Thai Theravada Buddhism has recently come under sharp criticism, bringing into question the long-held notions of Thai Buddhism as a "civic religion," its tolerance, and its role in relation to the Thai state.[11] This study examines how Thai Theravada Buddhism has played and continues to play a role in shaping perceived cultural and political—and even legal—reality.

How could proponents of Thai Theravada Buddhism speak so boldly of its rationality and things being "devoid of self entity" when it is itself an integral part of Thainess? What kind of political regime could ever take into account the "perpetual flux of natural forces incessantly interacting and changing"? What type of social and political context does Thai Thervada Buddhism provide for defamation-based adjudication?

In the aftermath of the *coup d'état* in September 2006, answers to these questions concerning defamation, *lèse-majesté*, and Thai Theravada Buddhism were put in bold relief.[12] The coup, which overthrew the democratically-elected government of then prime minister, Thaksin Shinawatra, helped solidify two opposing groups—the "yellow-shirts" (the People's Alliance for Democracy, or PAD, supporters of the monarchy, the military, and a limited democracy) and the "red-shirts" (anti-coup, pro-the United Front for Democracy against Dictatorship, or UDD, mostly Thaksin supporters). The backdrop to recent political events in Thailand—the protests against Thaksin in early 2006, the coup in September of that year, and the division in Thai society made so strikingly evident as society squared off into yellow and red—was the monarchy and the curious *lèse-majesté* law protecting it.

At first, the coup appeared to belong to the variety so common to the modern political environment of Thailand. Carrying out the coup was the awkwardly named "Administrative Reform Group under the Democratic System with the King as the Head of State" (later changed to the CNS or Council for National Security). The CNS began by simply dusting off martial law provisions from the last coup in 1991 and listed the typical, generic causes for the coup: political divisions, "widespread reported corruption," and political meddling in the bureaucracy. More pronounced and newly phrased, though, was the charge that the Thaksin administration was "also usually bordering on" *lèse-majesté*.[13] A little more than a year afterwards, the military-appointed National Legislative Assembly (NLA) considered a revision to the country's draconian *lèse-majesté* law. The NLA chairperson, Meechai Ruchupan, announced ominously that "three separate groups" were in a bid "to topple the institution of the monarchy." The first group was

> using the public stage to debate whether the institution of the monarchy should continue to exist. The group was critical of the monarchy and spread its opinions through articles and research, and presented the idea of imposing checks on the monarchy.

The second group was "anonymous" and was using "websites registered abroad" to create "a campaign" that "aims to attack [royal] individuals," "criticises behaviour," and "publishes unsuitable pictures and distorts facts." The last group "seeks to abuse the institution for self-interest and political reasons." A panel had been set up to investigate "ways to tackle national problems through legislation, particularly the four reasons cited by the *coup* makers for overthrowing the Thaksin Shinawatra government," including *lèse-majesté*. "Anti-monarchy activities," the panel advised, could be countered by

> setting the issue as a national agenda and appointing a panel to be in charge of such offences, ensuring the National Police Commission strictly enforces the law, and promoting the image of the monarchy institution, especially by creating understanding with the international community.

Beyond these efforts, the panel also recommended extending those protected by the *lèse-majesté* law to include the king's children and members of the Privy Council. The law would also "allow police and judges to ban publicity or criticism or comment on *lèse-majesté* cases in any media."[14]

Although the new military-inspired constitution (the country's 18th) was designed specifically to dilute the vote of Thaksin's rural base, Thaksin's former allies still won a majority of votes and formed a new government in December 2007. Within a few months, PAD had reassembled to protest. Currying support from both the palace and military, PAD supporters, now dubbed "yellow-shirts"—a colour connected to the king—staged an ongoing protest, and denounced from its around-the-clock televised stage any who displayed signs of anything less than pure royalist sentiments. For those perceived as committing *lèse-majesté*, the PAD demanded immediate arrest and rapid prosecution. Caught in the PAD's net was Chotisak Onsoong who had refused to stand up in a movie theatre when the royal anthem was played,

Jakrapob Penkair, a government minister; Jonathan Head, a Bangkok-based correspondent for the British Broadcasting Corporation (BBC), and "red-shirt" Daranee Charnchoengsilpakul who said something so dreadful that when she was locked up in July 2008, officials threw away the key.[15] Hoping to prompt the military to intervene and stage another coup, the yellow-shirts seized the Prime Minister's Office (called Government House). Thaksin himself, after being found guilty on charges of corruption, was in exile but still hoping to make a political comeback. The political discourse emerging from this situation seemingly pitted popular sovereignty against the role of the monarchy, and diversity of thought against national unity based on a century-old ideology of "Thainess."

This book questions this century-old construction of a particular kind of political polity and nationalist ideology subsumed within "Thainess," and suggests it is near collapse. The promoters of Thainess—principally and most recently the PAD and key state actors such as the military—are making a desperate attempt to "save the nation."[16] We approach the questions: What is "the nation" as they conceive it? And what are the mechanisms that they have created and maintained to protect it?

The 2006 coup was different than the previous 18 ones punctuating Thai history over the past 60 years. This coup and its aftermath laid bare the peculiar anatomy of the Thai body politic for closer examination; it exposed fissures which previously obscured a clearer view of this peculiar social, cultural, and political landscape. The landmark towering over this cultural and political backdrop is the monarchy and a set of defamation-based laws—most prominently, *lèse-majesté* and treason—that largely define the boundaries of "Thainess."[17]

Although it is not quite yet time for a post-mortem, we can make some preliminary forays into this phenomenon by dissecting a certain slice of time. A few particular months in late 2008 to early 2009 outlined rather sharply the contours of what I am calling a *defamation regime*—a state whose very mentality and central impulse are defined by its understanding and use of defamation-based laws. On 27 October 2008, Army commander Anupong Paochinda reminded the nation that "The monarchy is a revered institution" and it was reported that "[the] military will not tolerate attempts to smear the monarchy for political gain." The military's former communist suppression unit, the Internal Security Operations Command (ISOC), was "under strict instructions to monitor and report any suspicious activities that might tarnish the monarchy."[18]

The next day, the Information and Communications Technology Ministry announced a program costing as much as Bt495 million (US$15 million) that would block some 1,000 websites "containing lese majeste content."[19] One provincial governor said he had ordered officials to monitor community radio and cable television stations "around the clock" for *lèse-majesté* violations. The Metropolitan police chief of Bangkok reported that offenders who made "speeches against the monarchy in public places or via the mass media

. . . would face legal action without exemption." The Foreign Affairs Ministry added Bt600 million to its budget to "to shore up the country's image," and an undisclosed amount was given to the secret "Taskforce 6080."[20] A newspaper columnist said the coup "appears to have opened the floodgates" to "anti-monarchy movements," and a year after the coup, Taskforce 6080 was set up under ISOC to counter any public representations that implied the palace was behind the coup. Its main aim is to "dig for information about politicians who harbour ideas that expose a threat to the constitutional monarchy."[21]Believing that "involving the monarchy" in political conflict "was improper," an army spokesperson helpfully advised: "To show sincere respect to the monarchy, you should simply think well, speak well and do well."[22]

Unlike any time before, the crisis in Thailand has created a virtual epidemic of *lèse-majesté* cases, with court actions on 765 cases between 2006 and 2009—an average of almost 191 per year—an increase over the immediate previous decade when there was of an average of just five new cases per year.[23]

The judiciary is also protected by a defamation-based law, with a maximum seven-year imprisonment for anyone defaming or showing contempt of the court. On November 1, Thaksin was scheduled to address his supporters by phone from abroad at a political rally. The judicial branch reported that it would monitor Thaksin's speech to see if he criticized the court decision that had recently found him guilty of corruption. If Thaksin asserted that the court decision was "politically motivated" or that the judges were not "independent," he might be charged with insulting the courts. The president of the Thai Supreme Court (*san dika*) also cautioned the press about printing Thaksin's remarks, as offending publications could be also charged.[24]

In Thaksin's 10-minute address to the rally that night, one particular sentence—"No one can bring me home apart from royal kindness or the power of the people"—stirred instant controversy. The Supreme Commander of the armed forces reportedly "needed to check the full details" of the speech, and warned, "The armed forces will not stand idle if Thaksin's remarks are found to have offended the royal institution." For weeks after Thaksin's speech, debate centered on what Thaksin really meant. It took a day for the military to arrive at the conclusion that certain phrases in Thaksin's speech were "out of bounds," and vowed to "coordinate with the Lawyers Council in carefully examining Thaksin's remarks for lese majeste." A high-ranking military official, without a trace of irony, seemed insulted that the former prime minister wanted "royal clemency in spite of a guilty verdict by the court" (although all successful coup makers in the past 60 years have presented for approval from the king a self-administered amnesty for their own law-breaking).[25]

Could anyone say whether Thaksin had intended to insult the king or not? One academic from Chulalongkorn University cryptically said, "His remarks are open to interpretation. He might be asking the people in red [Thaksin supporters] to help bring him home. The plea for royal kindness can also be widely interpreted." Apparently, a good deal of attention focused on the part where Thaksin said that the guilty verdict had been "ordered by a person he identified by the vague Thai term '*khao*'" ["him," "her," or "them"]. In a panel discussion at the same university, a linguist decoded the true meaning of Thaksin's statement and made the following judgment:

> This term is ambiguous. But to me it is clear that Thaksin referred to one particular person, whom he implied wielded power over the judiciary. He could have chosen another term, *puak-khao* ["them"] if he really meant the judges or his opponents.

The linguist said Thaksin had threatened to name "his foes" in the future, and when he did it would become "public knowledge" that Thaksin felt the king to be one of them. The panellists said many parts of Thaksin's speech "could be regarded as lese majeste," and "felt" that the speech was "just one part of a recent underground movement to discredit and weaken the monarchy." A former deputy head of ISOC went and met Thaksin abroad "to directly ask him whether he is disloyal to the monarchy." The general divined Thaksin's loyalty to the throne through "his facial and eye expressions."[26]

All of this, according to a military official, was causing "discomfort to His Majesty the King." ISOC moved to remedy the situation a few days later. Its head, saying the king "has been weary for a very long time," insisted that "All parties must have the same goal to make the King happy." Accordingly, ISOC organized 1,000 people and launched a campaign to "make the king happy."[27]

The way that *lèse-majesté* is talked about in Thailand is odd. The military could not say whether Thaksin's statement was insulting to the monarchy before studying the text "in detail." If it was "found to have offended the royal institution," then the military would act. Words are "ambiguous." Within the world of *lèse-majesté*, the "real" meaning of something said is not at first apparent. It is all coded. It takes national security experts or linguists to unravel the layers of ambiguity. And then at some moment, the inner reality of the words—based on the intention of the speaker—suddenly becomes perfectly clear.

It was learned in mid-November that the opposition Democrat Party had forwarded yet another new draft for revision of the *lèse-majesté* law, one that would provide protection from defamation to other members of the immediate royal family, increase the punishment to a minimum of five years and a maximum of 25 years of imprisonment, and reverse a few centuries of jurisprudence by requiring those accused to prove their innocence.[28] Shortly after, the PAD seized the international airport, which led to the resignation of the prime minister (precipitated by a court ruling). A Democrat Party-led coalition, with military backing, then elected Abhisit Vejjajiva as prime minister. Facing economic turmoil due to the partial collapse of the US financial system, the new leader announced on his first day that protecting the monarchy was his administration's foremost priority. A few weeks later, an Australian writer and author of an obscure novel in English was found guilty of *lèse-majesté* and sentenced to three years' imprisonment. Shortly thereafter, Giles Ungpakorn became the first Thai academic to be formally charged with *lèse-majesté* for a book about the 2006 coup. A few weeks later while fleeing the country, he issued his *Red Siam Manifesto*, one of the first public expressions of Thai republican sentiment in half a century.

Lèse-majesté had become an international headline. To get to the bottom of this special defamation-based crime, two foreign journalists and I turned to the experts—the police who make the charge. We met with Police Lt. Col. Wattanasak Mungkandee, the officer who had dared to make the charge of *lèse-majesté* against a high government politician and Jonathan Head, a BBC correspondent based in Bangkok.[29] Our goal was to understand better the mechanisms of the *lèse-majesté* law whose 15-year maximum imprisonment is higher than seen anywhere in the world since the nineteenth century.[30]

Wattanasak met us out of uniform in a shopping mall cafeteria. Dressed in chalk-blue shirt, he was soft-spoken and his hand shook as he held his cup of coffee. We asked what constituted *lèse-majesté*. He said either "to take something untrue and say it" or to say something insulting. How is "insult" defined? Wattanasak admitted the definition was vague, and said that the average person wouldn't be able to know what it was. Only a person who had studied law—Wattanasak has a Master of Law degree—would be able to say whether something was insulting or not. He admitted that most police officers avoided *lèse-majesté* cases: "They don't want them at all. They are afraid of influence from the government" that may damage their careers. But after examining the evidence in these two cases, Wattanasak felt he had to make the charges, as no one else dared to. He wanted to set an example, so others would protect the monarchy.

He said that since the September 2006 military coup that had ousted Thaksin, there had been more cases of *lèse-majesté*. Although he had never seen any evidence, he was sure there was a conspiracy to topple the monarchy. Without explaining, he cited as an example the BBC case, where Head had said that the Thai people were worried about the question of succession. "Well, isn't it true?" I asked. "Yes," he admitted. But to say so in public? "No, it can't be done." It might cause an adverse reaction. A bit stunned by this admission, my colleagues and I repeated the question. He reaffirmed: "The truth can't be said." "Expressing an opinion like this," he stressed, "is forbidden under Thai law."

One of my colleagues asked why the *lèse-majesté* law was so severe when Thai adored the king. "Society has changed," he began. In the past, people were very strict in showing their loyalty to the monarchy. A friend of his had said that under the democratic system, the constitution should not compel people to show loyalty to "nation, religion and monarchy." His friend had argued the *lèse-majesté* law should be abolished so people would have the right to criticize the monarchy. Wattanasak disagreed. "When there is a crisis," he said, only "the monarchy can solve the problem." My colleagues were worried that they might inadvertently break the law with something they wrote. They asked Wattanasak if there were any official guidelines as to what constitutes *lèse-majesté*. There were none, he answered, and that it may not even "be possible to write such guidelines because [the law] is very broad."

The conclusion of our interview: The truth cannot be uttered and there are no rules in a regime under *lèse-majesté*.

1 The truth recently discovered

What is the set of defamation-based laws designed to do? What are these laws protecting? In what kinds of cases does the state feel the need to play a part? The laws that employ the "defamation principle"—laws involving insult, slander, and libel—are peculiar legally because they do not address the question of truth at all. They are crimes primarily of words adjudged by their potential effect, and according to the motives of their authors. There is no evidence in the normal sense of the word, no issue of alibis, material evidence such as fingerprints or DNA, or mitigating circumstances. There are but the words, and the suspected intention. If the crime of defamation succeeds, it succeeds in the minds of those who heard or read the scurrilous words.

First and foremost this class of crimes is only secondarily (or sometimes never) concerned with the truth of the words. Defamation is a crime designed primarily to protect reputations—of individuals, collective entities, companies, governments, national symbols, institutions; defamation is not designed to produce the truth.

In historical terms, society's acquaintance with truth in cases of defamation has been relatively recent. It is worth noting that it was only possibly in the 1735 John Peter Zenger trial that truth was allowed as a defense in libel suits. Zenger, a journal publisher in the British colony of New York, had published the following sentiment:[1]

> The Assembly ought to despise the smiles or frowns of a governor; that he thinks the law is at an end; that we see men's deeds destroyed, judges arbitrarily displaced, new courts erected without consent of the legislature; that it seems that trials by jury are taken away when a governor pleases; and that none can call anything his own longer than those in the administration will condescend to let him do it.

For these words, Zenger was tried for "being a seditious person; and a frequent printer and publisher of false news and seditious libels, both wickedly and maliciously devising" of the Governor of New York, whom he aimed "to traduce, scandalize, and vilify." Zenger brought "into suspicion and the ill opinion of the subjects of the king residing within the Province" the

Governor and all members of his administration. Specifically, on the 28th of January, Zenger "did falsely, seditiously, and scandalously print and publish, and cause to be printed and published, a certain false, malicious, seditious, scandalous libel entitled *The New York Weekly Journal*."

At the time, the common (and only?) defense was to deny responsibility in publishing the alleged libel. So it was with great surprise that Zenger's lawyer, Andrew Hamilton, freely admitted that his client had in fact published the libel, but added that he saw no reason "to deny the publication of a complaint, which I think is the right of every freeborn subject to make when the matters so published can be supported with truth."

With confession in hand, the prosecutor proclaimed:

> I think the jury must find a verdict for the king. For supposing they were true, the law says that they are not the less libelous for that. Nay, indeed the law says their being true is an aggravation of the crime.

But Hamilton countered with a revolutionary suggestion: if his client is to be found guilty, it must be demonstrated that "the words themselves" were "libelous that is, false, scandalous, and seditious or else we are not guilty." Therefore, Hamilton argued, he and his client would "prove those very papers that are called libels to be true." The Chief Justice protested, "You cannot be admitted, Mr. Hamilton, to give the truth of a libel in evidence. A libel is not to be justified; for it is nevertheless a libel that it is true." Why is it in cases of libel, Hamilton then asked, that truth could not be brought before the court? For all other crimes, such as murder or assault, it is. He knew, of course, that "it is said that truth makes a libel the more provoking." Why, he wondered, would a libel that is closer to the truth be punished more harshly than a libel that is a falsehood? How could the truth bring even greater punishment?

> For would it not be a sad case if the judges, for want of a due information, should chance to give as severe a judgment against a man for writing or publishing a lie, as for writing or publishing a truth? And yet this, with submission, as monstrous and ridiculous as it may seem to be, is the natural consequence of Mr. Attorney's doctrine that truth makes a worse libel than falsehood, and must follow from his not proving our papers to be false, or not suffering us to prove them to be true.

The Chief Justice read aloud from a law book:

> It is far from being a justification of a libel that the contents thereof are true, or that the person upon whom it is made had a bad reputation, since the greater appearance there is of truth in any malicious invective, so much the more provoking it is.

Hamilton asked the jury to take note that "we are denied the liberty of giving evidence to prove the truth of what we have published" and that "the suppressing of evidence ought always to be taken for the strongest evidence."

From our modern perspective, everything seems counterintuitive: the truer Zenger's allegation, the greater the crime and the greater zeal to suppress such truth. As we shall discover in this volume, as with most defamation cases, the focus always comes to rest on intention and potential effect. Hamilton asked what exactly was the "standard rule" in determining malice or a breach of the peace? Who is to say if the words in question are defamatory? Or that they "tend to the breach of the peace"? The prosecutor consulted a law text for the answer: it is libellous if a scandal "is expressed in a scoffing and ironical manner," in a way that "is expressed in direct terms." Concluded the prosecutor, "I think nothing can be plainer or more full than these words." Hamilton argued that there "still occurs some uncertainty," to wit, "what words are scandalous, and what are not," for the prosecutor has contended that the words in question "may be scandalous, whether true or false." When coming to intentions, Hamilton asked,

> How shall we know whether the words were spoken in a scoffing and ironical manner, or seriously? Or how can you know whether the man did not think as he wrote? For by your rule, if he did, it is no irony, and consequently no libel.

The Chief Justice chided Hamilton, "Do you think it so hard to know when words are ironical or spoken in a scoffing manner?" Hamilton answered, "I insist that the only rule by which to know is – as I do or can understand them. I have no other rule to go by but as I understand them." As such, continued Hamilton,

> [It] follows that these twelve men must understand the words in the information to be scandalous—that is to say, false. For I think it is not pretended they are of the ironical sort. And [only] when they understand the words to be so, they will say that we are guilty of publishing a false libel, and not otherwise.

The Chief Justice countered:

> No, Mr. Hamilton, the jury may find that Zenger printed and published those papers, and leave it to the Court to judge whether they are libelous. You know this is very common. It is in the nature of a special verdict, where the jury leave the matter of the law to the court.

Zenger's trial was less than a century after the abolition of the Star Chamber, the special court of the English kings notorious for its swift, arbitrary, and sometimes horrific punishments. "It is true in times past it was a crime to speak truth," said Hamilton and quoted the phrase that "*the practice of informations for libels is a sword in the hands of a wicked king*" (original emphasis).[2] Now, Hamilton argued in his final statement to the jury, "Truth ought to govern the whole affair of libels." He called to the conscience of the jury to make the right decision, so that all people

> will bless and honor you as men who have baffled the attempt of tyranny, and by an impartial and uncorrupt verdict have laid a noble foundation for securing to ourselves, our posterity, and our neighbors, that to which nature and the laws of our country have given us a right to liberty of both exposing and opposing arbitrary power . . . by speaking and writing truth.

Despite the Chief Justice's strong recommendation to the contrary, the jury decided in favor of Zenger and a new principle entered the world of the printed word: the truth can be told. In this long-ago trial, all of the dynamics that characterize defamation cases today were apparent: the degree to which the truth may be registered, the difficulty of reading the minds of people and discerning intention, the ever shifting sands of words and their meanings.

In the newly independent United States, it did not take long for measures to muzzle the press and suppress the freedom of expression to appear. Section 2 under of the *Aliens and Sedition Act* of 1798 must be one of the most outstanding expressions of a wide-reaching defamation measure:

> That if any person shall write, print, utter, or publish, or shall cause or procure to be written, printed, uttered or published, or shall knowingly and willingly assist or aid in writing, printing, uttering or publishing any false, scandalous and malicious writing or writings against the government of the United States, or either house of the Congress of the United States, or the President of the United States, with intent to defame the said government, or either house of the said Congress, or the said President, or to bring them, or either of them, into contempt or disrepute; or to excite against them, or either or any of them, the hatred of the good people of the United States . . . then such person . . . shall be punished by a fine not exceeding two thousand dollars, and by imprisonment not exceeding two years.[3]

However, Section 3 did allow an exemption:

> That if any person shall be prosecuted under this act, for the writing or publishing any libel aforesaid, it shall be lawful for the defendant, upon the trial of the cause, to give in evidence in his defence, the truth of the matter contained in the publication charged as a libel. And the jury who shall try the cause, shall have a right to determine the law and the fact, under the direction of the court, as in other cases.

In November of 1907, Abdul Hamid, the Sultan of Turkey, used an increasingly popular legal device to silence foreign critics. He instructed his ambassador to France to bring a *lèse-majesté* suit against the editor of *La Revue*, essentially libel of His Majesty. A few years prior, the newspaper had accused the Sultan, among other things, of being "responsible for the assassination of about 300,000 Armenians." Such a libel, the Sultan had calculated, should be worth 500,000 francs in damages. The editor of *La Revue*, M. Jean Finot, would, before a jury in Seine, have to "show cause why he should not apologize" to the Sultan. M. Finot had earlier heaped further abuse, claiming that "it is materially impossible to offend a personage such as the Sultan." Witnesses summoned to testify included Emperor Wilhelm of Germany, a wide assortment of ambassadors and government ministers, and even the French Prime Minister, Georges Clemenceau.[4] Eight years after initiating the suit, Turkey killed hundreds of thousands more Armenians.

Nearly a century after the Sultan sued for *lèse-majesté*, in early 2005, the Turkish writer, Orhan Pamuk, said in an interview that Turkey had killed 30,000 Kurds and 1,000,000 Armenians. The truth had to come out and Turkey had to face its own history, said Pamuk, telling the BBC that, "What happened to the Ottoman Armenians in 1915 was a major thing that was hidden from the Turkish nation; it was a taboo. But we have to be able to talk about the past."[5] A lawyer, Kemal Kerinçsiz, filed a complaint with the police, and, obligingly it seems, the Turkish government introduced a new penal code provision, Article 301, which read:

1 A person who publicly denigrates Turkishness, the Republic or the Grand National Assembly of Turkey, shall be punishable by imprisonment of between six months and three years.
2 A person who publicly denigrates the Government of the Republic of Turkey, the judicial institutions of the State, the military or security organizations shall be punishable by imprisonment of between six months and two years.
3 In cases where denigration of Turkishness is committed by a Turkish citizen in another country the punishment shall be increased by one third.
4 Expressions of thought intended to criticize shall not constitute a crime.[6]

The government then retroactively charged Pamuk for violation of Article 301 and for apparently insulting the armed forces of Turkey. A number of other writers were charged for violating Article 301 as well. In January 2006, the case against Pamuk was dismissed for technical reasons. Kerinçsiz was not satisfied, saying, "Orhan Pamuk must be punished for insulting Turkey and Turkishness, it is a grave crime and it should not be left unpunished." Later the same year, a Turkish-Armenian journalist was found guilty of Article 301, and then assassinated. Unable to persuade the court, apparently Kerinçsiz turned to other measures. He was arrested in early 2008 for being part of an ultranationalist group that allegedly planned to assassinate various public figures, including Pamuk.[7]

The law's wording, though, was legally nebulous. Admitted a Turkish government minister later, there were "certain problems" with the article. The government amended the law, changing "Turkishness" to "Turkish nation," reducing the maximum punishment to two years, and, requiring the Ministry of Justice to grant permission before a case could be filed.[8] This amendment was due in part to pressure from the European Union, to which Turkey had applied for membership. Some citizens of Turkey quite rightly challenged the hypocrisy of the EU by pointing out that many members had laws similar to Article 301. Germany's Section 90 punishes "Disparagement of the State and its Symbols" with up to three years' imprisonment. Article 292 of the Italian law code provides up to four years' imprisonment for "insult or vilification of the flag or any other emblem of the State." The 1999 Portuguese Penal Code Article 332 punishes anyone who "desecrates the Republic, national flag or the national anthem, the symbols or emblems of the Portuguese sovereignty" with up to two years' imprisonment. Denmark has even a broader clause, reading, "Anyone who publicly denigrates all the European Countries or European Nations or the Parliament of Europe shall be punishable by imprisonment of maximal 2 years." In five years between 2001 and 2005, Germany and Italy combined had 157 cases; from The Netherlands alone, 419 cases between 2004 and 2006. One Turkish observer concluded, if you want us Turks to drop Article 301, you drop yours first.[9]

Throughout this entire series of events in Turkey, the most obvious question was never asked: Did Turkey kill one million Armenians in the earlier part of the twentieth century, or not? For some intellectuals and citizens, the answer to this question can only be discovered by putting together the facts and confronting the painful truth. For others, though, facts are a distortion of a greater truth that speaks about a people and their history.

The Introduction discussed current *lèse-majesté* cases in Thailand, where the truth of the alleged slur is never considered. With Turkey, the question of whether hundreds of thousands of Armenians were killed or not is lost behind an insulted Turkishness. In the Zenger case, despite the admonitions of the judge, a jury of citizens decided for the first time that truth should in fact be considered in cases of libel. And although the American Revolution against the British was partly based on the principle of free speech, the new government was quick to qualify such freedom for state purposes.

This grand struggle between truth of facts and some greater truth of the nation, of the race, of religion, of a people, goes ever on.

Historical evolution of defamation

The cluster of crimes that use the defamation principle emerged in ancient times, a type of law that recognized a certain kind of sacredness providing legitimation for divine kings and religious, sacred realms. The first era for these laws was that of blasphemy, slander, and heresy, the latter of which was most notoriously exemplified by the Spanish Inquisition.[10] Truth within European medieval political regimes was provisional and ever shifting, in the end determined by power. Michael Hanrahan provides a description of how "slander" operated in fourteenth-century English society, noting that "profound limitations of interpretations" of what was said in society were dependent "on a provisional truth that only lasts as long as the power that can enforce it":[11]

> [T]he ability to secure the charge of slander and thereby resolve its inherent contradictions was typically contingent on power alone. Such determinations were almost always provisional and consequently susceptible to reversal – an instability that is the salient characteristic of slander itself. The ascendant faction in the various struggles of the period consistently mobilized slander to determine its opponents' attacks as false and defamatory, or to justify its own attacks or counter-attacks as truthful. Used in this highly and often undisguisedly, motivated way, allegations of slander consistently sought to marginalize competing accounts of events. But "slander", however defined by civic or royal authorities, always threatened to and often did enjoy a second life in the public sphere as a challenge to the official interpretation of events.[12]

The second age of defamation-based laws saw the emergence of absolutist states in Europe in the sixteenth through eighteenth centuries and the development of a distinct body of literature and commentary on *lèse-majesté* laws. In France, for instance, Cardinal Richelieu was behind revising provisions on offenses against the monarchy in the *Code Michaud* of 1629 "to include the composition, publication, and distribution of defamatory libels concerning political matters." Even with a law reinforced to protect the king, however, the pressures created in the formation of the absolutist state nonetheless brought the monarchy's role into question. As each interest of the various state factions—primarily church officials and magistrates—sought to appropriate or subtly coerce the royal institution, they collided, forcing the monarchy either to justify itself or be justified by others. The effectiveness of royal power had been measured by the awe and reverent silence it inspired. As the king's political role was increasingly debated, as jurists penned apologies justifying the application of the law, and as the king became unable to control the "verbal space" within the kingdom, the institution was inevitably diminished or desacralized.[13]

On the side of the apologist, the jurist Cardin Le Bret's *De Souveraineté du Roy* represents perhaps the first detailed explanation of the *lèse-majesté* law in France. For Le Bret, to speak disparagingly of the king was an offense against God

> because sovereign princes being vicars of God, his living images, or rather gods on earth as Holy Scripture calls them, their persons should be respected by us as divine and sacred thing(s) . . . so that one may say that when one insults the King, one insults God himself.[14]

Greater, then, was the crime of regicide. Le Bret wrote that because "the prince is the spirit that animates the state, holds its members together, preserves peace among all his subjects and causes justice to reign," regicide brought "confusion, disorder, brigandage, violence, and sedition which would end in the ruin and complete destruction of the state. This is why it may be said that this crime embraces all the other more horrible evils that men may commit."[15]

Although the king was armed with a strengthened law to protect himself, what proved to be his most formidable enemy—the public—began to take form in the early to mid-eighteenth century. Defining itself largely in terms of popular versus royal sovereignty, this emerging public left the salons and took to the streets.[16] As elite infighting weakened censorship, the public's alienation from direct participation in politics was channeled into "controversial literature and illicit publications." By the mid-eighteenth century, the king had already become "politically dysfunctional."[17] But the charge of *lèse-majesté*, ironically, was made with even greater vigor and reached further down into society than ever before. In the aftermath of the Damiens Affair of 1757, a spate of *lèse-majesté* arrests redefined the established order. After this point, members of the competing elite were apparently only rarely charged with that crime. Members of the public, quite often its humblest members, became identified as enemies of the state.

Among the one hundred persons arrested for *lèse-majesté* were:

> a *marquis*, a lawyer, a *huissier* [doorman; usher], a *greffier* [clerk of the court], a law student, a master locksmith, a master blacksmith, a journeyman and an apprentice hatter, a shoemaker and his wife, five or six domestic servants plus a jeweler's shopboy.

Dale Van Kley suggests that the French state was beginning to understand the hopeless dilemma it faced. Rather than risking further desacralization of the monarchy by bringing these cases to trial because of their "noisy, conspicuous character," Van Kley indicates that the "extrajudicial" method of imprisoning without charges was preferred.[18]

In England, treason was synonymous with offenses against the king and a vigorous printing industry fed the public with "news" in the form of the pamphlet, a precursor to the newspaper. The rapid spread of what Benedict Anderson calls "print capitalism" disseminated the printed word in various vernaculars (rather than Latin), resulting in new imaginings of political communities often at odds with the sacred hierarchies of the absolutist state. In a very broad sense, "truth" came to be understood within an imagined community constituted in the form of popular, vernacular text. Heresy and religious truth were mediated more through the sacred language of Latin. As such, the third age of defamation was in the form of "libel"; social and political truths were mediated and contested through the vernacular.[19]

Jürgen Habermas helps describe the milieu in which the public sphere emerged in local vernaculars. Truth and legitimacy, conceived within the public sphere, were set against those of the state ("The sphere of public authority") which attempted to maintain control of political discourse through the use of various libel laws. Growing out of the development of "the public literary sphere" of the coffee shops, this political public sphere "defined a space for discussion and exchange removed from the sway of the state." The public sphere was first and foremost "critical of the acts or the foundation of state power" whose emergence redefined the relationship between the state and the individual, creating a new kind of "publicness," or, what Habermas called a "peculiar" and historically unprecedented phenomenon: "people's public use of their reason."[20]

Roger Chartier, who uses Habermas's framework to understand eighteenth-century France, argues that the "exercise of public reason by private individuals was to be subjected to no limits, and no domain was to be forbidden." "The critical exercise of reason," he claims, "was no longer reined in by the respect due to religious or political thought . . . [N]o domain of thought or action" was excluded or "removed from critical judgment."[21] One key area of struggle for the public sphere was "in the context of the controversy in constitutional law over the principle of absolute sovereignty." According to Habermas, through time, a "rigorous concept of the law" emerged that "guaranteed not merely justice in the sense of a duly acquired right, but legality by means of the enactment of general and abstract norms." Laws came to be seen "as rational rules of a certain universality and permanence." An expectation that laws provide for the just "exercise of power" evolved. The "critical public debate" that resulted was "without regard to all preexisting social and political rank and in accord with universal rules."

Habermas contends that the bourgeois idea of creating "the law-based state" was actually an attempt at "dissolving domination" by "abolishing the state as an instrument of domination altogether." As a result, there emerged demands for "a set of basic rights" that concerned "the sphere of the public engaged in rational-critical debate." These rights included "freedom of opinion and speech, freedom of press, freedom of assembly and association, etc."[22]

Defamation-based laws—especially those on the "high" end—sedition, treason, blasphemy—generally declined in the face of popular sovereignty and became less of a locus for mediating truth in society. The French legal theorist Vidal predicted in the early part of the twentieth century that "political crimes" would decline as perpetrators would no longer be viewed as "a public enemy" and instead as "a friend of the public good." Such crimes were once considered as "graver and more dangerous" and "punished under the name of *crimen majestatis* (*crimes de lèse-majesté*), crimes against the divine right of governments" and tried in "exceptional tribunals."[23] But in the future the penalties for political crimes would become milder and "tried by a jury."[24] While Vidal's optimism proved tragically mistaken about the fate of "political crime" in the twentieth century (e.g. the Soviet Union, China, East Germany), he nonetheless accurately described the general decline of defamation-based laws in states where the public sphere thrived.

However, in some new nation-states—perhaps those imposing an "official nationalism"—the set of defamation-based laws were adapted to accommodate new nationalist imaginings. Most visible were those constitutional monarchies which used *lèse-majesté* law as a cornerstone of an official nationalism.

For instance, the German Empire exhibited a perfected set of defamation laws. In 1901, Ernest Schuster wrote:

> German law protects, or attempts to protect, every individual, whatever his station may be, against personal insults, and that the special provisions relating to insults directed against German sovereigns . . . are only of a supplemental nature, and are based on the same principles as those relating to the punishment of ordinary insults.[25]

This comprehensive approach to defamation explains why the German Empire saw what must be the most concentrated period of *lèse-majesté* cases ever—between 1885 and 1905, there were an average of 500 cases per year. The law allowed a maximum period of imprisonment of five years, but sentences typically ranged from a month or two to three years. The average sentence up to 1895 was almost six months.[26] Although the sentences seem relatively modest, the sheer quantity of those sentenced equaled a lot of jail time for Germans. One newspaper calculated in 1899 that in the previous decade, "as the price of the very limited amount of freedom of speech which exists in the Empire," German courts had, as a whole, condemned those found guilty of *lèse-majesté* to 2,600 years of imprisonment.[27] In one six-year period, a total of 248 persons under 21 years of age had been incarcerated for *lèse-majesté*, seven of them under 15 years of age.[28]

Lèse-majesté seemed omnipresent: in Hamburg, "a man scoffed" at a song the Emperor composed;[29] a 19-year-old girl was given two months "for merely criticising a picture of the Emperor" in a store window; a 17-year-old girl was given six months "because, in the presence of another girl, she tore down a portrait of the Emperor from the wall of her own room";[30] a drunk German-American was accused of calling the Emperor a "sheep's head" and deported (In his own defense, the accused countered that he had only said that the Emperor was merely a "blockhead");[31] little 13-year-old John Brodowski was given a week in jail;[32] a "popular music hall comedian" was ordered to stop making jokes about the Emperor;[33] in Dusseldorf, a deaf man was (somehow) given four months;[34] a worker of Beuthen was given one year;[35] a farmer who questioned the piety of the Emperor and court enjoyed a two-month jail stay;[36] two newspaper editors were found guilty of *lèse-majesté* for publishing an article from an Austrian newspaper that reported a tramp who died in Austria was really a son of a past German Emperor.[37]

The use of *lèse-majesté* by the German Empire reflect the most conservative and suppressive tendencies of the law adopted by authoritarian constitutional monarchies. These tendencies include: protections under *lèse-majesté* tend toward conflation and expansion; *lèse-majesté* serves as a self-protecting mechanism; cultural and political conditions of authoritarian structures partially determine the *lèse-majesté* law; and legal permutations make *lèse-majesté* both prone to abuse and seemingly impossible to change.

Without open and free debate, the law negated the usefulness of the main democratic body of the empire, the Reichstag. "The rule," wrote one observer, was that "[it] is absolutely necessary to the existence of a constitutional Government" that "representatives of the people shall not be questioned elsewhere for words spoken in debate." Instead, Reichstag members could not "express themselves freely about measures which personally affect their 'dread sovereign,'" and were forced to speak in a "very gingerly manner" when "expressing themselves." Limits on debate in greater society were deemed just as bad: "The debates upon the subject are deprived of the illuminating power which they would have if the discussions were free."[38]

A professor of history at Berlin University was accused of *lèse-majesté* and threatened with demotion for his views on German history. One commentator argued that academics should have "the right to speak critically of historical events," further expressing a worry that:

> [I]t would appear that any citizen, at the close of the nineteenth century, (excepting in Russia and in uncivilized countries,) should have the right to criticize the policy of the Government, and still more so a professor of history, unless he consents, against all the glorious traditions of the German universities, to teach with a gag in his mouth.[39]

The application of the lese majesty law in the German Empire ultimately proved counterproductive. One newspaper argued in 1897: "The law has been vigorously enforced, but it has been not only powerless to prevent offenses of this nature—it has, to a large extent, created a condition of affairs it was designed to guard against."[40] In the face of a government willing to employ *lèse-majesté* against its opponents, perhaps, precisely because of the abuse and what it represented, newspaper editors and pro-republican socialists set themselves against the government with the utter certainty they would be tried and jailed. Some showed remarkable perseverance and apparent alacrity in going to prison; upon release they committed the crime again and were re-imprisoned.[41] The effects of the *lèse-majesté* law were so severe, one observer feared, that Germans without foreign exposure were losing touch with reality: "Many of the things which are believed by the German at home to be necessary to the Teutonic edifice, when viewed with the same eyes from afar, seem archaic and useless."[42]

As a final point, it is interesting to note that even with an avowed republican party in the Reichstag, the bizarre dynamics of the *lèse-majesté* law made it impossible for any force in German society to revise it. In the end, it was the Emperor himself who ended *lèse-majesté* prosecutions. In 1904, the Emperor "directed the Ministry of Justice to deal liberally with all persons convicted of insulting him" and in 1906, he apparently pardoned all those in jail for *lèse-majesté*.[43] At least in the international press, reports of German cases of *lèse-majesté* virtually disappear.[44]

Defamation as discursive crime

Defamation-based crimes in the form of words (or other forms of expression that broadly might be called "art") are crimes of immateriality. This differs from the opposite, which holds for all other crimes that are defined by their hard reality and physicality. "Regular" crimes leave all the markings of an occurrence that happened in the physical world, at a certain time and place. Guns, fingerprints, bruises, hair, semen, shapes of wounds, tire tracks, blood, skin, footprints, traces of drugs, powder burns leave concrete evidence. Forensics experts, doctors, eye-witnesses, and coroners can attest that the crime did occur at such and such a time in such and such way. This is largely the world of *Law and Order* and *Crime Scene Investigation* where forensic science seems to unravel crimes as never before. For prosecutors, there are suspects and motives, circumstantial evidence, and alibis. Judges and juries must interpret the intent and letter of the law in relation to the physical evidence and testimonies presented. Almost never at question is whether the crime occurred or not. When the jilted lover's blade pierces his heart, the crime has already happened. When that heart stops beating, an even greater crime has occurred, whether anyone else is aware of it or not. With material crimes, someone did die, the money is gone, the tanks did roll down the street and train their guns on the parliament building. The questions are only whether those accused committed the crime or not, whether there were any mitigating circumstances surrounding the crime, and then what penalty should the defendant receive if found guilty.

But exactly when and where does the act of defamation actually happen? At what point does a piece of writing begin its treacherous journey from "opinion" to "defamation"? When it is conceived over time in the mind of the writer? When composed? Edited? Submitted? Read to colleagues? Read by the editor? Sent in an email? Printed? Distributed? When read by the newspaper customer?

When, upon being read, does the defamation cause the reader to lower his or her estimation of the reputation of the target of the piece? When the target is moved to press charges? When the offending piece is entered into the court record? When read by a judge? When "confirmed" as defamatory by "witnesses" or "experts" in court? When the judges mull over the "facts" of the case and see the malevolent effect of the defamatory words in their own hearts? When they somehow discern what the effect of the words would have on "the people" in general? Or when the judges finally hand down their judgment?

Defamation-based crimes are *discursive crimes* involving words, gestures, art, or graffiti: human expression adjudged as criminal.[45] The particular legal nature of discursive crimes describes three tendencies of historical and political significance: (1) an intersection between language, literature, and state power that creates a "state poetics"; (2) a confrontation between abstract political and social characterizations and state ideological formations that mark certain expressions as "subversive metaphor"; and (3) a contestation between official or politically and socially acceptable expression and the truth that affects the public sphere.

First, as discursive crimes, adjudication and commentary about defamation-based offenses create a system or a type of aesthetic mirroring literary criticism: laying out the components and dynamics defining "good" and "bad" literature. In the case of Siam (Thailand after 1939), the kingdom has developed a poetics defining the "good" and "bad" citizen or subject. This notion of "poetics" as a state function in Thai studies derives from Craig Reynolds and Andrew Turton. Reynolds, discussing the nineteenth-century poem, *Nirat Nongkhai* [No'ngkhai], argues that the poet violated court-inspired notions of literary standards and conventions. As much for its political subversion, the poem was condemned for literary infractions. The "elite and subaltern domains" were separated, Reynolds goes on, "in part by the definition of what literary products are acceptable to the elite." The "commentary" that emerges about "what poetry should be, how it should be read, and how it should function in society" is what Reynolds calls, "state poetics." Through this poetics, the Bangkok elite "sought to establish protocol of language and conventions for genres as a way of coding its own social identity."[46]

Turton takes this idea of state poetics and places it in contrast to an opposing "civic rhetoric" which attempts to stretch the boundaries of public discourse. Turton writes:

> [Civic rhetoric] refers to the way in which power intervenes to construct the agenda and rules of procedure for social debates, for the construction of knowledge. It refers to more than just language and speech; though if language is put into context, understood as statements, understood as also absence of things said, written, and discussed, and stretched to its physical limits, then we would return to a full sense of language as coextensive with social intercourse . . . There are, if you like, extremes: at the one end the very language-based of poetics, and at the other the excommunication and even physical execution for saying the wrong thing.[47]

Reynolds describes a "state poetics" as the standard by which the elite judges the appropriateness of certain works of art. Unlike other crimes, the discursive crime follows tenets of literary criticism: the text and its construction using metaphor, irony, construction of narrative, and even "performance." Expressed primarily in legal terms, state poetics is a coherent body of rules and conventions by which the state judges what is politically and culturally acceptable, and what is not. "Texts" are not limited to merely more conventional literary forms, such as poetry, but also include a wide range of new forms: offhand comments, gestures, critical essays, newspaper stories, academic theses, dictionary entries, movie scripts, cinematographic images, photographs, novels, and even socks.

Second, the site and what constitutes completion of the discursive crime are unique. Other crimes are completed upon their commission; crimes of defamation are completed when the poison of subversion enters the mind of the audience. When someone is killed by another, it is murder. But discursive crimes need an audience before the crime can occur. A book is not really literature until it is read. In a similar way, the discursive crime has not yet happened when the defamatory words are merely spoken or written. The crime obtains only if and when the words are communicated publicly. Theoretically, the crime of defamation becomes complete only when the defamatory words succeed in causing the listener to feel disparaging of the target—whether that is a private individual, the king, or the nation. It is true that the subversive crime begins in the heart of the rebel, but it ends in the mind of the one who hears or receives the subversive message. It happens when the mind of that person is, quite literally, *subverted* (or the court determines that a mind might have been subverted).[48]

The nature of the target of the discursive crime of defamation is a crucial factor. The target of physical assault is concrete enough: the human body. Defining "reputation," even of an individual, is an already difficult task, as is manifest within a specific social milieu constructed by individual perceptions. When the target is "the government," "a nation," "a religion," "the monarchy," or "a *people-ness*"—all abstractions, symbols, *subversive metaphors* that conjure up a complex mixture of emotions and imaginings—definition becomes essentially impossible. When discursive crimes are adjudicated, guilt or innocence is based on the feelings and interpretations others—judges or juries.

As we saw in the case of Zenger, defene attorney Hamilton challenged the assumption that "ironical" words are easily recognized—and thus so is the malicious intent of their author. The other end of the crime—the effect defamatory words would have on those who read them—Hamilton also challenged, when he asked by what standard can a judge determine whether words would "breach the peace"? This blurred landscape of meaning, of truth and metaphor, of intention and how words are understood, of effects that occur in the minds of readers, creates essentially a *poetics of subversion*: a system of rules, conventions, practices, mediums, and aesthetics whose purpose is to subvert the mind of the audience, to turn it against the existing *status quo*.

Third, and finally, discursive crimes are inextricably part of the public sphere. Habermas's argument might be summarized thus: the essential characteristic of the public sphere is that it is a space where private individuals (or non-state actors) exercise their reason together as a public, through a medium of debate and exchange of ideas. The public sphere is created essentially through discussion, either orally or written, and so it is discursive. A discourse on law, at one level or another, becomes central to the emergence of any public sphere as the struggle and guarantee of rights to expression are necessary for its rise, expansion, and perpetuation.[49] The discursive crime is the quintessential public crime, for it requires a public to be a crime, and, as a crime, it is brought to the attention of the public. Defamation represents a kind of restraint on freedom of expression. "While people may have the right to speak freely," writes Keith R. Evans, "they do not have a right to defame freely." A constitutional law lays out "certain rules of defamation" and "freedom of speech yields" to these rules "which act as a limitation on any constitutional guarantee."[50]

Although many factors influence a given society's access to truth and what is deemed allowable, its set of defamation laws must be one, if not the, most important.[51] As a general rule, we can posit that the stronger and more vigorously applied a given country's set of defamation laws, the less access that society has to truth or social and political characterizations. This is particularly true in the case of a *defamation regime*: a polity distinguished by the following indicators: frequent use of defamation-based laws by the state; little reluctance on the part of police to charge, prosecutors to try, and courts to accept defamation-based cases; little or no exemption from guilt allowed by courts; weak constitutional provisions ensuring freedom of speech (and the general strength of the rule of law supporting constitutional rule); little restraint on the part of citizens in accusing others of defamation-based offenses; the entire range of defamation-based offenses become criminalized; and severe, disproportionate punishments are instituted for defamation-based crimes. Fuller forms of these regimes intertwine defamation law and less tangible qualities such as nationalist ideologies and identities. As we saw above, the German Empire from the 1880s until 1906 was a splendid example of a defamation regime.

Under a defamation regime, defamation laws and their use not only can impair society's access to truth, but can actually play a role in transforming how such society perceives truth and reality. In such cases, we might say that without an alternative way for the public to exercise its reason, limitation of the rights to speech, expression, and thought make the rise of the public sphere problematic, if not impossible. The result is that such a society has a relatively more difficult time accessing and assessing truth.

The historical evolution of the public sphere makes better sense when it is juxtaposed against two other socio-political spheres—*the official sphere*

(Habermas's "sphere of public authority") and *the sacred sphere*. Rather than intending to provide a normative view of societies, I suggest we use this crude scheme to indicate the historical direction of Thailand as a constitutional monarchy. Thailand's experience differs from the rather typical historical trend of European constitutional monarchies from sacred formations to generally more authoritarian, and then to less authoritarian or liberal regimes (see Tables 1.1 and 1.2 and Figure 1.1). Two principles govern these sociopolitical spheres. First, truth is most obscured in the sacred sphere, and most accessible and open to debate in the public sphere. The official sphere can be drawn in either direction. Second, as the three spheres represent society as a whole, their relationship is inherently oppositional: when one sphere expands, another shrinks.

The state of exception and defamation regimes

The cycle in Thailand has become so familiar it seems normal: a coup is staged, the constitution is abolished, coup makers grant themselves an amnesty, a new constitution is drafted, new elections are held, the newly-elected government is perceived as increasingly corrupt, a crisis ensues; the next coup is staged, and so on. Each coup suspends normal juridical structures and procedures with the declaration of emergency provisions or martial law. Giorgio Agamben argues that this establishes the state of exception; Thailand is the exceptional example of the state of exception.

Agamben notes that the slow dissolution of law in Germany after World War I began with use of an old, seemingly innocuous Prussian law that allowed the police to "take into custody" persons deemed potential threats to state security, "independently of any criminal behaviour." Upon "proclamation of the state of siege or of exception," the government could invoke the principle of this law and suspend certain rights and juridical functions. Agamben emphasizes the exceptionality of such a situation by pointing out that the government used these provisions "many times" from 1919 to 1924, "sometimes prolonging it for up to five months."[52]

The Nazi government declared a 12-year-long state of the exception. Under such circumstances, "*The state of exception thus ceases to be referred to as an external and provisional state of factual danger and comes to be confused with juridical rule itself.*" Over such length of time, whatever had been perceived as the danger becomes generalized into a general rule. "Taking into custody" becomes part of the state of exception. When the state of exception itself becomes "the normal situation," the result is the concentration camp. Agamben writes, "*The camp is the space that is opened when the state of exception begins to become the rule*" and, in this case, the camp has "absolute independence from every judicial control and every reference to the normal juridical order." The concentration camp in Nazi Germany finally became "a permanent reality."[53]

Table 1.1 Legal indications in the sacred, official, and public spheres

Legal indication	*Sacred sphere*	*Official sphere*	*Public sphere*
Constitution:	nonexistent	provisional, if at all	the principal guarantor of rights; the highest law
Mechanisms protecting the constitution:	(not applicable)	weak or absent	strong and a central duty of citizens to protect
Highest judicial body and legal system:	extensions of the monarch and sacred order	have little or no effect on statutory or other legal measures	overturns laws or other measures in conflict with the constitution
The law:	preserves	primarily a weapon to ward off advances from primarily the public sphere, but secondarily the sacred sphere	an area of contestation, and a key guarantor of rights thereof necessary to the integrity of the public sphere
The justice process:	veiled behind a system of informers, secret courts	(police procedures, prosecutorial decisions) nontransparent and appears arbitrary	clear, transparent, and measured
The right to freedom of expression:	imagined by the state to exist because an enlightened Buddhist state would grant such right (in word)	"guaranteed" but nullified by statutory laws, national security laws, or other legal measures	primacy over statutory or national security laws
Criticism of regime:	allowed ideally, but in practice impossible, and merely a sign of moral turpitude of critic	a threat, often apparently guaranteed by the constitution but in practice severely limited	a duty of every citizen and requisite universal skill for expansion of the sphere
Crimes against the state:	tantamount to crimes against the monarch	threats in various forms that impinge on public order and morality	against the integrity of the constitution and laws which alone preserve the public sphere
Defamation-based laws:	(including *lèse-majesté*) part and parcel of a set of blasphemy-based laws	criminal offenses are part and parcel of a set of national security laws with heavy sentences	generally civil and fiercely contested

Exceptions to crimes “against” the state:	few, if any, and at the discretion of the monarch	weak and rarely granted	strong; the more public the person, the more he or she opened to criticism and scrutiny
National security laws:	absent	defined in cultural terms	(if any) strictly monitored by popular groups and bodies
“Truth”:	sacred, “truer,” more moral, and more real than what “generally true”	defined by the state	• defined through reasoned public discourse and made concrete through law and court decisions • an absolute defense in legal cases
The primary “mesh” obstructing truth:	*Lèse-majesté* which can completely obscure the truth	set of defamation-based laws	absent or liberally interpreted by police, prosecutors, and the courts
The state:	(and monarchy) inviolable and cannot be charged	effectively inviolable as no mechanism by which citizens can sue the government	legally culpable
Regime defended as:	a cultural trait of subjects	a limited democracy	a popular democracy
“The people”:	represented by the monarch and his or her representatives	the legal standard in defamation-based adjudications, but only symbolically, and only as represented by the court	the legal standard in defamation-based adjudications, as represented by people
The worth of each person:	carefully delineated and based on relative proximity to the sacred center	unequal and weighed in political and cultural terms; the higher the person, the harder for truth to penetrate	equal before the law

Table 1.2 Political and cultural indications of the sacred, official, and public spheres

Political and cultural indications	*The sacred sphere*	*The official sphere*	*The public sphere*
Sovereign power resides:	exclusively with the monarch	exclusively with the government in the name of the people	equally and exclusively with the people
Depictions of "popular sovereignty":	if any, assumed by the monarch	if any, assumed by the state/government	
"Popular sovereignty":	if any, represented by the crown	if any, represented by the state/government	implicit
Understanding of "political":	realm of deceit and selfishness	• atrophied; politics dirty and politicians selfish, immoral, and dishonest • strictly separated from "neutral" values, such as "academic," "government"	politics a direct expression of the popular will
Understanding of "power":	• in relationship to the sacred • moral and/or neutral when wielded by the monarch	• facile; immorally held by politicians, morally wielded by "neutral," "non-political" actors such as military leaders, the monarch • moral and/or neutral when wielded by the government	• it always plays a role in any kind of governance, domination, or unequal exercise • it may be neutral, but never the parties or forces wielding it
"The people":	understood as uneducated unaware, and dangerous; gullible and easily misled by unscrupulous parties	• uneducated, unaware, and dangerous in a concrete sense • the cause of failure to democratize • easily manipulated by a "third hand"	
Legitimized by:	"naming" and issuing of edicts, welfare of the kingdom	"re-establishing" order, abolishing past constitutional items, and issuing of new ones	the degree that a more equal and inclusive popular sovereignty created

Law:	sacred and generally inaccessible; an extension of the monarch's sacred realm	used a tool to preserve power unequally	seen as having sociological and political implications on relations of power and inequality
Intention in violations of defamation-based laws:	central in defining the traitor against the sacred; who is "evil"	central in defining the traitor against the state; who is "evil" or a "danger"	secondary to truth
Public discussion:	non-existent and instead take the form of innuendo, rumor, gossip	limited or outlawed	central to the strength and preservation of the public sphere, where truth and rights meet and determine future directions
Veracity of any particular, "generally true" event:	difficult, if not impossible, to verify	difficult to verify, given limits placed on accessibility, prosecutions of defamation-based crimes	relatively easily defined
The distinction between "opinion" and "fact":	subsumed and conflated into "truth"	strictly maintained; fact "real" and opinion "biased"	complex and nuanced
Mechanisms of government accountability:	absent or barely existent	weak	strong
Culture:	• primarily a part of the sacred regime and delineates various levels of rule and subjugation • dictated and protected by a set of "taboo" prohibitions • homogeneous, inherent, and obvious, moral and non-political	• properly defined by the state • expression of inherent traits of a race • homogenous • primarily a tool for creating "unity"	heterogeneous, political, and legally protected, encouraged, and support
Truth:	to be found in the sacred, handed down by spiritual masters, and expressed in sacred terms	• linear and not complex • accessible in reverse proportion to the strength of defamation-based laws	complex and emerges within a certain process

(Continued)

Table 1.2 Continued

Political and cultural indications	*The sacred sphere*	*The official sphere*	*The public sphere*
To question or criticize:	"the sacred" or even to see or speak the monarch's name prohibited	the government socially reproved, suspicious, and severely limited	the government a core function in strengthening and expanding the public sphere
Democracy:	portrayed as immoral, dirty, unwise	portrayed as immoral, dirty, unwise; its failure due to the lack of readiness of the people	–
Independent systems of representation:	forbidden or tightly controlled	dangerous as judged by degree of realism and extent of distribution	equal
Morality:	part of the sacral order	determined by the state	a private matter; shared "morality" based on common belief in the core values of the public sphere

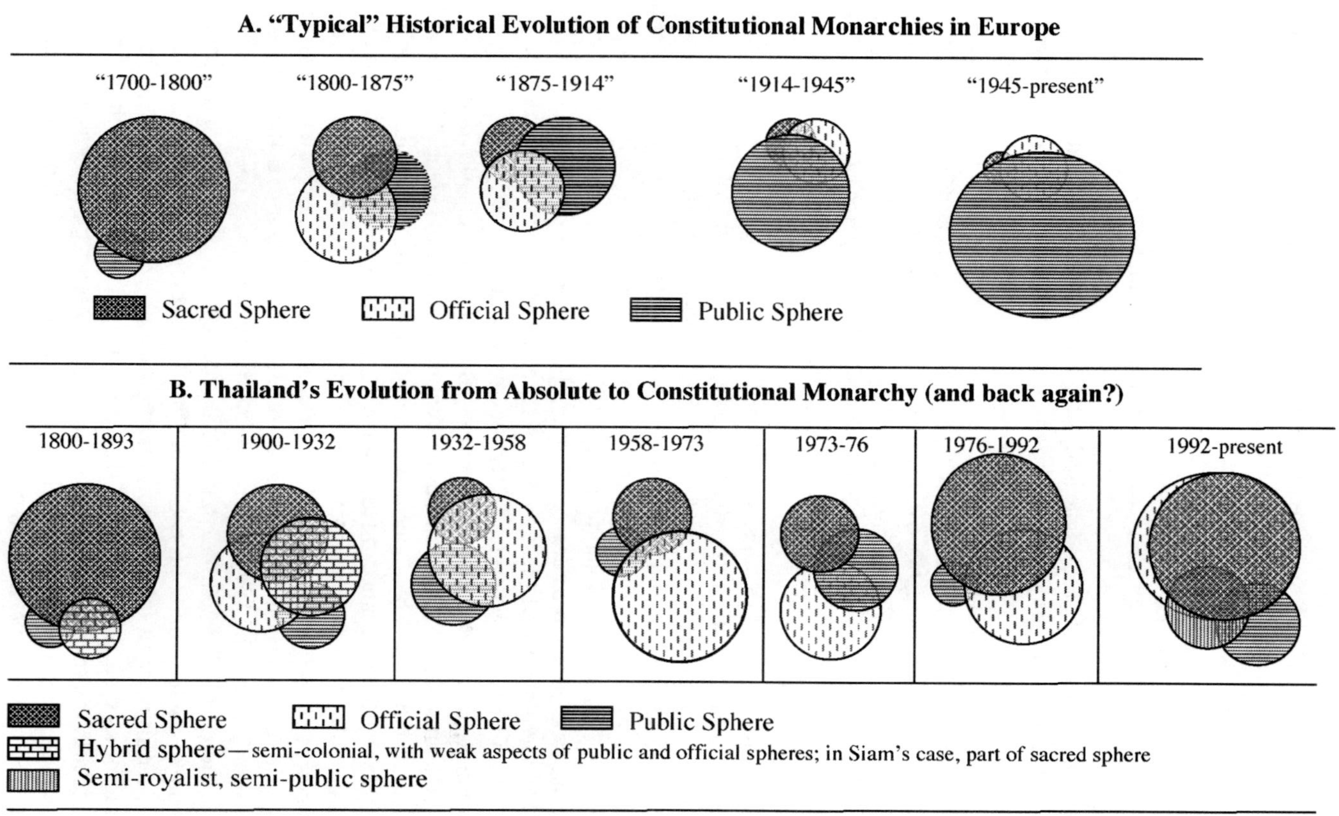

Figure 1.1 "Typical" historical evolution vs Thailand's historical (d)evolution.

The entire process is something like this:

1 The declaration of the state of exception in the face of a specific danger by a specific law that allows police to temporarily detain.
2 The danger becomes no longer a fact as such, but a generalized rule.
3 The specific law becomes a generalized practice.
4 The state of exception becomes the rule.
5 Finally, a space is created—exists—beyond normal law.[54]

Foucault's analysis of "the docile body" led him to the prison and insane asylum—state institutions providing continual surveillance. But, as Agamben points out, Foucault's frame of reference stays within the normal system of law. Agamben explores the state of the exception leading to the concentration camp. This process was not merely limited to Nazi Germany. In fact "in our age," he argues, "the state of exception comes more and more to the foreground as the fundamental political structures and ultimately (the stage of exception) begins to become the rule."[55] No clearer case of this can be suggested than the US government holding of "enemy combatants" in Guantanamo Bay.

How can Thailand's coups, self-granted amnesties, and torn-up constitutions be understood within the framework of the state of exception? If Agamben is impressed with the German Weimar government's declaration of a state of emergency and suspension of regular law for five months, and makes his maximum case with the twelve years of the state of exception under the Nazis, what would he make of Thailand, where the state of exception has reigned, to some degree or other, for as many as five decades?

Nazi Germany fused the defamation regime with the state of exception. A defamation regime generates a terrific force when it designates itself as encompassed by the state of exception. By ever invoking the defamation principle in defense of the state, a defamation regime can extend the state of exception infinitely. The state of the exception and the defamation impulse intersect in their reliance on discourse to substantiate their points: their common use of "indeterminate concepts" that create "the situation." It is no coincidence that the "content" of the discursive crime is most often the same indeterminate concept that undergirds the state of exception. If the situation is determined not by law or fact, but by an indeterminate concept, such as "peace and order" or "threat to national security," the state can claim, using the threat each defamation action conjured up before the public, to face a crisis requiring it to take extraordinary measures. In Thailand's case, these extraordinary measures come in the form of military coups which at once re-establish the state of exception and the defamation regime. Thus, by maintaining the crisis brought to light by the defamation action, the state of exception may also be maintained.

Origin of Thailand as a defamation regime

The beginning of Thailand's journey to becoming a modern defamation state can be dated with surprising accuracy: March 7, 1898. On that day, a certain Mr. J. J. Lillie, editor of the *Bangkok Free Press*, agent for the *New York Herald* newspaper in Paris, and British subject, attempted to send the following telegram:

> Severe fighting neutral zone Battambong province between Siamese troops Cambodians owing refusal pay taxes thousand troops operating rebels defeated several engagements heavy losses both sides.

Fearing that an international incident might cause European intervention and perhaps colonial takeover, the director-general of the Telegraph Department refused to send it "on grounds of misrepresentation of the fact." He then passed the telegram on to the Ministry of Public Works, whose minister sent it on to the Ministry for Foreign Affairs, with the recommendation that, "we must do something to justify our action, otherwise we expose ourselves to all his [Lillie's] systematic complaints which, if we have only to defend ourselves, would be too weak to the eyes of the world."[56]

The right to refuse to send the telegram was claimed by the Siamese government by virtue of Article 7 of the International Telegraph Convention which stated that a signatory may refuse to send "any private telegram which may appear dangerous to the security of the State or which may be contrary to the laws of the Country, to public order or decency." Lillie "formally protested," and said that he would "take all possible steps to prevent such disgraceful official tampering with prose messages." He then attempted to send another telegram, which read: "Herald Paris Siamese Telegraphs refuse cablegrams Franco Siamese incident allege false (Signed) Lillie."[57]57

In a letter to the British Legation, the Minister of Foreign Affairs, Prince Devavongse, explained that Lillie's telegrams "contained assertions of such nature that their spreading throughout Europe might appear dangerous for the security of the State" for "falsely representing an important province of the Kingdom to be in a state of anarchy or civil war." Moreover, the telegrams might have "falsely" caused "the European public to believe that there really had occurred some 'Franco-Siamese incident.'" While admitting that "although [they were] true," these allegations were "alleged to be false" by the Siamese government, "whose divulgence they want to suppress."[58]

The Siamese government depicted its actions against Lillie as "simply a measure of public protection against the dangerous, arbitrary & illegal use of a public instrument of correspondence." The government alleged that, in fact, it had already shown "excessive leniency" in allowing Lillie's earlier "offensive telegrams"—especially given "the serious danger resulting for the international relations of Siam from the publication of certain telegrams"—to be sent during the previous year to the *New York Herald* during the King's tour of Europe.[59]

Lillie was responsible for "insults against the Sovereign, the Government & the people of Siam." Had these telegrams been published, they would have constituted an "alarming communication whereby it was falsely asserted that Siam was in a hopelessly disordered state, that the rights of foreigners were systematically violated, and that there was no security either for persons or for their property." The Siamese therefore demanded the expulsion of such a foreigner who had made "such malicious and injurious use of the hospitality granted to him."[60]

As he was forcibly escorted and thrown onto an outgoing ship from Bangkok, Lillie might have wondered exactly how his report on troop movements in Cambodia constituted an insult to the king, the government, and the Siamese people. Were there troop movements? This is a question of fact. Was there any "truth" to his assertion that Siam was in chaos, that foreigners' rights violated, or that it was unsafe to live in Siam? Was this an expression of an opinion? Could it be proved one way or another? Whatever he might have been thinking, he no doubt had little idea that his expulsion by the Siamese government heralded a new age and, in some respects, the birth of a "nation." This brief and largely insignificant footnote in early modern Thai history was perhaps the first time the Siamese/Thai state protected its own representation *as state*. Lillie's expulsion was also no doubt the inspiration behind the government's issuance of an edict against defamation soon after, one which would serve as the model for all later measures concerning defamation. This edict, in turn, provided the foundation for laws that evolved into crimes against the state—actions, words, gestures—that caused the state to feel threatened and necessitated suppression. This first defamation edict in 1900 and a more finely enumerated number of defamation measures in the first comprehensive penal code in 1908 provided the modern legal apparatus that protected a kind of quasi-colonial, quasi-imperial sacred state.

In the early 1900s, Siam's use of defamation laws was on a par with neighboring colonial states. Over the succeeding decades, Siam followed a course similar to other constitutional monarchies following the overthrow of its absolute monarchy in 1932 and the ushering in of elements of democratic and popular sovereignty. It looked as though defamation-based-laws, and especially *lèse-majesté*, were playing a diminishing role in Thailand, with but a handful of cases in the 1950s.

But in 1958, Thai political history changed course with the establishment of a military-led defamation regime that used defamation-based coup decrees to suppress criticism. While in other constitutional monarchies *lèse-majesté* laws remained unchanged and the number of cases incredibly low, in Thailand, over the course of some 50 years, the numbers of cases increased from an average of less than one arrest, to 5 cases prosecuted per year, to the then all time high of 164 new cases received, and 82 cases adjudicated by the Thai Court of First Instance in 2009.[61]

The story of *lèse-majesté* around the world would be a quaint and occasional footnote in history were it not for the fact that this peculiar law and all of its bizarre dynamics have enjoyed a remarkable resurgence in Thailand, creating the richest concentration of the charge in recent history, with a punishment almost twice as draconian as any seen in centuries anywhere else. Never has such an archaic law held such sway over a "modern" society (except perhaps "Muslim" theocracies like Afghanistan under the Taliban).

Defamation-based laws as a field of study

The legal literature on the dynamics of defamation is old and vast, with works that long outlive their authors. The British jurist Clement Gatley may have died in 1936, but his 1924 *Gatley on Libel and Slander* has been continually updated and revised. Half a century later, in its seventh edition and more than 700-pages long, Gatley's work was now McEwen's and Lewis's *Gatley on Libel and Slander*. William Lloyd Prosser's *Prosser on Torts* became *Prosser and Keeton on Torts*, which was finally neither by Prosser nor Keeton, but by David Owen. This 1,286-page, 4lb classic, along with Gatley's work, is but one of hundreds, if not thousands, of books and articles dedicated to the question of libel and freedom of speech.[62] However, outside of the field of law, relatively few academics have focused on defamation. English-language scholarly work is focused almost exclusively on England and France prior to 1800.[63] There has been surprisingly little scholarly work done on defamation in post-colonial and developing states; the few monographs are often legal treatments of the law, rather than anthropological, historical, or political.[64]

Much of the scholarly work on Thai law in the late nineteenth and first half of the twentieth centuries was published in *The Journal of the Siam Society*, featuring, most notably perhaps, the work of H.G. Quaritch Wales and Robert Lingat. Up until a decade ago, few English-language scholarly pieces on Thai law had appeared, limited to a mere handful of articles and a single monograph, David M. Engel's *Law and Kingship in Thailand during the Reign of King Chulalongkorn*.[65] Thailand is also often omitted or underrepresented in Asian studies monographs on law.[66] Recent work by Engel and Frank Munger, however, promises to open whole new areas of Thai research and conceptualization.[67] In the field of history, Tamara Loos's *Subject Siam* must be one of the first scholarly pieces to draw heavily on the discourse of law as a centre of the contest for power.[68]

In Thai legal circles, defamation as a civil or criminal offense is of miniscule interest and has, over the past half century, created only a handful of typically brief articles.[69] In the leading law schools of Thailand, there is no separate course on defamation.[70] Lawyers and prosecutors interviewed for this study leave the impression that the role of Thai defamation laws in protecting reputations is generally more prominent than worries about the effects of its use on truth. For those in the field of law, defamation laws are seen as simply another set of laws within the criminal code that work in no way differently from other laws.[71] A fairly substantial book dedicated solely to the topic of defamation-based laws was in its second printing in 2001; another one examining personal defamation law remained in print in 2007.[72] Both are for the practicing lawyer, with relevant laws concerning defamation cases, court forms, and so on. Until a few years ago, despite its clear effects, the Thai *lèse-majesté* law received little attention from either scholars or journalists.[73] Defamation-based laws were only of marginal concern even to those in the legal field, and apparently of no interest to historians or social scientists. The absence of attention to this set of defamation-based laws and its historical and legal evolution seems to support the view that defamation is merely a legal side issue.[74]

However, by 2009 the number of defamation cases had quadrupled over a dozen years and the damages called for in litigations were astronomical, even in Western terms.[75] Despite the king himself seeming to criticize the frequent use of the *lèse-majesté* law in late 2005, the number of accusations and arrests reached unprecedented levels.[76] In response, a segment of the press, academics, and human rights activists have taken modest measures to bring the issue of the personal defamation and *lèse-majesté* laws to the attention of the public.[77] Both laws, it was argued, are prone to abuse, and therefore should be reformed or abolished.[78]

The argument and structure of this book

This book traces the evolution of a single legal and judicial principle through more than a century of modern Thai history. The first part of the book illustrates a number of historical, religious, and cultural factors that nourished an embryonic defamation regime. We begin by juxtaposing the development of "truth-producing forms" in the West against the specific qualities of defamation laws (which are not designed to produce truth in any form). On the one hand, I make the general observation that each form has its own practices and creates its own particular truths. Defamation, on the other hand, has a set of legal characteristics that sets it off from other kinds of laws.

We then take up the question of which premodern "truth-producing" forms existed in Siam and how they related to social and political formations. I make the case that Theravada Buddhism, as practiced in Thailand up through the mid-nineteenth century, exhibited two traits that relate to defamation. First, Thai Theravada Buddhism placed (and still places) a particular emphasis on intention, as do defamation laws. Intention is largely judged as good or ill depending on the perceived potential effect, as determined by those who have penetrating insight—religious saints, kings, and high officials. Ill intention may also be evident by the form of something said (e.g. coarse words automatically indicate bad intentions). Second, "truth" (or *dhamma*) in Thai Theravada Buddhism is apparent only to those of pure mind. The average person cannot see the truth through the entanglements of day-to-day living and is often deceived by the apparent reality of the world and the intentions of others. The notion that truth is only accessible to spiritually powerful people has an enormous impact on the use of defamation laws. A hierarchy of truth-holders is created, one that reflects rather well the class structure of Thailand.

As Siam was never formally colonized, this cosmological and religious formation was left relatively intact. In fact, this formation may have strengthened as the Thai nation-state centralized its power, as expressed in part through the creation of a modern law code and "rationalization" of the judicial system. Thus, although the outlook of the Thai elite retained many premodern elements, it was by the early twentieth century expressed in modern legal forms.

A third factor might have been the legal conceptual framework that the foreign advisors passed on to the Siamese government. If we can trust Foucault, these advisors would have been subject in their own legal education and work concerning the ideas and practices of social control and dangerousness. These three qualities—(1) a Thai Theravada Buddhist view of human nature that emphasized intention and a view of truth as hierarchical; (2) a new, centralized, powerful legal apparatus and forms; and (3) a focus on the need to control potential criminality and dangerousness of individuals—were key antecedents to the formation of the Thai defamation state.

The book then focuses on two genealogies of defamation in Thailand. The first is a straightforward chronology of the changes made in various defamation-based laws from 1900 to the present. Up until the late 1950s, defamation-based laws followed a course rather typical of other constitutional monarchies. Adjudication of personal defamation cases by Thai courts were generally in line with international standards; defamation of the state or government was generally trumped by legal saving clauses that allowed expression of opinions; and the *lèse-majesté* law, although still on the books, was rarely used. However, beginning in 1958, the military dictatorship installed a full-fledged defamation regime—expressed in national security terms—whose effects, even half a century later, still dominate Thai society and politics. Adjudication of personal defamation cases were often the purview of military courts into the late 1980s; since 1992, defamation cases more than quadrupled; and courts have allowed cases that are at variance from international norms. Defamation of the state or government was controlled by a military decree and enforced by political police (Special Branch or *santiban*). The maximum penalty for *lèse-majesté* has increased to levels perhaps unknown to the world for the past few hundred years; accusations of *lèse-majesté* have proliferated as nowhere else; and the range of who and what is protected by the law has expanded.

The key moment occurred when intensification of the use of defamation-based laws and principles was conjoined with a stabilized state of the exception. Drawing on the work of Giorgio Agamben and Carl Schmitt, Chapter 5 makes the argument that, under the doctrine of "the state of the exception," Thailand consolidated as a defamation regime. As Thailand moved into an eternal "Abnormal Times," legal impunity became institutionalized in the 1950s by the courts' decisions exonerating military coup-makers. It has since spread as the standard Thai *modus operandi*. The indeterminate aspects of defamation as a discursive crime have allowed the Thai state to identify its threats and define the crisis which then justifies an infinite extension of the state of exception.

Chapters 6–10 are concise histories of three key components of defamation: intention of the speaker, the target (a person, the government, a nation, a people, the monarchy), and the receiver ("the people"). Coincident with these key components of defamation, Thai Theravada Buddhist predisposition toward intention makes it, rather than the truth or acceptability of what was said (cf. Zenger), the focus of judicial deliberations. Intention in turn is deciphered from the perceived impact the discourse in question would have on a hypothetical public. Negative social or political impact indicates ill intention. The presence of malice nullifies any exemption from guilt on the grounds of expressing an honest opinion. Malice shows the morally impure state of the defendant and indicates either reckless disregard for, or ignorance of, the truth. This overlay of Thai Theravada Buddhism also arranges society into levels of people in corresponding to their proximity to the truth and, therefore, the credibility such persons are accorded. There is a near perfect correlation between merit, wisdom, and truth: those of great merit have the penetrating insight to recognize the truth and so can discern the intentions of others. The reverse is true as well: those of little merit (average folk) cannot recognize the truth or understand the intent of others.

Another component of the defamatory action is the target. Personal defamation was adjudicated fairly "normally" by courts up through the 1950s. Courts granted some leeway to citizens to criticize the government and allowed some exemptions in defamation of the state cases. After 1958, however, Thai society came under the rule of a military decree which enumerated the targets protected from defamation or criticism. The latent *lèse-majesté* law was revitalized and the punishment doubled in 1976. Despite a short renaissance of thought and expression during the so-called democratic period from 1973 to 1976, this first 30 years under the defamation regime tied defamation securely to official nationalism and thereby deadened social and political imagination. Shortly after this defamation decree was repealed, a military-imposed government amended the personal defamation law in the criminal code. Over the past 15 years or so, Thai courts have consistently allowed defamation cases where the target is a collective body ("the police," "the military"). Also at variance with previous and international practice, Thai courts have allowed little latitude to citizens commenting on public figures (particularly members of parliament, prime ministers, and other public officials), or in making certain representations of public events and actions. In particular, the *lèse-majesté* law has come to encompass greater and greater swaths of the public sphere, in many cases, making certain political comment impossible.

The final component of defamation examines a third key principle: that the offending words cause people to look down on the target. "The people" are the standard, the criteria, by which words are determined to be defamatory or not. Proof of the efficacy of the slanderous words would be testimony by an average citizen that the words did in fact cause him or her to have contempt for the target. And yet this principle runs in direct opposition to the hierarchy of truth mentioned above: "the people" cannot be trusted to recognize the effects of slanderous words or the intention of defamers. This task remains safely in the hands of judges (those of great merit), linguists, national security experts—indeed, anyone but "the people" themselves.

In the final section, we examine how the defamation law or principle affects Thai perceptions of "the enemy," "Thainess," "Thai history," and "Thai truth." In the 1930s, the Thai anti-communist law punished those advocating communism. An enemy of the state was the communist. But as the mechanisms of official nationalism focused on creating unity through the coinage, definition, and propagation of the idea of "culture," a shift became discernible by the late 1960s. The anti-communist law was culturalized, or perhaps better said, Thai-ified. The enemy was still the communist. But now communists were those who caused "people to lose their faith in religion or the traditions and customs of the Thai race." By the early 1980s, the Thai state was in full forward gear, generating various Thai culture schema designed to build loyalty of Thai official nationalism. However, Thai-ification became not merely an effort to reorient and reshape the imaginations of people living in Thailand: this effort embarked on a colonizing mission that took it into history, into the animal kingdom, and across national borders. *Thai* dinosaurs roamed the now-*Thai* landscape; *Thai* dogs exhibited superior Thai traits; foreigners also had to show respect toward Thainess.

Finally, we examine how defamation developed a sort of Thai "truth," as it appeared in politics, history, and art. In a vibrant defamation regime such as Thailand, the state plays a major role in arbitrating truth, resulting in an entire defamation power schema that, in turn, creates a certain social psychology.[79] The truth of a perceived insult or defamatory message is based on its "sting" rather than any consideration of what has been asserted. The depth of the sting determines the seriousness of its supposed effect on "the people." The sting pre-empts rational consideration of the actual content of the message. Thus, "real" truth can only have salubrious effects.

If something expressed publicly causes disunity, chaos, ruin, and a loss of faith in the state, it is a sign of malicious intent. The truth of something said or written can only be perceived by moral persons who themselves are unaffected by the defamation or insult. The central principle of defamation—the closer to truth, the greater the crime—results in a hierarchy of truth-delivery media—newspapers, movies, books—based on the danger they may pose in an uneducated society. Race and adherence to state ideology grant greater access to the truth—the more "Thai" and the greater the obedience to the dictates of "Thainess," the greater exposure to the truth. As a whole, the defamation apparatus outlines the borders of legitimacy as dictated by a certain use of language, and citizenship, as the state dictates what constitutes "the good citizen" and his or her relationship to the state. Over time an axiomatic, pervasive, and persistent "defamation thinking" develops—a type of worldview and authoritarian impulse that obfuscate even the most rudimentary forms of public truth.

I should make clear what I am not arguing. I am not arguing that Buddhism or Buddhists, or that Theravada Buddhism or Theravada Buddhists, necessarily have a tenuous grasp on political and social reality or truth.[80] Neither am I arguing that the Thai legal system as a whole cannot discern truth. For all crimes other than defamation, the Thai justice system functions, at least in theory, just like everywhere else. However, I am arguing is that Thai Theravada Buddhism, when given a fairly strong continuity with the past, provides a strong foundation from which a defamation regime may spring. I argue that, in contemporary Thai political and social discourse, there is in fact a difficulty in accepting, recognizing, acknowledging, or acting upon truth. Any vigorous and unrestrained use of defamation-based laws can skew the way that a society views truth and how it views itself culturally, socially, and politically.

As this introduction suggests, the direction and thrust of defamation always collide with the drive for truth. Defamation laws express state power. The contest is not between defamation laws and truth. Rather, the contest is essentially between power and truth. Various political formations dominate this contest through laws based on defamation. If a defamation regime is fully operational (as I argue it is in Thailand), a discernible cultural, social, and political effect occurs, one that shapes the ways society perceives truth.

With the state of exception extended infinitely, Thailand has fallen out of historical time and entered, with a captured and tortured truth, an eternal abnormal time. For more than a century now, truth has been on trial in Thailand. It has come time for us to judge its proceedings.

Part I

Defamation and truth-producing forms in Thailand

2 Regimes of truth, regimes of defamation

Each society has its regime of truth.
Michel Foucault

Defamation and the principles underlying its legal and political evolution represent the volatile combination—the explosive alchemy—between the twin discourses of power and truth, demarcating within the criminal continuum what can and what cannot be expressed in a given society. In this and Chapter 3, a number of conceptual foundations are laid. First, the journey toward the West's present understanding of its truths is described as quite gradual. The present-day features common to the juridical pursuit of truth—defense attorneys, prosecutors, rules of evidence, the credibility of witnesses—were assembled over a number of centuries. From the Church, the state assumed the role of moral guarantor and judge of the soul, while gradually replacing the victim of private wrongs, and developing a set of crimes perceived as against the political order, in which the state was victim, prosecutor, and judge. Second, an examination of the various components and unique characteristics of defamation-based laws and adjudication provides insight into the ways that certain kinds of truths or conceptual configurations emerge as a regime of defamation. Third, defamation laws and their adjudication are related in various ways to "the truth." Although this discourse is more familiar to media and law experts, the argument made in this book makes discussion of truth, opinion, and characterization unavoidable. We then apply these three inquiries—the historical development of truth-producing forms, particular social and political aspects of defamation, and the question of truth—to nineteenth-century Siam (Chapter 3).

Evolution of truth-producing forms in Europe

Foucault's provocative work provides an indirect way of examining the relationship between truth, power, and legal forms by focusing on structures rather than content:

> [T]ruth isn't the reward of free spirits, the child of protracted solitude, nor the privilege of those who have succeeded in liberating themselves. Truth is a thing of this world: it is produced only by virtue of multiple forms of constraint. And it induces regular effects of power. Each society has its regime of truth, its "general politics" of truth—that is, the types of discourse it accepts and makes function as true; the mechanisms and instances that enable one to distinguish true and false statements; the means by which each is sanctioned; the techniques and procedures accorded value in the acquisition of truth; the status of those who are charged with saying what counts as true.[1]

Foucault argues that the evolution of juridical forms was linked to the ways that various societies understood truth. If we are to understand "the forms by which our society defined types of subjectivity, forms of knowledge, and, consequently, relations between man and truth," Foucault argues, then we need to understand the evolution of various juridical forms. Juridical forms produced certain rules and practices that were "constantly modified through the course of history." Juridical forms, or judicial practices, according to Foucault, are:

> the manner in which wrongs and responsibilities are settled between men, the mode by which, in the history of the West, society conceived and defined the way men could be judged in terms of wrongs committed, the way in which compensation for some actions and punishment for others were imposed on specific individuals.[2]

Foucault examines the way that different juridical forms have their own systems of knowledge and approaches to truth. Generally speaking, he argues, "rational forms of proof and demonstration" involve a practice under which we understand how truth is produced, under what conditions it is produced, what forms it takes, and which rules seem to apply.[3]

The Greco-Roman development of "inquiry" led to "philosophical, rational systems" and "scientific systems" which were lost with the disintegration of the Roman Empire. Foucault contrasts this approach with the "legal" system the Romans encountered in their conquests of German tribes. In these areas, there was no public, legal practice. Legal action was a form of warfare, a "kind of duel," ritualized revenge between individuals, families, or groups. As such, there was no "crime," no victim, and no one representing the authority of society as a whole. It was always something between contending sides. The only function that a third party might have played was to affirm that the rules of engagement were followed. There was no third party seeking to discover the truth. There was no right or wrong, just winning or losing.[4]

In medieval times, this developed into what Foucault calls tests or games. The two parties agreed on the test and were compelled to honor the outcome. One "test" was when the one accused of a wrong brought together twelve witnesses, who had to be family members, who swore the accused had not committed the act. Innocence was determined more by "social importance" than by any attempt to get at the truth. Another test was done verbally. An accused person had to repeat certain kinds of formulas. Guilt came to the one who failed to utter the formulas correctly. Women, priests, and children could have another take the oral test in their place. If standing in for the accused, this representative—an early kind of lawyer—failed, the accused was found guilty. A third form of the test was oath taking. If the accused refused to make an oath, they lost. A fourth type of test was simple corporal punishment or what we would now call torture. If you walked on coals and two days later had no scar, you were innocent. If thrown into the water with foot tied to hand and the water "accepted" you and you subsequently drowned, you 'won," so to speak.[5] Foucault argues these kinds of tests "didn't have the function of designating or manifesting, or discovering the truth." They were "legal devices" and not "truth devices" (or truth devices securely within the realm of the miraculous).[6]

Small states developing in medieval Europe tried to re-establish the Greco-Roman approach, only for German law to return when they fell. In the twelfth century, though, the system of "inquiry" returned, but this time altered from the Greco-Roman form. In this newer version, the inquiry did not so much focus on the "knowledge of contents" as truth's "forms and conditions of possibility." No longer was legal action taken by two individuals on their own; now the contesting parties "submit[ted] to a power external to them, a judicial political power." Representing "the sovereign, king or master," the *prosecutor* emerged, acting as the injured party in the name of the victim. Eventually, the prosecutor—that is, the "political authority"—no longer just represents the victim, but actually replaced the victim as the injured party.[7]

New, too, was the concept of "infraction." The wrong was no longer between two individuals, but "against the order, state, law, society, sovereignty, and the sovereign." Moreover, as the injured party, the state demanded compensation, which created a new mechanism of fines and confiscations. The "administrative inquiry," presided over by a representative of political authority, became a truth-seeking procedure. The authority could pose questions, interrogate. It could also bring together a group of notable persons—recognized by their positions, wealth, age, and so on—to consider the matter. With no coercion from the authority, this group—an early kind of jury—was empowered to give a "collective opinion" on what was seen as the truth. The first full application of this method of inquiry occurred when William the Conqueror took control of the Anglo-Saxon lands of England. In order to understand the array of land-holding patterns, William set up a vast inquiry that, in the end, produced the *Doomsday Book*.[8]

But two other developments in the history of the West transformed this "administrative management" practice that "allowed political power to take control of judicial procedures" into a practice acquiring "extraordinary dimensions." First, a method of moving the time and space of the crime developed. A community might catch someone red-handed, presently involved in committing a "flagrant" act. Here the simple remedy was to catch and drag the scoundrel off to the authorities. But what if there was evidence of a crime but no one was caught red-handed? The inquiry itself took the place of the flagrant act. By convening persons under oath, to say what they had seen and knew, who could show they were in a position to know, who could affirm that something had in fact happened, the inquiry became "the indirect equivalent of the flagrant offence." This "major discovery," Foucault contends,

> was a new way of extending actuality, of transferring it from one time period to another and of offering it to the gaze, to knowledge, as if it were still present. The integration of this inquiry procedure, reactualizing what had transpired, making it present, tangible, immediate, and true, as if one had witnessed it, constituted a major discovery.[9]

Second, an adoption and adaptation of the Church's *visitatio* evolved. Bishops in the Middle Ages regularly visited the areas under their supervision. The bishop began with the *inquisitio generalis*, a general inquiry about what had happened since his last visit, what transgressions or crimes had been committed, and the general management of church affairs. The *inquisitio specialis* was convened if there had been transgressions or crimes. Foucault describes the double-pronged purpose and effect of the visit:

> The ecclesiastical inquisition was at the same time a spiritual inquiry concerning sins, transgressions, and crimes committed, and an administrative inquiry concerning the way in which the Church's assets were managed and the profits gathered, accumulated, and distributed, and so on . . . This model—spiritual and administrative, religion and political—this method for managing, overseeing, and controlling souls was found in the Church: the inquiry understood as a gaze focused as much on possessions and riches as on hearts, acts, and intensions. It was this model that was taken up and adapted in judicial procedure.[10]

Foucault warns that "the inquiry" as it emerged in Europe was not so much the adoption of rational practices as "primarily a governmental process, an administrative technique, a management method." It was first and foremost "a particular way of exercising power" that embodied not just the reorganization of judicial procedures but "a whole political transformation, a new political structure."[11]

Three long-term results where produced from this transformation. First, within the scientific realm, the inquiry established a set of techniques that led to the scientific revolution, a creation of knowledge about the world. This in turn, when combined with new emerging techniques of social control, led to the creation of the social sciences, the "science of man." Second, the inquiry became "permeated with religious categories" that transformed what had been a wrong between two individuals into a legal infraction against the state and a spiritual transgression against God and society. Hence, new categories such as transgression, sin, and culpability became part of the inquiry. "Doing injury to the sovereign and committing a sin," Foucault writes, "began to merge." The most notorious and extreme result of this development was witnessed during the Inquisition. And third, part of the inquiry created administrative and economic knowledge and procedures concerning "population, wealth, money, and resources." With such knowledge, kings of newly emerging states developed a system "to establish, secure, and increase royal power." The emergence of a political judicial system of course does not imply that Enlightenment thinking had necessarily had any effect on the degree of severity of the punishments meted out by the state. The 315 types of acts that could send an English subject to the scaffold in the eighteenth century, Foucault avers, made the "English penal code, penal law, penal system one of the most savage and bloody that the history of civilizations has known." Nonetheless, the emergence of the inquiry method up to the end of the eighteenth century represents the first great transformation in judicial forms and the truths they create.[12]

Now that we have a bit of an idea of some of what Foucault calls the "types of discourse" and "the mechanisms and instances" that define "true and false statements," we can better recognize "the techniques and procedures accorded value" in acquiring the truth, and "the status" of those who have the power to say what is true. The point of this brief foray into European history is to appreciate that judicial forms developed over many centuries. Evidence, testimony, and judgment were quite different from what we are accustomed to now. Each political form had its own judicial forms for discovering the truth. But by the time of absolutism, the state, and not private, contending parties, was the final arbiter of the truth. In Europe, the state had also absorbed the moral judgment of the Church and made crime an infraction against king and God.

Chapter 3 examines the relationship between the development of law and judicial forms and practices in nineteenth-century Siam and the truths that emerged from such relationships. Of particular interest in the case of Siam is the development of "infraction," the authority that abrogated to itself the right to determine what constituted an infraction and how the religious/moral quality of "sin" (and so, intent) bonded with infraction. But we will turn now to two important, related issues: the unique and cogent features of defamation as a law and its tenuous relationship to the truth.

Defamation as law

Defamation, a general category of law containing primarily slander and libel—saying or writing something damaging to another's reputation, respectively—is an imputation that "tends to lower [the other] in the estimation of others, or to expose him to hatred, contempt or ridicule, or to injure his reputation in his office, trade or profession, or to injure his financial credit." Courts begin with the assumption that defamatory words are damaging to reputation. Technically, if it is shown that the words were defamatory, the defendant is guilty, regardless of the truth of the statement. The proven damage to reputations, though, can be trumped by what are variously called "privileges," "exclusions," and "saving clauses." Standard privileges can exempt defendants—typically the media—from liability for expressions of opinion, fair comment and criticism, fair reporting, and neutral reporting. The media may also make defense against libel for showing that what was expressed was "not capable of defamatory meaning," was the truth, or was reporting on public officials or public figures. Proving the truth of what was said can serve as an absolute defense in civil cases in many countries, but such may not necessarily be the case in countries where defamation still remains a criminal offense.[13]

It should be noted here that although I am drawing from British and American thinking on defamation due to their long and rich experience in the area of freedom of speech, it would be a mistake to assume that in practice countries coming from the common law tradition are necessarily freer in practice.[14] Whether a country draws on common law or follows a derivative of the Napoleonic code tradition seems to make little difference in terms of free speech. For instance, "common law" Britain, the US, Ireland, and Sri Lanka rank 27th, 53rd, 1st, and 141st, respectively, on the Reporters Without Borders' Worldwide Press Freedom Index of 2006. Ratings for countries following a "civil code" tradition range in the same index from Finland (1st), France (35th), to Vietnam (155th).[15]

Another way to justify my focus on Anglo-American thought on defamation is to say that although Thailand clearly operates under a civil code system, there is nonetheless a perception among Thai jurists that Thai law is largely derived from the British. At least until recently, probably the majority of Thai studying law abroad did so in Great Britain and the authors of the two primary legal texts I use in this study point out that defamation thinking in Thailand is drawn from the British.[16]

Not many areas of law lend themselves so well to historical study as defamation. As a crime of words (and sometimes even thought), defamation occupies a special place in human society; our understanding of defamation has much to do with how we understand ourselves in society and under state control. It is the quintessential public act.

Criminality and accountability

A "wrong" has an ancient meaning dating back in English to the twelfth century. It still retains its original meanings today. But it was only with the development of states that "wrong" was used as an infraction against the state and was largely eclipsed by "crime." A person who feels they have been "wronged" by another party can no longer legally take care of the matter privately in a duel. One can still informally demand the other party "to step outside." But one can also resort to civil law to address the wrong. It is a case between two private parties where the state lays out certain rules by which the contest in court will be carried out. A person who feels wronged by another can also do nothing. "A wrong" only becomes a case when one party wishes it to be so.

Within a special class of civil law is the ancient wrong of slander. Persons who choose "to do injustice to [a person] by statement, imputation, opinion" or "to discredit or dishonour by word or thought," may be sued for defamation. Compared to other civil and criminal laws, defamation has a number of unique features. *Prosser and Keeton on the Law of Torts* describes the frustrating aspects of this law:

> It must be confessed at the beginning that there is a great deal of the law of defamation that makes no sense. It contains anomalies and absurdities for which no legal writer has ever had a kind word, and it is a curious compound of a strict liability imposed upon innocent defendants, as rigid and extreme as anything found in law, with a blind and almost perverse refusal to compensate the plaintiff for real and very serious harm.[17]

But the nonsensicalness, the "anomalies and absurdities," extend beyond those produced by the weighing of damage to reputations against a society's need for freedom of expression. Defamation itself plays a central role in determining the extent to which members of a society can write and read about one another.

There is an inherent tension between the two opposite poles of defamation: the need to protect reputation and the need for society to have access to certain facts and opinions. This tension is heightened when defamation is deemed a criminal act. Criminalizing defamation makes the offense one against society and the state, giving it the stigma of a crime and its offenders as criminals. As a crime rather than a wrong between two private citizens, libel takes on additional noteworthy characteristics. Within English law, the general crime of treason branched into attempted or actual physical acts against the state or king, sedition, or writing which incited disloyalty or acts against the government, and criminal defamation. The Criminal Libel Act of 1819 was applied for blasphemy and sedition. An 1888 amendment made prosecution of criminal libel allowable only with the consent of a judge. In other parts of the United Kingdom, such as Scotland, libel was no longer treated as a criminal offense.[18]

In order to increase the degree of accountability of public figures, in most democratic countries courts permit considerable latitude for public comment on their behavior. In standard legal practice in democracies, the principle is well established. Gatley writes:

> It is the duty of everyone, in the interest of public efficiency and good order, to bring any misconduct or neglect of duty on the part of a public officer or employee, or any public abuse, to the notice of the proper authority for investigations. Any complaint or information as to such misconduct, neglect of duty, or abuse, though volunteered, is privileged, provided it is made in good faith to the person or body who has the power or duty to remove, punish or reprimand the offender . . . In doing so he [the one bringing the matter to public attention] exercises an undoubted privilege which it is not in the public interest to penalize.[19]

In English law, exemption is given to defendants in both criminal and civil suits for comment on the conduct of public officials for "good order" and because it is in "the public interest." In 1964, the United States Supreme Court established a federal rule that

> prohibited a public official from recovering damages for a defamatory falsehood relating to his official conduct unless he proves that the statement was made with "actual malice"—that is, with knowledge that it was false or with reckless disregard of whether it was false or not.

Although this rule does not grant newspapers "absolute immunity" of libel suits from public officials, it is, as a rule "difficult for a plaintiff to show that a newspaper published a story with actual malice." In New York, for instance, "public officials" refer to all people who are "elected or appointed to office and who appear to have substantial responsibility for control over public and governmental affairs." The more public the figure is, the greater the burden is for showing actual malice. Such burdens are lessened for private persons involved in public matters and even more for libel of private persons involved in purely private matters.[20]

A further question has to do with to what degree criticism of public officials and institutions is given exemption as "fair comment" and whether statements made about them are more of a statement of fact or the expression of an opinion. Within legal circles, the initial difference between the two is easy to define: a fact is something that can be verified; an opinion is something that cannot be proved, or is not "falsifiable." This principle applies especially to the use of metaphorical speech or comment about collective bodies. In a case of defamation, it is mandatory that the plaintiff convincingly show that the defendant was speaking specifically about him or her and not someone else. If the defendant has made a general statement, or made a statement about a large number of people, it may not be possible for the plaintiff to prove that the defendant was speaking of him or her in particular. In some countries, such as the United States, collective libel suits are rarely, if ever, allowed.[21]

The intention, the standard, and the potential effect

A defamatory action has four related components: the defamer (and his or her intention), the defamer's words or "action," the potential effect such words are predicted to have, and the standard by which the crime is considered as completed. Mr. A says Ms. B. is a crook. Ms. C hears the words and believes Ms. B is a crook. The court considers the intent of Mr. A., the content of what was said (Ms. B is a crook), what a society in general would feel about Ms. B if the words were thought to be true, the judgement which either confirms or does not confirm that the words were defamatory, and the effect of such words on society.

As discursive crimes, no base of physical evidence exists which, when reconstructed, outlines the contours and progression of a crime. Only words in various and sundry phrasings inflict damage on a reputation. At best, the sole physical evidence is a piece of paper with writing on it. The rest of the crime is discursive interpretation and the weighing of one discursive interpretation against another that is more closely related to literary criticism (with a social and political twist) than "normal" legal adjudication. As such, there is a tendency for prosecution of defamation to pay special attention to what comprises the central piece of "evidence"—the intent or motive of the author. Guilt can in many cases be established if "malice of aforethought" can be proven—pre-meditated libel designed to injure another's reputation.

In some civil cases, it is the responsibility of the plaintiff "to prove actual malice in the popular sense of the term." However, in most civil cases of libel, where the truth of what was expressed can serve as an absolute defense, the focus is usually on "the tendency and consequence of the publication rather than the motive or intention" of the author or publisher. Libel is considered as a more serious form of defamation for "a libel written and published shows more deliberate malignity than a mere oral slander."[22]

But, with criminal prosecution of defamation, establishing intent becomes key. Gatley admits that "malice" once played a more central role: "There are dicta in some old cases to the effect that malice is 'the gist of an action of defamation.'" Malice, or "wrongful intention," is what a court "always presumes when a wrongful act is done without legal justification or excuse." In libel cases, the key distinction between guilt and innocence is often based on the question of the mental state or morality of the accused defamer. As an 1869 court decision on a libel case averred, "The sole question is whether he acted honestly and in good faith."[23]

Guilt in defamation cases is partially based on the legally nebulous quality of how "society" or "right-thinking people" would understand the offending words. In general, for defamation adjudication, Gatley states, the law places more emphasis on "the tendency and consequence of the publication rather than the motive or intention" of the defamer.[24] Nonetheless, intent and effect are intimately connected. The discursive crime of defamation becomes complete when the malicious intent of the words succeeds. That is, if the words were intended to cause a lowering of the good name of another, that effect can truly only be seen when the words are read and the heart of the reader is betrayed by the malicious intent of the words. How does a court determine this effect? Are there witnesses who, having read the words in question, attest to the fact that their estimation of the person so libelled is now lowered? Is it judges who use their own judgment in guessing how the average person would react to the words?

English law historically has left it up to juries to decide. Since defamation as a civil offense is based on the understanding of the allegedly offending words by the public, it is the public itself, through juries, who make the determination. English law has thus adopted as the standard "the view which would be taken by the ordinary good and worthy subject of the King," or by "right-thinking people generally" who are instructed to understand the words in question as they "are normally construed in their natural and ordinary meaning, *i.e.* in the meaning in which reasonable men of ordinary intelligence, with the ordinary man's general knowledge and experience of worldly affairs, would be likely to understand them." The test, according to an 1882 ruling, "is whether, under the circumstances in which the writing was published, *reasonable* men to whom the publication was made would be likely to understand it in a libelous sense."

Right-thinking people serving in juries may be of varying opinions on the matter. Barristers must contend with this reality in working to their clients' advantage:

> Ordinary men and women have different temperaments and outlooks. Some are unusually suspicious and some are unusually naïve. One must try to envisage people between these two extremes and see what is the most damaging meaning they would put on the words in question.

Juries are also instructed not to think in terms of how a particular group in society might view the words and instead reflect on the "community as a whole." An expression "which is merely distasteful or objectionable according to the notions of certain people is not defamatory." A distinction must be made between "merely a breach of conventional etiquette, and what is illegal, mischievous, or sinful—between, in fact, matters of taste and matters of crime."

In the end, the legal category of "right-thinking people generally" is not very precise. Gatley quotes a number of jurists on the point, all of whom agree that determining libel is "not one of construction in the legal sense."

The legal facts of the case do not prevail in a jury's determinations in libel cases; they are not really "a question of law." The only "fact" in the case is "the impression the words convey to the jury."

In England itself, criminal libel can be prosecuted for blasphemy, sedition, obscenity, incitement to crime, contempt of court, a challenge to a duel, or for words that may "provoke a breach of the peace." Although a party felt wronged by something published can call for criminal prosecution, Gatley advises that such a person "should content himself with his civil remedy." As "libel and slander are essentially personal wrongs," Gatley avers to the opinion of Lord Coleridge on the matter:

> There ought to be something of a public nature about a libel to justify the interfering of the Crown as representing the public in proceeding by indictment. The Crown was the prosecutor in the case of an indictment, and therefore an indictment for libel ought to be something which interested the Crown, which concerned the general interests of the public, and was likely to create a breach of the peace . . . but when it was clearly an individual squabble between two people . . . it was well settled law, that it ought not to be, and was not in point of law, a proper subject of indictment.[25]

The phrase, "likely to create a breach of the peace" is a curious one, for it requires prophetic powers and loose logic for a jury to predict what kinds of words might create such a breach. The jury has to determine a true "breach of the peace," what is in "the general interests of the public," and weigh such against the equally important general interest in the public to allow freedom of speech. This places defamation in a small class of crimes where a defendant can be found guilty for a crime that does not yet exist.

Defamation as arbiter of culture and politics

Not only can the standard by which defamation obtains vary, the conditions and circumstances surrounding any given case are particularly sensitive to political, cultural, and social pressures placed on a society in general. The perceived threats, phobias, and anxieties of a society, whether real or imagined, may play a key role in defining what is defamatory and what is not. Unlike certain actions such as murder, robbery, and rape—which all are constants as crimes—the laws using the defamation principle are, relatively speaking, subject to greater swings of what constitutes criminality than most other crimes. For instance, otherwise innocent words can become suddenly defamatory with reference to the circumstances in which they were uttered or written and in reference to the context in which they appear. Public opinion can play a role. The words used on one occasion about a particular person may not be defamatory, while the same words in different circumstances may be. As Gatley points out, "It is not possible to say that any particular imputation is defamatory, regardless of the circumstances of its publication. Whether or not it is so will vary with time, place and the state of public opinion." And determining liability will not be "a matter of law" as such, "but a matter of fact for the jury."

Unlike the litigation of other laws, legal precedents for defamation are "not of equal authority" for "the rule for the interpretation of words . . . is different in one age from what it is in another." Moreover, "words have different meanings in different places." Beyond this, there is the difficulty of determining what is defamatory in terms of interpretation. For a newspaper article, say, jurists are asked to understand not just the meaning of the words in question, but the overall context in which the words appeared. For instance,

> Words which are not in themselves defamatory may, from the whole context in which they are published, convey a defamatory meaning. Conversely, this or that sentence may be considered defamatory, but there may be other passages which take away their sting. If in one part of the publication something disreputable to the plaintiff is stated, but that is removed by the conclusion, the bane and the antidote must be taken together.[26]

Adjudication assesses and places value on the relative worth of reputations in society, injecting a certain kind of class bias. Defamation is called "the Rich Man's Tort" for two related reasons. The first is that, in general, the richer and more important you are (in your own eyes and those of others), the greater the worth of your reputation. In a similar way, the greater the reputation of the person (or of the medium covering you), the greater the potential damage to your reputation might be. The second reason is that money is necessary to sue someone for defamation; furthermore, it can cost a lot to be sued. The problem is compounded when, as in the United Kingdom, free defense counsel is available for all kinds of cases except defamation.[27]

The laws on defamation, in a general sense, control, shape, influence, and impinge on how societies within their public spheres give voice to their culture and history, give shape to their works of art, express political aspirations and ideals, provide the canvas on which societies reflect upon and recreate themselves. Culture may have a material base, but its expression is, at least in modern societies, quite often discursive.

To give one example of defamation's effects, there is a 1791 case where a recently deceased person was allegedly defamed. His family brought charges, but in overturning the lower court's decision, Lord Kenyon warned how much "history" could be obliterated by defamation:

> To say, in general, that the conduct of a dead person can at no time be canvassed: to hold that, even after ages are passed, the conduct of bad men cannot be contrasted with good, would be to exclude the most useful part of history.[28]

Truth, fact, opinion, comment

On an initial level at least, truth does not intersect with judicial considerations in a defamation case. It is tempting to claim that defamation has nothing to do with the truth, but it would be better to say that its movement as a law is in near diametric opposition to the truth. Defamation laws are not designed to produce truth; they are for protecting reputations. There is even the legal axiom applied to defamation that says that the closer the offending words are to the truth, the greater the crime. Defamation laws are not intended to establish and protect the truth yet at the same time their operation can affect the way truth is perceived.

The question of where truth, as such, resides is a matter of contention within the domain of law and media freedom and is not familiar terrain for most historians. Historiography is a battle between different interpretations of events and discourses, between ways of approaching different kinds of realities or truths.[29] The prominent Thai historian Nidhi Eoseewong has reminded us how important the way truth is perceived in various historical and political formations, and that it deserves serious consideration of historians.[30] Chaiwat Satha-Anand has been involved in a more systematic treatment of truth and how it is "managed" by various societies:[31]

> The ways in which a given society manages "truth" vary, reflecting how power works in that society . . . For example, the law of the land could be enforced to silence "undesirable truths" that come out of a research paper; social pressures could be mounted for a university to recall an advanced degree given to the author of a published thesis that many consider blasphemous to their local heroine; ideas of political reforms could be praised for their sophistication, yet regarded as too idealistic to be put into practice and therefore shelved, or a part of history deemed too ugly to face could be relegated to the realm of silence. In other words, "truth" management reflects how a society selects, presents, neglects, or suppresses certain "truths," which in turn, could reveal much about the reality of that society.[32]

In his study of the 1948 "Dusun-nyor incident" in Pattani in which 30 Thai policemen and somewhere between 30 and 600 Malay Muslims were killed, Chaiwat argues that the little-known monument to the incident speaks a truth that is "one-sided"—the death of the heroic, Thai Buddhist policeman, but speaks silence to the killed "rebels." The facts behind the incident are disputed, historical interpretations of the event, affecting the way it is remembered, and affecting its categorization—"rebellion" (from the Thai government side) or "uprising" (from the Malay Muslim side).[33]

Because defamation is an exercise of power over truth and representation, it is necessary for this study to lay out some way of approaching truth.

Although the treatment of truth here will be in no way definitive, it will hopefully be a starting point for discussion in Thai studies.[34]

Within the domain of defamation, there are (roughly) three categories of expression: fact, opinion, and fair comment, or, what is falsifiable, what is not falsifiable, and what is allowed.[35] In the smaller sense of fact (or "truth"), it is a statement of fact, and, as Chaiwat observes, facts are stubborn: "'factual truth' is . . . problematic because it cannot be compromised. If one 'factual truth' is right, its opposite cannot be. In this sense, 'factual truth' is deeply despotic."[36] In other words, facts are a kind of truth that is falsifiable: "Mr. A is a criminal" or "Turkish soldiers killed a million Armenians," or "There was a Jewish genocide." Either Mr. A has been convicted in a court of law and is a criminal or he has not. Turkish soldiers killed Armenians or they did not. Either there was genocide or there was not. In the first instance, the one accused, Mr. A, may sue for defamation to protect his reputation. The contention is falsifiable. In the second, the accused were actually soldiers serving under the Ottoman Empire. But the Turkish state represents this historical entity in denying the charge. In the third instance, *no one* has been accused of anything: it is a statement that attests to something that happened. However, victims, or families of victims, may try to sue. Only the first instance is clearly falsifiable. The second might be shown to be pretty much true. The third is more complicated, because it characterizes the actions of the Third Reich against Jewish people as a particular social phenomenon. While not denying that many Jews were killed, some may debate the question of whether it was "genocide" or not. So even within the category of "what is falsifiable," only one type is clearly actionable. While the second may be difficult to establish, those accused of it are surely all dead. The third instance comes perilously close to an expression of an opinion.[37]

The second category of defamation is "opinion," the whole indeterminate range of human expression, comprised of essentially "metaphors"—characterizations of social and political events and personalities, interpretations, analyses, predictions, guesses—sometimes in the form of satire or irony. Opinions are various arrangements of representations and facts that are not falsifiable and still open to debate. These expressions do not generally claim to be "the truth," but sometimes *a* truth, such as this Thai artist's response to monks who criticized his work: "The artist who tries to present the truth of the society has to face a lot of pressure from monks who think that they represent the purity of . . . Buddhism."[38] This is also what might be termed a legitimate expression of opinion. A good example is Noam Chomsky's contention that US involvement in Vietnam is best characterized as an "invasion." Certainly, Chomsky marshals certain facts to make argument that if the same criteria used in characterizing the Soviet invasion of Afghanistan were applied to the US entry into Vietnam, then "invasion" is more consistent.[39] This is an argument, an interpretation. Opinion can also be over what meaning to give certain events, as the "facts" are revealed over time. The US government claimed the North Vietnamese provoked the "Gulf of Tonkin incident"; years later, with the publication of the *Pentagon Papers*, "new" facts brought new interpretations of the events.[40] Another type of opinion is a statement of fact that is virtually impossible to prove one way or another, such as, "The government is corrupt." Can the government prove it is not corrupt?[41] In the same vein, I characterize Thailand as a defamation regime in this book: an interpretation supported by a particular arrangement of selected "facts."[42]

The third defamation category is fair comment. As mentioned earlier in this chapter, an exclusion sometimes given in defamation cases is the right to comment on issues and people in the public eye for the public good. Fair comment is allowed even if some or all of the facts are wrong, as long as the defendant can show she or he did not act with reckless disregard of the truth. Theoretically in Western democracies, any issue or any person defined as "public" can be commented on, with a general proviso that the more public the issue or figure, the more latitude given to comment. It is the duty and right of citizens to monitor the actions of all public officials, whether elected or appointed. In Thailand, the majority of defamation accusations concern members of parliament and the bureaucracy (see Chapter 7).

These three categories—what is true (falsifiable, facts), what is not falsifiable (opinion, characterizations, representations), and what is allowed (comment)—and the range they are given—largely demarcate the limits and possibilities of the public sphere. If the public sphere cannot gain access to the basic facts behind events or cannot experiment with different characterizations and metaphors, the narrative frameworks through which societies understand their political, historical, and cultural contexts are necessarily inadequate for the truth to come to the forefront. Fact, opinion, and comment are necessary for growth of the public sphere in which social and political imagination can flourish. When the three are creatively combined, "Truth" in the larger, capitalized sense can be approached: the kinds of truth that we sometimes encounter with art, fiction, poetry, or even academic writing. The limit on any one of the three defines to some degree the extent of a society's social and political imagination.

Modern academics are hesitant to approach the question of truth or reality; perhaps rightly so. Historians, especially those influenced by postmodernism, are familiar with the shifting terrain of meaning and truth and that today's facts and truths may be tomorrow's myths. They know that the exercise of power engenders different kinds of truths, that realities are multidimensional and socially constructed.

I propose here a study of the genealogy of the way that facts, characterizations, and truth have been and are viewed in Thailand. To start out, we examine the historical roots of juridical forms and perceptions of "truth" in nineteenth-century Siam.

3 Truth and treason in old Siam

This chapter examines a number of aspects of nineteenth-century Siamese history related to defamation. Each aspect not inconsequentially provides greater conceptual precision to the effects of Siam "not being colonized."

Conventional treatments of Thai history emphasize the fact that Siam was not directly colonized by Western powers, implying that, in the case of the Siamese, "modernization" was something essentially different (and better) than that of its colonized neighbors. However, this position is more assumed than demonstrated.[1]

First, traditional Siamese truth-producing forms were still widely practiced up until the end of the nineteenth century. While certain "superstitious" beliefs and practices were excised, the cosmology of traditional Thai Theravada Buddhism—its social stratification, views of reality, and views on the legitimacy of kingship—was left largely intact. The centrality given to *intention* within Thai Theravada Buddhism as a marker of virtue was retained in its premodern form. While some aspects of Thai Buddhism collapsed in the face of Western science, the view that the truth can only be perceived by those of great merit persisted.

Second, Siam was transformed from a premodern kingdom into a modernizing nation-state within a few short decades. While absolute monarchy was largely gone from the world by 1900, the Bangkok elite adopted a dual strategy that gave absolute monarchy a set of modern laws and procedures while preserving and creating a neo-sacred state for internal purposes. The type of polity created by this drive for a Theravada Buddhist kind of purity I call a *ritual purification state*.

Third, within the area of law, this transformation was achieved with the aid of foreign legal advisors employed by the Siamese government. These advisors brought with them not only certain notions about colonialism, but also the legal conceptual framework of Europe at the time. I argue that the primary contribution of these advisors was to impress upon the Siamese government the relationship between criminality and dangerousness. The premodern emphasis on intention and the needs of a centralizing, absolutist state, when mixed with this view of criminality and delineated by defamation-based laws, created a virtual science of treason to accompany the state's official nationalism.

Truth-producing forms in old Siam

The mid-nineteenth-century Siamese state developed somewhat similarly to European state systems. First, fragmented, localized justice systems throughout the kingdom and some of its tributary states meted out justice with a combination of methods, including inquiry, religious strictures, and trial by ordeal. From time to time, the capital reasserted legal sovereignty over outlying areas by re-collecting and re-codifying traditional laws and requiring local judges to refer to a common set of codes and procedures. Beyond specifying infractions and punishments, these law codes also defined the prerogatives legally enjoyed (or not enjoyed) by various groups within society—this class of nobles could inflict certain punishments on that class of "serfs" or "slaves," men held certain prerogatives in relation to their wives and children, and so on. The sovereign insisted on acting as the final arbiter on capital crimes, and only he (in the Siamese case, always a *he*) would have the prerogative to decide who should live and who should die.

Judicial sovereignty of the state—the ability to impose standardized judicial practices—depended on a variety of factors—the closeness of patron–client ties, the strength and influence of neighboring states and local centers of power, and simple geographical distance. If the state were to fall—as in the case of Ayutthaya in 1767, the center disappeared and judicial units reverted back to local control, only to be reassembled, to greater or lesser degrees, when a new state formed in Thonburi-Bangkok. Even within local power centers, judicial power diminished with distance; a "Little Tradition" system of justice was exercised on a village level, in which certain elders played the role of arbitrators.[2]

Upon establishing a new kingdom based in Bangkok, Rama I laid out two sets of laws to assert legitimacy. The first was a review and a purification of the monastic discipline codes. The second brought together the corpus of laws from the Ayutthayan period, but then adapted and supplemented them with new measures reflecting the political needs of the new regime.

The "codification" of the *Three Seals Laws* (*kotmai tra sam duang*) was completed in 1805.[3] Essentially "a set of religious and legal scriptures," *Three Seals* reflected a "purified" form of earlier codes.[4] In principle, judges were to cite *Three Seals* in deciding cases, but as Loos points out there is little evidence *Three Seals* served such a purpose or that copies were sent to courts throughout the land. Justice in areas far from the capital depended on the judgment of local rulers, even as late as a century later. Because *Three Seals* was not applied uniformly throughout the kingdom and its tributary states, and the actual codes were kept and preserved more as sacred writings, we begin to understand *Three Seals*' significance. Loos insightfully notes:

> From the 1780s until the 1880s, Siam's Buddhist kings dispensed justice or *thamma*, as a function of their position as monarchy. In theory, the king embodied morality as did the judges and legal magistrates throughout the kingdom. Justice, accordingly, sprang from the laws of the universal, moral truth to which the kings, judges, and other representatives of the king had access by virtue of their position rather than by virtue of their application of legal codes to case "facts."[5]

In addition to utilizing past codes, *Three Seals* was informed by the existing Thai "feudal" system, *sakdina*, which classified all subjects in terms of rank within society. The degree of criminality of certain acts and the severity of punishments were based on "status and gender." As a result, Loos argues, this "fluid" understanding of crime and punishment under *Three Seals* was "a complex mix of the social location of the individuals involved and the degree to which the acts upset the status quo."[6] Thus, the truth of a set of circumstances may have been as much based on the status of the parties involved as on the actual events.

As an example, we might look at the two laws that describe "capital crimes," the only crimes on which the king alone could pass judgment. According to Pallegoix's account from the 1850s, these were also the only crimes to which the death penalty was still applied.[7] But to say that there were only two capital crimes—*lèse-majesté* and rebellion—would be misleading, for in fact *lèse-majesté* and rebellion were general categories of "Capital Crimes" [*phra aiyakan luang*] and "Crimes of Rebellion" [*phra aiyakan krabot suk*] within the *Three Seals*.[8]

A short introduction to "Capital Crimes" explains that such crimes had to be punished "in order to stop the many sufferings of the subjects." For the most part, the more than one hundred provisions in this section of the *Three Seals* were directed specifically at those serving the king. In other words, the law targeted competing members of the elite class, who, among other things, "coerce, oppress, compel, persecute subjects, seizing their wealth, gold, children, wives, servants for their own use." Royal officials were admonished not to:

> swear at [slander] Representatives or Servants of the King, or alter the Royal Law, alter the Royal Edicts, Decrees, or Orders; or insert other words; or covet greatly a higher rank than one already has, or making oneself higher than the rank already conferred by the king; or boasting or daring, without fear, to not follow the King's Orders . . . or exceed the demands of the Order . . . or oppress or conceal the act of oppression and troubling the subjects . . . or transgress or conceal violations of this Law, who is fearless in overstepping the bounds of propriety, or oppressing the subjects.[9]

Punishment under the law was "The Punishment of Ten Instances":

1 (a) Beheading, (b) seizure of household, (c) taking away of rank, (d) scattering of all children, wives and servants, (e) seizure of property by the Crown.
2 Cutting off both hands and both feet and imprisoned without food until dead.
3 Given one, two, or three lashes with a leather whip or a rattan stick and publicly exhibited in a cage for one, two, or three months.
4 Fined fourfold and then made a grass cutter for the royal elephants.
5 Fined thrice and then expelled from royal service.
6 Fined twice and then publicly exhibited for three or seven days.
7 Fined once and property taken from the subjects returned to them.
8 Slitting of the mouth and then having it stuffed with a ripe coconut.
9 Warned and given a sentence, but not carrying it out.
10 Leaving worldly affairs.

A prototype of *lèse-majesté* is found in Provision 7:

> Whosoever dares, without fear, to impudently speak of the King, disparages of Royal Acts, Edicts or Commands, that person has transgressed the Royal Criminal Laws of the King and shall be punished with the Punishment of Eight Instances, namely:
>
> 1 Beheading and seizure of household;
> 2 Slitting the mouth and cutting off the ears, hands, and feet;
> 3 Given 25 or 30 lashes with a leather whip;
> 4 Imprisoned for a month and then made to cut grass for elephants;
> 5 Fined fourfold and made into a serf;
> 6 Fined twice;
> 7 Fined once;
> 8 Pardoned from punishment on the promise of good behaviour.[10]

How marvellous the elaboration of offenses and the range of punishments! And how unlike modern law codes. Since the king served as the focal point of the kingdom, every possible nuance and intricacy of offense against the king and his power was meticulously detailed. Two hundred two crimes, with 49 types of treason against the premodern state were detailed in these two sections. The degree of penalty for capital crimes had to be found in the heart, in the intention of the accused. By gauging such, the king could mete out the appropriate penalty. *Three Seals* in this sense was a form of judging the heart, a sort of premodern alchemist guide to treason. And the variations were myriad.[11]

In practice, courts were involved in little of what we would understand as dispensing justice; Loos calls them, "'corrupt' by the logic of modern law."[12] Pallegoix's 1854 account of Siam describes a typical scene from the main court of the kingdom:

> The place where justice is served is divided into several small halls in which there are platforms covered with mats on which are seated mandarins with their pillows to lean on. The crowd kneels on the tiles, and the judges treat affairs while drinking tea, smoking a cigar and chewing betel . . . They bring the accused before judges in session. They read the act of accusation and then interrogate the witnesses after having let them take the oath . . . The accused has the right to have certain witnesses eliminated for reasons of relationships or other reasons foreseen in the law. He can also produce as many witnesses in his favor as he can find . . . The two parties, each on their own side, offer money to the judges who purposely let the affair drag on for a long time . . . Almost always the parties who are battling mutually ruin each other. When they have nothing to give anymore, the judge drops them then and there. The best means to win a case is to promise a large sum to some influential person or other who takes charge of your affair. Almost everywhere justice is venal but perhaps more so in Siam than elsewhere.[13]

Craig Reynolds describes in his study of "Nirat Nongkhai," how Section 7 of the *Three Seals* mentioned above was invoked in an 1878 case. "Nirat Nongkhai" was a poem written by Nai Thim about the travails of Siamese soldiers during a military campaign a few years prior. It was written by order of a Siamese general who led the troops and the piece was circulated in court circles. Nai Thim, a servant in the retinue of another general, criticized the actions of the kingdom's regent, who had ordered the military campaign. In the proclamation condemning Nai Thim to punishment, he was accused of criticizing the regent "for dispatching the troops in the wrong season and not showing compassion for the troops, of altering the king's name, of setting one faction against another, and of using extremely vulgar language." Moreover, the poem magnified events troubling to the kingdom and was "contemptuous of state affairs and military authority"[14] In the end, Nai Thim was found guilty and ordered to be whipped and jailed, perhaps largely as a warning to the general who had ordered the poem's composition. Reynolds argues that the poem "carries a definite sense of injury to the kings and his ministers." The crime had to do with the status of the parties involved. That it even became a case was due to the standing of two members of the elite in conflict. The noble employer of Nai Thim, the poem's author, was not punished. The reason Nai Thim was, though, was because he had written inappropriately, he had used words as a commoner that should not be used with members of the elite. Reynolds conceives the rationale behind this case,

> a verbal attack on an officer or minister of the king . . . interpreted as an attack on the king himself. And, this attack is tantamount to violation of the sacred. The law on *lèse-majesté* is one of the ways the sacred qualities attributed to the king were defined and protected.[15]

Truth was not so much at issue as a complex mixture of political, social, and religious components. This case illustrates that defamation practices that emerged in Siam had to do more with relationship to monarchy, power, and status within the elite hierarchy than any sort of truth-seeking method.[16]

Taking oaths is one of the oldest tests of strength, a category of what Foucault calls, "the old magico-religious tests" in which a litigant invokes the gods and calls them to bear witness to the truth, demanding punishment if violating the oath. Below is a description of oath taking by N.A. McDonald, who served as a missionary in Siam in the 1860s (for full impact, best read aloud):

> The witnesses are taken out to a Buddhist temple, where the following ironclad oath is administered to them. "I, who have been brought here as a witness in this matter, do now, in the presence of the sacred image of Buddha, declare that I am wholly unprejudiced against either party, and uninfluenced in any way by the opinions or advice of others; that no prospects of pecuniary advantage or advancement to office have been held out to me. I also declare that I have not received any bribe on this occasion. If what I have now to say be false, or if in my further averments I shall color or pervert the truth so as to lead the judgment of others astray, may the Three Holy Existences before whom I now stand, together with the glorious *Tewadas* of the twenty-two firmaments, punish me. If I have not seen, and yet shall say I have seen; if I shall say I know that which I do not know, then may I be thus punished. Should innumerable descents of Deity happen for the regeneration and salvation of mankind, may my erring and migratory soul be found beyond the pale of mercy. Wherever I may go may I be compassed with dangers, and not escape from them, whether murderers, robbers, spirits of the earth, woods, or water, or air, or all the divinities who adore Buddha; or from the gods of the four elements, and all other spirits. May blood flow out of every pore of my skin, that my crime may be made manifest to the world. May all or any of these evils overtake me within three days, or may I never stir from the spot on which I now stand; or may the lightning cut me in two, so that I may be exposed to the derision of the people; or I should be walking abroad, may I be torn in pieces by either of the supernaturally endowed lions, or destroyed by poison serpents. If on the water of the river or ocean, may supernatural crocodiles or great fish devour me; or may the winds and waves overwhelm me, or may the dread of such evil keep me a prisoner during life at home, estranged from every pleasure. May I be afflicted with intolerable oppression of my superiors, or may a plague cause my death; after which may I be precipitated into hell, there to go through innumerable stages of torture, amongst which may I be condemned to carry water over the flaming regions in wicker baskets, to assuage the heat of *Than Tretonwan*, when

> he enters the infernal hell of justice, and thereafter may I fall into the lowest pit of hell; or if these miseries should not ensue, may I after death migrate into the body of a slave, and suffer all the pain and hardship attending the worst state of such a being, during the period measured by the sand of the sea; or may I animate the body of an animal or beast during five hundred generations, or be born a hermaphrodite five hundred times, or endure in the body of a deaf, dumb, blind, and houseless beggar every species of disease, during the same number of generations; and then may I be buried to narok (hell), and there be crucified by Phya Yam.[17]

And there was corporal punishment, or, in its newer terminology, torture, as a way of getting to the truth. Again, McDonald describes this fourth kind of test:

> They have also a way of extorting confessions from criminals, which is terribly severe. The first way is by the use of the lash or rattan. He first receives ninety stripes, and then, if he don't confess, he is allowed a respite of a few days and receives ninety more; and if he still holds out, he is allowed another respite, and receives ninety the third time. And one who can endure three times ninety without confessing is presumed to be innocent. They have also other modes, by putting split bamboos on their fingers, something like the thumbscrew of old. People often confess when they are innocent, from fear of the torture.[18]

Another truth-producing form, frequently remarked by foreign visitors, was trial by ordeal, by either fire or water.[19] One scene of the tale *Khun Chang Khun Paen* depicts a trial by ordeal by water dunking. The depiction is faithful to the procedures as laid out in *Three Seals*. But beyond that, we get a more familiar sense of how criminal offenses might have been handled in Old Siam. The scene, set in the Ayutthayan period, begins with a royal page, Khun Chang, beseeching the king to punish his rival, Muen Wai, for insulting him and ordering his retainers to beat him. Most importantly, Khun Chang claims that Muen Wai at one point in the altercation had said to him, "I'm not even afraid of your master" (presumably referring to the king). The king summons Muen Wai and asks him, "Exactly who is the 'master' of this Chang that you claim you don't fear?" Muen Wai answers that he said no such thing, but adds that if he had, he should be executed. He admits that Khun Chang had insulted and slandered him in public and addressed him "improperly." Moreover, Muen Wai claims that as a child Khun Chang had attempted to murder him and left him for dead in the deep forest.[20] In the inquiry before the king, each claimed to be telling the truth and would place his life on it, while accusing the other of making up and inventing things, lies, evil deeds, slander, smearing of reputation, and falsehoods. The king asks for the testimony of suitable witnesses (members of the nobility), admonishing them to not "take sides" or "be biased." A nobleman, attesting to the fact that he was not "taking sides, lying, or playing tricks," gives his account of the events.

The king ponders the matter. "The important point," he thinks to himself, "is the improper reference. The plaintiff's allegation is serious. If true, it's punishable by death. If not true, the plaintiff is liable to the same punishment." The king wishes he could use the handy truth-producing form of beating the truth out of the two of them. If only he could order the court "to use the stick, we'd sort truth from falsehood in no time." But Muen Wai's position forbids the king from using this method, as it may incur the displeasure of the people. The king asks the timeless question of "who'll know what's true and what's false?" The king tells Khun Chang, "If I went by the book, your head would be cut off" for lying "about the improper comment without fear" and for having "wrongly defamed" Muen Wai. The only way the king "can escape criticism" is to arrange for a trial by water. The king gives the order:

> Have the posts set up in front of the Royal Quay. Have both of them enter confinement tomorrow for seven nights until the day of the ordeal. Keep them under guard, and have them ready by one o'clock in the afternoon. Officials from every department will come to watch. *Phra* Khru, issue the summonses. Detain the two of them in the palace.

Upon hearing the order of the king,

> [officials] came out and sat in the main guardhouse to prepare and distribute the summonses. They sent for the posts belonging to the Department of the Capital, and had the prison warders store two of them. They defined the zone, created the court, had clerks write out the charges and testimony, and found judges to serve as neutral observers. "Do not let any food be sent from their homes. The court officers will provide the food for both of them. Get both the plaintiff and defendant to provide some thin white cloth to spread in the court for placing offerings, betel and pan in a well-made leaf tray, along with incense, candles, flowers, baisi, kaffir lime, soap nut, krajae, and sandal, all to be offered to Krung Phali. Have them wear upper and lower cloths in white. Lay out carpets and mats. Arrange the sacred thread. Place a bowl of rice, bowl of curry, water pitcher, spittoon, and water bowl under a shade, along with a flask of liquor, rice, a new wood stove, galangal, lemongrass, onion, garlic, dry chili, mortar and pestle, ladle, and chicken *phanaeng*. Arrange the same things at each place."[21]

On the day of the ordeal, the two litigants are taken to the river. Khun Chang ought to have been put upstream, as he was the plaintiff, but the judges decided that since Muen Wai was a noble, Khun Chang should be put in downstream from him. Their heads are pushed down, but Khun Chang shoots right back up, claiming,

> This fellow *Phra* Wai has knowledge. He blew something onto me. The power of the mantra gripped my heart unbearably, and my hair stood on end. Giving the defendant the upstream side allowed him to blow a mantra down to affect me.

After cursing Khun Chang as a "loudmouth" and wishing that he could "thrash . . . to dust" such a "great liar and tongue twister," the king has the trial done again, this time with Muen Wai downstream. Because one of the two litigants "was in the wrong," "he imagined snakes were twining round his body" and Khun Chang "shot above the surface shaking with fear." The truth had finally come out.[22]

In this account, the only "evidence" presented was conflicting accounts of things that had been said. The king quite competently challenges each litigant. But in the end he commands "neutral observers" to make sure the right procedures are followed as the litigants engage in a "test of strength." One of the two emerges victorious, strengthened by the truth. There were milder versions of trial by ordeal, especially in civil matters, such as disputes over loans. Litigants could race in a swim across the river or sit facing each other until one party's anger so overwhelmed him that he verbally attacks the other (thus proving guilt). The litigants could also have two candles of equal length prepared. The two candles were then lit at the same time. If a fly put out one of the candles or one went out on its own, then the case was lost, as the truth would then be known.[23]

A final point about traditional court procedure concerns "evidence." Present Thai usage of *lakthan* (or *phayan lakthan*—พยานหลักฐาน) is "that which is used to prove correctness or the truth."[24] At the time of compiling *Three Seals*, the modern term, *lakthan*, was not yet in use, at least as "evidence." Instead, "evidence" was primarily the account of witnesses (*saki phayan*, or *phayan*). An entire chapter of *Three Seals* with 67 provisions is dedicated to instructions concerning witnesses. One section discusses the oath that witnesses should take, specifying if they lie, let them "become crippled, deaf, and dumb," be "eaten by tigers if in the forest," struck by lightning, or have blood pour from their nose and mouth until dead.[25] Provision 24 instructs officials how to detect and resolve issues of falsified signatures or how to deal with hearsay evidence.[26] Another specifies, for example, that a husband cannot testify in disputes between his major and lesser wives.[27] One part instructs judges to consider the six characteristics of a witness in establishing basic credibility, such as if they have a domicile, many children, are of a just and virtuous character, and are revered by people in general.[28] It also defines a class of persons who cannot serve as witnesses, depending on their relationship to the litigants or their occupation. For example, retainers, relatives, friends, or those seeking revenge on one of the parties cannot be witnesses in the first instance; beggars, prostitutes, transsexuals, widows and widowers, fishers, or shoemakers in the second.[29] All the provisions relate to people and not to any other form of evidence. In other words, truth, if it was to come out, emerges from testimonies of witnesses.[30]

Truth and ritual purification in Thai Theravada Buddhism

Most ancient traditions were (and continue to be) part of what Max Weber defined as a "narrow tradition of knowledge." "Narrow" here means that the essentially single path to "knowledge" has limited accessibility. Truth can be accessed "only through prescribed methods of religious endeavour, by religious virtuosity."[31] Three key concepts of this "narrow" tradition of Theravada Buddhism are germane to this study: the nature of *truth*, the nature of *words*, and the nature of *intention*. All three—truth, words, intentions—form the heart of defamation-based crimes; therefore it is necessary to understand traditional views of these qualities and any transformation or reconfigurations that may have happened to them in modern Thai history.[32]

To appreciate the full impact of these changes, we need to review how the narrow tradition of Buddhist knowledge understood truth. Christine Gray describes the core of this cluster of beliefs:

> Theravada societies are organized around a single fundamental assumption and epistemological model: that the *dhamma* is primarily a hidden or immanent phenomenon that must be carefully "searched for" or "illuminated" . . . [and] is open to a very few exceptional individuals in society—monks and kings, to men of pure minds.[33]

Dhamma is part of "an invisible moral hierarchy or order of 'true morality,' *barami* or virtue." It is "revealed (illuminated) only through constant searching and mental purification," that is made known to humans gradually, "according to their level of purity." Purity is primarily achieved by ritual purification, by knowledge of authentic Buddhist texts, through mastery over specific meditation techniques, but may also be attained through public acts of generosity and other acts of "giving" or "renouncing."

Everyone is born into a particular karmic state that reflects in some way the accumulations of merit from previous lifetimes. Those in higher positions in society can credit their station in life to their success in accumulating merit in past lives. It is in higher positions that one is more likely to be able to dedicate oneself to seeking the *dhamma*. People "entangled" in day-to-day living are unable to cultivate the penetrating insight to "see *dhamma*" and at best may have fleeting glimpses of the *dhamma* through merit-making. Merit-making is an act of giving and relinquishing; the more that is given, the more merit, and accordingly, purity, is achieved. There is a clear connection between purity, the ability to see the truth, and merit-making. Impure persons cannot perceive the truth and the way to become purified is through merit-making or through nearness to sacred persons or objects.

Knowledge of the *dhamma* allows one to understand "all domains of social life." Trained in Pali, the "language of truth," a religious virtuoso gains "the right to interpret and "pronounce" *the* truth. With sufficient ritual purification, the religious virtuoso, with "penetrating insight," gains the "ability . . . to interpret the 'true meaning' or moral significance of activities" within all of society. With knowledge of the *dhamma*, the religious virtuoso is granted "credibility or veracity" in what he or she says.

There exists a rather radical division between visible and invisible worlds and between the kinds of people who can fully understand and act morally within the latter. On the one hand, in the "moral-celestial hierarchy" people are so "'entangled' in worldly affairs" that they are "unable to accurately foresee the consequences of their actions."[34] Such persons are the "hot-hearted" who exhibit the following qualities: They have unstill hearts, meaning they are "highly reactive" and cling to "sensory stimuli." They fear "demons, tigers, and other wild beasts." They are gullible and are "easily enticed by 'deceptive words' and by *apparently* virtuous or attractive phenomenon" [original emphasis]. They are unable to discriminate the moral qualities of others and "easily tricked by men who have an apparently pure exterior but an impure interior, i.e. evil minds or intentions." They lack virtue that draws others "to emulate their example." They are unable to communicate with beings of other realms, and cannot converse with angels or wild beasts, which they fear. Unable to speak Pali, they lack authentic understanding of the teachings of the Buddha which must be explained to them. They are distant from truth and are given to gossip and rumor mongering that result in chaos. They are incapable of "cultivating the penetration insight and wisdom necessary" to see the truth.[35]

On the other hand, there are "Cool-Hearted Men." At the top of the hierarchy, these "men of merit . . . have controlled their desires and are detached from the flow of day-to-day existence." Their "cool" and "peaceful hearts" do not react to the stimuli surrounding them. They possess a "pure mind which gives them the penetrating insight or wisdom that is necessary to perceive the causal roots of events." Their credibility allows them to "naturally command the obedience of others" without force. They fear nothing and have "strong hearts." They are in possession of "first-hand access to the 'truth' of the Buddhist teachings" through their knowledge of Pali and the royal language. They are separate from the "social process" which they can then "interpret . . . in a detached and accurate manner." They are "the most silent" and the mere sight of them and their great virtue can "create moral transformations" in men of lesser purity. They are in possession of "extraordinary powers of communication" that allow them to converse with "angels and tigers."[36] When speaking with lesser beings, they do so "at the precise level of understanding" of such beings. Their virtue is so great that they can say "but one word" and listeners understand them instantly. They are able to "read the hearts and minds of lesser beings, thereby are able to predict the *kammic* outcome of their actions."[37] Their opinions are unbiased. They do not take sides. They are *neutral*.[38]

There is also a third type—evil-doers—whose role in such a schema is clear. Evil-doers, those with malicious intent, may appear to be persons of virtue. They may have the knowledge and even some of the insight of meritorious persons. Ordinary hot-hearted people may be good but also easily confused and gullible. They cannot recognize the truth on their own. Evil-doers may recognize the truth, but intentionally distort and subvert the truth to satisfy their selfish desires. Using terms from the section of *Khun Chang Khun Paen* cited above, evil-doers twist the truth. They lie, invent and make things up, play tricks, and spread falsehoods. They smear the good name of others, defame, and slander.[39]

Of course, Buddhism allows for an infinite degree of impurity and insight between the most evil cur and the wisest religious virtuoso. What separates these two types of human is a graduated path to the truth. Only an "elite minority" can recognize *dhamma* as its hidden qualities are indiscernible to lesser beings. *Dhamma* is the exclusive preserve of those of pure minds."[40]

The cosmology underlying this notion of *the* truth is one where those of little merit are either evil-minded people set on creating chaos, or simple-minded people who cannot discern the truth for themselves and so are easily tricked by evil-doers. Religious virtuosi—monks and kings—are necessary to read the signs, to see the truth, and to interpret these for lesser beings. Kings are necessary to conduct a "constant purification of ritual" for order to be maintained, as "destruction of the ritual order connotes chaos." Able to understand "the nature and hidden structure of social events," kings can then "interpret social events and prescribe proper social practices." To avoid chaos, society must be hierarchically arranged, with renunciates and masters of meditation, those closest to the *dhamma*, at the top. Those who seek "material rewards" are too attached to "worldly things" and so are not credible. They are inflicted with "moral blindness" that makes them unable "to interpret social events."[41]

Monks, through renunciation and mastery of meditation, may approach sainthood and high levels of purity of mind. But kings, with power over the world within their grasp, have much to renounce, much more to sacrifice, and so the renunciation and sacrifice of the virtuous king, or *dhammaraja* "give rise to superior wisdom and insight . . . which enable him to 'see' *dhamma* . . . and interpret it for his subjects."[42]

Control over the right to interpret *dhamma* in traditional Theravada Buddhist societies establishes an "epistemological domination" within the realm that "enables the ruling elite to dominate men's perceptions of the world and their perception of *change*." The power of interpretation is given to "men of extraordinary virtue." They "can perceive the causal roots of an event instantly" and "judge the purity of heart" of others. They can "see into otherwise hidden hearts and minds of lesser beings" and they can read "signs of all sorts—words, acts, and events"—more deeply and "morally decode them." Only they can "determine the 'true' or full meaning of events" which also "entails a reading of the 'true' or complete intentions of men." A virtuous Buddhist king, in particular,

> is believed able to read the "hearts and minds" of men to a greater degree than ordinary men, and Buddhist saints, "mind readers," to an extraordinary degree. The king's great mental purity also endows him with the wisdom necessary to make authoritative pronouncements on the proper duties or codes of conduct of the nation's citizens, and the absence of a king-interpreter spells chaos.[43]

Words have both "material dimension and an invisible *karmic* dimension." The material dimension of words and their apparent and "true" meaning change through time. Their karmic dimension becomes manifest as they are part of *samsara*, or karmic process. As part of "the tangle of social existence," "talk" becomes part of the karmic cycle of cause and consequence, action and reaction. Because of the deceptive appearance of words and their tendency to become part of the karmic cycle, words and talk rarely bring out their true meanings. There is a "moral-semiotic 'depth'" of words in their "immanent or invisible meanings." The "true" meaning of words can be reached only by deconstructing them and, by so doing, understanding their "karmic causes and consequences."[44]

Since words (and actions) are an untrustworthy guide to the truth, their true meanings can only be ascertained by examining the person who used them. Since "mind" is the center of "Theravada belief about the cosmos," the true karmic effect can only be understood by ascertaining the "intent" of the mind or heart of the person who spoke or wrote.[45] Properly executed "perfect" or "complete" actions are "pure" actions that create "auspicious results." And pure actions are the result of "pure intentions."[46] As a result, "the morality" of acts involving words is "interpreted less as *an inherent quality*" of those words or the act of using them "than it is a function of the intention and religious practice" of such a person. It is "intention" that is "the most important determinative of *the karmic* outcome of an event."[47]

The results of this cosmological formation are a focus on form and a pronounced aversion to rationalistic or intellectual enquiry. Peter Jackson has argued that up through the nineteenth century the Siamese/Thai focus of Theravada Buddhism had been on "correct practice" (orthopraxy), rather than doctrinal truth (orthodoxy).[48] Jackson explains that, since the great doctrinal debates of Buddhism happened long ago, the emphasis of modern Theravada Buddhism has been "to maintain and faithfully reproduce the already laid down forms of practice and teaching, and preservation of the already fixed doctrines."[49] Thus, the reality of things is made accessible by "insight," which "is not of a rational character and cannot be arrived at by any logical analysis." The Buddhist categories of "thought conceptions" and "discursive thinking" are held as "lower meditative states" and cannot take practitioners to "the higher states" which "give way to suprarational wisdom." As a result, "reason alone" and "intellectual speculation" are not valued within the Theravada Buddhist tradition.[50] "Unrestrained rational enquiry," argues Jackson, was looked upon by the Buddha as bereft of any "spiritual benefit." The lack of "extrarational constraints" has "limited the development of an intellectual environment."[51]

In practical terms, the "knowledge" within this narrow tradition was expressed in the form of law codes and manuals which at first were jealously guarded by the elite. Most written texts, especially those of statecraft and religion, had a sacred quality to them. King Rama I had only three copies of the *Three Seals* made; one copy was given to the top judge, one the king kept near his bed, and the third was locked up in the royal library. The king might have wanted his dominions to follow the *Three Seals*, but part of its power was its limited accessibility.[52] Ironically, a foreigner and Thai nobleman printed the first copies of the *Three Seals* during the reign of Rama III (1824–51), thus making these laws available to local courts. Rama III, however, reconsidered, fearful that the profane act of printing would strip the laws of their sacred quality. He instead had the copies collected and burnt. Only in 1863 did King Mongkut (Rama IV) allow the *Three Seals* to be printed; over the next 33 years it went through ten printings. The printing press, Loos argues, made *Three Seals* "no longer a source of legitimacy and sacred power that had to be secluded." The printing of *Three Seals* "transformed" sacred scriptures "into a source of applicable and practical law." Loos points out by its final printing in 1896, the *Three Seals* was effectively replaced by a whole new legal and judicial framework.[53]

Related to the issues of printing and religious knowledge is Craig Reynolds's remarkable essay on Thai intellectual history, "Thai Manual Knowledge." Reynolds describes the forms of knowledge in premodern Siam and adds greater depth to the currently fashionable concept of local knowledge. Common to many Southeast Asian societies, a tradition of "manual knowledge" had been one of the primary ways by which knowledge and culture were transmitted. The Thai *tamra* combined both the sense of knowledge (*sastra*) and text (*tamra*) which one Thai commentator translated best as "authoritative text."[54] Primarily, though not exclusively, an aid for the elite, Reynolds describes the wide variety of knowledge captured within the *tamra* tradition. For elite, these manuals provided "knowledge that had to do with acquiring and exercising power, with waging war, with managing the constantly shifting balance of allies and enemies, with the art and science of governing."[55] Power was augmented through expertise in this kind of knowledge:

> Knowledge of spells, incantations, and the manipulation of cabalistic signs was a secret knowledge and jealously guarded lest it fall into the hands of rivals or enemies. Practitioners—teachers, astrologers,

> magicians—knew certain tricks to make their spells, incantations, forecasts, or prescriptions more effective than those of their rivals . . . some kinds of manual knowledge held a sacred, almost a magical, value.[56]

These texts were "arcane, even baffling to the uninitiated: verbal formulas; numerical tables and diagrams; cabalistic signs, calendrical charts; figures of lotuses; relic monuments, and other graphics filled with numbers."[57] Likewise, "the Theravada Buddhist canon, the *Tripitaka*, is the paragon of the manual format." Understanding the *Tripitaka*, though, depended on a "monastic or lay religious specialist" who could provide "exegeses of the Buddhist canon." The knowledge in religious manuals was so esoteric it could "be translated into useful forms" only with the aid of "a Buddhist authority—the monk, the guru, the teacher."[58]

The worldview described above has had immense consequences on how Thai society understands *the* truth. First, there is an implicit intolerance hidden in this view of reality. There need not be any debate over the dimensions or essence of truth or reality—the Buddha has already described it and followers work toward realizing that reality. Under this framework, the Christian "reality" is simply wrong, or only begins to touch upon the greater reality described by the Buddha. As issues of faith cloud their understanding, Christian methods are no doubt ineffective in approaching the true reality. Second, this view of *the* truth leads inevitably to a certain kind of educational approach and to the "authoritative text," which forms the basis of religious manual knowledge. Within Buddhism, in its "most popular" form, the basic primer is the *Vinaya*, the manual of monastic discipline which dates back to at least 1899.[59] The *Vinaya* is part of an expanded book by the Supreme Patriarch titled *Navakovda*: *Instructions for Newly-Ordained Bhikkus and Samaneras*. In the 1899 Preface, the author claims that the book presents a "method of teaching" and a "method of training:"

> The pupils should define and memorize all the clauses throughout this book . . . reading them through just once will not be enough to memorize them, so it will be necessary to repeat them over and over again in the same way as a chant . . . Those who are endowed with *sati* [consciousness] and *panna* [wisdom], and who make a great effort, can finish within the time limit while those who are moderately so endowed will finish at the end of the time limit. Those who are dull will not finish.

The Supreme Patriarch considers that, following memorization, the best method is to ask hypothetical questions about monastic discipline and then read over and sometimes compare various rules to find the answer. The third level is to gain "a wider knowledge." When a question is asked "the answer to which cannot be found in this book," the following example is given:

> "If a bhikkhu [monk] hits a child, what fault does he commit?" This

> cannot be decided from the Vinaya given in this book because it only mentions hitting a bhikkhu, which is pacittiya [a kind of "sin"]. For this sort of thing it is necessary to search in the large books of the Discipline, and once having found it, it will be immediately retained in the memory.

The author then suggests that pupils be given the same "saying of the Buddha," about which, with "thought and imagination," they can write an essay "to see for themselves" the truth in the saying. The point of such exercises is not to rationally assess the "truth" of the teachings, but to go through a process under which one understands the deeper truth(s).

The book is really a compendium of lists—list of rules that monks must follow, lists of the characteristics of the good husband, lists of what constitutes meritorious acts, lists of people with whom you should not be friends. The lists are not arranged by theme, but by numerological-driven "groups." For instance, the Three Jewels of Buddhism (Lord Buddha, Dhamma, Sangha) are followed by three "Values of the Three Jewels," "The Three Ways in Which the Lord Buddha Taught," the three "Bad Ways of Behavior," the three "Proper Ways of Behavior," the three "Bad Roots," the three "Things Which Worldly People Establish," the three "Conditioned Things," and so on. The *Vinaya* contains not a single sentence of analysis or commentary.[60]

This form of manual knowledge passed through the age of absolutism and continues to flourish in the present. Jaophraya Phra Sadet (Pia Malakun), a Thai nobleman of the early twentieth century, composed *Characteristics of a Properly Behaved Person* which Reynolds terms, "A fundamental text of the national curriculum." Reynolds asserts that, from this volume, Thai people who had been in school in the 1930s to 1950s often "could still remember the ten principles . . . neatness; do not act indecently (includes table manners, how to dress); show respect; behavior should inspire affection; be dignified; deportment that is pleasing to the eye; be good-natured; do not think only of yourself; act honestly and be trustworthy; do not behave badly (i.e., stay away from alcohol, opium, hemp, gambling)." Reynolds argues that "it is not difficult to see this manual of behavior as having been partially determined by a centuries-old adherence to 'proper behavior' and no more or less class-based than the monastic code of discipline that was one of its precursors."[61] Reynolds ends by asking whether "knowledge formatted in manuals . . . encourages orthodoxy and authoritarianism." He admits that this manual-approach may have historically "discouraged knowledge-seeking activities." Manual Buddhism is merely one form. Derived from this assessment, Michael Connors describes the "democracy education" efforts carried out to no particular effect over the past seven and a half decades, as something of a "manual democracy."[62]

Can we make any preliminary conclusions about the effects of Thai Theravada Buddhist notions of truth on Thai society as a whole? In his work on the nineteenth century, Nidhi Eoseewong depicts it as "truth-beyond-truth" [*khwam jing nua jing* – ความจริงเหนือจริง], (Buddhist or religious truth) vs.

"real truth" [*khwam jing thae*—ความจริงแท้] (truth of science and experience), arguing that "perhaps because of the influence of Buddhism," social phenomena were "accorded little importance . . . on the grounds it was something impermanent, constantly in flux, and thus not worth knowing, unlike the more permanent and indeed external 'reality' of the *thamma* [dhamma]" or what Nidhi has called, "Truth-beyond-truth." "In old Siam," writes Nidhi, "knowledge had been characterized by perfection; the highest truths were seen as eternal because they were not temporally conditioned. Knowledge of perfect truth was the end goal of all study." The arrival of Western science "would shake the Thai thought-world to its foundations." "Truth-beyond-truth" gave way to "truth revealed by experience." Siamese intellectuals of the time like Thipakorawong were forced to dismiss works such as the *Traiphum* (*The Three Worlds*) and argue that many elements in traditional religious writing were not be understood literally, but "metaphorically" [*khwam priap*—ความเปรียบ].[63] A new emphasis on logic [attathibai—อรรถาธิบาย] found and resolved contradictory aspects of Buddhist teachings, and led to a "return to the original texts" or the "'real truth'" of a more "authentic" and "uncorrupted" Buddhism. Siamese intellectuals of the age dismissed the Jataka tales [stories of the Buddha's previous lives] as "texts of countless fables and legends" and fantastical Buddhist commentaries as "dirty, nasty trash."[64]

Almost axiomatically most scholars looking at Siamese history of the nineteenth century make sense of this conceptual shift as a "traditional" thought-world challenged by a "Western, scientific" one.[65] Vandergeest, for instance, was perhaps too hasty when he wrote that "The pre-national orientation of associating dharma with the power to create social order by moral causality was displaced by that of the cause-and-effect relationship implicit in the mechanical laws of natural science." As European law became associated with the *dhamma*, "Buddhist and Brahman moral codes from the pre-national era were rejected."[66] Other historians have suggested, however, that while scientific knowledge about the physical world (and technology) was widely accepted, certain Buddhist beliefs and conceptual frameworks were divided into a separate domain of knowledge and largely retained. Reynolds points out that an 1860s Thai-language publication, while discounting the *Traiphum*'s explanation of natural phenomena, nonetheless perpetuated "the fundamentals of Theravada Buddhism" as the former made a distinction between the "natural world and the moral or religious world." Among the Bangkok elite, Western science may have prompted a "reevaluation of Buddhist cosmography," but, at the same time, "man's position in the universal hierarchy of animate existence . . . remained the same."[67] Nidhi argues that although "the idea of relative knowledge would emerge distinctly in Thai thought," certain elements of "the old vision of knowledge as something perfect has not really lost its hold on Thai society."[68]

From these findings, the following provisional conclusions can be drawn. The Thai system of knowledge developed a rather clearly demarcated bifurcation of truth and knowledge and of concomitant practices and disciplines. On the one hand, scientific epistemologies and procedures were effortlessly adopted *en masse* for the physical world. Whatever there was of Buddhist "science" completely disappeared. No "Thai" or "Theravada Buddhist" science came into existence, nor did "Thai scientific truth." There was also a sharp discontinuity between the judicial practices of the nineteenth century and those employed afterward. There is nothing particularly "Thai" about judicial and legal forms used in 1900 Siam that distinguished it from other countries.

On the other hand, a particularistic "Thai religious truth" continued to govern understanding of social and political phenomena, as informed by premodern Thai Theravada Buddhist notions of reality, described above. Modern Thai Theravada Buddhist distrust of the apparent reality of events or of words as a trustworthy vehicle of truth so permeates Thai social and political discourse that obvious, observable, facts are obscured by a focus on motives and the moral quality of the source. I argue for a significant continuity from premodern times to the present in precisely those judicial practices and views bearing a strong relationship to issues of truth and intention—those involving defamation-based laws. In this domain, Thai Theravada Buddhist notions of human and social truth moved from premodern to modern times largely unscathed. It is precisely within this set of laws that a whole complex of truth is conveyed to society.

In the face of greater egalitarianism and widespread education, the "narrow" traditions of Christian "knowledge" were delivered a massive blow by the Reformation and the Enlightenment. Egalitarianism and education recognized universal and individual access to truth through rational consideration and not through the Catholic Church. The shock of egalitarianism and universal knowledge was even more dramatic to the great kingdoms overthrown by European colonialism. In one fell swoop, the claims to divinity (and thus to power) of non-European, premodern kings and the entire complex of religious beliefs supporting such claims became utterly discredited. In Siam's case, though, the Theravada Buddhist system underpinning absolute monarchy became affirmed as the Thai elite (and their foreign advisors) developed a system that both preserved Siamese independence and froze Siam/Thailand within a "narrow" knowledge tradition. This Thai Theravada Buddhist knowledge system fostered a decidedly anti-rational and anti-intellectual framework that enfeebled the public's ability to exercise reason as it skewed conceptions of social and political truth.[69]

Truth in a Thai Theravada Buddhist sense is hierarchical. Four results follow: First, truth is largely inaccessible to ordinary persons. Hot-hearted persons lack purity and so, even when they witness a social event, they are unable to understand its true meaning. What seems clear and obvious to them might later be shown to be but an ephemeral phenomenon whose real meaning is hidden to those of impure hearts.

Second, wealth is a sign of greater access to the truth. Since, according to traditional Theravada Buddhism, wealth, regardless of how it is attained, is considered morally neutral, the elite have increased opportunities to donate at a more efficacious rate, and thus, increase their purity, thus, in turn, leading its members to gain greater insight into the truth.[70] Elite who do not seek the dhamma through extensive study of Buddhist texts can take shortcuts to increase merit by donating to temples and performing other public acts of generosity. The elite thus become, literally, sole owners of the truth, while the less fortunate are largely cut off from the truth and left to their petty gossip and rumours. In other words, ordinary people not only do not have access to the truth, but they also lack the mechanism (wealth) to gain more merit and greater access to the truth.

Third, the apparent meaning of words and actions is often hidden. Interpretations of words and actions are secondary to understanding the intentions of the actors involved. Otherwise put, words and what they create concretely in the world are but transitory phenomena, ever subject to change.

And, finally, the true meaning of things can only be understood by knowing the intentions of actors. All phenomena have been reduced down to a single indictor: intention. The work of noted Buddhist scholar and monk, P. A. Payutto, who underscores the importance of intention within Thai Theravada Buddhist conceptions, argues that intention is the key determinant of *karma:*

> Essentially *kamma* is **intention**, which includes volition, will, choice and decision, or the energy which leads to action. Intention is that which instigates and directs all human actions. It is the agent or prompting force in all human creation and destruction, therefore it is the actual essence of *kamma* . . . [original emphasis] . . . Intention is thus the volitional or conscious choosing of objects of awareness by the mind. It is the factor which leads the mind to turn towards, or be repelled from, various objects of awareness or mental concerns, or to proceed in any particular direction. It is the guide, the manager or the governor of how the mind responds to stimuli. It is the force which organizes the movement of the mind, and ultimately it is that which determines the numerous states experienced by the mind . . . Intention is the agent which guides our relationships with other things, and is the deciding factor for the direction and style of those relationships. Whether a person will act under the influence of unskilful tendencies, in the form of greed, hatred and delusion, or skilful tendencies, is all entirely at the discretion of intention . . . Human thinking is guided by intention. Intention is what fashions the thinking process and, through that, external conditions. Our way of life, whether on the individual level or the level of societies, both small and large, is directed by intention and the thinking process. It would not be wrong to say that intention, being the essence of *kamma*, is what decides our fate as human beings.[71]

It is only religious virtuosi with pure hearts—monks and kings—who possess the penetrating insight and wisdom to be able to read the hearts of others, to see their intentions. The most "real" aspect of things, the volition or intent of humans, is perceivable only by a very few "cool-hearted" people residing at the top of the hierarchy. It is the religious virtuosi who can see the hidden truth of words and the karmic effects they will create. They do not have to debate other aspects of a given act; they have only to read the hearts of men to understand all.

I suggest that the Thai Theravada Buddhist view of truth served as the basic framework for the emerging official nationalism of the kingdom-state, with the same lists, didacticism, particularism (and, thus, intolerance), and quasi-rational appearance as before (Chapters 6, 11, 12).[72] As a start, I have developed a cosmological framework and will explain how this, when engaged in the concrete world, manifested itself. I suggest below that a drive for purity, placed within a social and political context, turned the acts of premodern rulers into various acts of ritual purification.

Historians have typically depicted King Mongkut (1851–68) and his son, Chulalongkorn (1868–1910), as "reformers" during a period that saw certain changes in Theravada Buddhism and the arrival of "Western science." Mongkut is renowned for his legal and religious "reform." He is credited with reforming the Buddhist Sangha by eliminating superstitious beliefs and practices and establishing a purer sect of Thai Buddhism, Thammayudh. Western scholarship has generally depicted Mongkut's "reforms" as purifying Siamese Buddhism of "Hindu elements" and thus a sign of the king's "rationality."[73] Later, in response to the threat of Western colonialism, Chulalongkorn embarked on massive bureaucratic reforms, "rationalizing" the system of administration.[74] Western scholarship implicitly and explicitly understands that these two monarchs employed "Western science" to drive their reforms.[75]

Dropping this construct and making some rather obvious observations provide a clearer and more nuanced explanation of the relationships between Western science, these reforms, Theravada Buddhist conceptions of power, and legitimacy. Siamese kings successfully created the impression of "modernizing" by developing a sort of dual system—one for foreigners and the forms of legitimacy they represented, and another for Siamese subjects.[76] This dual approach, Gray argues:

> manages to satisfy ideological demands of indigenous and Western audiences alike: what looks like rational or "enlightened" behavior from the Western perspective can look like the perfect and encompassing behavior of religious virtuoso from the Thai, or like the activities of a deity, momentarily descended to earth.[77]

A fitting example of this dual approach comes from the famous account of King Mongkut and the solar eclipse. Eager to show his mastery of astronomy, he invited foreigners to accompany him to witness the eclipse. Foreigners became convinced of his "scientific" nature. It is ironic that Mongkut was later christened "the Father of Thai Science" for the accuracy of his prediction of the eclipse.[78] But descriptions of the actual event indicate a number of dissonant elements. The king gave "gold of the purest quality" to all of the foreign colonial officials, naval officers, and scientists joining the expedition. As the eclipse occurred, "The King gave money away to the members of the royal family and the high and low-ranking officials who accompanied him on the trip. Every one received the royal gift of money." Most remarkable, though, was what happened at the beginning of the eclipse: "The music therefore started the fanfare, and the King took his bath of purification."[79] Such was not the action of a modern astronomer and may have seemed inexplicable and surprising to the foreigners in attendance. But for his subjects, his astronomical skills proved he was a pure *dhammaraja* and his bath spread his meritoriousness over the kingdom.[80]

Westerners depicted the "fundamental differences and disharmonies" between the Theravada Buddhist cultural system and that of the West in a negative light and used those differences "as a pretext for domination." However, the Western-educated Bangkok elite appropriated this model of "cultural domination" and "internalized these pretexts in their own struggles for power, radically changing religion, economy, and the dynamics of legitimation in the process."[81] During the reigns of kings Mongkut and Chulalongkorn the "dual" model was developed and perfected—one for internal consumption with a truth based on "purity" as conceptualized through traditional Theravada Buddhism and one for external consumption which seemed to correspond to modern concepts such as capitalism, development, politics, and so on.[82]

Gray has noted that acts interpreted by Westerners in one way could also be understood in an alternative manner. Underlying many of Mongkut's actions was a Theravada-Buddhist-inspired drive for purity. Mongkut became a "cosmocrator" who introduced whatever practices deemed necessary to maintain the congruence between the social and the cosmic orders. For instance, he exercised his royal prerogative of "naming and renaming social practice—making (and remaking) 'the great classifications of social life'."[83] He underwent continual acts of purification himself and, in turn, he purified the realm.[84] In a similar way, King Chulalongkorn's "bureaucratic reforms" were, essentially, a "purification of the bureaucracy." While employing terms that pleased Westerners—"practical function," "efficiency," "practical utility," and "accurate budgets," Chulalongkorn actually elevated "the bureaucracy to the level of a Buddhist virtue or principle of purification." King Chulalongkorn "did not merely reform the bureaucracy, as his economic base expanded, he purified the *entire polity* as befits a Dhammaraja: the legal system, the ritual system, the temple system—activities which, taken as a whole, indexed his virtue as a Dhammaraja."[85] Concretely, these "bureaucratic reforms" increased the power and revenues of the monarchy immensely. With these new funds, he could engage in massive acts of "merit-making and monument-building" which, according to Gray, "were lavish to the extreme":

> The king purified the bureaucracy—clarified the "blurred" lines of administration—according to a new, more "modern" set of classificatory principles—those which promised order through the proper division of state into units with separate practical functions. This "purification" entailed the redistribution of the polity's resources . . . among a new consortium of elite—members of the royal family, the nobility, and powerful Chinese merchants.[86]

Deploying this framework of purification puts the premodern period of Siamese/Thai history in a new light, providing greater explanatory coherence for King Chulalongkorn's declaration of the Thammayuth movement as a separate sect in 1893, conferring royal titles on its leaders, as well as the Buddhist sangha "reform" act of 1902.[87] Employment of the framework of purification also allows us to posit a more consistent reasoning for administrative decisions[88] and for the work of another national Father, Prince Damrong Rajanuphap, the so-called Father of Thai History.[89]

Gray argues that many Western interpretations concerning these two reigns miss the point, as the reforms actually incorporated "Western symbols" into "Buddhist paradigms of purification." Gray maintains that Tambiah got close to the mark when noting that these reforms were not so much "modernizing" or "secularizing," but rather "reflect traditional purification patterns . . . that . . . enhanced [Mongkut's] soteriological claims."[90] Gray concludes that the actions of Mongkut and his successor were "historical movements and dynamics" best described as *buddhicization*, which she defines as "historical and cultural processes that position new beliefs and practices within an overarching Buddhist soteriological framework and which most often appear in the historical guise of 'purification,' a prerogative of kings."[91]

Describing this process as *buddhicization*, however, does not properly emphasize the primary impulse—*purification*.[92] Purification can be extended and deepened if we elevate it to the level of a state type and thus suggest that premodern Siam is best described as a *ritual purification state*: In its ideal formation, it is a kingdom/state whose primary purpose is to purify "itself" through a broad range of rituals—"it" connoting all government agencies and units, its "employees" (who are more like *adherents*) and, to a lesser degree, those the state "serves"—"the people."[93] These various government units in such a formation *may happen* to do what they are officially empowered to do, but almost as an afterthought, as the primary impulse is purification. State institutions are designed to purify; schools are not designed to educate.

We can recognize ritual purification in key moments of historical change, in major state-supported rituals and in the myriad day-to-day experiences of a country such as Thailand.[94] We will see various manifestations of the ritual purification state in this historical analysis, for it affects the legal basis of the Siamese/Thai kingdom-state (Chapters 5), it is specifically designed to create a sense of uniqueness (Chapter 11), and it generates a specific set of truths (Chapter 12). The ritual purification state is part of "the narrow tradition of knowledge;" its drive for purification creates both an internal hierarchy of purity (and access to truth) and a sharp separation between the roles taken by various social actors in the rites of purification.[95] In fact, this narrow tradition can only survive *because* of its exclusivity. The claims of absolute kings—especially before the advent of the printing press—of being universal kings would seem ridiculous were they made by modern kings. In the same way, the Thai ritual purification state could not survive—would not even make sense—outside of its narrow confines.[96]

A particular focus on intention and cosmological understanding of the nature of truth within a ritual purification state defined the Thai elites' world view just as foreign advisors filled the ranks of the Siamese bureaucracy. The question is: what ideological/legal baggage were these Westerners bringing with them?

Foreign influence in the service of the Siamese state

All historians of Thailand must somehow explain the significance of "Western influence" and how it affected Siam's transition to modernity. The tendency has often been to collapse "modernity" and "Western," "colonial" and "centralization," to see "Western" influence as a monolithic, ahistorical entity. In the process, we rarely get a good glimpse of the foreign advisors hired into the service of the Siamese state.[97] The most substantial and significant argument on the role of foreign advisors in Siam is advanced by Tamara Loos's *Subject Siam*. Foreign legal advisors served in the Siamese court in the 1850s through the 1930s (and in at least one case into the early 1960s). These advisers, Loos argues, "brought with them culturally specific concepts of justice, legal codes, and institutions that circulated throughout Siam, Europe, and colonized countries." Because of the power dynamics between the employer (the Siamese government) and the employee (the foreign adviser) due to the non-colonial status of Siam, Loos cautions that the impact of these advisers cannot be understood in "an exclusively national or dyadic colonial framework."[98]

Loos argues that these foreign advisors of the nineteenth and early twentieth centuries were part of a global elite during a time when "imperialism still operated hegemonically for most people." These advisors understood themselves as altruistically aiding Siam when in fact they were "participating in its subordination." They looked upon the Thai kings approvingly, "whom they described as benevolent and enlightened," and they shared the Siam elite's perception that the people in Siam were "passive, uneducated, and unprepared for democratic institutions." Loos concludes that examining the role of foreign advisers helps us better understand the complex interaction between colonialism and an indigenous elite engaged in a "global circulation of legal reform" and "qualify Siam's independence in subtle but profound ways."[99]

What are some of those ways?[100] Of all the foreign advisors, the "most important" was that of the general advisor, a post created in 1891. The general advisor "advised the monarch on legal matters regarding foreign relations as well as domestic reforms generally."[101] This advisor played a key role in codifying the criminal and civil codes.

There was a consensus among both foreign advisors and Siamese legal experts that it was crucial "to keep the codes culturally Siamese—that is, to incorporate Siamese law from [the *Three Seals*] to the extent that these laws suited Siam's changed circumstances."[102] Loos argues that most foreign advisers had little understanding of traditional Thai law, considerably slowing "the process of promulgating the civil codes."[103]

The criminal code was another matter. The framework for the criminal code came from a remarkable mélange of sources: the penal codes of Japan, France, Italy, Denmark, Hungary, Egypt, India, and others, as well as traditional Siamese criminal codes.[104] Loos mentions that the criminal code, drafted in English and then translated into Thai, "was adopted without a problem." But she also states that Prince Ratburi, King Chulalongkorn's son, found the translation of the code quite difficult, stating that: "The rhetoric is not very precise since the *farang* [Western] terms and Thai terms are not identical. Each has their own habits and disposition. To select accurately [a term] without excessive or incomplete meaning is, then, a supremely difficult task."[105] So difficult was the task that the prince created a "comparative edition" that shows, in Loos's view, that "the original Siam's modern laws required a Thai–Thai translation."[106][106] In the end, though, there was nothing particularly "Thai" about the criminal code.[107]

While still in his twenties, Prince Ratburi, was made the first effective head of the newly-established Ministry of Justice. With ten years abroad and a degree in law from Oxford, Prince Ratburi had a fine legal mind. He set up the first law school in 1897, where he taught for a decade. The sophistication of his legal writings shows that he was well versed in the trends of modern law in Europe as well as Thai traditional law.[108] The prince was perhaps too well trained: he learned the importance of an independent judiciary. Conflicts with his father over the issue ended with his resigning as Minister of Justice.[109]

But greater specificity is required: we must ask what intellectual and lawyerly baggage foreign advisors and the European-educated elite might have been bringing to Siam *at that time*. Foucault notes that a major shift in the factors and conditions surrounding penal law occurred in the late eighteenth and early nineteenth centuries. Legal theorists throughout Europe reached a common understanding about the meaning of crime. These theorists argued that crime, civil infractions, should be divorced from religion or morals and penal laws would "simply represent what is useful for society." "[A] clear and simple definition of the crime" should indicate that "it is something that harms society; it is a social injury, a trouble, a disturbance for the whole of society." Under these terms, the criminal becomes a "social enemy."[110] Through this redefinition, a revolutionary shift occurred, refocusing law from "the general defence of society [to] the control and psychological and moral reform of the attitudes and behaviour of individuals." Foucault writes that, between 1825 and the 1860s, "The direction of penal legislation was to veer away from what one might call the principle of social utility; it no longer focused on what was socially useful but, rather, targeted the individual." Rather than clearly defined penal laws and punishments recommended by theorists, a new space opened in which the individual became the focus of penal interest. The concept of "mitigating circumstances" allowed latitude for judges and juries to stipulate the rehabilitation regime for each individual on trial. By the end of the nineteenth century, criminology defined "danger" in terms of individuals. Rather than focusing on reparations needed to address a specific social injury, "danger" became a generalized state that looked at individuals' "potentialities" for criminality or to act against the state. The criminal was no longer defined as a representative of collective society; penology became the mechanism to control individuals. Foucault concludes, this transformation, in which the practice of inquiry was subsumed within "supervision and examination," gave birth to "the age of social control" and a "form of knowledge-power."

European-educated Thai elite and foreign legal advisers brought to Siam historically specific notions of criminality and dangerousness. In Europe, the focus on social control led to the creation of new institutions, such as the school, the asylum, the hospital. In Siam, Jackson writes, the "reforms" carried out under Chulalongkorn "mobilized an array of Siamese traditions into a coordinated phalanx of state power, transforming a field of cultural norms into a legally codified domain of surveillance, enforcement, and punishment."[111] However, the late-nineteenth-century contexts in Europe and Siam varied greatly. Possibly these notions of criminality and dangerousness did not lead to the building of new Siamese institutions, but blended into the growing discourse on political crimes and treason, marrying Western dangerousness and criminality with traditional Theravada Buddhist notions of treachery.

Siam entered the twentieth century with all the prerequisites necessary to establish a defamation regime. The pre-existing Thai Theravada Buddhist cosmology made moral virtue and intention the center of its truth-producing forms. Even in the face of modern science, this social and political hierarchy of truth was not supplanted; it was reinforced. Foreign advisors commended the efforts of the Bangkok elite to centralize the kingdom and christened as reforms the policies of this peculiar absolutist-colonial hybrid. The evolution of judicial forms in the West took centuries. The Thai state imposed a new judicial form in a few decades. By maintaining the kingdom-state's sacral center and by importing new scientific procedures in the service of absolutism, the Thai state achieved a remarkable feat: it combined the legitimation of the sacral absolutist system with the modern techniques and practices of science.

Whereas apologists for European absolutist, monarchical states reached a zenith in the seventeenth and eighteenth centuries, the Thai state created a twentieth-century version that gave defamation and treason laws an extra imprimatur of, essentially, blasphemy, a sort of Byzantine complexity of sacred rules, understandings, and procedures clothed in the parlance of modern law. Into this mix were tossed European notions of dangerousness and criminality.

Using a curious seventeenth-century English term, a hybrid of traditional art and modern science emerged what we might call *traitorology*.[112] Forged in the convergence of absolutism, sacredness, and colonialism, this branch of knowledge concerned itself with understanding the dimensions and nuances of treason, acts of betrayal, treachery, the "violation by a subject of his allegiance to his sovereign or to the state," or "any offence against the sovereign authority." *Traitorology*'s rules and procedures were made apparent through the use of a set of defamation-based laws and their adjudication, including, crucially, their medieval focus on intent and the moral state of the alleged perpetrator—creating a taxonomy of forms and manifestations of seditious expression.

In Europe, concern for danger and an impulse toward social control led to the development of a set of new sciences: sociology, criminology, psychology, and psychiatry. The Bangkok elite, however, generally eschewed these sciences and periodically outlawed their study. Instead, over the past century, Thai traitorology produced a remarkably vast body of theoretical literature that developed, by 1960 or so, into "a recognized department of learning," captured under the rubric of national security. The thrust of this branch of knowledge has been to meticulously observe, collect data, record patterns, analyze, and formulate public policy and laws designed to create and maintain particular understandings of "unity." The various bodies dedicated to this "science" are known well to the historian of Thailand and have received due attention: the various incarnations of the Ministry of Culture, the National Identity Board, and the National Security Council, all of which organize seminars and conferences and make vast and various contributions to the national education curriculum. While this discipline displays the trademarks of a modern science, combining aspects of sociology, criminology, linguistics, anthropology, the arts, and particularly history, its original impulse was, and persists today, centered on premodern knowledge concerned with treason.

These first three chapters have provided the foundation for the main body of the book. Chapter 1 followed the historical trajectory of defamation-based crimes and introduced the ideas of defamation regimes and discursive crimes.

Chapter 2 traced the development of truth-producing forms in the West and underscored their importance in the run-up to the emergence of defamation cases. This gradual evolution of judicial forms to discover truth was then counter-posed against the central thrust of defamation-based laws whose primary purpose was not to produce truth, but to protect reputations. We noted how study of the defamation law was particularly suited for understanding how societies communicate (or don't communicate) about politics, society, and culture. Since defamation involves an aspect of truth, we delved into the issue of how fact, opinion, and comment might be categorized and explained. Chapter 3 described various truth-producing forms still used in nineteenth-century Siam and noted that they did not appreciably differ from earlier forms of the West. The traditional Thai Theravada Buddhist notion of truth and reality, though, was shown to be quite different, especially in terms of perceived intentions of social actors. Intention, in turn, was related to accumulated merit which, in turn, provided varying levels of access to the truth. Combining Western notions of danger with the Thai Theravada Buddhist notion of truth and reality resulted in the birth of Siam as a defamation regime.

It is misleading to claim that something exceptional happened in Siam in 1900. Any number of the factors mentioned above were (and are) present in the historical record of other countries. Most defamation cases devolve, in one degree or another, to a question of intention; all non-"Western" countries were affected by "Western" influence in some way; all countries have certain continuities with their pasts; all countries have ways of dealing with truth. I adapt Benedict Anderson's framework from his reflections on power in Javanese culture by saying that "in their separate elements," nothing is particularly "unique" or "Thai" about these elements. Rather, I argue that these various factors, these premodern predilections, the historical contingencies surrounding them, did "in their totality[,] form a unique amalgam," that is "Thai."[113]

Part II

Genealogies of defamation and abnormal times

4 Chronology of Thai defamation-based laws

The Siamese government's altercation with M. Lillie (Chapter 1) no doubt provided the impetus for the passing of Siam's first "modern" defamation law, "The Royal Edict on defamation through falsely spoken or written words made known in the year 1900"[1] (hereafter referred to as "the 1900 edict"). The writing of this law was a significant effort on the part the Siamese state because it called for a "standardization of language and legal discourse." It was part and parcel of world-wide modernization, a movement of governments toward "simplification" and "legibility."[2] The edict itself was the result of a drastic simplification: in premodern Siam, there were the hundreds of ways to commit *lèse-majesté*, elaborated in tens of thousands of words (see earlier, p. 61). The comparable portion of the 1900 edict was a mere 71 words; the 1908 version 46 words. The 1900 edict spawned four separate lineages, as shown in Figures 4.1 through 4.7. In this chapter, I trace these different lines to the 2000s and explain in broad terms what changed in terms of legal wording, interpretations, punishments, and rationales. I also compare the inherent valuations granted by the state to persons and institutions: the prices, as it were, that the state levies for insults. What are the costs of a citizen's reputation? A government's? A monarchy's?

The impulse behind issuing the 1900 edict was a beginning, when the state woke to the legal consciousness of becoming a juristic "person," an entity that can describe what threatens it and justify its punishments. It was the start of a century-long process categorizing political crime, cataloguing cases, elaborating on its pain, silencing its opponents. In this sense, the 1900 edict represents the real birth of the Thai state. For the state, it was a case of "I feel insulted, therefore I am."

The 1900 edict

At the time of the edict's issue, the Siamese royal elite was beset by a specific set of pressures and alerted to certain opportunities. A peculiar mélange of forces created modern Siamese law—certain anti-colonial currents, certain internal colonial tendencies, a variety of Western legal advisors and traditional legal trappings—all in the context of the formation of an absolutist state (see Chapter 3). Members of the royalty had the very same year of the Lillie incident visited European capitals; Emperor Wilhelm II of the German Empire was visited in Berlin, whose government was in the midst of *lèse-majesté* epidemic, with an average of 500 cases per year.

Whatever the exact causes, the 1900 Siamese edict was drafted and made into law, presumably at the instigation of either Foreign Minister Prince Devavongse or Interior Minister Prince Damrong Rajanuphap with, perhaps, some of the foreign legal advisors.

The wording of the 1900 edict conceptually fell somewhere between the more archaic language of *Three Seals Law* (for instance, the titles of those protected) and the rather more typical modern language of the penal code (such as not starting with the "Whosoever dares to . . . "). The latter wording might indicate this set of laws was inspired more by traditional impulses than by modern jurisprudence.[3] Under the influence of Siam's foreign legal advisor, many criminal laws or edicts at the time were composed first in English and then reconstructed into Thai. The wording of the 1900 edict shares some similarities and some differences from the language used in the penal code issued less than a decade later. Nonetheless, it provides a glimpse into the mindset of the Bangkok royalty at the time.

The most obvious and important point is that the drafters placed all levels of defamation into a single provision, a single defamation package protecting people in various levels of society. Protected in the upper rung in Section 4 was "the reigning king of Siam or the major concubine, or the princes or princesses, or the kings, rulers, or presidents of foreign countries which share close, friendly relations with Siam" (Figures 4.6 and 4.7). The middle rung, Section 5, covered forsaking loyalty to the "present King, the King's ministers, or the government, or the royal customs of governance . . . or Ministers of the Royal Council, or the considerations and legal judgments of the courts and laws of Siam" (Figures 4.2, 4.3, 4.4). The bottom rung, Section 6, protected merely "persons" (Figure 4.1).

The infraction in Section 4 was defaming, using "intemperate words," and expressing something "truly defamatory." The infraction in Section 5 was sedition, a type of rebellion or treason (which I term "seditious rebellion"), rebellion with words, as distinct from the violent overthrow of the government (Figure 4.2). "To incite or encourage the people to forsake their loyalty," "to incite or promote the people to think of changing or altering the royal customs for the governance of Siam," and "to incite or promote the people to hate one another or create injury" were all expressly forbidden. Section 6 made illegal public expression intending "to defame another, or ridicule another person."

The three provisions of this edict protected the royal family, government officials and the governing system, and private citizens, respectively. Defamation laws are inherently status-sensitive: presumably, only people with some "standing" in society benefit from its protections. The range of such privileged persons in Siam at the time must have been rather small, numbering in

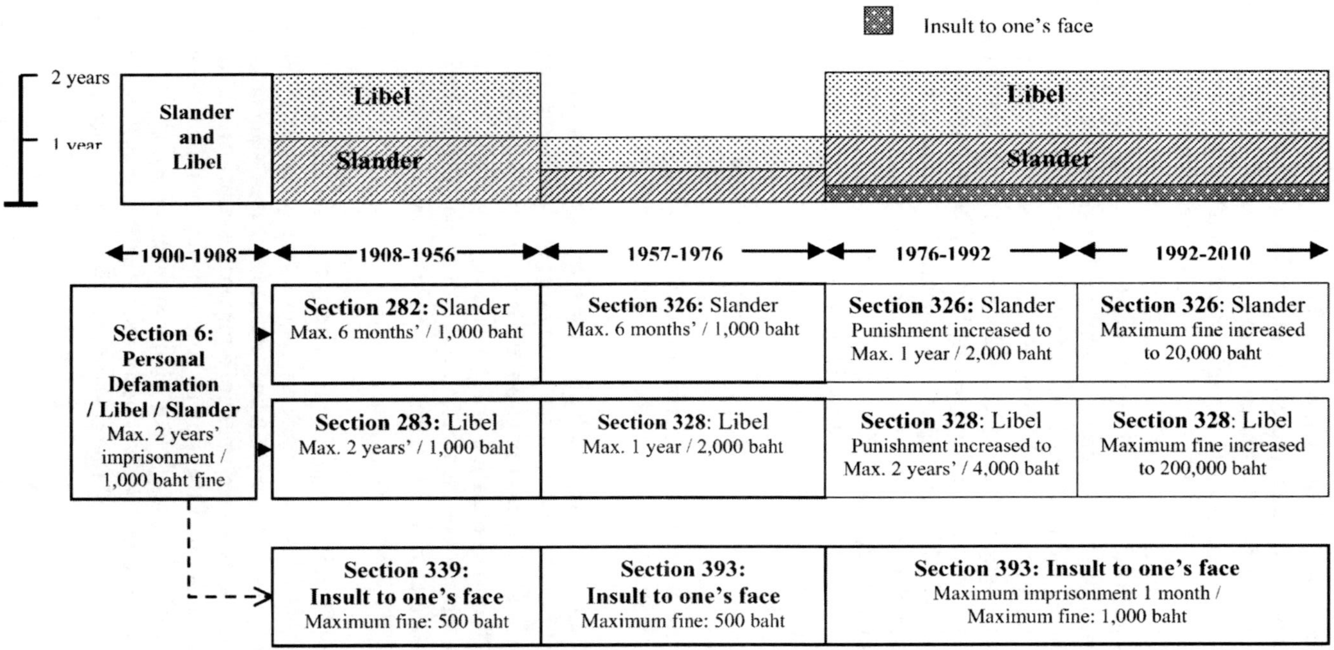

Figure 4.1 Chronology of punishment for defamation in Thailand, 1900–2010 (in maximum number of years' imprisonment and/or fine).

the thousands. The non-royal elite from within this group—principally the nobility—were among the first to feel the sting of lost privilege to the royalty under the absolutist state. Members of this group were certainly a target and they were given no greater protection under this law than the average citizen.[4] The growing number of educated (and generally low ranking) bureaucratic elite was a second target.[5] Those enterprising commoners who were formally or informally schooled and eager to make their views known through the new form of print media, such as Thianwan, became a third target group.[6] Pesky foreigners such as Lillie formed a fourth and final group. Only out of consideration of this last group might the Bangkok elite have hesitated in making the punishments any heavier than they were.

One of Siam's first legal primers, *Principles of Criminal Law* of 1904, discusses at length the principles of the 1900 edict. The author, Khunluang Phra Kraisi, a member of the elite who had studied in England and taught in Siam's country's first law school established by Prince Ratburi, begins by pointing out that, prior to the 1900 edict, "there was not really any law" covering specifically this kind of crime. The base principle underpinning this set of laws is the axiom, "The king is above the law. He cannot break the law." If the king is inviolable, the writer contends, we do not need to consider whether the king has acted legally or not. In the same way, royal servants (civil servants or *kharatchakan*), working under orders from the king, can also do no wrong.[7]

One of the most important types of rebellion, what I am calling "seditious rebellion," is the slandering of the king and government which, in law:

> must be taken quite broadly because it includes both actions and words, either through spoken words or any sort of written symbol which can be understood to be insulting to the *phra phu pen jao* [king-god] or government or the organization of the *banmuang* [country] to see the inciting of people not to have fear/be in awe of or to be discontented and without faithfulness or loyalty to, the king and the power of law or the organization of the *banmuang*.[8]

Khunluang Phra Kraisi admits that interpretation of this law "is rather slippery" and that "this type of law is different from other laws." "It is difficult," he confesses, "to draw a certain line" between what is "slanderous and what is not." Unlike the easy assessment of a physical assault against the government or king, defamation of the king or government can ultimately only be determined by looking at the intent of the speaker or writer. If the purported defamation were done "with honesty" and "without malicious intent," then it was merely criticism of the government. But one's sincerity, in this case, would be determined by posing the question: "Can the words [spoken or written] clearly be seen as encouraging the people to do wrong in any way and creating problems and a general resentment and dissatisfaction with the government or not?" Thus, posited somewhat vaguely, a specific government official could be criticized, if such criticism did not cause general discontent with the government. If general discontent came about, or if the criticism seemed to challenge the government system as a whole, then it was wrong. At the same time, criticism of an individual government official clearly carrying out the orders of the king was not allowed. Therefore, despite assurances that it was within the bounds of law to speak or write critically of the government, the possibility of any negative consequence of the words effectively prohibited any legal challenge to the government as an entity or officials in particular.[9]

In a rather coarse way, defamation measures give values to the reputations protected. We compare here not fines, but the most common shared aspect of life amongst humans—time—or maximum period of time an offender could be sentenced to jail. Under the 1900 edict, the reputation of the king, members of the royalty, heads of state of other countries, government ministers, the government, legal ways of changing the political system, the political system, and social unity were "worth" three years. The reputation of someone unfairly defamed (or "wronged" by a falsehood) was worth two years, and that of someone simply defamed (or, perhaps, "fairly defamed") was valued at one year. In other words, the reputation of the king or member of the royal family was a mere three times greater than the reputation of a wrongfully defamed person and 1.5 times greater than that of a defamed person (See Figures 4.1, 4.2, 4.4, 4.6, 4.7).

The gap in years of punishment between the king and a commoner was as narrow as it would ever be again. Figure 1.1 in Chapter 1 hints at why the Siamese government might have been so reasonable and measured in setting the punishments for this crime. Under this edict, this hybrid state was much more liberal than the premodern regime under the *Three Seals Law*, allowing, at least on paper, for expansion of the public sphere.

The 1908 criminal code and 1927 amendment

Eight years after issuing the 1900 edict, its three provisions flowered into eleven separate provisions in the first modern Thai criminal code and later became core sections in a slew of legal acts on the press, communism, the constitution, and the cinema. The first section of the 1900 edict evolved into seven provisions. Under "Outrages against the King and Kingdom" was Section 98: defamation of the king, queen, heir-apparent, and regent, Section 100: defamation of other members of the royal family, Section 113: defamation of the king, queen, or head of state of friendly foreign countries, and Section 115: defamation of flag or symbols of friendly foreign countries. Under "Offences against Governing" was Section 116: insult of officials. Under "Offences against Justice" was Section 151: contempt of the court. Under "Offences against Religion" was Section 172: defamation of religion (blasphemy) (See Figure 4.5). The second provision of the 1900 edict became Section 104: Internal Rebellion (seditious rebellion), which evolved further into various parts of Press Acts, the short-lived Constitution

Protection Act (1933–38), Bolshevik and Anti-Communist Acts (1927, 1933–46, 1952–2000), and less directly, the Cinema Act (See Figure 4.3). The third section of the 1900 edict, under "Offences against Freedom and Reputation" were Sections 282 (slander) and 284 (libel), and under misdemeanours, Section 339: defamation to one's face (insult) (Figure 4.1).

The 1908 code almost completely separated legal provisions concerning *lèse-majesté* from seditious rebellion (see a fuller version of the text in Appendices I and II). Sections 98 and 100 punish anyone who "displays malice or defames the King, the Queen Consort, the Heir-apparent, or Regent" or "the princes or princesses from whichever reign."[10]

How central and unique were these defamation-based laws? The author of the most recognized commentary on the 1908 criminal code, *Explanation of Criminal Law*, Ammatho Phra-inthapricha (Yian Lekhawanit) notes that all of the laws concerning defamation in the 1908 code in fact employ variants of the same Thai term, *min pramat* (หมิ่นประมาท). Although they all use the same term—combining the action of false defamation with insult—he warns that each law has its own "important principles and conditions." Section 282 on personal defamation, he said, provides the overall model for all the other laws concerning defamation.[11]

Unchecked defamation threatens peace and order of society. The seriousness of defamation, and the necessity of laws prohibiting it, provoked dire warnings from the author, who described defamation as an:

> unfair method that punishes that person, causing that person pain, bruising them in the same way as if doing violation to his body. The law does not allow anyone to punish anyone else, of any position or status, to their own satisfaction, as it is a path to revenge through force. It would cause disturbances in the country if the government does not try to solve matters such as these, even when it is believed to be a trifling, insignificant case. [Otherwise] this would bring serious events to come to pass.[12]

Incomparably more serious was *lèse-majesté* (*min phraboromdechanuphap*—หมิ่นพระบรมเดชานุภาพ). Ammatho quotes the Latin phrase, *"Crimen laesae majestatis omnia alia crimina excedit quoad poenum"* [The crime of *lèse majesté* is greater than all other crimes], considering it as any harm done to the king, whether physically or through words. Little legal distinction for either *lèse-majesté* or seditious rebellion was drawn between the actual commission of an act and merely attempting or planning such an act. Nor was it necessary to classify violators in terms of the ringleader, abettors, and so forth, "because it is the most serious crime." He quotes a Latin legal saying: "In matters of rebellion, there are no abettors, there are only principals." The principle of defamation became "considerably widened" in the case of the king "because it combines parts on slander and malicious gossip with the intention of injuring the honour of the king." Its components were "insult" or "words or actions which bring shame to another party, or cause them to lose their reputation or honour," "malicious gossip" which was "criticism that may bring damage to the good name or honour of another," and slander according to the general provision on defamation.[13]

Section 104 made clear that seditious rebellion was a public act (Figure 4.2). The law explicitly protected a new set of "damaged parties" from "disloyalty" or "insult": the concrete person of "the king," as well as the "government" and "the country." In three clauses, implicitly protected were peace and order, satisfaction of subjects, and royal laws. Now these entities were protected not just from defamation, but also from "insult" (*du min*—ดูหมิ่น). The new law provided greater abstraction both in terms of what constituted an illegal action and a target, and the wording placed emphasis on the effects of the words: "unrest" and "dissatisfaction" became illegal when they "cause[d] disturbances" (see Appendix II).

The seriousness of the damage caused was valued in terms of the length of the jail sentence. In terms of maximum time spent in jail, the reputations of the king and his immediate family were worth seven years, compared to three years for other members of the royalty, or the king, government, or country, respectively, two years for the reputation of a person untruthfully libeled, one year for a person libeled (even if the allegation was true), and six months for one slandered. On this scale, in terms of the value of reputations, the king's reputation became more than twice the value of the government or country and other members of the royalty. I might argue that this valuation represents an expression of absolute monarchy, in which the monarch had the premier position. As the subject of slander, the maximum difference between the worth of the reputations of the king and commoner was 14:1, 7:1 for the reputation of a person wrongfully libeled, and 3.5:1 for the reputation of one truthfully libeled, all significantly higher than the 3:1 and 1.5:1 ratios, respectfully, found in the 1900 edict.

In 1927, Thai legal history experienced a watershed, giving rise to three distinct lineages of defamation-based laws—seditious rebellion, sedition, and anti-communism (Figure 4.3). Two foreign advisors to the Ministry of Justice, the Frenchman René Guyon and the American Raymond Stevens were appointed to head the "Committee on the Prevention of Communism, Bolshevism and Other Dangerous Propaganda."[14] The committee recommended revision of Section 104 of the 1908 criminal code to afford "His Majesty's Government some power of control over revolutionary propaganda." Choosing not to specify by name "the dangerous doctrine and movements"—"communism" or "Bolshevism"—the committee laid out "the particular principles or qualities which have rendered such movements dangerous to the public security." Beyond advocating "the use of force and violence," communism "invariably attempts to arouse hatred and hostility to the Government, to stir up disloyalty and disaffection amongst the people, to arouse class hatred and to foment strikes and economic dissatisfaction." But the committee wanted the law phrased to have broader application so it "would apply to any political movement or theory which involves a menace to public

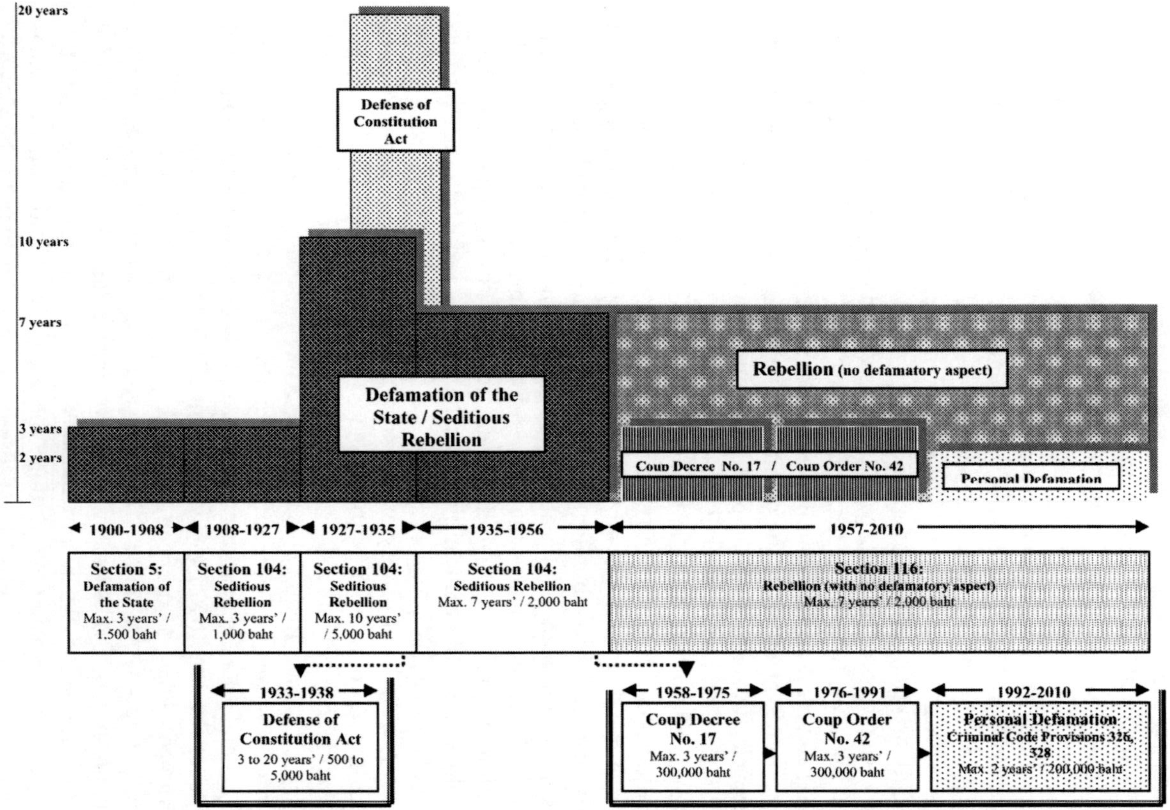

Figure 4.2 Chronology of punishment for seditious rebellion and acts against the constitution in Thailand, 1900–2010 (in maximum number of years' imprisonment).

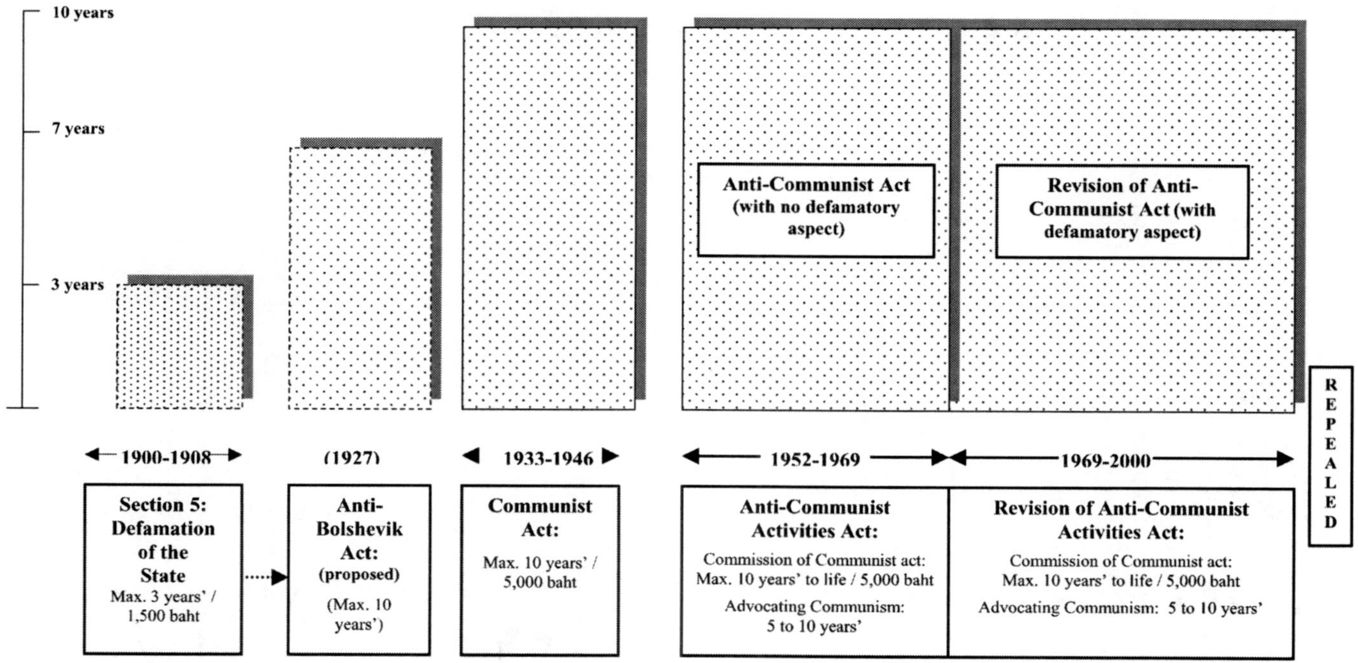

Figure 4.3 Chronology of punishment for communism in Thailand, 1927–2010 (in maximum number of years' imprisonment).

order." The committee felt that, unique to Siam, one of those menaces was public discussion about the form of the government:

> There is another danger in Siam, to wit: unwise and premature agitation for changes in the form of government. In the process of time there may be a general desire for some form of popular participation in government or some restraint upon the power of the Sovereign . . . There is danger accordingly that agitation of a political nature would lead to unrest and possibly premature attempts to secure some changes in the constitution of the country. This question presents real difficulties.

The report noted that the committee had also considered a "prohibition against public discussion of any changes in the government," but chose against such a "sweeping prohibition." Instead, it advised prohibiting "any arguments or methods which really advocate or incite to violence or which are intended to arouse hatred against the King or the Government or to stir up disaffection and class hatred." This distinction, the committee felt, would allow the government to "prevent and control" revolutionary agitation while granting "the freedom of opinion and freedom of discussion." History proves:

> that the attempt to prevent unrest among the people by sweeping prohibitions against any kind of public discussion of political principles not only fails but actually increases the danger. It would fan rather than allay any feeling of unrest. It would give the impression to the Siamese people and the world at large that the Government of Siam was very reactionary and would not even permit discussion of the principles of government or the possibility of any change . . . It would not, in fact, prevent discussion and unrest but would stimulate it.[15]

The draft laws proposed by the committee would afford the government the right to suppress actions or words not made "in good faith" and which "intended to stir up ill-will against the Sovereign and to arouse disaffection that may lead to disorder [*khwam mai sa-ngop*—ความไม่สงบ] (Chapter 5). Given the principles outlined above, the committee felt that the proposed law would not only be able to "prevent the spread of communism," but also prevent the "discussion or advocacy of any political theory" which is "intended to produce disorder and upset the security of the Government and the institutions of the country." Implicit for these lawmakers was that the law indirectly prohibited expression of republican sentiment (Chapter 8).

Retaining these three clauses of the 1908 version of Section 104 (see Appendix II), the committee sought "to broaden" the law to "cover every phase of dangerous revolutionary movements," by proposing rewriting the introductory phrase from merely: "Whoever appears before the people in whatever fashion, with intention for whatever results," to "Whoever commits any act, or whoever by words or writings or printed documents or by any means whatever, advocates or teaches any political or economic doctrine or system, intended or calculated [to]." The committee suggested replacing the following "create disloyalty or to insult the king, the government, or the country" with "bring into hatred or contempt the Sovereign, the Government or the administration of the State." The committee also advised adding two following clauses: "to bring about a change in the Government of Siam or the laws of the Kingdom, by the use of force or violence" and "to stir up class hatred."[16]

Adding these two clauses—concerning violent change and class hatred—was not a dramatic alteration from the 1908 wording. However, the committee continued to add four further areas. These additions severely punished not only individuals, but also, more importantly, (1) individuals involved with any organized group, whether association or labour union; (2) Extra punishment was reserved for "the chief, manager or an official" of any organized group or anyone attending a meeting of said group; (3) "If the purpose" of any said organization was "to bring about any change in the Government or the laws or institutions of the country" or "to coerce the Government or to intimidate the community," those found guilty could face up to ten years' imprisonment; and (4) The committee felt that in "extreme cases" life imprisonment or death should be the punishment if the offense was "committed as part of a plan to overthrow the Government or change the political or economic institutions by force or violence." The committee admitted the punishments were:

> more severe than in other countries. The situation in Siam differs materially from that of European countries. In those countries there exists a well-informed and politically trained public opinion and a large measure of popular government. In Siam, the bulk of the people are untrained in either economic or political thinking and therefore the dangers from unsound propaganda are greater. For these reasons the committee are of the opinion that heavier penalties are justifiable in Siam.[17]

While the committee held that the "security [*khwam mankhong*] of the Government" must "rest upon the consent and loyalty of the people," and that such loyalty could be won only by "the wise use of power for the benefit of the people" and not "by repressive laws," it nonetheless chose ultimately to recommend repressive laws. In the course of 25 years, punishment for criticism of the government had gone from a maximum of three to ten years.[18]

Early drafts of Section 104 included a saving clause, which provided exemption for "the publication of words or opinions which are free of bias and which are expressed for the public good in the criticism of the actions, considerations, or methods of the government or administration." This was dropped from the final draft.

Thus, in 1927, the most repressive modern Thai law, to date, was promulgated. Significantly, seditious rebellion was punished more severely than *lèse-majesté*. This "double coverage" represented a certain level of institutionalization of the monarchy, making seditious rebellion an act against an institution, not merely an act against the person of the king.

Overall, during this period, the sacred sphere of the monarchy shrank as the official sphere—representing the government/bureaucracy/military—assumed the defense of the monarchy and took on its own identity. The public sphere expanded modestly, perhaps due to inter-elite jockeying, a general conclusion drawn by Copeland.[19]

However, despite a greatly strengthened law to control public criticism, this impressive battery of laws failed to save the absolute monarchy. It was overthrown five years later when the official sphere, with the aid of the modestly growing public sphere, nearly extinguished the sacred sphere altogether.[20]

1935 amended provision on seditious rebellion

From the point of view of the law, the 1932 overthrow of the absolute monarchy was of surprisingly little significance. The new democratic government did not repeal absolute-monarchy-era laws restricting various freedoms. In the late 1930s under the Juridical Council, the main law-deliberative body, a committee was set up to amend the penal code to bring it in line with the new times. This committee finished its work in 1946; it took more than a decade before its modest changes came into effect. In the wake of a royalist attempt to retake control, the Protection of the Constitution Act was passed in 1933. Provision 3 forbade acting "in any way in opposition to or in order to have the people lose their faith in [*lit*. "lose the popularity of"—*suam khwam niyom*—เสื่อมความนิยม] or to be afraid of [*watwan*—หวาดหวั่น] governance under the constitution system of Siam."[21] Judging from the law at least, constitutionalism was initially taken quite seriously after the 1932 revolution, as violations brought imprisonment of three to twenty years.[22] Of course, the law was designed to imprison recalcitrant reactionaries who wanted to bring the absolute monarchy back. Although a repressive measure, the law clearly showed the "value" of the constitution in relation to the monarchy—maximum punishment for the former was twenty years' imprisonment, compared to *lèse-majesté*'s seven years, a ratio of nearly 3 to 1. Tellingly, it was repealed five years later.[23]

There were two other important developments during the 1930s and 1940s which showed a growing and vigorous public sphere. An amendment to Section 104 on seditious rebellion (as revised in 1927) nearly brought an end to *lèse-majesté*. In 1935, when King Rama VII (r. 1925–35) abdicated, Section 104 was revised in small ways—such as adding a suitably democratic "by the people"—and the clause, "to stir up class hatred" was taken out completely. The punishment was scaled back from a maximum imprisonment of ten to seven years. Most significantly, the post-absolute monarchy government recognized that democracy required the right of citizens to criticize the government and monitor its behaviour. In accordance to this new way of thinking, a clause was added:

> Provided that there shall be no offence under this section when the said words or writing or printed documents or means whatsoever will merely be an expression of good faith or amount to a critical and unbiased comment on governmental or administrative acts within the spirit of the Constitution or for the public interest.[24]

To illustrate the significance of adding an exemption, we can look at a 1932 case where a defendant was tried for rebellion under the revised criminal code of 1927. He had claimed that the king should be dismissed for ruling poorly and that he, the defendant, should rule in his place. Amongst his crimes, he abolished taxes on killing livestock and making local rice wine and cutting down trees for personal use. He also said that children who did not want to go to school should not have to. The prosecution argued that the defendant and his co-conspirators were "very audacious and dangerous subjects, causing the people to look down upon the king and become rebellious toward the governance by inciting the people to ignore the laws." He was sentenced to seven years' imprisonment.[25]

In contrast, a 1948 decision of Thailand's Supreme Court cited the newly revised Section 104. Mr. Chote Khumphan, a Member of Parliament campaigning for political office, had gone around Bangkok in 1946 saying, among other things, that:

> since getting the Constitution of 1932 . . . the people have still not gotten a truly democratic system of governance. It has been anarchy and dictatorship . . . under the power of administrators who acted as they wished. They have silenced the people, forbidding them from speaking or criticizing . . . [The government] has erected a lie, a sham Democracy Monument. Let us revile these dishonest ones . . . The revolutionary coup group [of 1932] came in wearing only underwear. Now they each have buildings and cars. . . . It's a fake democracy. Field Marshal Phibun is wicked for those around him resort to anything . . . The present prime minister [Pridi Banomyong] is even more accursed.[26]

The prosecution argued that the defendant, as a Member of Parliament, did not "have the power to act as he wished in respect to the law." It charged that the defendant, with "full intention" had "publicly proclaimed his contempt for the government and the administration of the kingdom before the people," and, as such, "might have created disorder or rebelliousness on the part of the people to the point of creating disturbances in the country." The Court of First Instance agreed with the prosecution, sentencing the defendant to two months in jail and a fine of 1,000 baht. The Appeals Court, however, judged that the defendant's words "had not caused contempt for the government and that his action was within the sincere spirit of the constitution and for the public good." It reversed the Court of First Instance's decision and released the defendant. The Supreme Court ruled that, under democratic principles, a person speaking publicly while campaigning for election might criticize the government. The court felt that while the words of the defendant were "not appropriate," he was not guilty, for "the people have a right to know about their system of governance since sovereignty rests with the people." As power ultimately belongs to "the masses," the "government can be criticized, whether favourably so or not." In making the ruling, the Supreme Court cited the final paragraph of the provision which stipulated that if the action in question was done within the spirit of the Constitution or for public benefit, it shall not be held as a violation.

Although there was no change to the *lèse-majesté* law after the revolution, the law could be and was read as indirectly allowing critical comment on the monarchy. The inclusion of this exemption (see above) allowed citizens to act "within the spirit of the Constitution" as well as to speak or act "for the public interest" or even if only to make an "expression of good faith." This exemption from guilt may have gone so far as to ensure that expressions deemed "insulting" to the monarchy were not violations of the law. These laws were in tune with the politics of the time, during a transition from absolute to constitutional monarchy. Any action done within the spirit of the constitution or for the public good was protected. By way of comparison, the laws of the 1908 criminal code protected the king without exception. This change indicates a shift in the position of the monarchy vis-à-vis the public sphere, allowing the people to more freely express their opinions.

Under the amended Section 104, the government and the monarchy were put on the same footing: the right to criticize either was given privilege when such criticism fell within the spirit of the constitution or was for the public interest. Such privilege was reflected in the government's apparent reticence to bring any cases of *lèse-majesté* to trial between 1932 and 1946, and a handful of cases between 1947 and 1957.[27] The only Supreme Court case that originated and was decided on in this 25-year period was in 1939. Advertising himself as a faith-healer, Pa Huchonhau claimed special powers. Calling the pocket knife he held in his right hand the "jewelled sword of state," he boasted that no one in the world could challenge him. Just by pointing at someone, he could make them crazy or die. He feared no one in the world, except his father, mother, Buddha, the *dhamma* [*thamma*], and monks. He was so powerful that he could call upon the king and the constitution to come and prostrate themselves before him. He was charged with *lèse-majesté* and for "telling a startling falsehood," for which the Court of First Instance sentenced him to one year and one month's imprisonment, respectively. In considering this first case of *lèse-majesté* to come before the Supreme Court after the overthrow of the absolute monarchy in 1932, the court concurred with the Appeals Court which judged that the defendant's words were "only words of boast, and there was no intention of showing vindictiveness or insult to the king." At worst, the defendant's words were merely "foolish and cowardly." As for the second charge, the defendant had said that he only wanted to heal people of various ailments without asking for payment, which, he admitted, did astonish people and brought greater numbers to him seeking relief from their sufferings. Since the Supreme Court felt that the defendant only wanted to "make people happy," it acquitted the defendant of both charges.[28]

In short, between 1932 and 1957 the legal space in terms of what could be said about the monarchy and the government expanded considerably. Criminalization of *lèse-majesté* and seditious rebellion were in retreat, and only a handful of cases were prosecuted in lower courts, averaging less than one case a year from 1947 to 1957.

In terms of seditious rebellion, the Juridical Council committee overseeing revision of the criminal code considered doing away with Section 104 altogether. Committee member and legal advisor René Guyon made the observation, shared by many on the committee, that Section 104 was the product of an absolute monarchy, implying that it was not suited to "a constitutional form of governing."[29] The committee held that there was simply no way to say how such a sweeping provision could be interpreted, but, regardless, it would restrict freedom of expression. On the one hand, of the seven cases of seditious rebellion and *lèse-majesté* to come before the Supreme Court from 1932 to 1958, only two resulted in conviction, compared to the perfect conviction rate of three such cases in the last fourteen years of absolute monarchy.[30] On the other, successive governments during this period were ready and willing to charge people with rebellion and/or sedition; of the 129 persons arrested for some form of rebellion or sedition from 1947 to 1957—an average of almost twelve a year—only 61 percent of these cases actually went to trial, with only five making it to the Supreme Court.[31]

Citizens from 1932 to 1958 had a fair amount of latitude in criticizing the government, either for specific allegations of wrong-doing of individual government units or officials, or for more general condemnations of the overall governing system, at least when compared with before the overthrow of the absolute monarchy (Figure 4.4). Discourse over laws and constitutions were now public and no longer part of a largely unassailable sacred state. Thus, a significant expansion of the public sphere came about, with some signs that it might come to dominate both official and sacred spheres, partially due to the successful maintenance of the integrity of the courts and laws (see Diagram 1). However, the official sphere expanded and became dominant, as military dictatorship became increasingly paramount, and some court decisions crippled the integrity of the courts and laws. Finally, a significant reduction in the sacred sphere (as opposed to the public sphere) occurred as the *lèse-majesté* law came close to elimination.

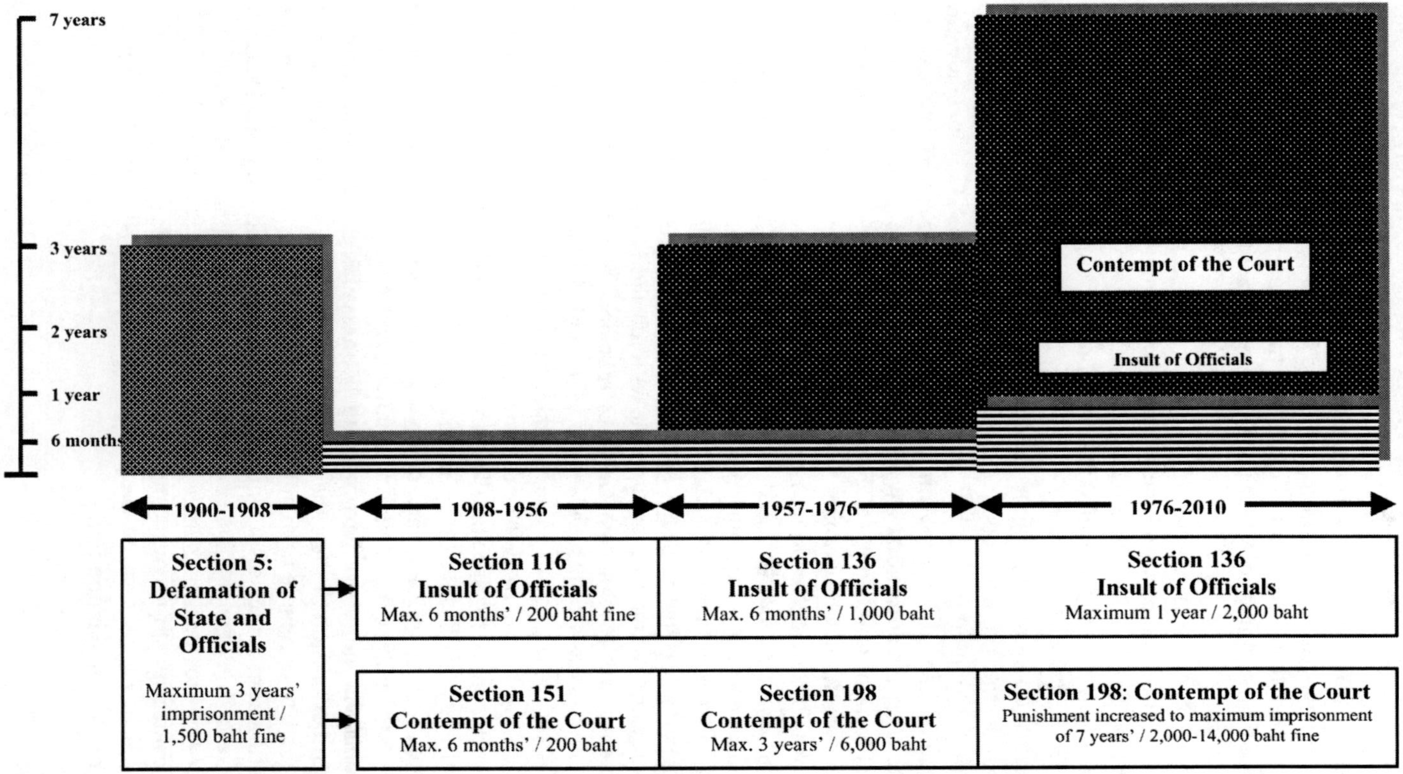

Figure 4.4 Chronology of punishment for defamation of officials and courts in Thailand, 1900–2010 (in maximum number of years' imprisonment and/or fine).

The 1957 revised criminal code

In 1957, the revised criminal code came into effect (hereafter called "the 1957 revised code). Overall, the corpus of defamation-based laws changed little.[32] The Criminal Code Revision Committee had proudly concluded in its final report of 1946 that sections on crimes against the state—in particular, Sections 98, 100, and 104—were "remodelled entirely in order to be at the same time more comprehensive and more coherent with the modern ideas."[33] However, the remodelling was modest and one change actually made the *lèse-majesté* law more comprehensive. Section 98, providing special protection for other members of the royal family, was cut. Section 100 was replaced by Section 112 which provided special coverage only for the king, queen, heir-apparent, and regent. The punishment was not reduced, and stayed the same as in the 1908 code. The Criminal Code Revision Committee became bogged down in its meetings over the difference between "insult" (*du min*—ดูหมิ่น), "insult to one's face" (*du min sung na*—ดูหมิ่นซึ่งหน้า), "defame" (*minpramat*— หมิ่นประมาท), "look down on" (*du thuk*—ดูถูก). There is no clue from the committee's records why in the end "insult" was added to "defame" in Section 112.

According to the earlier 1908 code, the law protected the king against defamation or threat. Jitti Tingsaphat's 1975 *Explanation of the Criminal Law Code* argues that "defamation" means "speech which makes people look down on or hate" the monarchy. While the 1946 Criminal Code Revision Committee concluded that it had drafted a law that did not provide protection to the monarchy as an institution, its inclusion of *insult* eventually did seem to do exactly that.[34] Adding "insult" gave greater latitude in interpretation and, Jitti argues, court decisions in which defendants were found not guilty under the old law code (such as the 1939 case) would have been reversed by the revised law.[35]

As the Criminal Code Revision Committee recommended, Section 104 on seditious rebellion omitted both references to the monarchy and elements of defamatory language (defame, show contempt). It did, however, retain exemption from guilt for acts "within the purpose of the Constitution or for expressing an honest opinion or criticism." The phrase, "to bring into hatred or contempt the Sovereign, the Government or the administration of the State" was completely cut. The new Section 116 on seditious rebellion became less a measure on defamation or insult of the state and accordingly less germane to this study (see Appendix II). However, seditious rebellion with defamatory aspects did remain in other laws, such as the 1952 anti-communist law and the 1941 print law and, most importantly, in a number of decrees issued by military juntas.

While the revised code made *lèse-majesté* more complicated through the insertion of "insult," it followed a more liberal path of reducing by half the maximum sentences for some of the other defamation-based violations, most importantly, slander and libel.

The 1958 coup decree

The criminal law code and the judicial system were largely wrecked by the constant upheaval of military dictatorships, especially after 1958. Special "coup decrees" superseded all other law. Somchai Preechasilpakul has written that because coup groups do not have a clear legal status, their coup decrees can have "far-reaching effects on the system of law" and are viewed by some Thai legal experts as having equal or greater standing than constitutional or code law.[36] One of the results is that while defamation of the state (seditious rebellion) had been more or less removed from the Thai criminal code, its spirit was resurrected in more comprehensive national security legal packages. Two coup decrees perfectly centered defamation-based laws in the heart of the Thai body politic. In fact, I will assert that the coup decrees on defamation represented the most significant development in this legal category since they were first assembled in 1900. The 1958 "Proclamation of the Revolutionary Group No. 17" (Coup Decree No. 17, see Appendix IV) announced that "the presentation of news and opinions by some newspapers has had an inappropriate character" and had, among other things, "been a Communist plot to disturb and undermine national security such as might gravely imperil the country and welfare of the people." In such a dire situation, the 1941 Press Law was insufficient. The first clause of the decree forbade publication of "any matter infringing upon His Majesty the King, or defamatory, libellous, or contemptuous of the Queen, Royal Heir, or Regent." This phrasing made an important modification to Section 112 of the revised criminal code. Instead of forbidding defamation or insult, the decree now prohibited voicing "any matter infringing" on the king, significantly contributing to the belief, that evolved over the succeeding half century, that making any reference at all to the king was wrong. Under this decree, the privileged space insulated from the public sphere was both extended and made less clear.[37]

Just as seditious rebellion and "defamation of nation" had been excised from the revised law code, Clause 2 of the 1958 decree put them back in, forbidding publication of "any matter defamatory or contemptuous of the nation or Thai people as a whole, or any matter capable of causing the respect and confidence of foreign countries in regard to Thailand, the Thai Government, or Thai people in general, to diminish." Put simply, this is one of the most pristine defamation-based constructions yet created, on a par with the Alien and Sedition Act of the United States (Chapter 1).

Clause 3 forbids reporting "any matter ambiguously defamatory or contemptuous of the Thai Government, or any ministry, public body, or department of the government without stating clearly the fault and matter." Clause 4 similarly forbids reporting "any matter ambiguously showing that the government or ministry, public body, or department of the government has deteriorated, is bad, or has committed a damaging offence without showing in what matter and particular."

Coup decree No. 17 remained in effect through the short semi-democratic hiccup of 1968 to 1971, was repealed in 1975, and then re-issued (with identical wording) as Order of the National Administrative Reform Council No. 42 (Coup Order No. 42) which remained in effect from 1976 to 1991. As such, this particular decree persisted through nearly this entire period of 42 years and represented a military-monarchy enshrinement of defamation-based laws.

The 1976 coup decree

One of the most profound moments in the biography of Thai defamation occurred in the aftermath of the massacre of students at Thammasat University on 6 October 1976. The new coup group cloned Coup Decree No. 17 when it issued Coup Order No. 42.[38] The coup group also promulgated Order of the National Administrative Reform Council No. 41 which singled out and reunified almost all defamation-based laws for the first time since 1900. "Coup Order No. 41" increased the punishment for all these laws. In a short rationale, the order explained that the current punishment of a maximum jail sentence of seven years for *lèse-majesté* was "not proper for the present situation" and increased the punishment from a minimum of three to a maximum of 15 years' imprisonment.[39]

In this single order, greater punishment was also to be meted out for defamation of the courts, of religion, of state officials, of national symbols, of countries with which Thailand enjoyed good relations, and of private individuals. The order did not explain why the previous punishments for these infractions were no longer "proper for the present situation." But those responsible for issuing this order understood there was some relationship between state power and defamation-based offenses, between the protection of the throne and the rights of the citizen. The defamation-based laws were the conceptual glue that held this amalgam together.

A pattern extends from the 1908, to the 1957, and 1976 punishments. For contempt of the court, punishment increased from six months to three years to seven years, respectively.[40] For religion, it went from two, to three, to seven years (Figure 4.5). For officials, it was six months, six months, and one year. For the flag and symbols of friendly powers, it went from six months, to one year, to two years. For slander, it was six months, six months, to one year. For libel, it was two years, one year, and then back to two years. Taking the percentage growth in the maximum punishment for each crime, the 1957 laws on average were 163 percent higher than in 1908. The punishments for 1976 provisions were almost 264 percent higher than those of the 1957 laws if factoring in the remarkable jump in defamation or contempt of the court (not including the latter, the jump was a much more modest 70 percent increase). Even more remarkable is the difference between the 1908 and 1976 punishments, which showed a 427 percent increase in maximum terms of imprisonment.

However, if Thai governments from 1932 to 1957 did not reduce the

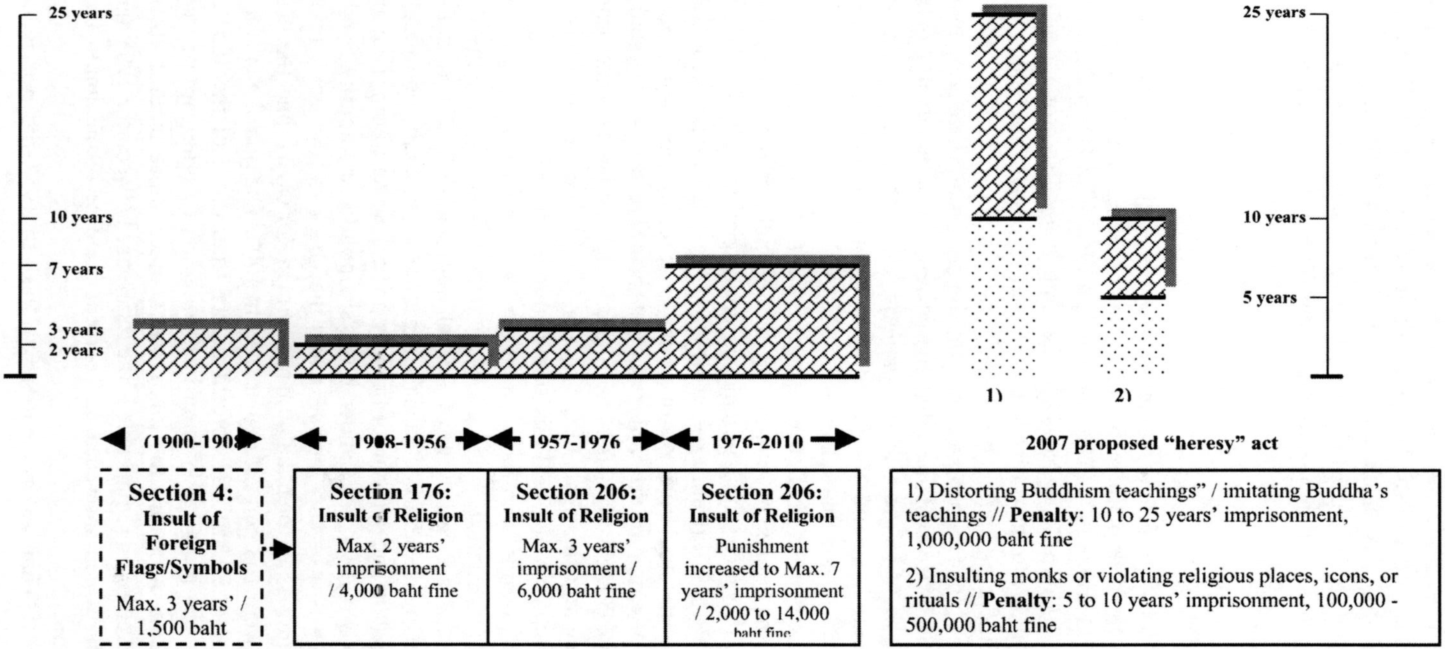

Figure 4.5 Chronology of punishment for insult of religion in Thailand ("heresy"), 1908–2010 (in maximum number of years' imprisonment).

penalties for crimes such as *lèse-majesté*, neither did they resort to charging citizens of them excessively. Between 1949 and 1956, there were on average a little over one *lèse-majesté* "incident" and less than a single arrest per year. The number jumped almost five-fold between 1956 and 1976 when the average annual number of *lèse-majesté* arrests and/or prosecutions was 5.3 and 4.9, respectively. Between 1977 and 1992, the average number of cases per year became 9.9, twice as much as in the 1960s and more than 1000 percent more than in the 1950s.[41]

Figures 4.1 through 4.7 show a sudden skewing of the comparative valuations of what or whom was protected. The value of the reputation of the monarch more than doubled. Suddenly the reputations of the courts and religion in 1976 became equal in value to that of the monarchy prior to the overthrow of the absolute monarchy. The increase in penalties for this class of crime was profound—and disturbing. The trend was going "the wrong way," so to speak—in Spain, for instance, the maximum punishment for *lèse-majesté* in the 1930s was eight years in prison, and two years in 2000, a reduction of 75 percent. Thailand bucked the global trend by significantly increasing the penalties for defamation-based crimes. But with the increase of punishments after 1976, Thailand began to take a path very different from most other constitutional monarchies. Thailand seemed to be going in reverse.

The 1992 amended provision on defamation

The last landmark in the chronology of Thai defamation laws occurred in 1992 when the fine for personal defamation was increased both in criminal and civil law codes and came in some ways to resemble seditious rebellion. In the 1957 criminal code, rebellion lost its defamatory inferences. However, seditious rebellion returned in 1958 with Coup Decree No. 17, in effect until 1975. This continued with Coup Decree No. 42, repealed in early 1991.[42] A little over a year later, the thread reappeared within the personal defamation law and its remarkably increased criminal fine. At one end of the continuum of defamation measures was *lèse-majesté* with its threat of a maximum 15 years' imprisonment; at the opposite end was personal defamation with a maximum two year's imprisonment. While seditious rebellion may have disappeared from the law code, *lèse-majesté* and defamation advanced from the far ends of the continuum toward the center. Both *lèse-majesté* and defamation began to cover what would have been deemed in the past as seditious rebellion.

Prior to 1976, with other mechanisms available to the government, the personal defamation law was not greatly used. From 1961 to 1973, an average of 333 cases of personal defamation were tried annually. This increased to 490 cases per year from 1974 to 1975 as Thailand experienced unprecedented political freedom. After the bloody massacre on October 6, 1976, the punishments of all defamation-based laws were increased. Personal

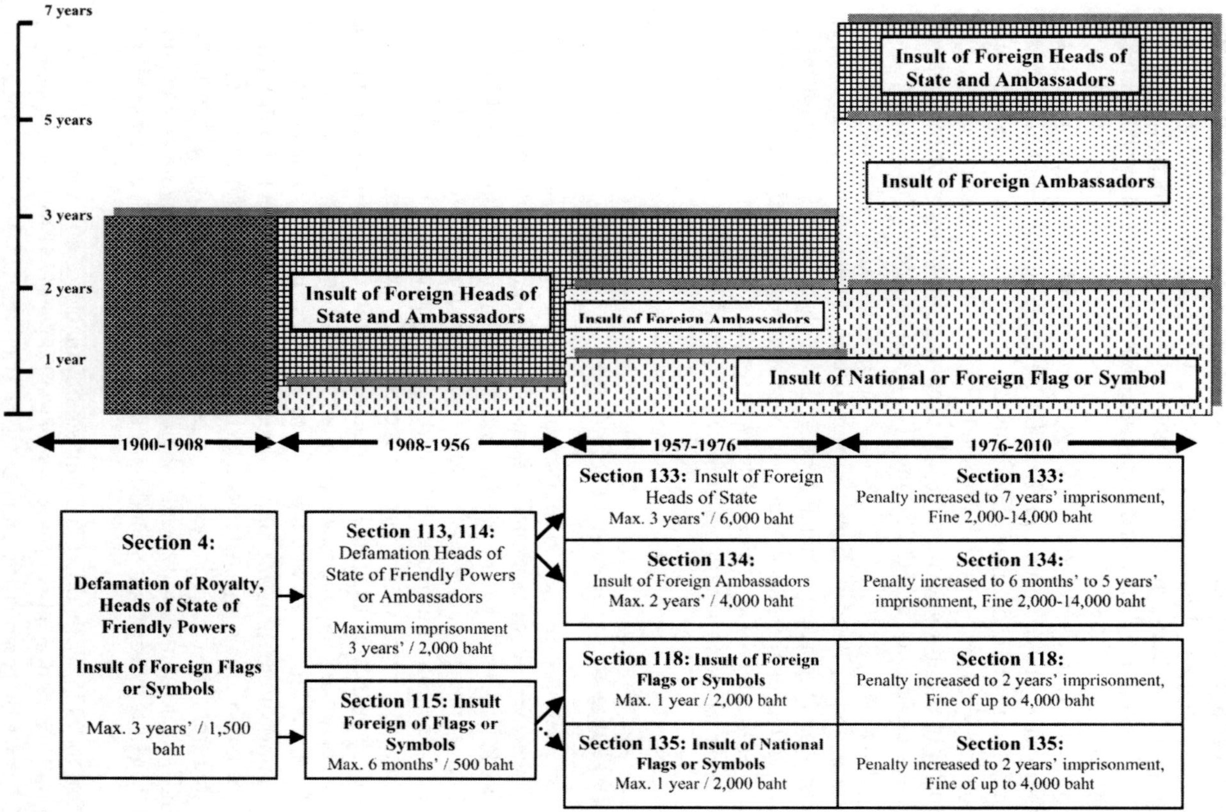

Figure 4.6 Chronology of punishment for insult of foreign heads of state, flags and national symbols in Thailand, 1900–2010 (in maximum number of years' imprisonment and/or fine).

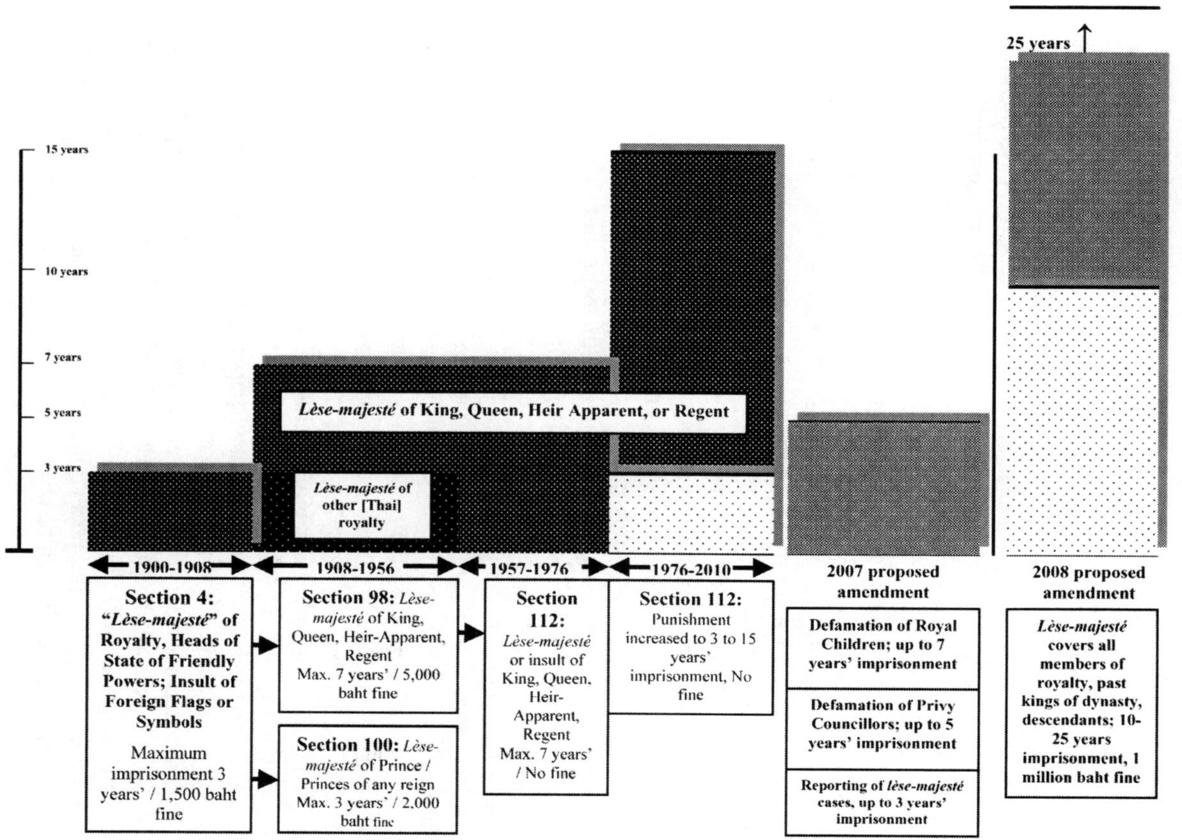

Figure 4.7 Chronology of punishment for *lèse-majesté* in Thailand, 1900–2010 (in maximum number of years' imprisonment and/or fine).

defamation penalties doubled. Slander could now be punished with a year of imprisonment and a 2,000 baht fine. The penalty for libel increased to a maximum of two years' imprisonment and a fine of 4,000 baht. This increase in penalties matched a surge in the number of arrests for defamation, with 862 arrests in 1977 and 931 in 1978, accompanied with a record high number of new defamation cases tried, at 686. But from 1979 to 1992—a 14-year period—the average number of new defamation cases tried dipped to an average of a little over 500 cases per year (see Figure 7.1).[43]

One reason the numbers stayed relatively low might have been that Coup Decree No. 42 of 1976, a split image of its 1958 predecessor, gave the Press Officer of Bangkok sweeping powers to close newspapers and forbid the import of improper foreign publications. However, this law was repealed in 1991 by the first government with a democratically-elected prime minister since 1976, a repeal which one scholar of the Thai media wrote, "seemed to symbolize the end of heavy-handed state intervention in the media."[44] The state was left with the archaic 1941 Press Law to control print, with fines largely at 1941 prices, so to speak.

Police Lieutenant Colonel Samphan Satthaphorn, the Press Officer of Bangkok through the 1980s, reminisced about his lost power when the Press Law of 1941 came back into force during my interview with him in August 1991.[45] He felt that the provisions of the press law were "too weak." Now in 1991, the press officer could only issue warnings or revoke the license of the publisher—the former being much too light a measure and the latter much too heavy-handed. Order No. 42, Samphan contended, could "make people scared," for the press officer was empowered to mete out a punishment of up to three years in prison and a fine of up to 300,000 baht.

The 1941 Press Law, he laughed, could impose a "200,400 baht fine" on a violator. He said that even the power of Phao Siyanon, the dreaded police chief of the 1950s, was limited by the Press Law of 1941 when dealing with newspapers. Only under extraordinary circumstances—such as a state of emergency or martial law—did the press officer's power increase, such as in the 1980s with the use of Order No. 42 which made, in Samphan's words, the power of the press officer "absolute."

But after Order No. 42's repeal, "newspapers [became] stronger than the press officer" who now had to coddle them and "be their friend." Samphan felt that this arrangement was "not very democratic." With little power, the press officer "had to listen to those who called" and who demanded he censure a publication. To free the press officer from political interference such as this, Samphan argued, "the press officer needs to become more powerful." Accordingly, Samphan's dream was a new law with some real teeth—such as imprisonment for up to five years for editors, he wistfully thought out loud.

And a new law was possible. The National Peacekeeping Council carried out a coup a short time after the repeal of Coup Decree No. 42 and put itself in a position to sail a new piece of press legislation through its military-appointed parliament. Samphan's dream law, which he was proposing to parliament, would also leave the phrasing about "order and public morals" vague, otherwise the press officer would have to spend days and days sitting in court, because, well, it is a vague idea and it would make for "more headache if you have to prove it." Samphan also knew that he had to work fast to get his bill through parliament before there were elections. "After elections," Samphan said dismissively with a wave of his hand, "forget it." He felt that his new bill would "better protect public opinion and the people," for it would allow the latter to take newspapers to court for personal defamation. He himself was scheduled to explain the virtues of this new law to parliament.

Samphan's dream only partially came true. Almost six months to the day after our interview, an amendment to the criminal law code came into effect. The rationale in the preamble to this amendment stated: "it appears at present that there are more and more of those committing defamation. At the same time, the rate of punishment is not appropriate to the prevailing conditions, causing violators of this offence to have no fear." The texts of the provisions, Sections 326 on slander and 328 on libel, were not altered. While maximum possible jail time for the two infractions remained the same, the penalties were increased. The maximum fine for slander increased ten-fold, from 2,000 to 20,000 baht, and for libel the maximum fine rose by a spectacular fifty times, going from 4,000 to 200,000 baht.[46] It must have been a proud and happy day for Samphan—25 February 1992 to be exact—when this amendment was signed by the military-appointed prime minister, Anand Panyarachun.[47] A report by Article 19 and the National Press Council of Thailand claims, "It is well-known that the 1992 amendment targets news media, since the maximum penalty would only be applied to a defamatory statement which was published or broadcast to wider audiences, i.e. through the media."[48]

The change in the law had a nearly instantaneous effect. The increase in the number of libel suits was so rapid that foreign observers began to question the level of press freedom in Thailand.[49] From 1993 to 1996, the average number of new cases per year jumped to 680, a 25 percent increase over the previous 16 years.[50] From 1998 to 2003, the average jumped another 70 percent to 1,160 new cases per year. Although Thaksin Shinawatra, prime minister from 2001 to 2006, was not the first to use the defamation law to silence his critics, he certainly became its indisputable master.[51] Deposing him though did not arrest the growing number of cases. The number almost doubled to an average of 2,200 cases per year for the five-year period of 2004 to 2008, with an all-time high of 2,694 cases in 2007. All told, the change in the average number of cases between 1976–92, and 2004–8—a 33-year period—was an increase of 410 percent, a remarkable development given that the global trend was for fewer cases of defamation and most certainly for criminal defamation.[52]

Lèse-majesté is at the other end of the defamation continuum. From 1992 to 2005, the average number of new *lèse-majesté* cases received by the prosecution department was a little over five. During the same 14-year period, the average number of cases prosecuted annually was 3.7. In some years, there were no new cases received (1993, 2002) nor any cases tried (2002).[53] But since the year of the coup, there has been an astonishing and troubling change. The average annual number of *lèse-majesté* cases from 2006 to 2009 received by the Court of First Instance, the Appeals Court, and the Supreme Court, respectively, was 100, 9, and 2; and the average annual number of cases successfully adjudicated was 53 in the lower court, and 10 in the Appeals Court. Since 2005, the Supreme Court has received 9 *lèse-majesté* cases, but has yet to hand down a decision on any of them. Comparing the average number of cases for the periods 1992–2005 and 2006–2009, there has been a remarkable 2,000 percent increase in new cases (see Figure 8.1). Given that the conviction rate for *lèse-majesté* cases averaged 94 percent for cases tried between 1992 and 2005, there must be literally scores if not hundreds of Thais serving prison time for the crime.[54] After interviews with editors of major newspapers in Bangkok, journalist Pravit Rojanapruk argued in 2008 that the law has over years of use created an entire system within journalistic circles about how to handle—or not handle—the threat of *lèse-majesté*.[55]

Operating with a particular notion of state poetics expressed within a narrow tradition of Thai Theravada Buddhism, the Siamese/Thai defamation regime essentially froze culture, society, and politics. This entire edifice is held in place by a modern-style penal code and judicial system. Throughout the twentieth century, the principle behind defamation-based crimes insinuated itself into a great number of legal acts, appeared in a broader range of defamation measures, and dictated more severe punishments. Even after a century, twenty-first-century Thailand remains locked in this framework. How can the historian or legal expert explain how a country that has become nominally more democratic since the overthrow of the absolutist state has become even more absolutist, authoritarian, and restrictive in terms of what people can say and write? How can this backward motion be accounted for?

5 Normalizing "abnormal times" and the "endless state of exception"

This chapter addresses the question: How can Thailand's succession of coups, self-granted amnesties, and torn-up constitutions be understood within the frameworks of the state of exception and defamation-based crime?

There is a sense in which premodern states were always in a "state of exception." Absolute monarchies, by definition, reserved the right to hand down judgments on certain kinds of cases and used special courts, such as England's Star Chamber. "Normal" legal practices, if any, could be trumped by the whim of the monarch. Euro-American law codes and procedures including some involvement of the public sphere, imply an expectation a "normally" operating juridical system. These "normal" practices and procedures are suspended when those holding or seeking state power declare a "state of exception."

If this formulation seems reasonable, we can conclude that, up until the overthrow of the absolute monarchy in 1932, the Siamese/Thai government was a state of exception. From 1932 until the present, Thailand's history has been punctuated with eighteen successful and attempted coups and eighteen constitutions—surely a world record. Each successful coup reconstituted the state of exception, each constitution (theoretically at least) re-set the nation and its laws back to "normal." Giorgio Agamben points out that the state of exception opens a legally fuzzy category. Carl Schmitt terms this category "general and indeterminate clauses" or "'indeterminate' juridical concepts," like "public security," "peace and order," and "state of danger." Agamben argues that a "concept such as the National Socialist notion of race" was a form of "indeterminate clause," "analogous to 'state of danger and 'good morals'." The foremost characteristic of such a clause or concept is that it "does not refer to any situation of external fact." Indeterminate clauses "had penetrated even more deeply into German and European legislation in the twentieth century," and "invasively into the juridical rule." These phrases "refer not to a rule but to a situation" in which legal concepts placed "certainty and calculability outside the juridical rule."[1]

The defamation regime and the state of exception intersect in "indeterminate" indistinct, legal concepts, such as "peace and order" or "threat to national security." I have emphasized the sensitivity of defamation-based crimes to the on-going political and social context (Chapter 2), to what is perceived as "the situation", which may take an issue out of the domain of fact and law and place it inside the realm of the defamation regime. This chapter traces the evolution of Thailand from a semi-legal constituted regime through its descent into the deeper realms of the state of exception. Though the cases of Nazi Germany and Thailand do not at first seem comparable, they in fact share important similarities.

Nazi Germany began to believe in its "indeterminate concepts"—such as racial superiority—and thereby claimed the state of the exception and took it to its logical end—the concentration camp. Few regimes can compare with Nazi Germany from 1933 to 1945 on this point. But Thailand is similar in that it possessed all the requisite components for an extreme state of exception—the development of laws used in extraordinary circumstances, the congealing of indeterminate concepts, and the military power to bring these into operation. The legal framework for the Thai sovereign to declare martial law passed into law in the 1910s. In the late 1930s, a Special Court was set up to try royalist rebels. A law to allow the state to pre-emptively place into detention anyone exhibiting potential criminality was discussed during World War II.[2] The indeterminate concepts of peace and order, public morals, anti-communism, and a bit later, Thainess, merged with a larger discourse intersecting defamation-based laws. From 1947 the military aggressively subverted the rule of law with coups, new constitutions, and military decrees delegitimizing the juridical order. The 1940s and 1950s saw the creation of a legal framework for defining emergency conditions, packaged under the delightful term, "Abnormal Times" [lit., "Not Normal Times", *wela mai pokati*—เวลาไม่ปกติ]. "Abnormal Times" is defined quite succinctly, while remaining vague, in Section 36 of the "Act on the Organization of Military Courts:" "when there is fighting or in times of war or when martial law has been declared."[3]

When full military dictatorship took hold over Thai society in the late 1950s, this legal framework—built for specific circumstances—was put into motion, eventually making "Abnormal Times" normal and a time without crisis extraordinary.[4]

Peace and order

The Press Officer of Bangkok in the 1970s and 1980s was not fond of going to court to justify taking action against a newspaper for endangering "public order" or "peace and order" because it was difficult.[5] No Supreme Court decision ever attempted to define the term, nor is there evidence of a definition of "public order" in any other laws employing the phrase, such as the Cinema Act of 1930 or the Press Law of 1941. Apparently, the issue was self-evident. Defamation laws are intended to protect against the potential effects of dangerous words and to preserve public order. Although government bodies have not defined "public order", it is often cited. Thus we can touch on a few examples where the term was discussed by legal officials and look at two court cases in which the question of public order played a role in the outcome.[6]

Traditionally, Thai kings' ultimate enemy was disruption of the "subdued peace" [*khwam sa-ngop rap khap*—ความสงบราบคาบ], a term still in use as late as 1927.[7] After 1932, perhaps because of its overtly oppressive and anti-democratic connotations, this phrase was replaced by "peace and order" [*khwam sa-ngop riap roi*—ความสงบเรียบร้อย], which serves as the legal standard in, for instance, the laws controlling the press and the cinema, often coupled with "of the people," or "public" and "public morality" [*sinlatham an di khong prachachon*—ศีลธรรมอันดีของประชาชน].[8] Carried over into the days of the constitutional monarchy was the notion that if words caused "turmoil unto disquietude," then a defendant could be found guilty of seditious rebellion. In a "consultation" of the Juridical Council in 1950, for instance, the legal advisor, the former Frenchman René Guyon (who Thai-ified his name into "Pichan Bulayong" during his five decades of service to Siam/Thailand), noted that the constitutional rights to freedom of expression were restricted if necessary for, among other events, "averting a state of emergency" and "maintaining public order or good morals." In Thailand, the legal advisor averred, censorship could only be imposed "by a special order which is issued for a limited period and only in very exceptional cases." The government could also invoke Section 104 on seditious rebellion to suppress news items that might "constitute a danger for the internal peace of the country and are likely to create unrest. If they are not forbidden and punished, the stability of the Government should be threatened permanently." Later that year, the government proposed an amended wording to replace the phrase "contrary to public order and good morals" to empower the press officer to prohibit news that "might infringe the liberty of another person or might cause a state of emergency or might be contrary to public order or good morals or might cause mental deterioration." Instead of having a single, vague phrase like "public order and morals," the proposed amendment would introduce three additional and equally vague phrases.[9]

In this attempt, the government set the foundation for pre-emptively moving against potential criminality. The government increased the number of conditions under which defamation-based laws might be invoked. It replicated the logic that made a potential crime equal to the actual commission of crime, all predicated on the word, "might," and, later the same year, included the possibility of "probable" infractions. Thus, the overall terms became vaguer and less determinate: a "probable" breach of the peace seems more serious, as if the danger were more immanent. In 1952, the government also used this logic to spread the sense of threat regarding communism; that was expanded from "communism" to amorphous and horrific possible eventualities, such as deprivation of liberty, state of emergency, mental deterioration, crisis—which in many cases had no correspondence in reality (or, as Agamben, writes, not of "actual fact"). These acts were not concrete, such as collecting arms, but quite often connecting seemingly unconnected to communism, such as questioning the relevance or truth of Buddhism.[10]

Throughout this period, the Juridical Council stayed the hand of the government, reminding it that Thailand was a democracy. In one of its consultations the Juridical Council's legislative advisor made the astute observation that often a government suppressed publications it "thinks [are] contrary to its own notion of public order (since public order is an extremely flexible expression which varies according to the principles actually extolled by the Powers that be.)."[11]

"Extremely flexible expression" was left for the government to decide. How could courts accurately "guess" the possible outcomes of these vague notions? The discursive space of public order expanded the government's reach as it compounded the lack of clarity. Thus, defamation-based crimes became positioned in an increasingly expansive and dangerous context, increasing the chances that cases would result in conviction and an evolution toward an even more comprehensive state of exception.

A Supreme Court decision in the pre-1958 period affirmed the applicability of defamation to specific circumstances. In 1940, the French government fell to Germany and Thai irredentists hungrily looked to "take back" areas "lost" at the turn of the century.[12] In Nongkhai province, on the Thai side of the Mekhong River across from Laos, a Mr. Jaeng Khroekham, at the early hour of 8 in the morning while in an opium den in the presence of ten others, chose to vent against the Thai government. A number of Thai policies irked Mr. Jaeng who was reported to have said, among other things:

> The district has announced that foreign money cannot be used . . . making the people upset . . . we can't save *kip* [the Lao currency] anymore. Doing like this makes trouble for the people. It is not just at all. The money we bring from foreign countries we have to use to pay our taxes. Our farms will be taken away completely to pay the taxes. This government has no justice whatsoever . . . Doing like this, all the people will die, will be damned, will all die a violent death.
>
> Last night the village headman rang the bell for a meeting of the villagers to tell the people that it was prohibited to use French money. If the government makes such an announcement, the people along the bank of the Mekhong River will be in trouble . . . The government is not fair. They announced that people cannot wear long-legged pants and must instead wear shorts. If the government doesn't allow them to use what they have, it must buy clothes for them to wear.

He was arrested and charged with seditious rebellion. The 1941 Supreme Court ruling, said that "taken one by one the words of the defendant may not be a violation of the law." However, when the words were put together, they became an offense because they *might* "have caused the people *along the border* to despise the Thai government because of the special time and incidents" (my emphasis). The people in the area were "anxious" about the "special" situation. Guilt in cases of seditious rebellion, the court concluded, "depends on time and place." In other words, had the defendant spoken the same words during the same period but in a less sensitive place or had he spoken the same words in the same place at a less sensitive time, then, given the court's deliberation, he might not have been found guilty. An "important consideration" in this case, the court clearly stated:

> was the particular time and place where the words were spoken because statements made in one place may not produce any serious results, but the same statements made in another place, which is experiencing an unusual situation, may produce serious or violent results. The prosecution argued that in this case, the words of the defendant were said to the "community" in an opium den along the Thai border with the country of Indochina at a time when there was a call for a return of the territory between Thailand and Indochina.[13]

The 1957 case of Kukrit Pramoj further illustrated this peculiar question of potential effect (also see Chapter 9).[14] After returning from study in England, this colourful personage of royal blood established the respected newspaper, *Sayam Rat*, played the part of the "prime minister" in Hollywood's *The Ugly American*, authored numerous books, set up a political party (the Social Action Party), and eventually became a real prime minister in the mid-1970s. One could argue that Kukrit and his brother, Seni, himself twice prime minister and stalwart of the Democrat Party, defined or at least were important constituents in the making of the Thai political system for the second half of the twentieth century.

Criticism of the government in Kukrit's newspaper column prompted charges of seditious rebellion.[15] At one point in the trial, prosecution witness Mr. Kawin Sunthornsarathun, Director-General of the Land Department, former head of the Department of Local Administration and Director-General of the Interior Department, testified. The prosecution showed the suitability of the witness's testimony on rebellion when it established that Kawin was "responsible for the happiness of the people and maintaining peace and order." The prosecutor's task was to establish the degree of guilt of the defendant. To what degree did the offending articles create rebelliousness? Under questioning by the prosecution, Kawin struggles to describe just how much rebelliousness the articles might produce:

> *Witness* feels that the articles beseechingly incited and provoked the people concerning various situations. They charged the government with being a troublemaker and many more things. It would make the people who read it believe it perhaps and make them angered . . .
> *Prosecution* asks how the writings would make the people feel.
> *Witness* says it would stoke the fire of rebelliousness.

> *Prosecution* asks if the nature of the use of words [in the articles] was usual or not.
> *Witness* says the words are of the nature that would cause rebelliousness to arise within the people and points out that . . . the contents of these writings are violent. They might induce the persons who read them to be in turmoil and be rebellious.
> *Prosecution* asks to what degree?
> *Witness* says reading the three pieces together, the degree of rebelliousness might be to the point of using force and creating disorder . . . [some parts of the writings] are not criticisms; they are accusations. If read, they might give rise to feelings of contempt and hatred for the government. And then, it might get to the point of using force, and causing a change.[16]

The 1941 and 1957 cases established the principle that the court becomes the arbitrator for deciding at what point a defamatory statement succeeds. In neither the 1941 nor the 1957 case did the words of the defendants cause disquietude. An expression of honest opinion or a normal criticism took on fearful proportions at a certain time. The court decided exactly when words became seditious and whether such words *might* cause a rupture in the public order.

In the 1967 edition of his work, Thai legal scholar Jitti Tingsaphat affirms the right of the people to criticize the "administration and bureaucracy in general." However, he adds, while "it is within one's rights to express an opinion, the limit is that one does not aim directly at disturbing the peace." A violation of the law occurs when "disturbing the peace" was the direct object of such words. Adjudicating this law by its effect—makes this law, at least to Jitti, faithful to its original intent.[17]

De-legitimation of law

Preserving a court system while continually degrading the rule of law—in particular constitutions—provided the "legal" framework for transformation of the state from a typical 1950s military dictatorship into a full-fledged defamation regime, a military-monarchy alliance ruled ultimately by the dictates and logic of defamation within the framework of the sacred state/state of the exception (Chapter 1). This was neither a preconceived nor inevitable plan of the military and monarchy, but this transformation extended from the logic that operates in Thai political culture. Thus, its emergence should be of no great surprise.

However, the evolution of these forms necessitated a steady erosion of the rule of law and acquiescence of the judicial system. From 1932 to 1958 each succeeding, successful group coming to power through coups established "legitimacy" through acts of ritual purification (Chapter 3). The peculiarly Thai practice of the ritual disestablishment of the existing constitution, the issuance of self-granted amnesties for the coup, and the re-establishment of a new and pure order, with some sort of constitution, evolved.[18]

From a Western perspective, this evolution could not be accomplished without the aid of the courts. We look at three cases from the 1950s which set within the historical record the legitimation of coups by the very institution that is supposed to preserve the integrity of the law—the Supreme Court itself.[19]

A 1952 case involved the attempted "Chief of Staff" coup of 1948. In this the defendants argued that they had not attempted to "overthrow" the government because the government in 1948 had come to power through a coup itself and so was illegitimate.[20] The court rejected this argument. Noting that the word "government" was not defined in the criminal law code, the court felt the term "must be understood by the general principle of law" which defines government as "an individual or group of individuals who exercise administrative power over the country and can maintain the peace and happiness of the country and whose authority is uncontested." Such a government, the court went on, is "the correct government according to the truth" and should be considered as such "in terms of criminal law." The Supreme Court ruled that an illegal government becomes legitimate once "people come to accept and respect it."[21] The only condition for legitimate rule was merely that the group has "administrative power." The Supreme Court made no mention of how that power was gained. The coup group did not need to be appointed by the king, be empowered by a constitution, or have approval from a democratically elected legislative body. The court added two non-democratic features that are hard to gauge, legally or otherwise, for the group making the coup: it had to "maintain the peace and happiness" of the nation and have uncontested authority. Who was to provide the measure of peace and order for the people's happiness? How was "uncontested authority" to be measured? What would or could be the form of contestation over power? How much of it did there have to be? Within what period? And "according to" what "truth"? Whose "truth"? The existence of this case suggests that some challenge to the authority and legitimacy of the coup government occurred. Nonetheless, the court found the defendants guilty.[22]

A 1953 case shows just how deliciously convoluted judicial adjudication became with many coups and new constitutions. After the democratically-elected government had been overthrown in a military coup in 1947, Prince Wiwatchai Chaiyan was appointed under the temporary constitution to serve as the minister of finance by the new government. In early December of that year, responding to reports that the ministry had been involved in opium smuggling, Wiwatchai made the affair public and dismissed a number of officials, including a Mr. Thongyen Lilamian, who became plaintiff in a case against Wiwatchai for illegal dismissal and personal defamation. The plaintiff argued that the defendant did not have the power to dismiss him, for he had been appointed minister of finance under the temporary 1947 constitution. The appointment was illegal because the constitution of the time was illegal because it was the result of an illegal overthrow of the previous government. If the appointment was not legal, neither was the dismissal. Moreover, after dismissing the plaintiff, the defendant persisted in damaging the plaintiff's honour and reputation by having his dismissal order broadcast over the Radio of Thailand, "with the intent of publicly disgracing the plaintiff." The plaintiff had even been arrested for public malfeasance and incarcerated for seven days. He was then released because "no wrong had been committed." He therefore sued for lost pay and pension to the amount of 99,249.50 baht, as well as an additional 50,000 baht for damages to his reputation and 2 percent annual interest.

In response, the defendant argued that his appointment as minister of finance had been approved by the King and parliament as stipulated by the temporary constitution of 1947. While this charter had been imposed through a coup, it was also "graciously granted by the King" and so legally replaced the 1946 constitution. A panel of the Supreme Court ruled that the coup group had successfully seized power. As such, this group had "the power to change, revise, repeal, and issue laws according to a revolutionary system in order to administer the country. Otherwise the country-nation would not be able to be established with peace." Thus, the temporary constitution of 1947 was "fully legal," in turn making the appointment of the minister of finance legal, which made his order of an official's dismissal within the ministry legal. The defendant was released and the plaintiff was ordered to pay court costs.[23]

What is ironic and makes the situation complicated is that by the time these cases from 1952 and 1953 got to the Supreme Court, the court had to affirm again and again the legitimacy of a constitution which had been legally replaced by another, which had itself since been overthrown. The military government had replaced the 1947 constitution with a 1949 constitution. The government then "illegally" abolished the 1949 constitution in a coup against itself in 1951 at which time the coup group revived an altered version of the 1932 constitution. The act was made "legal" when the government issued unto itself "The Amnesty-to-Those-Who-Brought-the-Thai-Constitution-of-1932-Back-into-Use Act of 1951."[24]

A third case, from 1954, involved a 1949 would-be coup group of 21 persons who argued that its attempted action was absolved by virtue of that same amnesty. In charging the defendants with rebellion (Section 104), the prosecution said the group had attempted a "change in the royal custom of governance in the kingdom." The defendants argued that their attempt to bring into effect a new constitution was not a would-be coup. The court had to answer two questions: First, if the defendants were charged with trying to overthrow the government, exactly what was the government? And, second, did the attempt by the coup group to set in place a new constitution amount to an attempt to change "the royal customs of governance"?

For the first question, the court defined "government" as that which "has been established according to the constitution which was announced to be in effect." Rather than going through the detailed and thorough exploration of what government might mean, as the Juridical Council had done in 1942, the court simply opened the official Thai dictionary which defined government as "an organization governing the country."[25] The court admitted that the 1947 government did come to power through a coup. But the "newly-established government took control and governed the land successfully and absolutely, and it maintained peace and order of the country-nation." For many years "it has been accepted and respected in general as the fully-constituted government." This case clearly laid the legal argument for legitimizing the violent overthrow of governments. The more successful the coup, the more it established its authority and silenced its critics, the more legitimate it was. Who, exactly, had come to "accept and respect" these governments? How was such acceptance or respect measured? The Supreme Court did not answer these troubling questions. Thus, the court laid the logical framework for dictatorship by providing legal legitimacy for military takeovers.

In terms of the second question, the court inconsistently began by ruling that a change in constitutions is a change in the "royal customs of governance" because "each constitution is a principle of governance of the kingdom, though each constitution has its own and different legal provisions." If this were not so, the court asked, then why would anyone want to bring in new constitutions? A change in constitutions is a change in the "royal customs of governance" one following the other, "like a shadow" is to itself. Therefore, the attempt by the defendants to establish a new constitution was a rebellion. Had the military government committed rebellion in the same way by forcibly reviving the 1932 constitution? According to the court, at first, apparently yes. But once the coup group had established power, the state of "rebellion" was nullified. Presumably in response, the defendants changed their tack by arguing that if the military government was not wrong in reviving the 1932 constitution, then neither were they. The court said that the action of the government was covered by the amnesty. The defendants then said that the amnesty should cover them, too. The court ruled, however, that "The Amnesty-to-Those-Who-Brought-the-Thai-Constitution-of-1932-Back-Into-Use Act of 1951" covered only those who voided the use of the 1949 constitution and not the 1947 constitution that was in effect when the coup plotters had been arrested.[26]

Any mechanisms of accountability became degraded by the amnesties that military groups invariably granted themselves. The coup makers recognized that every successful coup was illegal. A rather peculiar practice resulted, with power seekers performing what they perceived as an illegal act of overthrowing the existing government, then issuing an amnesty that retroactively made the act legal. Within this process the coup makers recognized that the constitution that had been in use had been so violated by the coup that it had lost its mandate and needed replacement. The first act of all coup groups was to abolish the present constitution; that earlier constitution's existence, if it remained in effect, made the coup illegal. Rather than retroactively suspending the constitution for the moment of the coup—during which the illegal act had been committed—and then putting it back into effect the following instant, the logic of Thai coups demanded that the constitution be erased. Thus, during this initial period the most prominent feature of modern Thai politics—the tedious pattern of crises solved by coups, the abolition of old constitutions, the granting of amnesties, and the drafting of new constitutions—began to punctuate Thai history.

This pattern seems inexplicable unless we look at the practice as ritual purification—a public act certified by Thai Theravada Buddhism that recognizes a sacrifice (staging a coup), acknowledges a necessary murder (the killing of a constitution), and rewards giving (a new constitution, a new political order).[27] What had the day before been the use of force to topple a government becomes magically transformed the next day through an amnesty into a meritorious act.[28] The former constitution was part of a past failed order. It could not be amended or suspended: it had to be purged.[29] Nor could the coup group simply make sure they were not charged by the police by virtue of an order establishing such. Instead, they must acknowledge they had been forced to act illegally and all parties must be exonerated.

The political order was reset. A new order was established by men of virtue (with guns). Their virtue allowed them to seize power not for themselves, but for the whole social and political order. However, they had to ritually purge themselves of the necessary violence by declaring an amnesty. A temporary constitution would do until sufficient time passed and other men of virtue could come and draft a new, permanent one. Hewison has called these solemn practices "serial-constitutionalism," a system in which the normal law is suspended and legitimacy is found in some flexible "sacred" place.[30] Those who took power have the right to issue laws. Once a military decree is made into law, Thai society as a whole becomes immobilized and unable to repeal the law. These decrees constitute a whole other class of criminal violations that trumps existing laws. Prior to 1958, this gradual evolution laid the groundwork for "Abnormal Times." The court decision in the 1941 opium den case (mentioned above) was based on the concept of crisis—in this case, World War II. The many coups and constitutions from 1932 to 1958 institutionalized "crisis" as a pervasive and serious situation beyond repair by "normal" mechanisms. And crises created coups. Once power was seized, martial law was declared and "abnormal times" began. Wrongdoers were tried.

Royalists who failed to reinstate the absolute monarchy in the 1930s were the first to be tried in "The Special Court."[31] During this period, leaders began to specify a certain kind of political situation that varied from the norm.

The underlying principle of "Abnormal Times" comes clear from discussions surrounding the draft of a 1944 bill that would "allow the confinement of persons who are a danger to the nation in times of emergency." The "Reason" was as follows:

> Because it appears that certain people are acting as an enemy to the peace and order and safety of the country-nation, who, if not confined, could cause disorder to the country through many ways. [*sic*] For one, in maintaining peace and order and the safety of the country-nation in times of emergency like this, it is necessary to have many methods in order to choose from to use [sic] that is fitting for the situation. It is not enough to depend on just one method. For this reason, it is fitting to have the method of confining persons who are a danger to the nation in order to prevent opportunities from being taken up that could be a danger to the nation.

The Section of the law most under debate was:

> *Section 3.*—When there is a case which appears to the Director of the Police Department that there is sufficient reason to believe that there is a person acting or having another person act, or making preparations to act, or conspiring to commit any act which will be a danger to the nation, the Director of the Police Department has the power to request of the committee appointed by virtue of this Act to order that such persons be confined in order to not give them an opportunity to proceed in carrying out such actions which are a danger to the nation.[32]

Adul Aduldecharat, the supreme commander of the armed forces at the time, pointed out that given that this was a time of war, "peace and order and public safety" were important. When peace and public order were not maintained, "chaotic difficulties . . . follow just as a shadow." He entreated the government to understand, "political crimes . . . are likely to involve methods or devices different from crimes that are not political" because of their "alternating complexity on many levels." It was often difficult, he went on to say, to present evidence of such crimes in court "as in regular criminal cases." When these crimes were allowed to "spread" and "widen," the situation would ultimately "explode." After that, it would be a "difficult matter to take things back to their original state." Conversely sometimes there might be enough evidence to take the suspect to court. But if the state lost, then that person could continue with their activities which might "create deleterious effects on the nation." In that case, there may even be more harm than good in taking the person to court. Therefore, the government must have "enough methods" to quell a situation such as this. In times of war, the government "must use methods which will prevent the most"—in this case, a psychological training school for the offenders. The head of the police would choose only those offenders who were "truly fitting and necessary." The school would retrain those people whose "way of thinking and acting" was "in their own interests and certainly against those of Thailand." For those who felt the name "psychological training school" was "not in accordance to noble feelings," the name could be changed. He concluded that "there [needed to be] a way to confine people whose actions or behaviour are a danger to the peace and happiness and safety of the country." This was not "internment" [*kak khang*], he emphasized, merely "detention" [*kak khum*].[33]

This draft was heavily debated by the Juridical Council. Prince Wan Waithayakorn, serving as special advisor to the Office of the Prime Minister, said the idea behind this law was to enable the government to confine people who "have shown themselves to be in opposition to the nation." In abnormal times such as these, Wan warned, there "must be an Emergency Measure for prevention." "It is the interning of a person," Wan went on to argue, "not because he has done something wrong but because some of his behaviour shows that this person is going to do something dangerous to the nation. We are holding here that interning the person first is a Measure of Safety."

One member commented that this law was "an idea of fascism itself." The chairperson of the committee questioned whether the measure would be against the Thai constitution which guaranteed that punishment could only be administered through a court. A "peculiar aspect" to this law was the way that persons merely suspected of something were to be confined as if they had violated the law. Another member said they were not talking about a "psychological training school" at all, but rather something more in lines of "a concentration camp idea" for the "concentration camp is for interning people who have shown themselves to be a danger to the nation." Wan agreed, saying that was why he believed "intern camp"[34] was a better term.

The government claimed the act was not in conflict with the constitution as confinement was not technically punishment. In war people were identified as "danger[s] to the nation," but insufficient evidence existed to bring the case to court. This person thus was to be sent off to the psychological training school in order to prevent a crime from happening. The representative from the Ministry of Justice argued that this measure sought to "confine the suspect first," thus conveniently stopping the crime from being committed.

Despite the objections, the law was passed in early 1945. Although not put into effect, drafting of the law established a key principle supporting special measures for "Abnormal Times."[35]

Instructively the more "democratic" government in power at the end of World War II strengthened martial law and allowed the military courts to intrude more deeply into civilian society. In 1944 and 1945, martial law was put in place. Crimes that, in "normal times," would be tried under the regular criminal courts could now be tried under military courts. These violations involved: the monarchy, Thailand's friendly foreign relations, civilian and military officials, official corruption, courts and judges, perjury in court, illegal associations, riots, public safety and communications, forging of money or official documents, and theft, robbery, purse-snatching, etc.[36] This list became the model military leaders later used to extend military jurisdiction over civilian life, most notably in 1951, 1958, and 1976. But beyond a list of cases to come before the military court annexed to the official declaration of martial law, a further 1945 revision to the law also specified that:

> any criminal cases which occur in an area where martial law has been proclaimed in which there are special circumstances concerning national security or public peace and order, the Supreme Commander of the Armed Forces may order that the adjudication of such cases be placed under the competency of the military courts.[37]

Later, the "Emergency Administration Act of 1952" empowered the prime minister to declare a "state of emergency" to "ensure the stability or safety of the Kingdom, public order and good morals, as well as the welfare of the people." Under this Act, the prime minister could declare curfew, empower officials to enter any premises between sunrise and sundown, and forbid meetings or publications. It also allowed the authorities to arrest and detain up to seven days "any person suspected of committing or attempting to commit any act endangering the stability or safety of the Kingdom." The mail and correspondence of such persons could be inspected when it was shown there were "suspicious circumstances," indicating actions that might prove "detrimental to the nation." Finally, the competent official could forbid anyone from leaving or entering the country, as well as ordering the immediate expulsion of any aliens from the country or forbidding them from doing business. The penalties are substantial. Violating curfew could bring a year in prison. Anyone attending a prohibited meeting or publishing anything forbidden could be imprisoned for up to five years. Anyone who left the country after having been forbidden from doing so could be imprisoned for up to ten years.[38]

The 1930s through 1950s thus laid the legal framework for "Abnormal Times," although it was not fully put into place before 1958. The decisions of the courts undermined the integrity of the entire judicial system. Short experiments with special administrative detentions and some attempts with military courts trying civilians were undertaken. Certain situations began to be imagined during which temporary "emergency" measures might be taken. But these various components of "Abnormal Times" were not yet put together in a more permanent way. Throughout this period cases were still tried publicly, defendants could still appeal cases, and the Supreme Court was still handing down decisions that had some legal weight.

From the first "permanent" constitution in 1932 to 1957, there were five constitutions—an average lifespan of five years. Despite the frequent attempted and successful coups, every government at least preserved the trappings of democracy—parliaments, law courts, some press freedom, and such. Accordingly, the entire process was open for the public to analyze, debate, and critique—the life-blood of any public sphere.

Militarization and the dawn of eternal "abnormal times"

"Abnormal Times" became a Thai legal term defined as a period of crisis during which normal political and legal functions of society were suspended and a temporary, specialized set of laws and procedures took effect to maintain security and peace until "Normal Times" could return. What might be criticism in normal times might be transformed into seditious rebellion in abnormal times. For military governments, abnormal times and states of emergency necessitated a special set of laws—martial law—and special courts.[39]

Judicial decisions of the 1940s and 1950s laid solid groundwork for subverting the rule of law. Redefining the Thai polity, though, required work in three additional areas: debasing constitutional law, subordinating criminal law to military coup decrees, and militarization of the civilian court system (having civilian courts serve as military courts).

During the 34-year period from 1957 to 1991 when the first democratically elected prime minister formed a government, even the appearance of democracy was removed—absolutely from 1957 to 1968, 1971–73, 1976–78, and from 1978–88. During only three brief periods—none lasting more than three years—were there any sort of apparent democracy—1968–71, 1973–76, and 1988–91. From 1957 to 1991Thailand experienced eight constitutions, with an average lifespan of less than four years. Each constitutional assembly was convened with a great deal of fanfare and solemnity.[40]

Discussion of the criminal code becomes largely moot because the justice system was, literally, overthrown. Criminal law, as with constitutional law, was made subordinate to, if not irrelevant by, coup decrees. The weak role of the Supreme Court in protecting rights diminished further. Serious consultations between the government and the Juridical Council on political matters were abandoned. The careful deliberations of the Council and their stern warnings in some cases against the government's plans to issue laws curtailing basic rights were lost. Forgotten, too, were the Supreme Court Decisions that had figured prominently prior to 1958.[41]

The fate of the Supreme Court was tragic and emblematic of the times. Its final political decision under the Sarit Thanarat government exhibited almost craven support of dictatorship; the courts as points or nodes of political mediation disappeared.[42]

"Proclamation of the Revolutionary Group No. 12," issued on 22 October 1958, which stated that "investigation authorities shall have power to detain the accused throughout the period of investigation without having to act in conformity with the provisions of law concerning the period during which an accused may be detained",[43] resulted in the arrest and detention in Lat Yao Prison of a large number of persons suspected of being communists or communist sympathizers.

Many detainees had no formal charges made against them and were never brought before a judge.[44] A group of the Lat Yao detainees, however, was able to appeal to the courts in January of 1959 after a new coup constitution came into effect. They argued that, as a new constitution had come into effect, the former proclamation was void and they called for the court to order their release. The Supreme Court denied their request on two grounds.

First, it ruled that Proclamation No. 12 was the result of a seizure of power on 20 October 1958. After that time, power was in the hands of the "Revolutionary Group" and any proclamations they made had the force of law.

Second, Provision 20 of the administrative constitution, which came into effect on 28 January 1959, addressed legal precedent, stating: "Whenever there is no constitutional provision or act covering a certain circumstance, it should be resolved by following the customs of governing Thailand under the democratic system [*phrapheni kanpokkhrong prathet thai nai rabop prachathipatai*]." What this meant, the court said, is that since the administrative constitution did not repeal any laws, then Proclamation No. 12, like all other laws previous to the constitution's coming into use, remained in effect. Moreover, the court ruled, the Revolutionary Group had granted itself an amnesty on 31 March 1959 which forgave it for its actions in October of the previous year. The amnesty also affirmed all the proclamations and orders made at that time as just and binding. Even if not, the Supreme Court could do nothing, for all of the suspects had been placed under the jurisdiction of the military court by the same proclamation. The petition was dismissed.[45]

This decision continued the coup-legitimizing decisions made by courts from the previous decade when the courts seemed to crumble in the face of the challenge that coups posed for the law. One can at once be sympathetic to the courts—how else, indeed, could they have ruled?—and incredulous that these bold usurpations of power eventually destroyed not only democracy in Thailand, but tore to shreds any meaningful sense of "law," juridical impartiality, or intellectual integrity of the courts. Through their rulings the courts effectively nullified themselves as "the last resort" of the people. Through their decisions, the courts advised those seizing power to utterly suppress and silence opposition or potential opposition from the start. The bloodier the coup, the greater the terror created, the more absolute the silence—and the more legitimate the power.

The court system became militarized. "Abnormal Times" necessitated the declaration of martial law, which continued in some areas of Thailand for decades and decades, if not up to the present. Crimes committed within areas under martial law were sent to the military courts. In actuality, most military courts were civilian courts operating under military court procedures. After 1958, cases that would go to these reconstituted military courts were, among others, national security provisions (including *lèse-majesté*, seditious rebellion, and other "high end" defamation-based measures (Provisions 107–35), public security (Provisions 209–39), sexual offenses (Provisions 282–83), offenses against life and physical security (murder, assault) (Provisions 288–300), and offenses concerning property and security (theft, robbery, etc.) (Provisions 340–57).[46] A number of articles and manuals were published to help judges and prosecutors understand how to operate and judge cases in military court style.[47] Military dictatorships favor military courts or tribunals for their quick administration of justice; additionally, decisions of a military court are not subject to appeal and defendants are often deprived of fundamental rights, such as the right to counsel or public trials.

In the first few years of this new court system, the percentage of criminal cases tried through the military courts was rather high.[48] From 1961 to 1963, of the 2,906 murder cases in 1961, 97.5 percent were tried in military court and, in 1963, 99.1 percent of them were.[49] Of the total number of 124,784 criminal cases tried in 1961, 28,748 cases, or about 23 percent were tried in military court and 14 percent of cases in 1962 and 1963. The percentage remained just under 10 percent through 1969 and dropped to 6 percent in 1971. With re-imposition of the dictatorship in late 1971, the percentages shot up again, tripling to 18 percent of cases in 1972, when even some unspecified misdemeanors were tried in military courts.[50] The percentage of criminal cases tried in military court edged higher to 22 percent in 1973, the last year of the dictatorship.[51] The percentage of new criminal cases in military court at first dropped in 1974 to 12.7 percent, then nearly vanished, at 0.8 percent of all criminal cases in 1975; it rose just slightly to 3 percent in 1976.[52]

Crimes defined as violations of national security laws—*lèse-majesté*, rebellion, insult of flags or other national symbols, insult of religion—were automatically sent to the extensive system of military courts or to militarized civilian courts. Unlike Thai Supreme Court Decisions which were generally public, most military court decisions were not publicly available and were often marked as "secret." As the discourse of national security spread and encompassed more and more of the public sphere, an entire dimension of Thai history was erased. Only occasional military court decisions were made public—such as the trial of *Phra* Phimontham (Chapter 10)—and a handful of Supreme Court decisions were released that considered national security issues.[53] In the first decade of this period beginning in 1958, a legal black hole devoured any instance of public consultation in the drafting of laws (there was no parliament) or public debate on law. Newspapers were shut down, silencing the most important vehicle for public discourse and oversight of the government. Not only did the public sphere shrink to pre-1932 proportions, but the necessary legal, political, and social scaffolding that supported the overall structure of the public sphere was razed to its foundations. The declaration of "Abnormal Times" animated an entire national security mechanism. The official sphere gained remarkable dominance over the public and even sacred spheres (see Figure 4.1). "Abnormal Times" meant not mere hegemony of the official sphere over a reduced civil society, but a near-total domination by the official sphere.

Even cases without obvious connections to national security, such as personal defamation, were tried in military court. Defamation served as a "fall back" charge in lieu of the more serious charge of seditious rebellion and received special attention from the state beginning in the early 1960s. Between

1961 and 1965, an average of 350 arrests were made annually for defamation. Of these, 248 led to convictions—a rate of 71 percent. During this same period, of the 15 arrests that led to prosecution in the military court, there was an 80 percent conviction rate. How could such cases end up under the purview of the military court, if there wasn't some connection between perceived national security and the reputation of some persons? Even including these 15 cases, defamation cases tried in military court accounted for only 1 percent of all defamation convictions during these years. In 1973, defamation cases mysteriously reappear in military court just as the military junta reached a crisis, representing a little over 1 percent of total defamation convictions. From 1974 to 1976, there were 13 arrests and nine convictions for defamation in military court, still less than one percent of all cases. The percentage of those arrested for defamation and tried in military court rose slightly to 3 percent in 1977. In 1978, when the number of defamation cases reached a high of 831—an amount not exceeded until 1998—the percentage of defamation convictions in the military court shot up to 19 percent and, in 1980, to 32 percent. An average of 71 percent of defamation arrests that led to trial before regular, non-military civilian courts led to conviction; in the military courts a more certain 89 percent of arrests led to convictions. In fact, in 1979, the conviction rate for defamation trials was a perfect 100 percent.[54]

After a decade of semi-democracy teetering on the edge of dictatorship, Thai society, beginning in 1958, was thrown into three decades of "Abnormal Times."[55] Abnormal Times were always exceptional because there was always a crisis prompted by enemies. In such circumstances, men of virtue (such as military generals) sacrificed their personal safety concerns to adopt extraordinary measures. Maintaining an aura of legality for initially "illegal" regimes created an atmosphere of legitimacy that made offenses against such regimes appear more serious. In other words, the more legitimate a regime claimed to be, the greater a crime, such as rebellion, represented.

One 1972 case illustrates the legal absurdities found during abnormal times. After ten years of strict military rule from 1958 to 1968, a new constitution was passed and elections for a parliament were held, only to be abrogated by an auto-coup on 17 November 1971. In response, three former members of parliament (MPs) submitted a petition to a court asking for charges of rebellion to be brought against the Revolutionary Council. The detailed response of the ruling junta deserves special attention, as it is one of the finest legal apologies for violence and coups ever issued in Thailand.[56] In the "Order of the Head of the Revolutionary Council No. 36/2515," dated 22 June 1972, the Prime Minister, Field Marshall Thanom Kittikhajorn, outlined the problem. The three former MPs charged the field marshal and 17 of his associates with rebellion. The military clique was accused of joining together:

> to use deadly force and threat to all of the people of Thailand, in order to overthrow the constitution, the effect of which was to cause civil

> politicians, the accused, and the Thai people throughout the country to become so fearful that they went along [with the overthrow of the constitution].

The military group was accused of then abolishing parliament, "which was the overthrow of the legislative power," an action which caused neither the MPs nor the "common Thai person to be brave enough to dare convene Parliament." The plaintiffs asked the court to punish Thanom and his 17 associates. Thanom claimed that there was "clear evidence" that the three former MPs, now defendants, "encouraged others to join them in appealing to the court" as the MPs had invited the media to attend. Thanom charged that in making an accusation and by inviting the media showed that what the MPs had done "was not the expression of honest opinions." Instead, the action was undertaken to:

> cause so much turmoil and rebelliousness amongst the people that it would cause disquietude in the kingdom, which is a violation against the security of the state, and constitute actions which are intended to oppose, obstruct, and overthrow the Revolutionary Council.

Thanom claimed that the authorities had been watching the three. Thanom's case asserted that the leader, Mr. Uthai Phimjaichon (who later headed a Constitution Drafting Assembly in 1997) had decided to make the charge because he "believed staging a coup d'état was unnecessary as there was a constitution." The parliament, then, "could have been ordered dissolved through constitutional means." But, by leading a coup and voiding the constitution, the military leaders put themselves in a state of "rebellion." Moreover, in their position as MPs, the three defendants were unable to perform the duties they had been elected to carry out.

The "National Security Maintenance Section" under the command of the Revolutionary Council and headed by the director-general of the police investigated this matter and issued the following in its report. It discovered that Uthai had often said, "Field Marshall Thanom Kittikhajorn had carried out the revolution for the sake of his own cronies and for those with power." The investigating authorities had to ask the question of whether the three accused had "made honest use of their rights" or whether they had acted "with the intention of causing turmoil and rebelliousness amongst the people, to the point of causing disquietude in the country and whether it was against, an obstacle to, or an attempt to overthrow the Revolutionary Council or not."

The defendants had defined three areas of allegation. The first area concerned three specific items the council wanted to refute. First, the council argued that the defendants had said that the coup was carried out "in the evening, before twelve," on 17 November. Although calling themselves the "Revolutionary Council," the council said that during the alleged time there had been "no revolution" at all. To say so "was to distort and misrepresent the truth in the interests" of the defendants' case. Second, the defendants went to criminal court where they were told that they would have to go and petition the military court. The defendants allegedly responded, "We don't know. That's for the courts to decide." This statement, the council's report said, was aimed at "having the people feel suspicious and have doubts about the status of the Revolutionary Council." These doubts would "result in causing turmoil, chaos among the people" because it would cause "the people to feel the Revolutionary Council had executed a coup [and would be in revolution forever] because in normal times one would start with the Court of First Instance and go up through to the Supreme Court." Finally, the suspects had said that the people "felt afraid and were compelled to go along" with the actions of the Revolutionary Council. But three months after the coup, it was "quite clear and evident" that the council "had not used force or violence, or threatened all of Thailand." In fact, it said, not "even one single person had been caused to feel fear." Moreover, on the evening that the coup had been staged, the council had made an announcement, "asking the people not to be worried, and the government officials to do their work legally as usual." To say that people were afraid when "the facts of the matter" were that no one was afraid was "to distort the truth in order to cause disquiet to arise in the country."

The second area of allegation the Order of the Head of the Revolutionary Council No. 36/2515 addressed was the charge made by the former MPs that the council had not "dissolved the parliament through constitutional means." Failing to do so, the order stated, was one of the reasons the suspects had charged the council with rebellion. The military leaders claimed that they had made it clear at the time why there needed to be a coup. In the order, they summarize that, in November of 1971, there were "both internal and external incidents" that "were fluctuating [and leading] toward a bad way" and that there was "a danger to the country-nation and the throne":

> The invasion by neighbouring countries had doubled in violence and intensity. There were incitements to support the creators of disquietude for the people in various places in the country, with the aim of changing the governance system to become another system which is not the democratic governance system with king as head of state. As far as internal problems in the county, it appears there were certain groups of individuals who exercise their constitutional rights, and some groups who advocate, undermine, and use influence to disturb and obstruct the administration of the government, such as inciting the people and various institutions to oppose and be rebellious toward the government, inciting students to go on protest marches and have labourers strike. Solving the aforementioned situations, if proceeding along constitutional methods, would likely not keep up with the pace of events. And so it was necessary to seize governing power in order to be able to solve these situations decisively and promptly.

The order goes on to say that the three accused persons, as members of parliament at the time, were "no doubt well aware" of the council's announcement to this effect at the time of the coup and "realized the necessity to proceed in addressing the situation of the country." Before the coup, the three had "heard the urgent discussions, asking for the government to proceed in suppressing the terrorists in an orderly and quick manner." The military leaders also admonished the three former MPs who, though trained in law, did not know that after a group had "successfully seized ruling power," it became "the highest governing power of the country." When "central, regional, and local administrative units" and "the people come to accept and respect the exercise" of such power, "it can be held that the revolutionary group is the government which is correct according to principles of political science and the science of law." In an almost comical admission of guilt, the council contended that "overthrowing the government" in this manner had brought it power "in exactly the same way as overthrowing a government legally." The Revolutionary Council then cited decisions of the Supreme Court from the 1950s, discussed above, that formed the basis of legitimacy for a series of military dictatorships throughout this period.

The Revolutionary Council also argued that the former MPs could not charge the council with having illegally dissolved parliament, for in the three months since the coup, an Administrative Assembly had been set up. This assembly and the administration overall had come to be "accepted and respected by the people both in Thailand and internationally." Charges by the three former MPs, therefore, were "not reasonable."

The third area of accusation concerned the question of who could serve as the damaged party. The three former MPs claimed they were the damaged parties as the parliament had been illegally abolished and this action affected them. However, the Revolutionary Council claimed that the three former MPs could not serve as the damaged party in this case. The council again admonished the three, saying that they were "well aware" of the fact that they did not have "the power to bring such a case to court on the charge of revolt." In criminal cases, only state prosecutors have such power. To reinforce this claim, the order mentioned a 1971 court ruling which disallowed Mr. Chumphorn Maninet, a member of parliament at the time of the incident, from bringing a criminal case to court as plaintiff. In this 5 November decision, a court ruled that:

> In terms of when a plaintiff cites his status as a representative of the common Thai folk according to the constitution, the court recognizes that such a representative of the citizens or a member of parliament has power and duties as far as the law stipulates. When there is no legislative law, the court sees that a member of parliament cannot serve as the damaged party and does not have the right to bring certain cases to court.

In other words, when a seizure of power has abolished parliament, MPs lose their special status and power as MPs. Thus, they have no more right to bring criminal charges against another as anyone else. They cannot claim to be a damaged party as MPs in a criminal case. Moreover, the military leaders claimed that no one, in fact, could claim to be "the damaged party." Section 25 of the 1968 Constitution of the Kingdom of Thailand stipulated that all Thai people are equal, the order claims, making any single, individual citizen equally unable to bring criminal charges against the military leaders for their coup as the damaged party, for there was "no damaged party." A member of parliament was equally not a damaged party.[57]

Apparently the courts agreed with this reasoning. In refusing to hear the case presented to it by the three former MPs, the criminal court, in the Decision of Red Case 1295/2515 [1972], ruled that, in a case such as this, "the nature of the damaged party" must be one in which such party "has legal status in order to receive special damages." In this case of a coup, the court ruled, "there is no collective quality to that violation" and so "the nature of the plaintiff is not one of the damaged parties."

For misrepresenting the facts, for claiming the parliament had been illegally abolished, and because the three former MPs could not serve as the damaged party, the order concludes, the attempt by the three to bring this case before the court "was not exercising the right" for "the expression of an honest opinion." It was an "intentional act" that sought to "mislead" the people to misunderstand that the coup carried out by the Revolutionary Council "was an act of rebellion which must be punished according to criminal law." Instead, the three former MPs should be charged with attempting to "resist and overthrow the Revolutionary Council," for sowing "suspicions" about the Revolutionary Council's rule, and for "intending to cause so much turmoil and rebelliousness amidst the people" that "disquietude" would result.[58]

If the actions of the three were to go unpunished, then, the order concludes, "the people" might have been "misled" to understand that "the Revolutionary Council was in effect still in a state of rebellion" which might have resulted in such doubt that the people might have acted in ways that were "against the law or the administration of the country." The actions of the three were thus "extremely serious." Thanom accordingly sentenced Uthai with ten years of imprisonment and the other two with seven years.[59]

In this decision, we have all the hallmarks of defamation-based state crimes : the lack of sincere intentions of the defendants (How could they possibly have been well intentioned if they publicly took this complaint to the court?); that the actions of the defendants would cause confusion and turmoil; that the actions would cause disloyalty toward the regime (How could anyone reasonably not have faith in a military government?); that the coup group had legitimate reasons for executing the coup (enemies, threats, breakdown of society); that somehow the coup was in defense of democracy.

This order made by the military government is rather remarkable, both as a defense of dictators and coups, and because of its close (and twisted) adherence to legal principles. One reason to quote extensively from this case is to show the awkwardness of the military government in trying to express the peculiar reasoning of the Revolutionary Council. The case was so bizarrely argued that one wonders why the Revolutionary Council bothered making it. It would have been better to say nothing at all. The Revolutionary Council might simply have referred vaguely to the threat to national security and summarily jailed the defendants.[60] But because defamation (in this case, seditious rebellion) is the ultimate public act, those prosecuting sometimes find themselves responding to the public.

This complex "network of legitimating laws and rulings" is so historically and legally encompassing that it has largely eluded the scholarly attention of both foreign and Thai academics. One of the few works that look directly at the phenomenon is Somchai Preechasilpakul's "Juridical Principles of Coups," which examines the origins of the legal breakdown and its effects on the Thai legal community.[61] Somchai makes the obvious—though rarely stated—point that forcibly overthrowing the government and constitutional order is a serious criminal infraction, quite clearly outlined in the criminal code. He argues that while "the Thai legal system has played a part in allowing a succession of *coups* to succeed to the present," its role in this respect has "never seriously been considered." He questions whether Thailand has made any progress in democratization given that this most basic truth remains largely unacknowledged, even (or especially) by leading legal minds in Thailand.

It is important that through the entire so-called transition from dictatorship to democracy in the past half century, the courts have yet to seriously challenge the core legality of coups and the laws the coup makers institute.[62] One Thai legal mind wrote,

> I wouldn't deny the point that there might have been a chance for change without the coup. I don't defend the coup . . . Certainly many people felt that we must resist the coup . . . [But] after two or three days . . . I had to accept . . . that there had been a coup . . . [the coup makers] had been able to seize power of the state fully and all sides accepted that they'd come in and were in power already . . . [the coup makers] had become the sovereign state power . . . If asked whether I like coups, do I support coups, I affirm that there is no legal person, especially legal persons involved in public law who are going to like coups and support coups. But we have to stand on the foundation of the truth that after there's been a coup, one has to move on. And many seeing the system like this [recognize] it as an opportunity to make change.[63]

Another legal scholar, Borwornsak Uwanno, makes the case that the king remained the sovereign power even after the absolute monarchy was overthrown, for the constitution that resulted became valid only after the king approved it. Somchai argues that this logic persists: because coup groups must seek the approval from the monarch to legitimize their act (which always abolishes the previous constitution) and to grant the amnesty forgiving the action, each coup essentially reasserts the ultimate sovereignty of the monarchy over any constitutional order.[64]

We should be careful not to see "rule of law" as *the* solution to Thailand's core issues of legitimacy and sovereignty. Munger reminds us the rule of law can just as often serve authoritarian as progressive regimes. Lev, too, points out that

> pressures toward constitutionalism and more effective legal process have advantages and suffer constraints quite different from those of old Europe . . . . [I]deas, in Asia as in Europe or anywhere else, take hold only when they *make sense domestically* and are *adapted to domestic purposes*.[65]

It is difficult to gauge when something "makes sense domestically" and if there are questions as to exactly *who* is adapting *what* to *what end*. One should also exercise caution in accepting the "cultural" traits of a given society at face value, for such quite-often superficial renderings may be merely state-sponsored and created "culture."[66]

We began this chapter discussing the "state of exception" and Thai "Abnormal Times." But I want to make clear the connection between the state of exception and defamation regimes. The motion toward the state of exception can be read backwards or forwards. If backwards, the severity of "the situation" is determined by "general and indeterminate clauses" (danger, crisis, threat to peace and order) captured in emergency decrees or martial law, which the state declares. In the latter, the sovereign power (the government, the state) declares a state of exception through invoking martial law, which in turn determines the indeterminate concept.

In Germany's case, the indeterminate concept of race was essential for the state's existence. Agamben claims that without it, "the National Socialist state could not exist." State power is not merely expressed by declaring itself outside the law; the essence of its power is in deciding when the state of exception prevails. The sovereign decides which situations are normal and which are not. The decision to declare a situation as normal or abnormal, writes Schmitt, "reveals the essence of State authority most clearly." Agamben describes the "the state of exception" as "willed"—the sovereign can create the situation that necessitates the state of exception:

> The sovereign no longer limits himself . . . to deciding on the exception on the basis of recognizing a given factual situation (danger or public safety) . . . he now de facto provides the situation as a consequence of this decision on the exception.[67]

Is it possible that Thailand's long acquaintance with the state of exception was the willed creation of the situation? By maintaining the situation (abnormal times) and the indeterminate phrases (public order, national security, Thainess) supporting it, Thai military governments were able to sustain the state of exception. When we realize defamation's particular sensitivity to time and place (= situation = indeterminate) and witness how abnormal times eventually became the norm, we can appreciate the close, intertwining relationship between the state of exception and defamation-based crimes and their adjudication. The crisis precipitates declaration of the state of exception. The state uses defamation-based law and its adjudication to both define the crisis and defend the state of exception.

The remarkable power created by the mix of the state of exception and the defamation regime, have seriously affected truth. As Agamben argues, when suspension of the law is prolonged, "fact and law are completely confused," and the distinction between "questions of fact and questions of law . . . has literally no more meaning."[68]

We can conclude with the paradox in the proposition that Thailand has always been in varying states of exception (the suspension of normal rules). Have the brief moments of suspension of the state of exclusion themselves been exceptional periods? Thailand might be the exception to the state of exception.

Part III

Components of defamation: intent, target, receiver

6 Intent and import

The next four chapters dissect the constituent parts of Thai defamatory action: the defamer, the words, the defamed, and the measure of completed action. This chapter examines the two pieces of evidence concerning the defamer—the words and their intent: the force that drove those words to be uttered in public or written and published. Chapter 7 studies the nature of the target of the defamatory action, beginning with the individual, and then rising up the scale to government officials, "government," and finally the nation and its symbols. Chapter 8 is a thorough examination of the most pristine of Thai defamatory targets: monarchy, and the peculiar nature of its protector, the *lèse-majesté* law. Chapter 9 ends this part with a look at what, at least theoretically, registers the successful completion of the defamatory act: that the people, having heard or read the words, look down on the insulted party.

Blasphemy laws in Europe were instituted to protect a kind of religious truth, as Nidhi calls it, "truth-beyond-truth." To insult the religion was to insult this truth-beyond-truth. Fostering teachings contrary to accepted religious doctrine was heresy, the teaching of falsehoods (claiming that truth-beyond-truth was not true). If one's sayings were deemed heretical, one's intentions were accordingly evil. The Spanish Inquisition tried to avert evil and, despite Catholic heresy trials against the likes of Galileo, the Enlightenment version of "the truth" (a secular one) largely eventually prevailed over the truth-beyond-truth of the religious realm. As defamation laws became distinct from blasphemy and heresy, they nevertheless continued to embody intention as an essential element, positing that bad intentions create lies and good intentions produce the truth. A coordinate step implied a connection between the feeling of defamation or insult and the untruth that produced it. In Europe, for a number of centuries, defamation cases with no particular religious overtones retained these associations; arguing a statement's truth was not permitted. The only points argued were who said or published it and whether the words would result in other people looking down on the one so defamed. Only in the eighteenth century could the truth be argued in defamation cases (see Chapter 1, John Peter Zenger), but even today the matter is far from over. Indeed, the charge of treason retains certain aspects of blasphemy which focus on insult that overwhelms questions of truth. I suggest that wherever either religious sentiment is strong or within a sacralized realm (which some constitutional monarchies might still be), the association between insult and untruth still holds.

In Western jurisprudence, intent, once considered "the gist of an action of defamation," no longer plays a central role in adjudication.[1] In civil cases in most countries, truth trumps malice. Even if malice can be convincingly shown, but the statement in question is shown to be true, there is no guilt. In Thailand, though, I argue that a more ancient (from the point of view of the West) view of a defamer as a malicious spreader of lies prevails. Intent remains the major determinant of guilt in defamation cases in Thailand. This assumption of intent is informed by a particular interpretation of Thai Theravada Buddhism which links good intentions and the truth and bad intentions and lies.

In Thailand, no space exists for well-intentioned persons to advance lies or malicious individuals to advance the truth. Words are inherently suspicious in Thai Theravada Buddhism, as their careless use produces unpleasant karmic effects. Determining whether words are careless or malicious requires looking at the intent of their author. Intent can be discerned by observing the effects of the words: "perfect" or "complete" words create favorable results, which indicates "pure intention." Conversely, words produced from ill intentions create negative results; they contribute to confusion, conflict, and chaos.[2] Veracity is also a key virtue within the Theravada Buddhist tradition. Perfect words are, of course, veracious. Therefore, veracious words reduce conflict and create harmony and unity; falsehoods inevitably lead to the opposite. Within a sacralized, Theravada Buddhist formation, the sacred head—a king—adheres to the royal virtues; he is a *dhammaraja*.

The fuzzy distinction between defamation and truth is reflected in the 1900 edict's name: "The Royal Edict on defamation through falsely spoken or written words." The assumption is that defamation is designed to punish those who "falsely" impugn others.[3] The edict also appears to give exception to sincere critics of the government. The rationale for the 1900 edict provides exemption for those who, among other things, "want to point out the inadequacies of the official work of the government, to have the government think of revising certain laws, or the royal customs dictating governing practices." Exemption is granted to those who have "good and sincere intentions" and speak "for the benefit of the country and people," but cancelled for those who are "stepped in love and hate," are "angry and resentful," or use "intemperate words." The curious link between truth, sincerity, and politeness gives exemption only to those who appear disinterested and dispassionate. Apparently, persons cannot have "good and sincere intentions" if they are biased and feel passionately. Truth thus becomes a function of a polite and altruistic society. Any hint of selfishness, vengeance, or bias on the part of the critic automatically transforms truth into an untruth. Intent is central to interpretation of this edict.

The author of the 1904 law textbook (see Chapter 4) avers that treason laws are based on the notion that "the king is above the law." To question an action of the king or to challenge this act's legality challenges his sacred claim to the throne as *dhammaraja*. The result of these propositions is that the king is good and, by extension, so is the state and government. To challenge him or to create "general resentment and dissatisfaction" is an act of bad faith, of ill intention. The essence of treason, then, is disloyalty to the king and state. Disloyalty can only be produced by an evil heart. Disloyalty is against the truth. Truth is loyalty.[4]

Intent under the Thai absolute monarchy

In his 1927 work, Ammatho argues that, in terms of defamation cases as a whole, it "must first be ascertained whether the defendant had honest intentions." Showing that the defendant had knowingly spoken or written something that caused the plaintiff to suffer a loss of reputation is not enough to prove that the defendant had ill intent. The plaintiff must also show that the defendant had reason or motive to act in such a way. Only a reason can convincingly show whether it is possible to say that the defendant had ill intent or not. Severity of punishment, says Ammatho, should be in proportion to the amount of malicious intent concealed in the defendant's heart but made apparent by some act. And if he or she had ill intent, then that person will be found guilty of defamation. Intent is key to understanding the crime of defamation. Ammatho separates intention into three aspects: "(1) intention to defame falsely; (2) intention to make it known; (3) intention to have it cause damage to the plaintiff."[5]

Ammatho gives the following example: If Mrs. A. says that Mrs. B. commits sexual improprieties with elephants and horses, this is not an imputation because those who heard such words would not believe them to be true. However, if Mrs. A. says that Mrs. B. has many lovers, people might believe such is true and so it is defamation. An example is the case where a person said of a woman, "When her husband is gone, the number of cocks [known to her] number in the hundreds and thousands." Such distinctions legally come down to intent: Did the speaker intend to have others believe this or not? If there was such intent, then there is defamation.[6]

Along with intent the "expression of an honest opinion" or "the expression of an opinion in good faith" are also generally excluded from defamation[7] According to Ammatho, such an expression is "an action that does not have the intention of causing unfavorable things to happen" and "is done with honest purpose, thinking that it is right and proper, or in order to be of good benefit to the masses." In other words, if "unfavorable things" happen as a result of words, then the words' intentions were bad. Ammatho says that the preconditions to expressing an "honest opinion" are good intentions and speaking in good faith. While the law gives an opportunity to people to express opinions "without fear of being in violation of the law," this "special power" is not absolute. The intent behind the expression of an opinion must be examined to ascertain whether they were "good or ill." If a statement is expressed "in good faith," there is no guilt. If it is expressed with ill intentions, it does not receive exclusion from guilt.[8]

English law grants a witness giving testimony before a court the full right to say anything, even if it is damaging to someone else's reputation, regardless of the witness's intentions. Ammatho argues that Thai law does not allow such a sweeping privilege: in Thai law, witnesses only have right to "voice something honestly." A witness speaking with ill intent about others may be defamatory. The result, he says, is that people under Thai law must "handle the truth with extreme caution." This applies to "fair comment" as well: exemption is given if personal defamation on the wrongful actions of authorities is of benefit to the public. The actions of government officials concern the public because such actions affect the public's welfare. Ammatho says the exemption is correct because it "gives the people an opportunity to criticize and chastise officials who have acted inappropriately, in order to have officials be cautious and not act illegally." An exemption is also given to individuals who comment on public affairs, including public personages. Such comment, though, writes Ammatho, must be "without bias" and must be made with a "sincere and honest objective," although it might damage someone's reputation.[9]

Ammatho notes no exceptions or saving clauses for *lèse-majesté* or seditious rebellion. In these cases, he argues, intent is "more important than anything else" for "only intention can make that action successful . . . intention can be considered as the act." While "motive or intention is enough to merit punishment," he advises that "there must nonetheless be external behaviour or signs" indicating intent, "because there is no way to know what is in a person's heart." Therefore, "in order to get to the truth underlying intentions, there must be something which can be held up as evidence which proves the truth of the behaviour." The evidence does not have to be substantial—"only enough to show the evil intent." A defendant can never argue that it "was a matter of necessity" because in cases of this type the stakes are so high:

> With offences against the king or country, one cannot argue that it was a matter of necessity for the one who committed the crime to expunge the guilt because it is a crime against the nation or against the land and damages the public. Necessity cannot become a defence. It must be held that the activities of the nation and of the king are more important than those of the individual. The former brings a great benefit to the people.[10]

Ammatho describes "internal rebellion" from Section 104 of the 1908 code as an act against the "rulers of the land or the authorities of the state." Here rebellion does not mean doing bodily harm to government officials "within a private capacity" or destroying public property, but rather displaying "a direct, malicious intent toward the country or the land." It might be acceptable to call for changes in the "royal customs and governing of the kingdom," but only "if it is done" in an "orderly" fashion "not upsetting to the government." If such change is accomplished by creating "great suffering in the land," then the perpetrator must be "severely punished." The central point is not whether "one thinks that royal customs should be changed," but rather if the act "is done with malicious intent" or encourages others to "have a mutinous heart which is capable of opposing the power of the land." Moreover, unlike other crimes, seditious rebellion does not necessitate that the actions "produce the desired results"—only that the actions have been conceived. If one has insulted the government, this is enough, regardless of "whether the people do look down on [the government]" or not. All that is necessary for guilt is that "a person incites or promotes such with the intention of having people look down on the king, government, or bureaucracy." Section 104, he says, is crucial, for the crime of insulting the king, government, or bureaucracy "must be punished."[11]

While Ammatho admits to no exemptions for *lèse-majesté* or seditious rebellion, he says that government officials could, at least theoretically, be made accountable through the exemptions given for personal defamation. If the accused have expressed an "honest opinion" in speaking in their own defense, "politely praising or criticizing any person or thing which in the natural course of things the public is speaking about," or "politely" recounting "any court proceedings or report of any meeting" are all exempt.[12] Truth may be introduced in one's defense when the expression was with "an intention of being a benefit to the public" or in accusing "an official of acting illegally within his official position and duties." Significantly, while the truth could completely absolve a person of guilt for personal defamation, there are no such exceptions for *lèse-majesté* or seditious rebellion.[13]

An early case from 1919, when Mr. Narin Phasit published some 3000 pamphlets and sent them out through the mail, illustrates this.[14] Among other things, the following words of the defendant were deemed defamatory:

> Officials who receive a monthly government salary do not pay attention or address themselves to ameliorating the problems of the people. Even more, Buddhism compounds the problem by leading people into ignorance, inherent in the practices of almost everyone. As a result, this is the state of the country and of Buddhism.

To determine intent, the Supreme Court divided the defendant's statements into seven distinct pieces:

1 That officials do not know of the troubles of the people;
2 That officials aware of the troubles simply ignored them;
3 That if officials were unable to fix [the troubles], they did not say so or were ashamed that they could do nothing. If so, they should resign;

4 The defendant's contention that he could be a provincial governor, minister, or advisor;
5 That the defendant used to be popular and enjoyed suppressing corrupt officials;
6 Buddhism leads people to ignorance;
7 If what the defendant said became known, would it be useful?[15]

The Supreme Court ruled that, by examining these seven components, the intent of the defendant could be discerned. First, the court did not simply pull out "a small point here and a small point there" but considered the defendant's words as a whole. Taken individually, the defendant's contentions might not be considered defamatory. But when items 1, 2, 3, and 6 "are read together," the defendant's words "can be construed as a criticism of the government that is sufficient to cause a loss of loyalty, and comprise an insult." Using this method of interpretation, the court ruled that the intent of the defendant is made clear. The court did not consider the defendant's contention that he had "acted with a desire to bring peace and happiness to the people, in the name of order." It upheld the two-year sentence.

Why did the inclusion of component 6 move this case beyond normal criticism into seditious rebellion, especially when Buddhism is not in any way protected under this law? Conversely, if the defendant had said everything *but* item 6, would this have been enough to constitute seditious rebellion? Or, what would have happened if he had written only item 6? It might be argued that even if Mr. Narin's criticisms of officials were severe, his touching upon Buddhism—a piece of the official nationalism and so taboo—provided a window into his malicious heart and tipped the scale into seditious rebellion.[16]

A decision of the Supreme Court of the same year, one from the province of Nan in the north, resulted similarly.[17] The defendant, Mr. Tan, had dressed up like an official and "went to the headman and people" of a particular district and told them that more than a thousand soldiers had been killed when the "flying ship" [an airplane] they were on crashed. Anyone becoming a soldier, Mr. Tan warned, would surely die in the same way. The prosecution argued that the words of the defendant constituted "inciting" those young men who had received their army enlistment papers "to scatter and flee" in fear. The defendant argued that this was not his intent at all. Rather, he had merely showed off to impress the women, as he was seeking a wife. After being found innocent in the Court of First Instance and the Appeals Court, the Supreme Court heard the argument of the prosecution, calling for a three-year sentence. In some homes the defendant had visited, witnesses reported that there had actually been young men who had been conscripted who, upon hearing the words of the defendant, did flee in fear. Because the defendant's words had turned the minds of some young men who fled, the Supreme Court ruled that "it was beyond a doubt that the words of the defendant clearly showed his intention of having people disobey the law."

Thus, the court declared it was not interested in what the defendant claimed to be his intent. The court felt his intent was clear by the result. It found him guilty and sentenced him to three months' imprisonment.

Intent after the end of absolute monarchy

Little change in the letter of the defamation law or its interpretation has occurred since the overthrow of the absolute monarchy in 1932. An amendment to the law on seditious rebellion in 1935 added an exemption to guilt for the expression of an honest opinion or comments made in the spirit of the constitution, but the 1957 code removed this. No change in legal thinking about "intention" occurred, whether for personal defamation or other more serious versions. As with Ammatho, Jitti Tingsaphat affirms that intention forms the core of defamation-based crimes.[18] As with any crime, defendants of defamation can claim they harboured no intent to defame. If the defendants can show they did not have any ill intent in saying what was said, they are not in violation of defamation by virtue of Section 59 of the 1957 revised code, which makes intent necessary for guilt of any criminal act. It reads:

> *Section 59.* – A person shall be criminally liable only when such person commits an act intentionally . . .
>
> To do an act intentionally is to do an act consciously and at the same time the doer desired or could have foreseen the effect of such doing.
>
> If the doer does not know the facts constituting the elements of the offence, it cannot be deemed that the doer desired or could have foreseen the effect of such doing.[19]

Jitti writes that intent involves the ability to foresee certain results occurring, and their very occurrence strongly suggests intent. Intent ensures guilt. From the defendant's "manner and words," the court can deduce intent. Jitti writes of the intent of those accused of defamation:

> To see this, the meaning of the words spoken must be understood. The court makes this judgment through application of the standard—solely the understanding of a common person—because intention in this section is intention in the action, namely, imputation. It is not the special intent to cause the person to lose their reputation, be disparaged of, or to be hated.[20]

Without looking at intent, Jitti says, it would be impossible to find someone guilty of saying, "Judge K. likes to eat eggs." If this were understood literally, there would be no defamation. But the true (Thai) meaning of the statement—that the judge takes bribes—can be understood only when looking at intent.[21] Jitti adds that the principle of "qualified privilege" applies to those who act in good faith or express a sincere opinion, meaning that if one "speaks in the belief that what he or she is saying is the truth as he or she understands it, even if that understanding is wrong," that person should not be found guilty of defamation.[22]

In regular defamation cases, Thai courts before and after 1932 started with a presumption of the defendant's ill intent. For instance, a decision from a 1938 case said that it is not the responsibility of the prosecution to prove intent by the defendant. From the beginning, "it should be regarded that there is intention already, except when the defendant is able to refute this assumption." In other words, anything judged as defamatory automatically provides its own self-evident intent. In a note following the decision of a 1937 case, a judge wrote that "the intentions of the defendant in giving meaning to the words should not be considered as important at all" because in cases of defamation "understanding of the people who hear them" is uppermost. Otherwise, the defendant could always claim he did not intend to defame. Furthermore, Thai courts, starting from an assumption that the words of the defendant are false, free the plaintiff from having to prove such. Hence, the nature of defamation cases seems to stack the case against the defendant from the onset.[23]

However, exemption could be claimed for defamation of particular kinds of persons. In a 1932 case, K. said that the actions of N., a politician, "were not morally justified." Jitti's summary of the case notes that the court reasoned that one's "morals" are important to an audience. If someone says that another does not have morals, "it is instantly understood [by those who heard it] that there is no morality in that person;" thus, the statement may not have been made "in good faith." But to say that the certain actions of someone are not morally justifiable depends more on the quality of those actions. The court judged that K.'s statement was an "expression of an opinion" and that it was a comment on "the actions of N.," which were a matter "concerning politics and the masses in general." As such, the court said, K. had the "right to voice his opinion, if without bad intentions."[24]

Jitti argues that intent should receive particular attention in *lèse-majesté* cases where courts are allowed to "interpret the law widely" and focus on "special intent" and actions that "show the dishonest thoughts of the one who acts." The same holds true for seditious rebellion. Jitti writes that the Thai law on seditious rebellion originally came from the English law on sedition, "which includes seditious libel and seditious intent." For this crime, Jitti argues, "intent is central," a matter the courts must decide from what was written. Affirmation of the right of people to criticize the "administration and bureaucracy in general," does not allow people to comment on any individuals in particular." If the criticism is too specific, it may become a violation showing contempt of officials. Just as in defamation cases, the outcome determines guilt. This law can be interpreted quite widely; intentions are discerned from the offending words. Although "it is within one's rights to express an opinion, the limit is that one does not aim directly at disturbing the peace." As such, "the true principle" is that, "if the words disturb the peace," the law is violated, provided that "disturbing the peace" was the direct intent of the words. Adjudication based on effect, makes this law, at least for Jitti, faithful to its original intent. Jitti's explanation does not differ markedly from Ammatho's. Between the writings of the two is a separation of some fifty years and the overthrow of the absolute monarchy. Nonetheless, the thinking appears to remain the same.

When do words or actions qualify as rebellion and how are they related to intent? Intent often nudges "normal" criticism into seditious rebellion, as the result moves from potentiality to actuality. The court is quite clear regarding an actual attempt to physically overthrow the government. In the 1954 case discussed in the last chapter concerning an attempted *coup d'état*, the Supreme Court explained that the provision on rebellion within the criminal law code was "drafted specially" and "the limits of the violation are much wider than for other kinds of violations." Thus, varying punishments for persons involved in the commission of a crime were put in place, depending on the level of each person's involvement. However, in rebellion, the law recognized no gradations between ringleader and followers. According to the law, all of the following are full violations of rebellion: "the preparation to revolt, the collection of force or arms, or the preparation thereof, or the conspiring to do so, or inciting the citizens to rebel, or when someone knows of another who is planning a revolt and helps conceal it." The reason for this "truly special provision," the court continued, was because "the law desires to suppress those who commit this offence from the very start."

This law addresses the physical actions involved in revolt. But what about treason that happens in the mind? When does the crime begin? And when does it become "successfully committed?"

In two separate cases from 1941, the Court attempted to answer these questions, at least partially. The Supreme Court discussed three possible ways to violate Section 104. One can act to:

1 bring into hatred or contempt the Sovereign, the Government or the administration of the State, or
2 bring about a change in the Government or the Laws of the Kingdom by the use of force or violence, or
3 bring about discontent and disaffection among the people, in a manner likely to cause disturbances.

The court argued that, in terms of (1), the king, government, and/or administration must have already been brought into contempt. In other words, the word or action of the defendant had to have already successfully caused another to feel contempt. Contempt cannot just be potential—it must be realized. If one set out to do something that would cause others to hold the government in contempt, but instead these actions or words caused others to feel contemptuous of the perpetrator, this would not be a violation. Intent in this case, at least from what the court seemed to be saying, would be irrelevant.[25]

However, according to the court, for (2) and (3), the results would be the opposite. In these cases, whether a change occurred in the government or whether disturbances occurred among the people was unimportant. Intent is the only important thing to consider here. The court even argued that what was exactly said was unimportant. The words were only important in so much as to whether they "come out as proof of intention to cause disturbances" or not. The court said this was "because the law views [the words] from the perspective of intention behind the action as significant and not the view of the violence or seriousness of the action." What, in the view of the court, qualified as having intent to create disturbances among the people? The court answered, an action that caused:

> the people to be dissatisfied with their position at the present time, with the government, with the governing system, with the economic system, or causing someone to hate [other] people, *e.g.* hating people of different classes or religion . . . [or] aiming to have the people resist the power of those who govern.[26]

In the opium den case discussed in Chapter 5, the Court of First Instance judged that use of violent, crude, or sarcastic words (or actions) tended to indicate the *de facto* guilt of the speaker, for such qualities were judged as not the product of honest intentions or something made in good faith.[27] The central point for the court was what and how the defendant complained about the government's decision to no longer accept Lao currency. What the court considered an indication of his ill intent was that he had "satirized the government" and employed "violent words." These words and actions, the court ruled, made contending that the defendant had expressed himself "in good faith" or through "normal criticism" impossible. The Appeals Court, however, reversed the decision, ruling that the defendant's words were "simply a normal expression of opinion or criticism concerning the workings of the government." Upon appeal to the Supreme Court, the prosecution argued that the defendant had "criticized the government and said that it upset the people with all it did." The defendant argued that he was not criticizing the Thai government, but the unjust governments of Indochina. The court examined the following question: "Had the defendant's criticism of the internal government been within the intent of the constitution or for the public good in any way, or was it merely an expression of a sincere opinion, a normal criticism of the conduct of the government?" The court felt the words of the defendant should not be excluded because of the "emphasis" on "satirizing the government." His "speech" or "idiomatic use" could not be seen as an "honest expression," and it was not "a normal criticism" because the "use of violent words show[ed] the ill intention" of the defendant. The defendant thus must be found guilty on this account. The court sentenced him to six months, with another third added on for good measure, totalling eight months of imprisonment.[28]

Another case, from 1946, immediately followed the death of King Rama VIII (r. 1935–46) who died under suspicious circumstances. A writer from *Prachathipatai* newspaper, Damri Patthamasiri, criticized the Prime Minister Pridi Phanomyong for declaring a state of emergency and imposing censorship on newspapers. Damri and a number of other journalists were arrested for rebellion. Apparently mocking the arrests and the possibility of being punished with execution, journalist Samphan Khanthachawana issued a challenge. Instead of using a pig's head for gun-shooting experiments (which the executioners in Thailand typically used for practice), Samphan was willing to present his own head. Given that the king had just died from a gunshot wound to the head, Samphan was thus charged not only with rebellion, but also with *lèse-majesté*. Although the details of this "revolt," are not perfectly clear, it appears that Samphan's principal crime was a lack of good taste—an obvious indication of ill intent.[29]

In 1956, during a brief moment of political freedom, Member of Parliament Thongyu Phutthaphat organized a protest demanding that the senate be abolished. A march ended with Thongyu and eight others initiating a hunger strike in front of the Prime Minister's Office [Government House]. The prime minister and others, in mock concern, had fancy food brought in, including such delicacies as shark fin, and delivered to the hunger strikers, along with a message that the senate would not be abolished until it was time. In response, the strikers put the fancy food in the middle of the street to be disposed of by vagrant dogs and returned to their protest. Not amused, Prime Minister Phibun Songkhram and head of police Phao Siyanon worried that anyone coming to see the government, including foreign representatives, would see this "horrible" scene. They had the protesters arrested. In an announcement published in the newspapers, the police department justified arresting the protesters for rebellion by saying that the group had tried, "though various methods, to overthrow the government and compel the government to abolish the senate." Moreover, the protesters had "used deceptive methods to make the populace misunderstand, in order to create disquiet and a serious situation in the country." The apparent crime: mocking the government. The first case mocked the dead earnestness of the government in jailing journalists. The second case implied the actions of the government were comparable to those of street dogs. Regardless of other factors involved, the arrest came precisely at the moment of ridicule. Malicious intent shows itself though the making of inappropriate jokes.[30]

The 1935 exemption to Section 104 on seditious rebellion (cited at the beginning of this section) lessened the focus of the courts on the question of intention. Only two of the seven cases of seditious rebellion that went to the Supreme Court prior to 1958 resulted in guilty verdicts. Even in those two cases, intent did not seem to be the deciding factor.

In its decisions, the Thai Supreme Court has consistently worked from the assumption that if something untoward has happened, it is possible to trace the transgression back to malicious intentions. A rendering of the components of a defamation-based crime in Thailand makes this clear:

- The first party uses certain potentially defamatory words.
- A second party, the target , feels his or her reputation defamed.
- A third party is present—the person or persons who hear or read the defamatory words.
- There is an effect, or possible effect, or no effect at all, as determined by a fourth party, the judges.

There are thus three steps or aspects to the defamation sequence: The first, intent, determines guilt. The second, the effect, makes the action complete concerning the first three parties. But it is the third, through the court itself, which actually completes and validates the meaning of the action.

The focus on effect reveals a key hidden aspect of defamation. Effect determines intent, and effect is seemingly determined by a successful completion of the crime—the person defamed is actually looked down upon by others. But in fact, it is not even necessary that this final and decisive stage is reached, as revealed in this 1973 Supreme Court decision which concluded:

> It is not necessary that [the defamatory statement] produce the result of causing the loss of reputation . . . That is to say, if the words spoken ought to be able to cause one the loss of reputation—and make [such person] insulted and hated by others—even if in truth those who heard it do not feel disparagingly or hateful of the one spoken of at all, it is still a successfully completed violation.[31]

This finding demonstrates an interesting tendency in Thai defamation cases. Not only is it possible that guilt can be determined solely on the effect of the words on listeners without reference to the truth or falsity of the defendant's statements—thus completely severing the case from the reality of what happened—it is not necessary that the words actually had any effect on the listeners. Guilt may be based not on the actual effect given words had on the listeners, but on the possible effect they might have had. The disturbing conclusion we can make about defamation adjudication in Thailand is: Intention at first glance seems to be determined by its effect; but then no, it is determined not even by its potential effect, but rather by no effect at all, as understood by a fourth party in the event: the judges.

The pattern of the intention-focused interpretation of defamation crimes from the time of the Thai absolute monarchy was resilient enough to survive intact to the present. In general, intention is seen as determining all the other conditions leading to guilt in defamation-based crimes. If the act of defamation happens, it arises from malicious intent. Criticism is a sign of bias, of ill-intent. An honest opinion cannot come from an interested party, or someone angered, or one who has sown chaos; thus. no exclusion is afforded from the reach of this law. Of course, all defendants argue that they did not intend to defame, but the actions, the results, the mere existence of the critical words in the first place, speak for themselves. Indeed, in the Thai context, a defendant's presence in a court answering charges of defamation or treason ensures guilt. It is only a matter of time before the traitorous heart, with its biases, impurities, maliciousness, its hatred and spite, reveals itself.

Intention within a modern Theravada Buddhist polity

It is no coincidence that the "narrow" tradition of Theravada Buddhism (Chapter 3) ultimately comes down to purity of mind, to intention, and to the fact that Thai courts have focused on intention in defamation-based cases. This "narrow" Theravada Buddhist link presents perhaps the most significant continuity between the past and present in Thai society. This reckoning leads to a particular way of giving value to different people in society while creating a cast of protagonists, antagonists, and audience. This system of valuation closely parallels the scale concerning numbers of years' imprisonment for particular defamation offenses afforded to different parties in society we used earlier (Chapter 4). That scale was directly connected to the aggrieved party's perceived (or self-perceived) proximity to truth, or truth-beyond-truth.

Gray writes that Theravada Buddhism employs an "opacity principle" that makes it "unthinkable" for a person of lesser merit to "correctly criticize the purity of intentions" of those closer to "*dhamma* or truth." Under this principle, "the intentions of men of superior wealth and religious purity are opaque or unknowable (invisible)" to lesser beings.[32] Within a Theravada Buddhist polity, only those of pure intention can see through the veils of confusion and recognize the true intention of others. The utter certitude that a defendant will be found guilty of defamation of any type in Thailand indicates that judges understand they can read the intention of defendants. According to a former Supreme Court judge, judges are not given training on reading intention or even on the special nature of defamation adjudication.[33] However, as we discovered in the cases examined in this chapter, motive or intent is established simply because the defamatory words exist. The words came into being only by virtue of the defendant's volition. The defendant chose to use such words and from their meaning motive can be surmised.

Gray notes that the Thai Buddhist cosmos is traditionally separated according to "wisdom": "Levels of the cosmos are identified with categories of persons marked by relative levels of detachment and hence wisdom and/or ignorance, and by distinct speech or communicative characteristics."[34] The particular focus on intent inherent in defamation-based laws and their adjudication, when combined with the pre-existing emphasis in Thai

Theravada Buddhism, gives shape to a particular configuration concerning truth and its holders. Within a Buddhist purity framework, those with the highest levels of merit, of pure intention, are closest to the truth; they are also best able to discern the intentions of others. McCargo has noted that what he has termed "virtuous rule" divides power holders into "good" people" and "bad" people, a schema that was apparent surrounding the events of May 1992 when the military killed unarmed protesters:

> Popular discourse and the media classified politicians [in 1992] as either "devils" (aligned with the military and forces of dictatorship) or "angels" (aligned with the opponents of dictatorship) The 1997 constitution reflected systematic attempts by its architects to create a framework within which good people could enter politics. A similar discourse followed the September 2006 military coup, which framed Thaksin Shinawatra as a "bad" figure, in contrast with the "good" royal servants . . . According to this notion of virtuous rule, those endorsed and supported by King Bhumibol were held to be dedicated to the best interests of Thailand as a whole.[35]

Drawing on similar conceptualization and on socio-religious terms commonly used in Thai political, social, and religious discourse, I offer a hierarchy of "truth-holders," categorized by respective proximity to the sacred center and by their use or relationship to defamation-based laws, in particular, the *lèse-majesté* law (see Figure 6.1).[36]

In this hierarchy, starting from the top, are *The Meritorious* (or *The Pure, The Neutral, The Virtuous, or The Charismatic*), *The Merit Seekers*, *The Lowly Meritorious*, and *The Demons*.[37] *The Meritorious*, a commonly referred-to category often tied to the idea of *barami* (charisma, prestige) and neutral (*khon bang klang*) occupies the top echelon.[38] Those considered politically neutral or, more accurately, entirely outside the realm of politics are included in this group. "Politics" (*kanmuang*) is understood here in an exclusively narrow sense as the dirty and corrupt practice of variously "interested" groups who parry for power through elections. *The Meritorious* do not become entangled in the dirty business of politics and assume power cautiously when there is no other choice. In a 1980 interview with the BBC, the king discussed his impartiality:

> We keep in the middle, neutral . . . in peaceful coexistence with everybody . . . We could be crushed by both sides, but we are impartial. One day it would be very handy to have somebody impartial. Because if you have in the country only groups of political parties, which have their own interests at heart, what about those who don't have the power, just ordinary people who cannot make their view known? They must have somebody impartial. And if one wants to destroy somebody who is impartial, one destroys oneself.[39]

THE MERITORIOUS
(*THE PURE, THE NEUTRAL, THE VIRTUOUS, OR THE CHARISMATIC*)

Accusing others of defamation-based crimes: Very infrequent direct use of defamation based law for first three groups; infrequent for last two
Accused of defamation-based crimes: Very rarely

Royalty, judges, Supreme Patriarch / leading monks / very high-ranking military and bureaucratic officials, some appointed "politicians"

THOSE IN THE SHADE OF CHARISMA
Accusing others of defamation-based crimes: Moderately frequently
Accused of defamation-based crimes: Rather infrequently

Leading businesspersons, members of upper echelons of society, successful former hopeful meritorious, most appointed "politicians"

THE MERIT SEEKERS
Accusing others of defamation-based crimes: Most frequently
Accused of defamation-based crimes: Very frequently

Educated middle class, most intellectuals, some segments of media and NGOs, some appointed "politicians," a few elected politicians, lower-level bureaucrats, a few exemplary representatives of "The People"

THE LOWLY MERITORIOUS
Accusing others of defamation-based crimes: Very rarely
Accused of defamation-based crimes: Very rarely

The Vast Bulk of "The People"

THE DEMONS
Accusing others of defamation-based crimes: Very frequently
Accused of defamation-based crimes: Very frequently

Most politicians, certain NGOs, certain media outlets, certain intellectuals, criminal types

Figure 6.1 Hierarchy of pure intentions and defamation.

The idea of *The Meritorious* above the fray began to coalese in the 1960s, as the sacred sphere was beginning its eclipse of the Thai official sphere. *The Meritorious* have pure intentions and meritorious behavior and are therefore the most trustworthy in holding power and the surest guide in determining guilt or innocence of defamation-based crimes. They infrequently formally accuse others of defamation-based crimes, but frequently allude to the existence of various groups of traitors and Demons.[40] They depend on *The Merit Seekers* to make charges of defamation-based crimes in their stead and sometimes, presumably, at their direction.[41] The uppermost three categories within the realm of *The Meritorious* are protected by special laws for acts of defamation: the royalty (up to 15 years' imprisonment), judges (up to seven years' imprisonment), and the Supreme Patriarch/Buddhism (up to seven years' imprisonment). The two lower groups in this category are allowed to sue for defamation in the name of their group [defamation of the military (1995), defamation of the police (1998)]. The prime representatives of this group are former judges, generals, and top bureaucrats who become advisors to the king on the Privy Council.[42]

The Merit Seekers who emerged in the 1960s and 1970s inhabit the middle tier, this consists of the educated middle class, most intellectuals, some segments of NGOs and the media, some "politicians" appointed in the aftermath of coups, a few elected politicians, some bureaucrats, and a small number of the more outstanding of *The Lowly Meritorious*.[43] They are those "seeking merit" by doing politically useful acts and pushing to gain greater proximity of the sacred center. It is easy to name examples of this group, for they are the most visible in Thai society. They include people like PAD leader Sondhi Limthongkul, politicians like Abhisit Vejjajiva, leader of the Democrat Party, Chulalongkorn University lecturer Dr. Tul Sitthisomwong, former social activists like PAD leader Pipob Dhongchai, and perhaps even Thaksin himself.[44] This group essentially forms the vanguard of those who make defamation-based accusations, especially accusations of defamation of the sacred center (perhaps at the behest of higher levels). Some *Merit Seekers* are especially prone to conspicuous and frequent declarations of loyalty to the throne and state. However, as they are in competition with each other, they are quick to label fellow *Merit Seekers* traitors or "un-Thai." They remain enmeshed in day-to-day life and thus prone to greed, selfishness, and delusion caused by consumerism, necessitating in many cases a periodic "return" to Buddhism and to pure intentions.[45] This group often feels close to "the People" or *The Lowly Meritorious*, and is eager to speak in its name. Members of this group often accuse Demons of defamation-based crimes and they frequently serve as the accuser and accused of defamation-based crimes.

The Lowly Meritorious are the vast bulk of "The People" who are born into less fortunate circumstances are sincere and naïve, and have little chance of elevating their status.[46] They are idealized by more meritorious groups even as they are deeply distrusted. This group is thought to be easily led astray by deceivers or a "third hand" (due to their low education) and are incapable of recognizing when they are manipulated.[47] This group serves as the primary subjects of merit-making of more meritorious groups. They are ostensibly the standard for deciding defamation cases (Chapter 9). This group is also identified as the reason for the failure of democracy. Members of this group have little reputation to protect and rarely accuse others of defamation. They are also infrequently accused of any type of defamation-based crime.

Finally, the *The Demons* comprise the bottom rung; those of base intentions who recognize the truth but choose to distort, misrepresent, or exaggerate it for selfish reasons.[48] In this group are many elected politicians, certain

NGOs and academics, and criminal types. The most prominent recent member of this group is former Thaksin Shinawatra, whose opponents, at various times, have likened him to Hitler and Satan. They are often portrayed as "third hands." As with *The Merit Seekers*, the politicians within this group are frequently accusers or the accused of defamation-based crimes.[49]

In order to illustrate graphically the changing relationships between these groups over time, I have constructed an alternative chronology of Thai history (see Figures 4.1 to 4.7, 6.1), based on perceived intentions, aspirations to the sacred sphere, and the evolving relationship between defamation-based laws and access to truth. While, certainly, the basic impulse within Thai political reality is authoritarian, more precisely if is seeks to purify and be purified, and through such purifications, to authenticate one's own purity and come closer to the truth. The simultaneous counter action is to impugn the intentions of others. Defamation-based laws are the tools used to do this.

In order to better explicate the changing dynamics between these groups, I return to the question of the cause of the 1976 increase in the protection given to courts under the 1976 coup decree (Chapter 4). The judges thus assumed an extraordinary role within the combined systems of defamation-based crimes and purity. Judges must see into the hearts of defendants and assess their intentions; they must either see the actual effect of the defendants' words or foresee the effects these words might potentially create. They are really the necessary "fourth party" who both complete and validate the defamatory sequence.

Defamation is a crime of words and words are untrustworthy guides to truth. Words change and have "hidden" meanings that create effects in the moral order. The true meaning of words and the true intentions of others can only be perceived by those of a pure heart. Judges, free from the entanglements of day-to-day living and pure enough to have penetrating wisdom, can pierce the cloak of the hidden heart. Judges have the power to assess exactly what every defamation case in Thailand comes down to: the defamer's intent. If the intent is malicious, these dhamma-seeing judges will recognize it. Judges, representatives of the pure king (not of the "hot-hearted" ordinary people), see and understand the two essential "hidden" aspects of defamation—the real intentions of the antagonist and the karmic effects those words have. Judges represent the king in a primary duty of the *dhammaraja*—dispensing justice. Thus, the extraordinary role of judges was given extraordinary protection in 1976, the year the sacred sphere became dominant over Thai society.

I conclude with two observations. When religious predisposition focuses on intent, discussion of the veracity or acceptability of content ceases. For truly, the presence or absence of malice does not affect the status of the message: either it is true or it is not, or it is an acceptable representation or it is not. In Thailand's case, the religious predisposition, communicated through Theravada Buddhism, created a hyper-attention to intention, judgment of intention, the endemic vilification of the other, lionization of the self, and reflexive accusations of treason—all without actually confronting message content. If one believes the person accused of defamation, then content is true and protests to the contrary are politically motivated. If one doesn't believe in the accused, content is false and protests to the contrary are motivated by wanton disregard for the truth and selfishness.

This observation leads to the second: focus on intent communicates something important about the way a defamation regime operates. The success or failure of a defamation regime does not stem merely from its skill in deflecting the motion of the political moment away from the question of truth, but more on its capacity to make the focus exclusively on the question of the author's intent and thereby obliterate the necessity of deflecting away from truth in the first place. This political formation throws the entire issue into the domain of the hierarchy of truth, where the truth of the matter is settled by the authority of those at the top. Determination of truth is unnecessary; what is key is domination over the authority to pronounce what is true.

7 The insulted and defamed I

From the individual to the nation

In January 1922, tram car drivers went on strike in Bangkok. One of the supervisors of the Tram Car Company, Mr. Hui, was overheard saying before a crowd, "Damn Thai nation! Why should I go reconcile myself humbly before them? Set a pot with [left-over] rice water in the middle of the road and tap on it. In just a second, here they'd come!" Two titled aristocrats who heard this filed a complaint, saying Mr. Hui had likened the Thai to "depraved animals" who are only on the look out for "rice water"—"the food of canines." Such words defamed the two plaintiffs as well as insulted "the common folk who have nationality as Thai," causing the Thai nation to "lose their good name and honour" and bringing "foreigners" to hold the Thai nation "in contempt."[1]

As news of the incident spread, eleven lawyers submitted a petition to the Prosecution Department demanding legal redress against Mr. Hui who had likened the Thai nation to "a canine." Such an invidious comparison was "deeply insulting" to their "land of birth." They asked that they, too, as members of the Thai nation, be included as plaintiffs in the case and for Mr. Hui to be charged with "defamation of the nation." The newspapers reported that Thai from all walks of life appeared at court "volunteering to add their names as plaintiffs" in the case, claiming that, "I am [of] the Thai nation, too."

When the trial opened a month later, Mr. Hui seemed to indicate that the charges could not be justified because although he was of Chinese heritage, he had in fact been born in Siam and was a Thai citizen. If being of Chinese heritage was a crime, he challenged the court to check the blood of the eleven lawyers and it would no doubt find many of them the same. The first plaintiff claimed that ever since he had known the defendant, he had never seen him wear Thai clothes. This lawyer also wanted compensation for lost business, for after the news of his position on this case had appeared, many of his Chinese and South Asian clients—he used the derogatory ethnic labels, *jek* and *khaek*—had stopped using his legal services. The second plaintiff claimed that Mr. Hui was "one who respected Chinese nationality greatly" and claimed that when he first knew Mr. Hui, forty years prior, he wore his hair long in Chinese pigtails and donned Chinese pants. If Mr. Hui had been upset with the tram drivers who were on strike, he could have said, "You damn tram car drivers!" But instead he reviled the entire Thai nation.

The prosecution brought forward a witness, Mr. Mali, to testify on its behalf. After affirming that his parents were both Thai, Mr. Mali reported that he had gone to where the workers were striking that day in search of work and heard Mr. Hui say words that meant "Thai people are dogs." After hearing such words, Mr. Mali was no longer interested in finding work there because he had been trained as a soldier and taught to "love the nation, king, and religion."

The Director-General of the Prosecution Department had to carefully consider who or what exactly was the damaged party. Could Mr. Hui be charged with Section 104 (seditious rebellion)? There was no precedent of such a case. Moreover, one of the principles of defamation is that what was impugned must be believable. The statement, "The Thai nation is a dog," was an "impossibility." Could those who heard it believe "it was true?" If not, there was no damaged party. Just as importantly, in cases of personal defamation, the number of persons claiming to be the damaged party must be "precise" and "limited." But what about "the nation"? In defamation cases, the damaged party must file the complaint. Eleven lawyers could claim neither to be "the damaged party" nor "representatives of the entire nation." In the end, the Prosecution Department was unable to pursue charges under Section 104 and instead tried Mr. Hui for the use of coarse language and insulting another.

In this case, the target proved impossibly large. The Thai nation was both abstract and concrete: too abstract to say who could possibly represent the nation appropriately and too concrete, for who in Siam could *not* represent the nation? The targets of defamatory actions range from the simplest—an individual person—to increasingly complex and abstract entities—the most eminent either the *nation* or a *people-ness*. *The police of this district* or *the police of this country*—two quite different aspects of *the police*, each with its own rules for defamation prosecution — are in between. The monarchy as target, for reasons to be elaborated later, deserves its own, separate consideration (Chapter 8).

Chapter 2 discussed the tension that plays between the criminality of defamation and the need for all societies to access truth and debate opinions. Private individuals are absolutely protected from defamation on items purely concerning private matters. Public figures, though, have limited protection; the more they thrust themselves into the public eye, the more likely any statement about them will be considered "fair comment." It is the right and responsibility of citizens to comment on public officials and elected representatives as their actions affect the public good. In many legal systems, the greater power a person wields vis-à-vis the public good, the less right such a person has to charge critics with defamation. These principles are fundamental to accountability and are essential aspects of the public sphere.

A different scale has developed in Thailand over the past century: in defamation cases, the more abstract and encompassing the target, the less truth can come to bear or opinions be allowed. In Thailand, whatever principles of defamation adjudication are observed for individuals, they evaporate in the face of greater abstraction: the public body, "the government," and the nation. These entities illustrate intermediate steps that evolve toward the perfection of the defamation model that culminates with the monarchy as the target of defamation, seen in the next chapter.

Defamation of the individual

In early 2009, Article 19 and the National Press Council of Thailand (NPCT) issued the most substantial critique of the personal defamation law in Thailand to date.[2] The report stated:

> Defamation, in both its criminal and civil aspects, is a key part of the legal framework that restricts speech critical of the government, businesses and prominent individuals . . . [The Thai] defamation law . . . represents a direct threat to freedom of the press and, indeed, anyone who wishes to criticise the government or those in power.[3]

Nothing is particularly unique about the wording of the past and present personal defamation laws in Thailand (see Appendix I). There is also nothing out of the ordinary about how the law is used in conflicts between two private persons. However, one specific aspect about the law's adjudication needs our attention. In a case of private defamation, the plaintiff must convincingly show that the defendant referred specifically to him or her and not someone else.[4] If the defendant made a general statement, or a statement about a large number of people, it may not be possible for the plaintiff to prove that the defendant was speaking of him or her in particular.

For instance, the 1927 law textbook cites the following as examples of statements that are too broad to be defamatory: "Most civil servants are corrupt. They like to embezzle Crown funds and to cause trouble for the people and citizens by suppressing them;" or "Lawyers make their living by cheating their clients. Can't find an honest one among them." Only those who showed "clear reason" why they believed the statements were directed at them personally could bring the case to trial. When a comment was directed toward a group, no single individual in that group could claim to have been defamed. Jitti Tingsaphat, in his 1970s text, worked from the maxim, "the larger the number, the harder it is to make a charge."[5]

Again, in a 1946 case, a government radio broadcast warned listeners not to believe the propaganda of the Democrat Party whose candidates were campaigning for election. A member of the Democrat Party sued for defamation, claiming the radio broadcast "was aimed, or might have been aimed, at the plaintiff and affected, or may have affected" him, the damaged party. The

Supreme Court reasoned that for defamation to obtain ("to successfully happen"), the defamatory statement "must be aimed at an individual in particular" and the plaintiff "must prove that he was that individual." The Supreme Court pointed out that even when saying that one in a group of three had committed perjury, none of the three can claim to be the damaged party. In this case, the Supreme Court concluded, the plaintiff had no legitimate claim as the damaged party and, therefore, the defendants could not be found guilty of defamation. The case was dismissed.[6]

In a 1955 case, a man complained in a newspaper that a doctor at Siriraat Hospital, one of the country's most prestigious, had sexually harassed his wife. The hospital's director, claiming to be the damaged party, sued for defamation. The Court of First Instance ruled that the article maligned the doctors at the hospital and may have caused loss of their reputations. The Court of First Instance also ruled that Dr. Chaloem, as director, was responsible for all the activities at the hospital and so could serve as the damaged party. Before the Supreme Court, the prosecution argued that all doctors at the hospital had been defamed by the article and were likely to receive damage from it. Therefore, the hospital's director, as a doctor there, had the right to file suit as one member of the damaged party. The Supreme Court ruled that it was the responsibility of the prosecution to "prove successfully to whom [the article] refers." As the article mentioned only one doctor, "there is nothing in the contents which show that the charges of the prosecution extend to every doctor." Additionally, there was nothing in the article to suggest that the single doctor mentioned was the hospital's director and so he could not serve as the damaged party.[7]

However, both the 1927 and 1975 law books opened the possibility that if an individual government official were defamed for something done within the performance of duty, his or her superior had the right to sue, for the damage to the intended target would also damage that government department as well and, in turn, the head of that department. Likewise, this might also apply to other juristic persons, such as a political bureau, a temple, a public company, an association, and a foundation.[8] This admission allowed for the resurgence of personal defamation after 1992, as will be seen below.

Until 1958 the adjudication of personal defamation in Thailand followed accepted international practices. Seditious rebellion as a criminal code violation also largely disappeared (Chapter 4). However, a strengthened defamation measure shared the stage with a slightly tamed seditious rebellion law under Coup Decree No. 17, in effect until 1975, and Coup Order No. 42, in effect from 1976 to early 1991 (see Appendix IV). No doubt the military and other national security groups kept a close watch on such measures: within a month of repealing Order No. 42, the government was overthrown by the military and new controls were placed on the press. The military government left nothing to chance upon returning power to a civilian government: the last session of the military-appointed legislature passed into law a revision to the personal defamation measure in the criminal code.

I had interviewed the Press Officer of Bangkok in 1991, just after Coup Decree No. 42 had been repealed. He waxed fondly about the days when he could strike fear in the hearts of newspaper editors (see Chapter 4). The locus of state power in controlling the media moved out of the Press Officer's hands with the repeal of this law.

I visited the Press Officer in Bangkok ten years later. Police Superintendent Suttipong Jangariyawong, the current holder of the position, looked surprisingly young and had been at it for a year. I wondered if things were as they had been before.[9] Had there been any political intrusion in his work? No. Had he made any warnings to newspapers about anything political? No. What had he done, then? To be precise, there had been four instances in the year when he had acted against newspapers. A picture of Burmese corpses from a military operation in Ratburi appeared on the front page of a newspaper—"not appropriate and may have adverse effects on foreign relations—the Burmese government may think it 'ugly.'" The photo of a woman who had been raped was on another front page—"exposing her to even greater shame." A crime magazine showed the torso of a woman who had been killed, cut up, and stored in a refrigerator. The breasts were visible. Finally, he had warned the *Bangkok Post* for printing a story, written by a monk, entitled, "How the Buddha died." How could this monk know? he asked.

In 1991, the state's role directly controlling news disappeared and was absorbed into personal defamation suits, police investigations, criminal court procedures, the caseload of prosecutors, and the courts—all acting in the service of power holders. According to Suchart Srisuwan, one-time editor of *Matichon* newspaper, this state of affairs "just started happening."[10] He explained that the end of the decrees imposed during the dictatorships came about since the early 1990s. The 1997 Constitution guaranteed press rights; only the 1992 re-strengthened defamation law limited those rights. Instead of using laws or other mechanisms to control the press, the state repositioned suppression to the responsibility of private individuals. Put another way, because defamation is a criminal offense, private individuals could draw upon state resources and power to silence the press and other critics.

One incident in 1997 neatly illustrates this change.[11] Deputy Minister of the Interior Chalerm Yoobamrung asked Legal Affairs Division Commander Pol Maj Gen Siripong Sappatanond, "What could be done with media which falsely attacks important government figures." Siripong then admitted that he "first informed" the minister "about the existence of Article 39 of the Constitution" at that time. Siripong interpreted Article 39 and the Printing Act to mean that courts had the power to "close down media which publish false reports or reports which are not useful to the public." The government then set up a "media monitoring committee" that "would analyse offending newspaper articles and radio or television reports and make an independent judgment whether they were appropriate or not." A "special one-day process" devised to "bypass normal lengthy procedures" would bring immediate results. Offending media outlets "would initially be hit with defamation suits" and "Repeat offenders would face indefinite closure, via a request by public prosecutors to the court."

These officials were apparently reacting to Article 39's wording: "Ambiguous or unclear allegations against any individual" that "were reported in a way that implied a clear message of the 'genuine matter' to the public." The police official responsible for this scheme, interestingly invoking the constitutional article protecting free speech, explained, "Reporting accurate information which is not useful knowledge for the public, or which is purely a personal matter for any individual, would also be regarded as a violation." The courts were ready to help. Criminal Court Chief Justice Pradit Ekmanee explained,

> If a media outlet carries a report which affects the order of society or damages economic or national stability, a court ruling could be sought to shut it . . . For example, if a newspaper publishes a false report that the government will devalue the baht, or that the country is going bankrupt, the government should be able to seek a court ruling to shut it down on the grounds the report is causing serious damage to the country's economy [and as a result] the public would panic and the report would scare foreign investors away.

Although the chief justice contended that "ordinary defamation cases would not warrant closure," this measure clearly placed court power into the hands of private individuals. An 8-to-2 decision of the Constitutional Court in 2006 confirmed this defamation law. The ruling, made against the Manager Group, reads: "Any press freedom has been enshrined in Articles 39 and 41 of the Constitution, media professionals and outlets are still responsible for any offences committed against personal rights and liberties as guaranteed by Article 34." Thus, "editors and newspapers were not exempt from criminal litigation for defamation."[12]

A 2004 case shows how deeply defamation has become part of the Thai political scene. In preparation for a censure debate, Thai Rak Thai Party government MPs set up a "lie detection unit" whose purpose was "to catch debaters who fabricate accusations and to bring defamation suits against them." Led by MP whip Wichit Plangsrisakul, the unit "would work closely with the party's legal advisers to keep watch for baseless, damaging claims against the eight ministers" targeted. Any opposition MP "making false accusations would face legal action."[13]

A survey of 324 libel cases that appeared in *The Nation* from 1997 to 2006 gives a clearer picture of how the defamation law was used (Figures 7.1 and 7.2)[14] Using these cases, I examined "defamation events," making no distinction between a threat and the actual filing of a defamation suit, as a threat can be as effective in silencing a critic as a court case. During this period, government officials—elected and non-elected—were twice as likely to accuse others of defamation as were non-governmental people. Of all government

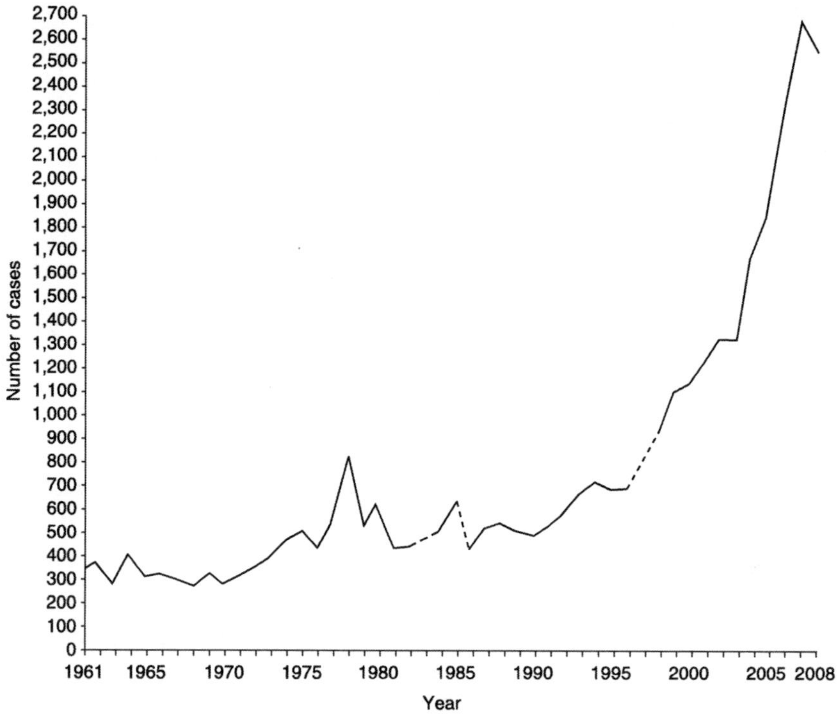

Figure 7.1 Annual number of criminal defamation new cases in Thailand, 1961–2008

Source: Thailand, Police Department (Krom Tamruat), *Rai-ngan prajam pi* (Annual Report of the Police Department); Thailand. Attorney General's Office (Samnakngan Aiyakan Songsut), *Rai-ngan prajam pi* (Annual Report of the Attorney General's Office) (Samnakngan aiyakan phiset fai sarasonthet, samnakngan wichakan) (each year individually from 1984 to 2005; year 1996 and 1997 are combined into a single volume). Thailand. Office of the Judiciary, *Annual Judicial Statistics, Thailand* 2005–2009.

officials, almost 70 percent of those accusing others of defamation were elected and, of all accusers, both elected officials and bureaucrats, including the police and military, made up more than 70 percent.[15] The single largest group of defamation accusers was government members of parliament (MPs). Other public and private figures—monks, movie stars, hospital patients—made up 57 percent of non-governmental defamation accusers (but still comprised only 17 percent of all accusers). Police and military personnel made up a significant percentage of overall defamation accusers, 14 percent in 2002 and almost a quarter of cases in 2003. Of all categories, the group least likely to accuse others of defamation was NGOs and social critics. It is clear that politicians and bureaucrats used the defamation law most readily.

Of those accused of defamation, there was nearly an even split between governmental and non-governmental figures. Among non-governmental entities, by far the largest group was the media, comprising 73 percent of the

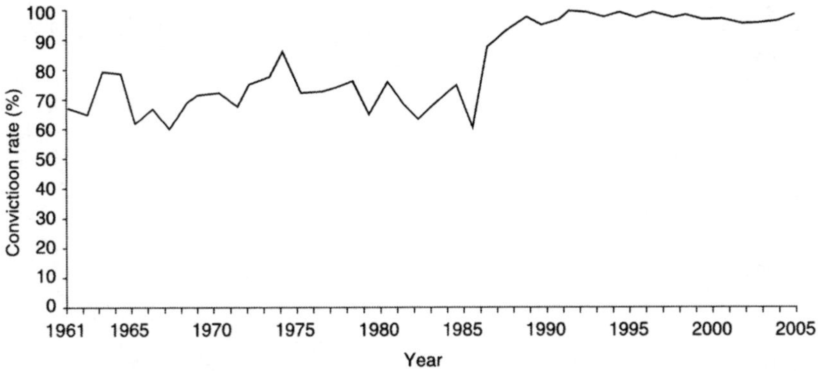

Figure 7.2 Annual conviction rates for criminal defamation cases in Thailand, 1961–2005

Source: Attorney General's Office (Samnakngan Aiyakan Songsut), *Rai-ngan prajam pi* (Annual Report of the Attorney General's Office) (Samnakngan aiyakan phiset fai sarasonthet, samnakngan wichakan) (each year individually from 1984 to 2005; year 1996 and 1997 are combined into a single volume); Thailand, Ministry of Justice, *Rai-ngan krasuang yuthitham prajam* (Annual Report of the Ministry of Justice), 2504–2527 (1961–1984).

total, followed by NGOs and social critics at 14 percent. Elected officials comprised 70 percent of those accused. Opposition MPs were 20 percent of those accused of defamation, while nine percent were government MPs, suggesting that MPs in current governments are more likely to use defamation as a tool in deflecting accusations. The police make up the second largest group of government officials accused of defamation, followed by the military. Combined, they made up 9 percent of all accused of defamation.[16]

Some observers have argued that Thai newspapers are frequently charged with defamation because the quality of news reporting is so uneven.[17] Some journalistic leaders feel that newspapers such as *Khao Sot* are "sleazy." Even Kiatichai Pongpanich, a respected Thai journalist, a senior editor at *Khao Sot*, and a key committee member of the Thai Journalists Association (TJA), agrees, saying that a lack of professionalism gets *Khao Sot* into trouble.[18] He admits that many items in his paper are "wrong . . . because sometimes we don't check anything. 'This is news. Just put it out'." Therefore, the newspapers are frequently sued for defamation. Managing editor of English-language *The Nation* and past chairperson of the Southeast Asian Press Alliance, or SEAPA, Kavi Chongkittavorn, believes the solution lies in improving Thai journalists' standards and making them more professional. Article 19's report on defamation points out that the nature of the newspaper business in Thailand makes editors and writers prone to defamation litigation:

> Highly sensational newspapers form an important part of the Thai newspaper market. These newspapers are issued under big banners, and depend on day-to-day newsstand sales rather than longer-term (monthly

> or yearly) subscriptions. They thus depend on generating big eye-catching headlines to draw attention. More often than not, these headlines are exaggerated and do not reflect the actual content of the story they announce.[19]

Another reason for the sheer number of defamation cases is that editors often publish stories in the public's interest but ones which they cannot prove.[20] Although an Official Information Act has been in place for ten years, the government still easily classifies many documents "secret." Making the Act work "depends on the government authorities or politicians" and there are always exclusions on the grounds of national security. "Everything can be interpreted as national security," says one editor, "items about the military, about politics, about governing—many things."[21]

Hyper-litigiousness grinds up newspapers' resources, shackles editors endlessly to time in court, and gives corrupt politicians at least temporary respite from imminent exposure, thereby depriving the public of the right to know. Despite frequent calls from Thailand's newspaper associations for the government to address the problem of defamation, there has yet to be a sustained effort. Suchart Srisuwan of *Matichon* newspaper contends that "The biggest problem [concerning press freedom] is the matter of these [defamation] cases . . . There are other problems, too, but in the end they're related to defamation."

Suchart points out that his newspaper has frequently won awards for its investigative reporting. Most of the award-winning stories uncovered scandals involving corruption. And almost all of these stories had initially provoked defamation suits against *Matichon*.[22] It is common for Thai newspapers to be facing a slew of charges from a single individual. "When there's someone charging us four, five, six times," he says, "it's got nothing to do with professionalism." Suchart recalls that one of the main culprits in the Bangkok Bank of Commerce scandal of the 1990s,

> brought four or five cases of defamation against us so we'd stop reporting the news. But we wouldn't stop. In the end when he was actually charged, he dropped the [libel] charges [against us]. This sort of thing happens a lot. This is not a matter of a lack of professionalism. There are some instances where we are defective, but they're a minority.

Editors are not surprised to have defamation charges brought against them; it is part of the newspaper business. Nor do many of those interviewed believe it should be decriminalized, as in the United States and made solely a civil offense. A number of editors who asked to remain nameless worry about the way defamation cases actually operate. Any politician or government official who feels aggrieved by a news report can turn to the court for relief. One-time managing editor of *Khao Sot* Thakoon Boonparn feels that defamation is primarily an issue between newspapers and the one defamed.[23] If truly defamed, the matter can be rectified in civil court. Why should there be a fine at all? he asks, and why so high? But beyond the possible fine, other costs mount. An editor sometimes has to post three separate bails—one with the police, one with prosecutors, and one with the court. Total bail can range from 100,000 to 200,000 baht or more. Add to this other fees of 100,000 and up front costs, and a typical case can cost up to 300,000 baht. When a paper is faced with, say, 20 or a 100 cases, "you can do the math yourself," Suchart remarked wryly, noting that these expenses "can be a problem for the account of a newspaper."

Defamation hearings on a given case are convened only one day every two or three months. The time demands are so onerous that some Thai newspapers facing many cases rotate editorship in order to distribute the burden of defamation cases. In Thai libel cases, the plaintiff does not assume "the practical burden of proving falsity." Instead, defendants have to prove the truth of their words. However, writes *The Financial Times*, "Such truth can be difficult to prove in court and may prevent potential speakers from rendering even truthful statements if they are concerned about their ability to prove the allegedly defamatory statements."[24] If newspapers eventually lose a defamation case in court, the financial burden naturally increases, sometimes to millions and millions of baht.[25]

Suchart of *Matichon* estimates that 80 percent of those bringing suits against newspapers are politicians and government officials and politicians, a percentage similar to our survey. The other 20 percent, he laughs, are those "related to politicians—their wives or provincial politicians . . . so 100 percent are political." Most plaintiffs seek neither vindication of their reputations nor monetary gain. In fact, Suchart estimates that 90 percent are settled amicably out of court—meaning apologies made and forgiveness granted, no retractions in the paper nor money paid. The primary objective of filing a lawsuit is to intimidate the newspaper into dropping coverage of a particular story. Once the story is no longer hot and the public's attention has been drawn elsewhere, nine times out of ten the plaintiff drops the case.

Although *Khao Sot* has its sensationalist side, it is precisely the paper's professionalism in other respects that draws the fire of officials and politicians. Kiatichai says his paper is recognized for its emphasis on "investigative reporting" that "dares to really reveal what's happening." The noted Buddhist scholar and social critic Sulak Sivaraksa concurs, saying he feels that *Khao Sot* is a "marvellous" newspaper and was one of the first to regularly carry issues covering the poor and the activities of the Assembly of the Poor.[26] Kiatichai makes the following observation:

> Nowadays the intentions particularly among politicians [is that] they sue you just for the sake of suing newspapers in order to stop the news. That's it. Nothing else. And then most of these cases are where they just compromise and settle out of court. But they give us a hard time, just to stop the news. Nothing more. Because they don't want the news to go on

> too much too long. Sue first. [He concludes:] We have a notion that in the newspaper business [you have] one leg in jail and one leg outside. You don't know whether the other leg will be in jail, too.[27]

Does the strategy of attempting to silence newspapers by filing defamation suits work? Suchart admits that, for smaller acts of corruption or local issues, defamation "is rather effective. In many instances," he comments, "even when we know it's true," newspapers, fearful of the burdens they might accrue, allow defamation charges to censor their news. But for larger, national cases, Suchart says, "we won't let the threat of defamation intimidate us. If they want to sue us, let them." Sometimes, though, editors feel battered by certain public figures who, in vengeance, bring tens of cases against a single newspaper. When this happens, editors often relent and stop carrying any news at all about these individuals. Frustrated, one of the editors bemoans, "No matter what we write, [a particular individual] charges us. So we have stopped covering him." Another editor offers: "If it's just one word, one sentence [about him], he'll just sue you anytime!" Do you cover this person any more in your paper? "No! Not even anything related to him!"[28]

When one editor was asked if he thought defamation could be used as a tool by those in power to silence critics, he answered that at the end of the day, the nature of the law can doom a newspaper:

> I understand [defamation] can be used as a tool. If there's someone crazy enough, it can be used as a tool for giving someone else a really hard time. Such as, suppose you don't want a newspaper to operate—just sue, 200–300 times. I wouldn't have to do anything else—just go appear in the court every day. I'm coming to such a state right now.[29]

Government prosecutors take cases to court "probably to avoid being accused of favoring the press," courts are likely to go straight to trial "as the evidence has already been screened by the State prosecutors," and criminal prosecutions of defamation can aid those seeking financial damages in civil court, all funded by government tax money:

> Thai law allows those who claim to be defamed to make use of the police and State prosecutors in pursuing defamation cases in court, which is tantamount to using State resources to redeem a personal interest. In Thailand, when an injured person files charges with the police, the latter investigate the case and gather relevant evidence. The Office of the Attorney General then decides whether the case is substantial enough to be prosecuted in court and, if so, it appoints a State prosecutor as plaintiff. As a result, the claimant is relieved of the burden of spending its own financial resources to pursue the case.[30]

Leading journalist Veera Prateepchaikul argued in 2004 that "that the state is too quick" in regarding journalists "as criminals." Calls to decriminalize the defamation law "have gone unheeded by this government and its predecessors. Governments always claim they need a working mechanism to protect the rights of the individual.[31] The Press Council of Thailand, in a meeting on "Use and Abuse of Libel Law," concluded that "the libel law was being used as a negotiating instrument by politicians . . . to shun individuals or groups criticising or scrutinising those in power." The Council suggested that the police "should act as negotiators," that "a court order a preliminary hearing before accepting a lawsuit for trial," and for litigation to be "limited to the civil court."[32]

This heavy, gratuitous use of defamation has led to increased self-censorship on the part of newspapers. TJA in 2006 depicted the threat to press freedom as heralding an "era of fear and hatred"[33] The International Federation of Journalists (IFJ) condemned, "Thai Prime Minister Thaksin Shinawatra's continued use of criminal defamation charges to silence media criticism of his government." A Human Rights Watch report on Thailand argued that the line between defamation and fair criticism was completely blurred, noting that "it's impossible to distinguish a libel suit from an attempt to silence the prime minister's critics. Thailand's once-vigorous free press is being slowly squeezed to death."[34] If Thailand had once been celebrated as the freest press in Southeast Asia, it was no longer, according to Reporters Without Borders. In its world-wide survey the Kingdom's ranking dropped from 59th in 2004 to 107th in 2005, 122nd in 2006 and to a low of 135th (out of 169) in 2007, putting it behind its Southeast neighbours Malaysia, Cambodia, and the Philippines, just below the Democratic Republic of the Congo, and only five places higher than Sudan.[35]

As the criminal law on defamation intends to compel social quietude, many editors felt a bias toward plaintiffs on the part of police, prosecutors, and judges. At a particularly turbulent time, from 1976 to 1982, the police made arrests on average of 81 percent of defamation incidents they investigated.[36] From 1986 to 2005, 87 percent of the defamation cases the prosecution department received were tried. Editors perceived that courts had to accept all cases of defamation, rather than consider the merits and grounds for each case at the outset. Kiatichai remarks that there is no alternative: "According to legal procedure, they have to accept all the cases."

There was a less than 5 percent chance that the case would be withdrawn or the defendant would have the chance to settle out-of-court.[37] If tried, conviction occurred in a remarkable 97 percent of cases. If prosecutors took the case from the police, 79 percent of defendants would be convicted.[38] Some editors expressed hesitation to approach the court alone. If they somehow caused offense, sooner or later they would run into the same judge in a future defamation case and be in trouble.

Newspaper editors placed their hopes on the 21 percent chance of acquittal and this was one reason why no editors dared to address the general problem of defamation when they were in court. A judge might take offense and cite them for contempt.

Despite the evidence cited above, one editor claimed that in "most cases," the plaintiff and the editor talk the issue through and "Charges are dropped and it disappears."[39] However, perhaps defamation cases have become so much a part of the life of newspapers that editors see them as normal. Kiatichai offers, "now we seem to have gotten used to these libel cases." They have become part of "the routine life of the media people."

Thailand's defamation law will probably not change any time soon. A perceptive editorial in *The Nation* celebrated a change in the press law of 1941 in late 2007, which would "do away with censorship and the once powerful press officers who could close down a newspaper or any publication."[40] In addition, the editorial called for an end to defamation as a criminal offense. To be "in conformity with the prevailing democratic atmosphere," the editorial continued to describe the history of the law:

> Criminal defamation laws have their origins in the need to maintain public order during a period when insults or attacks on reputations posed a real risk of endangering violence, in particular in the form of a duel. But this risk can no longer be applied under the present circumstances and, as a result, their public order roots should no longer be used as a justification for criminal defamation laws . . . the laws have been abused by politicians as a means to intimidate or to muzzle criticism against themselves by the media . . . efforts [of the National Press Council] have not been successful due to resistance from some sectors in society who strongly feel the need to retain the laws . . . to protect the reputation of individuals . . . The use of criminal law in defamation cases represents a disproportionate means of addressing the problem of unwarranted attacks on someone's reputation. It exerts an unacceptable chilling effect on freedom of expression, particularly in relation to statements regarding public figures or on matters of public interest . . . There is no denying there is a need to protect the reputation of individuals, just as it is necessary to protect free expression. The point is how to balance free speech with the need to protect reputation.

The editorial concluded with a call to completely repeal the law, or at least exclude imprisonment for convictions. "[T]he existing criminal defamation laws," the editorial wrote, "are out of time and out of place and go against the spirit of democracy."

Defamation of the official (body)

As in most countries, Thai government officials are protected from contempt, a form of defamation. Under the 1900 edict, criticizing a royal official was equivalent to criticizing the king, who was also the government, with up to three years' imprisonment. After 1908, royal officials were split into government officials (bureaucrats) and judges, with the maximum imprisonment dropping rather dramatically to six months while defamation of the government remained at three years. The distinction proved crucial in certain cases. In a 1923 case against the *Wayamo* newspaper, for instance, two defendants were charged with accusing government officials "indiscriminately of dishonesty and disloyalty." In responding to the charge, the defendants attempted to "call evidence to show that paragraphs which referred to all officials without distinction in fact only referred to one or two officials." However, the court ruled that such would not be permissible and condemned them for libel against the king and government.

Even while not explicitly provided for by the letter of the law, there was always some suggestion that citizens could express an honest opinion. The judge and foreign advisor in the case even affirmed this principle:

> It is universally admitted that the press makes for the welfare and progress of States by publishing useful information as to their administrations and on matters of public interest. Freedom is given to it to make fair comments and to publish bona fide criticisms on matters of public interest, but this must be done in good faith, for the public benefit and without malice.

A separate opinion on the *Wayamo* case, issued by Ralph Gibbins, the Adviser to the International Court, where this case was tried, makes a similar point:[41]

> Public interest in the Government and Administration of a State is a healthy sign of progress in civilization, and it is generally accepted that criticisms of Governments, and of officials in their official capacity are not actionable provided that such criticisms deal with matters of public interest, are fair, and free from malice. Sweeping condemnation of Governments or of officials do not however, fall within this description, and cannot be allowed.[42]

However, while an exception is made permitting criticism, in practice its use was inconsistent and rarely applied. The question of what constitutes a fair target of critical comment is not as simple as it first may seem, at least in a legal sense. This reveals a tension. The public is warned against making "sweeping condemnations" of the government (seditious rebellion), but is also called to make specific allegations. To be specific, though, risks violation of either insulting officials or defamation of private individuals.

The courts were protected from defamation or contempt by Section 151 of the criminal code and defendants were routinely punished. For instance, in a 1932 case Mr. Narin Phasit, in reference to another case, said, "The court is wrong and unjust.[43] The court deliberated the case and then concluded in a peremptory way to send me off to jail." The Court of First Instance ruled that, clearly, "the defendant intended to slander the court" and sentenced him to one-month imprisonment. The defendant appealed the decision, on the legal grounds that he had spoken the words with "the intention of causing benefit to the people, and that he had not acted insincerely," as provided in an exemption clause to personal defamation that "allows one to express an honest opinion for the benefit of the public." The Supreme Court ruled that this exception did not apply to contempt of court where the matter of words being spoken "sincerely or insincerely" did.[44]

Neither could the exemption clause for seditious rebellion be applied for contempt of government officials. In a 1937 case, the defendant, Luang Sikhanaphiban, had said of an "investigating officer": "What kind of authority are you for sure? You shouldn't be an officer to protect the peace of the citizens. You dare to unjustly investigate, out of spite. You dare to take false testimony. You've done this before." The court found him guilty and fined him 50 baht for both the crime and court costs. The Appeals Court felt the words of the defendant were "of ridicule" and not slander. The defendant was "just criticizing the methods of the authorities." The court felt "that the citizens have the right to criticize the methods of the authorities according to their own opinions." However, the public record in the end denied such a right. The Supreme Court reversed the decision and found the defendant guilty.[45]

In other words, specific contempt laws could be used when a citizen dared to criticize a particular government official or judge. As neither of these laws provided any exemption, personal defamation was not used. Of the 49 cases of personal defamation to reach the Supreme Court from 1914 to 1982, the plaintiff was a government official or judge in few cases. Cases of grave contempt or showing any sort of a "sweeping condemnation" of government could be tried as seditious rebellion. From 1958 to 1991, the coup decrees were used to suppress criticism, especially if the plaintiff was a politician who had no statutory protection. It was only in the early 1990s that defamation clearly absorbed certain features of seditious rebellion and became a favored tool for government officials and politicians to silence critics.

There were two aspects of this newly fortified personal defamation law of 1992, official defamation that contradicted a common legal interpretation: the use of personal defamation by public figures and collective defamation for government bodies. Prior to the early 1990s, neither of these practices had been allowed to any great extent and neither were, nor are, they allowed to such extent by international standards.

The newly amended "official defamation" law of 1992 was put to immediate use and eventually, eight years later, culminated in a sort of landmark case on issues of freedom of the press. The Supreme Court demanded in January 2000 that *Khao Sot* newspaper pay Narong Wongwan five million baht in punitive damages. In 1992, allegations that Narong had been denied a visa to the US for suspected involvement in the drug trade ruined his chances of becoming the Thai prime minister. In this “historic case against the media,” Narong demanded 100 million baht in damages and a retraction from four newspapers. The court’s decision apparently “rattled the affected newspapers” as the damages were “relatively high for defamation cases.”[46]

We may speculate that the guarantees for free speech in the 1997 constitution were stringent enough that officials and politicians had to fall back on the criminal charge of personal defamation, for, between 1996 and 1998, the number of new cases of defamation made a significant jump, increasing by 36 percent. The *Nation* noted that Pol Lt-Gen Seri Temiyavej, a close ally of the Democrat Party, “could eventually go down in the police force’s history as its most litigious officer” as he had filed 30 separate defamation suits against *Khao Sot* and said the number could go up to 50, claiming that the newspaper had attacked his character with “innuendo, insinuation and hearsay.”[47] Whereas an editor going to court takes away from the business of a newspaper, Seri shrugged off questions about how he could show up in court every other day during working hours by saying, “Going to court is part of my work too.”[48]

McCargo wrote in 2000 that rarely had prime ministers of Thailand used personal defamation laws when they became the target of criticism.[49] But things changed. Democrat Party Leader, Chuan Leekpai, was one of the first to use the law. In mid-2000, members of the Assembly of the Poor, led by villagers fighting against the Pak Mun dam, began a protest in front of Government House. Ignored by the government, villagers scaled the wall with ladders and entered Government House grounds. Repulsed and still ignored, villagers attempted again, but this time were dispersed with tear gas and beaten by the police.[50] A number of prominent academics and journalists condemned the use of force by the Chuan government. Nidhi Eoseewong compared the violence to the bloody crackdown on demonstrators by the military in May 1992, saying, “It is the same sort of dictatorship mentality, whether it’s from the military or what is supposed to be a democratically elected government.”[51] *Bangkok Post* columnist Sanitsuda Ekachai wrote in a piece entitled, “Tyranny goes by the name of Chuan”:

> Congratulations, Mr. Chuan. On the holy day marking the start of the Buddhist Lent of BE 2543 [2000], you went down in history as a civilian tyrant, a product of money politics in the guise of democracy. It’s your detached haughtiness and your contempt for the plight of the poor that did it.[52]

The action of the government was publicly condemned by 202 Thai academics nationwide, a number of Thai-studies academics from the United States, Canada, the United Kingdom, and Australia, 169 non-governmental organizations, and a variety of grassroots groups and networks.[53]

Prime Minister Chuan Leekpai responded by suing *Khao Sot* for its headline of 18 July which read:[54]

> CRUEL CHUAN
> [*CHUAN THAMIN*]
> SQUELCHES THE POOR ON MONK DAY
> [*PRAP KHON JON WAN PHRA*]

In filing the charge of criminal defamation, Chuan claimed that the headline in *Khao Sot* implied he was a "dictator" [or tyrant] and a "cruel person." Chuan felt "seriously defamed" and said that the paper "intended to mislead the public into thinking he was cruel and not supportive of democracy," for "ordering police to assault the poor villagers which in turn "seriously affect[ed] his image."[55] He said these representations were "completely false."[56]56 The suit submitted to the court also made the point that Thakul Uthaiwong, the editor of *Khao Sot*, "has already been convicted in a defamation criminal suit and is facing more than 50 other cases. This, Chuan noted, showed that Thakul "is a journalist without ethics and an immoral person who likes to present false reports to defame other people. He should be regarded as detrimental to society."[57]

Two legal principles come into play in this case. First, usually, the more public the figure, the less leeway is given for legal recourse to defamation prosecution. This holds particularly for elected public figures. Chuan as prime minister was the highest elected public figure in the land and responsible for public policy. In many countries, courts would have exercised great discretion in receiving the case. Chuan, a trained lawyer, was no doubt aware of this and of international standards and should have borne the criticism and responded to his critics by appealing to public opinion rather than resorting to the courts. Second, in most cases, the rule on the difference between an assertion of fact and an opinion is whether the assertion can be shown to be false. Is calling the leader of a country a "tyrant" falsifiable? Is it a statement that can be proved or disproved? Would "proof" require political scientists to testify in court about what exactly constitutes a dictator? In any case, the use of the word "tyrant" became part of the debate in larger society, suggesting that it was a depiction that should have been allowable.[58]

As we saw earlier in this chapter, Thai courts also had usually not allowed defamation cases where the plaintiff could not clearly show he or she was the damaged party. Prior to 1991, attacks on politicians were controlled by the Press Officer under Coup Decree No. 42. For personal defamation cases within the judicial system, Thai courts had fairly consistently upheld three standards: the right to criticize public figures, the falsifiability of actionable defamation cases, and little latitude given to collective defamation. After 1992, state agencies and politicians used defamation suits to silence critics. However, as defamation cases increasingly involved people exercising political power, the courts forwent such restraint, leading to the remarkable rise of defamation suits, as courts became the loci of political contestation. These cases became common.

In May 1992, government forces brutally suppressed demonstrators.

Harshly rebuked by the public, the military, while retreating somewhat from the Thai political scene, was nonetheless quick to take offense. On 5 January 1993, the following front-page headline of *Khao Sot* newspaper read: "14 Cruel Green Uniforms! 'We're the Big Man Soldiers' Attacked and Destroyed Bus with Gunfire! Slashed Away in front of 100s! 3 Injured and Killed for just a 5-baht Ticket!":

> There they go again! Shouting out, "We are soldiers!", a force of 14 wearing camouflage uniforms and armed with guns, Spartan knives, and clubs attacked and destroyed a Bangkok-Phetburi bus, taking out revenge for passenger fare of five baht. Automatic revolver unloads 18 shots into ill-fated money taker's head who died instantly. Another one is cut up and in serious condition. An unintended passenger gets embroiled and gets a Spartan knife through the collarbone and is in grave condition just the same.[59]

Army chief of staff General Wimol Wongwanich pressed charges of defamation against the newspaper for "maligning the Army, all of those now damaged who are in the service of the Army and who are under the jurisdiction of the Army." Soon, soldiers from districts and provinces from around the country—wherever there was a military camp—began filing charges, too. In the end, 62 charges were filed in 59 police stations—a record, according to the defendant in the case, *Khao Sot*'s editor at the time, Kiatichai Pongpanich.[60] The plaintiffs charged that the defendant sought

> [to] have all of people in general who read the aforementioned news understand that those who committed the crime . . . were soldiers under the jurisdiction of the Army and under the command of the Commander of the Army, all the damaged parties . . . because it is only Army soldiers who have green or camouflage uniforms.[61]

After five years and three months and a million baht spent on the defense, the case ended with the Appeals Court acquitting *Khao Sot*. Although the court had given the newspaper a fair amount of latitude, significant is the fact that the Court of First Instance had not dismissed the case in the first place on grounds that no particular army soldier could claim to be the damaged party. Thus began the era where the government representatives could file collective defamation cases against critics, thus preserving the continuity of seditious rebellion.

In a case involving the police, an economics professor from Chulalongkorn University, Sangsit Piriyarangsan, and a number of his colleagues issued results of a preliminary study about the illicit underground activities of the police. All fourteen police station chiefs in Bangkok filed personal defamation charges against the academics, apparently with the approval of the police director-general who "rejected the paper's findings as groundless." A police chief said: "I reserve my basic right to lodge a complaint with the relevant authority so the faults in his allegation can be proven." On the other side, a number of lecturers at the university drew up a petition supporting their colleague, arguing that "the research paper is presented to the public so that the problem will be rectified."[62] The next day, the Minister of Public Health, Snoh Thienthong, explained that no action should be taken against the researcher, for he had simply said what everyone already knew. He said police corruption "is very widespread and [everyone] knows it. So why should we lie and say it doesn't exist?"[63] With mediation from the prime minister, the issue was resolved when the university rector forced Sangsit to explain that "the study has not yet been completed and that its information may not all be accurate." These were the magic words. All of a sudden, the director-general of the police "no longer held any grudges" and now "the police respected the findings and admit that gambling dens did exist." For him, it "had been hard to swallow" the allegation that "all policemen at all stations took bribes":

> There are tens of thousands, perhaps hundreds of thousands of gambling arrests made by police. I'm not saying that there are no bad guys at all in the Police Department. I only question the research's findings that every single police station in Bangkok took bribes. Our lawsuits stemmed from concern that the image of good policemen would be tarnished.[64]

Finally (and a bit ironically), in 2000, activist Veera Somkwankid accused an unnamed Constitutional Court judge of accepting a free trip to Australia, compliments allegedly of Democrat Party secretary-general Sanan Kachornprasart, on trial for not properly declaring his assets.[65] Veera then made another charge that seven of the court's 12 judges had accepted 150 million baht in bribes to dismiss the corruption case against the politician. The newspaper reporter who broke the story claimed that he had learned of the information from a constitutional court judge who refused to stay at a party at which all the judges were to be propositioned with bribes.[66] On behalf of all 12 judges, Constitutional Court secretary-general Noppadol Hengcharoen filed a bundle of charges against Veera, most centrally, defamation.[67]

The legal principle specifies that libel charges can only be made when the damaged party is clearly identified. Neither a single judge, nor all of them, could make a clear claim to be the damaged party. As it turns out, prosecutors filed charges with the criminal court against Veera at the behest of seven specific judges "on charges of defaming seven Constitutional Court judges."[68] The case was not made any easier with seven specific judges having to show that they were precisely the seven unspecified judges alluded to by Veera. Nonetheless, Veera was found guilty.[69]

In a few cases, however, courts did affirm some of basic principles of free speech. In an August 1991 speech at a Thammasat University seminar reviewing the previous six months of rule under the National Peacekeeping Council

(NPKC), social critic Sulak Sivaraksa said the NPKC had cited corruption as a reason for the coup, only to become corrupt themselves. He admitted that the cabinet appointed by the NPKC was clean, but that was NPKC's intention—the NPKC generals wouldn't have to split the spoils with anyone else. Sulak also accused the then Commander-in-Chief of the army and deputy head of the NPKC, General Suchinda Kraprayoon of going to Burma to learn from the notorious State Law and Order Restoration Council (SLORC) how to stage a *coup* and that the NPKC's business relations with SLORC destroyed the nation's dignity. Finally, he charged that "dictatorial groups" such as the NPKC should be charged with *lèse-majesté* for subverting the the constitution that the king had granted. Sulak was accused of "oral defamation" by Suchinda. In addition, Sulak was charged for saying:

> This *coup d'état* by the NPKC is the greatest *lèse-majesté* . . . The NPKC had an audience with His Majesty the King the day they took power, which distressed the King very deeply. The Thai people were never aware of this . . . If they [the NPKC] had really been loyal, they would have done something to maintain the dignity of the monarchy and the nation.

The prosecution also claimed that Sulak had insulted and given a figurative "slap in the face" to the king when Sulak told a story of how the military detained the king when he returned from Europe in 1951, concluding, "The military always bullies the King."[70]

The court made short shrift of Suchinda's defamation case against Sulak. As something of a surprise, it observed that Sulak, as "an ordinary citizen," had "criticized and protested against those who seized power and abolished the constitution by accusing them of *lèse-majesté* and pointing out the five lies the NPKC used to justify its coup." The court even seemed to admonish Suchinda for pursuing the case in the first place:

> As an ordinary citizen, the defendant criticized and protested against those who seized power and abolished the constitution . . . Normally those who are involved in politics and public affairs need to listen to both praise and blame. As Suchinda was the deputy leader of the NPKC, he should have allowed himself to be criticized and resisted because of the coup. This kind of criticism is for the benefit of the country and people. As the quoted statement is an opinion or speculation, and not an affirmation, it is not strong enough to defame Suchinda.[71]

The court laid out an important legal principle concerning illegitimate rule and the right of citizens to speak against it. The court recognized the importance of the public's need to air its grievances against the government. The court quite frankly stated the obvious—the NPKC did in fact stage a coup—and for this action the NPKC should have expected it would, with reason, be "criticized and resisted." Compared with the Supreme Court cases of the 1950s and early 1960s legitimizing coups, this case seemed to be a step forward.

The defamation law reached a sort of apogee of absurdity or at least of disproportionality with the case of Supinya Klangnarong, the Secretary General of the Campaign for Popular Media Reform, when she made the claim that profits of Prime Minister Thaksin Shinawatra's company, ShinCorp, skyrocketed as a result of the Thaksin government's policies. The company sued her and the newspaper that printed Supinya's findings for a mind-boggling 400 million baht, about US$10 million at the time. Her acquittal, coming when charges of *lèse-majesté* and personal defamation in early 2006 were perhaps at a peak—was a blow to the Thaksin government and gave heart to the PAD protests—then a broad-based movement—calling for Thaksin's ouster. The court's verdict was heralded as a landmark case of free speech, as the court affirmed that Supinya and her co-defendants "were honestly expressing an opinion . . . for the benefit of the public, which is something that a citizen can do." Supinya had acted "honestly," the court said, in making comment, as the issue involved television and telecommunication airwaves which should be considered public property. Many international press freedom organizations were present at the hearing and the court's decision was seen as a significant step forward in ensuring freedom of the press; it was an important if not decisive blow to Thaksin.[72]

It would be reassuring to think that these landmark cases of Sulak and Supinya were part of an overall reorientation of the court's thinking on defamation or of the public's right to challenge the powers that be. However, within Thailand's legal system, Supreme Court cases do not carry much weight. Lower court decisions carry even less. It is not common for Supreme Court decisions to cite earlier Supreme Court decisions and it is extremely rare, if ever, for Supreme Court decisions to cite decisions of lower courts.[73] As a result, these two cases failed to become part of a more significant public record because the plaintiffs and prosecutors wisely chose not to appeal them.

The NPCT/Article 19's 2009 report on defamation litigation in Thailand makes clear that in certain respects, the Thai law on defamation does "comply with certain respects of international standards." At least the letter of the law allows, for instance, exceptions from guilt in defamation cases "by allowing fair and true comments on matters of public interest." But Thai law fails "to respect international standards" as it "does not prohibit public bodies either in the legislative, executive or judicial branches from initiating defamation cases. Thai law also does not require public figures to be more tolerant of criticism than ordinary citizens." As a result, the criminal defamation law has become "the main threat used by politicians and those holding public offices to silence their critics, and they tend to seek imprisonment rather than monetary compensation to punish their offences."[74]

Defamation of the government

The government identified itself as a target—indeed, became conscious of itself as an entity—in 1900. From that point to the end of the absolute monarchy in 1932, two clear dynamics about the nature of litigants emerged. The state began a process in which it reconstituted itself within a set of modern laws and judicial practices as a legal entity arrogating to itself the power and the right to arrest, charge, try, and punish its perceived enemies. Within this, the state acted as the police, the prosecutor, the damaged party, and the judge. It was a self referential system of "accountability" that seemed legitimate while, at the same time, remarkably skewing the administration of justice to the side of the state. As such, within the set of defamation-based crimes against the state, the conviction rate for the relatively few cases that made it to the Supreme Court was perfect prior to 1932: everyone tried for defamation of the government (seditious rebellion) was found guilty.

This unassailable record was due at least in part to the state's ability to evade legal responsibility or accountability. While the government, with the urging of its foreign advisors, appeared to steer clear of making "sweeping prohibitions" that would suppress any criticism of the government, it forbade critics from making "sweeping condemnations" of it. The impressive litany of exceptions provided for in the 1900 edict gives the impression that the government wanted an active, involved citizenry to root out and expose corrupt officials. But, in practice, the government was able to sue because either the condemnation was too sweeping, "The government is corrupt," or too specific, allowing the speaker to be charged with contempt of public officials, e.g. "This headman is corrupt." As we saw in Chapter 6, at some point Narin's comments simply crossed some line, from fair comment to seditious rebellion. This "line" became less, rather than more, distinct in the decades after 1932.

While defamation of private individuals is clear, "the government" as an entity is not. How can someone be charged with defaming "the government" if the "government" itself could not define exactly what it is? This issue is not as esoteric as it may seem, nor is it merely a matter of semantics. The answer, and the way it was debated in Thailand, makes a significant difference in cases of defamation-based crimes against the monarchy and state. Individuals, associations, companies, and certain other juristic persons can sue for defamation. But what if the target of the defamatory words is "the government," "the laws," or "institutions of the state"? Who will serve as a spokesperson for these entities? The Prosecution Department? The head of the allegedly defamed government agency? The monarchy? The prime minister? A member of parliament? And, at the governing end, who will decide exactly what these entities are?

The problem was illustrated by a 1939 case, when Mr. Mani was on his way to vote in parliamentary elections.[75] He stopped for a word with Mr.

Khunthong Suphap, who said, "We've had two elections already and I haven't seen any representative serve any purpose. The government does wrong. It shouldn't have dissolved parliament. It enacts crazy laws, forcing the people to pay unfair taxes." Upon hearing these words, Mr. Mani asked Mr. Khunthong to take back his words. When the latter refused, saying he had a right to speak, Mr. Mani went and reported the matter to the police. Mr. Khunthong was charged with saying things that would "cause the people to despise the government or officials." The Supreme Court upheld the Appeal Court's ruling that the defendant had spoken "in order to create contempt for the government" and sentenced him to two months' imprisonment.

But exactly which "government" was Khunthong creating contempt for? Was it "the government" that had just "dissolved the parliament" (the present administration), the one that had enacted "crazy laws" (the parliament), or the one that collected the unfair taxes (the bureaucracy)? Was it any one of these, or all three?

Over the next dozen years, "the government" tried in various ways to define itself through four Supreme Court cases and five Government and Juridical Council consultations. In the first case in 1941, a wife and husband both made statements which brought charges of rebellion against them. The police arrested the husband, Mr. Him Saelao, and put him in jail. The police then went to search his house. There, according to his wife, Mrs. Sin Saesai, the police found nothing. But when the police got back to the police station, they suddenly had evidence—in this case, illegal liquor. Or, so said the wife. This statement was seen as accusing the police of planting or making up evidence and thus was defamation of the government. In response to all of this, the husband was heard muttering, "These laws of Thailand just don't work." He, too, then was charged with defamation of the state. The words of the defendants, the prosecution charged, would "cause people to despise the royal officials of Thailand" and thus could lead to "unrest or rebelliousness among the people." The Appeals Court felt that the wife's words referred only to the "regular police" of the district who had arrested her husband. As such, her words were not intended to have "people believe that she was commenting on the police of Thailand in general." As for the husband, the court felt that his words "did not address anyone in particular" and so were not trying to "produce the effect" that the prosecution claimed. The Supreme Court upheld the decision of the Appeals Court, saying that the words of the husband "did not make people look down on government officials" in any way. In explaining its decision, the court argued that "government" was the various ministers who hold "temporary office" and decide the policies of the country. The "administration," on the other hand, was "the underlying governmental organization" which includes the "ministries, departments, sections, etc. taken as a whole." By way of example, the court pointed out that the government would not be defamed when someone said something that caused others to "despise just one unit or group" of the military or police, except if the one who spoke had "the aim of having the majority of the military or police be despised." In this case, the words of the wife referred to "just one group of police." In a similar way, the court said, the words, "The laws of Thailand just don't work," could not in any way "defame any portion of the administration" and so they did not violate Section 104, either.[76]

The Supreme Court took another stab at the definition of government in a case issued a few days later. The case involved incidents connected with a strike of *sam lo* or rickshaw drivers in 1939 in Lopburi province who, in a letter to the governor, said that "the head of the police had arrested *sam lo* drivers for trifling violations and with too great of severity," causing the drivers and their families to "fall into difficult times." The strike leaders were arrested and charged with seditious rebellion, using the argument that since the police were government servants, opposing them when they enforced the laws was tantamount to resisting the government, that is, rebellion. The Appeals Court felt that the defendants had organized a work stoppage not "in order to change the government or the laws of the land" but to "force the government" to do something. Before the Supreme Court, where the prosecution once again argued that the police were part of the official administration, the defendants were found innocent and the case was dismissed. In clarifying its decision, the court explained that a work stoppage which aimed to change or compel the government meant "trying to force the entire cabinet of ministers or particular cabinet ministers to resign." It did not mean that trying to "compel" the head of police in some district was an attempt to change or compel "the government." Although the police are "part of the whole, they still remain only [a part] of the bureaucracy [or administration] [*ratchakan phaendin*]," which is not "the same as the 'government.'" The government was the entire cabinet of ministers empowered by virtue of the constitution to set out political policies for the country. The administration had the responsibility of carrying out such policies through the various ministries. This, the court went on to say, did not include any particular police station which was not part of the administration as such. The Supreme Court thus laid out a principle: While the law stipulated that for an action to be a violation it must be against the whole, then any action against any smaller part of that whole is not enough to constitute a violation. When one acts against the smaller part, then it cannot be held that such is an action against the whole.[77]

In 1942, "the Government" initiated a set of consultations with the Juridical Council about what "it" was, exactly. The government was concerned that in giving lectures and making publications, a "certain government organisation always refers to itself as the government instead of using its own name." To rectify the situation, the government wanted the Juridical Council to help come up with rules "to the effect that on what matter the word 'Government' should be referred to and on what matter such government organisation should be referred to." The government said that the correct use of the term was no small matter, as it affected Section 104 which involved the "bringing into hatred or contempt the *Government* or *administration of the State*" (orginal emphasis).[78]

The lengthy discussions over the next twelve years are fascinating in their own fashion, and I but briefly summarize them here. The Supreme Court in 1941 concluded that the government was the cabinet of ministers holding "temporary office" and not any administrative unit. Accordingly, seditious rebellion was any effort to compel the cabinet of ministers, or, somewhat inconsistently, to take action against "the whole" (such as "the government"). In 1942 the prime minister concurred with this, as did the Juridical Council. While this body affirmed that neither the king nor the parliament was the government, it also, confusedly perhaps, argued that government may also mean a ministry or department when it was the "organ of execution" under direction of the cabinet of ministers. Overall, though, in the 1940s, the courts, government, and Juridical Council were restricting the range of what government should mean.

In contrast, three Supreme Court decisions of the 1950s stretched the meaning of "government" to include any force that has extended control over the administration and thereby has become recognized by the people as the legitimate power. One decision of the court tried to argue that a government that comes into power through a coup is not the government, at least initially. But once the coup group successfully establishes power, it, and the entire administration, becomes the government (see Chapter 5).

Although there were yet some inconsistencies, a general consensus from the 1940s considerations on "the government" did emerge.[79] "Government" referred to the Cabinet of Ministers who directed the affairs of the country. The Cabinet of Ministers, for its part, was the body appointed by the king, empowered by the constitution, and held the confidence of the parliament. The Cabinet of Ministers might speak as the government. The consensus also agreed that the government was not smaller administrative units, specific persons, the king, or even the Council of Ministers in such cases when its members were not carrying out their official duty. The central contrast was between the cabinet of ministers (the government) and the administrative organization (the bureaucracy) which carried out the government's policies, which might use the word "official" rather than "government" in reference to documents. The bureaucracy as a whole was not "the government" as neither is any part of it, such as "the police" or the parliament. Subunits of "the government" could, for instance, use the personal defamation law, but could not do so as "the government."

Given this, what was and what was not acceptable to say or publish? A person could say something that would cause a particular group of officials to be despised (although, in return, one might be sued for defamation). One could make a general assessment about the political system, such as stating that Thai laws are useless. One could not utter, though, something that was perceived as "against the whole" of "the government." A person could not say that that "the police" or "the military" are "corrupt" and thus cause others to look down on them—even if it could be shown that the majority of the police and military were in fact corrupt. What is clear is that laws and legal consultations were all expressed in democratic terms, with representative bodies and constitutions. Although Thailand in the early 1940s is today characterized as authoritarian, a level of adherence to basic democratic principles remained.[80] However, after the first successful military *coup* to overthrow an elected government in 1947, a discernible change occurred, with the emergence of new laws of exception and a tendency of courts to grant legitimacy to coups.

Thus, Supreme Court decisions of the early 1950s were highly undemocratic. In the 1952 "Chief of Staff" case, a group of officers argued that they could not have committed rebellion for the government in power was not legitimate. In the 1953 case, the court legitimized the 1947 coup (Chapter 5).[81] In this case, no attempt to separate the cabinet of ministers from the administration was made: they had become one and the same. "The police" were just as much "the government" as the cabinet of ministers. The only condition was that a given group (like a military coup group) had "administrative power," regardless of how that power was gained. This case might have set the precedent, as justified governments that came to power by coups. As such, all nuance was lost: coups consolidated all aspects of what government might mean into a single entity. The decisions conflated "government" with literally everything connected to it or which could be construed as a signifier for it.

One key contradictory aspect of seditious rebellion and the meaning of "the government" became clear in the 1957 case of Kukrit Pramoj (Chapters 5 and 9), who wrote a series of articles criticizing the US ambassador. These ultimately resulted in a charge of seditious rebellion. A description of the series, drawn from the police charge sheet, is as follows:

> The contents . . . from the first issue [of the magazine], there was a picture of a person holding a flag, and the poem, "Wake Up Thais" which had contents calling for the suppression of gangster types, and then the contents on page 4 are in the line of the government holding power like a troublemaker. It uses governing power oppressively and is habitually crooked. The rulers of Thailand understand that the Thai people forget easily . . . Those governing use power barbarically [as if] in the middle of the jungle. They use weapons to keep the citizens down. If anyone is stubborn, they will die.[82]

These articles were sufficiently alarming for a high-ranking government official to bring charges of seditious rebellion. Newspapers faithfully reproduced the court transcripts, giving us a rare look into the hearing. On 18 May 1957, the first day of the trial, newspaper accounts described a packed courtroom full of those wishing to hear the proceedings. The first witness for the prosecution was Police General Luang Chat Trakankoson, Head of the Interior Department and Chairperson of the Committee for Crime Suppression. He commented on the offending articles from the 10, 17, and 24 March editions of the *Sayam Rat Weekly Review* news magazine. To the prosecution's question about how the witness felt about the articles upon reading them:

> *Witness* says that in his feeling, it was about the belief of the people in the government. If it was in this form, the people would lose their respect for the government.
>
> *Prosecution* asks what the impact of the people losing their respect of the government would be.
>
> *Witness* says they would feel hatred and dissatisfied with the government and that government meant the present government.

The target was precise enough, seemingly—not just *the* government, but the *present* government. But was this clear? Later, under cross-examination by Seni Pramote, serving as defense attorney for his brother, the witness was asked again about "which" government. The elections had been held in late February. Technically speaking, after an election, the "government" is replaced by a caretaker government. It was the caretaker government that the articles seemed to speak of, as the articles were published in March. The witness agreed that a caretaker government was in place when the articles came out. Seni pushed the point. He asked the witness whether it would be abnormal for the people to think about overthrowing the government if in fact that government has ceased to exist following the elections. Would the people be a little crazy to want to overthrow a government that did not exist? This question by Seni brings up a crucial point that the letter of the law does not address. Is "a" government still "the" government after elections have taken place? Is it still protected by the law?[83]

This case shows that, during the period 1932 to 1958, despite the tendency of courts to justify coups and dissolve distinctions between "government," "the government," and "the administration," sufficient play in the term "government" existed for defendants of rebellious sedition to be found innocent.

The lack of clarity on this issue underscored the dramatic difference between defamation of the government (seditious rebellion) and defamation of private individuals. One member of the sub-committee at the Juridical Council said the term "government" seemed abstract and it was abstract in exactly the way that a person or a company could never be. The statement, "the Thai government is corrupt," is not difficult to understand. It means that there are people either in the government service or those who were elected who are engaged in some corrupt practice. But in a legal sense and in terms of defamation what "government" actually refers to becomes quite important.

If the definition of "the government" is difficult, how could the state ever truly try someone for insulting it? While it might have been complicated to say what "the government" exactly was, "the government" was not hesitant to charge citizens with insulting "it" while "it" was still deciding what "it" was.

With respect to the government as target of defamation, the public sphere expanded significantly from 1932 to 1958. The official sphere expanded as well, to a certain degree acquiring space from the public sphere, but mostly from the sacred (Figure 1.1). If there were certain tendencies or qualities that legitimized the sacred sphere, these were replaced with secular, authoritarian ones within the official sphere. But the public sphere ultimately was unable to make any long-term advances into the official sphere, as "the government" was able to avoid any clear legal definition of itself. While this helped a number of defendants of seditious rebellion to escape punishment, the long-term trend resulted in the definition of "the government" losing much if not all specificity, and for it to be easily interpreted as any words that questioned authority or the legitimacy it needed to protect.

Defamation of the nation and its symbols

We began this chapter with a case of defamation of the Thai people. A number of other rather abstract symbols and qualities are protected in Thailand by defamation-based laws.[84] For instance, in 1933 a newly enacted Defence of the Constitution law stipulated that Siamese citizens must look upon the constitution favorably. A provision of the national security laws forbids insulting symbols of the state, including the national flag.[85] As noted earlier, the military, with support from the courts, was an ascendant power in the 1950s. A mature authoritarian official sphere developed, replete with an organizational infrastructure, a conceptual and legal framework, and a fully formed cultural ideology. As a whole, the period marked a remarkable psychological expansion of the official sphere that enforced certain kinds of behavior, aspiring toward a hyper-regimentation of national life, and the outlawing of seditious thought. This psychological and physical space defining the official sphere is evident with the unthinking, uncritical routine of the twice-daily playing of the national anthem, when people in public areas are compelled to stand. "Public" areas include even the streets of Bangkok, where police force the traffic to come to a standstill. Quite often an unconscious code emerged that became integrated into Thai society, a behavior so ingrained that even when there is not the least threat of punishment, the behavior continues without anyone explaining why.

Such hyper-sensitivity became evident in a 1953 case involving a pair of socks. These socks were so threatening they became a matter of the police, prosecutors, and eventually the Supreme Court. Mr. Paen Ruangkham of Lampang bought some socks, put them on, and went out in public. Apparently an alert and patriotic citizen noticed something seriously amiss and reported it to the police. Mr. Paen was shortly thereafter arrested for insulting the national flag, for the socks bore a pattern of tiny Thai national flags. The police, under the direction of the prosecution, confiscated the socks. In the proceedings of the Court of First Instance, the prosecution argued that the defendant should be prosecuted according to the National Flag Act of 1936, which stipulated a punishment of not more than three months' imprisonment and a fine of not more than 200 baht. The defendant confessed to having worn the socks, but claimed he was unaware of the pattern on them and had no intention of insulting the flag. The Court of First Instance interpreted the provisions of this Act to mean that only the producer of the offending socks could be punished and so acquitted the defendant and ordered the confiscated socks returned to him. The Appeals Court overturned the Court of First Instance's decision, saying that the wearing of such socks was unconventional and peculiar.[86] It found Mr. Paen guilty of insulting the national flag, "a symbol of the Thai nation." However, for his confession, the court reduced the one month sentence and the 200 baht fine by one half. Given the threat the socks posed, the court ordered the socks once again confiscated. The Supreme Court took up the case because it was interested in the question of intent. As with the Court of First Instance, it, too, argued that the producer was at fault. It found the defendant innocent, released him, and ordered the confiscated socks once again to be returned. No report exists on whether a country-wide search was made to find the manufacturer of the socks.

This case involves one of the first court references to a "national security" item. What is one to do with something that by its very existence insults the nation? Do you put it in a locked box on a shelf? Do you burn it? Is it somehow less threatening if in the control of the state? If the producer was at fault, then there must have been something inherently wrong with the socks. Although the court found the defendant innocent because he did not act with intent, the socks should still have been "wrong," for the implication was that the manufacturer was still in violation of the law. And the defendant would no doubt have been found guilty if he had confessed to having full knowledge of their subversive design and intentionally wore them. As it was, the defendant was able to take the socks home. If he had then worn them intentionally in public, would he have been found guilty?

Did the state actually believe that the very existence of flags on socks was somehow so insulting that they had to be suppressed and the socks confiscated? Is it possible that offhand comments or the wearing of socks could be so threatening, of such intense interest by the state? What was charging the air with such a threat? It was and is the function of national security laws to energize social and political surveillance.

Through the 1940s and 1950s, the courts affirmed fairly consistently that no defamation case could be won when the plaintiff could not convincingly show that he or she had been specifically referred to in the defamatory statement. Thus, defendants in collective defamation cases were often found innocent. The court also showed some indication that the public would be given latitude in commenting on public officials or politicians. During the same period, though, "the government" came to encompass as much as it could, ranging from defamation of an individual government official or politician, to any administrative body, and to anything perceived as a "sweeping generalization" critical of the government. This pattern became permanent after 1958 when the military declared Thailand a state of exception. The previous careful considerations of the courts were lost. Seditious rebellion and defamation of the state and its symbols became less common charges after the late 1950s. However, in more diluted and dispersed forms, their essence remained within the anti-communist law through the 1980s and a series of military decrees until the early 1990s. Afterwards, these forms of treason became virtually synonymous with *lèse-majesté*.[87]

8 The insulted and defamed II

Monarchy and *lèse-majesté*

Thailand is unique in the seamless conjoining of the state of exception with the principles of the defamation regime codified in its *lèse-majesté* law. In this marriage both are perfected, for the product combines the suspension of all normal juridical theory, structures, and procedures while adopting the most fundamental and ancient axiom of defamation: "the greater the truth, the greater the crime." Thailand's use of the *lèse-majesté* law has become unique in the world and its elaboration and justifications have become an art. The law's defenders claim that Thailand's love and reverence for its king is incomparable. Its critics say the law has become the foremost threat to the freedom of expression. Barely hidden beneath the surface of growing debate around the law and its use are the most basic issues defining the relationship between those in power and the governed: equality before the law, rights and liberties, the source of sovereign power, and even the system of government of the polity—whether Thailand is to be primarily a constitutional monarchy, a democratic system of governance with the king as head of state, or a democracy.

An oceanic shift has occurred in Thai society over the past half century. In July 1957, speakers took advantage of a government policy to allow free speech in Sanam Luang, a huge field that stretches out from the Grand Palace. One man scandalously declared to a crowd of 200 that the king had killed his older brother in 1946 so he could take the throne. The speaker was thrown into jail for two years. Fifty-one years later to the month, a woman activist takes the stage at Sanam Luang and makes strident and personally offensive remarks about the Thai royalty. She, though, is locked up without bail for a year, subjected to a semi-closed trial, and then sentenced to 18 years in jail (both cases are discussed below).

Such harsh sentencing upset a fragile balance delicately (or perhaps better said, heavy-handedly) maintained since the overthrow of the absolute monarchy in 1932. To refer back to our schema of spheres (Figure 1.1), it can be argued that from the revolution in 1932 to 1957 the public official sphere expanded significantly at the expense of the sacred sphere, reflected in the few *lèse-majesté* cases and the general democratization of laws, such as revision of the criminal code and of the Press and Sangha Acts in 1941. These were part of what might be termed a "typical" evolution from absolute monarchy to democracy.[1] However, from 1960 to 1997 (for the time being discounting certain permutations created by the 1973 to 1976 period), Thailand diverges considerably from "typical" evolution. The strength of the public sphere undulated, but, in general, shrank. The official sphere expanded, but after 1976 becomes conjoined with the sacred sphere. The result was the emergence of a sacro-official sphere whose growth was not arrested until the movement for and the drafting and implementation of to date, Thailand's most democratic constitution in the late 1990s. As the public sphere began to enlarge at the expense of the sacro-official sphere in the first half decade of the 2000s, the forces constituting the sacro-official sphere struck back decisively with the 2006 coup and set out to pass laws that would expand the sacro-official sphere.[2]

This chapter traces the role of *lèse-majesté*, showing in broad strokes the evolution of a law that protected the king, queen, and heir-apparent to one that protected the institution and all that it has come to represent.

Freedom of thought and republicanism

In 1900, the monarchy was "the government." It slowly became a more distinct quality up until the revolution of 1932, which sharply demarcated the two entities and made the monarchy a target on its own. Lurid stories of debauched royalty instantly appeared in the newspapers.[3] The legal experts joining the deliberations of the criminal code revision committee in the late 1930s and early 1940s at first decided that the monarchy as an "institution" should be protected by law, but later concluded that the law should only protect king, queen, heir-apparent, and regent.[4] The committee also made clear that (what would eventually become in 1958) Section 112 of the revised criminal code should not be considered a *lèse-majesté* law *per se*; one member noted that "nobody uses *lèse-majesté* in constitutional monarchies."[5] The institution did not receive protection in the re-written Section 112 nor in the revised version of Section 104, in which the "Sovereign" was removed as a protected entity.[6] Nonetheless, misreading the times to come, the committee labored under the illusion that there was some legal way of commenting on the monarchy critically. One member stated, "The democratic system of governance places the highest power in the citizenry. If the king is no good, the citizens can have him removed [without specifying the mechanism]." To which another committee member responded, "If it's done constitutionally, then it's not against the law."[7] (The final version of the law can be read in Appendix III.)

Given the prodigious number of constitutions, constitutional drafting sessions should have been a natural place to discuss the constitutional role of the monarchy and other possible democratic forms. However, the topic was never taken up seriously, as illustrated by the discussions of the 1948 "Constituent Assembly." When the agenda for the day addressed the question: "Shall the Assembly confirm or not confirm that the regime of Thailand is a limited (constitutional) Monarchy?" newspapers said that many members preferred to leave off discussion of the topic because "to confirm a constitutional Monarchy was above doubt." While René Guyon reported that it "was certainly exaggerated" that discussion on the subject was "an offence to the monarch," no debate ensued and the session became "a touching occasion for the Assembly to manifest unanimously their loyalty to the king and their affection for the Throne." It was an opportunity, said some, for members of the assembly to "show that some republican tendencies were contrary to the real feelings of the people."[8] One member, suspecting that "there was an overwhelming majority in favour of the monarchy," added that he "would welcome any expression of republican sentiments. Then all would know who were the republicans." Another member spoke warningly of "reports of a republican movement in the country" whose members were "self-seekers."[9] This synopsis shows two important historical trends: the closure of debate about the future of the monarchy and belief that Thailand had an incipient republican movement. These two factors played into the long years of military dictatorship: defense of the monarchy unfailingly became the justification for virtually every coup from 1958 onward.[10]

The question of the legality of debating republicanism came before the Juridical Council in the early 1950s, which argued that not only was it illegal to have a political party that espoused republicanism, but it was illegal essentially to have republican thoughts. The author of the report, René Guyon, concluded that, according to the Thai constitution, "everyone is compelled to profess a religion" and be a monarchist for, "unfortunately the Constitution has omitted to proclaim also those freedom[s] of thought and conscience." The "omission" of such "fundamental principles of the United Nations Declaration on Human Rights" was "dangerous . . . because it may induce the commentators to contend that it is purposely that the freedoms of thought and conscience are not granted to the Thai." Such freedoms, wrote Guyon, "allow a person to have Republican belief in a Kingdom, or a Royalist to have Royalist belief in a Republic." The Thai constitution granted "full liberty of speech, writing, printing, and publication." However, he admitted, since "the freedoms of thought and conscience do not exist" in the constitution, this "full liberty is in fact restricted."[11]

In the early years of his reign in the 1950s, the king seemed to maintain a separation between his private life and when he acted in his role as king. But as he began to take a more public role, such as his tour of the Northeast in 1955, the line began to blur. In the same year, in probably the most notable *lèse-majesté* case of the decade, Yut Saeng-uthai, Secretary-general of the Juridical Council and assistant chairperson for the committee responsible for issuing the country's official news through the Department of Publicity, was accused of insulting the king for remarks he made on radio concerning a speech by king. As both the country's leading legal authority and with responsibility for providing information to the public, Yut said the following in trying to clarify the political role of the king: "The king ought not to comment on anything that is a problem or matter concerning the country's economy, politics, or society without going through a cabinet minister in the government." A member of parliament protested that Yut's words "cause[d] the people who respect and love the king to increasingly come to criticize [the institution]." One newspaper interpreted Yut's words to mean that "the king in a democracy is only a puppet which the government can manipulate as it wishes." This was wrong, the newspaper felt, because the king had the "burden" to be the provider of the people's happiness. If someone was doing evil, the king ought to be able to speak out without having to go through someone else. One newspaper even suggested that the *lèse-majesté* law was necessary in Thailand for the purposes of democracy, arguing that the current government was interested only in "ruling through power" and did "not want to listen to the people." Thus, restraint on the government's power would be supplied by the *lèse-majesté* law. Nonetheless, it seems absurd that Yut, a leading legal expert, while trying to explain the legal status of the king politically, was himself accused of *lèse-majesté*.[12]

The Thai government of the 1950s granted itself extraordinary powers to control the private thought of people. Such state aspirations were extraordinary and heralded the entrenching of a certain mindset that, despite the apparent movement of Thai society as a whole towards greater freedom, signified a persistent, darker and more authoritarian urge. The 1950s provided the conceptual base for Thailand's trajectory away from the model of other constitutional monarchies.

Protection of the institution of the monarchy

Beginning in the 1960s, *lèse-majesté* was transformed into something new. *Lèse-majesté* was no longer a defamation law protecting the reputation of a few important persons. This law and the institution it protected came to embody Thai culture, politics, and Thai society as a whole. Critics charged that the law was abused by unscrupulous parties using it to silence their opponents.

But the problem was not the law's abuse, but rather the law itself, the institution of the monarchy it supposedly protected, the nexus of relationships and power, the conceptualizations of culture and self, and the peculiar Thai style of politics that emerged.

The *lèse-majesté* law became inextricably linked to a constitutional provision maintained throughout the continuing procession of Thai constitutions, from the first in 1932 to the most recent in 2007. Section 3 of the 1932 version read: "The person of the King is sacred and inviolable";[13] and Article 8 of the 2007 version said: "The King shall be enthroned in a position of revered worship and shall not be violated. No person shall expose the King to any sort of accusation or action."[14] These provisions and the *lèse-majesté* law that supported them became more prominent over the second half of the twentieth century, whereas in most democratic constitutional monarchies, constitutional phrasings such as these became mere conventions and *lèse-majesté* laws fell into disuse. The difficulty for defenders of the law is to explain how the institution of Thai monarchy could be so utterly loved if it required the most repressive *lèse-majesté* law the modern world has known.[15]

In Chapter 7, I made the point that "government" came to encompass everything within the official sphere. Here, we examine how the monarchy in Thailand not only expanded the sacred sphere, but also gradually but decisively took over the official sphere. A fairly consistent trend from *lèse-majesté* cases can be discerned, from cases that referred personally to the king, queen, and heir-apparent, to cases where there was no reference to these three at all but rather to the monarchy, and finally to cases which, increasingly abstract, referred to the broad power structures of Thai society. The result—clearly visible from the early 1990s onward—was that *lèse-majesté* charges referred to words that no longer addressed the royal personages at all and sometimes had only the most tenuous connection to the monarchy.

In no *lèse-majesté* cases on record were defendants allowed to argue or enter into evidence anything about what they said was true or for the public good, and so should receive exemption. Truth, "sincere opinion," and "fair comment" have all been barred entrance to the sacred sphere where truth-beyond-truth is more powerful than any worldly truth.[16] The following instaqnces were all ones based on some disputed facts, and as such would have also been actionable as normal defamation cases.

The first Supreme Court decision to use the Thai phrase for *lèse-majesté* (*min phraboromdechanuphap*—หมิ่นพระบรมเดชานุภาพ) determined that comment or opinion provided exemption from conviction for *lèse-majesté*. In 1960, Kosai Mungjaroen referred in public to the 1946 death of King Ananda. He said "the younger brother killed the older brother in order to seize the throne" ["*Nong kha phi phua pen kan ching ballang.*"][17] The Court of First Instance ruled that the defendant's words impugned that "King Bhumipol did kill the king of the eighth reign who was the older brother of the present king, in order to gain the throne," that such words were "intentional," and that these words "sought to bring discredit to the power, reputation, and honour of the king in his revered position among the Thai people."[18] Accusing anyone of a crime is actionable. Kosai's words were an accusation of a wrong directly involving the king. While not denying he made the statements, Kosai claimed that his words were an expression of a sincere opinion, which provides exemption from guilt in personal defamation cases. The Supreme Court did not agree, saying that the expression of sincere opinion "does not mean that one could slander [others] in public places." Kosai was sentenced to three years' imprisonment, reduced to two years for his confession.

The accusation by the Sweden-based Thai National Salvation Movement, which in 1973 accused the king of "[responsibility] for the great loss of life" was a little less direct, but still perhaps actionable. The Movement claimed the king legitimated a dictatorship which suppressed the people. Thus, "the king is guilty of being a traitor to the nation and Thai people."[19] Authorities tried but were unable to prosecute. A third case was that of "Nine Reigns of the Chakri Dynasty," a 125-page book critical of the monarchy distributed in schools and various agencies in 1983. The publication accuses the Chakri kings, including the present king, of a host of crimes.[20] Again, for even ordinary defamation such would likely be actionable. Less direct than the preceding three was the final case. In 1988, a leader of the Democrat Party implied that the royalty was a lazy, morally slothful bunch (see Chapter 9).[21]

Other *lèse-majesté* charges could be classified as "insults," and so perhaps actionable as such—a Japanese man spitting while the royal anthem is played at a theatre, a university student muttering, "Hey, What song is this? I can't understand it" when hearing the royal anthem.[22] And then there were "inappropriate references" to royalty, such as *France Soir*'s 1967 publication of the Thai queen's measurements.

In the preceding cases, one can make the case that the wording of the *lèse-majesté* law seems to apply to them. It is more difficult with the next set, concerning assessments or opinions. The court (or police) had to decide which were honest opinions and which were not.

For instance, *Newsweek* was threatened with *lèse-majesté* in its 1967 report that said, in an area of heavy insurgency, the king "cautiously elected to remain inside his helicopter while aides handed out mementos."[23] In the same year American Larry Lomax made an assessment that "the king does not have enough charisma to unite the Thai people."[24] In 1982, *The Wall Street Journal* wrote the crown prince "appears to lack the intelligence, charisma, and 'common touch' necessary to secure the affection of the Thai people for the Chakkri Dynasty and reportedly has only lukewarm support within the Thai military. His image as a Don Juan also has damaged his reputation."[25]

Or there was the constant barrage of Sulak Sivaraksa's criticisms. In 1984, he commented that Thai kings should not be considered above criticism and the royalty should be thought of as common human beings: "It's just that I feel the King should be seen as a man with both power and humanity, with both bad deeds and good deeds; not good in every respect, that's my point."[26] Sulak also criticized the king's diploma-granting ceremony, saying that

> everyone is equal and should not have to crawl for diplomas from the King, or pay homage to car tires [referring to the practice of giving a *wai* toward the car transporting the king] . . . How can human beings manage to live in dignity when they have to pay homage to car tires?"[27]

And then there was the unfortunate case of Ms. Rattana Utthaphan, a student who wrote a personal letter to the king asking him to abdicate and enter politics.[28]

Although none of these comments would be readily actionable in a court outside Thailand, they nonetheless preserve a certain correspondence between the target of the opinion and some action or quality. These cases are neither insults nor assertions of fact. They are assessments, opinions, analyses, suggestions—key skills in any democracy—generally not leading to convictions. The foreign journalists had some issues of their publications banned and some made some apologies. Sulak was until recently too much of a risk to charge any more with *lèse-majesté* (see below, though, for his latest case). For her suggestion, however, Rattana was sentenced to six years in jail.[29]

Parallel to these normal *lèse-majesté* accusations and cases were ones where the correspondence between the person targeted and the precipitating action was distant and complex. A few examples will suffice. In a 1974 television interview, Kukrit Pramoj suggested that students petition the king on a question about the constitution. When asked by the moderator if this advice was "pulling His Majesty into involvement in politics," Kukrit answered, "If we have a king and we do not know how to make it beneficial, then it is like having a *jaret*."[30] A former head of the student council at Ramkhamhaeng University demanded Kukrit be arrested for *lèse-majesté*, for *jaret* "was a word that was low and dirty."[31] However, no one was quite sure what *jaret* meant. To solve the problem, the Santiban (or political police) opened a dictionary in front of reporters to find out. The police concluded that it meant an idol "that is placed in a ghost house and did not have the meaning that some had suggested, *ret* (to shit)." If the term *jaret* is a base thing, and then if it is connected to the king as a kind of equivalent, then perhaps *lèse-majesté* has happened. Here, then, is the beginning of a separation between an actor and an action.

Lèse-majesté showed up in the strangest places. In 1976, on page 16 in *Thai Rat* newspaper appeared a picture of the crown prince's fiancée singing the song "The Lao Moon" and standing between two princesses playing accompanying instruments. The caption said that through this celebration, students from Kasetsat University were able to raise money for the Sai Jai Thai (royal) Foundation. The next day in the same newspaper a picture of a seemingly foreign woman appeared, giving food to a dog next to a *khaen*, a Lao musical instrument. In the view of the rightist Village Scouts, the caption of the picture with the dog made some slanderous comparison between the king's potential daughter-in-law and the dog.[32]

Lèse-majesté also appeared in a boxing arena in 1978 where, prior to a match, a press agent said his boxer was protected by the king's charisma. The military court argued that such words should only be said by the victor of a bout after the match, when it would "spread the honour of the king."[33] *Lèse-majesté* reappeared in 1990 when there was an outcry over an announcement of a dismissal of a Ministry of Interior official on state-run radio. When confronted with criticism for making the dismissal public when a royal command of this type should have been published in the government gazette, Minister of Transportation Samak Sundaravej opined, "I feel His Majesty became a tool of the Government." Samak was then himself accused of *lèse-majesté* for saying the king was used as a political tool. The case was later quietly dropped.[34]

Incomparable *lèse-majesté*

In 1988, in response to a question posed by a provincial governor, a committee was set up by the Ministry of Interior to consider "tightening" the *lèse-majesté* law by revising the measure in the criminal code. Apparently there had been reports of traders using the king's portrait as a clock face. A high-ranking ministry official on the committee said that the law "should not be limited to written and verbal offences as at present."[35] These discussions thus widened the *lèse-majesté* law to include material artefacts as well as verbal and written items.

Many in Thai society criticize others for using the *lèse-majesté* law as a tool to silence their opponents. The law *is* used this way, but the problem goes beyond the law. The emerging and strengthening role of the monarchy complicates matters. Over the past half century, the active roles the king has played in politics and society collide with a public cognizant of its rights and committed to the right to comment and criticize what falls within the purview of the common good.[36] The situation becomes dangerous when the monarchy's role expands even while the myriad ways the monarchy touches on Thai society cannot be scrutinized. Thus, whole sections of Thai politics and discourse have been left unexamined or have been co-opted.[37] This situation helps explain in part why the number of *lèse-majesté* cases have remained so high (See Figure 8.1). The following cases illustrate some of these problems.

Although the king resisted calls for him to "constitutionally intervene" to dismiss Thaksin as prime minister in 2006, he did call for the judicial branch to play a more prominent role. The courts responded by annulling the April 2006 elections. The courts responded by annulling the April 2006 elections. Then there were many scholars and journalists who commented on possible palace involvement in the 2006 coup.[38] But the issue went beyond a mere question of playing a role in politics. Environmentalists and academics opposed to dams have had to tread a thin line, given that the king has been an enthusiastic supporter of this form of development. As a result, relatively few scholars have examined the role of dams in Thailand's development strategies. The small-scale farmers' movement that began in the 1980s, inspired by a Japanese organic farmer, was co-opted by the palace's promotion of the king's in the king's "New Theory" of farming which eschewed and sanitized the radical aspects of the movement. Likewise, the "Sufficiency Economy" concept is promoted as official state policy, blotting out the efforts of the social movement that had fostered its radical form.[39] The largest Thai conglomerate, the Crown Property Bureau, which reports directly to the palace, was, until recently, shielded from critical examination.[40] The immense wealth and power of the royal family and Crown Property Bureau holdings would, in other constitutional monarchies, be open to some criticism. In early 2007, a *Thai Post* newspaper reporter wrote, "Newspapers should not just investigate the stock transactions of ShinCorp more than the corruption of Thaksin Shinawatra, but [should] also go deeply into how the Crown Prince may be involved." The reporter was summarily dismissed.[41]

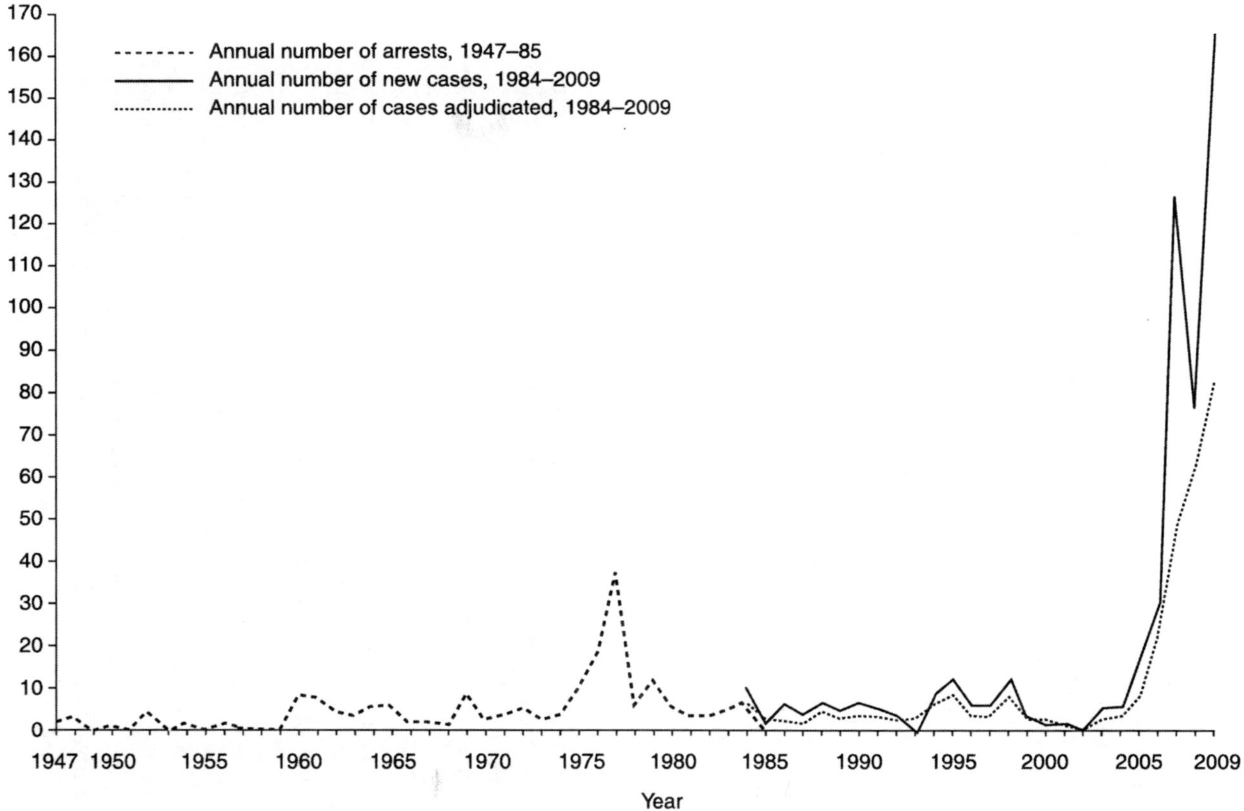

Figure 8.1 Annual number of *lèse-majesté* arrests, new cases, and cases adjudicated in Thailand, 1947–2009

Source: Thailand, Police Department (Krom Tamruat), *Rai-ngan prajam pi* (Annual Report of the Police Department); Thailand. Attorney General's Office (Samnakngan Aiyakan Songsut), *Rai-ngan prajam pi* (Annual Report of the Attorney General's Office) (Samnakngan aiyakan phiset fai sarasonthet, samnak-ngan wichakan) (each year individually from 1984 to 2005; years 1996 and 1997 are combined into a single volume).

Thailand. Somnak-ngan San Yuttitham, *Rai-ngan statiti khadi san thua ratcha-anajak prajam pi* (Annual Judicial Statistics).

In what one scholar has called the media's "reconciliation with the monarchy," the Thai media has assiduously avoided critically commenting on the monarchy.[42] The military-appointed legislative body of 2006–7 shepherded through a number of laws that have affected the media. A proposal by Borwornsak Uwanno gave the chief of police, under the 2007 Press Act, the power to forbid the import of any materials deemed offensive to the royal family. Banyat Tasaneeyavej, an appointed legislator and president of the Thai Journalists Association, cheerfully said, "We're not bothered by it because it doesn't affect our rights or freedoms in presenting the news."[43]

The effects of the law extend beyond the press to academia. Historian Thongchai Winichakul writes that the view of the monarchy as "above politics" has made it impossible to study Thai politics or history. Because scholars "have been penalised" or work "under self-censorship in order to avoid trouble due to the serious nature of the *lèse-majesté* charge," writes Thongchai, "the monarchy . . . has been able to escape the attention, let alone scrutiny, by most observers and scholars." The result is, "when we study and talk about politics," the monarchy—"a most crucial piece"—is omitted.[44] Kevin Hewison makes a similar point: "It seems that many scholars consider that the monarchy is indeed above criticism . . . The resulting self-censorship means that critical material on the current monarch has been ignored."[45] Michael Connors writes:

> The existence of *lèse-majesté* should not be seen as a minor blotch on an otherwise clean slate of political opening up. In the 1980s, liberalization was a limited affair, opening a political space for elite conflict and expression, bounded by the triad of nation, religion and monarchy. In villages, newspapers and in relations with the bureaucracy and capitalists, ordinary Thais faced the brute rule of superior power and the strictures of national identity and culture propagated by state ideologues and the palace. The stage-managed role of the monarch, the compulsory respect shown to the institution, and the pressure of social conformity left many people with a taste of bitterness which few felt confident to express. Such was democracy with the king as head of state.[46]

While certain freedoms have expanded, so, too, has the role of the monarchy in politics, development work, religion, and controversially, the monarchy's immense wealth. Kobkua writes that "By the early 1990s, the monarchy firmly installed itself at the center of Thai politics."[47] It had done so financially, too. *Forbes* reported in August 2008 that the king of Thailand is the richest royal in the world, with an estimated worth of $35 billion.[48] The *lèse-majesté* law shields this overwhelming, inescapable presence in Thai society, politics, and the economy. As a result, the operation of the *lèse-majesté* law in Thailand creates a black hole of silence in the center of the Thai body politic. Political and social discourse is relegated to the fringes as whisperings and innuendo. The centrality of the monarchy, in light of the king's growing infirmity, makes the looming crisis of succession even more ominous.[49]

Given the monarchy's extraordinary public role, it is not surprising that *lèse-majesté* has crept into deeper and deeper levels of society and appeared at times so absurd that even the king tried to put some restraint on its use, as evidenced by his birthday speech in December 2005.[50] Only once – in a panel organized by the Thai magazine, *Pajariyasan* – did legal experts, including a representative from the palace, sit down to critique the law. Some panellists attributed the abuse of the law to the timidity of the police, prosecutors, and courts, and their vulnerability to outside political pressure. Others pointed out that slander and libel cases were interpreted by courts very strictly, but with the *lèse-majesté* law—a special kind of defamation case—the courts interpreted cases broadly. One panellist argued that under this provision there "will be no end to [litigation]," extending to "insulting the royal palace, insulting the royal flag, the king's personal car, and everything." Other panellists suggested that *lèse-majesté* cases should be handled similarly to ordinary defamation cases. That is, the damaged party—the king or royal household bureau—should decide whether to press charges. One participant pointed out that malicious gossip thrived under the existing legal arrangements:

> These days, whenever someone cannot act openly, then they must speak in secret. When things are said "in secret," I can say there is no way that such things can be positive, because what we can say positively, we can say openly. So when there is such speaking in secret, it must always come out as damaging gossip. [With the law as it is, it] will always produce negative results. The law then becomes something that produces a negative image of the institution of the monarchy itself.[51]

The king's deputy principal private secretary, Tongnoi Tongyai, predicted in 1987, "The penalty for *lèse-majesté* offences is likely to be gradually commuted and its abolition is probable if the country's democracy keeps progressing," as in the United Kingdom[52] (Figure 8.1). Despite Tongnoi's optimism and clear-sightedness of this panel, exactly the opposite has happened.

Conflation of royalty and the institution of the monarchy under *lèse-majesté*

Over the past decade, the *lèse-majesté* law and what it protects have come to occupy increasing space within the public sphere. Its evolution has transformed the law into forms with little or no resemblance to other defamation-based laws. The tendency in the exercise of the *lèse-majesté* law in Thailand to conflate the institution of the monarchy with the person of the king has been compounded by an even greater conflation between the monarchy, Thai culture, and identity. As a result, charges of *lèse-majesté* have become at once both more common and difficult to explain.

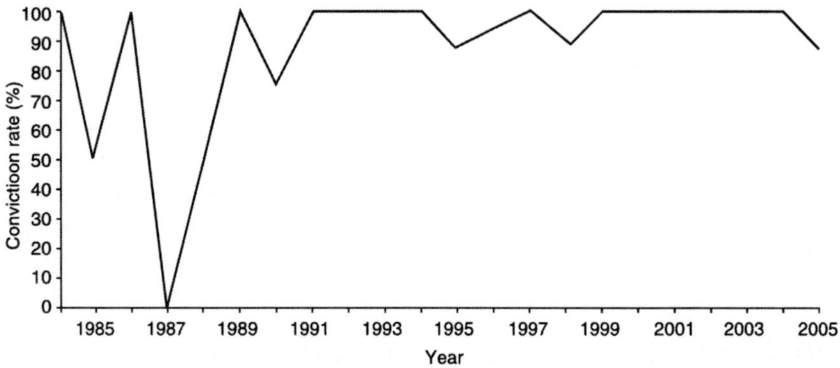

Figure 8.2 Annual conviction rates for *lèse-majesté* cases in Thailand, 1984–2005

Source: Attorney General's Office (Samnakngan Aiyakan Songsut), *Rai-ngan prajam pi* (Annual Report of the Attorney General's Office) (Samnakngan aiyakan phiset fai sarasonthet, samnakngan wichakan) (each year individually from 1984 to 2005; year 1996 and 1997 are combined into a single volume).

The 2005 "sticker case" illustrates this shift. Five members of the Democrat Party were charged with *lèse-majesté* for distributing campaign stickers, two quoting the king—"The King said 'The richer people are, the more they cheat,'" and "'Corrupt people will be cursed'"—and one quoting the queen—"The Queen said 'Poverty is no disgrace while evil and fraud are disgusting and shameful.'" Police investigators contended that "improper words had been added to one of the remarks"—"the richer people are, the more they cheat." If added, it would mean the stickers "had indeed been distorted." The police said they were going to check with the Office of His Majesty's Principal Private Secretary to see exactly what the king's words were. The Democrat legal team brought with them "photocopies of a news report" from 2004 which showed that Sumet Tantivejakul, Secretary-general to His Majesty the King's Chai Pattana Foundation, had related the king's words in a seminar. Nonetheless, the police had to check and see if the quotes distorted the words of the king and queen. Not only do these words not refer to the royalty, they were words of royalty themselves. They proved exactly correct; the case was eventually dropped.[53]

In 2007, Silapakorn University lecturer Boonsong Chaisingkananont's examination questions nos. 8 and 6 came under attack as *lèse-majesté*—"Do you think the monarchy is necessary for Thai society? How should it adapt to a democratic system? Please debate," and "How does the yellow shirt fever reflect problems in Thai society? Are they problems that need to be tackled? If so, how?" They were questions, but even as such, they seemed suspicious. In order to discover if they had any subversive effect, though, the police would have to see how students answered them. The police did seek to see the student examination booklets. This not only raised questions about confidentiality between teachers and students, it also alarmed Boonsong's former students who wondered if they had answered "wrong." That the case came about because of academic conflicts is immaterial; the police treated it as "real." Police reportedly dropped the case, though no official notification was provided to Boonsong.[54]

Jakrapob Penkair, a Thaksin supporter, made a speech at the Foreign Correspondents Club in Bangkok in August of 2007 entitled, "Democracy and the Patronage System of Thailand." The text of the speech shows it was an academic critique arguing that at least the present Thai form of constitutional monarchy was antithetical to democracy. When the text of the speech became public in March 2008, the opposition called for Jakrapop to step down from his position as Prime Minister's Office minister.[55] The exact items that might allegedly constitute *lèse-majesté* are not readily apparent. Much has to be read into his words to come out with a clear critique of the monarchy.

The police relied on a Chulalongkorn lecturer, Anan Lao-lertworakul, to uncover the meaning of Jakrapob's words. The resulting report, "Decipher a secret code – a dangerous attitude of Jakrapob Penkair," shows just how oblique Jakrapob's references were and how Jakrapob's words had to be construed to make them into *lèse-majesté*.[56] Anan focused on Jakrapop's use of "patronage" [*upatham*] and "patronage system" [*rabob upatham*]. Patronage, wrote Anan, has two meanings: the first of which Jakrapob defined as

> a system in which the different statuses of people in society are recognized, with some high status (big) people and some low status (little) people. The two groups of people help and support each other in a mutually beneficial way.

Anan claims this system is a "win–win" system in which both "the high-status" and "low-status" individuals benefit. This system, according to Anan, is "not based on the idea of equality but it is not in conflict with or entirely incompatible with the idea of democracy" for it is "not a political ideal" or "system of government": "It is merely a system of social relationships in society."[57]

However, Jakrapob used "patronage" in this sense only twice. Anan noted that Jakrapob was trained in political science, but chose to create his own definition. In 20 of the 21 other times Jakrapob used the term, the meaning was clear. Among other things, Jakrapob argued that patronage kept people from developing their "own capacity" to realize the need for democracy and that it was "in direct conflict with democratization."

Anan's analysis resulted in a mathematical formula, starting with the observation that "patronage" came from "pater," meaning "father." Anan says that Jakrapob called "King Ramkhamhaeng" (understood as the first "Thai" king in the thirteenth century) "Great Father Ramkhamhaeng." The "highly likely" reason that Jakrapob used the latter was "to cleverly insinuate to the listeners the concept **patronage = Great Father = king**." As Jakrapob defined patronage as a system in which "the monarchy gives patronage in the form of a tiny bit of assistance to the people in exchange for their loyalty,"

Anan deduced Jakrapob's "way of thinking" as: "**Patronage = Great Father = King**, and **Patronage System = King System = Monarchy**" [original emphasis]. Therefore, concluded Anan, Jakrapob's "monarchy" could be substituted for "patronage" and so he committed *lèse-majesté*.[58]

This example again illustrates that even when there is no reference to a royal personage, *lèse-majesté* may be alleged. Significantly, the charge might have been brought about by Jakrapob's criticism of Privy Council President Prem Tinsulanonda, who is not covered by *lèse-majesté* law. The connection can be seen from a reporter's question to Jakrapob after his talk: "Do you think a privy councillor is part of a monarch's surroundings?" The question was significant for it went to the core of a hotly-debated contention at present in Thailand: Is only the king's person or the monarchy and all that is perceived as its "surroundings" covered by the law?[59] In June, Jakrapob resigned. Jakrapob probably did his own calculations, and came up with his own formula: Criticism of the institution + suppression of red-shirts = *lèse-majesté* charge = better to go into exile. Following political upheaval in April 2009 and facing additional charges, he fled the country.[60]

This issue of exactly how many steps from the king or monarchy does *lèse-majesté* cover comes to the fore in the next case which, when it was first published, seemed to be missing something. *The Nation* reported in 2008 that a Democrat MP and leader of the anti-Thaksin People's Alliance for Democracy (PAD), Somkiat Pongpaiboon, had been arrested for *lèse-majesté* for "making improper comments about Rachawinit Secondary School, which is located on a land plot donated by His Majesty the King and has the emblem that contains the royal insignia."[61] The school was also located just beyond the boundaries of the PAD's around-the-clock demonstrations. Teachers claimed the blaring speakers from the protest disrupted the school and called on the PAD to move its rallies. As a kind of ethnic put-down, "Somkiat allegedly said the teachers could be Cambodians and the school could have belonged to Cambodia's Prime Minister Hun Sen." Thus, to attack a school whose land was donated by the king was worthy of a *lèse-majesté* accusation. When Somkiat said "the school could have belonged" to Cambodia, his infraction was even greater, given that the land had been the king's. When reporting to the police, Somkiat, using a peculiar phrasing, reportedly denied having said something that "*verged on insulting* the monarchy" [my emphasis]. The steps from the insult back to the king are: school is Cambodian → school's land donated by king → royal gift = king; therefore to insult school is to insult king.

Three types of new challenges to the law: freedom of thought, disgruntled royalists, and "republicanism"

In the past few years, three new kinds of challenges have emerged to the Thai *lèse-majesté* law: "different thinking is no crime," the spurned democratic Thai monarchist, and a fearless, unrepetant challenge.

The first kind of challenge is based on freedom of thought and expression.[62] In September 2007, Chotisak Onsoong and Chutima Phenphak refused to rise for the playing of the royal anthem in a movie theatre. Formal charges were placed against the two in April 2008. Police documents show that Chotisak had said, "Why must I stand up? There's no law forcing me to."[63] The threat of 15 years in jail seemed disproportionate to the action: had a Thai refusing to stand in respect quirkily challenged the century-long reign of *lèse-majesté* in Thailand? Chotisak, an activist and opponent of the 2006 coup, denied committing *lèse-majesté*. He said that his action was an exercise of his right to freedom of expression as guaranteed by the constitution. "Laws which violate human rights," he contended, "should be abolished." In his own defense, Chotisak launched "a campaign for the right not to stand while the royal anthem is played," under the rallying call (and tee shirt), "Not standing is no crime. Different thinking is no crime."[64] Within a week, more than 500 persons had signed a petition whose thrust went to the center of the *lèse-majesté* issue, claiming its utter incompatibility with democracy. The petition's complaint focused on "the use of *lèse-majesté* law to prohibit the individual's freedom of expression," and "the use of violence and harassment on those with different thoughts/political ideologies." The petitioners had a new vision for Thai democracy, in which democracy's "beauty" ought to be "that people can have the rights to think differently."

Following Chotisak's arraignment, hundreds of comments about the case hit the web boards of *Prachatai* and *Fah Diew Kan* websites, many in his support. Comments included comparisons of those who stand for the anthem with feudalists, instances of Thai wives instructing their foreign husbands not to stand at the cinema, and some sentiment that, given this sort of situation, the monarchy should be abolished. Though a bit indirect, these comments represented perhaps the first semi-public expression of anti-monarchism, if not republicanism.[65]

Exclaiming "I can't stand this," Khon Kaen's Sunimit Jirasuk went to the police to level charges of rebellion and unrest against the website owners.[66] Sunimit worried, "by allowing open discussion on the internet, both websites demonstrated their intent to be focal points of those who wanted to eliminate the monarchy."[67] Non-elected senator and the moderator of the rightist *Manager Online* radio programme, Kamnoon Sitthisaman, affirmed on 22 April that Thailand's democracy is "unique," a political form called, "Democracy with the King as Head of State." Over the past few years, Kamnoon averred, fomenting against this form are "some academics, Thai Rak Thai cohorts and members of anti-coup groups" who "promote just plain 'Democracy,' or 'People's Democracy.'" "This new idea," as evidenced on the websites in question, appeared as comments that are "many times [more] precariously offensive" as they "insinuate [against] the highest institution" in what Kamnoon called "unspeakable" ways.[68]

The authorities were faced with a conundrum. They had to stop the issue from spiralling out of control. But the options for charges were absurdly incongruous: as a violation of a 1940s national culture act, not standing at a cinema could bring a 100-baht fine and a maximum of one month in jail as compared with 15 years for *lèse-majesté*—a difference by a factor of 180.[69] At the same time, if the authorities pursued charges into an expanding circle of Thai society, the absurdity of the charge against Chotisak would become even more apparent, creating in turn more vehement opposition to the law and perhaps the monarchy itself. This case went to the core of the *lèse-majesté* question: Does the law protect the persons of the king, queen, and heir apparent, or does it protect the institution of the monarchy and all of its accoutrements, such as the royal anthem? Is it an insult to the monarchy or to the king not to stand? Or is it, as Chotisak contended, that different Thai should have the right to think differently?[70] A radio station in Bangkok "urged listeners to attack Chotisak when he was scheduled to appear at a panel discussion on *lèse-majesté* at Thammasat University," and provided personal information, his address, and telephone number.[71] Chotisak reportedly stopped going out in public.[72]

In connection with Chotisak's case, Jittra Khachadet, head of the union at Body Fashion Thailand Limited, a subsidiary of Triumph International, appeared on a television show to talk about pregnancy and abortion issues. On her tee-shirt was, "Not standing is no crime. Different thinking is no crime." *The Manager* newspaper and PAD picked up on the story and the issue was brought up in the parliamentary senate. Jittra's employers fired her and she filed suit for wrongful dismissal with the labor court. The court ruled that given "the spirit of the Thai nation is unlike the identity of other nations which is accepted [and] known well to be that the Thai people respect and revere the king." Jittra knew this, the court opined, as she knew that the show would be broadcast nationwide. As Chotisak was understood by members of society to be part of a Thaksin conspiracy to overthrow the monarchy, and Jittra wore a tee-shirt that supported Chotisak, then the company's reputation would be affected, and therefore the company had just cause in dismissing her.[73]

Sulak Sivaraksa represents the second type of challenge. He consistently affirms he is a monarchist; however, he said he would consider changing to republicanism if the *lèse-majesté* law were not removed and the monarchy could be held up to public scrutiny. He and the editor of *Fah Diew Kan*, Thanapol Eawsakul, were charged for distributing comments made by Sulak in an October 2005 interview—"Having A Monarchy Is Less Costly than a Presidency." Sulak said that the monarchy and related entities, such as the Crown Property Bureau, should be subject to public scrutiny and criticism.[74] The irrepressible Sulak commands considerable respect from both foreign admirers and among Thai activists. Sulak, who has been tried for *lèse-majesté* three times and accused of it much more frequently, has long been a vociferous critic of the monarchy and has sought to make it accountable and open to public scrutiny. He also actively tests the resilience of the law. Police must arrest him, but they and the prosecutors are reluctant to send cases to trial, probably because of the unpredictability of what Sulak might make part of the public record. Sulak is prone to speaking his mind regardless of the setting and says things in public that Thai say in privacy. As a result, the authorities have used other tactics, such as seizing and banning his books.

In a recent interview, Sulak pondered whether Thai should have the right to hold republican sentiments. He wondered whether he could remain a monarchist. Then he realized: Mustn't all Thai, by law, be avowed monarchists? What would it mean if someone such as Sulak said he was no longer one? Would that be *lèse-majesté*? Sulak's position is clear: "No monarchy is worthy of my loyalty unless I can criticize it."[75] Can an established Thai monarchist state he or she is no longer one?

Authorities label the third type of new challenge "republicanism," but no credible evidence has yet been made public showing any concerted, organized republican movement.[76] The case of Daranee Charnchoengsilpakul (better known as Da Torpedo), an anti-PAD activist, seems like a new challenge. In July 2008, she attacked those she alleged were behind the coup – Prem – but also the palace.[77] Some accounts said she accused the queen of criminal acts and threatened Her Majesty. Accusing someone of criminal acts is actionable in ordinary defamation cases, but the defendant must have a chance to prove the truth of their statements as part of their defense. The *lèse-majesté* law precludes such a chance. On the grounds of national security, Daranee remained incarcerated and was consistently denied bail in the year-long lead-up to her trial in 2009.[78] She was found guilty on three counts of *lèse-majesté* and received an 18-year sentence, the longest ever given for the crime in almost a century.[79] The court ruled that she "intended to insult and make threats to Their Majesties the King and Queen." When leaving the court, she said, "It is what I expected to happen." She said she will appeal.[80]

Just before his probable arrest for *lèse-majesté* in early February 2009, Chulalongkorn University Associate Professor Giles Ungpakorn fled Thailand, arguing that it was impossible to receive a fair trial for *lèse-majesté* in Thailand,

> It is clear that the charge is really about preventing any discussion about the relationship between the military junta and the monarchy. This is in order to protect the military's sole claim to legitimacy: that it acted in the interests of the monarchy.

As leaving, he issued a communiqué called the *Red Siam Manifesto* which outlined a strategy for returning democracy to Thailand.[81] The *Manifesto* expresses a preference for Thailand as a republic, since all institutions could then be scrutinized by the public. In response, the Thai government ordered internet providers to use filters to make *Red Siam Manifesto* inaccessible. Giles's act is one of the first public, frontal attacks ever made on the monarchy.

This incident demonstrates a "perfect" moment in the scenario of Thai defamation. The government tried to ban access to *Red Siam*, but, by that time, it was obvious that anyone who was interested and who had internet access could download it. Thammasat University lecturers Chawin Leenabanjong and Suwinai Pornnawalai questioned Giles's motives, claiming he acted in the name of deposed prime minister Thaksin and was part of a movement to "overthrow the lords." Their main contention was that when Giles spoke at a rally of "the red-shirts" (former pro-Thaksin and anti-dictatorship groups), his mask of neutral academician "was torn off."[82] With a racial overtone as Giles is "only" half-Thai, the two lecturers said that Giles "does not understand Thainess, does not understand the feelings of Thais, does not understand the cultural context of Thailand but instead . . . shows ingratitude to his Father who is the most revered of this country."[83] Panatda Disakul, a national security specialist of the Ministry of Interior, called *Red Siam* "inappropriate, untrue, and did not use the language of a gentleman." He suspected someone was behind Giles's action and said it was clear that Giles did not have good intentions and lacked "the feeling of Thai peopleness." Panatda concluded, Giles "should not have been born a Thai."[84] On the other side, groups of academics opposed to the use of the *lèse-majesté* law argued that Giles should be afforded the right to academic freedom.

In contrast to other democratic constitutional monarchies, in Thailand the public sphere has lost ground to the emerging domination of the sacro-official sphere, in which a given power structure employs state legal mechanisms and the sacred sphere to preserve and protect its power. Though Thailand is not a theocracy, a pervasive and extensive system of political taboos channels perceived criticisms into state-designated categories.

Once the absolute monarchy was overthrown in 1932, the king himself, King Rama VII (r. 1925–35), called Siam *prachathipatai doi mi phramahakasat tam ratthathammanuun* [democracy with a monarch according to the constitution" or, "constitutional monarchy democracy"—ประชาธิปไตยโดยมีพระมหากษัตริย์ตามรัฐธรรมนูญ].[85] A Thai historian from Chulalongkorn University was instructed not to use this phrasing and, until he used instead the ubiquitous "the democratic regime of government with the King as Head of State" [*rabop prachathipatai an mi phramahakasat song pen pramuk*—ระบอบประชาธิปไตย อันมีพระมหากษัตริย์ทรงเป็นประมุข] (the formulaic phrasing much loved by military coup leaders), he was told he would not be welcome to speak again.[86] When a Chiang Mai University lecturer signed a petition in support of Giles Ungpakorn's right to academic freedom, his department initiated an investigation that could have led to his expulsion.[87] Social and political commentary on the monarchy—which has typically been a call to redefine the role of the monarchy or reform the *lèse-majesté* law—is automatically understood as part of an organized republican movement. The expression of republican sentiment is understood no differently today than in the 1950s. Some of the participants at a seminar on the *lèse-majesté* law in March 2009, speaking about reforming the law, nonetheless felt that Chotisak's words were unacceptable for Thai society. No one I talked with felt quite sure whether by Thai law all Thai must be monarchists or if it was illegal to say in Thailand that one is not a monarchist.

Concealed behind the debates over *lèse-majesté* are issues unresolved since 1932. The *lèse-majesté* law has stymied debate over the role of the monarchy, political rights, and popular versus royal sovereignty.[88] Monarchy-ness has become involved in so many political and social issues that reaction is inevitable. In Northeast Thailand these days, without a trace of sentimentality or nostalgia, it is not uncommon to hear people say that after this reign, it may be time to abolish the institution. In 2002, constitutional and monarchy historian Kobkua Suwannathat-Pian wondered:

> Would the principle of constitutional monarchy as practised by the King be fundamentally affected by an emergence of a people's parliament? Would there be a clash of sovereign will: the throne's and parliament's? Would the monarchy retreat behind an official façade of pomp and ceremony?[89]

It was the military, with the palace's probable knowledge of, if not support for, the 2006 coup,that answered Kobkua's questions. One interpretation is that the Democrat Party-PAD-military-palace alliance had succeeded in routing out the Thaksin-era remnants of popular sovereignty.[90] The military-appointed legislature tried to usher in ultra-conservative legislation, such as a law against heresy and an increase of the penalty of *lèse-majesté* to a maximum of 25 years imprisonment (see Chapter 13). Prime Minister Abhisit Vejjajiva came into power in late 2008 promising to set guidelines for *lèse-majesté* cases and making protection of the monarchy his top priority. He seemed to fulfill his promise. The Democrat Party-led administration has achieved the dubious distinction as overseeing the highest number of *lèse-majesté* cases ever recorded in Thailand's modern history. In 2009, there were 164 new cases received by the lower court—a 115 percent increase over 2008, and even a 30 percent increase over 2007, a year of pure military rule. But most shocking is that the 2009 numbers represent more than a 1,500 per cent increase over the average annual number of new *lèse-majesté* cases in the previous decade of 1996–2005. Taking into account the conviction rate, minimum sentencing, and the fact that between 2007 and 2009, 192 people were tried for *lèse-majesté*, we are faced with the disconcerting probability that there may be as many as 170 political prisoners in Thailand at present serving time for *lèse-majesté*, the vast majority of which are unknown to human rights organizations or greater society (also see p. 112).[91] Such is the result of royal "liberalism."

Another interpretation of this extreme rightward shift is that it signals the ultimate failure of a century-long effort to impose a certain type of official nationalism. The enemy seems to grow in numbers, overwhelming the countryside and threatening the city. In desperation, intimidation and jailing of opponents seems the only option. But it will inevitably fail as suppression will tip the balance to the side of popular sovereignty. In the face of utter suppression, we may yet at once be witnessing the end of the defamation regime and the collapse of the state of the exception.

9 The people

A completed defamatory action must involve three parties. The defamer says something defamatory about the defamed person. Most importantly, a third party must not only hear or read the words, but also must be made to feel contempt or have a lower estimation for the one defamed. Sometimes the third party is specified, sometimes it is implicit. Section 282 of the 1908 Thai code specified that the defamatory words must "cause *people* to look down upon or hate such person" [my emphasis]. Section 326 of the 1957 law code said the offending words must "likely . . . impair the reputation of such . . . person" or "expose such . . . person to hatred or contempt." Implicit in this phrasing is "expose such . . . person to hatred or contempt" *by others, by society, by people*, or *by the public*. The question for this chapter is, in Thai law, exactly who or what constitutes this third party, the entity that has changed through its exposure to defamatory words and now thinks less of the person defamed. The question is of utmost importance, for if *the people* or *society* encountered the words, but thought no less of the person defamed, then there might be no crime.

British law specifies a single standard by which words are judged defamatory or not: how society or "right-thinking people generally" understand them (Chapter 2). Theoretically, it should be *society* or *the public* who determines innocence or guilt, as defamation is a socially determined offence. In practice, though, a judge or jury stands in the place of society or the public. Judges specify that members of the jury should not imagine how a specific group understands the words, or how they personally feel about the words. Instead, the members of the jury should somehow intuit how "society as a whole" would understand and feel about the words. No other kind of crime asks so much of a judge's or jury member's imagination. Thai courts have affirmed that the legal principle in defamation is that what was said must be "believed by the people as a whole."[1] Our task, then, is to understand how Thai juridical thought has conceived of this standard of "the people" and how these concepts bear on the adjudication of defamation-based cases.[2]

Michael Connors' book, *Democracy and National Identity in Thailand*, is a landmark study on how "the people" have been conceptualized and become the focus of state policy. Connors examines "the hegemonic productions of the elites and their project of subjecting people to imaginary forms of their own rule." Coining the term *democrasubjection*, he defines this state project as a "particular practice of power," a "meeting ground of hegemony and government" seeking to solve "the people-problem." It is

> any articulated project formed at the intersection of the ideological interpellation of individuals into citizen-subject status within the framework of the nation, and the governmental practices that take up raw material of people for productive reform.[3]

Connors approaches this topic by examining the various discourses concerning citizenship, governmentality, and sovereignty, and how they combined around the term "Thainess." This cultural and political process is central to understanding how defamation-based crimes are adjudicated.

In this chapter, we pursue a path similar to Connor's by looking at the various discourses created in Thailand around "the people," the contradictions formed around them as bearers of failed democracy, as the subject of elite concern (and distrust), and as the standards for deciding the efficacy of defamatory statements. "The people" are an anonymous category which Thai urban classes think of as simple, close to the land, and preserving "culture" from Western corruption. At the same time, "the people" have caused democracy to fail through vote-selling.[4] But these same "people" (or judges acting in their name) serve as the standard to measure whether words are defamatory or not.

The public

Defamatory actions must be public acts done within the context of a society. They cannot happen in private correspondence between two persons. The title of the 1900 edict, "Phraratchakamnot laksana min pramat duai kanphut ru khian thoi kham thet ok khotsanakan rattanakosin sok 118" [Royal Edict on Defamation through False Spoken or Written Words Made Known of the Year 1900] indicates that only "spoken or written words . . . that are *made known*" (my emphasis), translated roughly as "among/in front of a meeting of people," are defamatory.[5] *Publications*, by their nature, are obviously "public" and, when distributed, are automatically understood to be "in front of a meeting of people." In 1900, the government considered this nascent "public" as based in the capital.[6] The state was the sacred center: "Siam State Circle" [*sayam rat monthon*] or "City of Siam" [*krung sayam*].[7] Only Bangkok prosecutors could wield the charge of *lèse-majesté* or defamation of the government.

Such specification is absent from the *lèse-majesté* measures of Sections 98 and 100 in the 1908 code. Presumably, these crimes did not require a public. For section 104, though, the act needed to done "before the people." For personal defamation, the act only needed to happen "in front of two or more persons"—implying that a conversation between two persons was not enough. But three's a crowd, as the saying goes, and constituted a "public."[8]

Mr. Narin Phasit sent out 3,000 pamphlets outlining his criticism of government in 1919; this was considered "public" (Chapters 6 and 7). In the "Flying Ship" case of the same year (Chapter 6), the Supreme Court asked whether the defendant, Mr. Tan, had "appeared before the people" [*prakot kae khon thang lai*] or not. The court ruled that the intent of this law was not that it was necessary for the defendant to have "announced before all of the people throughout the land" [*prachachon thang ban thang muang*]. Taking the message throughout the village and talking with persons who testified that they did not know him was enough to call his "an act that is performed appearing before the people."[9]

Just as the young conscripts fled upon hearing of the dangers of the flying ship, a case from just after the overthrow of the absolute monarchy in 1934 illustrates how "the people" represent the ultimate standard for judging whether a statement was defamatory or not. A Mr. Phrom Miphetchalieow of Ayutthaya, the former capital of Siam, was accused of insulting religion by digging up various artefacts near an abandoned or at least unoccupied temple and stupa. The Court of First Instance found the defendant guilty and sentenced him to five years of imprisonment. The Appeals Court, however, found that the prosecution failed to prove whether the place where the defendant dug was an "active temple" for it was without an abbot or a regular group of believers who came to worship the statues of Buddha. The court ruled that this was more an archaeological site and reduced the sentence to two years of imprisonment. The Supreme Court upheld the Court of First Instance's sentence of five years. In clarifying its decision, the court ruled that merely the act of stealing or digging around a religious place was in itself "an insult to Buddhism." That there was no abbot connected to the temple or that there was no group of believers who frequented it was unimportant. For the court, the main question was: if some Buddhists passed by and saw the defendant engaged in such activities, how would they feel? The court affirmed that believers would determine the act constituted not an insult. At the same time, the court felt its duty was to assess Buddhist feelings in such cases. The court had to "consider the feelings of Buddhists in general—what they would have felt in their minds"—in ruling on whether the actions of the defendant were insulting or not. The court reasoned there was a difference between defaming a private individual and defaming a religion. In the first instance, a person merely "aims to destroy the good name of individuals directly." In the latter, the law is "aimed at protecting and preserving, and not allowing the feelings of insult to arise in the minds of that religion's believers." To allow these feelings could "destroy the tranquillity of the country."[10]

I should highlight a few things here. First, the audience, the public, is the ultimate standard of the crime. The way they "read" the crime determines if insult happened or not. However, in this instance, the court assumed the role of interpreting the insult as if it were directed at "the people." Representing "the people," the court did not have to call actual witnesses to determine how it felt about the defendant's actions.

The court's decision was based on a hypothetical or imagined situation, a fiction. No believers met at this temple. Even if there were, no "people" were called before the court to confirm the insult. The insult, as felt by "the people," is merely assumed.

Second, in this case it is clear that the court held that defamation of state, religion, or national symbols was essentially different from defamation of private individuals because it could affect more than a reputation: it could affect all of society.

The unprovable crime

Neither in the 1941 NongKhai opium den case (Chapters 5 and 6) nor in any other case of seditious rebellion or *lèse-majesté*, did the prosecution produce in court anyone who heard the seditious words and then became rebellious. In fact, it might have proven to be legal suicide for anyone to appear in court to testify to feeling rebellious or contemptuous of the government. This peculiar characteristic of defamation-based state crimes was exploited in the 1957 case of Kukrit Pramoj (Chapters 5 and 7). First, the prosecution tried to prove that the contents of Kukrit's articles could cause others to feel contempt for the government. Kawin Sunthornsarathun, a high-ranking government official, acting as an expert witness for the prosecution, attested to the subversive nature of Kukrit's publications:

> *Prosecution* asks that after reading the three items, what does the witness feel about the prosecution bringing this case to trial?
> *Witness* says he feels that all three items have to be read in succession. He has read them, and he feels aroused about the contents. The contents are dense even though he has read each one of them. He still has the same feeling.[11]

Two days later, though, Kukrit's lawyer, Seni, traped Kawin in cross examination when he made a curious admission:

> *Defense* says you've read the *Sayam Rat*. Did it cause you feelings of rebelliousness and a desire to overthrow the government? (*A huge outburst of laughter by people in attendance.*)
> *Witness* is silent for a moment and then answers, yes it did. (*People laugh.*)
> *Defense (mockingly)* It did make you feel rebellious!? (*People laugh.*)[12]

This case marked a legal precedent for Thai defense strategists. One condition for determining the guilt of a defendant was that the offending words caused "the people" to feel rebellious. Therefore, it would seem to strengthen the case of the prosecution if it could bring forward witnesses to testify to such. In this case, it is the defense who asks the question. The defense seemed to risk providing the prosecution with key "evidence" against its client. But it was a trap. If the witness said that after reading the offending words he or she did not feel rebellious, then this strengthened the defense case because it showed "the people" would not feel rebellious. If, on the other hand, the witness admitted to feeling rebellious, then that witness discredited himself for confessing to be a traitor. Those in attendance at the hearing are not shocked, they laughed. The defendant remained silent for a moment, sensing he was trapped, and made the "unpatriotic" choice by answering that he felt rebellious. Thus, the witness "proved" the prosecution's case while simultaneously undermining it.

This strategy was also used in the 1975 Pradoem Damrongjaroen case (discussed in detail below) when defense attorney and human rights lawyer Thongbai Thongpao cross examined prosecution witnesses who felt outraged by a poem that allegedly insulted the king. He asked them, "Having read the poem, has it caused you to have feelings of disloyalty to the king?" The witnesses had no choice but to answer no, reading the poem had produced no such effect on them. This admission strengthened the defense case and perhaps contributed to the defendant's acquittal. Since the poem, even in the testimony of the prosecution's witnesses, did not cause one "to look down on the monarchy or the person of the king," how could the poem have been *lèse-majesté*?[13]

"The people" vs. uneducated people

Many scholars have noted that the nineteenth-century Bangkok elite's view of the outlying provinces and dependencies was similar to that of their European counterparts in neighboring colonies. In a 1874 letter to the Governor General of India, King Chulalongkorn explained that Siam was attempting to bring order to the dependency of Chiang Mai, which was difficult because, "in regard to the Laos territories, which belong to Siam, the people are uncivilized, not well acquainted [with] what is right and wrong."[14] The 1932 revolution did not change the prevailing Bangkok view of "the people." The new democratic constitution stipulated that only after ten years of education could average citizens directly elect parliamentary representatives. The assumption was that uneducated people cannot practice democracy. In Thailand, as Connors noted, "the people" are seen as encapsulated in an ahistorical frozen state. They are a faceless, amorphous uneducated mass who could potentially be led by unscrupulous opportunists.[15]

To show how this discourse has played out with respect to defamation and *lèse-majesté*, we will look at a few examples from the first days after the revolution in 1932.

In the debate on one of the first press laws after the revolution, a member from the Northeast called for "fair play" for the publications of both the public and the government. He saw that the law established only to control public publications. This Northeast parliamentarian held that exempting government publications "could not be held to be fair." The head of the drafting committee for the law, *Phya* Manavaraj Sevi, said that government publications ought not to be subject to such a law because the government's publications "only contained official announcements, which had nothing to do with regular news or politics." As such they would not be subject to the law. Additionally, the staff involved with a government publication was "a permanent one," so the publication could not be closed. He warned in the end that:

> the administration should not be brought down to the same status as business enterprises of the people. If no difference was made then he feared lots of other customs would have to be altered as well, and then everyone would exercise greater liberty. Only bad results might be expected.

Another member of parliament (MP) declared, "there is no Government anywhere in the word which agrees to be brought down to the same footing as the people." The connotations of these statements are that "the government" was engaged in the task of ruling, which had nothing to do with the raucous politics of "the people."[16]

Another point of debate concerned the educational qualifications for newspaper editors. Section 17 of the same law stipulated that an editor must have completed secondary school. Some MPs thought completion of primary school was sufficient. One MP argued that it would be "disastrous" to require completion of secondary school given that secondary schools had not been set up yet in most of the country's provinces. The measure would also be unfair to women, few of whom would qualify as editors. A number of MPs pointed out that the level of education was not important in the newspaper business as "a newspaper man exercised a sense of judgment more than anything else" and "the discretion necessary to editors could not be taught in school as regards the kind of matter that should be published." And, to require a high level of education would put many editors out of work. He said if the same requirement were made of parliament, many MPs would lose their positions as well. One of the MPs from Bangkok made the point that such a requirement favored rich over poor, as did the present education system. However, the prime minister's views won. He argued that the "standard of knowledge would serve as a key to higher knowledge in all directions. All civilized countries adopt such a policy and it is time that Siam follows in their wake." The measure passed. More than sixty years later, the 1997 constitution of Thailand, the so-called "people's constitution," maintained a similar, clearly class-based, provision, requiring members of parliament to have at least a four-year university degree.[17]

In his work on citizenship, Peter Vandergeest describes the "pre-national" "hierarchy of morality identified with differential knowledge of the Buddhist and Brahman dharma" in which the masses "were constituted as a separate category of moral being, closer to nature (animal-like), more subject to desires, and less knowledgeable of the dharma."[18] Although this worldview was challenged and transformed to a certain extent, much of the perspective was retained, but within a new framework of "civilization" [*arayatham*], supplementing moral superiority through dhamma and education. Vandergeest translated an excerpt from a "Morals Reader" used between 1944 and 1958:

> In general, humans who have reached arayatham already are those who have responsibility. Their behaviour is right and follows the moral principles. They do not become angry, rebellious, or murderous; they do not fight and strike each other . . . they do not cheat anyone, make others angry, and many other such things which pupils study in the *Morals Reader*.
>
> Very simply, people who have arayatham are people who act like nobles [phudi] and are polite, because they have studied . . . they are determined to make the country progress upwards continually. But people who do not have arayatham are those without knowledge; they are close to animals; they only have the body of [human beings], while in their hearts they are still like animals, like those called "forest people" . . . Before people in our country were ruthless and cruel. There were many ruffians going around beating and stealing. . . . But now this sort of thing is almost gone, because we Thai have more arayatham. Thailand has progressed.
>
> But we should not boast that we are a nation which has progressed a lot already, because we still have many who are ruffians, who are savages. This group of people are exclusively those who have never studied, who do not know wrong and responsibility. Their hearts are like animals. Later when the pupils are grown up, these ruffians will be all gone.[19]

The people were the standard for proving seditious rebellion, yet "the people" were neither qualified to serve such a function, nor could they be trusted. This tension is easily seen in the 1957 Kukrit case. In a previous day's session, defense lawyer Seni Pramoj had established that prosecution witness Police General Chat Trakankoson felt that reading the articles would "give rise to feelings of contempt and hatred toward the government," causing "the persons who read them to be in turmoil and be rebellious" to "the point of using force and creating disorder." This day, high-ranking government official Kawin Sunthornsarathun (see Chapters 5 and 7), in a continuation of Seni Pramoj's earlier questioning, said:

> *Witness* says that the articles need to be considered and deliberated. For people who have an education like myself, reading it will not cause them to feel rebellious. But for people who do not have an education, they could misunderstand and go astray.

> *Defense* says excuse me! Do you mean like Police General Chat Trakankoson who testified that he had such feelings of rebelliousness? Does this mean that Chat has no education?! (*People laugh.*)[20]

Whereas the testimony of the first witness put into question his patriotism, the testimony of Kawin made patriotism, if not the privilege of the upper class, then at least something that can only be understood and appreciated by the upper class. The witness at once affirmed his own loyalty to the nation while suggesting a potential source of treachery in the form of the foolish People. The witness affirmed the legal condition indicating the guilt of the defendant—that "the people" were caused to feel rebellious by virtue of seditious words—and at the same time made clear his own innocence.[21]

The intimate form of democrasubjection[22]

After Sarit's 1958 coup, the palace pursued a policy that drew a wider range of bureaucrats, military, and middle-class people into the circle of royal merit. The king "multiplied the classes of decoration," awarded more royal titles, and personally handed out diplomas to every university graduate of state universities from this period until the present. Baker and Pasuk record that the number of "functions, ceremonies, and audiences attended by the king "each year to see" from 100 in the 1950s to more than 600 by the early 1970s.[23] "The people" were not privy to such merit-based attention: they were "the children" under a system which made the king (or military leader) "father (*phokhun*)" of the nation.[24]

However, they received increasing attention either through royal-supported projects or through counterinsurgency programs. One important program of the US-funded Border Police was the Village Scout movement. Initiated in 1971, the program was designed to secure the loyalty of rural border areas through a five-day initiation rite. Starting in 1972, the royalty became one of the most enthusiastic supporters of the program, stating that it protected "all that is worthwhile and has helped to sustain our nation."[25] In 1975 as the political situation seemed to careen out of control, urban Thai, even in Bangkok, poured both money and themselves into the Village Scouts program. In 1976, the numbers peaked with almost two million new initiates. However, in doing so the program was uprooted from its rural base and became a quasi-fascist force, with a significant village scout show of force in the violence on 6 October 1976. Nonetheless, from 1971 to 1985, more than ten million adult Thai went through initiation into the scouts. The original initiates of the village scouts were the rural population and especially those thought susceptible to communist propaganda. However, as Bowie shows in a case study in Thailand's north in 1977, while the rural poor made up almost half the population, they contributed only 8 percent of new initiates.

For this minority, the Village Scout initiation emphasized the image of the king as the head of the family. However, Bowie contends:

> the symbolism of the family is inherently contradictory; it is at once a progressive symbol of altruism and a reactionary justification for hierarchy and privilege. The ambiguous medium of symbolism allowed the real differences between planners and participants to be masked in a temporary imaginary convergence . . . The Village Scouts was a conservative movement that paradoxically sought to generate popular support among the poor majority of the society, not for social change toward a more egalitarian society, but against social change in favor of the existing social hierarchy. [26]

Bowie points out that the Thai state previously found it difficult to reach peasants. Compulsory education extended only to the fourth grade and most villagers had only a radio. In the 1980s, education expanded enormously, as did the reach of electronic media. The state had not yet identified a solidly successful method of drawing in the majority—peasants and laborers. Most people were still spectators or grateful recipients of government or royal project hand-outs.

As Thai society polarized in 1975, the royal family shifted to the right. According to Handley, this phase culminated when the palace essentially took power by proxy in October 1976 and presided over a virtual theocracy, or, as some Thai academics called it, a *dhammocracy*.[27] Dhammocracy, however, failed miserably. The Thanin Kraivichien regime lasted only a year. During this year the Internal Security Operations Command (ISOC) and the National Security Council recognized that the ideological construct of "Nation, Religion, Monarchy" had failed, for it was "too distant from the people" and did not provide them with a "common standpoint."[28] The work of these state intellectuals and national security experts, as Handley described it,

> tried to determine why the nation-religion-king and 'democracy with the king as head of state' ideology had failed to unite Thais. An important conclusion was that neither concept had given the peasantry any status or told them how they would benefit. The concept of the state had been wholly focused on the royals and their idealized view of culture. The solution was to redefine the Thai nation to reflect a more balanced mix of royal and rural importance.[29]

"Self-sufficient village life" was now recognized and celebrated "as defining Thai culture." Policy-makers in the late 1970s and early 1980s "paid more attention to the social, economic, and political hopes of the people themselves."[30] In other words, the state stretched the concept of culture beyond the walls of the palace into the hinterland. The King's memoir records this remarkable shift in official ideology:

> The King and People become one. The Throne and the Nation become one, and a profound meaning is thus given to the Throne. It becomes the personification of the Thai nationhood, the symbol of the Nation's unity and independence, the invariable constant above the inconsistencies of politics. [31]

To implant this ideology, the palace, the Special Branch Police Division dedicated to the protection of the monarchy (and reputation), and other state agencies developed increasing sophistication in depicting a favorable image of the king and other members of the royal family, a depiction Connors calls an "iron regime of controlled imagery."[32] The king became the "development king" and the "farmer king," working tirelessly to solve the people's problems.[33]

As Handley points out, by the 1980s even as the king "regularly intervened" in Thai politics, the scenario played out for the public was that of a *dhammaraja* "above politics," selflessly working for the benefit of his people. Whereas the king had a mixed relationship with the military from 1958 to 1973, the 1980s became "a new era of adulation for the throne, a real second revival . . . with the weight of the military and the private sector" solidly behind the throne.[34] Many photo opportunities were provided with a "huge expansion of the royal development projects," largely due to the support of the new prime minister, career general Prem Tinsulanonda.[35]

The *lèse-majesté* law ensured that "the Royal development projects receive[d] remarkable, wholly positive, and uncritical press coverage."[36] Handley remarks that the king also:

> returned to his earliest lessons on the throne, that ritual and public-spirited activities were the real source of his prestige. As he stepped up his ritual appearances, he also moved to rebuild the palace's circle of allies through the award of royal honors. These were especially meted out to top bureaucrats and military men, whose wives then received . . . coveted aristocratic titles. [37]

Writing about the 1970s and 1980s, Gray goes even further, arguing that "the royal ritual system quietly generates a new Buddhist aristocracy, selectively disguising the means by which it acquires its wealth and thus ensuring that Thai economy retains the attributes of Theravāda ontology."[38] In terms of the expanding circle of royal merit, the palace secured the support of significant segments of the upper and middle classes (see Figure 9.1). From 1980 onward, there were concerted efforts to expand the king's circle of merit to encompass "the people." The only way to address the threats to the present power structure was, by way of state media and shrewd marketing, to engulf the entire population into the circle.

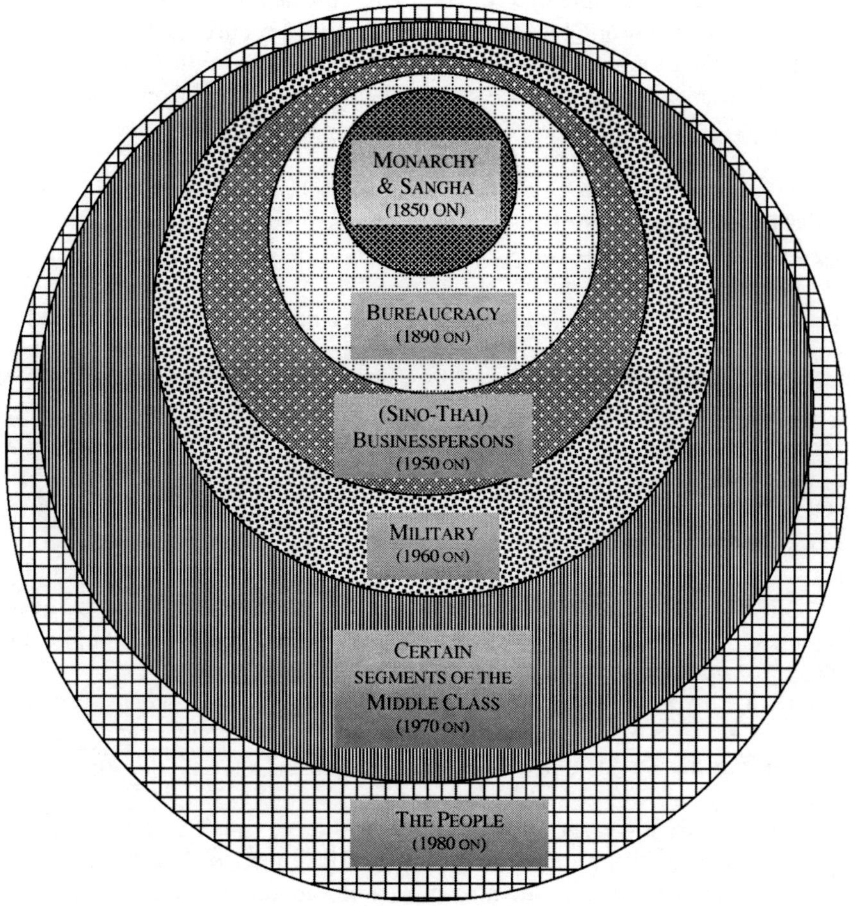

Figure 9.1 Circles of merit/purity.

Specialization in traitorology

From the 1970s onward, a clear science of Thai treason emerged, with its own categories of knowledge, its own methods of producing truth, and its own experts. In a 1937 case, one court felt that in defamation cases it was "capable of interpreting the words for itself, without needing anyone to explain the meaning to it."[39] We have seen earlier that when there was a question, legal experts, the police, and judges picked up the dictionary to make sense of things. Lawyers used the law to argue their cases. But beginning in the mid-1970s, knowledge of treason and *lèse-majesté* became the preserve of experts outside the legal field. Both the prosecution and defense increasingly depended on "expert" witnesses to inform the court as to the real meaning of words in question.[40] University faculty and other well-known cultural specialists became experts, but the emerging national security apparatus also brought its own formidable expertise to such cases.[41]

One of the first clear examples of this trend is illustrated in the celebrated 1975 case of Pradoem Damrongjaroen, a student newspaper editor. The paper published a poem which referred to "angels" or "groups of angels" who aided the upland people while ignoring the lowland peasants. The poem spoke of angels who brought farm animals, such as sheep, to upland people to win popularity. The prosecution argued that the use of "angels" was a metaphor for the royalty and, as such, constituted *lèse-majesté*.

The court said that two questions must be answered. First, to whom did "angels" or "group of angels" refer? Second, if "angel" or "group of angels" did refer to the king, then did the poem constitute *lèse-majesté*? In the first *lèse-majesté* case that drew on literary critics as expert witnesses, the court summed up the "important meaning" of the poem as follows:

> The hill tribes plant opium and marijuana and find ways to transport and sell it, and they mine for jewels and so are never in need and face no great problems because there are angels who come to visit them, donating cattle, sheep, and pigs to them to be raised. These actions of the angel or angels are for seeking favor. As for the people of the land or the rice farmers, it is difficult and they suffer and are poor. The hill tribes are going to prosper with the angels waiting to meet their needs, while there is no justice for the lowlanders.[42]

The prosecution attempted to show that the king had personally donated sheep in aid of the hill tribes. The defense argued that "angels" referred to government officials, as there were many groups which donated livestock to the hill tribes. As such, the poem did not constitute *lèse-majesté*. After hearing testimony about the royal projects conducted among the hill tribes, the court felt that it was clear that many groups, not just the king, had distributed various kinds of farm animals to the hill tribes.

The focus then moved to the question of the distribution of sheep. The court admitted that, from the testimony, it appeared that only the king donated sheep. Thus, the prosecution won its point. However, the court cautioned that the poem must be read in its entirety and a reader should not focus on the single word, "sheep." As this was a poem, its composition imposed restrictions in terms of form according to tonal and syllabic rhyme schemes. In short, the court argued, composing poetry cannot be thought the same as writing prose.

With the information derived from the initial two inquiries, the court then tackled the question of whether "angel" or "group of angels" referred to the king. It reasoned that since there were many groups which distributed livestock to the hill tribes, the poem referred not only to the king. Furthermore, the reference could not be to the king because the king did not act to win favor, as the poem claimed, but acted out of his personal compassion and kindness.

The last bit of evidence the court brought forward was that the prosecution had failed to show that the defendant had shown any sort of behavior or sign indicating lack of loyalty toward the king. For all these reasons, the court found the defendant not guilty.

The only factual point used in passing judgment was how many organizations distributed livestock. The other points were essentially an exercise in textual analysis—whether sheep were, for literary purposes, equivalent to cows and pigs; the significance of angel as singular or plural; whether poetry could be treated in as straight-forward a way as prose. As expert witnesses, the defense called Sulak Sivaraksa and Suchart Sawatsri, the first and second editors of the enormously influential *Social Science Review*. These two witnesses were brought in not as legal authorities or experts on *lèse-majesté* or livestock, but as literary experts. They suceeded in making their literary points, and Pradoem was acquitted.[43]

In a second 1975 incident, a newspaper columnist for *Dara yuk sayam*, Seni Soongnat, used the opportunity of a speech given by the Queen to make, allegedly, some veiled comments on Thai society. However, some observers construed that Seni made insulting comments about the king and queen.

To sort out matters, the prosecution employed university professors to tell the court the real meaning of the columnist's words. These experts held that:

> The writings implied that the king and queen accused or blamed the students and people for instigating unrest and were "non-humans," meaning evil persons, without principles, and always inciting irritating disquiet, attempting to separate the people by making them conscious of their station in life, trying to divide government servants by pointing out their distance from the people, supporting the police in suppressing people who have different thoughts.[44]

The Supreme Court disregarded the defendant's statement that he had not intended to insult the institution of the monarchy and upheld the Court of First Instance's sentence of two years' imprisonment for *lèse-majesté*.[45]

The 1988 trial of Wira [Veera] Musikaphong, though, was complex and featured many national security and cultural specialists.[46] Wira campaigned in the Northeastern province of Buriram in 1986 for a wealthy Democrat Party candidate who was running for office in the province but lived primarily in Bangkok. Wira made the point that one's birthplace should not be important because we cannot choose where we are born. In a moment of apparent rhetorical flourish. Wira uttered:

> If I could have chosen myself, why would I have chosen to have been born as a child of rice farmers in Songkhla? . . . If I could have chosen, I'd

> certainly have chosen to be born in the middle of the royal palace *[phrabormmaharatchawang]*. Then I would've been *Prince [phra-ongjao]* Wira. I wouldn't have had to come out here and stand in the hot sun and speak to you all. At this time, noon, I would have gone into an air-conditioned room, eaten a bit, *lain down* to sleep, and then gotten up at three . . . [but] one can't choose where one is born.

Later that day, in another speech, he restated:

> If I were a prince now, I would not be standing here, speaking, making my throat hoarse and dry. Here it is 6:30. I would be drinking some *intoxicating liquors* to make myself comfortable and happy. Wouldn't that be better than standing here talking and completely tiring out my poor *shin bones*?
>
> [emphasis indicates words to be used only with royalty]

Recordings of Wira's speeches were given to the police; he was arrested on two counts of *lèse-majesté*. At his trial, testifying for the prosecution was the Supreme Commander of the Thai Armed Forces, Athit Kamlang-ek; Sutsai Hatsadin, head of the paramilitary Red Gaurs; Samak Sundaravej, well-known rightist and later prime minister; and Phawat Bunnag, a royal under-secretary to the king. For the defense, was Chuan Leekpai, a leader of the Democrat Party and future prime minister, and Srisak Vallibhotama, noted lecturer on Thai history, archaeology, and culture. The cultural and linguistic points of contention revolved around the meaning of "palace" and "second-rank-prince." To whom was Wira referring was the crux of the case.

Samak said that as the singing of the king's song, the royal anthem, caused people to think of the king, referring to the palace caused them to think of the king as well. Phawat testified that the palace was a "place built by kings for the purpose of the king and queen to reside in, and to serve as the birthplace of princes and princesses who would one day come to the throne." Even if the king was not born in the palace, this witness held that he should be considered to have been born there because the palace represented "being-king-ness." Wira's wish to be born in the palace referred to the home of the present king. For the defense, Chuan testified on shadow puppetry in the South, attesting to Wira's sense of imagination and mastery of puppets. Srisak reflected on what "palace" could mean.

The second point focused on the meaning of "second-class prince." If the prosecution could show that Wira meant that the king was a second-rank prince, then it could strengthen the case against him. Expert witnesses again took the stand to discuss the exact meaning of "second-class prince." Accounts of genealogy, obscure manuals describing how degrees of royalty are assessed, and other evidence were produced.

A number of "experts" testified for the prosecution—university rectors, school directors, lawyers, and royal secretaries. Most prominent among these witnesses were members of the military, some who served as "national security" experts. As Senate member and Supreme Commander of the Thai Armed Forces, General Athit Kamlang-ek's qualifications had nothing to do with the greater meaning of words, legal understanding, or royal ranks. He was called to give the "security" assessment of the situation. He warned that Wira's remarks were meant to "persuade the people to lose their faith in the institution of the monarchy." Athit claimed that, if the people were led astray by Wira's words, it "would cause unrest among the people and destroy the security of the country." The people must rally around the king who serves as "the centre" that brings people together. Any loss of loyalty to the king would give an opening to the communists to infiltrate and destroy the Thai system of governance that has a king as head of state. He testified that, as head of ISOC, the military's anti-communist force, he had intelligence that placed Wira with communists. It was clear, then, that Wira's slanderous words against the king were part of a communist plot against the security of the nation.

The Supreme Court agreed and upheld the decision of the Appeals Court to convict Wira, although it reduced the sentence to four years.

These three cases differ from other kinds of defamation-based cases in that they assumed that the average layperson, or even judge, could not see their way through the intricate, layered meanings without an expert guide. These cases defined a significant moment in the history of Thai defamation-based laws and adjudication, for they marked the point at which one-to-one correspondence of what was impugned and the reputation of a concrete person was lost. In Wira's case, the defense pointed out that *lèse-majesté* should only concern direct and clear defamatory words directed at the king. It claimed that the prosecution's case concerning the "palace" was a "distorted interpretation" for the prosecution had quite "impossibly" used a "material object to refer to a person." This conflation of king and monarchy, monarchy and the state, and monarchy and the people (or nation) marked the beginning of the great age of *lèse-majesté* and soon became accepted practice (see Chapter 8).

While the cases of Wira and Pradoem involved words used poetically or metaphorically, expert consideration became extended to the most mundane of *lèse-majesté* cases. In the previous chapter I considered a case involving Samak Sundaravej who complained that certain parties used the monarchy as a political tool (p. 193). In Samak's case, a single police panel was insufficient. A second team was set up because, according to a high-ranking police officer, "the case had to be treated very carefully and opinions on legality had been sought from knowledgeable experts and academics."[47]

Ironically, *lèse-majesté* cases were apparently too important to allow the use of representatives of "the people" who were supposed to provide the standard. Instead, experts and, usually, military court judges were involved. In some cases, the testimony of ordinary people was expressly forbidden. In the 1978 case of Seni Soongnat the defense team tried to introduce non-expert witnesses to testify about the meanings and impact of the defendant's words—in other words, representatives of “the people” or “the public.” However, the Appeals Court intentionally did not make such testimony part of its decision. The Supreme Court ruled that, in such cases, only views of “wise persons” (*winyuuchon*),[48] expert witnesses, could be taken into consideration.[49]

Only with Wira’s 1988 case has the Supreme Court approved of the notion that members of the public could be legitimate witnesses in *lèse-majesté* cases. In a note attached to the decision, the court set a precedent by specifying that “average people” serving as witnesses could be taken into account when deciding *lèse-majesté*. The prosecution’s witnesses thus included peasants, local policemen, low-level government officials, and so forth. Also, the prosecution carefully pointed out that, after hearing the defendant’s words on the day of the crime, a “movement of some groups of people” [*prachachon bang klum mi khwam khluanwai*]—unnamed and unspecified—were going to protest the “act of the defendant which would cause disquietude in the land.” The people were at once a menace, the truly loyal, but still not quite a standard.

The problematic nature of “the people”

Seditious rebellion and *lèse-majesté* (and regular defamation) are public acts that require a public for them to obtain. No public, no crime. This principle was sorely tested in the 1922 case of Mr. Hui who said the Thai people were dogs (Chapter 7). For the crime to exist, people (Thai? Foreign?) had to hear what Mr. Hui said and then to look down contemptuously on the Thai. But the Thai people cannot be both the standard and the object, for this would result in the Thai people looking down on the Thai people, an impossibility (or at least hopelessly complicated). Perhaps this was the reason that the case against Mr. Hui was dropped.

Another quirk shows up in Wira’s 1988 case. The prosecution introduced a typed transcript of Wira’s speech made from a tape. Inserted in parentheses following the allegedly inflammatory words of the defendant, indicating the crowd’s response, were the words, “*siang ho*,” which can indicate either approval or disapproval, but is usually rendered as “boo.” The defense protested that these words should have been either “*siang ha*” (laughter) or “*prop mu*” (clapping), indicating the crowd’s approval. The defense insisted there was no protest at the time of the speech and that the listeners were in fact laughing and thought Wira’s metaphor good fun.

In response, the prosecution, not directly referring to this issue, embarked on a remarkable and dangerous legal line of reasoning. The prosecution took back its earlier contention that there was a “movement of people” outraged at the defendant’s words and explained the general lack of protest among listeners by implying the population of Buriram as a whole was involved in the crime of *lèse-majesté*. The prosecution claimed that the districts where Wira spoke were “pink areas” still under martial law, where a great deal of communist infiltration had occurred. The prosecution alleged that, had Wira spoken favorably of the royals, he would have cost his party votes. Therefore, Wira had calculated that by insulting royals his candidate would win the votes of this subversive population. That Wira's candidate won proved his guilt.

The defense turned this principle on its head and argued that Buriram's residents were good Thai citizens who loved the king. If Wira had spoken slanderous words of the king, then he and his candidate could not have won, for the people would not have elected them. But that he had said these words and his candidate was still elected proved that, in the eyes of the people of Buriram, he had not committed *lèse-majesté*, an opinion with which the Buriram provincial court concurred in finding Wira innocent.[50]

The implications of the prosecution's tactic are potentially devastating to the logic underlying the charge of *lèse-majesté*, a charge ultimately based on the hypothetical effect certain words would have on an unspecified collectivity. If the defense can show specific, actual (and favorable) responses of people to allegedly slanderous words, the logic of *lèse-majesté* cases begins to unravel. If the words of the defendant are judged to be *lèse-majesté* and the people laughed and clapped approvingly, then the people are guilty of *lèse-majesté*. But this cannot be so. The defendant cannot be found guilty because "the people," who are used as the ultimate standard to decide what constitutes *lèse-majesté* by the way they react to what is said, cannot, by definition, then also be guilty of that same crime. Or, put another way, when the Court of First Instance decided Wira's innocence, it implicitly affirmed the principle that laughing Thai listeners, by their laughter, proved the defendant's innocence. In the same way, when the Supreme Court, while introducing the principle that common people can recognize *lèse-majesté* when they hear it, judged Wira guilty, it also implicated the laughing Thai people of *lèse-majesté*, which is impossible.

In the last chapter we briefly introduced the case of Daranee Charnchoengsilpakul who, in July 2008 allegedly spoke harsh words in public against the monarchy and warned that the monarchy may come to the same end as in France and Russia. Deputy editor-in-chief of the *Bangkok Post*, Veera Prateepchaikul, wrote, "It was unthinkable that the audience was not offended by her offensive remarks. They just cheered her on and clapped their hands in joy." This was unthinkable because it went to the core of the *lèse-majesté* charge. We are always told all Thai love their king. As such, they serve as the standard for *lèse-majesté*. But what if some Thai cheer at the thought of violence done to the royals? It simply cannot be. They must be traitors, Veera implies. But what happens when, or will happen were, a substantial number of Thai seem to respond favorably to what is later judged as *lèse-majesté*? At what point do the traitors switch places with the patriots? Or, when can there be many kinds of patriots?[51]

This chapter suggested that the approach taken by the Thai state on the subject of "the people" has proven conceptually schismatic and sociologically schizophrenic. But it is possible that this quarter-century-old project of democrasubjection, under the weight of its own contradictions, may come to an end. Connors correctly points out that democrasubjection ultimately results in questions of popular sovereignty and citizenship. The people's role within the realm of defamation adjudication ultimately asks who shall be the bearer of their sovereignty: the people, or the state acting in the name of the people.[52] Connors satirizes the "meta-ideological insincerity" of the Thai elite's "baseless claims of popular sovereignty in the absence of a sovereign people":

> The people were the sources of sovereignty, but they were not yet able to divest it to legitimate representatives. The people were sovereign and yet this was an imagined state, needing state development and cajolement. The people were sovereign and yet rule should be according to enlightened elites. The people were Thai, but expressions of Thainess [were] to be cultivated, policed and socialized.[53]

In Thailand, the people are not seen as qualified to represent themselves; thus, those charged with the responsibility to represent both society and state are judges. No member of "the people" has ever been entrusted to attest to the failure of a defamatory statement. This is because such a statement never resulted in feelings of contempt for the defamed, or indeed, succeeded. "The people" remains a group distinct from the speaker—a government official, a national security officer, a linguist. Key to the Thai defamation principle is the reification and then gagging of "the people". If an actual member of "the people" happens to get around the interference and attested to something about a defamation case, such a person is inevitably accused of speaking for another (an influential person, not of "the people). The further up the defamation ladder (the top rung is *lèse-majesté*), the more "the people" become an object and the less "the people"are qualified to speak on their own behalf. "The people" are the standard, but never shall they speak.

We conclude this section with the observation that in Thai law and practice each constituent part of a successful defamatory conviction has fallen securely into place. Criticism of the government is tied to ill intentions. Intentions (ill or not) can only be read by pure hearts. In more than nine out of ten cases the pure hearts of judges see ill intentions. The targets in most cases become more encompassing. In individual defamations, past judicial practices are foregone and courts permit government units to mount collective defamation cases. Critics of public officials are given little leeway. When the target is the monarchy, defendants are absolutely denied the opportunity to claim exemption or to argue that what they alleged is true.

The state has been able to put a lock on expression, and truth is forced into exile.

Part IV

Thai enemy, Thainess, and Thai truth

10 Culture and traitor

The next three chapters draw out some larger implications brought about by Thai-based defamation laws and their adjudication. This chapter explores how the defamation principle in Thailand found a powerful expression in evolving anti-communism laws. Prior to the 1960s, the Thai anti-communist law had a strictly "political" focus. But, during the 1960s, when the concept of culture was added, the result became, in part, the emergence of Thainess as part of national ideology. Chapter 11 examines two related movements of Thainess. The first was within Thailand, making its way into Buddhism and even the animal kingdom, where Thai racial characteristics were identified. The second movement took Thainess abroad, where attempts were made to Thai-ify foreign perceptions of Thailand. Chapter 12 looks at the question of truth in news, art, and history and constructs a way of viewing "Thai" truth.

As background to this chapter, I wish to recall that often the juridical use of "indeterminate concepts" leads to the state of exception. Communism, an indeterminate concept initially quite clear and determinate, became the intermediate link between two well-used phrases in Thai law—"peace and order" and "national security"—and became in so doing increasingly less specific under the fully evolved defamation regime/state of exception. I then show how the initially separate trajectories of the concepts of communism and culture collided and conjoined, creating a single and forceful movement embodied in the term, "Thainess" and its nemesis—those who would question Thainess—the traitor.

Communism without culture

For many years, communism was the ultimate crime against the state in Thailand, occupying a special place historically. For their time (prior to 1976), the anti-communist measures were long the greatest of defamation-based crimes. In 1927, anyone who "advocates" any system that would "bring into hatred or contempt [against] the Sovereign, the Government or the administration of the State" could be found guilty of communism. A "chief, manager or an official" of any organization which sought the same could face up to ten years in prison, at the time making this infraction more severe than *lèse-majesté*.

But the most important contribution brought about by the law against communism was that it facilitated the expansion of the concept of "culture" from its humble beginnings in the late 1930s and early 1940s into the core of Thai nationalist ideology in the 1960s. To understand this transformation, I compare two cases involving communism, separated by 31 crucial years. The first example was palatably "communist;" the second something quite different. I will then examine what happened between the two cases, briefly mentioning Phibun Song Khram's culture programmes, his attempts to add "cultural" items to the anti-communist law in 1952, and finally the revisions to the anti-communist law in the late 1960s.

The first case took place in the Northeastern province of Sakon Nakhorn in 1935, where three men passed out pamphlets advocating communism. They were tried for violating Section 104 of the 1908 criminal code and the anti-communist law of 1933 for their "attempt to incite rebellion and aid in the spread of communism." Specifically, they were charged with distributing pamphlets that detailed the nature of communism. The prosecution argued that, since the final goal of communism was the overthrow of the government, the handing out of pamphlets on "many streets" might "bring people to look on Soviet Communism favourably." Investigators found that 82 pamphlets had been distributed and a red flag was discovered at a nearby temple. Both the pamphlets and the flag bore the hammer and sickle insignia. The Court of First Instance agreed with the prosecution and ruled, a little confusedly, that "a conspiracy to destroy the present government and establish soviets" was "a violent act even if force or violence was not used in bringing it about" and gave the defendants life imprisonment. The Appeals Court agreed with the argument of the defendants that it was "not clear they had a plan to destroy the government" or that "spreading pamphlets was part of such a conspiracy." However, it felt that the message in the pamphlets clearly intended to have people look down on the government and make them rebellious. As such, the defendants could be found guilty of distributing illegal pamphlets. Their sentences were reduced to ten years' imprisonment. In the appeal, the Supreme Court ruled that the defendants showed that they were well aware of the nature of the message printed on the pamphlets, as evidenced by their attempts to conceal them in their pants when arrested. The defendants had to prove their innocence if they were to maintain they were ignorant of pamphlet's contents. In conclusion, the Supreme Court said it was "simply impossible to know the intentions" of a defendant. One could only "look at behaviour in forming assumptions on motive." Even without knowing their intentions, the court ruled that the pamphlets "might create disturbances in the land and create hatred among social classes. This was inciting the people and aiding in having the people be disparaging of the law." The Supreme Court allowed the sentence to stand.[1]

This was a straightforward case with red flags, sickles, and soviets. The intentions, moral characters, and identities as Thai (or Lao? or Vietnamese?) of the defendants were not brought into contention. They advocated communism. The law forbade it. They were found guilty.

Bad monk = communist monk

The second case is more complicated. *Phra* Phimontham was a well-known Northeastern monk who had established himself at the important Mahathat Temple in Bangkok as an intellectual leader and social progressive. The Sarit Thanarat government charged him with engaging in illicit sexual intercourse in 1960 and being a communist in 1962. The monk was stripped of his titles within the *Sangha* (the official Buddhist hierarchy), disrobed, and jailed for four years before being tried in court. Given the monk's popularity, progress of his cases was widely followed.[2]

Unlike the 1935 Sakon Nakhorn trio, *Phra* Phimontham faced a litany of charges, all under the rubric of communism and national security: collecting arms and attempted sabotage, rebellion, and overthrow of the government and constitution; inciting monks to become communists; masturbating another man and having anal sex with him; inciting disunity in the *Sangha*; mingling with civilians in Germany; dressing inappropriately; saying the government used incompetent military persons to draft the new constitution and, moreover, was exploitative and a dictatorship and intervened in the internal politics of Cambodia and Laos; calling for a land reform and depicting China and Russia as good, saying the *Sangha* was under the orders of the government and that the monarchy was wasteful and the king should abdicate; calling the Buddha a liar; subverting Buddhism; saying that the Supreme Patriarch was crazy; teaching that past kings built stupas to deceive worshippers; and, finally, promoting a meditation method that hypnotized followers and made them more susceptible to communism.[3]

The core of the many charges brought against *Phra* Phimontham involved Buddhism. We look at four: destroying the Sangha, engaging in illicit sex, saying past kings were deceitful, and employing meditation as a form of communist brainwashing.

Destroying the Sangha

A central charge against *Phra* Phimontham was that he was the mastermind behind fliers that criticized the *Sangha*; said the supreme patriarch was crazy; said the *somdetphrasangkhanayok* (the equivalent of a "prime minister" within the *Sangha*) had made a hit list of monks in the *Mahanikai* sect to be purged and that the smaller but royal-backed *Thammayut* [Thammayudh] sect oppressed the larger but less influential *Mahanikai* sect; and called for the resignation of top monks from their posts in the *Sangha*. The intent of the defendant in spreading this flyer, the prosecution argued, was:

> to destroy the institution of the *Sangha*, bring down the government because it had appointed these people, incite the creation of disunity between the *Thammayut* and *Mahanikai* sects . . . [and] create chaos, disunity, [and] agitation among Buddhists, creating disparagement and rebelliousness within the *Sangha* and by the people, which is according to the plan and objectives of the communists.

Unfortunately, the only item the prosecution had to present for these serious charges was that *Phra* Phimontham had not been chosen to sit on the Council of Elders in 1960. No evidence existed to show that he had done anything related to the flyer. The court also examined the issue of whether *Phra* Phimontham had caused conflict within the *Sangha*, but here, again, it found nothing that led it to think so. There was one other charge which was only vaguely alluded to in the decision of the military court. It may be what the military court said it could not reveal, for such disclosure "would affect the institution of the *Sangha* and would stain the Buddhist elders and Buddhism." It was quite likely a reference to something related to the 1960 charge involving illicit sex.

Engaging in illicit sex

In *Phra* Phimontham's first trial, on 30 August 1960, the political police heard the testimony of Mr. Wirayut Watthananusorn who claimed that "beyond helping [me] masturbate, *Phra* Phimontham had once reached orgasm performing anal sex" with the witness, and "then never allowed anal sex to be performed on him again." A letter from the *somdetphrasangkhanayok* to the supreme patriarch a few days later explained the offense of *Phra* Phimontham's "engaging in illicit anal intercourse" and that this alleged incident probably led to his forcible disrobing and expulsion from the monkhood. Without specifying exactly what was at issue, this witness apparently recanted his testimony in court, claiming that he had been put under pressure by the political police to make false testimony in the first place.[4] *Phra* Phimontham was found innocent and re-ordained. But allusions were made to possibly similar charges in *Phra* Phimontham's second case, where the thrust of the charges as a whole focused on subverting Buddhism. But the connection had been made between sex-engaging monks as a sign of overall subversion of the religion, which in turn was tantamount to treason.

Past kings are deceivers

The court heard testimony about a 1956 incident in Nakhorn Pathom Province where a famous stupa is located. The prosecution charged the defendant with saying, "Past kings built the Nakhorn Pathom Stupa to deceive the people into prostrating themselves without putting any Buddhist relics in it," which was a statement that both "criticized kings" and "aimed to destroy the belief of the people, and have them stop giving respect to Buddhist relics." The defendant explained that in understanding and practicing meditation, one must work with that which is real, such as feeling [*arom*], something that "connects the mind of the individual with the outer world" [*ayatana*].[5] One, however, cannot take something unreal, supposed [*sommut*], or created [*banyat*], like a stupa. One could prostrate and pray before this stupa for a year and still not be successful (unlike with *vipassana* meditation.) The court judged that this was "a matter of religion between monks." The court did not agree with the prosecution that hearing these words would cause people to disparage religion, take away their faith, showed contempt for the king, or showed the defendant to be "an enemy" set on "destroying religion." As such, the court ruled that in this respect, the defendant "had not spoken in order to destroy Buddhism" as the prosecution had charged, nor insulted past kings.

Burmese Buddhist meditation as communist brainwashing

The prosecution argued that the defendant had given support to the "Meditation Center" in Burma and sent monks there to "receive training in meditation" who would then "bring [such training] back and spread it in Thailand." But this meditation practice "was in opposition to the principles of Buddhist meditation" for it was "deceitful" and "a trick" intended "to get people to believe in" communism, become communist party members, and to act "in accordance to the objectives" of communists. This meditation technique was a form of "hypnotising oneself and [one's] subconscious" that would then allow the teachers to "program the mind of the practitioners to believe that Buddhism was communism." This, the prosecution warned, "would not lead to the rise of wisdom and knowledge of the truth according to the principles of Buddhism."

The lead witness for the prosecution, citing a book by Professor Nittisat Phaisan, said that this meditation practice did not lead to "awareness" and was instead "established to brainwash those who practice it into believing that Buddhism is communism." The prosecution also introduced testimony by a certain Dr. Chian who said hypnosis was "a condition" that occurs under the direction of a hypnotist "that puts one in a sleepy state." Moreover, it was argued, persons engaging in this type of meditation would "separate themselves from society" and thus would not "oppose the progress of the communists."

In his defense, *Phra* Phimontham argued that Burmese Buddhism had "one of the strongest traditions of meditation practices," and that their use of such meditation practice at Mahathat Temple, where *Phra* Phimontham had been a monk, had become so popular that "foreigners and even the queen herself came" to practice it. Moreover, he did not so much consider it a "Burmese" meditation practice, but a "Buddhist" practice since it was from Buddhism that the practice sprung. The defense introduced the testimony of a monk who "specialized in meditation" and discussed various meditation techniques, quoted from assorted Buddhist texts, and affirmed that the meditation practice in question was indeed Buddhist. Another monk who had tried this meditation technique testified that he had achieved "excellent results" by experiencing "cool tranquillity" and feeling "happy." Even Sanya Thammasak, president of the Supreme Court and witness for the prosecution, testified that he had "benefited from his practice."

After reviewing all of the testimony presented by the prosecution and defense, the court ruled that the "meditation principles" were "according to *dhamma*" and did come from Buddhist texts. Not only monks in the Buddhist hierarchy, but also government leaders and compilers of Buddhist texts "all attested to the correctness of these meditation techniques." Moreover, the court examined Nittisat's book, and found that what was in the book, and its treatment of the meaning of the word "awareness" in a Buddhist context, was "in total agreement with the defendant's method of meditation." The court lashed out at the testimony of the high-ranking political policeman who served as the lead prosecution witness for having "painted a vague picture of the defendant brainwashing practitioners to believe that Buddhism is communism" and to "separate [them] from society in order that they do not oppose the work of the communists." When this witness was asked about the charges he had made, he admitted that he had no evidence for them. How could such a high-ranking policeman present such hearsay evidence? the court asked incredulously.[6]

While the court dismissed the case against *Phra* Phimontham, the basic contours of the case show a significant change occurred between 1935 and 1966. Before, distributing a pamphlet advocating communism could not even necessarily bring the charge of trying to overthrow the government. But by 1966, a monk making a theological point somehow seemed to substantiate a charge of communism. Both the list of specific charges constituting the degree of its violation and the list of effects it might have on society seemed more expansive. Over the span of thirty years, supporting communism had become more than a political act; it was an all-encompassing crime against the state. And, if it is possible to say that at some point in the piling on of charges concerning opposing the government, a given action or set of acts is transformed into a rebellion, then maybe it is also possible to say that at a certain point in the piling on of charges concerning rebellion, that it can be transformed into a threat against national security.

Evidently, the combination of all these charges was supposed to lend greater credence to the charge of communism. The logic seems to be: a monk who masturbates or dresses inappropriately does not respect religion. One who does not respect religion is willing to use religion as a tool. One who is willing to use religion as a tool could use Buddhism to spread communism. Ergo, a communist uses Buddhism as a tool to spread communism. Or, cutting some links from this chain: a monk who masturbates another is a communist. A relatively simple violation had been transformed into an act of treason. A small act which could create a charge so lengthy it required cataloguing, reflected an intention of the basest nature—that of the traitor—aimed at the destruction of the state and culture. Communism thus became an all-encompassing crime against the state, under the rubric of national security the ultimate source of betrayal.

The decision of the court, while freeing the defendant and apologizing, nonetheless affirmed that communism was odious, that Buddhism as practiced was good, that the Sangha needed unity, and that monks needed to know their place in the hierarchy.[7] It affirmed the connection between sloppy Buddhist practices (i.e., not being a good Thai culturally) with being the ultimate traitor, a communist.

Culturalization

"Culture" connects these two cases and periods. The first 1933 communist act concerning communism did not contain any "cultural" elements. It saw communism as an economic and political program designed to overthrow the government. The Thai word for "culture," *wattanatham*, was coined only in the late 1930s. Coining any word reveals both intentionality and a perceived need. This does not mean that "Thailand" did not have "culture" prior to *wattanatham* (วัฒนธรรม); there were older words approximating tradition and customs, *khanop thamniam* (ขนบธรรมเนียม) and *prapeni (*ประเพณี). As with other newly coined words of the day such as community (*chumchon*—ชุมชน), society (*sangkhom*—สังคม) or pubic (*satharanachon*—สาธารณะชน), *wattanatham* was created for a specific purpose: to provide the government with a new system of control, a new way of arranging and categorizing people and activities. At the same time, the country was renamed "Thailand." "Culture" constituted a new prescriptive framework under which the daily practices of the (former Siamese/now Thai) could be raised, modernized, and become more civilized.[8] In 1938, the Phibun Songkhram government initiated a series of "Cultural Mandates"—quasi-laws that, for instance, required officials to call various ethnic groups "Thai" in official documents and continued to mandate an entire body of "civilizing" practices for the nation. The government set up committees to develop a legal definition of culture and laws that would maintain such culture, culminating in the setting up of a Ministry of Culture. The results were a number of legal acts that outlined what Thai culture ought to be and provided for minor punishments to those who failed to follow the prescribed "Thai culture."

Many of today's Thai believe that the "invented traditions" of this period are authentic Thai customs.[9] The government's Thai culture project exposed a number of assumptions: that existing Siamese/Thai "culture" was inadequate and impure; that there was a single "Thai" culture uniting all "sub-ethnic" groups; and that the government's business included researching, designating, propagating, and enforcing correct observances of Thai culture. Thus, for Thai, "culture" became a homogeneous racial quality, properly defined by the state, enforced by legal means, and maintained through government bodies dedicated to preserving its "purity." A major aspect of this culturalization program was the general militarization and regimentation of social life.[10]

However, after a decade, "culture" had still not made inroads into the greater body of Thai law. The Communist Act of 1933 was scrapped in 1947, with efforts to revive it begun in 1950. By early 1952, in a "secret-very urgent" letter, the head of the cabinet of ministers asked the Juridical Council, to begin deliberation on a draft measure that would outlaw communism.

But apparently the Ministry of Foreign Affairs and the Juridical Council successfully convinced the government that, while the objective of a proposed law would be to suppress communism, the law should not specify communism. Documents from 1952 reveal that the name of the law was initially the "National Security Law." This was then changed to the "Law on Control of Subversive Activities."[11] An interesting "cultural" incident occured in the discussions between the prime minister and the Juridical Council on the various drafts. In January 1952 the crucial section of the law, Section 3, read as follows:

> *Section 3.*—In this Act, the words "subversive activities" mean any act, words, writings or printed matter by which any person or body of persons advocates or teaches:
>
> a) to overthrow forcibly the present social and economic order which is based upon the protection and preservation of private ownerships and upon fundamental rights and liberties constitutionally recognized to individuals; or
> b) to promote revolutionary unrest and struggle for the conquest of power by violence in order to replace the constitutional exercise of the democratic and parliamentary institutions by the dictatorship of a single political party even and especially if that party is a minority;
> c) to deprive of political rights [of] other classes than the class which has forcibly conquered power; and meanwhile to impose adhesion and support of the revolutionary party by terrorism, fear, sabotage, etc.;
> d) to promote economic transformations, by which private ownerships of property and means of production shall be abolished entirely or partly and shall be transferred to the State by way of confiscation or otherwise.[12]

Thus, this draft focused on the economic and political aspects of communism. In September, however, two months before the bill became law, the cabinet of ministers asked the Juridical Council to redraft the law so that it "directly opposes communism." Not only was the Juridical Council adamantly opposed to referring to communism directly; it also opposed the following revision of a portion of Section 3 as proposed by the cabinet of ministers:

> "Communist activities" means such activities: — . . . (b) compelling by terrorism or making sabotage; using any means whatsoever; *instigating children not to respect their parents; bringing about hatred between different classes of people; or publicating [advocating?] the people not to believe any religion*, with such purposes of adherence to help, support or attaining of such objects specified in (a).
>
> (my emphasis)[13]

The phrasing, "bringing about hatred between different classes of people" was similar to various versions of Section 104 of the 1908 code on seditious rebellion, but this must have been the first time that "instigating children not to respect their parents" or persuading "the people not to believe any religion" was proposed for a modern Thai law, much less accompanied by severe punishments. Under the proposal, the penalty might have resulted in imprisonment from ten years to life! Although the Juridical Council claimed the cabinet of ministers "directed" that these additional provisions—concerning religion, parents, and hatred between classes—be put into the draft of the act, it seems probable that, given Phibun's Cultural Mandates of a decade earlier, the prime minister himself was behind the move.[14]

Phibun also insisted that the law be directed against communism directly, another item which the Juridical Council vigorously opposed. Although the head of the Juridical Council at the time, Yut Saeng-uthai, "tried again and again" to explain the difficulty of ascertaining a precise meaning to the term, "communism," the prime minister insisted. René Guyon consoled himself with the observation that the final draft of the law sought to suppress activities and not thought itself (Chapter 8). Because of this, some of the legal objections that might be made against the law on the grounds that it violated the U.N. Declaration might be "averted." He hoped, though, that "the right of private opinion and private expression should consequently remain protected." To "prevent misunderstandings," he suggested to the government that "the definition of 'communist activities'" specified in the draft law "should be completed" with a clear exclusionary statement affirming the following right:

> Personal opinion and its expression shall not be considered as an activity within the meaning of this definition so long as no attempt shall be made for the purpose to gain supporters by propagating or disseminating a doctrine or carry on actions which might lead to internal disorders.[15]

The recommendation was ignored. At the last moment, for unspecified reasons, Phibun himself apparently removed the items on religion and children.[16] The draft became law on 13 November 1952. In the end, the final version of the law veered away from including culture and stayed more clearly within the bounds of economics and politics. But Phibun was at least able to pursue his culture program through the newly established Ministry of Culture *and* elevated the status of the World War II-era National Culture Institute to ministerial level. In effect, 1952 saw the creation of the anti-communist law and new efforts to make culture part of state policy, as two ministries became responsible for its maintenance and propagation.[17]

After seizing power in 1958, Sarit Thanarat and his Revolutionary Group continued the marrying of the political communism of the 1930s with the culturalization of communism under national security. Using the "Communist menace," Sarit's first act was to abolish the constitution and parliament. The coup group made clear that the communist threat was first and foremost a cultural threat. The "clear infiltration of Communism" was "everywhere" and it represented "the great danger attempting to influence the minds of the Thai people." Through political, economic, and social infiltration, communists were attempting "by every means to ruin the country, undermine the throne, annihilate Buddhism, and destroy every institution preserved by the Thai nation [attained] with such sacrifice." In addition, "some self seeking groups" had:

> taken advantage of the constitutional system to destroy the peace, to use their rights and liberties as tools to obstruct programs, create divisions, incite disunity in the nation, persuade the people to be enemies [of] one another, wanting to see only difficulties, deterioration, and final destruction of the nation.

The constitution had to be abolished for "its provisions were not binding enough to cope with the present situation." Soon a new constitution which was "strong enough to fight the dangers that confront the nation" would take its place. The proclamation stated the parliament also "ceases to exist as well" for it was no longer a "tool" right for the job. "New tools," the *coup* group claimed, "were necessary to improve the nation as desired."

One of those new tools was *watthanatham*. The Revolutionary Group maintained, "Most important of all . . . the king and Thai nation are inseparable," and the Group would use "its full strength and ability" to "do everything to keep the king in a revered position."[18] Citizens were called on "to cooperate with the Government to eliminate from Thailand, the nation's enemies, the Communists." If the communists persisted, the Revolutionary Group guaranteed "they will meet with retaliation more rigorous than has ever been known in the history of Thailand."[19] Although Coup Decree No. 17 did not use *watthanatham*, attacks that degraded the "Thai people" or "nation", could be construed as "cultural" (see Appendix IV).

These positions formed a bridge between the more "political" provisions of the 1952 anti-communist law and the more "cultural" provisions that would become explicit in its 1969 revision. As "abnormal times" became increasingly normal, "culture" moved toward the center of official ideology. The implicit connection between communism and violations of culture exposed in the 1966 *Phra* Phimontham case became explicit in the 1969 revision of the anti-communist law. The cultural aspects that Phibun had wanted to be included in the 1952 act finally became law seventeen years later, in a more direct and comprehensive way.

A key section in the 1952 law described "Communist activities" as those that sought "the overthrowing of a democratic form of government of which the King is the Head." Its counterpart in the 1969 revision described "Communist Activities" as those that sought to "undermine national security, the institution of religion, the institution of the monarchy, or the democratic form of government with the King as Head of State." The terms became more all-encompassing. "Overthrow" was replaced by "undermine," "a democratic form of Government" became "national security" including the institutions of religion and monarchy. The vague terms of the 1969 law lent themselves to a cultural interpretation, greatly widening the scope of the interpretation of "communist."

But Section 9 of the 1969 law takes us completely across the bridge; from this point culture became clearly identified as a concern of "national security." More importantly, Section 9 clearly draws out the cultural aspect. Below, the 1952 measure and then its 1969 revision:

> *1952 law, Section 9.*—Whoever shall provide support to a Communist Organization or Member in any of the following ways,
>
> 1 provide lodging, residence, or meeting place,
> 2 induce any person to become a member of the organization or group,
> 3 give money, or provide any other type of equipment, shall be punished with imprisonment from five to ten years.[20]

The 1969 revision lets the first two items in this provision stand unchanged, but adds an entirely new third clause, which outlaws anyone attempting:

> *1969 law, Section 9.*
>
> (3) to encourage any other person to lose their faith in religion, or any act which destroys the traditions and customs of the Thai race, or encourages any other person to lose their doctrine which has principles and practices in causing people to lose their faith in religion or the traditions and customs of the Thai race . . . shall be punished with imprisonment from five to ten years.[21]

A completely new phrasing became law, a newcomer to the set of defamation-based laws. The 1969 law described a successful defamatory statement or action against "religion" or the "Thai race" as: loss of faith, destruction of traditions and customs, and loss of principles and practices. There had been no hint of such wording in the communist law of the 1930s or in the 1950s text.

In 1969, "culture" became a legally defined set of beliefs and practices. Violations against culture could result in ten years' imprisonment. Since the law made no effort to define or specify "the principles and practices" or "traditions and customs," any "cultural" reference could be in violation. Nor was there any definition of "the Thai race." Exactly who was part of the "Thai race"? This wording contrasts with the 1935 Sakon Nakon case, where the defendants were in possession of literature extolling soviets stamped with red hammers and sickles, in the hopes of overthrowing the state: all "normal" communist things. Thirty years later, the charge of communism could be levelled at anyone who questioned or critiqued religion or who caused someone else to question traditions and customs. Phibun's 1952 draft included sections touching on religion (these were included in the 1969 version), but even his clause prohibiting those who instigate children to disobey their parents could have easily fit into this culturalized 1969 law.[22]

Most importantly, with this law came the fruition of an impulse as old as the Thai state itself: a law that in its provisions both created and consolidated a vision of the relationship between rulers and ruled, between insiders and outsiders, between those who love the nation and those who work for its destruction. The 1969 law created a "people-ness," the perceived blood-similarity of a certain "race" of people with certain shared traits. The law contained nothing about local traditions, dialects, or the protection of a diversity of cultures within the borders of Thailand. Instead, it was an expression of state-sponsored monoculture and of a single people. The defamation principle became fully realized.

The 1969 revision also reiterated, along with other laws of the time, the pretense that Thailand was governed by a "democratic form of Government with the King as Head of State." Despite the reality of tightly controlled military dictatorships, repeating this phrase over and over allowed the government and Thai society to somehow reconcile these two contradictory positions and believe that both could be true at the same time.

The 1969 revision also laid out a framework by which the state could designate "infiltrated areas," giving civilian officials power similar to that afforded the military under martial law, and regulating many key aspects of everyday life, especially in the countryside. This portion of the law, with later revisions in 1976 and 1979, greatly enlarged the scope and size of the initial anti-communist law. It allowed for the "anti-communist-ization" of Thai society. Section 14 designated each government-appointed provincial governor the "Provincial Director for the Suppression of Communist Activities." Each Provincial Director would be responsible to a regional director, who would also be the military commander of that region. Provincial Directors had the power to, among other things, order the handing over of all weapons; forbid meetings; demand employment and behaviour records from businesses; hold people "for questioning" for periods of up to fifteen days per time; forbid television or radio, or the use of public ways; check all printed matter and mail;, and set up controls over rice, food, and medicine. Anyone violating these regulations could be imprisoned for up to two years. Also, suspected persons could be held for up to sixteen months without being charged or brought before a judge. Military and police officials could arrest and search suspects without a warrant.[23]

The provisions of the anti-communist law and this intense focus on anti-communism combined to form the basis for the complete militarization of Thai society. Not only was one political vision and practice made compulsory, the state attempted to reach down into the minds of every citizen and regulate thought. Although much of this process was directly tied to "anti-communism," a greater, over-arching discourse on national security was forming.

The *Phra* Phimontham case and the change of state perspective reflected in the amendments of the communist act aid in explaining the drastic charges made against the "Bangkok 18"—the student leaders arrested in the aftermath of October 6, 1976. They were charged with: conspiring to commit communist acts; acting against the internal security of the state; *lèse-majesté* against the heir-apparent; assembling in a group of ten or more people to use deadly force with arms; causing chaos and confusion in the land; trespassing in the middle of the night; resisting and opposing state authorities engaged in the lawful execution of their official duties; murder and attempted murder of state authorities engaged in the lawful execution of their official duties; and the unlawful possession of firearms, ammunition, and explosive materials without a permit. The charge sheet against the student group explained that communism was a crime "of exceptional circumstance in regards to the security of the country and peace and order of the people." In "order to fulfil their objectives," during the period from 6 December 1973 to 6 October 1976, the defendants and many others had "both during the day and in the middle of the night . . . dared to incite, advise, instil, and propagandize to the people" that "the government was not good. It ruled oppressively and exploited the people. It was of capitalists and feudalists, and caused peasants, labourers, and poor people to receive injustices and inequality, causing the people to adhere to violence and fight." The defendants and many others "who had fled and were yet unapprehended" distributed pictures of "cultural progress" and information about the economy and society of the People's Republic of China. They had "propagandized" the view that a country under a communist system was "more advanced and progressive than Thailand which is under a democratic system." The goal of the defendants was:

> to have the people hate and disparage the government, to have the people have faith in communism, and in order to cause so much turmoil and rebelliousness among the people that disquietude would arise within the kingdom, and in order that the people break the laws, change the

> government through violent force, to seize the power of the state, which are not actions within the aims of the constitution, and which is not the expression of an honest opinion.

The defendants and others also "dared" to go into factories and hotels and organize the workers and conduct strikes "in order to create economic turmoil" and "changes in the laws." On 5 and 6 October, the defendants refused to end their demonstration at Thammasat University and disperse when ordered. Instead, the defendants and their associates attacked "the police, government authorities, and the people" with weapons and deadly force, "causing turmoil in the land." The defendants sought to "overthrow or change the constitution, to overthrow the legislative power, the administrative power, [and] the juridical power of the constitution." This was, in short, "rebellion." All of this was done, the charge sheet continued, against "the objective of democratic form of governance with the king as head of state" and for the abolition of private property and the confiscation of private land and the means of production without just compensation. These are the actions of communists, the charges concluded.[24]

The legal foundations for culture, organized around "Thainess," were now set. The succeeding October 1976 coup cleared away the underbrush of elected government and legitimate constitutions. Martial law transformed regular courts into military courts. The regime of Thainess could now begin.

"Thainess"

Culture, security [*khwam mankhong*], and identity [*ekkalak*], under the auspices of Thainess [*khwam pen thai*], came together as a nascent ideological formation in the late 1950s. The appointment of the first director of the newly-created 1959 National Security Council was none other than Wichit Wathakan.[25] Wichit served as the major architect for the cultural provisions under Phibun in the early 1940s. Phibun and some of his cronies fled the country in 1957 or were replaced by Sarit's people. Not only did Wichit survive the purge, but he emerged as Sarit's principal ideologue. Wichit popularized the terms, *kamphatthana* [development] and *patiwat* [revolution], in much the same manner as he, two decades earlier, had popularized *watthanatham* [culture]. Although the National Security Council concerned itself with all matters of "national security," military and otherwise, the appointment of Wichit as its first director—known more for his literary and cultural talents than military acumen—indicated that the military government implicitly recognized the connection between security, power, and culture.[26]

Not only did various institutions and agencies emerge to protect and preserve national security, but the subject of national security itself expanded well beyond military issues. Topics of articles from 1959 to 1988 in *Ratthaphirak*, the magazine of the National Defence College, connected national security to seemingly every conceivable issue, from human resource management to the railroad, from moral principles to bamboo.[27]

While the government set up a number of bodies to oversee merging security, development, and identity, the main ones were the National Identity Board (NIB) and the National Culture Commission of Thailand (NCCT). The NCCT was set up by an act of parliament in 1979 and NIB in 1980.[28] The latter determined the unique qualities of the Thai.[29] Connors argues that now "state actors addressed the people as specifically 'Thai', the attributes of which were exemplified by the king," thus producing an "intimate democrasubjection."[30] In Chapter 9 I noted that Connors describes "democrasubjection" as "subjection of people to imaginary forms of their own rule." If parliamentary democracy was denied to the people, then the people could partake "in their own rule" through their Thainess. The nature of Thainess was determined by the NIB and dictated by the NCCT, linking it to the discourse on national security.

In describing its origin, a NCCT booklet from the early 1980s stated that, although "it had been a tradition that culture and culture-related activities are the responsible domain of all governmental agencies, private sectors and common citizens," it was only during World War II that "the Government began to view culture as a key dimension in the process of nation building and decided to assume a more active role in cultural development." The booklet claims that the development plans of the economy after Sarit came into full power in 1958 "failed to incorporate the cultural dimension."[31]

The commission was necessary "because culture is something which shows the specific characteristics of the nation, and the uniqueness of the people in the nation which is the important root of the steadfastness and stability of the country-nation."[32] Therefore, the commission was the result of "the rediscovery of the interest and need to preserve, develop and strengthen Thai culture." The commission's membership came from the Ministry of Education, the Office of University Affairs, the Department of Local Administration (under the Ministry of Interior), and the Departments of Public Relations, Religious Affairs, and Fine Arts. In general, the work of the commission was to:

> formulate plans and projects; to promote and develop national culture; to draw on cultural heritage and bring its influence to bear on educational, economic, political and social development; and to cooperate and coordinate with governmental units, state enterprises and private sectors involved in the enforcement of culture and culture-related laws.[33]

In defining the cultural aspects of the National Economic and Social Development Plan for the early 1980s, the Commission established four programs: "Construction Programme," "Offense Programme," "Reinforcement Programme," and "Cultural Exchange Programme." Targeting "in-school children," "key public officials," and "all other citizens," the construction programme was "designed to encourage all citizens to generate new thinking which will result in new behaviour consistent with national development." However, "all that is new is to be based on traditional ideas and values." A "priority list of activities" for the "revitalization of five basic social values" included:

1 Self-reliance, diligence, responsibility
2 Moderation in spending and saving
3 Discipline, law and order
4 Adherence to religious teachings
5 Love of King, country and religion.[34]

In 1981, the Prime Minister's Office issued a directive announcing the government's commitment to culture. Because Thai culture "is an expression of the Thai identity, the foundation on which national unity and security are fostered," the government, "with vigour and commitment," needed to ensure "preservation and the promotion of Thai culture." According to this announcement, culture was "the reflection of national honour, pride and aspirations, the guiding principle for the people to lead noble lives conducive to self-development, to the development of society and of the nation." Two strategies were followed. First, the government would strive to "promote the preservation of Thai culture" in every way "so that it becomes an important tool for solving problems" encountered in development and "for [protecting] national sovereignty, for protecting tradition and religion from wanton destruction, for maintaining religious purity consistent with the concepts of moral and spiritual development of the people." Second, the government would "propagate Thai culture in all aspects" in order to "generate intellectual awareness on the importance of culture and its bearings on national identity, honour, unity and sovereignty."[35]

I end with a brief examination of a 1980s government booklet, "Guidelines in the Maintenance, Promotion, and Development of Culture of 1984." In sketching out the purpose of the guidelines, the government explained that "global society is changing rapidly in every area." Every society must adapt or it will be unable to solve its problems. Guidelines for "conducting life that is in line with the flow of change" are needed. The private sector, people, and the government would work out a "long-term policy" for "together carrying out cultural work."

As with the 1942 measure, these guidelines attempt a definition of culture. Among other things, the guidelines define culture as something that "results from the collective conduct and practices in a single and continuous line of the members of that society." The guidelines also admit to the possibility that culture could change: "if the members accept and adhere to a model of collective conduct and practice, such can be held to be the culture of that society." Having a common model of behavior might be a good thing when the "original culture" does not match the "conditions of time and place." In such circumstances, "that culture" might need "improvement, change, or development" in order to "make it more suitable and efficient in the modern age." There may be a diversity of cultural practices in a given society and differences may be tolerated as long as they "do not cause any damage to the collective society." "Culture," the guidelines go on to say, "is both the foundation and a tool in building harmonious and firm unity among the people." It "helps lead people to conduct themselves morally, to follow the *dharma*, and to be ready to face life collectively across the same land in both good and bad times. " Finally, the guidelines posit that culture is "identity" and

> the outstanding qualities of that nation . . . which has a part in helping the people in the nation to have a feeling that they are of the same group, which would give rise to love and unity which would have an effect on the unified force of the group and maintain national security.

The section on "Areas that should be developed in Thai culture," list "attributes" that are not merely in line with the thinking of Wichit, Sarit, and Phibun, but also in the tradition of lists and formulas within the Thai Theravada Buddhist tradition. The guidelines proclaim, that members of Thai society are:

> [to] follow in practice that which is correct and good and beautiful in matters of the official national culture collectively and locally as follows:
>
> 1 The raising and training of children in the family, the relationships in the family, in society, and with people of foreign nationalities.
> 2 Work, vocation, and using time usefully.
> 3 Cleanliness, healthiness, environment, nutrition, and medicine.
> 4 Thai language, communication, and literature.
> 5 Entertainment, sports, recreation and leisure, and mental health.
> 6 Conserving and protecting both material and spiritual cultural heritage such as the fine arts in the areas of sculpture, architecture, painting, literature, music, dance, archaeological sites, archaeological relics, historical sources, respectful/submissive politeness, and kindness.
> 7 Preserve the image [*phap lak*], reputation, and honor and pride of Thai culture in the world community.
> 8 Creativity and seeking of knowledge, growth academically, and handing down culture which is in accordance with Thai society.
> 9 The national religion, religions which have secured themselves in Thailand, philosophy, order and discipline, traditions and customs, popular values, and Thainess.
> 10 The institutions of the monarchy, politics, governance, ideology, and national security.[36]

This national security discourse was heavily supported by academics. Prasong Soonsiri, head of the National Security Council but who had no academic qualifications, shared his ideas on the relationship between Thai language and national security in a 1984 seminar.[37] Discourses on identity spread into all aspects of intellectual life as well. In a typical event, most of the papers produced for a 1985 National Identity Board seminar entitled, "National Identity and Thai National Development" linked identity, security, and development.[38]

It is misleading to simply say that security came to encompass more than just military issues. Rather, it is more accurate to say that national security, through the workings of the defamation regime within an endless state of exception, became the means by which the whole of Thai society was militarized and culturalized. If, in the 1960s, displays of nationalist fervor were largely organized by the government (as witnessed in the protests against the decision of the World Court decision in 1961 on a "disputed" temple on the Thai-Cambodian border), within forty years it had become a self-perpetuating mechanism.[39] The government did not need to re-establish the Ministry of Culture in 2002, for the entire polity had long been essentially a Ministry of Culture.

And, of course, "the communist" had never really been the ultimate traitor. The Thai system easily accommodated and absorbed the former communist rebels back into mainstream society in the late 1970s and early 1980s. The problems were not the outside influence of Chinese communists or shifting geopolitical configurations. In the 1970s, the Communist Suppression Operations Command (CSOC) re-geared to become the Internal Security Operations Command (ISOC). Who was the enemy now?

The revision of the anti-communist law in 1969 reflected an oceanic shift in the Thai body politic. When anti-communism became culturalized, the 1969 law began a journey that took it away from any reference to communism and instead reflected a newly constituted authoritarianism based on the principles of the defamation regime, juridically shaped within the emerging legal space of the state of exception, articulated by the state ideology of Thainess. Thongchai argues that this conceptual world was further propagated within a "discourse of national security" which,

> is undoubtedly a very effective paranoia put into Thai people's heads by the Thai state. The creation of . . . the enemy in particular, is necessary to justify the existing political and social control against rivals from without as well as from within. Without this discursive enemy, all of the varieties of coercive force, from a paramilitary organization on every border of Thailand to the professional army, would be redundant. In contrast to the general belief, the state and its security apparatus survive because of the enemy . . . The enemy must be presented, produced, or implicated and then discursively sustained. It is always projected—if not overtly *desired.* (original emphasis)[40]

This chapter has explained the general framework of coercion that put a discourse about the enemy "into Thai people's head." This discourse defined and defended, narrowed and isolated (and has been left with only) Thainess, against which it produced the most enduring enemy: those opposed to the official configurations of Thainess. Recent events have shown (discussed in the Introduction and Chapter 13), that the qualifications for entrance to full Thainess have narrowed. The following account from 2008 demonstrates this.

In the charge against Jakrapob Penkair (Chapter 8), the decipherer of his message centers on one passage in the transcript as proof of betrayal. Jakrapob was asked by a reporter whether he had claimed that Thaksin's loyalty to the monarchy was 100 percent. Jakrapob said, no, he had not said that. When asked to clarify, Jakrapob said that Thaksin had "*some*" loyalty to the Throne. In the police investigator's mind, this was proof of Thaksin's treachery, and, by association, Jakrapob's. The climax of a Chulalongkorn University linguist's unravelling of Jakrapob's speech comes when the linguist explains, "Only one sentence can explain it; all his intentions in saying other things were excuses" obscuring his real crime:

> People who have studied English or foreigners, even ordinary Thai children who study English in primary school can tell you that 'some loyalty' means 'partial loyalty' not 100 percent. In considering what Jakrapob said, you have to think about his attitude, and the attitude of the people behind him, towards the institution.[41]

To have anything less than absolute loyalty for the throne was tantamount to treason. It was—it is—all or nothing. Thai must be monarchists. Not being a monarchist is to be against the throne, and to be against the throne is not to be Thai.

11 Thai-ification and colonization

When Senator and Vice President of the Public Welfare Council of Thailand Somporn Thepsitha learned of the story in 1997, he was evidently touched, and felt it merited government attention. In Saraburi province, a mother dog had been poisoned, leaving behind eight puppies. They might have died, had it not been for the "unselfish" actions of "Jong," a 1-year-old male dog who, after eating, rushed over to the puppies and provided them with nutrition by throwing up what he'd eaten. When the puppies were done, "Jong" cleaned them up by licking their little mouths. Somporn said, "The council has praised many humans for their good deeds in the past, but this time, it is a dog's turn to have a heart as beautiful as a human's. The council will give 'Jong' a monthly salary of Bt1,000 so that his owner has money to feed him and his puppies." Then Somporn suggested: "The dog should be known as 'Amazing Dog' to mark the Amazing Thailand tourism campaign so people will know that Thai dogs can do good deeds, while *some expensive foreign breeds cannot*."[1] (emphasis added)

These kinds of stories are common in Thailand; they evidence a need to put Thai *something* in a positive light, especially in comparison with foreigners. Why, we might ask, did Somporn feel it was so important that "people will know" such things? What people? Thai? Foreigners? What purposes do these statements serve? What quality of mind do they show, and how did it develop?

I noted that seditious rebellion as a criminal code violation disappeared after 1957. Its essence was recaptured in 1958 in Coup Decree No. 17 (repealed in 1975) and then revived in Coup Decree No. 42 in 1976, which was in effect until early 1991. From 1991 seditious rebellion as a crime ended (Chapter 4). Seditious rebellion thus had a lifespan of about 91 years. By mid-1992, there remained but two vigorously pursued defamation-based crimes—personal defamation and *lèse-majesté*. But the spirit of seditious rebellion remained a *quasi*-social offense, connected to the notion of Thai uniqueness.

Seditious rebellion after 1991 no longer had to be a crime; it did not have to be, either, for by then the Thai population, and particularly the Merit Seekers (Chapter 6), had become thoroughly and irretrievably habituated to the logic and impulse of *defamation thinking*—of viewing external information about self/collective self in relation to collective self and the world focusing on the source of the information rather than its contents. Defamation thinking became a self-fulfilling cosmos of an endlessly repeating monologue (imagined as a dialogue) between the avatars of Thainess and those who appeared to offend it. "Thai-ification" describes the internal colonization of Thai race/ethnicity and its claimed attributes within the borders of Thailand. But beyond the geographical and conceptual borders of Thailand was the launch of a colonizing mission into the minds and lands of non-Thai. Thai individuals and the Thai government have engaged in a crusade to purify the minds of ignorant or evil-minded foreigners and to demand their obeisance to Thainess, to expunge any manifestations counter to the official view of Thailand anywhere. We might argue that, in the Thai case, the "state of exception" has exceeded the boundaries of the juridical system, spilled over into culture and notions of the truth within Thailand, and then finally (and rather incredibly) has resulted in attempts to export the state of exception abroad.

Uniqueness of Thai uniqueness

Thailand's uniqueness is expressed in ubiquitous phrasing that runs something like this: "Thailand means the Land of the Free; Thailand was the only Southeast Asian country to never be colonized by a Western power." Though scholars have punched holes in this formulation since at least the 1970s, the population as a whole has yet to seriously question it.[2] When this notion is linked to the development of Thainess in the late 1970s, the notion of Thailand's historical uniqueness was extended into the realms of religion, culture, and anywhere else it could find a grip. We can see this process as twofold: the first deepens and internalizes defamation thinking within the Thai population at large (in the form of Thainess); the second embarks into the extra-Thailand world and attempts to colonize foreign minds with a respect for the importance and antiqueness of Thainess.[3]

Within this context the excitement over the dog "Jong" can be appreciated. Over the past two decades, things "Thai"—Thai food, Thai culture, Thai products, Thai qualities—have become increasingly commodified. This has gone hand-in-hand with an "ethnicization," a Thai anthropomorphization of things. Dinosaur bones discovered in the Northeast led to the declaration of ethnically infused "Thai dinosaurs."[4] It has extended to the distant, nominally pre-Thai past; "prehistoric ruins" or "ancient temples" within Thailand's modern borders are now termed *Thai* prehistoric ruins and *Thai* ancient temples. After 1997, one might have guessed that "Thai-style politics" or "Thai-style democracy" would have gone out of fashion. But after the 2006 coup, these anachronisms were revived and once again celebrated.[5] Even the king's favorite dog became remarkable for its close adherence to proper Thai social etiquette.[6]

It is not difficult to trace the history of this drive. Thongchai has described the dual process in the late nineteenth and early twentieth centuries of the Bangkok elite's "civilizing mission" within Siam and the definition of self as separate from "the Other Within."[7] Many scholars of nineteenth-century Siam have recognized, implicitly or explicitly, the proselytizing component of King Mongkut's religious "reforms": his drive for purification and purity inherently created a sense of uniqueness and provided a vehicle for propagation.[8] There are King Rama VI's curious speeches (r. 1910–25) in one of which the King said, when addressing members of the upper and bureaucratic classes joining his Wild Tigers Corps, "I would like to persuade and plead to you all. You and I are the same. Can we for once think along the same lines? Please do not consider me a human being. Please think of me as a Thai human being."[9] Phibun Somgkhram's World War II administration pushed both its "Cultural Mandates," designed to instil a love for all things Thai (except embarrassing un-modern things like chewing betel nut) and irredentism that took advantage of a weakened France and Great Britain and "took back" areas of present-day Laos, Cambodia, Myanmar, and Malaysia as part of a great pan-Thai empire.[10]

This process of Thai-ification was most deeply ingrained into Thai culture with its forcible entry into the state of exception following Sarit Thanarat's 1958 coup, in which Thai and foreign things and ideas were placed in opposition to one another. This sentiment was best described by Sarit's foreign minister:

> The fundamental cause of our political instability in the past lies in the sudden transplantation of alien institutions on to our soil . . . If we look at our national history, we can see very well that this country works better and prospers under authority, not a tyrannical authority, but a unifying authority around which all elements of the nation can rally.[11]

Thus, it is no surprise that during this same period we find the first explicit Thai-ification programs. The *thammathut*, or "envoy of the Dhamma" program, initiated in 1964, sent monks on proselytizing missions as part of what Ishii terms "basically a Buddhist missionary or propagandist" effort. Monks engaged in "missionary activities" that "included preaching to villagers and giving guidance in Buddhist study and meditation techniques to officials, school children, convicts and others." The program's formative moment came when the head of a government agency working with hill tribes "discovered for himself the importance of Buddhism's role as a spiritual bond between Thais" and set the hill tribes as one of the program's primary targets. Despite lack of success, the program indicates this growing expanse of what and who should be Thai-ified.[12]

McCargo argued the view of uniqueness permeates mainstream Buddhism: "Rather than advocating the universalism which some have seen as the essence of Buddhist teaching, most Thai monks and Buddhist thinkers have preferred to espouse a particularistic worldview, placing Thailand at its centre." The leading voice of Thai Buddhism is Dhammadipok (Prayudh

[P.A.] Payutto), whose writings "contrast the positive aspects of Thai Buddhism with negative features of other cultures, especially western culture."[13] Such examples lead to a conceit about the uniqueness of all things Thai—incomparable with anything or anywhere else in the world—yet understandable only to Thai.

Something of a Thai-driven "universalism" has developed between Thai Buddhists and science. Tambiah recounts that in the nineteenth century, decidedly unscientific aspects of Thai Buddhism were played down.[14] However, more recently, writers such as Prayudh Payutto and foreign scholars of Thai Buddhism have gone to great lengths to show science in Buddhism: a belief that the Buddha perfectly described the nature of the world, human society, and scientific psychology and, only now, is Western science catching up.[15] Prayudh writes, "Another aspect of long interest to the Buddhist has been the scientific nature of Buddhism. There is a usual claim, and also a pride among the Buddhists that Buddhism is the most scientific of all religions."[16] Within the framework we describe here, such statements are attempts to say that Buddhists can apprehend reality and the truth better than others. When this sentiment is tied to the belief that Thai practice the most authentic Buddhism, or the interesting contention that the Buddha actually lived in Thailand (rather than India), then the inference is that Thai Buddhists are closest to Buddhist truth, which is really just scientific truth, as shown in this remarkable claim from a website:[17]

> Buddhists are closer to the real truth of the world as described by science; Thai Buddhists are the closest to real Buddhism and the Buddha. Therefore, amongst the world's peoples, Thai have the greatest apprehension of truth.

This formulation suggests one of the most prominent (and contradictory) features of the defamation regime: defamation thinking (which has a tendency not to look at the truth of the matter) is strongest in societies that feel in possession of a rather exclusive channel to truth and reality.

We turn to a stunning example of defamation thinking in the events surrounding the 1993 edition of the UK-published *Longman's Dictionary* whose entry for "Bangkok" read,

> [T]he capital city and main port of Thailand. It is famous for its TEMPLES ... and other beautiful buildings, and is also often mentioned as a place where there are a lot of PROSTITUTES." [original emphasis].

A furor ensured when this definition was revealed to the Thai public. Speaking for all Thais who were "appalled and outraged at this inappropriate description," the Thai ambassador to Great Britain contacted the publisher and requested that Longman make a "correction" of this "extremely unfair" characterization. Minister of Interior Chavalit Yongchaiyudh lashed out at the definition as "unacceptable to the 50–60 million Thais." Angry students protested in front of the British embassy, burning the book in effigy for "unfairly building a morally and ethically bad image of the Thai people." The Special Branch's Bangkok Press Officer charged that the book "offended Thai people's moral standards," citing the Press Act of 1941 in banning the book from Thailand.[18]

Longman representatives explained that the Dictionary sought to "set words in their cultural context" by "draw[ing] its information from a wide range of sources." In doing so, the definition "intended to reflect the popular meaning of words," and thus developed "a commonly held image of the capital abroad . . . The definition of each word is in accordance to what it is, and not what one wishes it to be."

The crime in this case was, essentially, defamation of the nation. As with any defamation charge focusing on insult rather than truth, the characterization was seen as unfair. And of course, the discussion of the truth never became the issue. Longman made its case. Longman's position was rejected not because it was untrue, but because it tainted the image of Thailand.[19]

Abhisit Vejjajiva, Democrat Party member and government spokesperson at the time, engaged in a lively line of defamation thinking. First, he attacked the source country: He suggested a Thai dictionary define England as "a former colony hunter that killed scores of natives." London could be defined "as a place full of prostitutes," and England as having terrorist groups such as the Irish Republican Army. Then, he made a sociological observation: "Maybe the West does not have much of a prostitution problem. That's because their sexual behaviour is more promiscuous and they don't have to pay for it." He questioned the academic credibility of the dictionary: The definition "shows that the dictionary has a very low academic standard." Then, he provided a profit-driven explanation: Longman used a "sensational angle" as "News is largely about something that is not normal. It is not the general situation of the country." He cited his personal experience: "I have never known anyone who knew Thailand look at us that way."[20] But what seemed worse of all was the publisher's apparently hostile intention: Longman "did not understand the Thai Government's concerted effort to solve the problem."[21]

Abhisit's response to Longman focused on three aspects: (1) England's hypocrisy; (2) its morality; and (3) selfishness, malice, and deliberate misrepresentation of English culture. Abhisit's final comment above asserts evil or ignorant intent (how could Longman say such things when the Thai government was so sincere?), combined with, strangely enough, an implied confirmation of the truth of the dictionary's contents. The Thai police used a defamation-based law to ban the book (which also made it illegal to even possess it).[22]

But even if the law had not been used, the incident shows how deeply entrenched defamation thinking had become in defining Thailand. The final scenes of the drama show two other impulses of the defamation regime: in the end Longman bowed to the pressure, apologized, and promised to remove the definition. All was good again (see a similar outcome to the Sangsidh case in Chapter 7).[23]

In the final scene the Thai cabinet of ministers resolved to commit itself to Longman's education: the Minister of Foreign Affairs said, "The ministry will give special attention to child prostitution in its efforts to give the publisher a better perception of the government's continuing attempt to curb the flesh trade."[24] This response shows how defamation thinking reframes issues in ways that miss the original point, as Longman never mentioned child prostitution.

Who or what was protected in the outrage over the Longman definition? Were Thai fearful that foreigners reading the definition might misunderstand Thailand? Should the definition have omitted reference to prostitutes and instead depicted Bangkok as "a place where the government earnestly fights against child prostitution"? Did the protesting citizens fear that they might become subverted by a definition in an English dictionary? Prostitution-less (and misunderstood) Thailand became the hero of this drama. Longman was the villain, the insensitive, ignorant foreigner. The climax came when the hero stood up for his dignity and defiantly put the flame to the book. But who was the audience? And why was the performance even held?[25] A pseudonymous op-ed in *The Nation* framed the objective of the defamation accurately. Dr. M denounced the government's "image-defending" as deflecting attention away from the real problem—prostitution:

> The trick is to inflate the insult so that it looks like Thailand as a whole has been disparaged. The publicity is crucial: Thailand's image, reputation, collective-face gets hit so big so that everyone can see them. This foreign agent makes a perfect target because it can't defend itself, and as an outsider it makes it easy to rally all Thais together in the orgy of abuse.[26]

Imagined audience

Chapter 8 discussed a 1978 *lèse-majesté* case concerning a press agent who said that his kick-boxer was protected by the king's charisma. The case revealed an odd detail. The agent's words were in *Thai*. The newspaper that published the agent's words was a modest *Thai* language newspaper in a Northeastern city. The case was heard by a regional *Thai* military court. The court ruled that stating that a king was responsible for a victory, as a way to honor the king, was acceptable. But to say something about the king prior to the match was unacceptable because "there was no surety of who would win and who would lose." If the boxer lost, though, the court said, "it would cause some of the people to misunderstand and be confused about the charisma of the king, *including foreigners as well*"[27] (emphasis added).

This statement reflects a peculiar construction of the Thai worldview. The court inferred that it understood and was clear "about the charisma of the king." Some Thai might not be. But why include foreigners? What might foreigners "misunderstand or be confused about?" The inclusion reflected an assumption by the court that foreigners were following the case. Two questions come to mind: first, how would they? Even the report of the case to a national audience was in a Thai language newspaper, *Matichon*. Second, even if the case was reported in an English language newspaper, why would foreigners be particularly interested? Why was it necessary for them to understand?

In Chapter 9, I discussed the 1934 case of insulting religion in which a man was tried for digging in temple ruins in Ayutthaya. He was found guilty.[28] The court reasoned that even if no Buddhists had seen him, *had* they seen him, they *would have been* offended. The court decision evidences a certain quality of imagination, that an insult would be felt by imaginary worshippers who were not there in either time or space.

The court decision seems predicated on an imaginary dialogue running underneath Thai society, an internal one that preaches to Thai the importance of unity and preserving Thainess and another, possibly a monologue, that intones the virtue of things Thai to a supposed foreign audience.

I look at four examples out of many, all born of the same impulse, all with the objective of demanding foreigners understand truth, Thai style.

The first was in 2001, when Myanmar's *New Light of Myanmar* newspaper published three articles by Ma Tin Win of the Myanmar's Institute of Education, two of which prompted official Thai protests.[29]

One of the articles "How did opium arrive at the Golden Triangle region?," was apparently written in response to Thai accusations that the Myanmar government supported opium cultivation. What the Thai government found offensive were probably the following sentiments expressed in Ma Tin Win's piece: "As Siam (Thailand) had permitted the British to trade opium and to move it in the country at will, it is sure that it would grow poppy in the Golden Triangle area," and "Even the most inferior king of our nation had never let the nation fall under total subjugation without a fight though your king Maha Mongkut had done so. We have never signed any agreement with any nation to import opium."[30]

Another article, "Never been enslaved, but real slave," implied that King Mongkut was forced to acquiesce to British demands to sign an unfair treaty in 1855. Ma Tin Win claimed King Mongkut "thus gave away the country to keep his throne," commenced a relationship of "Neocolonialism" to the West, and so became effectively enslaved. But, "As King Mongkut was on the throne of Siam, there was no one who would say that Siam was enslaved. Its people would not know it. But it is a real slave. It is nothing else but a slave."[31]

After the last article's publication, the Thai Foreign Ministry charged that the articles had "gone beyond the accepted bounds and norms of behaviour by thoughtlessly affronting the most revered institution of the Thai nation. That has provoked deep resentment among the Thai public, which will inevitably cause severe damage to Thai-Myanmar relations."[32] The Burmese

Ambassador was summoned to hear a "strong protest" and the Thai Foreign Ministry demanded that "such an abomination" not occur again. The ambassador responded that the articles did not reflect the Burmese government's position. Later, the Thai parliament discussed the articles behind closed doors. Former deputy foreign minister Sukhumbhand Paribatra of the opposition Democrat Party called on the government to demand an "official and unconditional apology" as the articles "distorted history, included intolerable *lèse-majesté* elements," and were "flawed by ingrained prejudice and total disregard for historical accuracy."[33]

This Thai government reaction showed again the same level of discomfort at the thought of foreigners somewhere misunderstanding something about Thailand. The mere existence of the article, unread by Thai eyes, seemed offensive. That foreigners might have thoughts implying defamation of the Thai monarchy seemed wrong. Foreigners, too, had to understand Thai truth.

This same issue holds in our second case. That foreigners could presume to depict Thai history in any negative way was galling. This is best illustrated by the continuing discourse over Anna Leonowens, her books, the novel, the two cinematic dramas, and the musical.[34] Margaret Landon adapted her 1943 novel, *Anna and the King of Siam*, from Leonowens's *An English Governess at the Siamese Court* and then *Romance of a Harem* (1870, 1873, respectively). Landon's books then provided the basis for the movie of the same name in 1946, which was then turned into the 1956 musical *The King and I*, which then led to the 1999 non-musical adaptation, *Anna and the King*.[35] The original story has also spawned a series of works by foreign scholars on the king in question, King Rama IV (King Mongkut, r. 1851–68). These works tend to vilify Leonowens for her scurrilous account, impugning that she was a "two-faced widow of little class or breeding who caused immense embarrassment to the nation."[36]

Anna and the King has always been a lightning rod for cross-cultural misunderstandings and differences, and a fair amount of Thai and foreign scholarly effort has been expended on setting the record straight. One Asian newspaper mentioned in 1998 that Leonowens's volume has been a "widely disputed account" and that "scholars insist there are distortions" in the current script, with the highly improbable contention that the movies and play were "accepted as gospel in the West." The newspaper account goes on to state that it was King Mongkut "who began modernising the country with its first major contacts with the West while cunningly keeping at bay the European colonists who were carving up the rest of the region."[37]

However, Anna was not an issue in 1947 when the movie, *Anna and the King of Siam*, opened in Bangkok. Remarking that it was the "first time in Siamese history" that "evening dress was required in the cinema," *Time* magazine effused that many of those attending "arrived in shiny new Dodges and Buicks." "Almost all" of "Bangkok's elite" had apparently "read and discussed" Leonowens's account. The article stated, with surprisingly precise figures, "[l]eading Siamese critics and historians had taken pains to point out that it was more than 75% inaccurate." "The criticisms," *Time* confided, "only made the movie more of a treat, because most Siamese had expected the royal family to ban it altogether, or censor it beyond recognition." The regent, who represented and took care of the king's affairs when the king was still not of age to fully take the throne, "after careful consideration," left the movie untouched, saying, "The people want to see the film in its entirety, and in a democracy the people are the best judges." The verdict of the audience? *Time* reported it was "*sanuk dee*" or "very entertaining."[38]

This tolerant and almost playful, though still reverent, attitude toward the monarchy changed as the monarchy began to ascend in importance from the mid-1950s onward. Though not as *sanuk dee* as before, the royalty, after a private showing of the filmed musical version of *The King and I* in 1956, reportedly said that it contained "nothing harmful." In an appeal to the Thai government's Movie Censorship Board (MCB), Twentieth-Century Fox movie production company pointed out that members of the Thai media, without having seen the movie, said Yul Brynner, the actor who played the role of the king, "received audiences without wearing a shirt" and many parts were insulting. In the end, Phibun Songkhram, both prime minister and minister of interior at the time, prohibited the movie in Thailand.[39]

Fox argued that Phibun had no authority to make such an order and wanted the MCB to reconsider. Fox promised that if the movie were approved, an expert would check the script before subtitles were added and provide a special introduction, explaining that the movie's objectives were not to "insult the Thai people, government, royal family, or the king in any way." Twentieth-Century Fox averred that, compared to the non-musical version of the story, the movie *Anna and the King of Siam*, released to favorable audience response in Thailand in 1947, the 1956 version "raises the dignity of the Thai king, equal to helping to spread to foreign countries the Thai way of life in the past, and especially a story about the power of the Thai kings in the past."[40]

In a letter to the MCB on 9 September 1956, Phanuphanyukhon, a member of the Thai royalty, argued that although he did not feel satisfied with Fox "because it was a movie about a Thai king and Thai people which deviates [from the truth]," he nonetheless felt that it should be shown for a number of reasons. It sought to create fantasy and the characteristics of the people, the scenery, costumes, and Thai geography "were created with the intention of deviating from reality, not with the intention of having people understand the true conditions of the Thai people of Thailand." He suggested that the musical was better than the previous movie and even better than the book on which it was based.[41] He said the movie caused "many Americans to become interested in Thailand" and that as far as he knew, "this interest did not include looking down on [Thailand]." In conclusion, he said that

> Even if this movie in the eyes of the Thai would damage Thailand, the harm would be most likely only in foreign countries which they [the authorities in Thailand] could not control. It would not be damaging in Thailand because every Thai person was likely to understand that *farang* [Westerners] were ignorant and that the movie deviated from the truth considerably. The damage then would be to the *farang* themselves.

If it turned out that Americans came away from the movie believing that Thai were "narrow-minded and uncivilized," it would be "more deeply damaging to the Thai than if Thai people saw the movie." However, the MCB, in a 1965 re-vote, did not agree and the film was banned five-to-four.[42]

In the late 1990s, Twentieth Century Fox tried once more. It employed two royals, Supinda Chakrabhand and her sister to work over the script. Supinda complained that the original draft "was unfair to Thailand. It was a total defamation of Thai royalty." However, even with her help, the Film Board of Thailand (FBT) still turned it down, because, according to a newspaper account, "certain scenes were factually inaccurate or culturally implausible or potentially insulting to the Royal family, the institution of Buddhism or Thai people in general." In response, Twentieth Century Fox redrafted the script to give it "a new cinematic treatment," allowing Thai historians and other scholars "carte blanche to extensively revise" it. After three attempts, the script was still rejected. The grounds for objection were as follows: for "Dialogue which humiliates Siam and Buddhism," for a ship captain saying that "Siam is uncivilised, unlike Bombay and Singapore," for Louis (Leonowens's son) comparing "the sound of Buddhist monks chanting" with "bees in a beehive," and for an Indian nurse worrying that she would "be in the hands of a 12-year-old child" if King Mongkut were to die. "Inappropriate dialogue and acting" included the king's daughter dropping fruit on the king's head from a tree, the king addressing his children as "dear child," for the princesses calling Leonowens "dear ma'am," and for "eye contact" between Leonowens and King Mongkut "in a romantic scene." "Inappropriate characterization of King Mongkut" included the king saying Leonowens's crinoline was like a "moving snail" and the king speaking "in broken English without the use of verbs and articles," while at the same time attempting to use "big words" like "scientific" and "endeavour." The character of Louis is chided for making fun of the way the king walks and talks and by comparing him to Queen Victoria. The character of the king's daughter was "inappropriate" since it depicted her as "speaking English inaccurately." It was thought inappropriate that 11-year-old Prince Chulalongkorn would use "big words" like "imperialist" and "school teacher." Finally, moments of "Inappropriate setting and atmosphere" included depicting "an assassination attempt" in a Buddhist temple, vendors selling "reptiles like crocodiles," and having rubber trees in a scene of a northern Thai city because "they only grow in the warmer South."

With the aid of "five [unnamed] Thai historians," the scriptwriter tried once more. A press release from Twentieth Century Fox said "It's been a primary goal of the studio and filmmakers to ensure the cultural and historical accuracy requested by the local government." An aide to Supinda claimed this fifth script was "totally different from the version rejected previously" and Supinda herself said that in this version "King Mongkut will now be shown as a far-sighted person who used diplomacy, not military force, to keep threats from the colonial powers at bay." The historians would ensure, said an FBT member, that this version would be "in the interests of authenticity and historical accuracy." Supinda hinted at treasonous motives if the script were rejected this time, saying "it will look like somebody is allowing our history to be abused outside the country." Incredibly, Warner Brothers wanted in on the action, asking at the time for permission "to make an animated version of *The King and I*."[43]

However, *Anna and the King* was again banished. Even though academics had their hands in this version, the script was finally and forever banned because it "intentionally tries to undermine the monarchy and seriously distorts Thai history." The movie was filmed in Malaysia and the eventual video was also banned. When the police arrested a couple for selling CDs of the movie, it was unclear whether they would be charged with having banned material or *lèse-majesté*.[44]

The assumption made in both the Myanmar and *Anna and the King* cases is that Thai history is not disputed and the official version is the truth. Anything not in accordance with this characterization is not only defamatory, but, because it is defamatory, it must be a lie. Therefore in these cases it is never quite clear what separates inappropriateness from distortions from truth. As this study has argued, this is because there is no separation. The reasons for rejecting the scripts tend to conflate inappropriateness and inaccuracy. In total confidence, the FBT experts could state categorically that no such words or actions, or anything like them, ever took place. Of course by 1999 the reign of King Mongkut was well beyond any living memory.

There is little chance that any Thai historian could ever develop the script of a movie depicting King Mongkut in any fashion. The Thai-produced epics *Suriyothai* or *Ban Rajan* were historical movies covering periods safely in the murky past.[45] The FBT did not accuse these movies of portraying the past inaccurately, perhaps because the experts who condemned *Anna and the King* were the same ones consulted in making these movies. These movies were "genuine" from the beginning. No Thai has criticized the decision of the FBT or expressed discomfort with the state defining "history." Nor was there an analysis of the documents from that period to show that Leonowens was wrong. The truth had already been established regardless of facts or alternative possibilities. The depiction of the king by Anna Leonowens was insulting and demeaning. She was a low class woman given to flights of fancy and she intentionally depicted King Rama IV in a bad light. Because she was bad, her version of events was necessarily untrue.

A final case comes from halfway around the world. In 2002, Sherry Levin, owner of St. Jack's restaurant in Philadelphia, was suddenly "besieged by phone calls from angry Thai residents and officials." Threatening phone calls included dire warnings from Thai officials who said they would "stop issuing visas to Americans" and a UN official's promise to take up the matter with the Thai Ministry of Defence. The Thai government ordered its ambassador to the United States to raise the matter with the State Department. The Ministry of Foreign Affairs warned that there might be "possible repercussions on bilateral relations." The governor of Pennsylvania and mayor of Philadelpha were called upon to act. Both refused.

The cause of all the ruckus? An ad depicting Thailand's current King, Bhumibol Adulyadej, "as an urban hipster with bleached highlights and stone-encrusted glasses" was at the center of this furore.[46] Levin who could not believe the response, was quoted as saying, "Wow, you guys really have to lighten up." She said the ad was "just harmless fun." The threats, she said, "just seems so out of proportion." After phone calls from city officials and the State Department, she dropped the ad. "This has all been fun, but it was just getting too bizarre," Levin said. "I don't think now would be a wise time to run the ad again, unless I really wanted to agitate people, and that was never my intention."[47]

The lesson: for the parts of other cultures that intersected with Thai culture, it would be solely and strictly on the terms of the Thai defamation regime.

The 2006 coup as democracy

The events surrounding the September 2006 coup highlighted the deeply entrenched mechanisms of the defamation state. In addition to abuse of defamation-based laws, particularly *lèse-majesté*, a pervasive denial about the actual state of affairs became apparent, from the status of the coup to the violence in the South. A number of events during a one-month-and-a-half period—from early August to mid September 2007—illustrates this point. The military officers executing the 2006 coup were organized under the Council for National Security (CNS). In 2007, as it prepared to celebrate its one-year anniversary in power, its deputy director, General Phasit Sonthikhan, voiced some startling thoughts. He was reported to have said, "The only way to ensure that future democratic governments are not ousted by military coups is to give the armed forces a clear role in politics." Otherwise, the general warned, "the country cannot escape from coups." This sentiment makes it appear that democracy in Thailand has to ensure a role for non-elected persons (this would, of course undermine democracy). Remarkably, Phasit then went on to give a few instances where the military played a political role: in addition to "some African countries," he held up the decidedly undemocratic example of Burma.[48] Thoughts such as these no doubt failed to reassure those in Thailand and abroad about the country's smooth return to democracy. The military-appointed government had presided over the drafting of a new constitution which was coming up before Thailand's first-ever national referendum. Once the constitution passed, new elections would be held. At this point, Thailand's track record since 2006 had not been very encouraging:

- The early 2006 elections had been nullified on technical grounds.
- The military overthrow of an elected government had been internationally condemned..[49]
- The National Legislative Assembly (NLA), the Election Commission, the constitution-drafting committee, and the Constitutional Tribunal had all been installed by the military after the coup.[50]
- The Constitutional Tribunal had issued an order dissolving Thaksin's Thai Rak Thai political party and banned 111 of its executives from politics for five years.[51]
- Thirty-five provinces were under martial law during the period before the constitutional referendum.[52]
- There were indications of military involvement in lobbying for the new constitution.[53]

Nonetheless, a spokesperson for the Ministry of Foreign Affairs hoped that foreigners understood that Thailand was moving in the right direction, saying, "The next general election would be a key factor contributing to foreign countries' decision to normalize ties with Thailand."[54]

No doubt convinced of the Thai government's sincerity and "so the international community could be certain in the knowledge the poll is conducted in a free and transparent manner," the European Union (EU) offered to send a team to monitor the December elections.[55] Friedrich Hamburger, EU ambassador to Thailand, said, "This offer was made logically, to a friendly country that wants to return to a democratically elected government."[56] This was a normal gesture. Many governments in transition, such as Nepal, welcome international bodies, including the EU, to observe the elections.[57] The mandate of the EU monitoring teams "is to collect and verify information concerning the election process, to analyse the observations and, then, after the elections, to publish their findings. They have no authority to change, improve or correct any shortcomings that may occur in an election."[58]

An outbreak of defamation fever immediately resulted. To the perceived insult of Thailand being akin to a "failed state" and thus needing to be monitored, Prime Minister Surayud Chulamont and CNS chairman General Sonthi Boonyaratkalin rejected the offer. Sonthi turned it into a matter of the "third hand" and the evil intentions of the EU; he wanted to "get to the bottom of the matter so as to understand what has triggered a move for foreign supervision of the polls." Surayud misconstrued the offer as a desire of the EU to "interfere."[59] Foreign Minister Nitya Pibulsonggram retorted: "We in Thailand have a track record across history. We are not a failed state or on any watch list. We are mature. We can solve our own problems. I don't think we need anybody to teach us how to vote."[60] Secretary-general to the Election Commission (EC), Suthipol Thaweechaikarn said the EU's offer was "'degrading,'" putting Thailand into the category of a 'failed state'." EC chairman Apichart Sukhagganond said the proposed memorandum of understand (MoU) would make Thailand a "colonial state" and was concerned that the EU team members would "poke their heads into the polling booths."[61] Election commissioner Sodsri Satayathun felt, "allowing the EU to observe could 'do more harm than good to the country'" and that stipulations under the MoU "would send 250 officials to rural villages to spy on the election process."[62] Many NLA members opposed signing a MoU with the EU, claiming that the new constitution "requires any agreement having a bearing on sovereignty to be debated and approved by parliament." The doyen of dictatorship and NLA president, Meechai Ruchupan, intoned: "It is improper to supervise our election process unless we sign a (reciprocal) agreement which allows the [Thai] EC to supervise the EU's election," mis-comprehending the point that Thailand's last elected government had been deposed by a military coup.[63]

A *Bangkok Post* editorial approved of this outrage, saying that the types of expressions quoted above were "valid and justified." Writing as if there were some confusion somewhere in the world about Thailand, the editorial argued,

> Thailand may still be seen as being under military rule in the eyes of the international community. But it is definitely not a "failed state" or a "crisis state" that should require the presence of EU officials to perform a task beyond the role of an observer.[64]

A friendly gesture on the part of the EU turned into outrage at the suggestion that Thailand was a failed state or that the EU would presume to trample on Thai sovereignty. Indeed, this was an imaginary debate between Thai and Thai perceptions of the EU. It was imaginary because the EU had never suggested anything like it was accused of: it had maintained throughout that its mission was to monitor and that such monitoring was normal for states holding elections after political disruptions. The EU made no comment on the Election Commission, the quality of its work, or the capacity of the government to carry out the elections. As some observers noted at the time, Thailand had played "the nationalist card" over the issue of elections and the EU.[65] However, under the auspices of the defamation thinking, the focus shifted to the words and their perceived effect. Krit Garnjan-goonchorn, the Thai ambassador to the United States, reportedly felt, "the issue of international observers" triggered an impression of Thailand as a failed state." As a result, "We are not happy because it hurts our dignity."[66]

As the controversy with the EU was unfolding, CNS chairman General Sonthi ordered 93 Thai diplomats stationed in 61 countries "to explain to the international community that Thailand is serious about national reconciliation." Worried about foreign media reportage that was "unconstructive and unfavourable to Thailand's image," Sonthi said the diplomats should explain the present political situation, and that their "explanations would help to restore the international community's confidence in Thailand." He did not think the coup "put the country in a negative light," for it was "bloodless" and "acceptable to most people."[67] Prime Minister Surayud, for his part, planned to use his participation in the United Nations General Assembly "as a forum to convince the international community about the return of democracy to the kingdom" and to emphasize that "His government had upheld the principles of good governance from the day it took office." But he also would "meet leaders of several other countries . . . on the sidelines of the assembly to explain to them in person how hard his government has worked to end the country's political crisis."[68] The problem in Surayud's view was the image, and not the reality.

The defamation impulse engages in a three-step process. The first step was development of a Thai perception that there was a *misunderstanding*: the *Other* (foreigners) do not understand. *Others* did not understand that the coup was executed in the name of democracy. The generals and the meritorious people they appointed to the cabinet of ministers, the NLA, and the constitution drafting committee were committed to working for the nation, unlike the evil ones (Thaksin) who had worked for selfish ends.

Whether the coup was a "good coup," and the extent of palace involvement in the coup have been debated elsewhere.[69] The argument that exceptional circumstances justified a coup-for-democracy, or the denial of any palace involvement, was part and parcel of the defamation state and its skewed perception of reality: the coup and all it spawned was an exception to the rules.[70] From the perspective that the coup was good and justified, the offer from the EU was an affront, for it suggested that coups are a dramatic break in the progress of democracy.

The second step of the process was to create an *imagined dialogue* that impugned intentions, conjured up accusations (never actually made), and then fantasised in horror about the implications: loss of sovereignty, colonial state, foreign spies. This imagined dialogue targeted the domestic audience and was mainly a diversionary tactic that worked from the principle, the greater the perceived insult, the greater the diversion. The louder the public cry of insult, the more the reality of a coup could be obscured.

The third step of the process was to convert foreigners to this way of thinking. Since foreigners could not understand the true nature of the coup and the Thai concept of virtuous rule, then they had to be engaged not in public forums, but in private discussions. The focus became image and how to repair it, not addressing the deeper cause (such as the coup itself). It is ironic, perhaps, but also predictable, that incidents such as this become self-fulfilling prophecies. By not allowing outside monitors or by not addressing the issue of impunity (the coup makers included an amnesty for themselves in the new constitution), Thailand made its way into the "warning" category of a "failed state" index.[71]

This chapter has noted how the notion of uniqueness (Thainess) has gone hand-in-hand with the state of exception and how such conceptualizations have been defended or justified by defamation thinking. The cases examined involved questions of fact (are there a lot of prostitutes in Thailand?), of representation (the king as New Age icon), and of depictions (is Thailand a failed state?).

In these examples, the issue was primarily between Thailand and non-Thai. In his "Performative State," Peter Jackson describes the split Thai psyche embedded in "the regime of images," with one part performing for the outside world and the other acting within a closed "Thai" conceptual world. Within his conceptual framework, where effect is the exercise of power, Jackson argues that the present

> trenchantly conservative regime of power continues to draw strength by mobilizing widespread desires for international recognition, deploying for contemporary political benefit the pleasure produced when Thai performances of civilization and modernity are acknowledged on the international stage.[72]

This chapter described this inner Thai world, suggesting that the performance for the outside world has an imagined audience. The Thai state appears concerned about what foreigners think and this perception is often referred to in popular and official state culture. But the Thai state does not really engage the outside world so much as attempt to convert it. When outsiders speak admiringly of Thailand, such outsiders are sensitive and have an appreciation for Thainess and Thai uniqueness. When a critical voice is heard, it is quickly concluded that the outsider simply does not understand or, worse, has evil intentions. The performance of the state, to use Jackson's metaphor, is to an empty stage. The key condition is that the internal audience overhears the performance. The defamation state is now nourished on the "vast reservoirs of emotional energy" that animates "an apparatus of power directed against the Thai population and it continues to operate today as a highly effective means of silencing domestic political critics."[73]

12 Defamation and truth

A number of conditions have to be in place for defamation laws and their adjudication to have great social and political impact. In Thailand, at least up to the 1950s, the outcome of the majority of defamation cases had negligible social or political effect. Adjudication of personal defamation cases followed established norms. The Thai Supreme Court laid out standards and criteria on a par with the rest of the world concerning the distinction between an opinion and a fact. A 1936 Supreme Court decision, for instance, clearly spelt out such difference. Broadly speaking, the court said anything that can be proven as true or false can be considered to affirm or deny a fact. An opinion, on the other hand, is something which "each person" might have in "accordance to only their feelings and thoughts," which might prove to be "contradictory," "without beginning or end," and of which "the truth or falsity cannot be proved." Saying someone is a thief, for instance, is a statement of fact because it can be proved. But suggesting that one "does not see anything wrong with stealing" is an opinion "because its truth or falsity cannot be proved" and depends on one's own "principles." However, instances where a defendant can find exclusion through citing the expression of an opinion are few, for in most cases the words are inevitably an affirmation of a fact.[1] Jitti Tingsaphat says further that in certain cases even an opinion can be defamatory when, as if it were a statement of fact, it is made with "clarity and certainty" and "without ambiguity or vagueness."[2]

When both litigants are average citizens with no political connections and the matter is tried in civil courts, there are no collateral effects. Under the same conditions, however, when defamation is made a criminal offense, the state becomes involved in mediating what is defamatory; this, in turn, places the state in the role of determining some level of truth. The state plays a larger role when the offense is criminal and one or both of the litigants are politicians, civil servants, or otherwise influential people. When criminality and the importance of the target are placed within a defamation regime under the state of exception, the result can alter that society's view of truth.

Defamation thinking, as delineated in the last chapter, is the long-term effect of living under a defamation regime: focus on the truth of the issue is lost in deliberations on the perceived intent of the defamer or critic and the estimated impact the words might have on society. This penultimate chapter examines truth, reality, and perception within the context of the principles underpinning the defamation regime in Thailand. I have made the argument that pre-existing conceptions of truth within Thai Theravada Buddhism were relatively unchallenged and left largely intact because of Thailand's non-colonial past (Chapter 3). I have also noted that over the past century, the defamation regime has strengthened (rather than weakened, unlike in more democratic constitutional monarchies) (Chapter 4). The most significant shift was the 1958 coup, which solidified certain juridical trends that undermined the rule of law and sent Thailand spiralling into the state of exception—a state especially suited for the permanent establishment of the defamation regime (Chapter 5). As part of this, I ask the reader to recall the distinctions between "fact, opinion, comment," how these qualities are handled by defamation-based law and adjudication, and, most importantly, how each are conditioned by various exclusions (Chapter 2). We should also bear in mind how the identity of the target affects defamation adjudication and how such adjudication impacts greater society. When all these factors are considered, we can approach with more precision how defamation adjudication and thinking affect perceptions of Thai social, cultural, and political reality.

I look at "truth" in this chapter within three areas: news, art, and history, and then lay out a set of principles of truth under which Thai society has operated. I conclude with an exploration of the greater implications these principles have on Thai society.

Thai perceptions and conceptions of social and political truth have been little studied.[3] Annette Hamilton argues that state censorship and control of the media does not necessarily mean that the public cannot find out the truth; only that truth has to arrive in more circuitous ways. Knowing that media are tightly controlled, "only provides an even more fertile ground for the proliferation of rumours, gossip, and the circulation of information, criticism and sometimes wild imaginings." The result is "an unofficial discourse" that "ensures that even the forbidden may be available, and that which cannot be said may be expressed in other ways."[4] But "news" coming from within this "hidden dimension" cannot be brought out for public scrutiny, so questions about "the interpretation of 'the real'" arise: "what is 'truth' and what is 'fiction' are by no means clearly separated."[5]

Truth in news

We can begin by re-introducing Police Lt. Col. Samphan Satthaphorn, the Press Officer of Bangkok who oversaw the enforcement of Order No. 42 from 1976 to 1991 (Chapters 4, 5 and 7).[6] During this period, he personally issued 61 separate orders covering 73 instances in which newspapers violated Order No. 42. Samphan characterized his power over newspapers as "absolute." So it was disturbing when, in the interview I had with him, this colorful and gracious interviewee admitted with a laugh, that if one did not know the politics behind each instance where the press officer ordered closure or issued a warning, then one might assume that "there is a real standard" behind them.

This became even more troubling when Samphan confessed further that the specific clause from Order No. 42 indicating how a given article violated the order was in many cases arbitrarily attached. I asked if he believed that a newspaper's accusation of a high-ranking military man involved in "unofficial activities"—corruption—or seeing prostitutes in Europe would seriously "cause people in general and foreigners to lose their faith in Thai people or the Thai government," Samphan revealed that "sometimes, this is only a sentence . . . we just make a sentence to make a charge."[7]

Samphan claimed that perhaps as much as 50 percent of the time someone in the government called him and demanded that he act against this or that newspaper. Given these admissions, my attempt to try to find some sort of hidden standard or rule governing the use of Order No. 42 seemed hopeless. It is a fact that, behind almost every instance of its use, there was a story of competing factions, political parties, and intrigues.

Samphan admitted that his job as press officer was no joy. If he failed to act, offended government officials and politicians complained. If he issued too many warnings or closed a newspaper, he incurred the wrath of the press. If he tried to please one faction, he offended another, and so on. He cited one particular case. In 1988, two newspapers, *Matichon* and *Sayam Rat*, published stories claiming that the military had aided illegal lumbering operations in a particular province, an allegation attributed to a high-ranking policeman. Once the matter became public, the policeman denied making such a statement, but a Member of Parliament, Chamni Sakset, maintained it was true. *Naew Na* newspaper actually specified that certain military persons from the Fourth Army region were involved in these illegal operations. For his part, Samphan went to speak with Chamni and ask him whether what he said was true or not. Chamni said that this information was revealed in a closed session of parliament by an influential policeman. When the matter became open knowledge, the military was "angry" and demanded that Samphan, as press officer, take action. Although Samphan claimed that he had "checked" the story, he had not gone to the province nor had he talked with this policeman "because he [this policeman] was senior." "So," said Samphan, "we kept quiet." Was the allegation true? Samphan admitted he did not know. But neither did it matter, because the case was "involved with politics." In the end, *Naew Na* received a warning for publishing "false" news, "stirring up agitation," and "causing disquietude." Later in the interview, Samphan confessed that with a case involving many different political factions: "Sometimes, I tell you the truth, everything is not clear if [it is] true or false."[8]

I found it difficult to discuss any case with him in which we did not have to resort to a discussion of the various factions involved. But he said that he had to try to follow "policy." If someone called from the government, what could he say? Most of the time he had to go along with it or else he would not have been able "to stay." Even so, he claimed that, whatever the case, the press officer had to "follow the law." When Supreme Commander of the Thai Armed Forces, General Arthit Kamlang-ek, was reported by a Thai newspaper to be traipsing around Europe with a Thai beauty queen (a former Miss Universe), and he called the police and said, "What the hell are you doing letting them print something like this?"—the press officer was unable to do anything because the incident was alleged to have happened abroad.[9]

Can I not suggest that "political" maneuverings are involved in every public action in Thailand? Having said this, though, does not necessarily mean that the actions of the press officer were random or that they were merely actions demanded by those in power. Despite his words, other things Samphan said indicated that the press officer did work with some sort of standard. He admitted that, in more than half the instances where he issued a warning or order for closure, the matter was something he himself had found in the newspapers. If his job were merely "political," then why would he have ever done anything unless ordered to do so by some faction?

With great exactitude, however, Samphan could discuss how the king's picture should be positioned on a page. It always had to be above photos of any other person and not too close to something inappropriate, such as a photo of a "toilet or something like that." Within royalty, whose picture was higher did not matter. Also, the facing page was irrelevant. He claimed that these guidelines came from "the law," which he said obligated everyone "to obey and respect the king and queen. That is our morality, or you can say, our culture, or our folkways." I asked, which law? The law on insulting royalty, Section 112 of the criminal law code, Samphan answered. But when I pointed out that no such guidelines were in that provision, he admitted that there were no exact rules. Instead, he claimed, when looking at the position of a picture of royalty in a newspaper, "we must look deeply inside his feelings [of the one who put the picture there]. What is he thinking? But if in the situation I decide that he did not really intend to do something [bad] like this, okay, we give them a pardon."

There were also instances where Samphan fully realized the politics behind an incident, yet he also had convictions about what he was doing. In one 1990 case, *Phaya Khrut* newspaper published a story about labor unrest at the Port Authority of Thailand. In the story, the writer quoted a mob ringleader using such words as *mung* [an impolite form of the pronoun, "you"], *ai* [a derogatory prefix placed before a name or noun], *dirachan* [beast], and so on. The ringleader had even used this crude and impolite language with the high-ranking ministry official who went to resolve the labor dispute. In his warning to the newspaper, Samphan, in his position as Press Officer of Bangkok, felt that the use of such words in reference to a ministry official was:

> not appropriate and impolite, and was not of a good form of the written language which the mass media should use in commenting on the facts which it then reports to the people for them to read. It is true that the mass media has a right to comment and report, but it should be within

> the framework of the law, morality, [and] national culture. The media should use polite contents that do not incite, are not severe or violent, and which do not arouse the feelings of those criticized. It should be reporting that shows rational reasons so that all sides have understanding and accept correctness for the sake of unity of all groups, and to prevent conflicts from happening.[10]

Samphan expressed outrage at the newspaper's use of such vulgar words. He worried that "small kids" would read it and misunderstand. In English, he struggled to express his conviction, saying that the moral aspect is the base, a universal base, and from that develops folkways, and then on to culture, and finally to law—a "law of morals." Whatever the case, more than just "politics" is going on. Or, there are certain standards that lie beneath "politics" largely determining the form those politics eventually take. For our purposes, how do those "politics" come to influence the "Thai" way of interpreting public and political truth and reality?

To answer this question, I look at how "the truth" was viewed in a number of instances. Again, my premise is that, as in defamation, truth is not the primary criterion. And even with personal defamation, the truth can become a criterion when it can be shown that it serves the public interest. In what is essentially defamation of the state and nation, there is no saving clause, no way that the truth can assert its primacy in the matter. Truth—something which was largely irrelevant—was not the ultimate measure. Rather, the ultimate measure was the results of truth: effect and danger.

We start with depictions. In October of 1977, a number of newspapers made references to the bloody events of 6 October 1976. On 1 October, *Tawan Sayam* published a story mentioning that many people fear what "dire events" may occur in the "accursed month" of October, which had seen the "great calamities" of 1973 and the "serious events" of 1976.[11] The press officer sanctioned the newspaper for violation of Provision 6, prohibiting publication of:

> any false matter of a nature tending to panic, worry, or frighten the people or matter tending to incite or arouse disorder, conflict with public order or morality, or prophecies concerning the fate of the nation which might upset the people.[12]

Ten days later, *Tawan Auk Parithat* attacked the government, which had come into power through a coup, for its poor performance in terms of human rights, particularly concerning the fate of the student leaders arrested on 6 October 1976. The press officer said that, this story, along with photographs of the student leaders, was deliberately published "in order to persuade those who read it to have a feeling that the court and those governing were not giving justice to" the student leaders and instead were "bullying [them]." The newspaper was also condemned for an article assessing the nation's labor situation negatively. The press officer said that the article was "written to arouse confusion and incite those who use labour to have feelings of hatred for the government through making the accusation that Thailand is always being sanctioned by world labour organizations for having no democratic rights for the people who use labour."[13]

On the second anniversary of the events of 6 October 1976 and after a general amnesty had absolved both the student leaders and the military and right-wing groups, the newspaper *Khon Num* published a cartoon depicting the deaths and injuries from that day. The press officer censored the newspaper for having "the intention to revive nonsense, find faults . . . of having intentions that are ignoble, despite this issue having already quieted down through the amnesty which most of the people, including the students, are satisfied with." Publishing such a cartoon, the press officer concluded, intentionally acted "to have people misunderstand and hate the government."[14]

In these examples, prophecies were seen as dangerous, mentioning injustice and the government in the same breath was dangerous, and a cartoon that distilled the events of 6 October 1976 to deaths and injuries became a danger necessitating a response from the state.

A similar principle was used with coverage of the "rice standard" in late 1982 and early 1983 which the government regulated in the interests of rice farmers. One newspaper, *Naew Na*, published a headline which the press officer felt said, "the government was lying and had pushed down the price of rice." Press Officer Samphan said that this was "false" or "of the nature that might cause the people to be startled or worried, or create fear." While this newspaper's statement might have had an element of opinion to it, Samphan was forced to admit that a related story by *Sayam Rat Sapda Wijan*, under the headline, "Government has deceived the people, criticism from academics" was in fact "reporting of the news." Nonetheless, Samphan went on to say that the story could well cause readers "to misunderstand" the government's measures over the rice price "were not working," which in turn might "incite some groups of people, such as rice farmers," which could result, finally, in "creating disquietude."[15]

In this second example, what is reported is certainly not an opinion, but an account of something that happened. That the press officer himself made this point gives it credence. But because of the effect the article might have had, it had to be condemned.

So far I have discussed specific events that verifiably happened. But what about more general conditions that were sometimes verifiable and sometimes not? References to the military have been harshly sanctioned many times. For instance, a 1980 article appeared in *Sayam Nikorn* discussing maneuvers by the military to have the mandatory retirement age extended so that the highest ranking generals could remain in power.[16] The press officer attacked the article as, "malicious, derisive, and contemptuous of the government in an ambiguous way." Moreover, he said, some parts were "false," while others "revealed official secrets." These various charges added up to being "against public peace and order and good morals of the people."

In 1983, *Matichon* newspaper published an article pointing out there were two large factions within the military—one under the supreme commander, and the other under the head of the army. This article, wrote the press officer, implied that "the military is not unified" and that it has an internal "conflict," which again pointed to "disunity in the military." Disunity in the military reflected "the weakness of the Minister of Defence," which could lead to "the possible ruin of the government" and even to the ruin of "the military and nation."

In a final case concerning the military, a 1989 article appearing in *Sayam Rat* mentioned that the military was seeking ways of "infiltrating" people it trusted into high positions within the government. The press officer criticized this as "malicious, mocking, [and] ridiculing of a department in the government."[17]

The overall impression of these articles about the military was that the military had interests outside its primary duty of defending the country. A general tried to lengthen his term to hold onto power. The military had factions. The military tried to get its people into political positions. These described a general state of affairs concerning Thai governance. Together they constituted a critique that the Thai government was under the control of factions and individuals who pursued their own interests. In this sense, this issue was not confined to the military.

A 1989 *Dao Sayam* article implied that the appointment of a governor was a matter of politics and not accomplished with the cool objectivity needed for good government. An article the same year in *Naew Na* reported on a system by which police could buy higher positions. The not-very-startling article earlier that same year in *Sayam Rat* noted that the police, politicians, and civil servants had come under the influence of powerful godfathers. This sentiment, the press officer said, "slandered and ridiculed" these groups, as well as being "malicious, mocking, and ridiculing of the Thai government or units of the government in an ambiguous way without specifying exactly where the wrong was." A government divided along personal factional lines, amenable to the highest bidder, and manipulated by money could never sincerely serve the needs of the people. Therefore, the articles were simply wrong.[18]

Samphan had been the press officer for these cases. His understanding was that they were pure politics—or it at first appeared. When *Naew Na* reported that positions within the Police Department were available to the highest bidder, the minister of interior called the head of the police and was very "upset," complaining that if the press officer let articles like this be printed, it would "make trouble for the police department." I asked if the report was true. With a laugh, Samphan said, yes, the report was true, but the prices are higher than those reported! And would such a report cause the people to feel "anxious and worried?" I asked. He answered, "No, no, no."

Then I asked about the accusation reported in *Sayam Rat* that politicians and many people in the government were under the influence of godfathers. Samphan explained that many people in the Chatchai Choonhavan government's cabinet of ministers were known to be godfathers. Many people wanted to know why the government would choose such people to serve on the cabinet. Well, were they godfathers? "Yes," said Samphan, but "you're not supposed to" report it "like that." The press officer had to consider that reporting a story "like this" was "not good and would make the people understand that our cabinet, or foreigners read it—it's not nice! But it's true! It's true, but you cannot prove it."[19]

More than "politics," the mechanism in press suppression here was intended to protect the image of the government as good, free of politics, and serving the people's interests and needs. Since this image was sincerely believed, at least on some level, the press officer or any other government official had little compunction closing a newspaper, censuring a television show, or banning a book when it infringed on this image.

When the newspaper *Siang Puangchon* noted in July of 1977 that Narong Kittikhachorn, the former and hated head of the police who fled the country with his father Thanom in October 1973, had returned to Thailand, the press officer censured the publication for he felt it was intended to create disquietude and disorder.[20]

When asked about an incident such as this, Samphan emphasized that the press officer must adhere to the government's policy. When a publication might "affect" or have "an impact on the government," the press officer must act. At that time, the policy of the government was to forbid Narong's return. Thus, when Narong did return, the report had to be suppressed. As for the newspaper, "when you print it, [it doesn't matter if] it's true or not." The people in the government "don't care. They don't want this kind of news [pounding his fist] to be printed. That's all!"

At another point in the interview, Samphan described the principle further:

> If you are talking about the government, we are under the government so we must do something to protect the government and make the people look on the government as good. Always, we don't want the people to look at the government as bad.[21]

Samphan cited an example. *Matichon* regularly covered the activities of the Buddhist "sect," Santi Asoke. The group, whose Buddhist monks were expelled from the Buddhist *Sangha* (the official Buddhist hierarchy), created a political and religious movement. This movement spawned, among other things, almost self-supporting alternative communities based on simple living, organic foods, and herbal remedies. Its political party, *Phalangtham* (Moral Force) for a short period dominated Bangkok politics.[22] Given the movement's immense popularity, Santi Asoke always aroused the suspicion of the authorities. An article in *Matichon* caused Samphan to respond with a warning, saying that the story "might cause misunderstandings to arise between the involved parties, and will bring an even wider expansion to the conflict and might affect the unity of the nation."[23]

In discussing this case, Samphan explained that there was an ongoing conflict between Santi Asoke and the *Mahatherasamakhom*, or, (Supreme) Council of (Buddhist) Elders, the latter of which Samphan likened to "the king of Buddhists" or "the government of the Buddhist Sangha." Samphan said that the Council of Elders and Santi Asoke did not share "the same ideology." Since the Council of Elders was under the authority of the government, naturally the government supported the council. Santi Asoke, on the other hand, was "like the outlaw," Samphan concluded, saying that "is the problem." So why not ban all news concerning Santi Asoke, I asked. Samphan responded that it was not that *Matichon* wrote about Santi Asoke, it was that *Matichon* was "always writing something wrong." If this was published, people "will believe it and maybe misunderstand," Samphan responded. Misunderstand what? "Misunderstand that Santi Asoke is better than Supreme Council of Elders or something like that." Stories about Santi Asoke were okay, he went on, but not stories that compared the two. To point out that followers of Santi Asoke ate only one meal a day, while saying that the Council of Elders had "really good food" was not okay. It would be all right if the story said that Santi Asoke had just one meal and that they ate vegetarian. But to then say that the Council of Elders [and all the monks in the official *Sangha*] ate twice "would cause people to understand that Santi Asoke is better. But for the government, the Council of Elders is the best."[24]

Finally, it was not only inappropriate to say that the government had failed in something, or make a comparison which would place something of the government in a bad light, but also even future actions of the government had to be protected. In 1989, for instance, *Matichon* published a story which questioned whether certain industries under construction along the eastern seaboard—a sort of investment zone—might have the same detrimental impact as similar industries had in Japan. In Japan, many people had fallen sick from the disease, "*minamata*."[25] The newspaper reported that Thai people were becoming afraid that mercury leaking into the sea might cause the same health risks. Samphan censured the article, saying that such a report "was false and not correct according to the truth." Moreover, it "might cause people to be startled, worried, or afraid, or [might] spoil the reputation of the economic policies of the country." Samphan said that the minister of industry had told him that such a thing could not happen in Thailand. If an article like this were printed, it would "make people too scared about the future." Therefore, the contents necessarily had to become "false."[26]

Truth in art

Annette Hamilton describes the intriguing "double reality effect" in media portrayals of reality and their reception by Thai audiences. She asserts that the art form of "realism" is too real for many Thai. An inversion between truth and reality in media and artistic portrayals of social reality is common practice in Thailand:

> Traditionally the means of "telling the truth" was to narrate through conventional fabulous forms, where stock characters depicted events which could be used to understand "the real" of contemporary life. Where a story is presented "realistically" the result is an identification of the fictional protagonist with real people and events . . . in contemporary Thai film and television . . . [s]tories which can be read as political are presented through a fantasy historical past, while viewers identify film and television narratives as depictions of real events and identify the stars with the characters they play. "Fiction" and "reality' run into each other in the popular imagination.[27]

This section examines how presentation of society—in movies, novels, television, all subsumed under the category "art"—is affected by defamation-based law and thinking. Many rules or practices surrounding art also apply to the following topic of history.

The first law concerning the cinema in Thailand was the Cinema Act of 1930, which, as with the newspapers, forbade anything that might be against public order and morals.[28] In 1972, Section 8, Proclamation of the Revolutionary Group No. 205, forbade showing any movie that "that might cause contempt for government or nation." Section 9 banned any "political" content in movies that might "adversely affect governance or incite the creation of disquietude in the country."

In 1991, the document, "Guidelines for Checking Movies of the Ministry of the Interior" detailed violations with more exactitude. The three areas of violation were "noble morality, culture, and traditions of the nation," "peace and order and security of the nation," and "politics and governance related to foreign relations." In the first two areas, items in a movie which do the following were forbidden:

1.1 show contempt or insult to things of worship, through any action that is false or distorted toward religious principles, and would cause bad feelings toward any religion;
1.2 matters which are obscene;
1.3 actions of cruelty toward any person or animal; but if it is an action which refers to education or research for the benefit of humans, and is not cause for influencing others to act accordingly as an example, or to break the laws of the land, then it can be done.
2.1 to ridicule, mock, scorn or insult the institution of the Thai monarchy, or any action which is capable [of] or could be the cause of such feelings of ridicule or scorn and insult;
2.2 clear expression in the nature of insult to the state or nation or government, or inciting to cause disquietude in the land;
2.3 matters which are felt will serve as an example in instilling bad traits, leading people to evil behaviour.[29]

The law also established the Movie Censorship Board (MCB; also called the Film Censorship Board), whose editing handiwork can be admired in theatres throughout the country. Unlike newspapers that were warned or closed after having printed items deemed dangerous, movies are subject to censorship, scissors, and Vaseline, so that viewers never get to see the "bad" movie or "bad" scenes. Foreign movies that might be banned never appear in a Thai theatre. The crime, so to speak, is never committed, or never allowed to be committed. The censor's cuts are stored in a room at the Licensing Bureau of the Police Department and incinerated every ten or so years at a nearby Buddhist temple's crematorium. Hence, it is difficult to exhibit concrete instances of what the state deemed as cinematically dangerous.[30]

In 1991, according to the the Assistant Director of the MCB, Police Lt. Col. Nikhom Intasen, the board's membership had long been dominated by police personnel. However, under pressure from the Association for the Promotion of Thai Movies, the composition of the board had become more diverse, with police replaced by representatives from such government units as the Publicity Department, the National Culture Commission, and the Ministry of University Affairs. If the film concerned youth, a special representative from the Ministry of Education might attend. A movie about Buddhism might have a representative from the Department of Religious Affairs; a movie about politics, the Ministry of Foreign Affairs; a film about the army, a representative from the Ministry of Defense, and so on. With a minimum of six members present, the board, viewing around 300 movies per year, votes to either ban the movie outright (only two to three movies per year in 1999, according to Nikhom), or to require certain edits. If the movie company was dissatisfied with a decision of the board, it could appeal, or go to the courts, apparently a circumstance so rare that in 1991 Nikhom could not recall a single instance of it ever happening.[31]

Nikhom granted that the phrasing, "against order and public morals" was broad. He felt that the board was given "wide discretion" in making its decisions. However, the board did employ a set of guidelines, including a prohibition of anything "distorted or false" about any religion, of anything "obscene," or shows cruelty toward people or animals. However, these were just guidelines and quite often the board allowed showing such things if it felt that doing so would provide an illustrative example. Therefore, rather than thinking of the guidelines "prohibiting" anything, Nikhom advised it might be better to say that the guidelines spoke of the overall impression or message of a movie. Thus, it might be acceptable to show youth drinking liquor if the message were clearly critical of such actions and showed some negative consequences stemming from them.

The standard for assessing each item was not clear, Nikhom went on. In terms of obscenity, for instance, he used the standard of whether the material was sexually arousing or not. On the one hand, even if there were no nudity, such sections might be edited out or "smudged over" with Vaseline. On the other hand, if an instance of nudity was not sexually arousing, then it might not be cut.

In the view of the Director of the National Film Archives of Thailand, Somchat Bangjaeng in 1991, the laws controlling cinema had "depended on the period" and had always been "very wide." The original standard in the 1930 law prohibited the showing of any movie that was "against public order and morals." Censorship had apparently begun quite early. Somchat noted that a 1925 silent movie made by an Indian-German joint production team, *The Lion of India*, had been banned in Siam because its depiction of the Buddha differed from the way the Buddha's life was understood in Siam.

The guidelines referred to by Nikhom were apparently closely followed. For instance, no government official, soldier, policeman, or Buddhist monk could be shown in a negative light.[32] Nor could there be depictions that might lead to the moral degeneration of youth, such as a scene showing a boy gambling. Among the scenes Somchat could remember being censored from Thai movies, was a scene of a place of prostitution, cabaret dancers in front of Thammasat University, and someone selling marijuana in a slum."[33]

Although the interview with Somchat was carried out in 1991, the MCB has continued to watch over the morals of the Thai nation to this day. The most recent case, which would have been released in Thai theatres in 2007, involves Apichatpong Weerasetthakul's critically acclaimed *Syndromes and a Century*. The MCB demanded four scenes be cut from the movie. Apichatpong refused; the MCB refused to return the reel and said it would make the cuts itself. Despite protests from various movie organizations, the movie was not approved and has yet to appear in theatres in Thailand, despite glowing reviews from critics.[34] One of the scenes slated for the knife showed, for less than a minute, a Buddhist monk strumming on a guitar; another scene showed a doctor who, upon kissing his girlfriend, experienced a swelling in the loins. Evidently, proper monks do not play guitars and professional doctors do not get erections, even when provoked. Depictions to the contrary present a clear threat to the peace and order of society.[35]

Somchat confirmed that, up until 1991, a political movie had never been made and then shown in Thailand. He said that up to that time some exceptions had touched on politics or political issues, but never a movie with a strong political message.[36] A few that came close, though. What Somchat called, "a truly political movie" was made from a book serialized in the newspaper. However, production was finished in the politically repressive year following 6 October 1976 and was never released. Another movie, *Thongpan*, recounted the story of a family relocated away from their farmland due to the construction of a dam. Featuring some of the leading intellectuals of the day (it was made during the open period between 1973 and 1976), it ended with the disintegration of the farmer's family. This movie has remained "private" and was never released in the theatres; thus it never came under consideration by the Movie Censorship Board.

More recently, movie critic Kong Rithdee called Bhandit Rittakol's 2001 film *14 Tula songkhram prachachon* [14 October, the People's Fight (Moonhunter)] "the last large-scale [*sic*] 'political film' made in Thailand."[37] With screenplay by Seksan Prasertkul, the movie tells the story of the October 1973 student uprising and Seksan's own flight to the jungle to join the communists. Director Patchanon Thammajira's *Colic: Baby Sees a Ghost* (2006) is a standard-fare Thai horror movie. A screaming baby is diagnosed as colic, but the baby does not stop crying because ghosts related to the 6 October 1976 massacre are present. In the end, the parents find peace when they make offerings to the fallen at the 14 October Monument.

Somchat contended, "Thai movies were at a disadvantage to foreign movies" in terms of showing violence. While a violent Thai movie does not pass the censorship board, a similarly violent foreign movie does gain approval. This was because, Somchat felt, foreign films are seen by the MCB as "distant" from those watching them. A Thai movie is "close" to its Thai viewers and so violence is censored. Even Chinese movies, which are sometimes particularly violent, have been allowed. Put another way, Somchat felt that Thai violence is more dangerous to a Thai audience than foreign violence.[38]

When asked to compare movies with other forms of the media, or why a bad monk could be discussed in the newspapers but not depicted in a movie, Somchat said he did not know for sure. He felt that the state looked upon movies "as a form of entertainment," and generally "lacking in value"—and, from his position as head of the archives—as something that did not need to be preserved. At the same time, however, Somchat noted that when the state feared a movie might affect something, "it was rather strict in censoring." Because movies and television "are the closest to reality," Somchat said, they have always been tightly controlled by the government. Since the early 1950s until the late 1970s, writers, journalists, and politicians were often subject to arrest. Since, in his estimation, 90 percent of Thai movie scripts came from novels, the intimidation and arrest of writers in general may have had an effect on movies. Added to that is the possibility that a completed movie could be censored outright, thus losing quite a bit of money, and it becomes clear that movies would tend to remain exactly that—a form of entertainment.[39]

Distilling the views of the press officer, the movie censor, and the film archivist, it is possible to begin to fashion a continuum on which we can place various vehicles of expression—movies, documentaries, fiction, newspapers, and television—in terms of their potential dangerousness.

Newspapers and movies attract the most government concern. Newspapers are dangerous because they are *supposed* to be real; movies are dangerous because they *appear* to be real. When opinion dons the garb of objectivity, as in the printed word of a newspaper, it may lead those learning of such an opinion to conclude that it is a fact. People can therefore be fooled by newspapers when a newspaper pretends to present a fact, when it is actually peddling an opinion.

Movies are the opposite. Movies are fiction clothed in such a way as to appear as if they were fact. Thus, people may become confused and take fiction as true. Newspapers are fact become fiction; movies, fiction appearing as fact. For precisely this reason foreign movie violence is given greater leeway in the eyes of the censors—foreign violence, although seeming more real, would (or does, in the eyes of the MCB) not confuse its viewers because foreigners are seen as more violent. This posture actually helps to preserve the government's contention that Thailand is a peaceful society—because foreigners are more violent in movies. Violence in newspapers—especially gruesome photos of victims of murder or road accidents—is not particularly an issue, especially when its presentation is stripped of all political context.

Given these qualities of movies and newspapers, each deserves control by the state. Before the spread of television sets throughout the country, radio, followed by newspapers and movies, were the only media to reach into the village. From its very inception, television has remained securely under state control. Even after the 1997 constitution, more than a decade passed before the semi-independent Thai public television station was established that provided any semblence of balance to the strongly pro-government stations.[40]

Literature, as opposed to newspapers, has never apparently been viewed as much of a threat by Thai governments. Samak Sundaravej, minister of interior in the year following the events of 6 October 1976, not only banned but also made possessing any of 204 books a crime; not a single one was a novel or collection of short stories of a Thai writer. The ministry seemed concerned about more standard "academic" works, such as translations of Marxist works like *Leninism-Marxism on Socialist Theory as Science*, or indigenous, non-fiction pieces such as Thirayut Boonmee's *Analysis of the Struggle of the Lao Dong Party*, or even works inspired by liberation theology, such as Pablo Friere's *Pedagogy of the Oppressed*. Few, if any, banned works involved poetry or fiction.[41] As a whole, according to *Sarakhadi* magazine, 1,057 books have been banned in Thailand since 1950.[42]

The Thai state's apparent relative lack of concern about the revolutionary potential and danger of literature cannot be attributed to low Thai readership rates. The preamble to Samak Sundaravej's order made clear that the state was worried about certain books. It empowered the minister of interior to "confiscate and destroy" any printed materials which might "cause the destruction of national security." Clause 2 of the order prohibited anyone from having in their possession:

> any type of material which presents the news, articles, or writings which express an opinion which, if communicated through any means, would cause disunity in the nation or direct the readers to have faith in and look upon communism favourably, or cause disorder, turmoil, or rebelliousness among the people, or would have the people violate the laws of the land.

Although the order gave a grace period for possessors to voluntarily hand over such materials, after that, violators could be imprisoned for up to one year and fined as much as 2,000 baht. If any troublemaker were to suggest that this order or any other anti-communist propaganda put forth from the government at the time violated this law, the measure provided a saving clause:

> The above does not apply to printed documents or materials which are of the administration or of the authorities or instructors of ministries, bureaus, or departments who have the duty to provide education in the ending or suppression of communist activities or in the defense of the Kingdom, all of this being for the performance of one's duties.[43]

When the military junta promulgated this order, it might have been considered the crowning day for Thai books. At long last, Thai books were taken seriously enough to prohibit. But it might also be thought the day Thai literature died, for largely the same reason, for no Thai creative literary works made the list. How could movies be so dangerous, if most were made from novels, yet the novels themselves were not deemed as dangerous? What about these different genres made one so dangerous while the other did not merit attention? Where was Khamsing Srinawk (Lao Khamhom) whose sly and biting satires were influential in the radical "Literature for Life" movement? Where were Sriburapha's works, one of the first "committed writers," who was jailed for rebellion and communism for four years for his involvement in the 1950s "Peace Rebellion" and who then finally fled to communist China when Sarit crashed into power and jailed most active intellectuals?

Part of an answer may come by returning to the continuum between "reality" and "fiction" and its relationship to danger. Perhaps literature is not "realistic" enough to be dangerous. Literature is thought of as more clearly a form of fictional entertainment. Newspapers' "non-fiction" writing (as opposed to novels and short stories) appeared more "real" and so required heavier scrutiny by the government's intelligence and censorship services. Non-fiction writing appearing in news print was seen as the most effective tool in swaying people's loyalty away from communism. Sriburapha was not dangerous as a writer; he was arrested for his activism, not for his literary vision. The same was true of Khamsing. His writings did not seem to concern the government. His resistance to the repressive regime following 6 October, his leadership in the Socialist Party, and reports that he agreed to serve as prime minister in a provisional Thai government to be set up in Laos, however, did.[44]

Truth in history

I have suggested that "history" from within the sacred sphere is nearly impossible (Chapter 11). Only semi-mythical characters from a misty past can be depicted, precisely because there is little detail. The closer we move to the present, the more impossible, from the point-of-view of the sacred sphere, history's task becomes as substantial documentation exists. Hence, the movie script of a movie about Rama IV cannot be written to meet the needs of both the historian and the sacred sphere. Truth about the monarchy will not emerge from a variety of different treatments or from a multiplicity of perspectives. A monarchy, any monarchy, because it exists at least partly in the sacred sphere, cannot be depicted from multiple views; it simply cannot be depicted at all. Especially in Thailand, the kings of the Chakri dynasty will be sequentially treated with laudatory odes: not depictions from real life, but edificatory snippets, bloodless moments of praise so blinding that it washes away any hint of irony or satire. Thai history will have no dictators, no massacres, no corruption, no coups. . .

In the Official Information Act of 1997, media and private citizens were given the right to request information from 8,000 government agencies. Apparently the act is well used, with submission of large numbers of requests for documents and a well-established appeal system for those who encounter problems. However, many have experienced problems from intransigent bureaucrats inured in a "culture of secrecy" who obstruct efforts to release documents, often citing "national security."[45] Exclusions for reasons of national security are not new. The exclusionary space of national security developed with the beginning of the modern Thai state one hundred years ago. What is new is the insidious connection of national security to a concept of "privacy" and, as it were, defamation.

Using the Official Information Act, newspapers and an organization representing families whose relatives were killed in protests against attempts by the military to hold on to power in May 1992 requested government documents that would reveal who was behind what the *Nation* newspaper called "one of the darkest chapters of modern Thai history."[46] There was no response for months after the request was made, and no reason given. For years, the Ministry of Defense (MoD) maneuvered and delayed. Even the prime minister, Chaun Leekpai, who was also acting as Minister of Defense, claimed he could do nothing. The Supreme Commander of the Armed Forces felt "disclosure would do more harm than good." The MoD finally promised to release a report that had been commissioned in 1992.[47] Then, in the months prior to the report's release, officials pretended that the report was going to reveal startling information. The views of various military generals had to be canvassed on the advisability of actually making the report public. Finally, in May 2000, with much hoopla, the MoD released the 600-page report on the events surrounding the May 1992 crisis.[48]

The report turned out to be, in the eyes of many, a whitewash of events. Relatives of those who died in those days "express[ed] deep disappointment" over the report's failure to lay doubts to rest. Military officials had censored all names of military officials and units and key information on military actions during the period, citing "national security" and "invasion of privacy." In fact, 60 percent of the report was deleted.[49] Although much information and all specificity in terms of names had been blacked out, the Defense Ministry attached a note " warning . . . that if those who receive the information want to further publicise it, they must do so at their own risk." Defense Ministry spokesman Sanan Kachornklam said that anyone publicizing the report "may be subject to libel lawsuits." The Official Information Office said appeals could be made against the extensive censoring if those made the report "incomplete or incomprehensible" and incapable of serving the "public interests."[50]

How can an officially generated and sanctioned report be censored on the grounds of privacy? In the Official Information Act of 1997, "personal information" is defined as:

> information relating to all the personal particulars of a person, such as education, financial status, health record, criminal record or employment record, which contain the name of such person or contain a numeric reference, code or such other indications identifying that person as fingerprint, tape or diskette in which a person's sound is recorded, or photograph, and shall also include information relating to personal particulars of the deceased.[51]

The definition says nothing to indicate that the order to shoot civilians (or others, for that matter) is a personal matter. Why has the elucidation of an official matter become so difficult? Why have we not heard about those responsible for the October 6, 1976 massacre? In any case, there is no reason to think that, with time, truth about May 1992 will finally be presented. The fear of defamation used today to justify denying knowledge will extend beyond any of our lifetimes.[52]

Among the earliest government rules on the cinema was the banishment of any movie that "might affect the administration of the country or create disquietude." As a result, history has not been served well in Thai movies. An example of a movie never made came from a script written by a Thammasat University teacher of cinema on the life of Field Marshal Sarit Thanarat. However, rather than making a movie only to have it banned, this teacher sent the script to the Movie Censorship Board for prior approval, which it did not receive. The reason given, as Somchat of the film archives understood it, was that it would show "dictatorial power" with direct reference to the military, which the board felt "maintained the democracy of the country."[53] Thus, making and showing such a movie might "cause people to hate the military and it could cause disunity." Somchat thought that inserting a disclaimer at the movie's end, claiming that the people and events were fictional would not have worked in Thailand because everyone would know to whom the movie referred.[54]

When asked about this script, Police Lt. Col. Nikhom Intasen of the Movie Censorship Board confirmed that the board had rejected the script on grounds that it "was critical of a leader of the country" and showed "bad things" that were of a "personal" or "private" nature. As such, the movie-maker would be liable to charges of personal defamation made by the former dictator's relatives. Nikhom continued to say that, had the script been a "political history" of Sarit, a "history of the work that had been done" under him, and "how he helped develop the country"—in short, as he said, "the good things"—then that would be all right. But the script talked about his many, many minor wives. This was "personal" and so the script was rejected.[55]

Because of this approach, whole swaths of Thai history are lost. Not because the original documents are not there, but because these documents only peripherally appear in society. This does not mean that no Thai person talks about, say, the events of 6 October 1976. Groups, efforts, and individuals constantly try to bring these issues to the attention of society. But, if such attempts actually try to bring agency to history—that is, names of those responsible—they quite often result in a defamation case. This was discovered by Ji (Giles) Ungpakorn when he accused Samak Sundaravej of involvement in the 1976 massacre at Thammasat University.[56] It is a tribute to the success of the sacro-official sphere that these small, personal, efforts persist, reflecting confidence that the shrunken, enfeebled public sphere is largely irrelevant. No reckoning with the truth occurs on the national stage. However, those who dare call for even personal satisfaction face charges of *lèse-majesté*, rebellion, or defamation.[57]

History is the victim of defamation for it de-peoples the past, making the past devoid of names, attributions, and responsibility. The bad past becomes personal, with no names. History becomes magically mechanized by anonymous action, movements of undifferentiated masses and mobs, and shouting in the night, without actual agency, without people doing things. No blood, no shootings, no orders, no death appear in the military's report on the 1992 uprising. All that happened was the movement of dark forces, gangs, factions, rumors, behind the scenes maneuvering, and the prompting of masses on the streets to march toward their own suppression.

The official history is that of bright, shining faces, of great men whose names ring out as their accomplishments are proclaimed. It is ever the glorious times of a happy people: the general reaches down and pats a child on the head; the grandma, smiling, raises her hands in devotion and obeisance.

Defamation-based law drives the hard history of Thailand into darkened streets, making it a fugitive, always on the run, meeting in shadows and sustained by rumor. There are sometimes signs that critical commentary may appear, but if it does, it is always in a coded language. It is necessary to call in the virtuous interpreters who are familiar with a special set of landmarks scattered throughout this political landscape. Beware for those who travel through this dangerous topography unguided.

This is the realm of *lèse-majesté* and defamation, from which truth and history were banished a half century ago. What remains in this sacred thought-world is the reified, coded language of *lèse-majesté*, which only the meritorious can discern and then interpret for others.

For instance, many interpreted the king's 2005 birthday speech to mean that the king was opposed to the use of the *lèse-majesté* law. However, a reading of the king's speech indicates that the precise meaning is not clear.[58] Aspects that might be confusing are proclaimed as an indication of great wisdom. A pattern emerges. The more critical the situation, the more concentrated and focused the code.

Another instance was when, as a new government formed in late September 2008, Privy Council President Prem Tinsulanonda "presumed every Thai citizen would want to see peace and a return to normalcy" and "Everybody should work together to pull the country through the quagmire." He suggested that government leaders should "study His Majesty the King's remarks, which might provide them with clues for resolving the conflict."[59]

This discussion of truth in news, art, and history suggests an answer as to why little truth gets to the public sphere. However, I have also hinted that, on another level, events are mulled over by individuals and small groups, privately. Hamilton, perhaps too optimistically, suggests:

> Precisely because everybody knows the news is not really what is happened . . . watching the news becomes a major act of cultural interpretation. Stories as portrayed on "the news" provide the substance for interpersonal conversations between intimates, who may re-interpret or deconstruct "what is happening" through commonly-held beliefs about the nature of power and the hidden narratives which are used as explanatory frameworks.[60]

Thailand's official depiction is of a nation based on "unity, infused with Buddhist values, upheld by a proud military tradition, and under the beneficent influence of a monarchy ever-responsive and compassionate to the needs of the people." News from outside Thailand "asserts the universality of corruption, ruthlessness and power," while the official view shows Thailand is the exception. In practice, Hamilton argues, the positive image created by the Thai media is counterbalanced by "the truth of local existence," peopled by corrupt officials, a military that celebrates its impunity, and a justice system responsive to the powers-that-be. Thailand is, as with many other countries, part of an "anarchistic, disordered world full of unscrupulous power-holders and unpredictable spiritual forces."[61]

Principles of truth under defamation

This chapter has discussed truth and its relationship to the news, movies and literature. Truth in Thailand sets the criteria for the degree a medium is dangerous for society, a continuum of danger. The more realistic the medium, such as newspapers, the more truth is suppressed, denied, or controlled. At the same time, Thai rather freely discuss in private what they would never say in public. This response—knowing the truth but not saying so publicly—creates an almost schizophrenic reality, one segregated into two mutually exclusive realms.

We have the testimony of the Press Officer who admitted that the question of truth was peripheral to his work in enforcing Coup Decree No. 42. From this most pristine product of defamation thinking, we can assemble a lexicon of truth perversion, falsity, and contempt, categorized and arranged in ascending intensity:

1 Various Dimensions of Truth Perversion, from less to more: "ambiguity"/"exaggeration of the truth"/"distorted from the truth"
2 Various Dimensions of Falsity, from less to more: "inaccurate"/"differs from the truth"/"not the complete truth"/"false/"false nature"/"wrong"/"false and which is not correct according to the truth"/"no basis in truth"/"against the truth"
3 Various Dimensions of Contempt, from less to more: "mocking"/"ridiculing"/"derisively"/"contemptuously"/"maliciously"

Protected entities are: His Majesty the King, the Queen, Royal Heir, or Regent, the Thai Government, or any ministry, public body, or department of the government, the nation or Thai people as a whole (and in general), and Thailand. Everything in this language focuses on both truth and insult, yet, all is confessed as contrasting with truth.

What are the long-term effects of the repeated application of these frameworks upon Thai society as a whole? Would the mechanisms that search for, and attempt to make clear, "truth," in the form of "facts" (at least in a "Western" sense), become enfeebled? Would an alternative regime of truth emerge and by what principles would it operate?

Taking in the breadth of this discussion some provisional conclusions can be made. about the nature of truth as conceived in Thai society over the past century, within the framework of defamation-based laws and their use. The following eight principles essentially describe a defamation regime under the state of exception.

PRINCIPLE ONE: THE DEGREE OF TRUTH IS BASED PRIMARILY ON ITS SUPPOSED EFFECT.

Truth is assessed on the level of effect. Truth in and of itself does not create distrust in the government, a bad reputation for the country, chaos, or disquietude. The defamatory words are false because of the negative implications they may spawn: "(the words may) cause the people to misunderstand or cause them to not have trust in the policies of National Administrative

Reform Council," "spoil the reputation of the economic policies of the country," "cause possible ruin of the government, including the military and nation." These falsehoods are intended to "incite disquietude," "stir up, arouse, incite and cause disquietude," "cause incitement leading to the rise of disquietude and internal disorder in the country," "incite, causing the destruction of unity," and "affect the unity of the nation." "The people" are easily disoriented and such words cause them "to be startled and cause fear," or "to become startled or worried, especially and exceedingly affecting national security." These false words might even "cause foreign countries to lose their faith and trust in Thailand, the Thai government, or the Thai people in general."

PRINCIPLE TWO: TRUTH IS SUBORDINATE TO THE MORAL QUALITY OF THE SOURCE, AS DEFINED BY "INTENTIONS."

The greater the insult that comes through reading the defamatory words, the more suspect the intentions of their author. Implicit in the letter of the law or charges made by the police is the assumption that the author knew the truth of the matter; but, driven by malice, he or she recklessly disregarded it. Words such as "ambiguous," "distortion," "exaggeration," and "misrepresentation" have a relation to truth, but an imperfect, perverted one. Ridicule, mockery, and derision are types of contempt, which automatically make the actor malicious and the words untrue.

PRINCIPLE THREE: TRUTH IS ONLY TANGENTIALLY BASED ON THE "TRUTH" OF THE CONTENTS, OR THE ACTUAL TEXT.

Most cases of defamation in Thailand omit an evaluation of whether what was said was true or not. This principle is adhered to absolutely in *lèse-majesté*, where it is illegal to argue the truth of what was said. This also holds for seditious rebellion when it was explicitly illegal (up to 1992) and remains true for today's collective personal defamation suits. Little room is available for figurative or metaphorical truth, especially when delivered in the garb of insult, ridicule, satire, or mockery.

PRINCIPLE FOUR: THE DEGREE OF INSULT IS EQUAL TO THE READER'S OWN LEVEL OF UNDERSTANDING TRUTH.

As defamatory words are often couched in insinuations and indirect references, only a person with greater access to truth can perceive the potential damage of the insult. Thus, the police who handle *lèse-majesté* cases are not themselves swayed by the malicious sentiments, nor are prosecutors, judges, the educated classes, or the good citizens who bring the matter to public attention. However, these groups can imagine for "the public" or "the people" the degree of insult the latter would feel (once it has been explained to them). This principle can also be applied to Movie Censorship Board members, who are not aroused by sex scenes in the movies they view, but can predict how the public might be aroused, and so excise such scenes.

PRINCIPLE FIVE: TRUTH IS HIGHLY CODED AND ONLY THOSE WITH SPECIAL ACCESS TO IT CAN DECIPHER IT FOR OTHERS.

The truth of any given political, social, cultural—or even economic—situation is not as it appears. Nothing can be taken at face value. The reality is below the surface where real actors and forces determine the outcome of history. Just as we saw in the *lèse-majesté* case of Jakrapob (Chapter 9), judges and the police could not understand or discern the truth on their own until a traitorology expert explicated and delved into the core of the matter—determined by the quality of intent. The truth-givers are always providing coded messages to greater society about what is really going on and it is up to the wise and prudent among them to discern it.[62]

PRINCIPLE SIX: TRUTH IS JUDGED ACCORDING TO A CONTINUUM OF THE DEGREE OF REALISM AND THE EXTENT OF ITS DISTRIBUTION.

Truth exists, but only in obscure forms for normal people. Truth is diluted to the degree that it is exposed to society and is believable. Television records reality and its coverage is most widespread, so the state must monopolize it. Within this continuum of representation, newspapers have broad distribution and communicate "facts" and therefore must be controlled. Movies are occasional reality-related events that trick viewers into believing they are merely recording reality, so they must be regulated. Non-fiction books and novels are the least widespread and the least "realistic" and therefore are allowed to present more concentrated forms of truth.[63]

PRINCIPLE SEVEN: DEEPER TRUTH IS REVEALED BY A LEVEL OF EMOTION CULTURALLY IMPENETRABLE TO "NON-THAIS."

The first four principles do not operate in other, non-Thai, cultural contexts. The degree of insult felt when encountering a defamatory statement is not in relation to facts, but rather in relation to a created, imagined, and maintained set of culturally, perhaps even "racially," defined notions or mantras of Thainess: "All Thai love their king," "Thai love their king more than other people love theirs," "Thai don't kill Thai," "We lost territory to foreigners," "Thai are peace-loving," "We don't have racial issues like the West does," and so on. These statements are, in effect, the essence of the "narrow" Theravada Buddhist tradition now reconstituted in "cultural" terms (Chapter 11) and creates a hierarchy of cultural purity—"Thai Truth"—to which persons of various positions have varying access (See Figure 9.1).

PRINCIPLE EIGHT: CRITICISM AFFIRMS THIS REGIME OF TRUTH, AND IS ESSENTIAL FOR ITS EXISTENCE.

Because this regime of truth is based on a belief in uniqueness, outside criticism does not threaten but rather affirms it. The more "Thailand" perceives itself "besieged," the more confirmation is bestowed to this regime of truth.

A number of conclusions can be made about the nature of defamation regimes. First, this categorization of Thai perceptions of factual or representational truth describes the core tenets of any defamation regime, but is best exemplified by the Thai case. The Thai defamation regime in the state of exception creates a unique *Thai Truth*, one focusing on effect, on intention rather than actual contents, in which conventionally understood truth is ignored or vehemently denied.

This leads to a startling conclusion: there may well be no documented instance of a defamatory statement actually proven in Thailand. The truth-interpreters of Thai society (The Meritorious) recognize and decode the malice of defamatory actions and predict their effects on those less wise, but are themselves unaffected. More importantly, they discern how media has varying effects on people and, in the people's name, censor or ban such items to the degree that such media are realistic. At the same time, these wise people claim that only Thai can truly understand the unique relationship Thai have with the world and Truth. Finally, the utter truth of this Truth is proven when it comes under attack by the Demons or ignorant foreigners. In fact, the more it is attacked, the truer it is.

This truth system creates a sort of *partisan exceptionalism* which posits that the validity of one faction's truth is based on its superior, higher moral qualities. Although another faction may do and say exactly what that faction does, what that faction does is right and what the other faction does is wrong. The acts of one's faction exemplify its moral courage. The other faction acts with impunity.

An example of this common Thai social and political phenomenon occurred in mid-2008. When the police did not push fast enough on Jakrapob's case, the PAD claimed the police acted in a partisan manner. But PAD made no cry when the police quietly stopped pursuing the *lèse-majesté* case against PAD leader Somkiat Pongpaiboon: This was justice.[64] A non-partisan approach could have declared that *lèse-majesté* should not be used against anyone, or that the police should move quickly on every case. Under the current Thai truth system, however, such "consistency" or "logic" is nonsensical and reveals a dangerous naïveté.

When a defamation charge has been made, its efficacy, its potency automatically and instantly obtains. As such, positing that such charge is "politically motivated" is no longer meaningful, just as it is for people who really know the truth of a particular matter and keep it private. To see everyone else as partisan allows for a belief that "neutral parties" can enter the discussion and sift through the confusion of a crisis and make sense of it for all. The public sphere is privy only to the partisan murmurings of those in power. Regardless of what people say in private (or perhaps precisely because they say so only in private), the public sphere under partisan exceptionalism withers.

Partisan exceptionalism is a form of extremism, but, as Carl Schmitt wrote, in the state of exception, "All law is situational." This is another way of saying, "All is permitted" if the situation warrants it. The result of the mechanisms of the defamation regime in the state of exception is not merely militantly anti-democratic; it becomes nihilism. But, contradictorily perhaps, this nihilism claiming to possess the truth is nonetheless willing to delve into the depths of a reverse subterranean hierarchy of enemies (Chapter 10) and authoritatively pronounce them traitors to Thainess.

13 Conclusion

This study shows "that the ostensibly 'soft' phenomena of culture have moulded the 'hard' realities of political power throughout Thai history."[1] Defamation-based laws and their adjudication have created a series of oppositions that define Thainess and Thai culture. This structure of meaning was cemented into place and strengthened in the ahistorical, half-century-long "state of the exception." It was sustained by the notion of Thai uniqueness and resulted in degradation of the truth, which might be better viewed as a narrowing of social and political imagination

Thailand as defamation regime

First, this work has made the argument that the emphasis on intention so prevalent in Thai defamation cases comes from pre-existing Thai Theravada Buddhist cosmology. This view of human nature and society remains largely unchanged by Western colonial depredations and changes since. Historians agree that the arrival of Western science shook the foundations of Thai society. Cosmological and philosophical pre-scientific claims were marked as incorrect and rather unceremoniously tossed aside to make way for scientific claims to the truth. One gets the impression the traditional Thai Theravada Buddhist worldview collapsed. That is largely true for the empirical sciences, which were appropriated wholesale from the West.

However, many historians have also noted that members of the Bangkok elite retained a Theravada Buddhist perspective on human nature.[2] Thongchai suggested that, for internal consumption, King Mongkut appropriated astronomical knowledge and used Western science to strengthen his claim to royal charisma.[3] Gray has noted that much modern historical work on Thailand, at least until recently, viewed Mongkut's religious reforms and Chulalongkorn's modernization as positive and rational. She argued against that position, noting that these nineteenth century and early twentieth century movements were purification rituals that reinforced Thai conceptions of the righteous king, the dhammaraja.[4] Similarly, Jackson has made the case for "semi-coloniality," arguing that European "imperial power," in relation to Siam, "took in the semi-colonial conditions of informal empire, when Asian economies and legal systems were forced to conform to Western norms while political regimes, education systems, and cultural production remained in local hands."[5]

I argue that Thai culture experienced discontinuity in terms of empirical science and continuity in terms of a Theravada Buddhist outlook. Nidhi has pointed out that the 1893 Crisis sparked by French colonial aggression did in fact shake up the Bangkok royal elite, to the extent that it marked the end of one historical epoch and the beginning of another.[6] Thongchai has argued that what really sent Chulalongkorn into a period of depression was not so much the "the loss" of Siamese territory as the lost claim to royal charisma. Thai history, or at least what Thongchai terms as the royalist version of Thai history, has emphasized the colonial threat and the adept ways Bangkok royals navigated through such difficult times.[7] What I suggest here, along the lines of Gray and others, is a history that examines internal Siamese dynamics, rather than the arrival of Western science or colonial ships.

The Thailand-as-unique thesis is quite tempting, but perhaps for reasons not usually cited. Siam was unique for it retained a view of human nature that focused on purity of mind. Those with fortunate past lives accumulated merit and were born into positions of power and respect in this one. Those with much merit could perform ritual purifications to give them the penetrating insight to see the real truth of situations and people. The traditional path to purity of mind was determined by a succession of rebirths leading to the present fortunate birth. Today modern education has become one of the paths legitimating people born with such insight. Those with many years of educational training share the upper echelons of wisdom with senior monks, judges, and the king. There are many paths heading to the same expected outcome: loyalty to the state and a fervent belief in its utter righteousness (and one's own righteousness through rank and association).

The result of this particular Thai Theravada Buddhist view of truth is a focus on intention. "Purification" serves as an historical trope because of its intimate connection to our understanding of defamation in Thailand. Purification makes truth clear; impure minds cannot see the truth. Truth in a traditional Theravada Buddhist context is closely related to intention. From Siam/Thailand's emergence into the modern age a hierarchy of truth and access to truth was established, bringing about a connection between pure minds, truth, and defamation.

During the reign of King Chulalongkorn, those in power identified defamation as meriting special concern. Drawing both from previous notions of treason and modern notions of a sovereign state, the defamation regime was officially established. This regime set into motion mechanisms to legally conceptualize the components and dynamics of defamation—intent, target, effect, and standard. Whereas intent can be substantiated in various ways for crimes which can be adjudicated normally, intent is the primary determinant of guilt or innocence in trials of defamation-based crimes.

Thailand would not be a defamation regime if defamation cases, even with the focus on intent, resulted in a fair number of acquittals. These acquittals would be a sign that exceptions, such as considerations for expressions for the public good and so on, held some sway in court. But defamation cases in Thailand are overwhelmingly judged against the defendant—up to 95 percent for conviction rates of over the past twenty years, for instance, for the entire range of defamation court cases.[8] This percentage would not be so daunting if crimes of defamation did not touch on questions concerning the exercise of power and the state. However, defamation-based crimes, especially *lèse-majesté*, do bear on these central issues For some cases of personal defamation, and virtually all cases of seditious rebellion and *lèse-majesté*, the crime is seen primarily as one of loyalty to the state of identity.

Defamation charges are based on a set of indeterminate, fuzzy clauses either in defamation laws themselves, or in the prevailing political or legal conditions, such as "Abnormal Times". The strength of the defamation regime is partially based on the inherent and intentional indeterminacy of what it protects. We noted that the reputation of an individual protected from libel is somewhat clearly demarcated. But precision diminishes as that person or the institution becomes more highly elevated in the national hierarchy of state bodies, from "the police", to "the government" itself, to "monarchy" (and "this form of government"), and finally to abstractions such as "nation," "national security," and "public order." Antoon de Baets has noted the concern free speech organizations have about "broad definitions" of defamatory targets, for "Public bodies and conceptual entities are so broad and vague that they can be said to be always under attack, and the more abstract they are the more arbitrary and fanciful the charges become."[9]

Nazi jurist Carl Schmitt noted that sovereignty grants the state the power of "determining definitively" these issues of indeterminacy. State power is not evident in how the state defines these values, but rather in how the state determines when they apply and in what situations they receive exception.[10] Schmitt argued that ultimately these indeterminate values and the situations they described could not be "factually determine[d] in any definite manner." Schmitt points out that "liberal constitutionalism" tends to "spell out in detail" the meaning and conditions of the indeterminate values that underpin the state of exception.[11] That's why he preferred dictatorship.

Two conclusions can be drawn from this discussion about the nature of defamation regimes:

First, we can posit a contrast between liberal and democratic, and authoritarian regimes in terms of defamation. Democratic states strive to create an increasingly precise jurisprudent tradition concerning the right to free speech. This may take place in the form of abolishing laws or specific clauses not in conformity with constitutional provisions, decriminalization, social or judicial restraint, or a systematic judicial reform that strengthens the applications of exclusions for fair comment, sincere opinion, or expression made for the public good. These are all indications of an expanding public sphere and a corresponding shrinkage of official or sacred spheres. Contrastingly, authoritarian and sacred regimes work against greater specification in the application of defamation laws, expanding the scope of defamation targets, rarely granting exemption from guilt, showing little restraint in accepting cases, and making little effort to amend or abolish laws in conflict with the spirit of the constitution.

Thailand clearly falls in the latter category. The number of new cases of personal defamation steadily increased each year, with major jumps in the late 1990s and another between 2004 and 2007 (See Figure 7.1). There is no indication that the state has seriously considered decriminalization of libel, or that it even perceives the rapid number of defamation cases (and convictions) as a problem.[12] *Lèse-majesté* cases have proliferated as never before since the heating up of political conflict in late 2005. From 2006 to 2008, Thailand saw an unprecedented number of *lèse-majesté* cases in its courts, with the Supreme Court receiving six cases, the Appeals Court receiving 32 cases and successfully handing down decisions on 40 others, and the Court of First Instance hearing almost 200 cases of *lèse-majesté* cases in 2007 and 2008 alone—dwarfing figures from the historic high of 1977 when there were 36 arrests for *lèse-majesté* (of which only seven were eventually prosecuted). But 2009 deserves special recognition, with an astounding 164 new cases of *lèse-majesté* received by the lower courts.[13]

This study suggests an analysis of defamation-based laws and adjudication—and the ramifications thereof—provides a key gauge measuring the level of democratisation in Thailand. That defamation laws and adjudication have been applied over the years in greater doses and increasing strength challenges scholars who optimistically trace "Thailand's trajectory toward greater democratisation" over the past few decades. The chronology of defamation in Thailand has few bright spots and portends a dark future. Thaksin Shinawatra used the personal defamation law with abandon. The rise of the People's Alliance for Democracy (PAD), especially in its post-May 2008 incarnation, was largely based on hunting down and exposing those its leaders perceive as betraying the monarchy and Thainess. The Democrat Party's rise to power was based on its support for the PAD and its shared propensity for trumpeting its loyalty to the throne and smearing of the patriotism of its enemies.

The authoritarian urge behind defamation-based accusations is easy to trace. Personal defamation cases tripled between 1997 and 2005. The upward trend became noticeable once the Democrat Party came to power in 1997 and especially when Democrat leader and then prime minister Chuan Leekpai chose to use the personal defamation law to punish government critics. By charging critics with defamation he contradicted the nearly universal standard in democratic countries of allowing comment on high-ranking public officials—even if these comments were technically defamatory. The courts and state prosecutors could have failed an instrumental role either by using discretion and discrimination in accepting personal defamation cases filed by public figures, or by establishing a custom of genuine jurisprudence in cases of defamation-based adjudication. When they failed to do so, the way was clear for Thaksin's unprecedented abuse of the defamation law, filing tens if not hundreds of cases since 2001 and demanding astronomical amounts in damages. The courts did nothing to stop this trend. As a result, accusations of defamation have become integral to Thai political life, weakening the public sphere and negating other possible optimistic developments in Thai democratisation.[14]

Outside of personal defamation, the trend is even more worrying. Under Sarit Thanarat's regime, the Sangha Act was stripped of its democratic elements. A coup-installed legislative body amended the Act in 1992, providing special protection to the Supreme Patriarch, the leader of the official state-sponsored Buddhist hierarchy, and to Buddhist monks in general that began to resemble a heresy law:

> *Section 44 Bis.* No person shall defame, insult or express aggression against the Supreme Patriarch. Any person who violates shall be liable to imprisonment for a term of not exceeding one year or to a fine not exceeding two hundred thousand Baht or to both.
>
> *Section 44 Tri.* No person shall impute any group of monks [*sic*], causing disgrace or disunity. Any person who violates shall be liable to imprisonment for a term of not exceeding one year or to a fine not exceeding two hundred thousand Baht or to both.[15]

In 2002 I wrote, perhaps too optimistically, that Thailand had no heresy law.[16] That same year, the Education Ministry and the House Committee on Religion, Arts, and Culture both introduced (unsuccessfully) legislation that would have provided even heavier punishments for criticism of state Buddhism.[17] A year after the 2006 coup, the military-appointed National Legislative Assembly (NLA) actually considered a draft law called, "The Support and Protection of Buddhism Act." The law would have meant imprisonment for 10 to 25 years and fine from one half to one million baht for anyone found guilty of "distorting Buddhism teachings" and up to ten years and a half a million baht fine for insulting monks or violating "religious places, icons," and "even rituals." Had this passed, Thailand would have become a religious state, with state-appointed theologians deciding on correct Buddhist teachings. While it is fortunate that the draft was shelved with little debate, that it was even considered shows that the authoritarian urge based on defamation is still strong.[18]

Two recent proposals for amending the *lèse-majesté* law also give little reason to be optimistic about increasing democratization in Thailand. The Introduction of this book related the account of the National Legislative Assembly's attempt to strengthen the *lèse-majesté* law. If passed, the amendment would have extended the number of personages protected by the law (the king, queen, heir-apparent, and regent if there were one) to include the king's children and members of the Privy Council.[19] This amendment would not have made the law more precise, but instead would have expanded the "indeterminacy" already inherent in the law. In October 2008, Piraphan Saliratviphak of the Democrat Party (later Minister of Justice) proposed an amendment to the *lèse-majesté* law to outlaw defamation or insult of "members of the royal family" [*phraboromwongsanuwong*]—including relatives, descendants, and past kings of the dynasty, impose a Bt500,000 to Bt1,000,000 fine, increase the penalty from three to 15 years to five to 25 years, and place the burden on the accused to prove innocence.[20] This proposed amendment would complement the NLA-passed Computer Crimes Act under which *lèse-majesté* offenses are punished with imprisonment of a minimum of three and a maximum of 20 years.[21]. The military government of 2007 had previously set the high for new cases of *lèse-majesté* at 126. The Democrat-led government came charging into power after spending a year introducing to parliament more severe penalties and promising to enforce internet-related *lèse-majesté* laws.[22] The Democrat Party did a superb job of it. It presided over an all-time high of new *lèse-majesté* cases at 164 (see Figure 8.1), the first jailing under the Computer Crimes Act, and the longest sentence given for *lèse-majesté* since at least the 1970s. The first computer criminal was Suwicha Thakhor, an oil rig engineer who posted a YouTube video clip deemed offensive to the monarchy. He was sentenced to 20 years in prison (cut in half to 10 years for his confession).[23] And a defiant Daranee Charnchoengsilpakul (Chapter 8) was given 18 years, an incredibly long sentence for a word crime in a nominal democratic society.

A heresy law, a functioning and often used *lèse-majesté* law, and a 20-year prison sentence for a difference in belief or something deemed insulting, in the twenty-first century, in a country that makes pretensions of having progressed democratically, does not make sense.[24] In terms of religion, Duncan McCargo has called for a rethinking of the way that Thai Buddhsim is viewed by scholars, especially in light of the mobilization and militarization of Buddhism in the South of Thailand:

> Thai Buddhist studies are too often pervaded by a set of simplistic and rarely challenged assumptions: Buddhism is a peaceful religion, Thailand is a tolerant country guided by the exercise of metta (loving-kindness) and characterised by religious freedom, while Thai Buddhists enjoy harmonious relations with people of other religions . . . [Attacks on Malay Muslim civilians in the South] revealed the extent to which hard-line nationalist discourse and anti-Muslim sentiments were becoming increasingly overt and mainstream elements of Thai Buddhist identity and thinking.

Concludes McCargo, rather than providing a force of compassion and understanding, "Thai Buddhism was becoming increasingly particularistic, more and more national and very markedly less civil."[25]

The second conclusion that can be drawn from this study is that judges are given extraordinary power to shape the contours of Thai politics through adjudication of defamation cases. The courts are a public body that cannot be criticised.[26] Even legal experts are unclear about exactly what comments can be made concerning the courts. Court decisions examined in this study suggest that it may be illegal to say that the courts are unjust. This is not a moot question because a perceived insult can result in up to seven years' imprisonment.[27] Chulalongkorn University lecturer Naruemon Thabchumpon was found guilty of contempt of court for saying that court and police in Lampun province had acted unjustly. She was sentenced to a year in jail and fined 14,000 baht.[28] One law lecturer claims that once a final decision is handed down, court judgments can be critiqued, although few scholarly pieces do so.[29] A former Supreme Court judge opined that court decisions can be critiqued, but warns that such critique must employ "academic principles."[30] Klausner proposes there is a "unique historical bond between the Crown and the judiciary" that makes the courts untouchable:

> Unlike other civil servants throughout the government bureaucracy in various Ministries, all judges, after their trainee status has been completed and prior to assuming their position as full fledged judges, must pledge an oath of loyalty to His Majesty and be royally appointed by him. In addition, every judgment made in court must be rendered "in the name of the King".[31]

This study suggests the centrality of judges and courts in forming the basic contours and outcomes of certain political, social, and cultural practices. The courts hold much power over Thai society and how its citizens may speak of one another. The courts are not easily checked by other government agencies and the public seems to be denied any critical role. Minor efforts to introduce a jury system in Thailand have not succeeded.[32]

Historically, Thai courts have played little role as agents of social and political change. A political analyst noted: "Up to now, the courts have played a very limited role in Thai politics compared to other democracies. There are no precedent-setting judgements punctuating Thailand's political history."[33] Thongchai has pointed out that "there is no significant critical study of the politics of the judiciary." He has argued,

> The judicial system has a long and solid record of siding with whoever is in power. But they do so quietly, rarely engaging with politics overtly. They always know the winds, so to speak. Heroic actions were not impossible but are rare. Its undistinguished history suggests that the judiciary is not at all an independent body to counter abuse of power. Indeed the lack of an independent judiciary is probably one of the most serious problems of Thai democratization that has escaped serious attention.[34]

Since the king deemed the April 2006 political situation "a mess" and called on the courts to fix the crisis, the courts have exerted uncharacteristic influence over Thai politics, leading to a *judicialization* of Thai society.[35] The new 2007 constitution makes Thailand what might be called a *judge-ocracy* or *curiocracy*, with committees dominated by judges who select members of so-called independent agencies such as the National Human Rights Commission (NHRC) and the unelected members of the senate. Court rulings (or silence) have been met with growing controversy. Courts annulled the results of the general election in April 2006 on a technicality, dissolved the ruling political party and banned its executives from politics for five years twice—once in 2007 and then again in 2008, essentially disqualified two prime ministers, selectively granted or denied bail to various suspects, and were largely silent and therefore seemed to condone the coup. There were even allegations that some high-ranking judges were behind the coup. As a result, many Thai have lost faith in the judiciary system.[36]

Newspaper columnist Chang Noi witheringly described the underlying spirit of the draft of the new constitution in 2007: "Fear and loathing of elective democracy is the dominant theme of the new draft constitution. Never again, the drafters hope, should real power be based upon the people's vote."[37] Sensitive of the criticism that judges were given immense power, Supreme Administrative Court President Aklarathorn Chularat tried to soothe public fears that high-ranking judges "would lose their neutral role and select only former and active state officials with close connections to them." Aklarathorn reportedly "expressed confidence in the judges' impartiality in their role" and that for his own part "he would only select those with high capability, good knowledge, and acceptable performance and qualifications, and vowed not to let politicians interfere in the selection process for independent bodies." Assured Aklarathorn, "We are duty-bound to select the best people."[38]

Aklarathorn's vision was fulfilled with the selection of new NHRC commissioners. Politicians did not interfere. The judge-dominated committee received 133 applications for NHRC commissioners on 8 March 2009 and, within two days, forwarded seven names to the senate. The Asian Human Rights Commission (ARC) warned that "the selection process of the new commissioners has been rushed, non-transparent, undemocratic and contrary to the basic principles that the NHRC is supposed to represent."[39] However, behind closed doors the Senate approved the nominees. One observer in dismay renamed the NHRC "the Anti-Human Rights Commission" as the seven selected comprised "a top cop, a judicial administrator, a civil servant, an industrialist, an academic, a former senator, and a road safety advocate." None of Akarathom's "best people" had any "good knowledge" about human rights or were recognized in the field, four had no conceptual understanding of human rights at all, and one had been under investigation for possible human rights violations himself. Concluded an Asian human rights observer, "A more ugly lot of rights commissioners would be hard to find."[40] Brad Adams, Human Rights Watch Asia director, said in a press release, "Instead, inexperienced and unqualified people were placed on this commission in a way that clearly broke the rules. The best thing these members can do for human rights is to step down."[41] The appointments were a disaster and embarrassment, caused by a deeply flawed selection process stipulated in a distressingly anti-democratic charter that depended on top judges. Such are the bitter fruits of what McCargo has called "virtuous rule" (see below).

The century-old Thai defamation regime reached perfection when under the auspices of the 2007 constitution parliamentary rule was replaced with judiciary rule. This state of affairs is the culmination of a process began in 1958 with the undermining of the legal regime, further legal depredations following the coups of 1976, 1991, and 2006, and the advent of the military-installed National Legislative Assembly and constitution-drafting committee providing the final pieces. The NLA proposed a series of legislative defamation-based measures to provide more comprehensive protection of the three pillars of Thainess—monarchy, religion (Thai Theravada Buddhism), and the courts (representing the pillar of nation). If realized, Buddhism and the monarchy would be protected by measures stipulating maximum punishments of 25 years, in addition to the present maximum punishment of seven years' imprisonment for contempt of the courts, a penalty that gives it the same weight as the monarchy prior to 1976.

From the perspective of defamation, Thailand has yet to realize democracy under constitutional monarchy. The defamation laws were not substantively revised to reflect the change to democracy in 1932. Since 1976 at least, Thai defamation laws have shifted the country into reverse, with laws more draconian than under the absolute monarchy.

Thailand as the state of the exception

This study has shown how the literature on sovereignty and the "state of the exception" directly relate to defamation. But this literature refers indirectly to the type of legal and political milieu in which defamation regimes thrive. Up until the 1950s, Thailand might not have been a full-fledged defamation regime. On the one hand, I argued that the courts and the Juridical Council were hesitant to expand the range of indeterminate clauses such as "peace and order" and allowed some latitude to those criticizing the government. At the same time, on the other hand courts lent legitimacy to the violent overthrow of the government, refused to overturn amnesties that military coup groups wrote for themselves, and acquiesced to a succession of torn-up constitutions. Sarit Thanarat and his military clique took power in the late 1950s and established the defamation "state of the exception," initiating more than a half century of a legal indeterminacy that strengthened and solidified the defamation regime. This regime's spell over Thai society now appears permanent, evolving into an "eternal abnormal time."

Carl Schmitt's work eerily, but with great accuracy, described not the German Third Reich so much as present-day Thailand.[42] Schmitt states that he built a "general concept in the theory of the state . . . not merely to a construct applied to any emergency decree or state of siege." This theory was based on the deceptively simple phrase, "Sovereign is he who decides on the exception."[43] Schmitt wrote in the early 1920s when the Weimar Republic expressed the "general norm, as represented by an ordinary legal prescription."[44] Ultimately, Schmitt argued, "the test of whether an emergency exists cannot be a juristic one." The state of exception is not primarily a legal prescription, although its effects may have a juridical effect. Sovereignty was a "concrete application," meaning that the leader is the one:

> who decides in a situation of conflict what constitutes the public interest or interest of the state, public safety and order . . . The exception, which is not codified in the existing legal order, can at best be characterized as a case of extreme peril, a danger to the existence of the state, or the like. But it cannot be circumscribed factually and made to conform to a preformed law.[48]

Schmitt's work made sense only when a normal regime of law is established to which an exception can then be instituted.[45] It can be argued that an absolute monarchy is by definition already a state of exception. When did a regime in Siam first express this type of logic? It is not too difficult, then, to argue that Siam as a level regime was already in a "state of exception" in 1900 under King Chulalongkorn.[46] The king was sovereign, yet there was no exception since no normality (in this sense meaning some level of popular sovereignty or what Schmitt calls "constitutional liberalism") had yet been established.[47]

Siam's "legal order" was established during the period 1893 to 1908 and it was the king who determined "the public interest or interest of the state" and "public safety." Such determinations were made in the language and within the framework of premodern conceptualizations of danger. This situation of the Thai elites was inherently contradictory, a state of what Michael Herzfeld has called "crypto-colonialism" (see below). The Thai elite were both humiliated by, and eager to work with, Western colonial powers. Thongchai correctly notes that, in 1893, Chulalongkorn became depressed due to the monarchy's loss of prestige.[49] Thus, the "emergency" suggested itself before a "normal" regime of law (in Schmitt's sense) had been constructed.

Accordingly, the framework of modern Thai law was established within a time and on the basis of the "state of exception." How else can we read Schmitt's meaning when he says, "The precise details of an emergency cannot be anticipated, nor can one spell out what may take place in such a case, especially when it is truly a matter of an extreme emergency and of how it is to be eliminated"?[50] The events of 1893 were not anticipated, nor were the contingencies or dangers spelled out in law. Thai modern law was established according to an incredible mindset (the loss of royal charisma) and conditions (an absolutist state with a number of colonial models at hand). These historically contingent conditions made the "state of exception" the norm within Thai law.[51]

The "state of the exception" suggests the larger question of accountability and impunity. To what or to whom must the sovereign (meaning the one with the power to declare the state of exception) be held accountable when declaring the "state of exception"? In constitutional systems, the constitution lays out the guidelines for its own suspension. Schmitt felt that constitutions muddy the issue of who is sovereign, for actions are "subject to controls" and "hampered in some way by checks and balances." The sovereign is the person "who must decide whether the constitution needs to be suspended in its entirety."[52] In Thailand, it is the generals who carry out the coup and the monarch validates it. If generals had to "consult a senate or the people" before launching the coup, they would not be sovereign. It is necessary to state the obvious: in Thailand "the people" have never been sovereign. Any pretensions to the contrary have regularly ended when the tanks once again roll out onto the streets.[53]

In 1932 a constitutional order was established when the absolute monarchy came to an end. Until 1958, various declarations of emergency were made, but, as Schmitt wrote, "not every extraordinary measure, not every police emergency measure or emergency decree, is necessarily an exception." Thai courts generally went about their adjudications normally. But in a number of instances (Chapter 5), Supreme Court decisions laid the groundwork for the "state of the exception." The Supreme Court apparently did not, as the embodiment of "day-to-day" jurisprudence, "confront the extreme case disconcertedly" as Schmitt theorized, but rather approached these cases with eager acquiescence.[54]

However, prior to even being asked to do so, the courts essentially affirmed the core principle of the state of exception according to Schmitt:

> *the existence of the state is undoubtedly proof of its superiority over the validity of the legal norm* [emphasis added].

Instead of leaving the norm alone, the Supreme Court reconfigured the norm, so that the political order could accommodate the basic form of the exception, the coup: "unlimited authority, which means the suspension of the entire existing order",[55] in which "the state remains, whereas law recedes." This was not a case, as Schmitt wrote, "[where] the norm is destroyed in the exception," but rather, one where a norm is moved decisively to embrace the exception.[56]

Two other aspects in the theory of the "state of the exception," both of them in relation to Sarit Thanarat and his predecessors, might apply to Thai history. Schmitt carefully differentiates between chaos and the exception. While "[T]here exists no norm that is applicable to chaos," Schmitt nonetheless affirms that "anarchy and chaos" are conditions in which "the juristic sense still prevails even if it is not of the ordinary kind."[57] Within the Thai Theravada Buddhist polity, chaos is the karmic effect of actions and words of ill-intentioned persons. If unchecked by persons of virtue who have penetrating insight, all will come to ruin. Chaos precedes and heralds the coming of the sovereign, the one who will make the decision "in absolute purity," the decision that "frees itself from all normative ties and becomes in the true sense absolute."[58] Increasing selfishness and chaos prompt the coup; Buddhist ritual purifications define post-coup actions—voiding the old constitution, granting an amnesty, convening the wise to create a pure new constitution.

The coup itself is a modern phenomenon, conditioned by a historical sense of "normal rule of law."[59] If the Enlightenment was rationalistic and "rejected the exception in every form," the Thai coup is the re-entrance of the sovereign and the miracle. The rationalistic "theology and metaphysics" that underpin the "modern constitutional state . . . banished the miracle from the world" and

> rejected not only the transgression of the laws of nature through an exception brought about by direct intervention as is found in the idea of a miracle, but also the sovereign's [or military general's] direct intervention in a valid legal order.[60]

Within this formulation, *the decision* is the key factor. Schmitt writes that the state of the exception is "a reduction of the state to the moment of the decision, to a pure decision not based on reason and discussion and not justifying itself, that is, to an absolute decision created out of nothingness."[61]

This drama is easy to see in modern Thai history. The military makes the decision to act, declares itself the sovereign, and invokes the state of exception. If chaos eventually ensues, then the king steps in to solve the crisis. Quite often the supporting role goes to "the people," who demanded miraculous intervention by the military or the king (such as protests leading up to the 1957 coup, or the call by the PAD for the king to intervene in 2006, or the PAD's attempts to provoke a coup in 2008). That the king is considered semi-divine and that the military has overwhelming physical force contribute to the sense of these events as miraculous.

Thak's descriptions of one of the key components of Sarit's approach to power is appropriate: Sarit's *decisiveness*.[62] Still today, Sarit is thought of fondly for his decisiveness. Sarit established this formula when acting against arsonists and eulogizing his own pure intentions:

> I have decided that prompt and decisive action must be taken immediately, especially in the case of fires . . . Therefore, I am forced to act with ultimate decisiveness [*det khat*] What is right or wrong, I and I alone will

> take responsibility for carrying out policies that I deem most correct and which will lead to the happiness of the people. Please accept and take notice of this.
>
> . . . decisiveness is the only instrument that can help the nation achieve progress.
>
> Whether it is just or not I do not fear. I only hold on to the thought that with every breath I take, I think only of the happiness of all Thais. This is my highest wish which has led me to make this drastic decision.
>
> I will assume sole responsibility if there is any.[63]

This was peculiar phrasing: Sarit accepted full responsibility, after having absolved himself and his cohorts of responsibility for overthrowing the government. Moreover, he made this statement as sovereign, a hollow claim to full responsibility made with knowledge that "no higher authority could review the decision," and so no possibility of consequences.[64]

Every miracle must overcome adversaries. For Sarit, communists were the enemy. For the PAD, the military, and the palace, the most recent enemy was Thaksin. Many Thai applauded PAD for bringing more of the public into the process and holding the government more accountable. But one of PAD's principal achievements has been rather to draw out and develop the politics of hatred.[65] PAD, in a cosmological expression and not merely rhetorical flourish, called its opponents "creatures from hell" or "demons."[66]

Schmitt points out that the state of exception is not declared on juridical grounds, but rather on "philosophical-historical or metaphysical convictions," thus underscoring the importance of understanding more precisely the sovereign's state of mind.[67] To Schmitt, political theory is essentially a kind of theology that expresses deep-seated beliefs about the nature of humans. In Thailand, though, this cosmology is arranged by perceived levels of merit according to Thai Theravada Buddhism (Chapter 6), and its conservative expression is intrinsically opposed to democracy and the public sphere.[68] PAD rhetoric does not create dialogue; it is a stage for denunciation on theological grounds.[69] Schmitt derided the bourgeoisie as the "discussing class," torn between privilege, financial interests, ideas of liberalism, rule of law, and greater rights extended to all.[70] The "state of the exception," taken to its logical end in Thailand or elsewhere, does not end with democracy and the expansion of the public sphere. Instead, it leads to accusations of treason, theological condemnations, and an acceptance and even celebration of impunity and authoritarianism. As Schmitt states, "Dictatorship is the opposite of discussion."[71] Perhaps the full expression of Thai Theravada Buddhism as a political theology is uniquely Thai, but Thailand's political configuration today shows it remains, nonetheless, a child of the European Counterrevolution.

The state of the exception is merely another manifestation of the belief in the uniqueness of Thai culture and political institutions. It is expressed in the ideology of Thainess, whose roots go back to the establishment of the defamation state in 1900. It evolved into a set of interlocking schematics whose various parts manifest themselves in Thai historiography, popular culture, national security considerations, and so on.[72] These schematics create and perpetuate what Thongchai lays out as the core historiographical premise of the Thai "royalist-nationalist ideology":

> Siam was under threat from European powers . . . its independence was in jeopardy. The rapid modernization and reform of government were measures for the defense of the country's independence . . . With skilful diplomacy, the Chakri monarchs saved the country, though not without sacrifice and pain.[73]

This century-old model expresses the dynamics of Herzfeld's "crypto-colonialism," in which certain countries not formally colonized by European powers become enmeshed in an "ironic predicament" that becomes "articulated in the iconic guise of aggressively national culture" and

> the aggressive promotion of their claims to civilizational superiority or antiquity, claims that almost always appear disproportionate to their political influence. One begins to suspect that they have been placed, or place themselves, on high cultural pedestals that effectively isolate them from other, more brutally material forms of power.[74]

In such cases, the anthropology of such countries lacks "major theoretical traditions," perhaps because the Thai elite in the crypto-colony of Siam had a hand, with the applause of admiring foreign advisers, in creating its own anthropological and cultural "theoretical" tradition that depicted Thailand in a certain way. The "image" became "the outcome of some careful impression management at the level of state-supported institutions" which allowed the elite to "consolidate their authority."[75] In Thailand, this tendency was reinforced with an "official discourse" substantiated by the development of a Thai "national character." The solidification of this national character type came about by the late 1930s with renaming the country "Thailand," the propagation of the newly coined word for "culture" (Chapter 10), and embarking on irredentism to "reclaim" areas from the French and British during World War II.[76] These manifestations fed into American influence during the cold war, when communism became "incompatible with civilization" and the quintessential "un-Thai" charateristic. At the same time, the "resentment" of perceived "elite emulation of Western models" caused a "reaction" through "antimaterialist religious" movements opposed to "Western and materialist morals and models." The elite "resist domination" and use "civilizational discourses to enhance their own power, at the cost of collective subjugation of their country to a global cultural hierarchy," and "by deploying a world-dominating discourse about 'culture' in defense of their perceived national interests and specificity."[77] On the level of anthropological theory, Thailand as a subject had been "ambiguous and frustrating" because Thainess is based on "[t]he opposition between colonizer and colonized."[78] Herzfeld argues that it is time to dismantle such dichotomies, to "reveal the presence of other hegemonies, harder to disassemble precisely because they have been well concealed . . . The world is no longer made up of colonizers and colonized alone, nor was it ever so simply split."[79] But Thailand remains stuck in that world, even though it maintains it was never (directly) "colonized." The centerpiece of its history is, strangely, something that never happened.

"Thai" truth within "a society of whisperers"[80]

This study suggests that truth under a defamation regime becomes a difficult proposition. The origins of the defamation regime are found in the logic of blasphemy and heresy, not in social and political forms that produce truth. I propose that the rather uninterrupted historical hold of Thai Theravada Buddhism, under state control and with a tendency to depend on truth from spiritual masters, has resulted in creating a relative disregard for obvious facts and truths. In Thailand, even the most mundane truth often plays a secondary role to image and reputation.

Theravada Buddhism provides a strong foundation for a defamation regime places intent over the substance of communication. Jackson has argued that state power emerging within this type of formation focuses on "the management of aestheticized 'surface' performances" which are part of a historical legacy that creates "the legitimation of political authority."[81] This pre-existing tendency was crystallized with the militarization of Thai society as it fell into eternal "abnormal times"—which extended even into periods when the military had largely removed itself from active politics. When married to the modern legal order of the defamation regime, this perspective on truth and exceptionality flourished.

Thailand stands at one end of the continuum of defamation regimes, where its defamation laws—especially the *lèse-majesté* law—have banished truth from the public sphere, where truth is translated in a complex world of signs decipherable only by modern-day People of Virtue. Truth exists in the margins and veiled worlds of the private sphere, hidden deep within the national institutions of rumour and gossip.

Borwornsak points out that intent is a key component of defamation-law adjudication such as *lèse-majesté*.[82] But it can be argued that focus on intent is the core of the problem in the first place. The existence of a defamation case suggests that the words are defamatory. If defamatory, then the intent of the defamer was malicious. "Evidence" of ill intent extinguished the possibility of claiming exclusion. Under these self-fulfilling circumstances, given the exceedingly low possibility of acquittal, one conclusion a society might draw is that much of the nation is in fact peopled by huge numbers of ill-intentioned citizens. That intent has been the near-exclusive focus of Thai defamation adjudication obscures the question of the veracity of the allegations of the defamatory statement. Defamation litigation is a form of subterfuge. It *appears* to be about the truth, when in fact it is about reputation. When the defamation case is about something alleged as a fact, all the litigation maneuvers—allegations of the defamer's impure motives, the possible effect the words might have on society if believed—do not alter the truth of what really happened.

Truth in a defamation regime requires privileged access available only to the righteous (and, usually, in the Thai case, "educated"). Truth is also, one might say, *ethnicized*—part and parcel of Thai culture and Thainess—indiscernible to the outsider. This particular juxtaposition of truth and Thainess, within a milieu of abnormal times, thrives, becomes actualized by its perceived threats. The truth of defamation owes its existence to the enemy. Even some erstwhile progressive Thai academics cannot resist the lure of Thai Truth and have "embraced a blend of racial nationalism, nativism, anti-Westernism and anti-capitalism."[83] Purveyors of this kind of truth must ferret out any and all manifestations of insult, even outside the borders of Thailand.

The suspension of "Thai" history

The pre-existing and rather clear historical focus of Theravada Buddhism on the issue of intent created a fertile soil in which defamation could flourish. Notions of truth are funnelled through this political, legal, and cultural skein, resulting in a particular "Thai" worldview and specification of certain dynamics within Thai history. The ritual purification of the state, as a historical trope or as a unit of analysis, parallels quite closely the journey of defamation through Thai history.

For the sake of argument, let us construct an alternate Thai history in order to pursue the themes of this study to their logical ends. Defamation laws and their adjudication—particularly treason and *lèse-majesté*—provide the foundation; "Thainess" or the official nationalism/royal-nationalist model become the building blocks; the state of the exception provides a structure; and "purification," "unity," and "crisis" provide for the social and political dynamics within.

Politics, constitutions, democracy, power, unity, and impartiality (or neutrality) inform the view of history from within this particular worldview.

Politics in Thailand is viewed as the naked grasping for power, the clinging to self-interest, the perilous karmic domain of words and talk. When Sarit seized power in 1957, he clearly indicated a coup was not a political act when he said, "I have nothing to do with politics." The king himself has made this kind of distinction, saying in 1974, "I became King when I was quite young. I was 18, and very suddenly, I learned that politics is a filthy business."[84] Politicians become entangled in their own selfishnesses. Politics causes bias and clinging and therefore results in divisions.

Constitutions are suspect for they are mere words. They try to set certain principles that, if adhered to too strongly, cause one to lose perspective, as all is transitory. It is better to have the essence of the constitution captured within The Meritorious, the persons of virtue.

Democracy is a highly imperfect form, as ordinary people do not have adequate merit hence, wisdom, to understand the real intentions of "better educated," closer-to-the-centre, people of merit. Ordinary people are not citizens, they are merely "the people" [*prachachon*], often wilful, resistant to the correctly-intentioned admonitions of those higher in the hierarchy, and easily misled. Elections do not result in the election of virtuous people. The Meritorious are a better fit as representatives of and for the people.

Power can only be exercised by persons who are impartial and have good intentions.[85]

Unity is the outcome of the correct use of power. In looking at Thai political conservatism, Hewison noted that "discipline and unity are closely linked to law and order and authority."[86] Discipline is necessary for "humans are imperfect and need controls."[87] Unity is taken as the ideal state of harmony and an absence of problems, subversion, or crime.[88] Since ascending the throne, the king has emphasized the need for unity. Lack of unity equals chaos, causing society to "degenerate and become confused and unstable, and possibly collapse altogether."[89] The presence of "political conflict" is a sign of disunity, the king has said, and will bring "utter destruction of Thailand. It will mean that the Thai Nation which the Thai People have built up for so long will turn into an insignificant country."[90] The king, no stranger to hyperbole in depicting Thai society on the brink of utter ruin, said in 1974, "Each and everyone must work together . . . , sharing common aims and objectives. Should any group fail in its duty . . . the entire nation may collapse and be destroyed."[91] If unified, Thainess would remain intact. Inscribed on an amulet given out by the king in 1965 were the words: "The Thai people can preserve Thainess by consciously striving for unity."[92] With unity achieved, a system of rights imposed from the outside is neither necessary nor legitimate. Since society is so prone to falling victim to evil doers, people cannot effectively preserve their rights. Only the king can truly ensure rights. As a personal secretary to the king has claimed, "Our Monarchy is far too deep-rooted and thoroughly involved in the protection of the individual's rights to be done away with."[93] The *impartiality* of virtuous rule is the only way to counter the evil doers.

In a recent work on legitimacy within the context of the troubled South of Thailand, Duncan McCargo aptly described this political ideal as "virtuous rule," based on the idea of "the virtuous Buddhist kingship, or *dhammaraja*":

> According to this construct, rule is legitimate if the ruler is good. The idea that politicians and other leaders may be divided into "good" and "bad" people is a pervasive one in Thailand and has been framed by the moralistic tutelary discourse that characterizes speeches by King Bhumibol and his network.[94]

Despite the pretense of adhering to ancient forms, development of this concept of virtuous rule is relatively new, formed with the establishment of the absolute monarchy when it was still clearly understood that the Siamese state ruled over an ethnically, culturally, and religiously diverse polity at the end of the nineteenth century.

Two largely contradictory policies were pursued at that time by the Siamese state. The first of these policies defined Siam vis-à-vis the European colonial powers. There was a certain arbitrariness to the present borders of Thailand; they were what remained after the European powers parcelled out Siamese-controlled areas to themselves. The European powers and the Siamese elite applied a variety of techniques and measures to demarcate boundaries. Simultaneously, the Siamese elite and European powers ethnically and racially classified the people within these boundaries (now Thailand, Laos, Vietnam, Cambodia, Burma, and Malaysia) into citizens. In the case of Siam, the push was for an internal religious, linguistic, cultural, administrative standardization that created the impression that the kingdom was a unified and unitary state.

Machinations by the Siamese elite with respect to this standardization are not hard to find. Siam carried out its first census in 1904, just as the government expunged and replaced ethnic terms in the names of administrative units (*muang lao khao, muang lao phuan*) with compass point designations (Northeast, Northwest). Grabowsky noted that "Lao ethnicity was henceforth negated," and attributed this redesignation to preventing race from becoming "a tool for further [French and British] expansion."[95] Item 7 of the "Explanations" to the census, using a newly developed "racialist" logic, described the reason the Lao are really Thai and not "real Lao":

> [T]here does exist a case where a separation [into different races] is not feasible. That is how to separate Lao from Thai, for even among the general population itself there are no discernable traits which can be used to differentiate Thai from Lao. If we speak about languages, Lao and Thai languages are of the same stock . . . If we base our supposition on well-known facts, then the people we call presently Lao were actually Thai and not Lao . . . There are still people of real Lao race, i.e., [the people] we call "Lawa" . . . the real inhabitants of Northern Siam, before the Thai came to rule the country [who] . . . are still living in small areas scattered all over the country. Since it was not reasonable to distinguish them, it made no sense to divide the Thai by taking the Lao as a separate group . . . Therefore, in the detailed census the Lao had to be registered as Thai.[96]

In 1904, when calculated along the lines of a largely mono-ethnic Siam, "Thai" made up 85 percent of the population. But if the "Lao" became their own "race", "Thai" would no longer make up the majority of a very hetero-ethnic Siam.[97] Education and administrative policies strictly enforced policies to make this ethnic unity real. The 1960 census avoided the question of ethnicity entirely, noting (triumphantly, perhaps) that 98.2 percent of the population were Thai nationals and 97.8 percent over five years of age could speak Thai.[98]

At the same time, it is no coincidence that the rebellions against centralization in the South, North, and Northeast in the first decade of the twentieth century were the same places where the Communist Part of Thailand was most successful in the 1960s and 1970s, or that these were the same areas under contention by the Assembly of the Poor, and, to a certain degree, where support for Thaksin and opposition to the 2006 coup forces were strongest.[99]

This suggests the possibility of a historical narrative organized along ethnic lines, where the Thai state, representing "Thainess," works to maintain the myth of ethnic unity, juxtaposed against resurgent non-Thai ethnic identities struggling for greater local autonomy.[100]

A second policy pursued by the Siamese state towards the end of the nineteenth century was to define the civilizing elite vis-à-vis the less civilized people in Siam: a way of arranging society hierarchically so that the elite could preserve and expand its power and legitimacy. The first policy, noted above, said, "We are all Thai." This second one, stemming from Theravada Buddhism, said, "Sovereignty belongs to those who are superior spiritually." This imagined hierarchy was contradicted by the diversity on the ground and the remarkable level of privilege and power wielded by the elite. Defamation laws, centered around the monarchy, were created to preserve this imagined unity.

After the 1932 overthrow of the absolute monarchy, the ensuing struggle between royal and popular sovereignty threatened this imagined unity. From 1932 to 1958, limits were placed on royal power, a precarious accommodation between the military and the royalty was forged, and the foundations of a permanent state of exception were put into place. We might call this a period of intermittent states of exception. Defamation laws eased slightly. The contending political forces left just enough room for history to "move," for agency to appear; the question of popular sovereignty was not yet resolved.[101]

Then, for nearly half a century from 1958 to the present, Thai history has gone into suspended animation—beginning in 1958 to 1973, and restarting from 1976 to now. The myth of unity was strengthened ideologically by Thailand-as-unique-historical-case and the establishment of a permanent "state of the exception." Accordingly, defamation laws were applied with ever-greater frequency and heavier punishment. Defamation of the state and seditious rebellion were effectively subsumed within *lèse-majesté*. The lack of rule of law, legitimacy, and breath-taking acts of impunity became so systematized that they emerged as celebrated unique characteristics of "Thai democracy."[102] Within its suspended state, "Thai history" harkens back to an imagined unity. In this pseudo-historical scheme, no "events" occurred, for history was not supposed to go anywhere. "History" happened in the mythical past and was no longer necessary. "Coups" in a general archetypal sense did happen, but not specific coups, for they were quickly erased, transformed into acts of of necessity, deprived of attribution. These were not quite "events," but more affirmations of the essential unity (or its enemies), where the actions of the ill-intentioned are meticulously recorded. Their condemnation was celebrated as affirmation, as was occasionally, their tearful regret as they had become conscious of their wickedness and begged for re-admission to the realm of Thainess. Those who refused to capitulate in court were locked up and lost to the world.

Thai "history" is more akin to a melodrama which, by its nature is plot-thin and peopled by caricatures. Thai "history" is not designed to progress, but rather to show the unfolding of the moral qualities of the characters and to deliver justice to good and evil. Thai "history" aspires to the epic, but always ends up turgid, pedantic, and prosaic.

In its suspended state, verifiable historical events are erased or obscured. The facts surrounding an event are unavailable, they inevitably become muddled and part of the enduring mystery of truth slowly unfolding itself to those who can see. Thai truth strengthens Thai unity. Defamation laws strike at the treasonous ill-intentioned, the un-Thai one who seeks to undermine the myth of unity. Laws based on the defamation principle propose a contest between contending forces in terms of those who, on the one hand, "sacrifice for the country" and "strive for unity," and those who, on the other, "divide the nation," "act with dishonest motives," "pit one group against another." The devilish characters are those who speak evil of the throne, or sow doubts about the government in general amongst the Thai people, or whisper calumniations in the ears of foreigners. The devils make dire prophecies about the kingdom-nation, causing people to panic. They speak vulgarly and ridicule culture. They sell out the nation by passing secrets on to non-Thai. To the meritorious, this is the work of the hot-hearted, enmeshed in the world of senses and illusion. If these hot-hearted ones were to succeed, then all would fall into chaos and ruin.

When evil forces have the upper hand in history, they bring about the reverse side of unity: the disunity created by "the crisis," the precursor to the declaration of the state of the exception. When Schmitt developed his theory of sovereignty, he was thinking of the suspension of normal law for a few months under the Weimar Republic of the early 1920s. Hitler extended the principle and stretched the state of exception from 1933 to 1945. But Thailand has perfected the form, stretching it to such an extent that the "eternal crisis" has become a central and perhaps intractable aspect of Thai political culture.[103] Crisis has become a prominent feature of the Thai political and cultural landscape, always the reasoning for yet a new constitution. Defamation adjudication is part of an attempt to cover the cracks and re-establish a semblence of unity. As unity is never total, though, Thai society is ever under the pressure of a "crisis mentality," under a never-ending siege.

The official model of nationalism, created in the early twentieth century, was most fully realized when the penalties for defamation laws were increased in 1976 (Chapter 4). Penalties for defamation and insult of the three core entities of Thainess—nation (represented by the courts), religion, and monarchy were dramatically strengthened. Courts and religion were given the same level of protection as the king had during the period of absolute monarchy. Under the aegis of "Thai-style democracy" the penalty for defaming the monarchy more than doubled in comparison to its level even under absolute monarchy. This expansion of the sacred and official spheres came at the expense of the public sphere.

Conventional Thai historiography has focused on external events or forces as the principal antagonistic agents creating and driving events. Western colonialism threatened Siam and the kings responded wisely in ways that preserved Siam's independence. The protagonistic agents of history, the kings, react in efforts to *preserve*. Nidhi, as paraphrased by Jory, believes, "Thai historiography as it has been produced over the last two centuries originates out of a desire on the part of the Thai elite to define a Thai self that is periodically threatened by outsiders."[104] Even critics of royalist historiography, such as Anderson, nonetheless leave the impression that Thai history is externally driven when they periodicize Thai history after 1960 as "the American Era."[105] While taking into account external factors, Gray's work suggests a multi-layered, intensively "internal" reading of Thai history.[106] This study has adopted a similar approach, examining the historical construction of legal and nationalist discourses within a cultural framework as a way of representing more comprehensively the recent historical experience of Thailand. Thai society may have modernized materially and physically, but its cultural and religious orientation has not. Instead, the experience of centralization has considerably narrowed Thai psychological frames of reference. The "crisis of Thai identity" may not be so much the confrontation between "Thai" and "Western," but a more schizophrenic one of a "Thai" identity versus another, long suppressed, internal identity or identities.[107]

Reckoning with history

Thaksin's coming to power in 2001 and the coup of 2006 set in motion historical forces that make the decade-long delay in completing this book fortunate, for these events laid bare the underlying dynamics behind modern Thai history. The coup and its aftermath caused an ideological implosion that threatens to rather unceremoniously shove Thai history out of its half-century-old suspension and, perhaps, lead to its reckoning. Previous coups were either brutally efficient in silencing society (those of 1958 and 1976) or accepted without much initial opposition (1991). The 2006 coup was different. It caused immediate opposition and cracked whatever unity might have been represented by the fading ideals of the October Generation[108] decisively into two—anti-coup (those against the 2006 coup) and pro-2006 coup (or at least coup-tolerant).[109] Those against the coup divided into pro- and anti-Thaksin groupings. The ethos of the People's Alliance for Democracy (PAD/

Yellow-Shirts), in early 2006, began as something of a forum for a diversity of conservative and progressive thought, and then decisively veered to the right. The PAD advocated limited democracy, fomented anti-foreignism and a deep distrust of the poor, and linked itself to the elitist Democrat Party, military, and monarchy. Pro-Thaksin and anti-coup groups coalesced around the United Front for Democracy against Dictatorship (UDD/Red-Shirts). Court rulings since the coup banned many political party leaders from involvement in politics for five years. Even with a new constitution designed to dilute the rural vote, remnants of Thaksin's Thai Rak Thai Party formed a coalition government in early 2008. The new leader of the party was Samak Sundaravej, an avowed rightist who was a prime mover in the crackdown at Thamamast University in 1976. Many leftist students fled to join the Community Party of Thailand, but then eventually returned to make their way into politics. Many of these avowed leftists of the October Generation joined up with Thaksin's Thai Rak Thai Party. And so it was no small irony that rightist Samak and leftist Thai Rak Thai party members now found themselves in the same government, facing off against another group of the October Generation in PAD. Meanwhile, many others of the October Generation had made their way into the NGO movement that seemed so promising in the late 1990s. But even in the countryside, the coup caused a schism, and the people's movement lost direction and desultorily drifted into obscurity.[111]

With all of these peculiar alliances and political configurations, Thai history no longer made any sense. Or maybe better said, the illusion of a progressive, democratic movement evaporated, revealing both a core authoritarian mindset amongst the elite and intellectuals, part and parcel of a shared project to keep Thai society and history in suspension, and subject to systematic social injustice. Thongchai painfully records the capitulation of prominent members of the October Generation, now what Thongchai calls *apichon* [อภิชน, or literally, "the privileged people"] and espousing views equal in thrust and content to Sarit and his "Thai-style democracy," or more officially, "Democracy with the Monarch as Head of State."[112]

Many leading Thai intellectuals and officials hold to the concept that Thailand has slavishly "copied" the West. In this view, Thai politics and society should, Thongchai summarizes, "be based on Thai intellect and culture."[113] Thailand should have a system of government that does "not copy the West," but instead suits "Thai conditions." It "must grow on Thai soil because Thais eat rice, not wheat."[114] An unnamed participant at a human rights seminar in Bangkok recently was pessimistic that the human rights community in Thailand would ever recover:

> There can only be hope when they talk about [rights] principles [which are not selective] and criticise [the situation and fellow human rights defenders]. [They] should discuss whether they want to stick with the universal notion of human rights or have Thai-style human rights, like those who talk about Thai-style democracy.[115]

The majority of people in Thailand, who live on the other side of this political divide, have become incredulous and enraged. They elected Thaksin into power in April 2006; the election was annulled by the courts. Then the entire election apparatus was thrown out with the coup in September. In 2007, a military-appointed constitutional tribunal disbanded the party they had elected into power in 2006. The *apichon*, "the privileged people", wrote a constitution better suited to their interests. However, even with new ground rules, the majority again elected a new government made up of Thaksin followers. The new prime minister was then kicked out of politics in August 2008 by a court ruling. The new party the majority had put into power was disbanded by a court ruling in December. Tempers seethed in the North and Northeast, as it seemed that everything was being done to thwart the will of the majority. Sovereignty, apparently, was not to be with "the people."

Much of Thongchai's work critiques the construction of the nationalist-royalist narrative of Thai history, which is based on the view that Thailand is unique because it was not colonized. Another set of conservative, elite presuppositions extending from Thongchai's formulation is perhaps not as explicit: *Thailand is unified because it was not colonized; its essential unity is based on ethnic and cultural homogeneity organized around the monarchy.*[116] Aided by modern technologies, the monarchy has become the most prominent feature of Thainess in the past fifty years. As Jackson writes:

> The resacralization of the monarchy is indeed part of the return of magic in Thailand, but in this instance conservative political regimes have had as big a role as imaging technologies, playing upon the residual supernatural charisma of the King to bolster authoritarianism. Since the regime of Sarit Thanarat in the late 1950s and early 1960s, a conservative and often authoritarian state-sponsored project of monarchical resacralization has been reinforced by the marketized technological return of magic in Thai popular culture.[117]

But political pressures have come even to threaten somewhat indirectly "monarchical resacralization." For the first time ever, persons close to the king—his privy councillors—have come under sustained attack by the UDD for allegedly masterminding the 2006 coup. In the opposite camp, the PAD and Democrat Party have forged an alliance based on committing themselves to move against perceived threats to the monarchy. Accusing others of *lèse-majesté* and denouncing those who seek to amend the law have become the hallmark of PAD ideology. The Democrat Party has made defense of the monarchy the centerpiece of the party's policies. As the number of *lèse-majesté* cases investigated and acted upon skyrocketed in 2009, the foreign press highlighted the law and its abuse and began to critique the Thai monarchy as never before. The issue became public.[118] A number of prominent international academics weighed in on the issue, including Noam Chomsky, Immanuel Wallerstein, Charles F. Keyes, and James C. Scott.[119] Thai academics set up a two-day public symposium in early 2009 to discuss the legal, historical, media, and human rights aspects of the law, advertised as first of its kind in Thailand.[120] A law professor from Chiang Mai University even proposed doing away with the law altogether.[121]

Lèse-majesté had been forced into the public sphere. Defenders of the institution and the law have had to deal with the critique in a measured and reasonable way, rather than labelling any suggestion that the law be amended as a sign of disloyalty, treason, and being un-Thai. The most prominent of these defenses was written by Borwornsak Uwanno, a chief architect of the 1997 constitution and a leading Thai legal mind.

The gist of Borwornsak's argument—at more than 3,300 words, the longest piece ever written in English (and probably Thai) by a Thai on the subject—is that Thailand adheres to international legal standards in limiting free speech if such may harm society.[122] The Thai people's relationship to the monarchy is unique and an expression of its particular ethical and cultural character. The *lèse-majesté* law exists as the result of a "societal consensus" and therefore Thailand, as part of its right to self-determination, should be allowed to use the *lèse-majesté* law without the judgment of other countries. The Thai monarchy's relationship to society is different from other constitutional monarchies for it "has a long history dating back to ancient times, [it] has an exalted religious and social status . . . [It] has close bonds with the people, who love and respect [it] for the monarch's contributions to their well-being":

> Thais have seen not only these images of magnificence, which reflect the continuity of Thai history and tradition, but also those of the King and Queen and their children sitting on the ground and conversing in plain language with ordinary people in remote, harsh areas of the country where no one wanted to go. Royal development projects, which today number more than 3,000, were thus initiated, reflecting the monarchy's closeness to the people . . . The bond between the Thai monarchy and the Thai people is unique. It is not one between the Head of State as a political institution and the people as holders of sovereign power. It is a special relationship with certain characteristics that may be difficult for foreigners to appreciate.[123]

One problem with Borwornsak's argument is the assumption that "Thailand" or "the Thai people" came to some sort of "societal consensus" about *lèse-majesté* and other defamation laws. In fact, the original *lèse-majesté* law was written during the absolute monarchy, all the punishments for defamation-based laws were increased after a coup by military decree in 1976, and the personal defamation law was revised by a military-appointed body in 1992, as was the passing of the Computer Crimes Act in 2007.[124] The law did not come from social consensus at all; its increased punishment and use are the product of dictatorship and authoritarianism.

The eternally troubling question for Thailand over the past half century has been: if the monarch is universally loved by all Thai, then why is there a *lèse-majesté* law at all?[125] Academics and journalists, both Thai and foreign, commonly take it as fact that all Thai revere the monarch. In fact, "the people" are often used as a pretext to end discussions on reforming the law. In 2007 for instance, former prime minister Anand Panyarachun said:

> [Y]ou have to go by the will of the people . . . I think you have to respect the thinking and customs of the people in this country . . . I am sure that the King does not mind whether the law exists or not, but the Thai people never, never tolerate criticism of the King . . . I believe that the Thais are more royalist than the King.[126]

This assumption is continually voiced but never demonstrated. There has never actually been a poll, since conducting one is unimaginable and the effort itself would probably be deemed *lèse-majesté*.[127] Even if there were a poll, the result is predictable—with the possibility of a 15-year jail sentence, who would ever admit otherwise?[128] Many academics affirm that the public expression of republican sentiments is illegal in Thailand, a conclusion reached by the Juridical Council in the 1950s. Republican sentiment had never been publicly expressed perhaps by a Thai until Giles Ungpakorn did so in his 2009 manifesto.[129] Despite the Thai state's repeated assertions, evidence of an actual, organized republican movement has yet to be made public. New are the signs of cracks in the half-century-old construction that has conflated criticism of the monarchy or those closest to the king with *lèse-majesté*. Leading members of the Privy Council—"charismatic, extra-constitutional" figures—former prime ministers, generals such as Prem Tinsulanonda and Suryud Chulanont — are under direct public attack. The UDD accused both of direct involvement in the September 2006 coup and demanded their resignations from the Privy Council.[130] Many UDD backers say openly that the institution of the monarchy needs reform.[131] Even Daranee Charnchoengsilpakul, whose infraction of *lèse-majesté* was apparently so terrible, appeared to be a monarchist when she said, "I do not want to topple the monarchy in Thailand. What I want is a sustainable monarchy like in the United Kingdom and Japan."[132]

The rigid and awkward construction of "democratic regime of government with the King as Head of State," a phrasing not coincidentally linked to another *bon mot*, "Thai-style democracy," is enshrined in Article 2 of the 2007 constitution. It is counterbalanced by Section 45 which guarantees freedom of expression "except by virtue of the provisions of law specifically enacted for the purpose of maintaining the security of the State, . . . maintaining public order or good morals or preventing the deterioration of the mind or health of the public."[133] Section 116 prohibits force or coercion in attempting to change laws. Can Thai citizens peacefully organize to change from a "democratic regime of government with the King as Head of State" to merely a "constitutional monarchy"? Is it legal to suggest redefining the role and powers of the monarchy? The Thai government has conflated questions such as these and criticism of the monarchy with republicanism—any criticism of the monarchy is seen as republicanism in the eyes of the monarchists. Popular sovereignty dictates that power ultimately resides with the people. But how can the popular will be assessed when the *lèse-majesté* law threatens 15 years' imprisonment?

A year after the coup, the Thai state faced a new kind of threat: a couple arrested on charges of *lèse-majesté* for refusing to stand up when the royal anthem was played in a movie theatre. The couple initiated a campaign with the motto, "To think differently is not a crime."[134] Or is it? Is it a crime to think and speak differently in Thailand?

The present course of the state and the stated objectives of the Democrat-led government may eventually provoke more talk of republicanism and, possibly, reform of the Thai monarchy. As the state strains to control critical comment of the monarchy, the eventual backlash may increasingly envision the possibility of a future Thailand with no monarchy.

With history suspended, there is no "event" to refer to and reconsider. This entire period—from Sarit's coup in 1958 to the crackdown on rioting in April 2009—is filled with historical confrontations to which no resolution has ever been reached by Thai society as a whole. There has yet to be any sustained attempt to deal with any significant historical event that led to death, bloodshed, or impunity over the past half-century: whether it is treatment of the Muslim populations in the South of Thailand and the Tak Bai incident; the repression of the Sarit regime; the deaths in the run-up to, and during, the 1973 uprising; the massacre at Thammasat University in 1976; the crackdown on the May 1992 uprising, the extra-judicial killing of more than 2,500 suspected drug dealers during Thaksin's time in power; the 2006 coup; or the 2008 and 2009 PAD/UDD demonstrations. Defamation-based laws have largely hampered efforts to approach these historical events in any sort of sustained or broad-based way. These laws create a sense of eternal suspension.

Dealing with the past in some way allows history to move forward. Although Thailand has been spared the degree and scope of violence experienced in other nearby countries, truth needs to make an entrance. What is the truth that is evaded?

The obvious answer to the question of the incessant calls to Thai unity is that there is an understanding, at some level, that no such unity ever existed and that even the appearance of unity has come at a terrible cost. Defamation laws mask the fissures and cracks in this unity. The Thai state (and perhaps some scholars) has taken the intellectual, social, and political silence created through the application of the national security/defamation laws as "proof" that Thai culture has created unity.

Michael Ignatieff has written that the Truth Commission of South Africa could be "a model for other societies seeking to rebuild their ethical order and reckon with the past."[135] World War II had its Nuremberg Trials, New

Zealand, Australia, and Canada have begun the process of bringing truth of their treatment of indigenous populations to light, and some European countries have mounted modest efforts to deal with their colonial past. The United States has yet to do the same with its indigenous peoples or to respond as a society for the history of black slavery (but at least it does have its first Black American president); Cambodia is slowly dealing with its killing fields of the 1970s. These society-wide confrontations with historical truth shift social memory as a whole. Ignatieff writes "In all these processes, the essential problem is how to balance peace and justice, forgetting and forgiving, healing and punishment, truth and reconciliation."[136]

Chaiwat Satha-Anand has noted that a movement toward democracy is occasioned with a push for collective remembrance. Around the world, intimidated and silenced societies, after sometimes decades of entrenched military dictatorships, entered into an psychological and epistemological fog, no longer able to state the most obvious truths. New democracies have moved to dispel the fog hovering over their pasts, "reclaiming and transforming public space into a space of memory where 'truths' about traumatic pasts can be confronted."[137]

The long-term effects of impunity, military rule, and the principles of the defamation regime on Thai society's perception of truth should not be underestimated. Obfuscating the truth over decades can attenuate language itself and imagination as a vehicle for conveying historical, social, religious, and political realities and possibilities. Languages are living things, and, as George Steiner reminds us, they also "can decay and they can die." Steiner describes the symptoms:

> Actions of the mind that were once spontaneous become mechanical, frozen habits (dead metaphors, stock similes, slogans). Words grow longer and more ambiguous. Instead of style, there is rhetoric. Instead of common usage, there is jargon. Foreign roots and borrowings are no longer absorbed into the bloodstream of the native tone. They are merely swallowed and remain in alien intrusion . . . the language no longer sharpens thought but blurs it. Instead of charging every expression with the greatest available energy and directness, it loosens and disperses the intensity of feeling . . . In short, the language is no longer lived; it is merely spoken.[138]

Twelve years of Nazism damaged the German language, perhaps beyond repair. "Something immensely destructive has happened to it," argues Steiner. "It makes noise. It even communicates but it creates no sense of communication." Germany retreated from the trenches of World War I with an imagined sense of humiliation, a perception it had been betrayed, and with a desire for revenge. Hitler came to power because

> [He] heard inside his native tongue the latent hysteria, the confusion, the

> quality of hypnotic trance. He plunged unerringly into the undergrowth of language, into the zones of darkness and outcry which are the infancy of articulate speech . . . He sensed . . . a rasping cadence, half nebulous jargon, half obscenity.[139]

In a not completely dissimilar way, the Siamese elite, too, felt humiliated in the face of Western imperialism. Anderson has argued that the "conservative ideology" of elite in European colonies was largely discredited and "has been in epistemological shock and on the political defensive." As a result of struggles against colonialism, these societies "inherited a political vocabulary and rhetoric that is essentially radical-populist, if not left-wing in character." Contrarily, because Thailand was not directly colonized, its elite have maintained "a calm, self-confident conservative ideology" that discredits progressive political rhetoric.[140] Kasian has reflected that the lack of Siamese colonization "sterilised Siam of a nationalist mass movement and its possible radicalisation." Western colonization "could perversely have contributed to the politicisation and conversion of many more Thais to nationalism and even communism."[141]

That the ideological model constructed by the promoters of official Thai nationalism has been so remarkably resilient for more than a century is a testament to their intelligence and savvy. At the same time, the intricacy of this construction and its current fragile and precarious state are also amazing and alarming. If any of the defamation components or dynamics were altered, the entire system could come crashing down. This might explain why the elite so desperately clings to it now.

> If the monarchy were to re-create itself into a more liberal form, or
> if the *lèse-majesté* law were even only slightly altered; or
> if the exceptions to defamation crimes were taken more seriously by the courts, or
> if the courts at least used criteria other than intent to determine guilt, or
> if "the people" expressed their diversity in more powerful ways (or representatives of "the people" decided defamation cases by jury), the logic of the defamation regime could crumble, causing the entire edifice to come tumbling down.

The cleavages in Thai society—class, race, ethnic, religious, regional, and political—so long papered over and held together by incessant calls for unity and a century-old construction of an ossified national identity, are no longer deniable or manageable. The linchpin is the *lèse-majesté* law. The law's use does not indicate the strength of the Thai state but rather its utter desperation. Borwornsak exalts not so much the monarchy as the law itself, making the claim that "the *lèse-majesté* offence" is itself "a distinctive character of Thai democracy amidst the global democratic movement."

Also striking about Thai society is the gap between core Buddhist teachings and the immense fetishism created around Thainess, the persistently anti-rationalist clinging to its constructs, and the sterile and romanticised resistance to "change." With great clarity, Ajahn Chah said:

> Nothing is certain. There is nothing in this world that is a certainty. This is the truth. The things that aren't true are the things that change, such as beauty. The only truth it has is in its constant changing . . . We "invest" our minds in material things in this way. When they are destroyed or damaged we suffer because we have clung to them as being our own. The Buddha tells us to see that these things are simply constructs of nature.[142]

As the "Thai" state shows signs of breaking apart, the advocates of Thainess and Thai-style democracy have fallen into a Buddhist-like nostalgia. After extensively explaining the important legal principles underlying the *lèse-majesté* law, Borwornsak seems to then just toss it all up in the air when he says, "As the Buddhist law of impermanence states, everything, the lese majeste offense included, arises, exists and perishes, as the society's ethical and cultural norms evolve also in accordance with this same Buddhist law. Nothing is permanent. 'The only permanent thing is impermanence.'"[143] Thus, rather than engage in perpetuation of the impermanent, it might be better to work towards constructive change.

Borwornsak's thinking reflects the zigzagging course of Thai politics since 1932, bouncing from the one extreme of flexibility ("Everything changes, so there needs to be continual changes in constitutions") to the other of belief in the undying reality of Thainess, meanwhile imagining that oscillating between such extremes is the Buddhist "Middle Way."[144] The personal experience of millions speaks to the wisdom and benefit of Thai Theravada Buddhism for individuals and certain social situations. But that same Buddhism, when applied to politics, creates enduring instability, remarkable income disparity and contempt for the less privileged, hostility towards difference, and a politics fraught with animosity and acrimony.

As we come to the end of this 110-year survey of defamation-based laws in Thailand, I note that these laws have played a key role in the construction and protection of a certain model of social and political control. Defamation has become the self-perpetuating mechanism of a wounded national ego, calling for boycotts and condemnations, with an internal apparatus of purification which has ossified Thai "culture" into a mythical time.

Thailand may continue to allow *lèse-majesté* and other defamation-based laws to consume everything, at the probable cost, in the end, of the monarchy itself. By creating narrowly understood demands of authoritarian loyalty, the ultimate end of defamation-based laws is not loyalty or love, but intolerance, violence, and destruction. Those who wield these laws bring destruction to democracy, narrow the public sphere, and create a precarious and fragile unity born of repression. The effects of defamation-based laws on the perception of truth have been devastating. These laws obscure truth, scar the past, result in endless accusations and counter-accusations of treason, and divide society into categories of patriots and enemies. This is one possible end to this history.

Jory points out that the "current political struggle" is really "a battle over the future of the monarchy in the Thai political system." Thai history and the writing of that history (historiography) are constrained by the law protecting the monarchy. Should conditions under which the *lèse-majesté* law operate be eased, limits placed "on the writing of Thai history [will] start to unravel" and a "new era" of Thai historiography and politics may yet emerge.[145] This other possible narrative of Thai history comes from groups who question conventional history or who believe that alternative, broad-based futures are possible for a new "Siam."[146] In this view, Siam could become a multi-ethnic society respecting ethnicities and local customs and languages. Would "Thailand" or "Thai history" make sense any longer without the example of Sukhothai shining in its past? Within Siamese society, indeterminate terms such as "the Thai," "the Thai people," "Thai society," or sayings similar to, "Thai don't kill Thai," would all . . . what? "Thai" truth would no longer make sense. But so much psychological, social, and cultural capital has been invested on maintaining the defamation state and its "Thai" truth that such a change seems doubtful.

There are good reasons for clinging to the Thai defamation state, for after a century, nothing else has been allowed to evolve "out there" to replace it. No principles, no rule of law, no identity other than Thainess exists in this space, the space defined by the "Western" notion of the imagined community that is the nation-state. Can a new unity emerge from the celebration of diversity, democratic values, and respect for difference?

Whether Thai society can or cannot change, or even whether it will ever have the choice, remains to be seen. History cannot remain suspended forever. The Great Reckoning may yet come. Meanwhile, the Ghosts of Forgotten History hover in deadened skies. For those who have seen them close up, their visages are tortured and fearsome. They are not revengeful, though: they thirst for justice which may mean just a tear from the society that bore them. Society below turns its back and bides it time. And true enough, their wails do become fainter as years pass by. In their long and saddened wait, the Ghosts begin to understand: "History shall not be for Us." They may linger no longer, they may just dissipate, unobserved, become lost to the world, be truly forgotten.

Or, against all reasonable expectation, there materializes some persistent and stubborn public will that breaks the silence and sets itself to see things through. The Great Reckoning may yet happen, and history will be jolted out of its suspended state. The Ghosts of the Dusun-nyor massacre, 6 October, Black May, and Tak Bai may perhaps take heart when they hear finally the sounds of a grieving society below. They have had their day of tears. They are healed, and the Ghosts of Forgotten History are at last free. With their release, History, itself healed, can move forward once again.

All of this may come to pass, when Truth finally has its day in court in Thailand.

Notes

Introduction: the defamation dilemma of Thailand

1 Antoon de Baets, "Defamation Cases against Historians," *History and Theory* 41(3) (Oct., 2002): 346. See also Antoon de Baets, *Censorship of Historical Thought: A World Guide, 1945–2000* (Westport, CT: Greenwood Press, 2002) and Derek Jones, ed., *Censorship: A World Encyclopedia* (London: Fitzroy Dearborn, 2001).

2 De Baets, "Defamation Cases against Historians," p. 346. Unfortunately, De Baets does not attempt a way of defining "public interest," a term that is highly specific to the political culture of each country.

3 Ibid., p. 358.

4 Ibid., p. 346.

5 The only Thai historian to be formally charged with defamation was Morakot Jewachinda. His book, *The Images of Pridi Banomyong and Thai Politics, 1932–1983* (Krungthep: Khrongkan Ho Chotmaihet Thammasat, 2543 [2000]), was originally published in 1987. In 2007, Nongyao Chaiseree, a former university rector charged Morakot with libel for saying in the book that Nongyao had "disrespected" Pridi. See, "Historians Back Academic in Defamation Case," *Nation*, 28 Feb. 2007. Other Thai academics, have suffered worse fates. See Chapter 12, note 57.

6 Patrick Jory, "Historiography in Thailand from 1945 to the Present," in Axel Schneider and Daniel Woolf, eds., *The Oxford History of Historical Writing*, Vol. 5, *1945–Present* (Oxford: Oxford University Press, forthcoming).

7 Buddhadasa Bhikkhu, *Handbook for Mankind* (Bangkok: Mahachula Buddhist University Press, n.d.), p. 20.

8 Ibid., p. 28.

9 Ibid., p. 29.

10 Ibid., pp. 31–32.

11 Duncan McCargo, "Buddhism, Democracy, and Identity in Thailand," *Democratization* 11(4) (Aug. 2004): 155–70, Duncan McCargo, "The Politics of Buddhist Identity in Thailand's Deep South: The Demise of Civil Religion?" *Journal of Southeast Asian Studies* 40(1) (Feb. 2009): 11–32, and Duncan McCargo, "Thai Buddhism, Thai Buddhists and the Southern Conflict," *Journal of Southeast Asian Studies* 40(1) (Feb. 2009): 1–10; Marc Askew, "Landscapes of Fear, Horizons of Trust: Villagers Dealing with Danger in Thailand's Insurgent South," *Journal of Southeast Asian Studies* 40(1) (Feb. 2009), pp. 59–86; and Michael Jerryson, "Appropriating a Space for Violence: State Buddhism in Southern Thailand," *Journal of Southeast Asian Studies* 40: 1 (Feb. 2009): 33–57.

12 For a variety of sources on recent events in Thailand, see the following: Marwaan Macan-Makar in his "Letter from South-East Asia," available at: www.ipsnews.

net/new_focus/marwaan, accessed 2 June 2009, and Bangkok Pundit, available at: www.bangkokpundit.blogspot.com/, accessed 2 June 2009; for analysis, see Michael K. Connors and his "Sovereign Myths," available at: www.sovereignmyth.blogspot.com/2008/02/democrats-did-not-win-majority-in-party.html, accessed 2 June 2009; Thitinan Pongsudhirak's regular column in *The Bangkok Post*, available at: www.bangkokpost.com/; and New Mandala, available at: www.rspas.anu.edu.au/rmap/newmandala, accessed 2 June 2009.

13 Administrative Reform Group under the Democratic System with the King as the Head of State, "Initial Statement," 19 Sept. 2006, available at: www.news.bbc.co.uk/2/hi/asia-pacific/5361756.stm, accessed 29 Nov. 2007.

14 *Nation*, 8 Oct. 2007.

15 *Nation*, 22 and 24 July 2008; *Bangkok Post*, 25 Feb. 2009

16 The PAD slogan on saving the nation, staving off "tearing apart the land." See Michael K. Connors, "Article of Faith: The Failure of Royal Liberalism in Thailand," *Journal of Contemporary Asia* 38(1) (Feb. 2008): 159–60.

17 The French term, *lèse-majesté*, means to defame or insult the king (or other member of a royalty), and is variously rendered as *lèse-majesté*, *lese majeste*, lese majeste, or lese majesty.

18 *Nation*, 28 Oct. 2008. The Communist Suppression Operations Command (CSOC) was more generically renamed Internal Security Operations Command (ISOC) in the 1970s.

19 I will use the rate of 33 baht to one US$ throughout the book, the approximate conversion rate during 2007.

20 Marwaan Macan-Markar, "Don Challenges Lese-Majeste Law – Risks Jail Term," 27 Jan. 2009, available at: www.ipsnews.net/print.asp?idnews = 45566, accessed 29 Jan. 2009.

21 See, Wassana Nanuam, "Taskforce 6080 Tracks Down Those Who Would Impugn," *Bangkok Post*, 2 and 29 Oct. 2008.

22 *Bangkok Post*, 30 Oct. 2008.

23 From 1996 to 2005, there were 50 total new cases of *lèse-majesté* sent for prosecution in Thailand, and 31 cases finished. Attorney General's Office (Samnakngan Aiyakan Songsut), *Rai-ngan prajam pi 2539/40–2548* [Annual Report of the Attorney General's Office, 1996/97–2005] (Samnakngan aiyakan phiset fai sarasonthet, samnakngan wichakan), as compared with 397 cases of *lèse-majesté* brought to the Court of First Instance between 2006 and 2009, with 213 decisions handed down. These numbers do not include the 36 new cases received by the Appeals Court or the 8 cases taken by the Supreme Court for the same period, Thailand, Samnakngan San Yuttitham [Office of the Judiciary], *Rai-ngan sathiti khadi tua ratcha-anajak prajam pi (ph.s. 2549, 2550, 2551, 2552)* [English title provided is *Annual Judicial Statistics, Thailand 2006, 2007, 2008,* and *2009*, respectively]. The numbers from the Office of the Judiciary do not include the large number of *lèse-majesté* "cases" still under investigation by police, nor an unknown number of court cases stemming from violations of the Computer Crimes Act.

24 *Bangkok Post*, 1 Nov. 2008. Thailand's judicial system has three levels: a lower court or Court of First Instance (*san chan ton*), an Appeals Court (*san uthorn*), and the Supreme Court (*san dika*). In Thai citations, Supreme Court decisions are referred to as *dika*, with the case number and year. In this study, Supreme Court decisions (*kham phiphaksa sandika*) are cited as "Thailand, Supreme Court, Supreme Court Decision [case no.]/[year]." Note: In transliteration of Thai into Roman letters, I am following the system used in Chris Baker and Pasuk Phongpaichit, *A History of Thailand* (Cambridge: Cambridge University Press, 2005), p. ix, as well as their rendition of Thai names.

25 *Bangkok Post*, 3 and 4 Nov. 2008. The Lawyers Council is variously called

the Council of Lawyers, a professional association representing lawyers in Thailand.

26 *Bangkok Post*, 3, 11, and 12 Nov. 2008.

27 *Bangkok Post*, 11 Nov. 2008.

28 Thailand, Government, Parliament, "Lek rap 115/2551 wan thi 29 t.kh. 2551, somnakngan kekhathikan sapha phuthaen ratsadorn; banthuk lakkan lae hetphon, prakop rang phraratchabanyat kaekhai phoemtoem pramuankotmai aya (chabap thi . . .), ph.s. . . . " [Received no. 115/2008, 29 Oct. 2008, Office of the Secretary-General to the House of Representatives; "Notes on the Principle and Rationale, Accompanying the Draft Act to Revise and Amend the Criminal Code (No. . . .), of . . . Year].

29 Interview, Police Lt. Col. Wattanasak Mungkandee, Bangkok, 28 Oct. 2008.

30 See David Streckfuss, "Thailand's Tough Law," *Dateline Bangkok* [Foreign Correspondents' Club of Thailand Magazine] (Second Quarter 2008), pp. 20–23.

1 The truth recently discovered

1 Text of the court decision comes from www.law.umkc.edu/faculty/projects/ftrials/zenger/zengeraccount.html, accessed 21 Aug. 2008.

2 Neil Postman, *Building a Bridge to the Eighteenth Century* (New York: Vintage Books, 1999), pp. 3–4.

3 Available at: www.lexrex.com/enlightened/laws/alien_sedition.html, accessed 7 May 2009.

4 *The New York Times*, 21 Nov. 1907.

5 "Author's trial Set to Test Turkey," available at: www.news.bbc.co.uk/2/hi/europe/4527318.stm, accessed 3 May 2008. See also, Sabrina Tavernise and Sebnem Arsu, "An Identity Forged from a Painful Past," *Bangkok Post*, 13 Oct. 2007.

6 "Turkey: Article 301 is a Threat to Freedom of Expression and Must Be Repealed Now!," Amnesty International Public Statement December 1, 2005, available at: www.amnestyusa.org/document.php?lang = e&id = ENGEUR 440352005, accessed 8 Mar. 2009.

7 "Pamuk Case Dropped as Minister Says 'I Have no Authorization for Permission' The Ministry Left the Decision of Whether to Proceed," *Zaman*; "Turkish Court Drops Charges against Novelist," *The Independent;* "Turkey Drops Charges against Author," www.Scotsman.com News; Reuters, Canadian Press "Orhan Pamuk: We are all Responsible for Dink's Death," *Hürriyet*, 21 Jan. 2007.

8 "FM Gul. Changes Must Be Made to Article 301," *Hürriyet*, 25 Jan. 2007; "EU Welcomes 301 Amendment but Calls for More," *Today's Zaman*, 30 Apr. 2008.

9 Metin Yilmaz, www.my.telegraph.co.uk/metin_yilmaz/blog/2008/04/15/article_301_turkish_penal_code_and_democratic_and_free_penal_codes_in_the_eu_countries_, accessed Nov. 3, 2008.

10 Hanrahan reminds us that in fourteenth-century England, slander "was understood to be a spiritual offence" and tried by ecclesiastical authorities. In fact, the Church had made claim to all cases of slander. Michael Hanrahan, "Defamation as Political Contest during the Reign of Richard II," *Medium Aevum* 72 (2003), p. 261, 273, endnote 12.

11 Ibid., p. 272.

12 Ibid., p. 260.

13 As one dismayed official exclaimed, "Today, it is the very foundation of the constitution and the order of the state that is called in to question. The different degrees

of authority and power, the rules and extent of obedience, the mysteries of state are discussed indiscreetly before the eyes of the common people." Jeffrey Merrick, *The Desacralization of the French Monarchy in the Eighteenth Century* (Baton Rouge, LA: Louisiana State University Press, 1990), pp. 25–26, 37, 85–86, 167.

14 See Cardin Le Bret, *De Souveraineté du Roy* (Paris, 1632), as quoted in, William F. Church, *Richelieu and Reason of State* (Princeton, NJ: Princeton University Press, 1972), p. 274.

15 Church, *Richelieu and Reason of State*, pp. 178–79, 185–86.

16 For detail and explanation about the hundred persons arrested for *lèse-majesté* as "the public," see Roger Chartier, *The Cultural Origins of the French Revolution* (Durham, NC: Duke University Press, 1991), particularly Chapter 2, "The Public Sphere and Public Opinion," pp. 20–37.

17 Jeffrey Merrick, *Desacralization of the French Monarchy*, pp. 21, 25–26, 37.

18 Dale K. Van Kley. *The Daniens Affair and the Unravelling of the Ancient Régime, 1750–1770* (Princeton, NJ: Princeton University Press, 1984), pp. 226–70.

19 Richard Streckfuss, "News before Newspapers," *Journalism and Mass Communication Quarterly* 75(1) (Spring 1998): 84–97. The rise of defamation was coupled with printing and with the rise of the novel, which might have created a demarcation between "truth" and "fiction," as suggested by Davis: "the distinction between fact and fiction, self and other, inner and outer began to collapse in an entirely new way and with significant consequences." Lennard J. Davis, *Resisting Novels: Ideology and Fiction* (New York and London: Methuen, 1987), p. 5, as quoted in Annette Hamilton, "Rumours, Foul Calumnies and the Safety of the State: Mass Media and National Identity in Thailand," in Craig J. Reynolds, ed., *National Identity and Its Defenders, Thailand, 1939–1989* (Clayton, Victoria: Centre of Southeast Asian Studies, Monash University, Monash Papers on Southeast Asia, No. 25, 1991), p. 348. A possible avenue of research might look at the connection between power, the state, defamation, emerging concepts of truth, and what Benedict Anderson calls "print capitalism." See Benedict Anderson, *Imagined Communities: Reflections on the Origin and Spread of Nationalism* (London: Verso, 1991).

20 Jürgen Habermas, *The Structural Transformation of the Public Sphere: An Inquiry into a Category of Bourgeois Society* (Cambridge, MA: The MIT Press, 1991). For much of this discussion, I depend on Roger Chartier's interpretation of Habermas. See Roger Chartier, *The Cultural Origins of the French Revolution* (Durham, NC: Duke University Press, 1991), particularly Chapter 2, "The Public Sphere and Public Opinion," pp 20–37.

21 Chartier, *Cultural Origins*, pp. 22–23.

22 Habermas, *The Structural Transformation of the Public Sphere*, pp. 52–54, 81–82.

23 Georges Vidal, *Cours de droit criminel et de science penitentiare*, 5th edn. (Paris: Arthur Rousseau, 1916), pp. 110–12, as quoted in Robert Ferrari, "Political Crime," *Columbia Law Review* 20(3) (Mar. 1920): 312.

24 Vidal also recognized that political crimes (and quite often defamation-based ones) are of a separate order, one "dependent on time, place, circumstances, the institutions of the land, and it is often inspired by noble sentiments, by disinterested motives, by devotion to persons and principles, by love of one's country." Vidal, as quoted in Ferrari, "Political Crime," pp. 312–13.

25 Ernest J. Schuster, "Lèse-majesté in Germany," *Journal of the Society of Comparative Legislation* 3(1) (1901): 41–45.

26 *New York Times*, 23 Jan. 1898.

27 *New York Times*, 5 Feb. 1899.

28 *New York Times*, 23 Jan. 1897.

29 *New York Times*, 22 Nov. 1894.

30 *New York Times*, 6 Nov. 1898.

31 *New York Times*, 21 Dec., 1898.
32 *New York Times*, 26 Feb. 1899.
33 *New York Times*, 22 Jan. 1899.
34 *New York Times*, 10 Oct. 1900.
35 *New York Times*, 28 Oct. 1900.
36 *New York Times*, 5 Oct. 1902.
37 *New York Times*, 18 Oct. 1903.
38 *New York Times*, 14 May 1897.
39 *New York Times*, 3 Jan. 1899. In fact, historian Ludwig Quidde was boycotted, dismissed from his teaching position, and jailed for three months for having made "satirical allusions" about the Kaiser in an immensely popular literary piece. Quidde was later given the Nobel Prize in 1927. Antoon de Baets, "Defamation Cases against Historians," *History and Theory* 41(3) (Oct., 2002): 349.
40 *New York Times*, 23 Jan. 1897.
41 See, as a sampling, *New York Times*, on 23 Jan. and 16 Oct. 1897: 6 and 13 Nov., 18 Dec. 1898; 3 Jan. and 5 Feb. 1899
42 *New York Times*, 12 Dec. 1902.
43 *New York Times*, 11 Nov. 1904, 26 Aug. 1906.
44 The last reported case in Germany appearing in the *New York Times* was on 10 June 1906, when a newspaper was "confiscated" for poking fun at the relationship between Emperor William I and Austrian Emperor Franz Josef.
45 I thank Thongchai Winichakul for coming up with this phrasing.
46 Craig J. Reynolds, "Sedition in Thai History: A Nineteenth-Century Poem and its Critics," in Manas Chitakasem and Andrew Turton, eds., *Thai Constructions of Knowledge* (London: School of Oriental and African Studies, University of London, 1991), pp. 28–31.
47 Andrew Turton, "State poetics and civil rhetoric: an introduction to 'Thai constructions of knowledge'," in Chitakasem and Turton, *Thai Constructions of Knowledge*, p. 10.
48 It is curious to note that for perfect completion of the discursive crimes of treason, *lèse-majesté*, or sedition (defamation of the state), affirming the efficacy of the defamatory words constitutes a crime in itself.
49 Seyla Benhabib, for instance, designates the Habermas model of the public sphere as "discursive public space" and contrasts that with the "agonistic public space" of Hannah Arendt, and a "liberal model of public space as public dialogue." Habermas's public sphere comes into existence, says Benhabib, through a public and "practical discourse." See Seyla Benhabib, "Models of Public Space: Hannah Arendt, the Liberal Tradition, and Jürgen Habermas," in Craig Calhoun, ed., *Habermas and the Public Sphere* (Cambridge, MA: The MIT Press, 1992), pp. 73–98. A number of scholars have commented that Habermas's public sphere does not actually correspond to any society, past or present. See, for instance, Nancy Fraser's "Rethinking the Public Sphere: A Contribution to the Critique of Actually Existing Democracies." Also see Keith Michael Baker's discussion of the historical specificity of Habermas's theory in his "Defining the Public Sphere in Eighteenth-Century France: Variations on a Theme by Habermas," both in Calhoun, ed., *Habermas and the Public Sphere*, pp. 109–42, 181–211.
50 Keith R. Evans, *The Law of Defamation in Singapore and Malaysia*, 2nd edn. (Singapore: Butterworths Asia, 1993), p. 3.
51 Although I would not define the United States as a defamation regime, freedom of speech in America is limited by what Herman and Chomsky define as "flak": "negative responses to a media statement" that

> may take the form of letters, telegrams, phone calls, petitions, lawsuits, speeches and bills before Congress, and other modes of complaint, threat,

> and punitive action. It may be organized centrally or locally, or it may consist of the entirely independent actions of individuals.
>
> (Edward S. Herman and Noam Chomsky, *Manufacturing Consent: The Political Economy of the Mass Media*, New York: Pantheon Books, 1988, p. 26)

I thank Ms. Supara Janchitfah of *The Bangkok Post* for directing me toward "flak."

52 Giorgio Agamben, *Homo Sacer: Sovereign Power and Bare Life* (Stanford, CA: Stanford University Press, 1998), pp. 167–68.

53 Ibid., pp. 168–69, original emphasis.

54 Agamben writes:

> The sovereign no longer limits himself, as he did in the Weimar constitution, to deciding on the exception on the basis of recognizing a given factual situation (danger or public safety): laying bare the inner structure of the ban that characterizes its power, he now de facto provides the situation as a consequence of this decision on the exception.
>
> (Ibid., p. 170)

55 Ibid., p. 20.

56 "Letter," from Bidyalabh, Ministry of Public Works, to Chaw Phya Abhai Raja, 8 Mar. 1898, in Thailand, National Archives, "m.r. 5 y./1 bet set k. yuttitham, (farang wiwat kap khon thai) Ruang nai roemti Mr. lili kae khong nangsuphim" [Miscellaneous, Ministry of Justice, (Westerner Disputes with Thai People) The Matter of Punishing Mr. Lillie in Rectifying Newspaper]. (Hereinafter referred to as "NA, m.r. 5 yau/1 bet set k. yuttitham.")

57 "Copy of Memorandum," from Siamese Telegraph Dept. to J. Lillie, Esq., Bangkok, 7 May 1898, and "Copy No. 93/116," to D.G. of Telegraphs, from J. Lillie, 8 Mar. 1898, in, "NA, m.r. 5 y./1 bet set k. yuttitham."

58 It is not clear to what extent exactly Siam was involved in this province. Although Damrong Rajanuphap, Minister of the Interior, publicly claimed that there was "not a single Siamese troop" in Battambong, this letter to the British Legation appears to contradict his statement. But the contradiction seems to go deeper than that. If it was in fact "an important province" of "this kingdom," then why couldn't Siamese troops be there? Otherwise, it would appear to be a "Cambodian" and not "Siamese" province. It is also interesting to note that the Siamese government recorded the reception of the following telegram sent from a "Russel" in Battambong to Lillie in Bangkok three days following Lillie's attempt to send the first telegram on the matter: "Governor returned. Great war finished. All he could get hold of massacred. Rest fled. Afraid Cardamon business gone." See "Telegram," sent from Battambong on 10 March 1898, received in Bangkok on 12 Mar. 1898, in, "NA, m.r. 5 y./1 bet set k. yuttitham." The view of foreign advisors about the questionable character of Lillie and the fact that he had been involved in a number of libel litigations, brings in the entire question of European views on libel at the time. For two accounts on Lillie, see Walter E. J. Tipps, *Gustave Rolin-Jaequemyns and the Making of Modern Siam* (Bangkok: White Lotus, 1995), pp. 291–94, 372.

59 "Copy No. 69/13706," from Devavongse, Minister for Foreign Affairs, to George Creville, H.B.M.'s Minister Resident & Consul General, 10 Mar. 1898, in, "NA, m.r. 5 y./1 bet set k. yuttitham."

60 "Draft Decree sent by Chow Phya Abhai Raja to Creville," n.d., in "NA, m.r. 5 y./1 bet set k. yuttitham."; Thailand, Government, "Prakat kan khap lai ok" [Announcement of Deportation], *Prachum kotmai prajam sok* [Annual Collected

Laws], Vol. 16, r.s. 116–17 [1898–1900], pp. 157–58. Dated "11 March r.s. 116, the 10,713th day of this reign." (Hereinafter referred to as "PKPS" with the corresponding volume number, year of publication, and page number[s].)

61 Thailand, Police Department (Krom Tamruat), *Rai-ngan prajam pi 2520–2532* [Annual Report of the Police Department, 1950–1959], Thailand, Samnakngan San Yuttitham [Office of the Judiciary], *Rai-ngan sathiti khadi tua ratcha-anajak prajam pi (ph.s. 2549, 2550, 2551)* [English title provided is *Annual Judicial Statistics, Thailand 2006, 2007,* and *2008,* respectively]. Numbers for 2009 were even higher. See note 23, p. 317.

Elsewhere, the past half-century has seen a mere spattering of *lèse-majesté* cases here and there, although the law remains on the books for most, if not all, constitutional monarchies. Europe has seen a few *lèse-majesté* cases over the past decade, but the utterances were either illegal already, or pointlessly tasteless. In a recent case in the Netherlands, for instance, a Dutch man was jailed for four months for drunkenly screaming insults about the queen, and saying he "wanted to put a bullet through her head." Available at: www.thecheers.org/news/Europe/news_17756_A-man-has-been-jailed-for-four-months-for-insulting-Queen-Beatrix.html, accessed 3 Jan. 2009. In 2007, a Dutch court fined a man 400 euros for calling Queen Beatrix a "whore" and "described several sexual acts he would like to perform on her." Available at: en.wikipedia.org/wiki/Lese_majeste#cite_note-9, accessed 2 June 2009]

62 Robert McEwen and Philip Lewis, *Gatley on Libel and Slander*, 17th edn. (London: Sweet & Maxwell Limited, 1974); William Lloyd Prosser and W. Page Keeton, David Go. Owen, *et al.*, eds., *Prosser and Keeton on the Law of Torts*, 5th edn. (St. Paul, MN: West Group, 1984).

63 See, for instance, Simon Burrows, *Blackmail, Scandal, and Revolution: London's French Libellistes, 1758–92* (New York: Manchester University Press, 2006), M. Lindsay Kaplan, *The Culture of Slander in Early Modern England* (New York: Cambridge University Press, 1997), or Hanrahan, "Defamation as Political Contest," pp. 259–76.

64 See, for instance, Keith R. Evans, *The Law of Defamation in Singapore and Malaysia* (Singapore: Butterworths Asia, 1993), p. 3, or Jill Cottrell, *Law of Defamation in Commonwealth Africa* (Ashford: Ashgate Publishing Company, 1998). In Asia as a whole, very little work has been done by indigenous scholars on defamation. Most work focuses on media freedom, such as Cet. 1, ed., *Kebebasan pers dan pasal-pasal penghinan* [Defamation and Freedom of the Press in Indonesia] (Jakarta: Dewan Pers: UNESCO, 2005), Yi-Ling Teo, *Media law in Singapore* (Singapore: Sweet & Maxwell Asia, 2003), Antonio P. Coronel, *Libel and the Journalist* (Quezon City: AFA Publications, 1991), R. Ramamoorthy, *Law of Malicious Prosecution and Defamation* (Bombay: N. M. Tripathi, 1976).

65 See, for instance, Michael Vickery, "The Constitution of Ayutthaya: An Investigation into the Three Seals Code," in Andrew Huxley, ed., *Thai Law: Buddhist Law* (Bangkok: White Orchid Press, 1996), pp. 133–210; Frank C. Darling, "The Evolution of Law in Thailand," *The Review of Politics* 33(3) (Apr. 1970): 197–202, David M. Engel, *Law and Kingship in Thailand during the Reign of King Chulalongkorn* (Ann Arbor, MI: University of Michigan Center for South and Southeast Asian Studies, 1975), and William J. Klausner, "Law and Society," available at: www.thailawforum.com/articles/lawwilliam5.html, accessed 28 June 2008.

66 In Routledge's 2009/10 Asian Studies catalogue, for instance, under four titles—*Regulation in Asia, New Courts in Asia, Legal Education in Asia, and Administrative Law and Governance in Asia*—only 4 of 64 articles concern Thai law and legal institutions (as compared to Indonesia with seven). See www.routledge.com/asianstudies, accessed 2 June 2009.

67 See David M. Engel, "Landscape of the Law: Injury, Remedy, and Social Change in Thailand," *Law and Society Review* 43(61) (March 2009): 61–94; *Culture and Power in Traditional Siamese Government* (Ithaca, NY: Southeast Asian Program Publications, Cornell University Press, 2001), and David M. Engel, "Globalization and the Decline of Legal Consciousness: Torts, Ghosts, and Karma in Thailand," *Law & Social Inquiry* 30 (2005): 469–514, and Frank Munger, "Culture, Power, and Law: Thinking about the Anthropology of Rights in Thailand in an Era of Globalization," available at: www.thailawforum.com/articles/Culture.html, accessed 28 June 2008, Frank Munger, "Constitutional Reform, Legal Consciousness, and Citizen Participation in Thailand," *Cornell International Law Journal*, 40(455) (2007): 455–75, Frank Munger, "Globalization, Investing in Law, and the Careers of Lawyers for Social Causes: Taking on Rights in Thailand," *New York Law Review* 45 (2009): 745–802, and Frank Munger, "Environmental Rights in Thailand: A Role for 'Cause' Lawyers?," paper prepared for the 4th International Conference on "Law in a Changing World," Thammasat University, 9 Dec. 2008. Also see Peter Leyland, "The Emergence of Administrative Justice in Thailand under the 1997 Constitution," in Tom Ginsberg and Albert H. Y. Chen, eds., *Administrative Law and Governance in Asia* (London: Routledge, 2009), pp. 230–56.

68 Tamara Loos, *Subject Siam: Family, Law, and Colonial Modernity in Thailand* (Bangkok: Silkworm Books, 2002), and Tamara Loos, "Issaraphap: Limits of Individual Liberty in Thai Jurisprudence," *Crossroads: An Interdisciplinary Journal of Southeast Asian Studies* 12(1) (1998): 35–75. Also see the excellent piece by Thanet Aphornsuwan, "Slavery and Modernity: Freedom in the Making of Modern Siam," in David Kelly and Anthony Reid, eds., *Asian Freedoms: Journeys of an Idea in the Context of East and Southeast Asia* (London: Cambridge University Press, 1998), pp. 161–86.

69 One of the first Thai scholarly law articles on defamation appeared in 1957 on defamation of the dead: Chalut Sawatdithat, "Mua phu tai thuk min pramat" [When the Deceased Are Defamed], *Dunlapha* 4(11) (ph.y. 2500): 875–88. Following in 1958 were three pieces on who could serve as damaged party in defamation cases: Suthin Loetwirut, "Phu sia hai nai khwam phit thana min pramat" [The Damaged Party in Defamation Cases], *Dunlapha* 5 (2501), pp. 3–19, Wijit Wijan, "Min pramat phu tai" [Defamation of the Deceased], pp. 92–94, available at: www.library.coj.go.th/Article/data/d5_2_6.pdf , accessed 4 July 2009, and Phaibun Phianrujop, "Minpramat phu tai" [Defamation of the Dead], pp. 311–16, available at: www.library.coj.go.th/Article/data/d5_5_5.pdf, accessed 4 July 2009. A 1959 article written by a Supreme Court judge Pramun Suwanasorn, "Min pramat" [Defamation], *Dunlapha* 6(1) (2502): 2–18, affirms the principle, "the truer [of what was said], the greater the infraction" in cases of defamation. Also in this period was Banyat Suchiwa, "Min pramat" [Defamation], *Bot Bandit* 27(1) (2513): 149–53 and the somewhat longer piece on defamation of officials, in Choke Jarujinda, "Du min jao phanak ngan" [Insulting Officials], *Bot Bandit* 28(4) (2514 [1971]): 917–34. More substantial, though no less conventional, is another Supreme Court judge's 1972 treatment of defamation: Sanchai Satjawanit, "Min pramat—du min" [Defamation—Insult], *Bot Bandit* 29(2) and 29(3) (2515 [1972]): 366–89 and 541–73, respectively. Without exception, these are all flat pieces dissecting the various components of defamation and citing Supreme Court cases, with no analysis whatsoever. More recently there has been Visanu Khrua-ngam, "Seriphap nai kan sadaeng khwam khit hen" [Freedom for Expression of Opinions], *Warasan Kotmai* 11(4) (2524 [1981]): 570–76; Jitti Jaroencham, "Klao doei sujarit phua khwam chop tham" [Speaking in Good Faith for Fairness], *Warasan Aiyakan* 16(179) (2536) (1993): 68–73; Jiti Jaroencham, "Yang mai thung khanat du min" [Not Quite Yet an Insult] 16(189) (2536) (1993): 127–30; Narong Jaihan, "Thot lae kha sia hai nai karani min pramat" [Punishment and Compensation in

the Case of Defamation], *Warasan Nitisat* 2(3) (2534) (Sept. 1991): 450–52. The only historical treatment of the law, its adjudication, and its effect on greater society is David Streckfuss, "The Poetics of Subversion: Civil Liberty and Lesè-Majesté in the Modern Thai State," Ph.D. dissertation, University of Wisconsin, 1998, particularly Chapter 2. If defamation in Thailand has been of minimal concern to scholars, freedom of speech has received even less attention. For an example, see Visanu Khrua-ngam, "Serriphap nai kansadaeng," above.

70 The two Thai legal scholars primarily used in this book are Ammattho Phra-inthapricha and Jitti Tingsaphat: Ammattho's 1926 *Kham athibai kotmai laksana aya phak 2 ton 1* [Explanation of Criminal Law, Part 2, Section 1] (Krungthep: Rongphim Sokkanaphattanakorn, 2469), and Jitti's 1967/1975 and revised 1988–89 editions: Jitti Tingsaphat (1967), *Kham athibai pramuan kotmai aya (phak 2 tonn thi 1)* [Explanation of the Criminal Law Code, Part 2 Section 1] (Phranakhorn: Rongphim thai phitthaya, 2510 [1967]), Jitti Tingsaphat (1975), *Kham athibai pramuan kotmai aya (phak 2 ton thi 2)* [Explanation of the Criminal Law Code, Part 2, Section 2 and Part 3] (Krungthep: Samnakngan opphrom suksa kotmai haeng nettibandittaya sapha, 2518 [1975]), Jitti Tingsaphat (1988), *Kham athibai pramuan kotmai aya phak 2 ton thi 1* [Explanation of the Criminal Law Code, Part 2 Section 1] (Krungthep: Samnak opromsuksa kotmai haeng netibandittayasapha, 2531 [1988]), and Jitti Tingsaphat (1989), *Kham athibai pramuan kotmai aya (phak 2 ton 2 lae phak 3)* [Explanation of the Criminal Law Code, Part 2, Section 2 and Part 3] (Krungthep: Samnakngan opphrom suksa kotmai haeng nettibandittaya sapha, 2532 [1989]). My justification for depending mostly on these two sources is because they were both, if not *the*, standard law textbooks of their day; they are historical documents in themselves. Information is drawn also from the 1950s text of Yut Saeng-uthai, *Kham athibai kotmai laksana aya r.s. 123* [Explanation of Criminal Law [Code] 1908] (Krungtheip: Winyuchon Publication House, 2005), as well as leading contemporary texts, in particular Khanit na Nakhorn, *Kotmai aya phak khwamphit* [Criminal Law Criminal Offence Section], 3rd edn. (Samnakphim mahawitthayalai thammasat, 2532 [1989]), and 9th edn. (Krungthep: Winyuchon Publication House, 2006), and Kiatkhajorn Wajanasawat, *Kham athibai kotmai phak 1 (chabap phim khrang thi 10)* [Explanation of the Criminal Code, 10th edn.] (Krungthep: Samnakphim phon(la)sayam printing, 2551 [2008]). For the purposes of English translation, we have primarily used Dunlayasatpathiwet, Luang, *Pramuan kotmai aya phrom duai khamplae phasa angkrit* [The Criminal Code Accompanied with English Translation, as Compiled by Suchat Jiwachat] (Krungthep mahanakhorn: Samnakphim nitibannakan, 2516 [1973]), and its 1985 edition (Krungthep mahanakhorn: Rongphim jaratsanitthawong, 2528). One of the best for citations to articles covering various areas of criminal law is Twekiat Menakanist. *Pramuan kotmai aya chabap ang ing* [The Criminal Law Code, reference edition] (Krungthep: Winyuchon Publication House, 1997).

71 Interview, Stehen Frost, Bangkok, 21 May 2007; interviews with National Human Rights Commissioner Surasee Kosolnavin, Bangkok, 5 July 2006; and Khon Kaen, 9 May 2007.

72 Prinya Jittrakaranathikit, *Khwam phit thana min pramat-du min sung na* [The Crime of Defamation and Slander], 3rd edn. (Krungthep: Samnakphim nititham, 2538 (1995)); Suphon Issarasena, *Kandamnoen khadi minpramat* [Carrying out Defamation Cases] (Krungthep: Nitibanyakan, 2546 (2003)). In addition, there were two graduate theses written on defamation: Amnuai Khiewkham, "Minpramat thang aya: suksa chaphao het thi tham hai mai tong rap phit" [Criminal Defamation: A Study Specifically on Reasons for Exclusion from Guilt], thesis, Faculty of Law, Thammasat University, 2532 (1989) and Duan Jitrakorn, "Minpramat nai thang aya" [Criminal Defamation], thesis, Faculty of Law,

Thammasat University, n.d., a limited edition of a cremation volume: Pramun Suwannasorn, "Min pramat" [Defamation], in, *Anusorn nai ngan phraratchathan phloeng sop nai pramun suwannasorn* [Commemoration in the Royally-sponsored Cremation of Mr. Pramun Suwannason] (Krungthep: Hanghun suan jamkat Siwaphorn, 2524 (1981)), and even a play written by King Rama VI on contempt of court: Phrabatsomdetphra Mongkutklao jaoyuhua, *Bot lakhorn ruang minpramat san tobta chuai amnat lae nam yok ao nam bong* (Krungthep: Khurusapha, 2506 [1963]).

73 The only Thai-language monographs devoted solely to *lèse-majesté* were accounts and court findings of the 1975 Pradoem case (Naeow ruam nak kotmai phua prachachon, klum naksuksa kotmai klum mai, Rai la-iat khadi prawatisat min phraboromdetchanuphap "Thung chao fa jak kha chao din" [Details of the Historic Case, "From the People of the Sky to the Slaves of the Land"] (Krungthep: Naeow ruam nak kotmai phua prachachon, 2518 (1975)), and the 1988 Wira Musikapong [Somchai Jenchaijittarawanit, Khadi prawatisat min phraborom detchanuphap: Wira Musikaphong tit khuk phro kanmuang! [A Historic Lèse-majesté Case: Wira Musikaphong Jailed Because of Politics!] (Krungthep: Samnakngan phua sawaengha khwamyuttitham nai sangkhom, 2531 (1988)). The first notable attempt was in 1987 when the journal *Pajariyasan* invited legal scholars and royal councillors of the Privy Council to comment on the law. See "Khwamphit thana min phraboromdetchanuphap kap kan pokkhrong rabop prachathipatai thi mi phra maha kasat pen pramuk" [The Crime of Lèse-majesté and the Democratic Governance System with the King as Head of State], *Pajariyasan* 14(6) (Nov.–Dec. 1987): 12–45. The issue was touched upon again in 1993 in Chamlae kotmai khruangmu khong kanmuang banthuk kansammana Ruang "ja kae panha kanchai kotmai pen khruangmu thang kanmuang dai yang rai" [Cutting Out Laws (Used as) Tools of Politics: Proceedings of the Seminar, "How to Solve the Problem of Laws Being Used as Tools of Politics"], Bangkok, Law Faculty, Thammasat University, 22 Dec. 1992 (Krungthep: Asornmuangnit, 2536 (1993)), and then little or nothing on the topic for more than a decade. English-language contributions to the critical examination of *lèse-majesté* probably started with Craig Reynolds's 1991 historical piece, "Sedition in Thai History: A Nineteenth-century Poem and its Critics," in Manas Chitakasem and Andrew Turton, eds., *Thai Constructions of Knowledge* (Southampton: School of Oriental and African Studies, University of London, 1991), pp. 15–36. Reynolds admits that "even in historiography," the subject of *lèse-majesté* "has been neglected." Since then, there have been only a few longer pieces, including David Streckfuss, "Kings in the Age of Nations—The Paradox of Lèse-Majesté as Political Crime in Thailand," *Comparative Studies in Society and History* 37(3) (July 1995): 445–75, and David Streckfuss, ed., *Modern Thai Monarchy and Cultural Politics: The Acquittal of Sulak Sivaraksa on the Charge of lèse-majesté in Siam 1995 and Its Consequences (*Bangkok: Santi Pracha Dhamma Institute, 1996). Passing reference to *lèse-majesté* is made in Roger Kershaw, *Monarchy in South-East Asia* (London: Routledge, 2001), Tamara Loos, *Subject Siam*, Shigeharu Tanabe and Charles F. Keyes, eds., *Cultural Crisis and Social Memory* (London: Routledge-Curzon, 2002), Michael Kelly Connors, *Democracy and National Identity in Thailand* (London: RoutledgeCurzon, 2003), Maurizio Peleggi, *Thailand: The Worldly Kingdom* (London: Reaktion Books, 2007), and Kobkua Suwannatha-Pian, *King, Country and Constitutions: Thailand's Political Development 1932–2000* (London: RoutledgeCurzon, 2003). By February 2009, the number of critical newspaper and magazine articles on the topic had skyrocketed. To list just a few, see Grant Evans, "Modern Monarchy and Inviolability," *Bangkok Post*, 13 Feb. 2009, Jon Ungpakorn, "Another Nail in the Coffin of Thai Femocracy," *Bangkok Post*, 10 Oct. 2007, Thongchai Winichakul, "Lese Majeste Law Still Problematic,"

Nation, 11 Oct. 2007, C.J. Hinke, "Thai Means Free: FACT Coordinator CJ Hinke Comments on Lese Majeste," 29 Apr. 2008, available at: www.prachatai.com/english/news.php?id = 619, accessed 12 July 2008, Frank G. Anderson, "Thai Traditions: Lese majeste in Thailand," *Khorat Post*, 2 May 2008; and Nidhi Aeusriwong [Eoseewong], "Hitler's Moustache and Protection of the Institution," and Meechai Ruchuphan, "Meechai's Liberal Thoughts: Are We Still Thais?," in Niyom Rathamarit, ed., *Focus on Thai Democracy National and Local Issues* (Bangkok: King Prajadhipok's Institute, 2006), pp. 319–25, 578–81, 584–87.

74 The question has to be asked: If the interpretation I am making—that the effects of these defamation-based laws have been so pervasive within Thai society that large portions of cultural, social, and political truth have become seemingly inaccessible—why has this phenomenon not been more visible, especially to the historian? On what evidence or at least from what indications are these suppositions made? The 1900 edict, for instance, has been mentioned only by the legal historian David M. Engel and was not apparently even worthy of note by the long-serving foreign general adviser to the king at the time, Gustave Rolin-Jacquemyns. See Tipps, *Gustave Rolin-Jaequemyns*, pp. 291–94, 372. As for English-language academic work in the post-war period, neither "libel" nor "defamation" appear in any of the indexes of the major academic monographs, except for Duncan McCargo's *Politics and the Press in Thailand: Media Machinations* (London: Routledge, 2002).

75 As Chang Noi caustically points out, the going rate for a high-end politician's reputation was a mere 500 million baht [more than ten million dollars]. Despite Chang Noi's guarded optimism, there does not seem to be a trend of Thai courts deciding to "quietly reject" defamation cases. Chang Noi (pseud.), *Nation*, 29 Apr. 2006. See also, *Nation*, 31 May 2005; and *Bangkok Post*, 1 May 2005.

76 The king himself seemed to indicate that the law is a problem, calling for the law to be used sparingly. The king said:

> In referring to what they said in the newspaper, in radio and television that they will not criticise what the King does and says, do not criticise, actually I want them to criticise because whatever I do, I want to know that people agree or disagree. If they do not say, it can be seen as good . . . Actually I must also be criticised. I am not afraid if the criticism concerns what I do wrong, because then I know. Because if you say the King cannot be criticised, it means that the King is not human . . . if you rule out all criticism as a violation, the damage is done to the King or the King is not a good person.
>
> (*Nation*, 5 Dec. 2005)

For a critical commentary on the speech and how it was interpreted, see sanpaworn.vissaventure.com/log/243/the-kings-speech-can-do-no-wrong, accessed 10 Nov. 2008.

77 The Press Council of Thailand, for instance, issued its "white cover report" on the personal defamation law in 2004, entitled, "Necessity to Reform the Use of the Defamation Law" ["khwam jam pen thi ja tong patirop kan chai kotmai min pramat"]; see "Summary of the Academic Meeting" [Sarup kan prachum wichakan], 7 tulakhom [October] 2547 (2004), akan samakhom nak khao nak nangsu phim haeng prathet thai. *Fah Diew Kan* magazine devoted much of two issues in 2006 and 2008 to the question of *lèse-majesté*, with a fair number of Thai academicians and human rights activists weighing in. See, in particular, Thanapol Eawsakul, "Min phraboromdechanuphap nai sangkhom thai" [*Lèse-majesté* in Thai Society], *Fah Diew Kan* (Apr.–June 2006), pp. 67–81; and Somchai Preechasilpakul, "Min phraboromdechanuphap" [*Lèse-majesté*], pp. 148–57, Pravit Rojanaphruk, "Kotmai min phraboromdechanuphap lae kan sensor tua eng" [The

Lèse-majesté Law and Self-censorship], pp. 158–70, Thongchai Winichakul, "Kan khui ruang sathaban kasat to satharanachon pen sing thi pen pai dai" [Talking about the Institution of the Monarchy to the Public Is Something Possible], *Fah Diew Kan* 6:1 (Jan.–Mar. 2008) pp. 94–103. Thai defendants in *lèse-majesté* cases have generally defended themselves by claiming their loyalty to the throne or by arguing it was a matter of academic freedom. For more details on the latter, see Niphon Jaemduang, comp., *Phiphaksa sangkhom thai phiphaksa s. siwarak: khumu suksa kandamnoen khadi aya laksana khwam phit thana min phraboromdechanuphap lae min pramat* (sathaban santiprachatham, 2539) [A Judgment on Thai Society, a Judgment on S. Sivaraksa: A Handbook for Defence on the Criminal Charge of Lèse-majesté and Defamation] (Pracha Santi Pracha Dhamma Institute, 1996). The law is increasingly mentioned in Thai academic works looking at related topics, such as the recent publication of a Thai-language book critiquing royally supported projects, with a surprisingly provocative English title of *The Royally Initiated Project: The Making of King Bhumibol's Royal Hegemony*, but less direct Thai title. See Chanida Chitbundid, *Khrongkan an nuangjak phraratchadamri: kan sathapana phraratcha-amnat nam nai phrabatsomedetphrajaoyuhua* (Krungthep: Munnithi khrongkan tamra sangkhomsat lae manutsat, 2550 (2007)), p. 214. The law is mentioned in passing in a number of Thai works, for instance, in Sutthachai Yimprasert, *Phaen ching chat thai* [Contest for the Thai Nation] (Krungthep: Samnakphim 6 tula ramluk, 2550 (2007)), p. 390.

78 A very thorough piece on media freedom in Thailand, including sections on defamation and *lèse-majesté* is a joint publication by Article 19 and Forum-Asia, *Freedom of Expression and the Media in Thailand* (Dec. 2005), available at: www.article19.org/pdfs/publications/thailand-baseline-study.pdf, accessed 19 May 2009. A more recent report specifically on defamation was written by Sinfah Tunsarawuth for Article 19 and National Press Council of Thailand, entitled "Impact of Defamation Law on Freedom of Expression in Thailand," Mar. 2009 [draft copy].

79 Turkey might also be a strong candidate for a defamation regime. For certain similarities with Thailand, see Ayşe Gül Altinay, *The Myth of the Military-Nation* (New York: Palgrave Macmillan, 2004), pp. 13–32.

80 Although this work does not delve into the connection between personal practices of Theravada Buddhism and political movements, future study might show certain tendencies particular to Theravada Buddhist states. Certainly, there are those Buddhists who feel uncomfortable about the way that Buddhism is used and fear the intolerance of some of its adherents may bode ill for Buddhism in the long run. For instance, see Sanitsuda Ekachai's heroic stand against those who would make Buddhism the national religion (*Bangkok Post*, 1 Nov. 2007). Although she herself is a Buddhist, she counters Buddhist chauvinism, as in her *Keeping the Faith: Thai Buddhism at the Crossroads* (Bangkok: Post Books, 2001). Another example is Stanley J. Tambiah who has questioned the role Buddhists have taken in Sri Lanka. See Stanley J. Tambiah, *Buddhism Betrayed? Religion, Politics, and Violence in Sri Lanka* (Chicago: University of Chicago Press, 2002). Also, please see note 92, p. 340.

2 Regimes of truth, regimes of defamation

1 Michel Foucault, "Truth and Power," in James D. Faubion, ed., *Power* (New York: The New Press, 2000), p. 131.

2 Michel Foucault, "Truth and Juridical Forms," in James D. Faubion, ed., *Power* (New York: The New Press, 2000), p. 4.

3 Ibid., p. 33.

4 Ibid., pp. 34–37.

5 Ibid., pp. 37–38.
6 Ibid., p. 39. Foucault notes that sometimes "the community intervened"—when the community as a whole felt itself to be the injured party—and demanded compensation of some sort. See p. 35.
7 Ibid., pp. 36–40.
8 Ibid., pp. 43–45.
9 Ibid., p. 47.
10 Ibid., pp. 46–47.
11 Ibid., p. 48.
12 Ibid., p. 53.
13 Robert McEwen and Philip Lewis, *Gatley on Libel and Slander*, 17th edn. (London: Sweet & Maxwell Limited, 1974), pp. 5, 13–19; Norm Goldstein, ed., *The Associated Press Stylebook and Briefing on Media Law* (New York: Basic Books, 2004), pp, 341–56.
14 It should also be added that American and British libel laws are significantly different. In an article about the California legislature passing a bill restricting the right of British subjects from suing American publications for libel, *San Francisco Chronicle* writer Bob Egelko nicely sums up the difference: "One difference between British and U.S. libel law is that a U.S. plaintiff must prove that the defamatory statement was false. In Britain, once the plaintiff shows that a statement would harm his or her reputation, the defendant must prove it was true." Available at: http://sfgate.com/cgi-bin/article.cgi?f = /c/a/2009/05/15/MN7I17KKT6.DTL, accessed 2 June 2009.
15 Available at: http://www.rsf.org/article.php3?id_article = 19388, accessed 14 Nov. 2008. Article 19 provides a map which shows that an overwhelming majority of countries in the world still hold defamation as a criminal offense, regardless of which legal tradition they come from, with Napoleonic code France and Cambodia both considering decriminalizing the offence, while common law Britain, South Africa, and Malaysia are not. Available at: http://www.article19.org/advocacy/defamationmap/map, accessed 14 Nov. 2008.
16 The question of the most important influences on Thai legal thinking is an important and deserves its own study. Until 1960, Britain graduated many of those featured prominently in the present volume: Prince Ratburi, *Phra* Kraisi, Ammattho, the Pramoj brothers, Jitti Tingsaphat, and Sulak Sivaraksa. The two most important exceptions were Pridi Banomyong, who finished in France, and Yut Saeng-uthai, who finished in Germany.
17 See also Article 19's "Handbook" which examines international standards and practices for defamation, available at: http://www.article19.org/publications/law/the-handbook.html, accessed on 14 Nov. 2008, as well as "Defining Defamation: Principles on Freedom of Expression and Protection of Reputation" Reporters Without Borders, 2000. Available at: http://www.article19.org/pdfs/standards/definingdefamation.pdf, accessed on 14 Nov. 2008.
18 "Criminal Defamation Laws and the Right to Freedom of Expression," Joint Amicus Brief of Interights and Article 19 in Constitutional case N 16/98, available at: http://74.125.153.132/search?q=cache:http://www.bghelsinki.org/fe/suggestions_en.html /accessed on 23 May 2009.
19 McEwen and Lewis, *Gatley on Libel and Slander*, pp. 487–88.
20 Goldstein, *Associated Press Stylebook*, pp. 348–50, 356.
21 An American legal scholar, for instance, points out that "Under current defamation law, a group member has no cause of action against the publisher of the defamation unless the group is very small or the defamatory statement applies specifically to the plaintiff." In some states, "small group" is limited to 25 persons. See Ellyn Tracy Marcus, "Group Defamation and Individual Actions: A New Look at an Old Rule," *California Law Review* (*71 Calif. L. Rev. 1532*, Sept. 1983),

Another legal scholar points out that a "more stringent formulation denies recovery" unless the plaintiff can show that "the recipients of the defamatory matter are *likely to identify* some, if not all, of the [members of the group] as intended objects of the defamation" [original emphasis]. Jeffrey S. Bromme, "Group Defamation: Five Guiding Factors," *Texas Law Review* (*64 Tex. L. Rev. 591*, Nov. 1985). However, elements of collective defamation can be captured within defamation-based national security laws. See Thomas D. Jones, "Group Defamation under British, Canadian, Indian and Nigerian Law," *International Journal on Minority and Group Rights* 5 (1998): 281–335.

22 McEwen and Lewis, *Gatley on Libel and Slander*, pp. 6, 75.

23 Ibid., pp. 5–6, 140.

24 Much of the following discussion is based on McEwen and Lewis, *Gatley on Libel and Slander*, pp. 8–23 and 43–57.

25 McEwen and Lewis, *Gatley on Libel and Slander*, pp. 9–10.

26 Ibid., pp. 54–55.

27 Mark Stephens, "The Ban on Legal Aid for Defendants in Libel Cases Needs to Be Overturned after *McLibel*," *The Lawyer* (Feb. 2005), p. 13; interview, Stephen Frost, Bangkok, 21 May 2007.

28 McEwen and Lewis, *Gatley on Libel and Slander*, pp. 10–11.

29 Jory writes, "The problem postmodernism poses for Thai historiography is its undermining of any attempt – whether liberal, Marxist, or royalist – to claim to represent a 'true' interpretation of the Thai past." While Jory is certainly right to say there is good reason to be suspicious of "the notion that historical truth may be attained through the use of reason and the rules of evidence, or what was formerly known as the 'historical method,' as influenced by the positivist 'scientific method'," truth—even when it is that merely of "events," nonetheless needs to be reckoned with on some level. Patrick Jory, "Problems in Contemporary Thai Nationalist Historiography," available at: http://kyotoreview.cseas.kyoto-u.ac.jp/issue/issue2/article_251.html, accessed 23 Jan. 2008.

30 Nidhi Eoseewong, *Pen and Sail* (Chiang Mai: Silkworm Books, 2006), p. 250.

31 The "truth management" project was first described in Chaiwat Satha-Anand, "Sangkhomsat kap kapkaenjatkan 'khwam jing' nai sangkhom thai" [Social Science and "Truth" Management in Thai Society], *Sangkohomsat Parithat* [Social Science Review] 19(2) (1998): 44–55.

32 Chaiwat Satha-Anand, "The Silence of the Bullet Monument: Violence and 'Truth' Management, Dusun-nyor 1948, and Kru-Ze 2004," in Duncan McCargo, ed., *Rethinking Thailand's Southern Violence* (Singapore: Nus Press, 2007), pp. 174–75.

33 Chaiwat, "The Silence of the Bullet Monument," pp. 30–33.

34 This is not to imply that foreign and Thai historians are uninterested in the truth, but rather that many of them use a more Foucauldian approach which speaks of how different types of power-knowledge discourses produce certain "truths" specific to that discourse and not generally falsifiable as such. See, for instance, Attachak Satayanurak, *Kanplianplaeng lokkathat khong chan phunam thai tangtae ratchakan thi 4 – ph.s. 2475* [Change in the Worldview of the Thai Governing Elite from the Fourth Reign to 1932] (Krungthep: Samnakphim julalongkorn mahawitthayalai, 2538 [1995]). A little more directly to the question of truth is Attachak Satayanurak, *"Mu thi sam" nai prawattisat kanmuang thai* ["The Third Hand" in Thai Political History; author's title: "Truths" and Dealing with "Truths" in the Context of the "Third-Party Culture" (1957–the Present Time)] (Krungthep: Khrongkan jatphim khop fai, 2549 [2006]). Two works on the Thai media touch on the question of truth. Annette Hamilton provides an excellent piece on reality and truth as depicted by the Thai media and as received by ordinary Thai. See Annette Hamilton, "Rumours, Foul Calumnies and the Safety of the State: Mass Media and National Identity in Thailand," in, Craig J.

Reynolds, ed., *National Identity and Its Defenders, Thailand, 1939–1989* (Clayton, Victoria: Centre of Southeast Asian Studies, Monash University, Monash Papers on Southeast Asia, No. 25, 1991), pp. 341–79. Duncan McCargo's monograph makes a number of references to how the Thai media's view on objective reportage and the separation between news and comment affect the kind of information reaching Thai audiences. See Duncan McCargo's *Politics and the Press in Thailand: Media Machinations* (London and New York: Routledge, 2002), pp. 33–37, 40–42, 139.

35 Antoon de Baets "Defamation Cases against Historians," *History and Theory* 41(3) (Oct., 2002) examines the crucial issue of how to distinguish between truth and opinion in defamation cases against historians:

> Identifying the truth value of statements is not simple. Usually, courts distinguish two types of statements: facts and opinions. Proving facts is dependent on at least three factors. First, time: In some countries, it is not legally possible to prove the truth of statements about facts from the distant past (in France, older than ten years) . . . It implies, however, that proof of the non-defamatory nature of a given statement cannot invoke the facts themselves. Second, those in charge of proof: In some countries, such as the United Kingdom, the burden of proof is on the defendant, not on the complainant. Third, the intention: The factual claim must be meant as such and not, for example, as satire. Considering these factors, it is clear that judges and historians can diverge considerably in their weighing of facts and, hence, truth conceptions. Opinions (or "comments" or "value judgments") are not susceptible to proof because they do not fit a true/untrue scheme and therefore enjoy greater legal protection than facts.
>
> (De Baets, 2002, pp. 347, footnote 5)

In this study, I take a slightly broader sweep, placing what De Baets calls "historical truth" into the category of "fair comment" as "historical representations."

Within Thai studies, McCargo argues that, as a vestige of authoritarianism, these categories have become complicated. McCargo examines in detail how "news" and "comment" are perceived and produced by Thai language newspapers (McCargo, 2002, pp. 33–37, 40–42, 139). See Chapter 12 in this volume for further discussion on this point.

36 Here Chaiwat is drawing on the work of Hannah Arendt ("Truth and Politics," *Between Past and Future: Eight Exercises in Political Thought* (New York: Penguin Books, 1967). Arendt juxtaposed "rational truth" ("contested philosophical opinions on society and the world") versus "factual truth." Chaiwat, "The Silence of the Bullet Monument," p. 32.

37 These potentially falsifiable characterizations make a difference: Turkey's admittance to the European Union may depend at least partially on whether it admits that millions of Armenians were killed and whether it will accept the term "genocide" to describe the phenomenon. See http://www.atour.com/~aahgn/news/20001003f.html, accessed 3 Feb. 2009]; also http://turkofile.wordpress.com/2008/07/12/turkey-the-eu-and-the-armenian-genocide, accessed 8 Feb. 2009.

38 Somsak Raksuwan, *Political Monsters*, published on the occasion of the exhibit, "Political Monsters" by Somsak Raksuwan at Jamjuri Art Gallery (Bangkok: Amarin Printing, 2007).

39 Noam Chomsky, "Afghanistan and South Vietnam," in James Peck, ed., *The Chomsky Reader* (New York: Pantheon Books, 1987), pp. 223–26.

40 Edward S. Herman and Noam Chomsky, *Manufacturing Consent: The Political Economy of the Mass Media* (New York: Pantheon Books, 1988), pp. 206–10.

41 A similar assertion was made by Deputy Prime Minister Suthep Thaugsuban, who alleged that the "ambition" of former Prime Minister Thaksin Shinawatra "was to be the country's first president." Although Thaksin's lawyers filed a defamation suit against Suthep, it is hard to imagine how the contention could be proved or disproved (*Nation*, 6 Feb. 2009).

42 Postman's critique of "social science" and "social historians" is particularly relevant here. He writes:

> The stories of social researchers are much closer in structure and purpose to what is called imaginative literature; that is to says, both a social research and a novelist give unique interpretations to a set of human events and support their interpretations with examples in various forms. Their interpretations cannot be proved or disproved but will draw their appeal from the power of their language, the depth of their explanations, the relevance of their examples, and the credibility of their themes.
>
> (Neil Postman, *Technopoly: The Surrender of Culture to Technology* (New York: Vintage Books, 1993, pp. 154, 156)

3 Truth and treason in old Siam

1 Benedict Anderson was one of the first foreign scholars to question the actual significance of Siam's non-colonial status in his "Studies of the Thai State: The State of Thai Studies," in Eliezer B. Ayal ed., *The Study of Thailand* (Athens, OH: Ohio Center for International Studies, Southeast Asia Program, 1978), pp. 193–247. Thongchai has called the three axioms—"Siam was under threat from European powers; its independence was in jeopardy. The rapid modernization and reform of the government were necessary for the defense of the country's independence. With skilful diplomacy, the Chakri monarchs saved the country, though not without sacrifice and pain"—as forming "the foundation of the royal-nationalist ideology of Thai history" and much Thai historiography serves to "reinforce . . . the master narrative of Thai history." See Thongchai Winichakul, "Siam's Colonial Conditions and the Birth of Thai History," paper presented at the conference, "Unraveling the Myths of Southeast Asian History," 24–26 Nov. 2006, forthcoming. Works in the same vein covering this period have included Thongchai Winichakul, *Siam Mapped: A History of the Geo-body of a Nation* (Chiang Mai: University of Hawaii Press/Silkworm Books, 1994), much of Craig Reynolds's work, and Attachak Satayanurak, *Kanplianplaeng lokkathat khong chan phunam thai tangtae ratchakan thi 4 – ph.s. 2475* [Change in the Worldview of the Thai Governing Elite from the Fourth Reign to 1932] (Krungthep: Samnakphim julalongkorn mahawitthayalai, 2538 [1995]). Beyond Engel, there has yet to be a sustained examination of legal structures and epistemology in premodern Siam or an analysis of exactly what was transformed in terms of law in this period, although there are a number of works that touch on the subject: Andrew Turton "Thai Institutions of Slavery," in James L. Watson, ed., *Asian and African Systems of Slavery* (Oxford: Basil Blackwell, 1980), Peter A. Jackson, "The Performative State: Semi-coloniality and the Tyranny of Images in Modern Thailand," *Sojourn* 19(2) (2004): 219–53, Christine Gray, "Thailand: The Soteriological State in the 1970s," Ph.D. dissertation, the University of Chicago, 1986; David Streckfuss, "The Mixed Colonial Legacy in Siam: Origins of Thai Racialist Thought, 1890–1910," in Laurie Sears, ed., *Autonomous Histories, Particular Truths: Essays in Honor of John R. W. Smail* (Madison, WI: Center for Southeast Asian Studies, 1993), pp. 123–53, and Neil A. Englehart, *Culture and Power in Traditional Siamese Government* (Ithaca, NY: Southeast Asia Program Publications, 2001). Also see the intriguing piece, Akiko Iijima, "The 'International

Court' System in the Colonial History of Siam," *Taiwan Journal of Southeast Asian Studies* 5(1) (2008): 31–64.

2 Chatthip Nartsupha, *The Thai Village Economy in the Past* (Chiang Mai: Silkworm Books, 1999), p. 10.

3 *The Three Seals Law* itself was drawn from ancient Indian codes, but with a more pronounced Buddhist character. See Yoneo Ishii, *Sangha, State, and Society: Thai Buddhism in History* (Honolulu: Hawaii University Press, 1986), pp. 44–45.

4 I draw heavily from Loos's impeccable treatment of *Three Seals* (Tamara Loos, *Subject Siam: Family, Law, and Colonial Modernity in Thailand* (Bangkok: Silkworm Books, 2002), especially pp. 32–40, 179–85). A chronicle covering the period describes the rationale for the codification as for the benefit of "the common people":

> a king who governed a kingdom had to rely on the laws for rulers from ancient times that earlier kings had proclaimed as a basis for making judgments on judicial matters concerning the common people. However, these laws, too, had become greatly confused, unclear and contradictory, for there were greedy people who had not been the least ashamed to sin and who had made changes as they saw fit in the laws in order to allow for the judgments they wished. They had blemished the justice of the kingdom.
>
> (Thiphakonwong (Chaophraya), *The Dynastic Chronicles, Bangkok Era, the First Reign, Vol. One: Text* (translated and edited by Thadeus and Chadin Flood), Tokyo: The Centre for East Asian Cultural Studies, 1978, pp. 276–77)

5 Loos, *Subject Siam*, p. 34.

6 Ibid., p. 38.

7 Jean-Baptiste Pallegoix, *Description of the Thai Kingdom or Siam* (Bangkok: White Lotus, 2000), p. 193.

8 I retain the Thai conceptual categories in the laws. The term, *kabot*, is perhaps closest to the English "treason," which includes acts of rebellion, treasonous words—seemingly, anything that went against the king. The term *kabot* is still used in Thai legal parlance, although the translation into English seems awkward. See Stanley J. Tambiah, *World Conqueror and World Renouncer* (Cambridge, MA: Cambridge University Press, 1976), pp. 102–31. For discussion of *kabot* as a legal category, see Thawee Kasiyaphong, "Kabot" [Rebellion], *Warasan Kotmai* 3(1) (Jan.–June 2520 [1977]): 105–16. The article has also a bizarre Pali treatment of treason.

9 Khana Nitisat, Mahawitthayalai Thammasat, *Pramuan kotmai ratchakan thi nung julasakarat 1166, phim tam chabap luang tra sam duang* lem 2 (PKRI) [The Three Seals Law, vol. 2] (Krungthep: Rongphim ruankaew kanphim, 2529 1986]), pp. 369–70.

10 Ibid., p. 375.

11 Ibid., pp. 369–494.

12 Loos, *Subject Siam*, p. 39.

13 Pallegoix, *Description of the Thai Kingdom or Siam*, pp. 190–91. Also see Loos, *Subject Siam*, p. 39. I have had experience with such a system still intact in the Northeast. In 2004, I witnessed a villager "judge/arbitrator" (*tulakan*) resolve the issue of a foreign guest who suspected she might have been molested during a homestay. Taking up an entire day, the *tulakan* called in various parties, compared "testimony," asked the accuser how she felt the situation could best be resolved, brought the parties (and their representatives—in this case, other students and the parents of the alleged wrongdoer) together, and finally reached an agreement. Had

it failed, the *tulakan* said, the matter would have been turned over to the police to resolve (Personal experience, July 2004).

14 Reynolds, "Sedition in Thai History," pp. 25–26; also in revised form, Craig J. Reynolds, "A Seditious Poem and Its History," *Seditious Histories Contesting Thai and Southeast Asian Pasts* (Seattle: University of Washington Press, 2006), pp. 80–101.

15 Reynolds, "A Seditious Poem and Its History," p. 94.

16 There is no indication, for instance, that King Chulalongkorn engaged in any investigation into the circumstances of the poem's composition, but rather merely drafted the order of the poet's condemnation, in relation to how the poem offended the monarch. See Reynolds, "A Seditious Poem and Its History," pp. 94–95.

17 N.A. McDonald, *A Missionary in Siam (1860–1870)* (Bangkok: White Lotus Books, 1999), pp. 25–26.

18 Ibid., p. 27.

19 Chris Baker and Pasuk Phongpaichit, *Khun Chang Khun Phaen* (forthcoming). I thank Chris for sharing the ongoing draft with me.

20 Interestingly, the altercation was at the time a criminal offense, which meant committing violence, assault, seizing property, or putting into chains, and so was to be resolved in the criminal court. But the attempted murder was in a different class of offenses, including robbery, stealing "wives, children, . . . servants, elephants, horses, boats, carts, cattle, buffalo, cloth, noodles, vegetables, duck, chicken, or any other article," as well as using "filth-eating spirits" or making "love philters." Such crimes were dealt with by the "Department of the City."

21 Baker and Pasuk point out that the procedure depicted in *Khun Chang Khun Paen* is in the precise fashion as laid out in *Three Seals*: "The law went to great lengths to ensure that the two parties would prepare for the ordeal in the same way:

> Judges (*tralakan*) will detain both parties; buy chickens from the same place; buy beeswax; undyed thread; soap nut; kaffir lime, new rice pot, new curry pot, upper cloth, lower cloth, all from the same place; materials for a baisi, also from the same place; the judges will detain both parties; have them dress in white upper and lower cloths; remain in confinement for three days without walking outside; have the judges cook rice for them, and look after them. . . . Do not allow anyone to talk with either party, or else that party will lose. If either party goes outside, that party loses.

22 The reader will have to buy the book to find out what happened next.

23 See, "Phisut damnam/lui ploeng," [Proof by Water Dunking and Trial by Fire] matra 5/6," in Mahawitthayalai wicha Thammasat lae kanmuang, *Kotmai tra 3 duang chabap phim* lem 1 (kae khai mai) [*Three Seals* Law, Vol. 1, newly revised] (Krungthep mahanakorn: Sathaban pridi banomyong, 2548), pp. 324–25.

24 Ratchabanditayastan, *Photjananukrom* (Krungthep: Aksornjaroenthat, 2539), p. 879.

25 Mahawitthayalai wicha Thammasat lae kanmuang, *Kotmai tra 3 duang chabap phim* lem 1, p. 294.

26 "Matra 24," Ibid., p. 306.

27 "Matra 13," Ibid., p. 301.

28 "Prakat Phraratchabanyat," Ibid., p. 296.

29 "Prakat Phraratchabanyat," Ibid., p. 297.

30 "Laksana phayan," Ibid., pp. 292–319.

31 Max Weber, *Sociology of Religion* (Boston: Beacon Press, 1963), pp. 163–70. I use the term loosely, cognizant that Weber's entire construct of charisma and its inapplicability to Buddhist saints has been challenged. See Stanley J. Tambiah,

The Buddhist Saints of the Forest and the Cult of Amulets (Cambridge: Cambridge University Press, 1984), pp. 321–34.

32 The Thai cosmology, *Traiphum* or *Three Worlds*, is, according to many scholars, key not only to understanding the premodern Thai world-view, but does much to explain current social and political phenomena. Swearer, for instance, writes,

> Within its hierarchical framework of various human, heavenly, animal and demonic realms, the text focuses on a central figure, the universal monarch (*cakkavatti*), exemplified by the Buddhist king, Dharmasokaraja. . . . That King Rama I . . . commissioned a new recension of the *Traiphum* testifies to its longevity and utility as a charter for order and stability at the beginning of Thailand's modern era, also a time of political and social disruption.
>
> (Donald K. Swearer, "Center and Periphery: Buddhism and Politics in Modern Thailand," in Ian Harris, ed., *Buddhism and Politics in Twentieth-century Asia*, London: Continuum, 2001), p. 196)

Craig Reynolds also attests to its foundational importance, saying that it "classified and ranked all animate existence on the basis of merit" and "established 'rules' for the social hierarchy in premodern Siam," making it essentially "a 'theory' of premodern Siamese society," Craig J. Reynolds, "Thai Manual Knowledge: Theory and Practice," in *Seditious Histories Contesting Thai and Southeast Asian Pasts* (Seattle: University of Washington Press, 2006), pp. 220–21. Jackson says Buddhist works such as the *Traiphum* have, in Thailand, "retained an especially high degree of symbolic significance and relevance to political actions activities and debates," Peter A. Jackson, "Re-Interpreting the Traiphum Phra Ruang: Political Factions of Buddhist Symbolism in Contemporary Thailand," in Trevor Ling, ed., *Buddhist Trends in Southeast Asia* (Singapore: Institute of Southeast Asian Studies, 1993), p. 64. See Frank E. Reynolds and Mani B. Reynolds (trans.), *Three Worlds According to King Ruang: A Thai Buddhist Cosmology* (Berkeley, CA: Regents of the University of California, 1982).

33 Christine Gray, "Thailand: The Soteriological State in the 1970s," Ph.D. dissertation, The University of Chicago, 1986, p. 49. Christine Gray draws on a wide variety of historical texts, commentaries, and modern scholarship, one of the most important of which is *Traiphum* or *Three Worlds*, to make her case. For the core of the following discussion, I draw from Christine Gray's underused dissertation. It is a surprisingly open work, considering the period and would no doubt have caused some stir had it been published in the early 1980s. The work served as a primary source for Paul Handley's *The King Never Smiles*. I would like to take exception to the criticism of Handley's book, heard in passing, that he was inadequately informed about Buddhism and the concept of the *dhammaraja*. Handley makes extensive use of Gray's framework. Her dissertation work was done under the supervision of Frank Reynolds, one of the premier scholars of Theravada Buddhism. Handley was faithful to Gray's text and Gray, presumably, was faithful to Reynolds' work. In this context, see Paul Handley, *The King Never Smiles* (New Haven, CT: Yale University Press, 2006).

34 Gray, "Thailand: The Soteriological State," p. 24.

35 Ibid., pp. 53–55.

36 Tambiah recounts the story of Acharn Mun, a famous forest monk of Thailand's Northeast who, in his meditation practices in the forest, encountered wild animals. Tambiah explains the process by which meditation masters tame the wild beast:

> Firstly, the meditating monk pacifies the animals, and even wins their protection, by the practice of compassion ... which flows from the monk and envelops the animal. Secondly, a monk like him achieves the capacity to communicate with the animals, not merely through being able to interpret their noises, but also because an *arahant* is versed in "language of the mind, which is supreme to all the languages in the Three Worlds.
>
> (Tambiah, *Buddhist Saints of the Forest*, p. 88)

37 Gray, "Thailand: The Soteriological State," p. 55. From Acharn Mun's biography, it was said that "He showed his ability for mind reading ... He was aware, without seeing or hearing about the incident, that a monk-disciple had fallen in love with a tribal girl" and knew "by his clairvoyance" that this monk

> would not be able to resist it because of the action of his *karma* ... The Acharn also showed he had powers of clairaudience ... He also gave instruction "to such invisible beings as ghosts, demons, terrestrial and celestial angels and the higher angels" ... The Acharn once had a remarkable vision concerning three elephants.
>
> (Phra Acharn Maha Boowa Hyanasampanno, *The Venerable Phra Acharn Mun Bhurudatto Thera, Meditation Master* (trans. Siri Buddhasukh) (Bangkok: Mahamakut Rajawidyalaya Press, 1976), as quoted in Tambiah, *The Buddhist Saints of the Forest*, p. 100)

38 Gray, "Thailand: The Soteriological State," pp. 53–54. This celestial schema is roughly described by Attachak in "The Third Hand," which describes how the just exercise of power is a moral act in which the enlightened powerful are required to show compassion and act justly. Attachak, though, attributes this model only indirectly to Buddhism as he describes the relationship between the state and the monarch, and the ruled. See, in particular, "Concepts of State and Monarch," in Attachak, "*Mu thi sam*," pp. 6–15. Buddhist kings who practice the Ten Virtues are the most prominent examples of this group. For a detailed description, see Patrick Jory, "The *Vessantara Jataka, Barami*, and the *Bodhisatta*-Kings: The Origins and Spread of a Premodern Thai Concept of Power," *Crossroads: An Interdisciplinary Journal of Southeast Asian Studies* 16(1) (2002): 167–74.

39 The terms all come from Chapter 34 of Baker and Pasuk, *Khun Chang Khun Phaen*.

40 Gray, "Thailand: The Soteriological State," p. 49.

41 Ibid., p. 72. This cosmological hierarchy is described quite nicely in Peter Vandergeest, "Constructing Thailand: Regulation, Everyday Resistance, and Citizenship," *Comparative Studies of Society and History* 35(1) (1993): 136–39.

42 Gray, "Thailand: The Soteriological State," p. 11. Also see, Ishii, *Sangha, State, and Society*, pp. 44–46, for a fuller discussion of *dhammaraja*.

43 Gray, "Thailand: The Soteriological State," pp. 59–60.

44 Ibid., pp. 56–57.

45 Ibid., p. 51.

46 Ibid., pp. 257–58.

47 Ibid., p. 56.

48 Peter A. Jackson, "Introduction," *Buddhadasa: A Buddhist Thinker for the Modern World* (Bangkok: The Siam Society, 1989), pp. 33–49.

49 Ibid., p. 34.

50 Ibid., pp. 37–39. To eschew discourse is apparently not just a Thai approach to Buddhism, but part of an older, Theravada Buddhist tradition. Ishii remarks that the Sri Lankan Buddhist scholar Buddhaghosa wrote 137,000 lines of Buddhist

commentary, with "no debate or argument whatsoever" and with "no development of dogma." Ishii, *Sangha, State, and Society*, p. 11.

51 Jackson, "Introduction," p. 34. "Debate" within the Thai Theravada tradition seems similar to Foucault's description of the medieval "dispute" which dead-ended as an inquiry form in the West. Foucault writes,

> The dispute was a confrontation between two adversaries who used the verbal weapon, rhetorical procedures, and demonstrations based essentially on the appeal to authority. One appealed not to witnesses of truth, but to witnesses of strength . . . the more authors one of the participants had on his side, the more evidence of authority, strength, and gravity he could invoke, the greater were his chances of winning.
>
> (Michel Foucault, "Truth and Juridical Forms," in James D. Faubion, ed., *Power*, New York: The New Press, 2000, p. 51)

52 Loos, *Subject Siam*, p. 33. Foucault notes the connection between power and knowledge in premodern political forms: "political power always implied the possession of a certain type of knowledge. By the fact of holding power, the king and those around him held a knowledge that could not and must not be communicated to the other social groups" (Foucault, "Truth and Juridical Forms," p. 31).

53 Loos, *Subject Siam*, pp. 39–40.

54 Reynolds, "Thai Manual Knowledge," p. 218.

55 Ibid., pp. 218–19.

56 Ibid., p. 219.

57 In a similar way to Foucault describing the eventual dead-end of alchemy as a truth-seeking device, these "magical" texts and the teachers promoting them either fade with the death of their inventor, or are passed down through a disciple network of the initiated. Foucault, "Truth and Juridical Forms," p. 50.

58 Reynolds, "Thai Manual Knowledge," p. 220.

59 Reynolds, who translated the autobiography of the first Supreme Patriarch of modern Siam, dates the first publishing of the *Vinaya* to 1916. It may, though, have appeared in various, less complete versions earlier. A new edition seemed to come out annually, with the fifth edition issued in 1899; at that rate, the first edition would have come out in 1895. Prince Wachirayan was made head of the Thammayudhnikai order in 1892 and set out with Prince Damrong to create "the curriculum for monks and novices" through "standard textbooks." It was likely that at least an earlier form of *Vinaya* had been compiled at that time (Maurizio Peleggi, *Thailand: The Worldly Kingdom*, London: Reaktion Books Ltd, 2007, p. 110). The English translation, which seems assiduously faithful to the Thai version, is subtitled, "Standard Text for the Dhamma Student, 3rd Grade." For a painful and delightful description of *Vinaya*, see Reynolds, "Thai Manual Knowledge," p. 237.

60 Somdet Phra Maha Samana Chao Krom Phraya Vajirananavarorasa, *Navakovda*: *Instructions for Newly-Ordained Bhikkus and Samaneras* (Bangkok: Mahanakut Rajavidya Press, 1993), pp. vi–ix, 36–42. With eight editions in a few years, the author acknowledges that readers have been "variously satisfied." The ninth edition of 1904 includes more Pali words; the 1910 twelfth edition daringly adds "Groups of Two." In the Preface to the first English edition of *Navakovada*, the Supreme Patriarch in 1969 writes, that "teaching and learning have changed considerably" since the book first came out and "the information is brief and concise with little or no explanation" (Somdet Phra Maha Samana Chao Krom Phraya Vajirananavarorasa, pp. xi–xiv).

61 Reynolds, "Thai Manual Knowledge," pp. 235, 238.

62 Connors, *Democracy and National Identity in Thailand*, pp. 46–51; Reynolds, "Thai Manual Knowledge," p. 239. Connors does not use this term, but he seems perfectly in line with what Reynolds describes.

63 Craig Reynolds writes that information about the physical world in *Traiphum* was no longer "unquestioned" and was "shaken by explanations offered by Western science." Craig Reynolds, "Buddhist Cosmography in Thai Intellectual History," in Craig J. Reynolds, *Seditious Histories Contesting Thai and Southeast Asian Pasts* (Seattle: University of Washington Press, 2006), p. 175. [161–84]

64 Nidhi Eoseewong, *Pen and Sail* (Chiang Mai: Silkworm Books, 2006), pp. 249–53, and Nidhi Eoseewong, *Pak kai lae bai rua* (Krungthep: Amarin kanphim, 2527), p. 392.

65 See, for instance, Peter Jackson who writes, "Mongkut's ethical and rationalist interpretation of Buddhism created a divide between the traditional metaphysical interpretations of the religion's teachings and those views which were more influenced by scientific thinking," Jackson, "Re-Interpreting the Traiphum Phra Ruang," p. 73.

66 Peter Vandergeest, "Constructing Thailand," pp. 142–43.

67 Reynolds, "Buddhist Cosmography in Thai Intellectual History," p. 183.

68 Nidhi, *Pen and Sail*, p. 249.

69 Ishii could not have underscored this point more clearly. He notes that Cambodia, Burma, and Laos had all experienced a half century of colonialism, whereas "only Thailand managed to preserve its political independence; only the Thai king's authority as 'defender of religion' remained intact; and only Thai Buddhism has come to the present without severance from its traditions." Whatever this particular type of Buddhism was, the now truly absolute Thai king could, "in a little less than two decades . . . establish a system of government that extended to every corner of the land," and enforce it. Ishii, *Sangha, State, and Society*, pp. 67–68.

70 Ishii cites village research done in the Northeast of Thailand that shows this essentially class aspect of merit: "the villagers accumulate 'merit' in order to be reborn with an outstanding ability and resources that will provide a higher position [in the next life]" Ishii, *Sangha, State, and Society*, p. 15.

71 P.A. Payutto, *Bhikkhu, Good, Evil and Beyond: Kamma in the Buddha's Teachings* (Bhikkhu Puriso, trans.) (Bangkok: Buddhadhasa Foundation, 1993), pp. 6–7, 10, 60; also see pp. 20–24, 46–49, 61–62, 74, and 76.

72 In his scathing critique of Thai Buddhism, McCargo has noted that "most Thai Buddhist monks" have eschewed a universalistic position in terms of Buddhism and have instead chosen "to espouse a particularistic worldview, placing Thailand at its centre." Modern Thai Buddhism is dedicated to "the preservation of orthodoxy and the maintenance of the established order." "Far from being a religion particularly compatible with democratic ideas," writes McCargo,

> Buddhism in the Thai context has become an authoritarian religion, intolerant of dissent and unwilling to accept critical voices. Indeed, the sangha hierarchy are complicit in creating a climate of fear that curtails serious intellectual debate about religious issues; they work closely with the state security apparatus . . . Thai Buddhism, in other words, offers misleading messages and images to the wider world. Religious tolerance is a virtue little practised (or even understood) in Thailand; while prominent Buddhists may generally adopt a tolerant view of other religions, they typically adopt a narrow, even bigoted, view of Buddhism itself. Thai Buddhism is in fact intensely hierarchical.
>
> (Duncan McCargo, "Buddhism, Democracy, and Identity in Thailand," *Democratization* 11(4) (Aug. 2004): 156, 166)

73 Gray, "Thailand: The Soteriological State," pp. 253–56.

74 David K. Wyatt, *Thailand: a short history* (New Haven, CT: Yale University Press, 1982), pp. 208–12.

75 Buddhism's progressiveness, and its status as a civic religion, has been challenged by Duncan McCargo recently. See Duncan McCargo, "The Politics of Buddhist Identity in Thailand's Deep South: The Demise of Civil Religion?" *Journal of Southeast Asian Studies* 40(1) (2009): 11–13.

76 Gray, "Thailand: The Soteriological State," pp. 244–45, 275–78.

77 For instance, Westerners interpreted Mongkut's travels among his people as a sign of egalitarianism. For the internal audience, though, his travels brought men "flocking" to hear his sermons and produced "a host of miracle stories of the type that are found in the life of the Buddha." Gray, "Thailand: The Soteriological State," pp. 256, 260–61.

78 See Thiphakonwong (Chaophraya), *The Dynastic Chronicles, Bangkok Era, the Fourth Reign, Volume Two: Text* (trans. and ed. Thadeus and Chadin Flood) (Tokyo: Centre for East Asian Cultural Studies, 1978), pp. 532–39; Patrick Jory, "The King and Us: Representations of Monarchy in Thailand and the Case of *Anna and the King*," *International Journal of Cultural Studies* 4(2) (2001): 206. Thongchai makes the interesting point that King Mongkut is also considered the "Father of Thai Astrology." Thongchai Winichakul, *Siam Mapped*, p. 47.

79 The noteworthy event, recorded by chronicler of the first and fourth reigns, *Chaophraya* Thiphakonwong, recounts this fusion of Western science and traditional knowledge:

> The King himself had personally calculated the coming of the eclipse . . . in the coming year of the Dragon, the tenth year of the decade, the year 1230 of the *cula* era [when] there would be a solar eclipse whereby the sun would be totally eclipsed . . . The King had calculated this event by using the old astrological texts of Siamese and Mon, as well as many old American and English texts. The King had made use of all these texts, to come to one and the same final conclusion. . . . He calculated on charts that the actual point of the eclipse would be at eleven degrees, forty-one minutes, forty seconds north latitude, at a spot only fifty-one geographical minutes west of Bangkok.
>
> French scientists "also discovered that an eclipse could be witnessed in Siam," and were welcomed by the King to join his party. Thiphakorawong noted, however, that the French scientists (unlike the king) "were unable to locate the precise avenue of the sun's path." Thiphakornwong (Chaophraya), *The Dynastic Chronicles, Bangkok Era, the First Reign, Volume Two: Text*, pp. 533–34.

80 Mongkut's actions upon returning to the capital require some explanation. Although perhaps suffering the onset of the illness that would soon kill him, the anger of the king at those who did not "understand" the true nature of the eclipse is curious. The chronicles record that the king's first piece of business was to question the "famous astrologers" of the court about the eclipse. When they could not answer, Mongkut "was furious" and "ordered that they were all to be sent to scrub stones" in the palace for a day, then imprisoned for eight days, during which "each of them was to wear a chain made of shells from the large fresh water snail on his neck," and food was to be served "to them on coconut shells and on fibrous coverings of the area nut." When the "women palace guards" described the eclipse as covering an inch and a half of the sun, the king said that using such measurement showed "that these ladies did not know the correct way to speak, despite the fact that they were ladies of the palace." They were ordered to scrub stones as well. Then Mongkut "expressed his anger towards the members of the royal family and

the noblemen . . . because they had not sent him any report on the nature of the solar eclipse that was seen in Bangkok." The following day, when the king asked high-ranking monks about the eclipse and each "gave a different answer," "the King [became] very angry." All told, the fanfare at the eclipse, the purification bath, the gifts of gold and money, and the anger (and punishments) suggest that the king viewed the eclipse (and his own accuracy at predicting its place and time) as more than a mere event of scientific note, but rather an auspicious occasion, which the king felt others did not recognize. Thiphakornwong, *The Dynastic Chronicles*, pp. 540–41. Also see, Gray, "Thailand: The Soteriological State," pp. 254–56, 268.

81 Gray, "Thailand: The Soteriological State," p. 68.

82 Many scholars have read the nineteenth-century Buddhist *sangha* "reforms," based on purifying Buddhism of its accumulations of superstition, as a move toward Western science. The case can be made, however, that these changes were rather away from Western science and toward a reformulated re-sacralization of Buddhism for the purposes of absolutism, dressed up in modern philology and textual criticism. Patrick Jory, for instance, does not come to this conclusion, but the gist of his excellent piece on Siamese scholarship's relationship to colonialism can certainly be read in this alternate way. He writes that King Chulalongkorn's opinions on Orientalist Buddhist works were not merely the "scholarly musings of a bookish monarch," but should rather "be understood in the context of the colonial threat to the kingdom's independence and indeed to the monarchy's survival" (p. 3). Jory is surely right to say that the Siamese court's involvement in re-interpreting the meaning of the Jataka stories was "a new conception of authority" (p. 24) which, though, is not to say that it was necessarily more "scientific" or "Western." See Patrick Jory, "Thai and Western Buddhist Scholarship in the Age of Colonialism: King Chulalongkorn Redefines the Jatakas," *The Journal of Asian Studies* 61(3) (Aug. 2002): 1–28.

83 Gray, "Thailand: The Soteriological State," pp. 253–54.

84 Mongkut's actions make better sense according to this interpretation. Tambiah argues that Mongkut's religious "reforms" resulted in an "obsession with orthodoxy in detail of practice" which was "really part and parcel of the preoccupation with the separation of the true canon from its impure adhesions." Another aspect was Mongkut's attempts to purify the Buddhist canon, a task which "inevitably involves a puritanical cleansing of the stables and the removal of impurities." Tambiah depicts many of Mongkut's actions as "contradictory." But the contradiction may be of Tambiah's own making, for in the end, Tambiah placed this drive for purity within a framework of Mongkut's "rationalism." Tambiah is forced to conclude that Mongkut's approach "looks contradictory" when confronted with the fact that "rational" Mongkut "created new forms of worship." Tambiah is forced to dismiss this phenomenon as "common to revitalizing movements" (p. 214). Tambiah, *World Conqueror and World Renouncer*, pp. 211–14. How can the person making Buddhism more rational (in this sense, more open to scrutiny and criticism) create new forms of "irrational" king worship? A "rational" ruler might have instituted reforms which reduced the "magical" aspects of the monarchy as well. The answer to the question actually leads back to Tambiah's initial explanation: the "reforms" were actually part of a Theravada Buddhist purification scheme, one which automatically magnified the importance of the dhammaraja. Also in this respect, see Anderson's comparison of Chakri and Meiji reforms, Benedict R. O'G. Anderson, "Studies of the Thai State: The State of Thai Studies," in Eliezer B. Ayal, ed., *The Study of Thailand* (Athens, OH: Ohio Center for International Studies, Southeast Asia Program, 1978). pp. 200–11.

85 Gray, "Thailand: The Soteriological State," pp. 277–78.

86 Ibid., p. 279.

87 Ibid., pp. 280–83, 288. Also see Ishii's more detailed account of the "reforms," Ishii, *Sangha, State, and Society*, pp. 82–93.

88 Chulalongkorn initiated a purification of "the people," especially those who were not fully "Thai." His half-brother, Prince Damrong Rajanuphap, renamed Lao provinces and even renamed the entire region of the Northeast as "Isan," meaning, "northeast" (of Bangkok). The results of the first census of the country in 1913 were a bit of a conjuring trick: Lao were unable to register their "ethnicity" as Lao, but were forced to declare themselves as "of the Thai race." The population was now cleansed.

89 Some of Damrong's "revisions" expunged ethnic tags from historical chronicles. In fact, Damrong seemed to be involved in all these various reforms—whether administrative, educational, or religious. See Ishii, *Sangha, State, and Society*, p. 68. It is no wonder, then, that Sulak writes, "Damrong's entire career was in fact to create a new awareness of Siamese identity, not only through administrative reform, but also out of this concern for education, research work, and the national museum and library." Of course, Damrong was not creating "Siamese" identity so much as a Thai identity, an effort that links him directly with Phibun Songkram's nationalist programs in the late 1930s and then again with the programs of bodies like the National Identity Board (Chapter 10) in the early 1980s. Sulak Sivaraksa, "The Crisis of Siamese Identity," in Craig J. Reynolds, ed., *National Identity and Its Defenders, Thailand, 1939–1989* (Clayton, Victoria: Centre of Southeast Asian Studies, Monash University, Monash Papers on Southeast Asia No. 25, 1991), pp. 45–52. Terwiel has a more balanced view of the creation of nationalist thinking, noting that it began in the late nineteenth century and continued rather consistently onward. See B.J. Terwiel, "Thai National Identity: Popular Themes of the 1930s," in the same Reynolds volume, pp. 133–56.

90 Gray, "Thailand: The Soteriological State," p. 255.

91 Ibid., pp. 127–28, 253–55.

92 Gray's description of this process as "buddhicization" or my naming it "ritual purification" assumes a strong Buddhist element in its construction. Niels Mulder may get closer to the mark by arguing that "Thai Buddhism" might better be called "Thai religion," giving more weight to the animist belief system that preceded Buddhism in Thailand (Niels Mulder, *Inside Thai Society: Interpretations of Everyday Life*, Amsterdam and Kuala Lumpur: The Pepin Press, 1996). He writes that:

> Over the ages, the tension between the teachings of Theravada Buddhism and Thai animistic practice was resolved by appropriating those elements of the Buddhist doctrine that are compatible with animistic thinking and basic human experience. As a result, the institutional and ritual expression of Thai religion appears to be very Buddhistic, but its characteristic mentality is not so much interested in the Theravada message of moral self-reliance as in auspiciousness, worldly continuity, and the manipulation of *saksit* (supernatural "sacred") power. Consequently, Buddha images became seats of such power and the practice of merit-making [is] turned to ensuring prosperity.
>
> (ibid., p. 19)

Also see Jackson, "The Performative State," p. 222.

93 The connection between the Thai Theravada Buddhist drive for purity and state formation has not been addressed either by Southeast and South Asian Buddhist literature or that on state formation. Indeed, there are few works that even recognize the drive for purity as a focus of research. See, for instance, Trevor Ling, *Buddhism and the Mythology of Evil: A Study of Theravada Buddhism* (Oxford: Oneworld Publications, 1997) or Ishii, *Sangha, State, and Society*. Otherwise,

purity and purification belong more to anthropology and most often pre-state societies, especially in its relationship to taboo, such as Mary Douglas, *Purity and Danger* (London and New York: Routledge, 2005) or Bronislaw Malinowski, *Sex and Repression in Savage Society* (London and New York: Routledge, 2001). One exception is Anne Ruth Hansen's recent work which features purity/purification as one of its central themes. See, *How to Behave: Buddhism and Modernity in Colonial Cambodia, 1860–1930* (Honolulu: University of Hawaii Press, 2007). However, her work does not (and was not intended to) give any sense of how this drive for purification played a role in the events to come in Cambodia, such as the rise of the Khmer Rouge. In Thai studies, there are few works that link present political practices with premodern forms, in the manner of Ben Anderson's "The Idea of Power in Javanese Culture," *Language and Power: Exploring Political Culture in Indonesia* (Jakarta: Equinox Publishing, 2006), pp. 17–77. However, Stanley Tambiah's work on forest monks does make this link between purity, society, and the political order. See, for instance, Stanley Tambiah, *World Conqueror and World Renouncer*, pp. 162–75, when he notes that "act[s] of purification of the sangha were a frequent and endemic feature" (p. 170) of Theravada Buddhist kingdoms. In another work, he argues that traditionally times of political or environmental crises in Theravada Buddhist polities created "all the more a need to recharge and fortify monarchical legitimacy and creative powers by tapping the purity and charisma of the untarnished forest ascetic" (p. 77). When threatened by British colonialism, King Mindon of Burma turned to purification as the answer: He "leaned toward more self-denial, greater self-discipline, and a zeal for purification as a counterbalance to diminished kingship" (p. 64). The biography of Acharn Mun, a Buddhist saint, was still important (in 1984) for Thai society:

> For the Thai people today—as in the past—the *authenticity* of a *bikkhu*'s life as a renouncer . . . who has transcended worldly attachments . . . is a vital exception. And today there is a crisis relating to the established *sangha*, the institutional monastic communities and centers of worship, which have long enjoyed the patronage and protection of the government and whose authenticity is in question at the same time as the *legitimacy* of the political authorities is in question in the face of internal domestic tension and external political threats.

Also, see "The Path of Purification: the ascetic practices," pp. 28–37 and 346–47, in Tambiah, *Buddhist Saints of the Forest*. Jackson also places Thai Theravada Buddhism at the centre of Thai state legitimation, thus explaining the continued importance of the Thai religious-literary work, *Three Worlds*, which "has retained a political potency up to the present day . . . because of its political association with the ascribed historical sources of the political and cultural identity of the modern Thai state," Peter A. Jackson, "Thai-Buddhist Identity," in Craig J. Reynolds, ed., *National Identity and Its Defenders, Thailand, 1939–1989*, p. 193; and Peter A. Jackson, "Re-Interpreting the Traiphum Phra Ruang," pp. 64–100. Duncan McCargo's clear-sighted piece on Buddhism and the state addresses the reticence of particularly non-native Buddhologists to address the darker forces within Theravada Buddhism which have played in state formation. McCargo, "Buddhism, Democracy, and Identity in Thailand," pp. 155–70. Indeed, the record for Theravada Buddhism and modern democracy is not very encouraging: Cambodia saw the rise of the Khmer Rouge; Thailand is comfortably authoritarian; Myanmar is authoritarian, but Buddhist monks from time to time organize against the regime; Sri Lanka's most vociferous proponents for war against the Tamils are the Buddhist political parties. However, Buddhism does not play a prominent role in the literature of state formation and state building.

94 I combine elements of Christine Gray's "ritual purity" and Clifford Geertz's "theatre state" in developing this concept of the ritual purification state. See Clifford Geertz, "Centers, Kings, and Charisma: Reflections on the Symbolics of Power," in Joseph Ben-David and Terry Nicchols Clark, eds., *Culture and Its Creators: Essays in Honor of Edward Shils* (Chicago: The University of Chicago Press, 1977), pp. 150–71. Gray argues that "epistemological domination . . . enables the ruling elite to dominate men's perceptions of the world and the perception of change." One of the forms this may take is "ritual purity" which "is the source of men's ability to pronounce authoritatively on the 'true meaning of things'," and is the "source of elite's ability to prescribe dhamma (appropriate rules of conduct) for citizens," and a "medium through which men gain the right to name and rename social practice," Gray, "Thailand: The Soteriological State," pp. 22–3. Craig Reynolds describes Geertz's conceptualization as

> [a] culture of ceremonialism [which] acted as a magnet at the center, exerting a pull on the subject population, thus explaining political authority and the obedience of subjects without reference to bureaucracy or economics, or to violence or coercion. Geertz's concept of power is not one of command-and-obedience but one that privileges the capacity of pomp, drama, and display to order human affairs. Ceremony puts people in their places, particularly in relation to divinity, and thus orders existence. . . . Ceremony, drama, and display are not illusory; they do not conceal the ordering function of the state. They enact it.

See Reynolds' description of Geertz's concept, and its critics, in Craig J. Reynolds, "Paradigms of the Premodern State," in *Seditious Histories Contesting Thai and Southeast Asian Pasts* (Seattle: University of Washington Press, 2006), p. 44. Geertz said that within the theatre state, "the state drew its force, which was real enough, from it imaginative energies, its semiotic capacity to make inequality enchant," Clifford Geertz, *Negara: The Theater State in Nineteenth-Century Bali* (Princeton, NJ: Princeton University Press, 1980), p. 123. "The enchantment of inequality," writes Reynolds, "helps explain the attraction of monarchical authority and of public office throughout Southeast Asian history" (p. 44).

The ritual purification state certainly draws principally from Geertz's conceptualization, but adds more specificity as to the exact drive and focus of certain performances within the theatre state. But unlike the theatre state, a ritual purification state organizes ritual actions and occasions where there is not a simple divide between actors and spectators. In this case, it is essential that the "spectators" participate in the ritual action for the goal of the action (purification) to obtain. All participants, to one degree or another, derive "merit" from their participation, depending on each participant's proximity to the center. While government officials and persons of status certainly derive the lion's share of merit, especially in certain state-sponsored ceremonies in which ordinary citizens have a more passive role, ordinary people partake in a range of daily rituals which provide a fleeting glimpse of the truth. For instance, millions of children throughout Thailand sing the national and royal anthems at schools every day. Whereas a quite lackadaisical attitude can be taken by teachers in terms of lesson plan creation, pedagogy, punctuality, or even attendance in the classroom, when it comes to performing some school or government ritual or the morning flag raising, everyone is in attendance and suddenly solemn and serious. For a moment (at least theoretically), the hearts of these little subjects are freed from the entanglements of day-today living. This occasion gives their momentarily pure hearts access to a greater dharmic truth (of the nation). In a given week, at least in upcountry schools, so much more time and effort is placed on these ceremonies, the actual purposes of the school becomes clear.

95 Jackson performs a "remodulation of the apparatus" of Geertz's theatre state to fashion what he terms the "performative state." Since the beginning of the twentieth century, the Thai elite have essentially been engaged in a "civilizing" performance for the outside audience and an inner performance that has sought to legitimize the monarchy and existing power structures. The ritual purification state is compatible if not complementary to Jackson's performative state. The former gives more specificity about the method and content of the latter's performance. See Jackson, "The Performative State," pp. 236.

96 See Chapter 12, principle 7. Many have assumed (including this writer) and have written that various military-led Thai governments were *authoritarian* or that certain aspects of Thai political character are so. But all of the various components of a given cultural or political phenomenon somehow never neatly fit into this Western-generated description. If Thailand were authoritarian or at least effectively so then the schools would be strict, but students would learn, people would follow the laws. But Thailand is not authoritarian or totalitarian. Its basic impulse is toward purification. It is the result of this *impulse* that is authoritarian.

97 We learn from Benedict Anderson how the Bangkok royalty became familiar with and adapted colonial-style administration in Siam. Thongchai, Baker and Pasuk, and Peleggi have advanced much more nuanced arguments about the nature of this "influence." See Anderson, "Studies of the Thai State," pp. 209–15 and Chris Baker and Pasuk Phongpaichit, *A History of Thailand* (Cambridge: Cambridge University Press, 2005), pp. 47–80.

98 Loos, *Subject Siam*, pp. 47–48.

99 Ibid., p. 53.

100 While refusing, apparently, to reduce these advisors to being simply "part of the homogenizing machinery of European capitalist modernity," Loos is somewhat hard pressed to clearly spell out the "subtle but profound ways" that these advisors concretely affected a particular issue and, instead, becomes a bit muddled with postmodernist constructs. All the leads she initiates are intriguing, to be sure, but often leading to nothing concrete.

101 Loos, *Subject Siam*, p. 52.

102 Ibid., p. 65.

103 Ibid., p. 62.

104 Even before foreign advisors played a prominent role, in 1869 the young King Chulalongkorn was already aware of possible advantages a modernized criminal code. Kullada Kesboonchoo-Mead writes that "the king showed an early inclination towards absolutism by instigating a survey of how modern states raised and distributed their resources." After reviewing "the constitutions of Britain, British India and the Second Empire of France," the king ordered the "Code Napoleon" to be translated, which

> told the king how an absolutist state with full control over its resources and territory functioned. It went on to explain how power in the absolutist state was concentrated at the centre and how the centre controlled the periphery; the centre was to have full control over the collection and distribution of resources.
>
> (Kullada Kesboonchoo-Mead, *The Rise and Decline of Thai Absolutism* (London: RoutledgeCurzon, 2004, pp. 51–52)

105 Quoted in Loos, *Subject Siam*, pp. 62, 67.
106 Ibid., p. 67.
107 Loos tantalizes us with her observation that there may be some significance to the fact that the lead in drafting the codes was often given to the Siamese elite. Draft provisions were often drawn up first in Thai and then later translated to English. This was a reversal of the process in colonial regimes where laws in the colonial language were the starting point and indigenous terms had to be adapted or coined to fit the "Western" forms. At the least, Loos argues, many Thai laws of the period did reflect Siamese elite priorities. Loos's point sounds reasonable, although she does not show convincingly that the difference was significant. Loos, *Subject Siam*, p. 65.
108 Ibid., p. 51. Khun Luang Phaya Kraisi, who finished at the prince's law school in 1897 and went for further training in England, is the author of one of the first Thai legal textbooks, cited in Chapter 4.
109 Kullada, *Rise and Decline of Thai Absolutism*, pp. 111–17.
110 The following discussion comes from Foucault, "Truth and Juridical Forms," pp. 53–59.
111 Peter A. Jackson, "The Performative State," p. 238.
112 *Oxford English Dictionary Online*, available at: http://www.oed.com.
113 Anderson, *Language and Power*, p. 19.

4 Chronology of Thai defamation-based laws

1 Thailand, Government, "Phraratchakamnot laksana min pramat duai kanphut ru khian thoi kham thet ok khotsanakan rattanakosin sok 118" [Royal Edict on Defamation through False Spoken or Written Words Made Known of the Year 1900], *PKPS*, Vol. 17, r.s 118–19 [1898–1900], pp. 20–21.
2 James C. Scott, *Seeing Like a State* (New Haven, CT: Yale University Press, 1998), p. 2.
3 Loos makes the point that the codification of civil law, given its close relationship to social codes, was tied closely to language and categories of premodern Siam. The codification of the criminal code though was relatively speaking more straight-forward. Tamara Loos, *Subject Siam: Family, Law, and Colonial Modernity in Thailand* (Bangkok: Silkworm Books, 2002), pp. 65–68.
4 Chinese merchants were probably not the target, as they had generally accommodated themselves to the existing elite structure. The target was certainly not the mass of multiethnic peasants of no "public status" recently unbound from (Thai) feudal ties. The peasant uprisings that erupted in the periphery of the kingdom over the following decade were not forms of defamation. They were rebellions that could be handled through conventional forms of armed suppression. Charles F. Keyes, *Thailand: Buddhist Kingdom as Modern Nation-State* (Boulder, CO: Westview Press, 1987), pp. 54–56, and Chatthip Nartsupha, "Ideology of Holy Man Revolts," in Andrew Turton and Shigeharu Tanabe, eds., *History and Peasant Consciousness in South East Asia*. Senri Ethnological Studies No. 13 (Osaka: National Museum of Ethnology, 1984), pp. 111–34.
5 Members of the Siamese royalty had done their best to limit enrolment in the new schools to other members of the royalty; failing that, they tried to keep membership restricted to the upper classes. Only when the growing bureaucracy needed more qualified persons were they forced to admit *khon lew* (literally, "bad people," but understood as "people of base or common stock"). Kullada Kesboonchoo-Mead, *The Rise and Decline of Thai Absolutism* (London and New York: RoutledgeCurzon, 2004), pp. 117–20; Chris Baker and Pasuk Phongpaichit, *A History of Thailand* (Cambridge: Cambridge University Press, 2005), p. 74.

6 Kullada, *The Rise and Decline of Thai Absolutism*, pp. 117–20; Baker and Pasuk, *A History of Thailand*, pp. 74–76.
7 Phrakraisi (Thiam), Khunluang, *Lak kotmai aya* [Principles of Criminal Law] (Krungthep: Rongphim kong lahuthot, r.s. 122 [1904]), pp. 18–20.
8 Ibid., p. 37.
9 Ibid., pp. 35–40.
10 Ammatho Phra-inthapricha, *Kham athibai kotmai laksana aya phak 2 ton* [Explanation of the Criminal Law, Part Two, Section 1] (Krungthep: Rongphim sokkanaphattanakorn, 2469 [1926]), pp. 510–40.
11 Ammatho, *Kham athibai kotmai laksana aya* [Explanation of Criminal Law] (Krungthep: Rongphim Sokkanaphattanakorn, 2470 [1927]), pp. 1345–46. In the Criminal Law Code of 1908, a single word, *min pramat* is used in almost all of these various laws, all with different aspects. Sections 98, 100, and 113, in English, use the word "insult" and "defame," Sections 116 and 339 use the English word, "insult," and Section 282 uses the English word, "defame." From "Note" at the end of Thailand, Supreme Court, Supreme Court Decision 363–64/2473 [1930], *Pramuan khamphiphaksa san dika 2473* [*Collected Decisions of the Supreme Court*, 1930], p. 213. (Hereinafter *Collection of the Decisions of the Supreme Court* will be referred to as "PKSD"). We draw from a Thai legal lexicon, Uthai Suphanit, comp., *Sap kotmai thai nai adit lae patjuban* [Thai Legal Terms in the Past and Present] (Krungthep: Samnakphim prakaiphruk, 2526 [1983]).
12 Ammatho, *Kham athibai kotmai laksana aya* [Explanation of Criminal Law], p. 1410. Jitti writes that since the basis of defamation has always been to "cause the one so defamed to become angry and revengeful," it could be a cause for "the rise of disquietude and disorder in the country." Ironically, the closer to the truth the defamatory statement, the more discord it creates. See Jitti Tingsaphat (1975), *Kham athibai pramuan kotmai aya* [Explanation of the Criminal Law Code], p. 2237.
13 Ammatho, *Kham athibai kotmai laksana aya* [Explanation of Criminal Law], p. 536.
14 The following section shall draw from Thailand, Juridical Council, "Report of the Committee on the Prevention of Communism, Bolshevism and Other Dangerous Propaganda," n.d., in Thailand, Juridical Council, "Rang phraratchabanyat kaekhai pramuan kotmai aya ph.s. 2470" [Draft of the Revision of the Criminal Code Act of 1927], in *Ruang set* [Finished Matters], Vol. 19. The original document is ten pages long but not numbered.
15 Thailand, Juridical Council, "Report," in *Ruang set* [Finished Matters], Vol. 19.
16 Thailand, Juridical Council, "Penal Code Amendment Act B.E. 2470," in *Ruang set* [Finished Matters], Vol. 19.
17 Ibid.
18 If the committee had succeeded in its earlier proposal, the punishment would have been incomparably greater, with the possibility of life imprisonment.
19 Matthew Copeland, Chapter 4, "Political Journalism," in "Contested Nationalism and the 1932 Overthrow of the Absolute Monarchy in Siam," Ph. D. dissertation, Australia National University, 1993.
20 Baker and Pasuk describe the desperation of the absolutist government of the time:

> Resentment spread to senior levels of the bureaucracy. The government reacted by drafing an anti-Bolshevik bill, but then modifying it to combat a wider range of dissident opinions. Serious offences incurred the death penalty. More papers were closed. Some journalists were intimidated with threats or violence. Immigration laws were used to deport many critics.
>
> (Baker and Pasuk, *A History of Thailand*, p. 118)

21 Translating *watwan* as "to be afraid" might be too mild, as McFarland renders its noun form as "apprehensive fear" and the Thai–English online dictionary as "apprehension; panic; scare; terror; dread." Available at: http://www.thai2english.com/search/หวาดหวั่น+, accessed 29 June 2009; George McFarland, *Thai-English Dictionary* (Stanford, CA: Stanford University Press, 1944), p. 925.

22 The law empowered the Ministry of Interior, "for the sake of public peace," to detain or restrict persons who violated Provision 3 to a "defined area" for up to ten years. Persons thus restricted could later appeal to a special committee. If they could prove that they were "not opposed to the governing under a constitutional system" and "will propagate and support, with a pure heart, the constitutional governing system," the committee could recommend to the Cabinet of Ministers that such persons be released.

Unlike most laws which go through a fairly long process of draftings and considerations by the Juridical Council, little documentation on this measure is contained in the bound volumes at the council. Thailand, Government, "Phraratchabanyat jatkan pongkan raksa ratthathammanun ph.s. 2476" [Defense of the Constitution Act of 1933], in *PKPS*, Vol. 46, 2476 [1933], pp. 418–20. The same measure appears in Thailand, Government, *Ratchakitjanubeksa* [Royal Gazette] on 12 Nov. 2476 [1933].

23 This act was repealed in 1938 without much comment. See, Thailand, Government, *Ratchakitjanubeksa* [Royal Gazette], Vol. 55 (22 Aug. 2481 [1938]), p. 288. During its short lifespan, the law was used fairly frequently, especially along with rebellion or sedition charges. In the "Special Court," it was part of the charge in Thai Noi, "Kabot nai sip pi 2478" [Sergeant's Revolt of 1935], in *25 Khadi kabot* [25 Cases of Rebellion] (Krungthep: Rongphim ratthana kanphim, 2513 [1970]), pp. 164–68, and Thailand, Supreme Court, Supreme Court Decisions 118/2479 [1936], *PKSD 2479*, pp. 149–54 and 456/2478 [1935] 19 th. s. 763, *PKSD 2478*, pp. 763–73.

24 Thailand, Government, "Phraratchabanyat kaekhai phoemtoem kotmai laksana aya ph.s. 2478 (chabap thi 3)" [Amendment to the Criminal Law Code of 1935], in *PKPS*, Vol. 49, 2479 [1936] (20 Aug. 2478 [1935]), pp. 46–76. For some reason it does not seem to appear in the Royal Gazette until later. See Thailand, Government, *Ratchakitjanubeksa* [Royal Gazette], Vol. 61, Part 6 (19 Apr. 2479 [1936]).

25 Thailand, Supreme Court, Supreme Court Decision 612/2475 [1932], *PKSD 2475*, pp. 564–68.

26 Thailand, Supreme Court, Supreme Court Decision 631/2491 [1948], *PKSD 2491*, pp. 759–65.

27 There may have been some *lèse-majesté* cases settled in the Court of First Instance prior to 1947, but as Ministry of Justice and police records from the period are incomplete, it is difficult to say with certainty. Judging from the 1939 case, any such cases may have been treated very leniently by the courts.

28 Thailand, Supreme Court, Supreme Court Decision 1081/2482 [1939], *PKSD 2482*, pp. 1650–53.

29 Thailand, Juridical Council, "Report of the Meeting of the Sub-committee on the Consideration and Revision of the Criminal Law Code," Meeting No. 298, 9 Apr. 1942. p. 5. René Guyon was employed in the early part of the twentieth century as a legal advisor to the government, a position he held until the late 1950s.

30 One of the last successful defenses in a *lèse-majesté* case was the 1995 acquittal of Sulak Sivaraksa. For more on the case, see David Streckfuss, ed., *Modern Thai Monarchy and Cultural Politics: The Acquittal of Sulak Sivaraksa on the Charge of Lèse-majesté in Siam 1995 and Its Consequences* (Bangkok: Santi Pracha Dhamma Institute, 1996).

31 Krom Tamruat. *Rai-ngan prajam pi, 2490–2500* [Annual Report of the Police Department, 1947–57].

32 The revised criminal code was enacted in 1956 and the code came into effect on 1 January 1957. When legal scholars refer to the revised code, they refer to the act; here we shall refer to it as the 1957 revised code, when it went into effect.

33 One member pointed out that the crime of simply throwing a stone at the king should not be punished with execution because the original law protecting the king was written in the time of the absolute monarchy. Claiming that they were archaic and not an "objective observation," the committee decided to tone down the Thai version of the provisions concerning the king which had always begun with "Whosoever dares to . . . "—a remnant of the *Three Seals Law*—and eliminate the word, "dare" [*bang at*]. JC, "Report of Meeting No. 7," 3 June 1939, Vol. 1, p. 13.

34 Nidhi Eoseewong suggested the committee revising the criminal code after the 1932 revolution intended that *lèse-majesté* protect the institution of the monarchy rather than the person of the king, thus limiting its incursion into the public sphere. At the same time Nidhi notes that the sacred sphere has seemingly expanded. I would argue instead that the effect of the revision committee's work provided the basis for the expansion of the public sphere. See Nidhi Eoseewong, on the panel entitled, "Kotmai min phraboromdetchanuphap kap khwam mankhong khong rat" [The Lese Majesty Law and Security of the State], Khrongkan prakatsaniyabat kotmail mahachon, khana nitisat, mahawithayalai thammasat, et al., "Lak miti kotmai min phraboromratchanuphap" [Symposium on Legal Dimensions of the Lese Majesty Law], 21–22 Mar. 2009, Thammasat University.

35 The other laws within this set are: Section 118 on insulting flags or symbols of the state, Sections 133 and 134 on insulting foreign royalty or heads of state, or foreign ambassadors, Section 135 on insulting flags or symbols of other countries, Section 136 on contempt of government officials, Section 196 on contempt of courts, Section 206 on insulting religion, Section 326 on slander, Section 328 on libel, and Section 393 on insult to one's face. Jitti Tingsaphat (1975), *Kham athibai pramuan kotmai aya* [Explanation of the Criminal Law Code], p. 2163. A rather refreshing way of presenting criminal law, Khanit's approach breaks from the rather staid model. While still drawing from the more expansive, analytical work of Jitti, Khanit does make some interesting points about the nature of defaming the royalty and the problem that truth plays in such a situation. See p. 630–31. Also, see his treatment of crimes against the state and national security laws as a whole: Khanit na Nakhorn, *Kotmai aya phak khwamphit*, pp. 625–87.

36 Somchai Preechasilpakul, "Lak niti ratthaprahan" [Juridical Principles of Coups], in *Ratthaprahan 19 kanyayon* [The Coup of 19 September] (Krungthep: Fah Diew Kan, 2550 [2007]), pp. 190–202. Somchai recounts how some of the leading lights of Thai law, such as Yut Saeng-uthai, Vissanu Khrua-ngam, and Borwornsak Uwanno, have justified giving coup decrees higher legal weight than any other type of law. Vissanu wrote that "Within the hierarchy of law, an analysis of the contents of coup decrees" in terms of their "legal status and ranking," shows they have preeminent legal weight: "Coup Decree No. 2 (20 Oct. 1977) is of the same rank as the constitution, because it abolished the Constitution of Thailand of 1976"; "Coup Decree No. 10 (7 Nov. 1977) is of equal standing of the law codes because it revises and amends" such codes. See Vissanu Khua-ngam, *Kotmai ratthathammanun, phim khrang thi 3* [Constitutional Law, 3rd edition] (Krungtheip: Samnakphim Nitiban, 2530[1987]), p. 755, and Somkhit Loetphaiboon, "Kanprapprung prakat khong khana patiwat" [Addressing Coup Decrees," *Raphisan* vol. 1, (Apr.–June 2536 [1993], p. 45.

37 Thailand, Government, "Proclamation of the Revolutionary Group No. 17," *International Translation Law Directory* (n.p., 1958), pp. 612–13.

38 Thailand, Government, "Kham sang khong khana patirup kanpokkrong phaendin chabap thi 42 long want thi 21 tulakhom ph.s. 2519" [Order of the National

Administrative Reform Council No. 42, issued 21 Oct. 1976], in *Phraratchabanyat kanphim ph.s. 2484* [The Press Act of 1941] (Krungthep: Sut phaisan, 2531 [1988]), pp. 48–50.

39 Thailand, Government, "Khamsang khana patirup pokkhrong phaendin chabap thi 41 long want thi 21 tulakhom ph.s. 2519" [Order of the National Administrative Council No. 41, issued 21 Oct. 1976], Thailand, Government, *Ratchakitjanubeksa* [Royal Gazette] Special Issue, Vol. 93, Part 134, p. 46.

40 The remarkable 1400 percent increase in protection of the courts requires comment. It is probably no coincidence that it was during this period that the court had abandoned any pretense of judicial integrity and became "the last [meaningless] resort" of the people. Thus, the courts were given king-like protection. The same might be said for Buddhism. When monks advocated the killing of communists, Buddhism received king-like protection.

41 The statistics from the [Thai] Police Department and the Prosecution Department do not perfectly correlate. The police statistics list cases by incidents, arrests, cases sent to the court (1949–77), and cases received by the court (1949–77). The Attorney General's Annual Report begins in 1984. These statistics more accurately indicate how many cases were accepted by the prosecution department.

42 Thitinan Pongsudhirak, "Thailand's Media: Whose Watchdog?" in Kevin Hewison, ed., *Political Change in Thailand: Democracy and Participation* (London: Routledge, 1997), p. 222.

43 The surging number of defamation arrests in 1976–869 cases—may have played a role in its inclusion in the military decree increasing the punishment for slander and libel.

44 Duncan McCargo, *Politics and the Press in Thailand* (London and New York: Routledge, 2002), p. 12.

45 Interview, Lt. Col. Samphan Satthaphorn, Deputy-Superintendent of Sub-Division 3 of the Special Branch of the Police Department, Bangkok, 21 Aug. 1991. The interview was in English and I have smoothed out some of the phrasings for readability.

46 Article 19's report on defamation in Thailand makes the point that the maximum punishment for defamation is equal to that "causing physical injury," while the maximum fine for the latter is only 4000 baht. No maximum or minimum is stipulated for civil damages in defamation; civil suits for defamation are usually adjudicated after criminal proceedings have ended. The maximum amount awarded to date was in the 2000 case of politician Narong Wongwan v. Naew Na newspaper. The plaintiff demanded 100 million, the court of first instance awarded ten million, and the Supreme Court reduced the amount to five million baht. See, Sinfah Tunsarawuth, "Impact of Defamation Law on Freedom of Expression in Thailand" (a joint report carried out by Article 19 and the National Press Council of Thailand), Mar. 2009 [draft copy], pp. 1, 6, 9–10.

47 Thailand, Government, Parliament, "Criminal Code Amendment, (No. 11), B.E. 2535," *Ratchakitjanubeksa* [Royal Gazette] Vol. 109, Part 13, (25 Feb. 2535 [1992]), pp. 1–2. A detailed explanation for the amendment can be found in Thailand, Government, Parliament, "Ekasan prakop kan phijarana rang phraratchabanyat kae khai phoem doem pramuan kotmai aya, (chabap thi . . .) ph.s. . . . ," Sapha nitibanyat haeng chat, a.ph.[92] / 2531 [1988]. The date might suggest that discussions about the amendment had begun well before the measure became law. An academic apologist supporting the new law wrote that without more severe penalties, the law "would not cause fear to violate the law when compared with the benefits of presenting such news." He averred that, even with heavier penalties, the government still needed to "improve the process of the application of the law"—arrest, investigation, and court hearing—so that the violator is "truly punished." The core objective of the law—"to threaten and block those who would violate the

law"—would have a two-fold effect. First, "the people in general will have their rights of reputation protected." Second, having such a serious punishment for violators permitted "the ability to control the behavior" of those in the media and make them "more responsible in presenting the news." Rather than restricting press freedom, the law will help the Thai people because they will have more "trustworthy" news and "develop the quality of journalists" so that the news they make public is "correct." There was no reason to fear, he concluded, that the law "will become a tool of the state to restrict freedom of the media" as long as "the authorities apply the law honestly and those in the media present news honestly according to the truth." See Narong Jaihan, "Thot lae kha sia hai nai karani min pramat" [Punishment and Damages in the Case of Defamation], *Warasan Nitisat* 2:3 (Kanyayon 2534 [Sept. 1991]), pp. 450–52.

48 Sinfah, "Impact of Defamation Law on Freedom of Expression in Thailand," p. 1.

49 1994 Human Rights Report: THAILAND, available at: http://stockholm.usembassy.gov/human/human95/Thailand.htm, accessed 12 Nov. 2008.

50 It should be noted that the statistics from the Office of the Attorney General group together "Offence[s] of Disclosure of Private Secrets and Defamation," Sections 323–33 of the 1957 Thai criminal code. However, arrest or prosecution disclosing private secrets seems rarely used. So we can assume that the vast majority of cases within this category are slander and libel. Records are unavailable for 1983, and the 1996 and 1997 figures from the Attorney General's *Annual Report* are combined into a single volume, although the number of cases suggests a single year's total. Averages counted the 1996–97 as a single year, and do not include 1983.

51 See *Nation*, 18 July 2000.

52 Sinfah Tunsarawuth, "Impact of Defamation Law on Freedom of Expression in Thailand" (a joint report carried out by Article 19 and the National Press Council of Thailand), Mar. 2009 [draft copy], p. 5. It might be helpful to give an idea about the frequency of slander and libel as criminal offenses in other countries. In Norway, in 1997, for instance, a rather surprising 1052 cases were reported. Even more remarkable is the fact that after investigations, cases dropped by the prosecution, and so on, only eight cases went to trial: two resulted in fine, four in "conditional imprisonment," and two "unconditional imprisonment." Norway, Government, Statistics Norway, available at: http://www.ssb.no/straffkjede_en/tab-2002-06-18-03-en.html, accessed 12 Dec. 2008). In Spain, in 2005, 113 crimes "against honor" went to trial. Nine were dropped, 103 resulted in a fine or less than two months in jail, and three resulted in imprisonment from 6 months to four years. Spain, Government, Instituto Nacional Estadística, available at: http://www.ine.es/jaxi/tabla.do, accessed 15 Aug. 2009.

53 Thailand. Attorney General's Office (Samnakngan Aiyakan Songsut), *Rai-ngan prajam pi* (Annual Report of the Attorney General's Office) (Samnakngan aiyakan phiset fai sarasonthet, samnakngan wichakan) (each year individually from 1984 to 2005; year 1996 and 1997 are combined into a single volume). Until 2005, the Attorney General's Office provided the best statistics on criminal cases in Thailand. However, this section of their annual report was dropped after 2005.

54 Thailand, Samnakngan San Yuttitham [Office of the Judiciary], *Rai-ngan sathiti khadi tua ratcha-anajak prajam pi (ph.s. 2549, 2550, 2551, 2552)* [English title provided is *Annual Judicial Statistics, Thailand 2006, 2007, 2008*, and 2009, respectively].

55 Pravit Rojanaphruk, "Kotmai min phraboromdechanuphap lae kan sensor tua eng" [The *lèse-majesté* Law and Self-censorship], *Fah Diew Kan* (Apr.–June 2006), pp. 158–70.

5 Normalizing "abnormal times" and the "endless state of exception"

1 Giorgio Agamben, *Homo Sacer: Sovereign Power and Bare Life* (Stanford, CA: Stanford University Press, 1998), pp. 171–72.

2 The 1907 "Martial Law" was apparently the first of its kind for Thailand, passed at the end of the reign of King Chulalongkorn (King Rama V, r. 1868–1910). It could be proclaimed "whenever there are events which necessitate" it in order to "maintain peace and order without danger." The only special powers martial law gave military authorities were the right to search any premises at any time, to evict anyone from a prescribed area, to require people in such an area to turn over their arms and ammunition, and to transfer jurisdiction of certain crimes to military courts. Thailand, Government, "Kot aiyakansuk rattanakosin sok 126" [Martial Law of 1907], *Pramuan kotmai prajam sok 126* [Annual Collected Laws], pp. 314–16.

3 "Ph.r.b. thammanun san thahan ph.s. 2498" [Act on Organization of Military Courts of 1955], available at: http://www.kodmhai.com/m4/m4–7/H7/H-7.html, accessed 10 June 2009.

4 Only at the beginning of abnormal times in the 1960s were any studies done on the topic—two brief articles, both of the same title. To my knowledge, no legal or academic work on "abnormal times" as such exists. See Nom Sisanphang, "San thahan nai wela mai pokkati" [Military Courts in Abnormal Times], *Dunlapha* 5(12) (Dec. 2501): 807–9; Surat Rattana-udom, "San thahan nai wela mai pokkati" [Military Courts in Abnormal Times], *Dunlapha* 6(3) (Mar. 2502): 192–95.

5 Interview, Lt. Col. Samphan Satthaphorn, Bangkok, 21 Aug. 1991.

6 The question has been examined by a number of Thai legal scholars, but has not been examined or critiqued in a public forum. See Ukrit Mongkhonnawin [Dr.], "Khwam sa-ngop riap-roi lae sinlatham an di khong prachachon" [Peace and Order and the Public Morality], *Bot Bandit* 32(1) (Jan. 2518): 11–32.

7 See, for instance, Thai-language drafts in "Penal Code Amendment Act B.E. 2470," in Thailand, Juridical Council, *Ruang set* [Finished Matters], Vol. 19.

8 Here we forgo what could be a lengthy discussion of the definition of "public morality". For a consideration, see "Public Order and Morality," in Chapter 7 of Streckfuss, "The Poetics of Subversion: Civil Liberty and Lesè-Majesté in the Modern Thai State," Ph.D. dissertation, University of Wisconsin, 1998,

9 Thailand, Juridical Council, "Letter," to the Secretary-General of the Juridical Council from the Secretary-General of the Council of Ministers, Re: Freedom of the Press according to the Constitution, 5 Apr. 2493 [1950], "Tentative Press Amendment Act in 2493–2496 (1950–53)," in Thailand, Juridical Council, "Tentative Amendment Acts to the Press Act (1947–1952)," in *Ruang set* [Finished Matters], Vol. 331.

10 See Chapter 10 for a fuller discussion of this point.

11 Thailand, Juridical Council, "Opinion of the Legislative Adviser re: the freedom of Press according to the Constitution," 22 Apr. 2493 [1950], "Tentative Press Amendment Act in 2493–2496 (1950–53)," in "Tentative Amendment," in *Ruang set* [Finished Matters], Vol. 331.

12 During World War II, Thailand "took back" parts of British Malaya, Burma, Cambodia, and Laos. See Scott Barmé, *Luang Wichit Wathakan and the Creation of a Thai Identity* (Singapore: Institute of Southeast Asian Studies, 1993), pp. 163–71.

13 Thailand, Supreme Court, Supreme Court Decision 209/2484 [1941] 25 th. s. 291, *PKSD 2484*, pp. 291–98.

14 See Chapters 7 and 9 for further discussion of this case.

15 In late February 1957, Prime Minister Phibun Songkhram held elections and the

media reported that the elections had been "dirty." The American Ambassador to Thailand, Max Waldo Bishop, apparently told Phibun that he should use the word "disorderly" rather than "dirty" in terms of the election. It was also reported that Bishop said that ballot boxes had been snatched in American elections in Chicago, just as they had in Bangkok. In response, Kukrit published an editorial about in his newspaper, apparently calling Bishop a "gangster" or "low life." As a result, Kukrit was charged with defamation of a representative of a country with which Thailand enjoyed good relations. After a few weeks in the courts, it was dismissed. However, during the trial, Kukrit published more in his newspaper. The contents of those articles brought charges of rebellion. This second case was eventually also dismissed. Newspapers faithfully reproduced the court transcripts, giving a rare look into what actually was said during the hearings. For an excellent account of the people and events in 1957, see Sutthachai, *Phaen ching chat thai*, pp. 362–99.

16 "People Listen to Examining of Witness in Kukrit Rebellion Case, Laugh at Prosecution Witness to Merriment Until Court Warns, Witness Educated, Having Read Does Not Feel Rebellious," *Sayam Rat*, 28 May 2500 [1957].

17 Jitti Tingsaphat (1967), *Kham athibai pramuan kotmai aya* [Explanation of the Criminal Law Code], pp. 902–10.

18 Amnesties in Thailand have been little studied. One of the few pieces is Pattana Chaiyaset (Roi Tho), "Kotmai nirathosakam kap phu tham kanpatiwat ru ratthaprahan" [Amnesty Laws and Those Engaging in Revolt or Coups], *Warasan Aiyakan* 4(45) (Sept. 2524 [1981]): 9–13.

19 Readers may consult Appendix V for the list of "permanent" and interim Thai constitutions to make sense of the following cases.

20 The "Chief of Staff" coup, which never got beyond the planning stages, involved "a number of army general staff officers." David A. Wilson, *Politics in Thailand* (Ithaca, NY: Cornell University Press, 1962), p. 130.

21 Thailand, Supreme Court, Supreme Court Decision 1153–54/2495 [1952] d. 832, *PKSD 2495*, pp. 832–42. Many of the same cases examined in this chapter have also been examined in a similar article by Somchai, "Juridical Principles of Coups."

22 On this point, see Michael K. Connors, "Article of Faith: The Failure of Royal Liberalism in Thailand," *Journal of Contemporary Asia* 38(1) (Feb. 2008): 151.

23 Thailand, Supreme Court, Supreme Court Decision 45/2496 [1953], *PKSD 2496*, pp. 55–67. The court consulted international law on what constituted a legal government. A note following the opinion by Yut Saeng-uthai, an expert in German law and later head of the Juridical Council, said that the 1947 coup was similar to the 1918 "revolution" in Germany. The German Supreme Court, ruling on the legality of its new government, said that the laws it issued were: "complete and legally binding because, even though the government which issued the law arose through a revolution which used force, it has been still able to substantiate its own position of power. Therefore, constitutionally, there must be an acceptance of the power of such a government." In another ruling, the German Supreme Court emphasized that:

> It was not possible for the power of the new government which has arisen through revolution to not be accepted and approved constitutionally nor was it possible for such power to be denied because the legality of its occurrence is not at all of any importance to the nature of the power of the government. The state cannot operate without the power of state once the former power has been completely eliminated. At that moment, the new power is able to function successfully and is able to replace the old power.

If a coup group is able to secure power, it then has "the power to make laws," "proceed fully" in all respects, and

> eliminate groups of the people who are opposed to it through the application of means of the power of that government which is successful and absolute. Just this is enough for the power of the government to be true and to be sanctioned legally.

These various opinions of the German Supreme Court, the writer says:

> show that a revolution or *coup d'état* is at first illegal but whenever the perpetrators have successfully and fully carried out the revolution or *coup d'état*, they are then able to legitimize their power as true, through the suppression and pacification of the former government or group of individuals who are opposed to it, and thus are able to have state authority and [exercise] the highest power in the state. Therefore, they are in a position that enables them to grant a new constitution, repeal the original laws, and enact new laws according to their wishes.

Yut cites the following sections from the Decisions of the German Supreme Court: vol. 99, p. 187; Vol. 100, p. 27; and from the "Criminal Section" of the Decisions of the German Supreme Court, Vol. 53, p. 68; Vol. 59, p. 157, quoted in Thailand, Supreme Court, Supreme Court Decision 45/2496 [1953], *PKSD 2496*, pp. 55–67.

Yut's analysis appears close to the thinking of Carl Schmitt. Did Schmitt's writing influence Yut's thinking? Did Yut perhaps even study under Schmitt himself? Was Yut a conduit of fascist legal thought into Thailand? These suppositions are possible, given that Yut finished his doctorate in law in 1931 and was at Berlin University in 1932, just as Schmitt's ideas on sovereignty were coming to the fore. Yut Saeng-uthai, *Kotmai aya phak 2–3* [Criminal Law, Books/Sections I-II] (Twekiat Menakanist, ed.) (Krungthep: Somnakphim Mahawitthayalai Thammasat, 2540 [1997]), unnumbered preface section.

24 "Amnesty Act B.E. 2494 [1951], Granted to Persons in the Course of Reviving the Constitution of B.E. 2475 [1932]," issued on 31 Dec. 1951. To get a sense how a self-administered post-coup scenario played out recently, see David Murray, *Angels and Demons* (Bangkok: Orchid Press, 2000), pp. 175–80, 196. For a military legal take on the issue, see Phattana Chaiyaset, "The Amnesty Law," pp. 9–13.

25 Judges turning to dictionaries is not uncommon for defamation-based adjudications, See State of Illinois, Appellate Court, "Docket No. 79712–Agenda 12–March 1996"; KIMBERLY BRYSON, Appellant, v. NEWS AMERICA PUBLICATIONS, INC., et al., Appellees; Opinion filed October 24, 1996.

26 Thailand, Supreme Court, Supreme Court Decision 1513–15/2497 [1954] d. 1319 m. 113, *PKSD 2497*, pp. 1319–50.

27 For greater elaboration on the idea of the ritual purity state, see Chapters 3 and 13.

28 Sarit Thanarat said that the apparent coup was not one at all. Rather it was a revolution. See Thak Chaloemtiarana, *Thailand: The Politics of Despotic Paternalism* (Chiang Mai: Silkworm Books, 2007), p. 107.

29 One wonders if these old constitutions of Thailand are actually "torn up," as the Thai phrase, *thuk chik* (ฤูกวซ่ก) would infer.

30 Hewison is not sure if he is the one who came up with the term, but said in personal communication that the term drew "on the old joke that if you wanted to get the Thai constitution in a library you had to go to the serials section." A constitution at first apparently inspired great hope. A pamphlet from the mid-1930s advised all Thai to "Respect and venerate the constitution which is the thoughtful and pure soul of nation." As each spurned constitution was thrown out

for a new one, by 1958 one wonders about the pamphlet's writer's concern for "the soul of nation." Had the soul of nation been so abused that it warranted love no longer? See B.J. Terwiel, "Thai National Identity: Popular Themes of the 1930s," in Craig J. Reynolds, ed., *National Identity and Its Defenders, Thailand, 1939–1989* (Clayton, Victoria: Centre of Southeast Asian Studies, Monash University, Monash Papers on Southeast Asia No. 25, 1991), p. 148.

31 Thailand, Government, "Phraratchabanyat jat tang san phiset ph.s. 2477" [Special Court Establishment Act of 1933], in *PKPS* Vol. 46, pp. 410–11; Thailand, Juridical Council, "Rang phraratchabanyat jat tang san phiset ph.s. 2476 kaekhai phoemtoem ph.s. 2478" [Draft of the Special Court Establishment Act of 1933, as revised in 1935], in *Ruang set* [Finished Matters], Vol. 158; and, Thailand, Government, "Phraratcha kamnot jat tang san phiset phua phitjarana phiphaksa khadi khwam phit thana khabot phai nok phraratcha-anajak ph.s. 2483" [Royal Decree Establishing a Special Court to Judge Cases of Violating the Law of External Rebellion of the Kingdom of 1940], in *PKPS* Vol. 54, pp. 142–44. The most famous case coming from the Special Court was in 1939, of those proroyalists who had been arrested for rebellion. Apparently, though, it was the last use of the Special Court. See Thailand, Special Court (San Phiset) (issued by Krom Khotsanakan, *Khamphiphaksa san phiset ph.s. 2482 ruang kabot* [Judgment of the Special Court of 1939 on the Case of Rebellion] (Krungthep: Krom khotsanakan, 2482 [1939]).

32 Thailand, Juridical Council, "Banthuk lakkan lae hetphon, prakob rang phraratchabanyat kakkhum phu pen phai kae chat nai phawa khapkhan ph.s. 24." [Notes on Principle and Reason, with draft of the Act for the Confinement of Persons Dangerous to the Nation in Times of Emergency of 19. .], 20 Dec. 2487 [1944], in "Draft of Act," in *Ruang set* [Finished Matters], Vol. 393.

33 Thailand, Juridical Council, "Banthuk ruang kieowkap rongrian opprom jitjai" [Notes Concerning the Psychological Training School], confidential [*lap*], from "Adul, Supreme Commander," 23 Oct. 2487, in "Draft of Act for the Confinement of Persons Dangerous to Nation in Times of Emergency, ph.s. 2488 [1945]," in *Ruang set* [Finished Matters], Vol. 393.

34 Thailand, Juridical Council, "Rai-ngan prachum kammakan rang kotmai (kammakan kong thi 1), khrang thi 367/2487" [Juridical Council Committee, Report of Meeting on Drafting of Law, Law Drafting Committee No. 1], Meeting No. 367/2487 [1944], 18 Dec. 2487 [1944]; Thailand, Juridical Council, "Rai-ngan prachum kammakaan raang kotmai (kammakan kong thi 1), khrang thi 368/2487" [Juridical Council Committee, Report of Meeting on Drafting of Law, Law Drafting Committee No. 1], Meeting No. 368/2487 [1944], 19 Dec. 2487 [1944]; "Draft of Act," in *Ruang set* [Finished Matters], Vol. 393.

35 Thailand, Juridical Council, Letter from the Secretary of the Cabinet of Minister to the Secretary of the Juridical Council, Secret [*lap chapho*], Subject: Detaining persons who are a danger to the nation in times of emergency, 15 December 1943; "Rang phraratchakritsadika khuapkhum phu ja pen phai kae chat nai phawa khapkhan, ph.s. 24. .," from the original draft of "Draft Edict for the Detention of persons who will be a danger to the nation in time of emergency," 30 Oct. 2487 [1944], in 1, "Draft of Act," in *Ruang set* [Finished Matters], Vol. 393; and, Thailand, Government, "Phraratchabanyat kak khum phu pen phai kae chat nai phawa khapkhan ph.s. 2488" [Act for the Confinement of Persons Dangerous to the Nation in Times of Emergency of 1944], 12 Jan. 2488 [1945], in *PKPS* Vol. 58, pp. 74–78.

36 Thailand, Government, "Phraratchabanyat kot ayakansuk (chabap thi 3) ph.s. 2487" [Martial Law Act (No. 3) of 1944], in *PKPS* Vol. 57, pp. 860–65. See also the measures from the following year as the government strained to place more and more legal space under the jurisdiction of the military courts, Thailand,

Juridical Council, "Confidential-Urgent Letter," from Duan Bunnag, Secretary-General of the Juridical Council, to Secretary-General of the Council of Ministers, 23 Jan. 2487 [1944], and "Rang, Ruang hai san thahan mi amnat phitjarana phiphaksa khadi aya bang praphet tam bot banyat haeng kot ayakansuk" [Draft, Giving the Military Court Power to Consider Certain Types of Criminal Cases as According to the Legal Provisions of Martial Law], in "Hai san phitjarana phiphaksa khadi tam phraratchabanyat kot aiyakansuk" [Courts Trying Cases According to the Martial Law Act], in *Ruang set* [Finished Matters], Vol. 393/8.

37 Thailand, Juridical Council, "Matra 7, Phraratchakamnot kaekhai phoemtoem phraratchabanyat kot ayakansuk ph.s. 2457 ph.s. 2488" [Section 7, Royal Edict amending the 1914 Martial Law Act of 1945], in "Tua baep bang matra kieowkap kot ayakansuk" [Some Model Provisions Concerning Martial Law], n.d., in "Amnat san rawang chai kot aiyakansuk" [Power of the Courts When Martial Law Is In Effect], in *Ruang set* [Finished Matter], Vol. 439/3.

38 "Emergency Administration Act B.E. 2495" [1952], *International Translation Law Directory* (n.p., 1958), pp. 81–83.

39 The phrase is mentioned in a handful of Thai Supreme Court cases, but never defined. See Thailand, Supreme Court, Supreme Court Decisions 1559/2506 [1963]; Decision 1155/2506 [1963]; Decision 321/2507 [1964]; Decision 1978/2522 [1979]; Decision 1959/2524 [1981].

40 None of the keen observers of Thailand and constitutionalism have attempted to place Thailand's serial constitutionalism, or the ritual that attends it, within any sort of conceptual framework. Kobkua Suwannathat-Pian, perhaps the premier historian on Thai constitutions, writes that the change of constitutions reflects the changing elite power group configuration and, so,

> It was not surprising, therefore, that every time power changed hands from one faction to another, there was a real need to abrogate the extant Constitution and to write a new one, to find a new method of manipulating the electoral institution and electorate, and to keep an elected Government pliable to the will of the new faction in power.
>
> (Kobkua Suwannathat-Pian, *Kings, Country and Constitutions*. p. 7)

41 Sutthachai's detailed historical account from pre-1947 until 1957 describes the effects spawned by the coup in 1947, which worsened through the decade. He notes, for instance, that the coup effectively ended "constitutionalism," as the swapping of governments through the ten-year period made "the constitution" essentially meaningless. However, he does not address the overall effects of the coup on law itself. See Sutthachai, *Phaen ching chat thai*. pp. 100–103.

42 Handley claims that the courts in the early 1970s were "still a stronghold of integrity and independence." Actually, it seems that the courts had capitulated much earlier. See Paul Handley, *The King Never Smiles* (New Haven, CT: Yale University Press, 2006), p. 206.

43 Thailand, Government, "Proclamation of the Revolutionary Group No. 12," issued 22 Oct. 1958, in *International Translation Law Directory* (n.p., 1958), p. 609.

44 Thak records that immediately after the coup in 1958, "mass arrests" of suspected Communist sympathizers and newspaper editors were carried out. Some of these might have been arrested by virtue of Coup Decree No. 21 that empowered the government to round up all those generally defined as "a menace to society and the common people" and "eliminate" them, meaning they were put through a "social purification process" that attempted to redeem them from their evil ways. Of the 7539 arrested from 1958 and 1963, 2743 were held for a three-day detention, while another 4738 were held indefinitely in "reform institutions."Thak

Chaloemtiarana, *Thailand: The Politics of Despotic Paternalism* (Chiang Mai: Silkworm Books, 2007), pp. 96, 121–22.

45 Thai Noi, "Kabot lat yao pi 2501" [Lat Yao Revolt of 1958], pp. 363–67. The Supreme Court made a similar ruling in 1962 when it said that Proclamation of the Revolutionary Group No. 21, which gave power to the authorities to "investigate and arrest individuals who conduct themselves as hooligans and to hold them while investigations are going on for not more than 30 days," had the power of a law even though it had neither "been passed through the Parliament or through a Legislative Assembly" nor signed by the king. Once power was seized by the Revolutionary Group, anything its head ordered "must be held as law, even without the Royal Signature or approval from the Parliament." See, Thailand, Supreme Court, Supreme Court Decision 1662/2505 [1962], *PKSD 2505*, pp. 1405–8.

46 Thailand, Government, *Ratchakitjanubeksa, (chabap phiset)*. lem 75, Section 85, 27 Oct. 2501 [1958]; [Coup Decree No. 16], pp. 5–6, and [Coup Decree No. 17], pp. 7–10. Some of the provisions involving defamation were not included in this special set of provisions, such as insult of religion, contempt of court, and personal defamation laws, suggesting that they were perhaps not seen as important. However, the opposite might be true, as an entirely separate provision was given to all the defamation-based offenses, either indirectly or indirectly through Coup Decree No. 17.

47 Martial law and military courts had such an active role during this period that many legal scholarly articles discussed their dynamics. In English, there are short and technical discussions about the military court system in Thailand by, Samran Kantaprapha, "Military Judicial System of Thailand," *Military Law Review* 14 (Oct. 1961): 171–81, and Sming Tailangka, "Military Judicial System of Thailand," *Military Law Review* 64 (Spring 1974): 151–58. In Thai, see Atthakaiwanlathi, Luang, and Suk Frunawin, "Rabop aiyakan lae san thahan" [System of Prosecution and the Military Court], n.d.; Prathin Phattanatham, *Kantamnoen khadi aya nai santhahan* [Prosecution of Criminal Cases in the Military Court] (Krungthep: Baphitthakanphim, 2525 [1982]); Samran Kanphrapha, "Arai nai san dika thahan" [What's in the High Military Court?] *Dulapha* 25(6) (Nov.–Dec. 2521 [1978]): 20–37; Sanchai Satjawanit, "San thahan tam prakat khong khana patiwat" [The Military Court According to the Decree of the Revolutionary Council] *Botbandit* 28(4) (2514 [1971]): 876–79; Ura Wangomklang, "San thahan nai wela mai pokkati" [The Military Court in Abnormal Times], mimeographed, Rongrian nai roi Phrajulajomklao, n.d.; Fuang Ratchataphan, "Khadi thi san phonlaruan tong yok fong tae san thahan long thot dai" [Cases that Civilian Courts must dismiss but which the Military Court can rule on] *Bot Bandit* 21(2) (Apr. 2506 [1963]): 265–68; Uan Monthianthong, phontho, "San thahan sung phrae saphap jak san phonlaruan" [The Military Court when Changed into a Civilian Court], *Bot Bandit* 23(4) (Oct. 2508 [1965]): 821–43; Chuchoet Raktabut, "Amnat phitjarana phiphaksa khong san thahan" [The Power to Consider Cases of the Military Court] *Dunlapha* 7(8) (Aug. 2503 [1960]): 958–61. The military courts were called into action by virtue of a declaration of martial law around which another body of expert knowledge grew. See, for instance, Jarunee Thanarataphorn, "Kot aiyakan suk lae khet amnat san yuthitham mua mi kanprakat kot aiyakan suk" [Martial Law and Jurisdiction of the [regular] Courts When Martial Law has been Declared], *Dunlapha* 28(6) (Nov.–Dec. 2524 [1981]): 81–110.

48 Statistics are drawn from Thailand, Ministry of Justice, *Rai-ngan krasuang yuttitham prajam pi ph.s. 2504–2509* [Annual Report of the Ministry of Justice, 1961–66] (Ronghim sahakorn khai song haeng pratehet thai, k.t.m., n.d.); Thailand, Ministry of Justice, *Rai-ngan krasuang yuttitham prajam pi ph.s. 2510–2516* [Annual Report of the Ministry of Justice, 1967–73] (n.p., n.d.); Thailand,

Ministry of Justice, *Rai-ngan krasuang yuttitham prajam pi ph.s. 2517–2519* [Annual Report of the Ministry of Justice, 1974–76] (Rongphim ruangtham, k.t.m. 2523 [1980]), Thailand, Ministry of Justice, *Rai-ngan krasuang yuttitham prajam pi ph.s. 2520* [Annual Report of the Ministry of Justice, 1977] (n.p, n.d.); Thailand, Ministry of Justice, *Rai-ngan krasuang yuttitham prajam pi ph.s. 2521* [Annual Report of the Ministry of Justice, 1978] (n.p, n.d.).

49 Though, by 1965, the overwhelming number of murder cases were tried in regular criminal courts. Thailand, Ministry of Justice, *Rai-ngan krasuang yuttitham prajam pi ph.s. 2504–2509* [Annual Report of the Ministry of Justice, 1961–66].

50 From 1961 to 1966, no misdemeanors went to military court. In 1972, 14 misdemeanor arrests were tried in military court out of a total of 396 cases; in 1973, 6 out of 324

51 The percentage of criminal cases tried by military court was 11 percent in 1964, 8 percent in 1965, and 9 percent in 1966 and 1967, respectively. In 1967, there were 125,370 cases tried, 9 percent in military courts; 9 percent of 1968's 121,641 total cases were tried in military court, 8 percent of 1969's 123,667 cases, 7.5 percent of 1970's cases, 6 percent of 1971's 133,831 cases, 18 percent of 1972's 149,388 cases, 22 percent of 1973's 171,460 cases.

52 These numbers are not small. The number of criminal cases tried in military court in 1974, 1975, and 1976, were 16,666, 935, and 4,026, respectively.

53 Between 1919 and 1958, 17 seditious rebellion cases were tried by the Supreme Court, and only 1 from 1959 to 1989. Of the hundreds of *lèse-majesté* cases originating after 1958, only three made it to the Supreme Court.

54 Thailand, Ministry of Justice, *Rai-ngan krasuang yuttitham prajam pi ph.s. 2522* [Annual Report of the Ministry of Justice, 1979].

55 For the effect of coup decrees on the normal regime of law, see Somchai Preechasilpakul, "Juridical Principles of Coups," pp. 190–202.

56 "Uthai Phimjaichon 10 pi Anan kap Bunkoet khon lae 7 pi," [Uthai Phimjaichon 10 Years, Anan and Bunkoet Each Get 7 Years], Chao Thai, 24 June 2515 [1972], in Thailand, National Archives, "p. 2/2515/3, Karani Nai Uthai Phimjaichon Nai Anan Phakpraphai lae Nai Bunkoet Hirankham adit s.s. yun fong ho na khana patiwat" [The Case of Mr. Uthai Phimjaichon, Mr. Anan Phakpraphai, and Mr. Bunkoet Hirankham, former MPs, taking the Revolutionary Council to Court].

57 It is ironic that the Revolutionary Council at once made the claim that it had not carried out a revolution, that coups are not a form of rebellion, and then cite a provision in the very constitution that it had abolished.

58 The order quotes from a criminal court decision that suggests the interesting possibility of the population at large charging a military government which came to power through a coup. If the three former MPs were able to charge the Revolutionary Council, then:

> There may be other individuals who, as damaged parties, could charge the Revolutionary Council for the same thing, or even charge it for other civil or criminal damages. An example of this would be if the citizens of each province [charging the council] with their representative serving as plaintiff, or citizens in the provinces charging that the revolution of the Revolutionary Council caused them damage, and it could become all the people [making such a charge] on their own, without going through their representatives. It could be called, "nation-wide litigation," if it were possible. Instead of bringing peace and order to the country, this [possibility] would cause a state of utter confusion and unrest, and all sorts of difficulties would follow.

59 It may seem a bit troubling that the leader of the Democrat Party, Seni Pramoj,

visited his fellow party members in prison and remarked that being so jailed was not a cause for sorrow as it was "a common matter." He compared the three to a troublemaker who "has to accept being hit sometimes." See "In Prison for Political Crimes No Loss, Goes to Visit and Console in Jail," *Chao Thai*, 29 June 2515 [1972].

60 Worse is the detrimental effect a decision like this had on Thai society. As George Steiner argued, the Nazi manipulation of the German language and the bizarre logic and incongruities caused by rationalized brutalizations led to a degradation of the German language so great that Steiner wondered if any sense can be made in German again. With the contortions caused to "what is generally true" in these justifications and just straight denials of truth, one must wonder if Thai is beyond the point of repair. See George Steiner, "The Hollow Miracle," in *George Steiner: A Reader* (New York: Oxford University Press, 1984), pp. 207–22.

61 Somchai Preechasilpakul, "Juridical Principles of Coups," pp. 190–202.

62 Some minor, indirect rulings have made the point that coup decrees, at least in some areas, cannot be contrary to provisions of the constitution. See Thailand, Supreme Court, Supreme Court Decision 913/2536 [1993], available at: http://www.thaijustice.com/webboard.asp?sub = 0&id = 758216, as discussed in Somchai, "Juridical Principles of Coups," pp. 194–95.

63 Surapol Nitikraiphot, *Thai Post* [Thai-language newspaper], 15 Octo. 2549 [2006], as quoted in Somchai, "Juridical Principles of Coups," p. 197. Somchai makes the point that having rationalized the effective legitimacy of the coup, many of these leading lights of the Thai legal world then find accommodation with and serve the new coup-imposed system.

64 Somchai, "Juridical Principles of Coups," p. 198, and Borwornsak Uwanno, *Kotmai mahachon 2: kanbaeng yaek kotmai mahachon – ekachon lae phatthanakan kotmai mahachon nai prathet thai* [Public Law 2: Dividing Public/Private Law and Development of Public Law in Thailand] (Krungthep: Nittitham, 2537 [1994]), p. 253.

65 Daniel S. Lev, "Introduction," in *Legal Evolution and Political Authority in Indonesia: Selected Essays 3* (The Hague: Kluwer Law International, 2000), as quoted in Munger, "Globalization, Investing in Law, and the Careers of Lawyers for Social Causes," p. 753. Emphasis added.

66 Munger is right to rap Reynolds for too easily accepting the "fundamental values underlying the political discourse of constitutional monarchy in Thailand" and other scholars who use generalizations like "Buddhist value." See Munger, "Globalization, Investing in Law, and the Careers of Lawyers for Social Causes," pp. 766–67; and Frank E. Reynolds, "Dhamma in Dispute: The Interactions of Religion and Law in Thailand," *Law and Society Review* 28 (1994): 433–55.

67 Agamben, *Homo Sacer*. pp. 170–72.

68 Ibid., pp. 170, 172.

6 Intent and import

1 According to McEwen and Lewis:

> The state of mind . . . of a person who publishes a libel . . . is immaterial in determining *liability* except when the occasion is privileged, in which case the plaintiff has to prove actual malice in the popular sense of the term. The law looks at the tendency and consequence of the publication rather than the motive or intention of the publisher.
>
> (Robert McEwen and Philip Lewis, *Gatley on Libel and Slander*, 17th edn. London: Sweet & Maxwell Limited, 1974, pp. 5–6; original emphasis)

2 Christine Gray, "Thailand: The Soteriological State in the 1970s," Ph.D. dissertation, The University of Chicago, 1986, pp. 55, 257–58.
3 Thailand, Government, "Phraratchakamnot laksana min pramat sok 118 [Royal Edict on Defamation of the Year 1900], pp. 20–21.
4 Phrakraisi (Thiam), Khunluang, *Lak kotmai aya*, [Principles of Criminal Law], pp. 35–40.
5 See section on "Ill Intentions," in Ammatho Phra-inthapricha, *Kham athibai kotmai laksana aya* [Explanation of Criminal Law], pp. 1386–92, 1398.
6 Ibid., pp. 1352–53.
7 In Thai law, the word *sujarit* is used, meaning "faithful; trustful; trustworthy; virtuous; conducting oneself well; good; upright (in dealing with others)," [George McFarland, *Thai-English Dictionary*, p. 871]. In legal parlance, *sujarit* is used to approximate the English, "in good faith," which is its usual translation. In recent Thai legal parlance, though, this term is sometimes interchanged with the word *borisut* meaning, "innocent" or "pure."
8 Ammatho Phra-inthapricha, *Kham athibai kotmai aya* [Explanation of Criminal Law], p. 1398.
9 Ibid., pp. 1382–84, 1401–2, 1411–14.
10 Ibid., p. 531.
11 Ibid., pp. 541–45.
12 Sections 283 and 284, ibid., pp. 1397, 1409.
13 Although the records of 1908 to 1917 Supreme Court cases are not easily retrievable, few if any cases of the exemption were applied in cases prior to 1932 coming before the court. For instance, Ammatho's 1927 volume on Thai case law cites mostly hypothetical, rather than real, court cases when discussing personal defamation and its exemptions.
14 Thailand, Supreme Court, Supreme Court Decision 445/2462 [1919] 3 th. s. 272, *PKSD 2462*, pp. 272–77.
15 I have reworded some of these items for clarity.
16 For more on this remarkable figure, see Peter Koret, "The Gestation Period for Miracles: The True Story of a Siamese Man's Attempts to Create World Peace and Million-Ton Bread Ovens," unpublished manuscript.
17 Thailand, Supreme Court, Supreme Court Decision 586/2462 [1919], *PKSD 2462*, pp. 368–72.
18 Jitti Tingsaphat (1975), *Kham athibai pramuan kotmai aya* [Explanation of the Criminal Law Code], Sections 1155 and 1156, pp. 2197–2200.
19 Dunlayasatpathiwet, Luang, (1993), *Pramuan kotmai aya*, p. 25. It is possible to go deeper into the subterranean mind and its relationship to the world. For instance, note the intriguing wording of Section 62:

> Whenever any fact, if really existing, will cause the doing of any act not to be an offence, or the doer not to be punished [*sic*], or to receive less punishment and even though such fact does not really exist, but the doer understands mistakenly that it really exists, the doer shall not be guilty.
>
> (Dunlayasatpathiwet, p. 26)

Beyond this, the question of "actual malice" becomes very interesting when applied to defamation cases. Actual malice obtains when the "doer 'knows' the facts comprising the external components of the crime" and "desires" the action to "create effect." As the "facts" really exists, the doer shall not be guilty" (Dunlayasatpathiwet, p. 26). But since the "facts" of defamation cases are often based on discursive rather than "actual," material, ascertainable factors—both the "facts" and "effects"—are placed in a special relationship, perhaps unlike any other law or crime. See Kiatkhajorn, *Kham athibai kotmai aya phak 1* [Explanation of Criminal Law, Part 1], pp. 148–57.

20 Jitti Tingsaphat (1975), *Kham athibai pramuan kotmai aya* [Explanation of the Criminal Law Code], pp. 2197–2200.

21 Ibid., pp. 2197–2200.

22 Ibid., pp. 2216–17. This exclusion apparently does not apply to expressing opinions about the courts. In a 1932 case, a defendant, upon hearing the decision handed down by the court in a first case, uttered, "The court is wrong and unjust. The court deliberated the case and then concluded it in a peremptory way to send me off to jail." With these words, the court felt that it "is clearly seen that the defendant intended to slander the court." The exclusion in the defamation law which allows the expression of an opinion in good faith for the benefit of the public does not apply to the law concerning contempt of the court. See, Thailand, Supreme Court, Supreme Court Decision 573/2475 [1932], *PKSD 2475*, pp. 539–41.

23 Thailand, Supreme Court, Supreme Court Decisions 1059/2481 [1938], *PKSD 2481*, pp. 1288–94, and 607/2480 [1937], *PKSD 2480*, pp. 691–95, respectively; Ammatho, *Kham athibai kotmai laksana aya* [Explanation of Criminal Law], p. 1410.

24 The following cases, Thailand, Supreme Court, Supreme Court Decisions 317/2475 [1932], 399/2486 [1943], and 645/2503 [1960], respectively, are summarized in Jitti Tingsaphat (1975), *Kham athibai pramuan kotmai aya* [Explanation of the Criminal Law Code], p. 2229–30.

25 Thailand, Supreme Court, Supreme Court Decision 97/2484 [1941] th. s. 119, *PKSD 2484*, pp. 119–26; and, Thailand, Supreme Court, Supreme Court Decision 209/2484 [1941], *PKSD 2484*, pp. 291–98.

26 Thailand, Supreme Court, Supreme Court Decision 97/2484 [1941] th. s. 119, *PKSD 2484*, p. 126, and Supreme Court Decision 209/2484 [1941], *PKSD 2484*, pp. 291–98.

27 Thailand, Supreme Court, Supreme Court Decision 209/2484 [1941] 25 th. s. 291, *PKSD 2484*, pp. 291–98.

28 This point was also made in the 1957 case of seditious rebellion of Kukrit Pramoj described earlier in this chapter. His defense lawyer asked permission from the court to show one of the prosecution witnesses the offending articles. He then asked, "You've read some parts of the articles in this newspaper, or together all, and reading some parts might bring one to understand the meaning in a different way, right?" The witness answered that it "depends on the nature" of what is read. For example, in "reading a book, one must look toward the intention of the writer . . . one must read it at once and in its entirety."

29 Thai Noi, "Kabot sawannakhot pi 2489" [Death of King Revolt of 1946], pp. 203–10.

30 The case was eventually dismissed by the courts. Thai Noi, "Kabot hai pak pi 2499" [Hyde Park Revolt of 1956], in *25 Khadi kabot*, pp. 359–62.

31 Jitti cites the Supreme Court Decision [3397–98/2516 [1973] where the court made this distinction. Jitti Tingsaphat (1975), *Kham athibai pramuan kotmai aya* [Explanation of the Criminal Code], Sections 1141 and 1142, pp. 2170–72.

32 Christine E. Gray, "Hegemonic Images: Language and Silence in the Royal Thai Polity," *Man* 26 (March 1991): 49.

33 Unnamed source.

34 Gray, "Hegemonic Images," p. 48.

35 Duncan McCargo, *Tearing Apart the Land: Islam and Legitimacy in Southern Thailand* (Singapore: Nus Press, 2009), p. 16. Also see David Murray, *Angels and Demons* (Bangkok: Orchid Press, 2000).

36 Patrick Jory argues that the Thai Theravada Buddhist cosmological order goes into decline and belief in the king as a bodhisatta "was replaced by national-dynastic historical narratives." "[T]he concept of *barami* survives in Thai political discourse only as a relic of the former moral-political system of belief." I argue that this system is, in essence, still intact, though perhaps not in name. See Patrick Jory, "The *Vessantara Jataka, Barami*, and the *Bodhisatta*-Kings: The Origins and Spread of a Premodern Thai Concept of Power," *Crossroads: An Interdisciplinary Journal of Southeast Asian Studies* 16(1) (2002): 179–80.

37 This schema is derived primarily on the basis of merit, based on a variety of sources, including Phra Thammpidok, *Photjananukrom phutthasat chabap pramuan sap* [Buddhist Dictionary]; Gray, "Thailand: The Soteriological State"; Stanley J. Tambiah, *The Buddhist Saints of the Forest and the Cult of Amulets* (Cambridge: Cambridge University Press, 1984), pp. 294–96, and Tambiah, *World Conqueror and World Renouncer* (Cambridge, MA: Cambridge University Press, 1976), pp. 15–17; McCargo, *Tearing Apart the Land*, p. 15; and Lucien Hanks, "Merit and Power in the Thai Social Order," *American Anthropologist* 64 (1962): 1247–61. Neil Englehart says the king "plays an important role as a kind of capstone to the social and political order. He serves as a reference point, defining the pinnacle of karma in human society and assuming a position of supremacy in social as well as political terms. All lines of patronage and all social hierarchies ultimately terminate with the king" (pp. 13, 23). The system is partially created according to words of the Buddha from the Pali text, T.W. Rhys Davids, trans., *The Questions of King Milinda*, vol. 1 (Delhi: Motital Banarsidass), 1975 [1890], p. 101, as quoted in Englehart, *Culture and Power in Traditional Siamese* (Ithaca, NY: Southeast Asia Program Publications, 2001), p. 21: "Beings have each their own Karma, are inheritors of Karma, belong to the tribe of their Karma. Have each their Karma as their protecting overlord. It is Karma that divides them up into low and high and like divisions."

Meritorious Persons or Persons of Virtue, *phu mi bunbarami* (ผู้มีบุญบารมี) represent the highest echelon. The very top rung of this level are the *phu mi bunyathikan* (ผู้มีบุญญาธิการ) and the second rung is for those who depend on the *phu mi bunyathikan*–Those in the Shade of Charisma, or *phuyu tai rom barami* (ผู้อยู่ใต้ร่มพระบารมี). The second level belong to the Merit Seekers, or *phu sawaeng ha bunbarami* (ผู้แสวงหาบุญบารมี). The third level is for the majority, the Lowly Meritorious, or *phu mi bunbarami noi* (ผู้มีบุญบารมีน้อย), or *buthuchon* (ปุถุชน, *var*. of *prachachon* (ประชาชน). The bottom level, at least within the human realm, is inhabited by The Demons, or *tua man* (ตัวมาร, พวกมาร). See also, Phra Thammpidok, "Puthuchon" [as distinct from *arayachon*], and "Man" [demons who obstruct the fulfillment of good], in "*Photjananukrom phutthasat chabap pramuan sap* [Buddhist Dictionary], pp. 175, 231–32.

38 As part of the category of *phu mi bunbarami*, Patrick Jory describes *phu mi bun* as "leader heroes whose authority derives from their practices of self-perfection" or "'accumulation of *barami*'." See Patrick Jory, "The *Vessantara Jataka*, *Barami*, and the *Bodhisatta*-Kings," p. 161. This group is perfectly described by McCargo as making up "network monarchy" whose members carry out the king's working through proxy:

> The monarch intervened actively in political developments, largely by working through proxies such as privy councillors and trusted military figures; and the lead proxy, former army commander and prime minister Prem Tinsulanond, helped determine the nature of coalition governments, and monitored the process of military and other promotions. At heart,

network governance of this kind relied on placing the right people (mainly, the right men) in the right jobs.

(Duncan McCargo, "Network Monarchy and Legitimacy Crises," *The Pacific Review* 18(4) (Dec. 2005), p. 501)

39 Quoted in Paul Handley, *The King Never Smiles* (New Haven, CT: Yale University Press, 2006), p. 274. This sentiment is nicely expressed by the Ministry of Foreign Affairs when responding to an article, "A right royal mess," *The Economist*, 4 Dec. 2008. The ministry's spokesperson goes to great length explaining exactly how the king is "above politics" and has maintained "steadfast political neutrality." As such, any criticism to the contrary is unfair and justifies the use of the *lèse-majesté* law. See "*Economist* articles contrary to the facts." Fortunately for the police, the Thai distributor of *The Economist*, Asia Books, voluntarily agreed to not distribute this issue (*Bangkok Post*, 9 and 13 Dec. 2008). If the police had resorted to banning the publication, they would have had to cite the offending passages, a practice that has sometimes resulted in charges of *lèse-majesté* levelled at the police department itself. See David Streckfuss, "Kings in the Age of Nations—The Paradox of *Lèse-Majesté* as Political Crime in Thailand," *Comparative Studies in Society and History* 37(3) (July 1995): 461–62.

40 When Privy Councillors Prem Tinsulanond and Surayud Chulamont were accused of backing the 2006 coup, Surayud chose not to press charges of defamation, as it might have seemed unfitting for a privy councillor to do so. He also may have chosen not to also because, unlike *lèse-majesté* cases, the court might have been forced to consider the facts behind the charge of involvement in the coup. *Bangkok Post*, 29 Mar. 2009.

41 One of the formal tasks of the Privy Council is to review the kingdom's *lèse-majesté* cases. One unnamed source insisted to me that it was the prerogative of the Privy Council—and not the king's—that certain cases of *lèse-majesté* were either dropped or maintained. See, for instance, the case of Bundith Aniya, who was found guilty of *lèse-majesté* and sentenced to 32 months in jail. Given his age and no criminal record, the court placed Bundith on probation. However, the Political Prisoners in Thailand website said, "The secretary of the Privy Council, the plaintiff in the case, is said to have appealed the case to a higher court, not wanting Bundith to have probation. This appeal was apparently being heard in the closed courtroom." Available at: http://thaipoliticalprisoners.wordpress.com/pendingcases/bundith-arniya, accessed 2 June 2009.

42 A second tier of *the Meritorious* consists of those who depend on graces and favor from those in the highest rung: Those in the Shade of Charisma, or *phuyu tai rom barami* (ผู้อยู่ใต้ร่มบารมี) is more general. If the prefix, *phra* were added to charisma, or *barami* (พระบารมี), this phrasing would mean specifically those dependent on the king, best translated as: Those in the Shade of His Royal Charisma. The group might include, in no particular order, leading businesspersons, members of the upper echelons of society, most "politicians" appointed in the aftermath of coups, and former members of *The Merit Seekers* who have successfully shown their loyalty to the sacred centre and gained admittance. Some businesspersons gained royal support in the 1950s, while others were granted royal titles, beginning in the 1960s, for their support for royal-recognized ceremonies. Groups in this category are meritorious, though they can become subject to greediness. They are moderately frequent accusers of defamation-based crime, especially by former Merit Seekers as they gain recognition and occasional admittance to this level. A more visible member of this group is Meechai Ruchupan, who regularly makes his expertise available after *coups* to help organize and lead efforts of the new military-installed government, or Prasong Soonsiri, former head

of the National Security Council and more recently was head of the constitution drafting committee that ended its work in 2007.

43 The term *sawaeng bun* is adapted from a framework suggested in Gray, "Thailand: The Soteriological State," pp. 18, 49, 388–422. Gray speaks of the "three-way race for virtue" between the military, monks, and king in the 1950s. Later, she describes the "search for dhamma" epitomized by the religious pilgrimage. I have combined these two Buddhist impulses and placed them within a merit framework.

44 For many of these may not publicly accuse others of *lèse-majesté*; indeed, they may be critical of the role of the monarchy in politics. But they are public members of groups or movements that actively manipulate the law. Members of the Democrat Party, though not often formally charging others with *lèse-majesté*, are supportive of others, such as the leaders of the People's Alliance for Democracy (PAD) in 2008, doing so. Abhisit Vejjajiva and other members of the Democrat Party have a long history of using defamation-based laws, such as Abhisit's leadership in condemning the Longman Dictionary in 1993 (Chapter 11). In 2002, he deplored the Thaksin government for not acting more decisively with the *Far East Economic Review*, saying that if Thaksin "wished to safeguard the image of the institution," a letter of protest to the publication "should have at least referred to 'lese majeste' but this was nowhere to be found," *Bangkok Post*, 3 Mar. 2002 (see also *Nation*, 21 Mar. 1998). More recently, Democrats urged the police to pursue the *lèse-majesté* case against Jakrapob Penkair more vigorously, and proposed a much stricter law (*Nation*, 19 Nov. 2008). (Abhisithas rarely, if ever, sued opponents for libel.) Others in this group, who might have been anti- or at least non-monarchists, now justify "using" the monarchy as part of their struggle against Thaksin because the "monarchy had used us" for all these years (unnamed source).

45 I am thinking here of Nidhi Eoseewong, *Pen and Sail* (Chiang Mai: Silkworm Books, 2006), p. 253, but the impulse toward purity is examined as well in Gray, "Thailand: The Soteriological State," and Tambiah, *The Buddhist Saints of the Forest and the Cult of Amulets* and *World Conqueror and World Renouncer*.

46 The *Lowly Meritorious*, or *buthuchon*, is surprisingly exact. McFarland defines the term as "a man of the lower class or of low character; a common or ordinary man; one who is yet unconverted, as opposed to one who has entered the Eight-Fold Path; a worldly, natural or unsanctified man; a sinner." McFarland, *Thai-English Dictionary*, p. 484. This definition is mirrored in the official Thai dictionary, "those who have not become *phra-arayabukkhon*," in Ratchabandittayasathan, *Photjananukrom chabap ratchabandittayasathan ph.s. 2542* (Krungthep: Nanmi Book Publishing, 2546), p. 702.

47 Attachak argues that the idea of "The Third Hand" was consolidated under dictatorship. This "Third-Hand" culture, he writes, "is so deeply rooted in the Thai culture of thinking that it emphasises smooth relationships between the state and the people . . . a conflict between the state and the people is not supposed to take place." If there is such conflict, "then it has to have been incited by a 'third' party'," Attachak, *Mu thi sam [The Third Hand]*, p. 45.

48 The term, "demons" is a familiar Thai epitaph. Drawing from the People's Alliance for Democracy (PAD), a number of other terms are commonly used in attacks: traitors (*khon kai chart*), betrayers of the land (*thorayot to phean din*), evil persons (*khon chua rai*), creatures from hell (*sat narok*). This language is easy to find in the PAD lexicon. See, for instance, two pieces from 22 Nov. 2008: available at: http://www.manager.co.th/Politics/ViewNews.aspx?NewsID = 9510000138489, accessed 15 Mar. 2009, and http://www.manager.co.th/Politics/ViewNews.aspx?NewsID = 9510000138509, accessed 15 Mar. 2009. Similar language is also used in premodern texts. Jory records that "King Rama I's accession to the throne in 1782 was likened to the *boddhisatta*'s defeat of Mara (the embodiment of evil and

delusion"), Jory, "The *Vessantara Jataka, Barami,* and the *Bodhisatta*-Kings," p. 169.

49 Members of a certain subcategory of this group are perhaps well-intentioned but seriously misinformed persons whose words and actions may have an evil impact or aid evildoers. This might include media outlets, such as *Fah Diew Kan*, and intellectuals who presume to compare Thailand's political culture or "impose" Western concepts. These misinformed persons include Thai intellectuals living outside Thailand, such as Thongchai Winichakul, whose contributions are often summarily dismissed because he "does not understand what is really going on," or foreign scholars of Thailand who simply cannot know what is happening.

7 The insulted and defamed I: from the individual to the nation

1 "Mr. Hui and the Thai Nation," *Sayam Ratsadorn*, 29 Jan. 2465 [1922] and, "The Matter of Mr. Hui, Defamation of the Thai Nation," *Sayam Rat*, 21 Feb. 2465 [1922]. I must thank Matthew Copeland for supplying me with a copy of this wonderful case.

2 Article 19 is a non-governmental organization who "fights for all hostages of censorship, defends dissenting voices that have been muzzled, and campaigns against laws and practices that silence," source: http://www.article19.org/.

3 Sinfah Tunsarawuth, "Impact of Defamation Law on Freedom of Expression in Thailand" (a joint report carried out by Article 19 and the National Press Council of Thailand), Mar. 2009 [draft copy], pp. 1, 3.

4 Thai newspapers often refer to individuals by nicknames or initials – Dr S., Mr. K., Mrs. B. – making suits for libel more difficult.

5 Ammattho Phra-inthapricha, *Kham athibai kotmai aya* [Explanation of Criminal Law], pp. 1367–70; Jitti Tingsaphat (1975), *Kham athibai pramuan kotmai aya* [Explanation of the Criminal Law Code], p. 2167. For brief details of Supreme Court Decisions 1636/2522 [1979] and 448/2498 [1955], see Jitti Tingsaphat (1975), *Kham athibai pramuan kotmai* [Explanation of the Criminal Law Code], p. 2184, and, Jitti Tingsaphat (1989), *Kham athibai pramuan kotmai aya* [Explanation of the Criminal Law Code], p. 2372.

6 Thailand, Supreme Court, Supreme Court Decision 56/2490 [1947], *PKSD 2490*, pp. 40–44.

7 Thailand, Supreme Court, Supreme Court Decision 1325/2498 [1955], *PKSD 2498*, pp. 1269–75.

8 This list, sketched out in 1927, is doubtlessly not limited to these. Litigants through the years have included the Democrat Party (a political party), the metropolitan police, and various government divisions, such as the Aircraft Department in 1931. Ammatho Phra-inthapricha, *Kham athibai kotmai aya* [Explanation of Criminal Law], pp. 1367–71; Jitti Tingsaphat (1975), *Kham athibai pramuan kotmai* [Explanation of the Criminal Law Code], pp. 2164–65.

9 Interview, Police Superintendent Suthiphong, Press Officer of Bangkok of the Police Special Force, Bangkok, 23 Feb. 2001.

10 Interview, Suchart Srisuwan, editor of *Matichon*, Bangkok, 23 Feb. 2001.

11 "New Process Could Close News Outlets" and "Pradit Offers Courts' Help to Police Media," *Nation*, 8 and 9 June 1997, respectively. The New York-based Committee to Protect Journalists (CPJ) immediately expressed dismay with the project, calling the media-monitoring scheme "disturbing." *Nation*, 16 June 1997.

12 *Nation*, 11 Sept. 2006.

13 *Nation*, 14 May 2004. From my earlier survey, probably five cases of defamation were filed against opposition MPs in connection with the censure debate.

14 For this survey, I used most if not all defamation cases published in *The Nation* and *Bangkok Post* during the period. "Cases" here includes both threats to sue (a

relatively small number) and actual cases where someone was sued. The totals, however, are far, far off from the actual number of cases during the period under study. This can be partially justified by noting that defamation cases are already biased toward the wealthy—those who have both the means to pursue such cases and feel that their good name is worth protecting. Naturally, the most "important cases" end up in the newspaper, as they deal with famous or public persons.

15 This is consistent with the findings of Article 19's report. See Sinfah, "Impact of Defamation Law on Freedom of Expression in Thailand," p. 5.

16 The results of this survey are not very different from those discovered by the Press Council of Thailand in a survey covering the period Feb. 1999 to May 2003, that showed that 41 percent of the defamation cases brought against the media in Thailand were made by politicians, 19 percent by civil servants, and 13 percent by police, 13 percent by "media professionals," 6 percent by "businessmen," 4 percent by the "general public," and 7 percent by "celebrities." See Article 19 and Forum-Asia, *Freedom of Expression and the Media in Thailand* (Dec. 2005), p. 79, available at: [http://www.article19.org/pdfs/publications/thailand-baseline-study.pdf, accessed 19 May 2009.

17 Duncan McCargo, *Politics and the Press in Thailand* (London and New York: Routledge, 2002), particularly Chapters 1, 2, and 5. Also, interview, Kavi Chongkittavorn, managing editor of *The Nation* and president of the Thai Journalist Association and chairperson of the Southeast Asian Press Association, Bangkok, 15 Feb. 2001. Kavi has more recently recognized defamation as a key problem; see Kavi Chongkittavorn, *Nation*, 10 Mar. 2009.

18 Interview, Kiatichai Pongpanich, senior editor of *Khao Sot* newspaper, Bangkok, 22 Feb. 2001.

19 Sinfah, "Impact of Defamation Law on Freedom of Expression in Thailand," p. 2.

20 Interview, Kavi Chongkittavorn, Bangkok, 15 Feb. 2001.

21 Sinfah reports that in recent years the Official Information Act has made access to government documents easy, although journalists rarely use it, personal communication, Sinfah Tunsarawuth, 21 Mar. 2009. Newspapers do not take precautions, either. Sinfah reports,

> Most Thai newspapers do not take precautionary measures to protect themselves from being sued for defamation. Most newspapers, even the more established ones which employ full-time in-house lawyers, do not consult their lawyers before publishing stories that could be seen as defamatory. Editors argue that time pressure prevents them submitting their stories to be read by their lawyers before publication. Many newspapers only employ lawyers once they have been sued.
>
> (Sinfah, "Impact of Defamation Law on Freedom of Expression in Thailand," p. 2)

22 Article 19 reports that of 2007, *Matichon* "was facing 48 criminal and civil defamation cases in court, some of which included record-high damage claims." Sinfah, "Impact of Defamation Law on Freedom of Expression in Thailand," p. 3.

23 Interview, Thakul Boonparn, managing editor of *Khao Sot*, Bangkok, 22 Feb. 2001. He is now the editor of *Khao Sot*, as distinct from Thakul Uthaiwong, one-time editor and now adviser to the newspaper.

24 *Financial Times*, Dec. 9, 2005.

25 Small and medium-sized newspapers were most vulnerable to punitive damages in defamation suits. *Naew Na* newspaper was essentially bankrupted by a defamation suit. Sinfah, "Impact of Defamation Law on Freedom of Expression in Thailand," pp. 9–10.

26 Interview, Sulak Sivaraksa, Bangkok, 21 Feb. 2001.
27 Interview, Kiatichai, 22 Feb. 2001.
28 Anonymous source.
29 Anonymous source. See also the sad description of the fate of Aroon Lanlua and other mentions of defamation, in McCargo, *Politics and the Press in Thailand*, pp. 110, 115, 130–31.
30 Sinfah, "Impact of Defamation Law on Freedom of Expression in Thailand," pp. 7–8
31 *Bangkok Post*, "Journalism Is Not a Criminal Pursuit," 6 Sep 2004.
32 *Nation*, 8 Oct. 2004. More recently, Article 19's report on defamation recommends that the standard practice is "when an injured party asks State prosecutors to file a defamation case on his or her behalf, the court does not hold a preliminary hearing to weigh the merits of the case." Sinfah, "Impact of Defamation Law on Freedom of Expression in Thailand," p. 4.
33 Available at: http://www.tja.or.th/modules.php?name = News&file = article&sid = 398, accessed 29 June 2008.
34 Available at: http://www.hrw.org/en/news/2004/08/31/thailand-libel-suit-deepens-assault-press, accessed 12 June 2009.
35 Thailand recovered slightly in 2008, with a rank of 124. Reporters sans Frontières, "Annual Worldwide Press Freedom Index," 2002 to 2008, available at: http://www.rsf.org/en-classement298–2002.html, through http://www.rsf.org/en-classement794–2008.html, accessed 9 June 2009.
36 Krom Tamruat, *Rai-ngan prajam pi, 2619–2525* [Annual Report of the Police Department, 1976–82].
37 Statistics from the Office of the Attorney General seem to be at variance with Article 19's report on defamation which estimates that "about half" of the newspaper "group's cases are settled before the court makes any ruling, while the other half proceed through to a final court verdict." Of the 1,451 defamation cases disposed of by courts in 2005, 90.7 percent led to conviction, 2.8 led to acquittals, 0.5 percent were "withdrawn," and 6 percent were disposed of by some "other" means. One explanation may be that if the *Matichon* editor's estimate is right, half the cases are settled on the mere threat of litigation, suggesting that defamation-related offenses in a given year may be *twice* the number in official statistics! Thailand, Attorney General's Office (Samnakngan Aiyakan Songsut), *Rai-ngan prajam pi 2548* [Annual Report of the Attorney General's Office, 2005] (Samnakngan aiyakan phiset fai sarasonthet, samnakngan wichakan).
38 It should be noted here that a 97 percent conviction rate is surprisingly lower than the overall conviction rate for all crimes in Thailand. In 1997, the conviction rate for the 488,222 cases tried was 98.4 percent and the acquittal rate was 0.7 percent (the other 0.9 percent were either withdrawn or disposed of in some "other" way). In 2003, for the 444,383 cases in which courts rendered a decision, the conviction rate was 98.56 percent and the acquittal rate was 1.44 percent. For 2004 and its 388,566 court decisions, the conviction rate was 98.64 percent and the acquittal rate was 1.36 percent. Thus, the conviction rate for defamation was higher than crimes of malfeasance in office (96.14) and murder (86 percent), but lower than for violations of military service (99.97) and prostitution (99.75). Thailand, Attorney General's Office (Samnakngan Aiyakan Songsut), *Rai-ngan prajam pi, 2539–2540, 2546, 2547* [Annual Report of the Attorney General's Office, 1996–97, 2003, 2004] (Samnakngan aiyakan phiset fai sarasonthet, samnakngan wichakan).
39 One explanation for this broad divergence between editors and statistics of cases that are withdrawn might be they include threats to sue as well. See note 37 above.
40 *Nation*, Oct. 18, 2007. In a similar vein, Somchai Krusuansombat, former president of the Thai Journalists Association, said,

> At this time there are no more civilized countries in the world where defamation can lead to imprisonment. All such laws have been abolished but there are still fines, sometimes of large amounts. That's how it is in the modern world. Putting someone in jail is old-fashioned. If [those countries] have abolished [criminal libel], why do we still need it?
>
> (Interview, Somchai Krusuansombat, *Thai Post*, Bangkok, 20 Oct. 2002)

41 Under extraterritoriality, special international courts were established to try cases where litigants were under foreign jurisdiction.
42 "The Case Against the 'Wayamo'," n.d., no name of newspaper, in "1923 Wayamo Case," in Juridical Council Archives, "Press 1932–34," Vol. 134.
43 This is the same Narin mentioned in a 1919 case in Chapter 6.
44 Thailand, Supreme Court, Supreme Court Decision 573/2475 [1932], *PKSD 2475*, pp. 539–41.
45 Thailand, Supreme Court, Supreme Court Decision 1127/2480 [1937], *PKSD 2480*, pp. 1183–87.
46 *Nation*, 20 Jan. 2000.
47 *Nation*, 23 June 1999.
48 David Streckfuss, "Truth Is Jailed under a Defamation Regime," *Nation*, 30 May 2005.
49 McCargo, *Politics and the Press in Thailand*, p. 16. Let there be no question that Thaksin Shinawatra developed into a world-level user of defamation laws. He and his administration wielded the libel law as never before. Thaksin personally brought at least 40 suits against his arch-rival, Sondhi Limthong in 2005–6, which probably represented 5 percent of all cases for the year. (This figure was calculated by FACT: Freedom Against Censorship Thailand in 2006; the figure may be considerably higher now). (Personal communication with CJ Hinke of FACT). Also see http://en.wikipedia.org/wiki/Censorship_in_Thailand#cite_ref-57, accessed last 10 June 2009.
50 *Nation*, 17 July 2000.
51 *Nation*, 18 July 2000.
52 *Bangkok Post*, 20 July 2000.
53 *Nation*, 23 July 2000, *Khao Sot*, 18 and 23 July 2543 [2000].
54 In this case, the headline reflected the sentiment of many in Thailand and abroad concerning the actions of the Chuan government. The word "cruel" [*thamin*] is the same adjective used to refer to "Black May" 1992, thus bearing special significance. "Monk Day" is equivalent to the Christian "Sunday." The day is calculated by the lunar calendar rather than being a set day of the week. To do something violent on "the Sabbath" seems worse, especially since this Monk Day was the first day of the three-month Buddhist Lent. It does not seem to be a highly inflammatory headline, given the context. *Khao Sot*, 18 July 2543 [2000].
55 *Nation*, 21 July 2000.
56 *Khao Sot*, 18 July 2543 [2000].
57 *Nation*, 21 July 2000. On the face of it, Chuan's attack on Thakul's moral character—something fairly consistently deemed defamatory by the Thai Supreme Court over the decades—seem far harsher than *Khao Sot*'s "debatable" comment on the character of a political leader in the aftermath of the arrest of villagers, which at least is within the realm of normal comment and airing of views on a public issue. In the end, the court found Thakul and other newspapers guilty of defamation for calling Chuan a dictator, sentencing Thakul to six months in jail (the sentence was suspended for two years and Thakul never spent time in jail in this or any other case) (Personal communication with Thakul Uthaiwong, 1 June 2009). For more on this point, see "Chapter Two," in David Streckfuss, "Poetics of

Subversion: Civil Liberty and *Lèse-Majesté* in the Modern Thai State," Ph.D. dissertation, University of Wisconsin-Madison, 1998), and Article 19 and Forum-Asia, *Freedom of Expression and the Media in Thailand* (Dec. 2005), particularly pp. 71–89.

As a lawyer, Chuan must have been aware of how in other democracies libel is little used by prime ministers or presidents. Chuan, as the quintessential "clean politician," used the defamation charge a number of times (see *Nation*, 5 Oct. 2001, 10 Feb. 2004). To his credit, Chuan only requested that the offending newspapers apologize publicly (and the offender go to jail) rather than seeking monetary damages. In 2001, Chuan sued *Matichon* newspaper and magazine for publishing, "Chuan did not pay adequate attention to the welfare of his wife and son and that his son would 'feel the warmth only when Chuan Leekpai faced difficulties and scandals that he needed to build public image'." The Supreme Court in 2005 ruled that "though the plaintiff is a politician and used to hold key political offices, and hence, the plaintiff can be regarded as a public figure, such statements are of the plaintiff's family affairs. It does not have anything to do with his duty as a politician and not benefit the public." Article 19 notes from the judgment:

> The ruling clearly shows that even if the subject of a report is a public figure, what has been written about him or her might not be seen as a matter of public interest. Thai courts tend to see statements criticising personal matters as defamatory. The defamation provisions in the Penal Code do not allow the defendant to prove that the defamatory statement is true if the statement relates to a personal matter and proof of truth does not benefit the public.
>
> (Sinfah, "Impact of Defamation Law on Freedom of Expression in Thailand," p. 11)

58 For an opposite view, see Sopon Onkgara, "The Urban–Rural Divide Grows Dangerous," *Nation*, 30 July 2000 and 6 Aug. 2000.
59 Thailand, Appeals Court (San Uthorn), "Khamphiphaksa," khadi mailek 3065/2541 [Judgment, Case No. 3065/1998, Appeals Court, 6 November, 1998], p. 2.
60 Interview, Kiatichai Pongpanich, Bangkok, 22 Feb. 2001.
61 "Khamphiphaksa," khadi mailek 3065/2541, pp. 1–4.
62 *Nation*, 3 Aug. 1993; *Bangkok Post*, 4 and 5 Aug. 1996.
63 *Nation*, 4 Aug. 1996.
64 *Bangkok Post*, 6 Aug. 1996; *Nation*, 6 Aug. 1996.
65 Thai judges take an oath to, and are appointed by, the king, and thus become representatives of the Crown. They are thereby shielded by the contempt of court law from being sued. Constitutional Court judges are not representatives of the Crown and so may be sued. However, as individuals or in the name of the Constitutional Court, they may sue critics for personal defamation, as in the case of Veera Somkwankid detailed below. Also see Chapter 13.
66 *Nation*, 16, 20, and 22 June, 26 July 2000.
67 *Nation*, 26 July 2000.
68 *Nation*, 7 Aug. 2000 and 22 Feb. 2001.
69 Veera was convicted of defaming the court in 2003 and sentenced initially to a 30-month prison term. The court suspended the sentence, due to Veera's "past social contributions," *Nation*, 10 May 2003. Constitutional Court judges also sued newspaper columnist Prasong Soonsiri for defamation. Prasong alleged in 2002 that the eight judges who had acquitted prime minister Thaksin Shinawatra of concealing assets in 2001 had accepted bribes to find Thaksin innocent (*Nation*, 15, 16, 17 Oct. 2004). The lower court acquitted Prasong of defamation. Prasong pointed out that not just he had won, but also "Society won." The Southeast

Asian Press Alliance (SEAPA) called this "a landmark decision that should strengthen the cause of free expression in Thailand." Nonetheless, the court also found Prasong guilty of contempt for using "impolite language" and sentenced him to one-year imprisonment and a fine of 7,000 baht (the jail time was suspended for two years) (*Nation*, 3 Dec. 2004). Prasong appealed, but lost in Dec. 2008. The case is pending with the Supreme Court (*Nation*, 10 Sept. 2008). Available at: http://www.seapabkk.org/news/2004/12/20041203.html, accessed 14 Dec. 2008.

70 *Nation*, 3 Aug. 1993; *Bangkok Post*, 4 and 5 Aug. 1996.

71 Thailand, Criminal Court, "Decision of the Court," Black Case No. 1901/36, 26 April 1995, in David Streckfuss, ed., *Modern Thai Monarchy and Cultural Politics: The Acquittal of Sulak Sivaraksa on the Charge of lèse-majesté in Siam 1995 and Its Consequences* (Bangkok: Santi Pracha Dhamma Institute, 1996), pp. 28–31.

72 *Nation*, 16–17 Mar. 2006. See also Sinfah, "Impact of Defamation Law on Freedom of Expression in Thailand," p. 5.

73 In the hundreds of Supreme Court Decisions examined in the course of this study, I never encountered any Supreme Court decision that cited a lower court decision as part of a decision. However, as we saw in Chapter 5, international law is occasionally cited.

74 Sinfah, "Impact of Defamation Law on Freedom of Expression in Thailand," p. 4. Article 19 recommends: "The law should clearly define public figures and matters of public interest, and require these people and matters to tolerate more scrutiny by news media than ordinary citizen and private matters" (p. 15).

75 Thailand, Supreme Court, Supreme Court Decision 346/2482 [1939] 23 th. s. 440, *PKSD 2482*, pp. 440–43.

76 Thailand, Supreme Court, Supreme Court Decision 97/2484 [1941], *PKSD 2484*, pp. 119–26.

77 Thailand, Supreme Court, Supreme Court Decision 143/2484 [1941] 25 th. s. 176, *PKSD 2484*, pp. 176–84.

78 Thailand, Juridical Council, "Letter," 5 March 2485 [1942], from the Secretary-General of the Council of Ministers to the Secretary-Gen. of the Juridical Council, Subject: On what occasion the word 'Government' should be used," and "Draft Note," n.d., in, "Ruang kan chai kham 'ratthaban'" [On the Use of the Word, "Government"], Vol. 360, Part 9. Original emphasis.

79 For more discussion of this topic, see Streckfuss, "Poetics of Subversion," especially Chapters 5 and 7. I use six sets of documents from 1942 in making this summary analysis: Thailand, Juridical Council, "Rai-ngan kanprachum kammakan rang kotmai (anukammakan chut thi 3)" [Juridical Council Committee, Report of the Law-Drafting Committee (Sub-Committee No. 3)], Meeting No. 96/2485 [1942], 16 March 2485 [1942], Vol. 360, Part 9; "Rang prakat samnak nayok ratthamontri Ruang kan chai kham wa 'ratthaban'" [Draft Announcement of the Office of the Prime Minister on the Use of the Word, 'Government'"], n.d., and "NOTE Concerning the interpretation of the word "Government," 20 March 2485 [1942], Vol. 360, Part 9; Juridical Council Committee, "Report of Meeting No. 108," 25 March 2485 [1942], Vol. 360, Part 9; "Rule for Using the Word "Government," n.d., and "Rules for Using the Word, 'Government,' from The Secretary-General of the Council of Ministers to the President of the Council of Ministers, 30 Apr. 2485 [1942], from the "Department of the Secretary-General of the Council of Ministers," Vol. 360, Part 9; and "Draft-Memorandum on word 'Government,'" 27 March 2485 [1942], Vol. 360, Part 9.

80 Of course, characterizing Thai governments as basically authoritarian is nonetheless accurate. Phibun did issue "authoritarian" measures. See Baker and Pasuk, *A History of Thailand,* p. 126.

81 Thailand, Supreme Court, Supreme Court Decision 1153–54/2495 [1952] d. 832, *PKSD 2495*, pp. 832–42, and Thailand, Supreme Court, Supreme Court Decision 45/2496 [1953], *PKSD 2496*, pp. 55–67.

82 "People Listen to Examining of Witness in Kukrit Rebellion Case, Laugh at Prosecution Witness to Merriment Until Court Warns, Witness Educated, Having Read Does Not Feel Rebellious," *Sayam Rat*, 28 May 2500 [1957].

83 "People Overcrowd to Listen to Hearing in Trial of Rebellion Case, Prosecution Witness on the Contents of Kukrit Writing, Sounds as if Warning to Government to Stop Being Enemy of the People, To Not Have Protest Marches, To Beware of Communists," *Sayam Rat*, 19 May 2500 [1957].

84 As part of national security offenses within the criminal code, there have been relatively few cases of "defamation of the nation" and even fewer have advanced to the Supreme Court. Generally, cases that might be so interpreted have been present in other statutes, such as the anti-communist laws, as described in Chapter 10, but most likely they have been subsumed under *lèse-majesté*.

85 Thailand, Supreme Court, Supreme Court Decision 2097/2497 [1954], *PKSD* 2497, pp. 1853–55.

86 In Thailand, feet are considered the dirtiest and lowest part of the body; intentionally pointing the sole of one's foot at someone else is considered a grave insult. Though the court never explicitly addressed the question, there must have been something doubly wrong with wearing such subversive socks.

87 As the archetypical traitor to the state—the communists—disappeared, the *lèse-majesté* law provided a new way of identifying enemies. Human rights lawyer Thongbai Thongbao remarked in the 1990s, "They don't charge people with being communists anymore—they use the *lèse-majesté* charge," in Paul Handley, *The King Never Smiles* (New Haven, CT: Yale University Press, 2006), p. 447. A newspaper headline nicely makes the connection, in reference to the Jakrapob case, "faces treason and lese majesty accusation," *Nation*, 29 May 2008. Actually, Jakrapob did not face "treason" (Article 116 of the criminal code), but only *lèse-majesté*.

8 The insulted and defamed II: monarchy and *lèse-majesté*

1 A very useful comparison of the 1902, 1941, and 1962 Sangha Acts is provided in Yoneo Ishii, *Sangha, State, and Society: Thai Buddhism in History* (Honolulu: Hawaii University Press, 1986, pp. 67–120.

2 At least judging from *lèse-majesté* prosecutions as a crude indicator, the annual number averaged almost six in the 1990s, while in the first half of the 2000s, the average was not quite three, indicating the relative reticence of the Thaksin government to use the law. See note 90, p. 377.

3 One observer alleged the following two actions would have been suppressed earlier: One newspaper carried a story about one particular prince who had accepted a 50,000 baht bribe. Another ran a headline about a royal: "Greedy for Sexual Intercourse." When accused, Thawat Ritthidet found no relief with parliament which declined to take action as the new constitution affirmed the king was inviolable. In "Letter" from the office of the Samakhom kammakan rang haeng sayam [Siam Drafting Committee], Juridical Council, "Nai Thawat Rittidet," 4 Oct. 2476 [1933], in relation to *Raingan kanprachum sapha phuthaen ratsadorn* [Report of Sessions of the House of Representatives], Session 121/2476 [1933], (saman)[general session], "Prathan sapha an nangsu nai thawat ritthidet ruang thuk ha wa minphraboromdetchaanuphaap" [House Speaker Reads Letter of Mr. Thawat Ritthidet on Being Accused of *lèse-majesté*], pp. 580–90.

4 Apparently, thinking of the monarchy as an institution was a new way of understanding not only the monarchy, but also the government itself, as evidenced in the

uncertainty on the part of committee members on how to translate the English word "institution" into Thai (it was later coined as *sathaban*). Thailand, Juridical Council, "Rai-ngan kanprachum anukammakan truat phitjarana kaekhai pramuan kotmai aya," khrang thi 156, 28/1/82, lem 11 [Juridical Council Committee, Report of the Meeting of the Sub-committee on the Consideration and Revision of the Criminal Law Code, Meeting No. 156, 28 Jan. 1939, Vol. 11], p. 8.

5 Thailand, Juridical Council Committee, Report of the Meeting of the Sub-committee on the Consideration and Revision of the Criminal Law Code, Meeting No. 150, 3 Jan. 1941, p. 8

6 Since the committee was never able to define "the Sovereign" (as an institution), "the Government," or "the administration of the State," as specified in the Section 104, it dropped them and settled on prohibiting those who sought to "to bring about a change in the Laws of the Country or the Government by the use of force or violence."

7 Thailand, Juridical Council Committee, Report of the Meeting of the Sub-committee on the Consideration and Revision of the Criminal Law Code, Meeting No. 151, 10 Jan. 1941, p. 4.

8 Pichan Bulayong [René Guyon], "5th Meeting of the Assembly for Drafting the Constitution," 21 July 2491 [1948]," in Juridical Council Library, Vol. 218, "Constitutions," "Part IV Rapports (personnels) of the Legislative Adviser as Observer on Behalf of the Government," pp. 1–2. A newspaper article of the meeting reported under the headline "Loyalty to Throne" that the session showed "an impressive demonstration of loyalty to the Crown" as "members greeted with resounding applause and passed unanimously a call for a vote on the perpetuation of constitutional monarchy in Siam." The newspaper article has no citation.

9 "Loyalty to the Throne," in Thailand, Juridical Council, Vol. 218, "Constitutions," n.d.

10 Nattapoll noted that academics have avoided the question of the monarchy's role after the 1932 revolution. Theories such as "the bureaucratic polity" have obscured the key role the monarchy played in destabilizing governments until 1957, after which the monarchy took a commanding position in the political sphere, one maintained to the present. See Nattapoll Chaiching, "The Monarch and the Royalist Movement in Modern Thai Politics, 1932–57," unpublished manuscript.

11 Thailand, Juridical Council, Pichan Bulayong [René Guyon], "Interpretation of the Constitution and the Declaration of Human Rights as Far as Communism is Concerned," 2 Apr. 2494 [1951], in "Kotmai pongkan khommiewnit," in *Ruang set* [Finished Matters], Vol. 452.

12 *Chao*, 11, 16, and 24 Feb. 2499 [1956]; *Sayam Nikorn*, 11 Feb. 2499 [1956]; *Sayam Rat*, 12 Feb. 2499 [1956]; *Prachathipatai*, 12 Feb. 2499 [1956]; *Khao Phanit*, 11 Feb. 2499 [1956]; *Chao Thai*, 12 and 14 Feb. 2499 [1956].

13 *The Constitution of the Kingdom of Siam, B.E. 2475*, in Thak Chaloemtiarana, ed., *Thai Politics: Extracts and Documents 1932–1957* (Bangkok: The Social Science Association of Thailand, 1978), p. 98.

14 *Constitution of the Kingdom of Thailand B.E. 2550 (2007)* available at: http://www.isaanlawyers.com/constitution%20thailand%202007%20-%202550.pdf]. The wording of the 1932 constitution concerning the role of the king did not change until the 1949 constitution, which first used the phrasing still employed in Section 8 of the 2007 constitution. The 2007 constitution also included the phrase, in Section 2: "Thailand is a democratic state with the King as the Head of State." See T*he Constitution of the Kingdom of Siam, B.E. 2475*, in Thak Chaloemtiarana, ed., *Thai Politics: Extracts and Documents 1932–1957* (Bangkok: The Social Science Association of Thailand, 1978), p. 98.

15 Under the German Empire, the maximum imprisonment for *lèse-majesté* was five years; in Tsarist Russia and Spain of the 1920s, a maximum of eight years; even under the Japanese emperor, the penalty for *lèse-majesté* was a maximum of five years' imprisonment (although this might have been longer during World War II), see David Streckfuss, "Thailand's Tough Law," *Dateline Bangkok* [Foreign Correspondents' Club of Thailand Magazine] (Second Quarter 2008), p. 22.

16 Information on accusations and cases during this period is uneven. A few cases are available through the published decisions of the Supreme Court. The most detail is available in those few cases when defendants or their backers published the proceedings of the cases in books (the 1975 Pradoem and 1988 Wira cases, for example). A number of cases were only briefly mentioned in the Thai press, while other cases did not show up in the Thai press at all and are available only through outside sources, such as Amnesty International.

17 The word, *min phraboromdechanuphap* combines the Thai word, *min*, "to look down on," with the sanskritized *phraborom* (perhaps, "the sacred supreme") and *dechanuphap* ("majesty"). Many Thai scholars and activists make the point that Thailand traditionally had no *lèse-majesté* law and that its formulation was quite recent, or that Thailand even today does not have such a law. This is curious, given what we saw in the *Three Seals Law* and the court's clear acknowledgment that Provisions 98 and 100 of the 1908 code and section 112 of the 1957 code are, in fact, *lèse-majesté* provisions. See, for instance, an account of a seminar by Thanapol Eawsakul, "Min phraboromdechanuphap nai sangkhom thai" [*Lèse-majesté* in Thai Society], *Fah Diew Kan* (Apr.–June 2006), pp. 67–81.

18 Kosai also said, the killing of Rama VIII was accidental (*"len pun an pen kan ko hai koet ubatihet"*). Thailand, Supreme Court, Supreme Court Decision 51/2503 [1960], d. 73, *PKSD 2503*, pp. 73–78; also see Jitti's commentary on this case, Jitti Tingsaphat (1967), *Kham athibai pramuan kotmai aya* [Explanation of the Criminal Law Code], p. 892.

Kosai's allegation was repeated in an English account of the death of Rama VII, called *The Devil's Discus*, which became the subject of a charge in 1964 as copies of the book were seized by police from book shops in Bangkok and shipments of the book were confined to port warehouses in 1964. " . . . Calls for Banning from Entering Thailand," *San Seri*, 23 and 26 May 2507 [1964].

19 " . . . books criticizing the king," *Sayam Rat* newspaper, 20 Nov. 2516 [1973].

20 *Nation Review*, 12 and 19 July 1983, *Bangkok Post*, 20 Aug. and 30 Dec. 1983; "Raktham Rakthai" [Saman Kongsuphon], *Kao Ratchakan* [Nine Reigns], "2nd edition," (n.p., n.d.).

21 Somchai Jenchaijittarawanit, *Khadi prawatisat min phraboromdechanuphap: Wira Musikaphong tit khuk phro kanmuang!* [A Historic *lèse-majesté* case: Wira Musikaphong Jailed Because of Politics! (Krungthep: Samnakngan phua sawaengha khwamyuttitham nai sangkhom, 2531 [1988], pp. 28–29, 35.

22 *Nation*, 10 Dec. 1976; *Bangkok Post*, 11 Feb. 1977; Thailand, Supreme Court, Supreme Court Decisions 1294/2521 [1978], *PKSD 2521*, pp. 1581–82; and 3243/2529 [1986], *PKSD 2529*, pp. 222–37; *Prachatai*, 25 Apr. 2008. Available at: http://www.prachatai.com/english/news.php?id = 617, accessed 15 June 2008. The Thai *national* anthem is played twice daily. Convention and a misdemeanor law demand that those in public rise to attention during this period. A person not standing could have a small fine levied. The *royal* anthem is played prior to certain public functions and always prior to showing movies.

23 "*Newsweek* Report Refuted," *Bangkok Post*, 7 Nov. 1967; "'*Newsweek*' Writer Apologizes to Their Majesties," *Bangkok Post*, 9 Nov. 1967; "*Newsweek* Magazine Protested for Article Which Was Completely Counter to Facts," *Kiattisak*, 8 Nov. 2510 [1967]; "Report in Response to the American Publication *Newsweek*," *Sayam Nikorn*, 9 Nov. 2510 [1967].

24 "Foreign Newspaper [in Foreign Land] Insulting, Doesn't Know High from Low," *Deli Niew*, 26 Nov. 2510 [1967], *Sayam Rat*, [no date].
25 "Thais Ban Asian *Wall Street Journal* for Story Critical of Monarch," *Washington Post*, 23 Jan. 1982.
26 Sulak Sivaraksa, *Siamese Resurgence* (Bangkok: Asian Cultural Forum on Development, 1985), pp. 416–18.
27 Sulak was found innocent of the charges from this case in 1995. See "Decision of the Court," Black Case No. 1901/36, 26 Apr. 1995, in David Streckfuss, ed., *Modern Thai Monarchy and Cultural Politics: The Acquittal of Sulak Sivaraksa on the Charge of lèse-majesté in Siam 1995 and Its Consequences* (Bangkok: Santi Pracha Dhamma Institute, 1996), pp. 28–31.
28 See Amnesty International, *Amnesty International Report, 1987–88* (London: Amnesty International Publications, 1988).
29 Of course, the period from 1957 to 1992 in Thailand in terms of law and rule of law was quite dire, as the basic mechanisms of law were either not functioning or were under heavy influence of the military. Many opponents of the government were summarily killed. For instance, the "case" of Kasem Prathumwiang of Udorn Thani who, it was said, set out to "create malice for the government, the tradition of political governance, and the economy of Thailand and to have the people look favourably upon communism." He criticized the king by saying: "We should not have a king because he lazes around and consumes a big salary without having to do a thing. And that money comes from the sweat and labour of the poor people." He therefore called for the monarchy to be abolished. His "trial"—a conversation with Sarit Thanarat–-ended with a bullet in the head. See "*Lèse-majesté*, Internal Rebellion, and Red Cases," *Sayam Nikorn*, 20 Aug. 2502 [1959], Luckier (but not that lucky) was Phromneet Banthip, a 24-year-old rubber worker in the south, who apparently said that Thailand should abolish the monarchy and set up a republic. He disappeared into the military court system with an eight-year sentence. See Amnesty International, *Amnesty International Report 1984–85* (London: Amnesty International Publications, 1985).
30 Thailand, National Archives, k/p7/p3/2517/3 Momratchawong Kukrit Pramot thuk klaoha chai thoikham min phraboromdetchanuphap [Kukrit Pramoj Accused of Using Words [that Are] *Lèse-majesté*] (30/10/17–5/11/17).
31 "Student Calls for Arrest of Kukrit for Insulting the King" (unclear, either *Chao Thai* or *Phim Thai*, 30 Oct. 2517 [1974].
32 "Harsh Photo Caption, lèse-majesté of Royalty," *Deli Niew*, 14 Dec. 2519 [1976]; and " . . . Order for Arrest of *Thai Rat* for *Lèse-majesté* of Daughter-in-law", *Deli Niew*, 15 Dec. 2519 [1976]. It is unclear whether an arrest was ever made.
33 One wonders why the court was so concerned whether foreigners correctly understood the charisma of the Thai king. See *Matichon*, 8 Sept. 1978.
34 Two police investigation teams looked into the matter. A high-ranking police officer said that "the case had to be treated very carefully and opinions on legality had been sought from knowledgeable experts and academics." *Bangkok Post*, 23 Aug. and 3 Sept. 1990; *Nation*, 24 Aug. 1990.
35 *Bangkok Post*, 10 and 12 June 1988.
36 See, for instance, a retrospective of the royal family's role in society in "Working Royals," Foreign Correspondents' Club of Thailand (FCCT), *King of Thailand in World Focus* (Singapore: Didier Millet, 2008), pp. 118–53.
37 Annette Hamilton, "Rumours, Foul Calumnies and the Safety of the State: Mass Media and National Identity in Thailand," in Craig J. Reynolds, ed., *National Identity and Its Defenders, Thailand, 1939–1989* (Clayton, Victoria: Centre of Southeast Asian Studies, Monash University, Monash Papers on Southeast Asia No. 25, 1991), pp. 341–79.

38 See, for instance, Michael K. Connors, , “Article of Faith: The Failure of Royal Liberalism in Thailand,” *Journal of Contemporary Asia* 38(1) (Feb. 2008): 124–42.

39 Chang Noi (pseud.), “What Does the Sufficiency Economy Mean for This government’s Policy?” (1 and 2), *Nation*, 30 and 31 Oct. 2006. The king’s concern over increasing the self-reliance of the poor is strange in light of the king’s own wealth—consistently among the top ten richest royals in the world. See the *Asian Sentinel*’s “How Thailand’s Royals Manage to Own All the Good Stuff,” 2 Mar. 2007, available at: http://pages.citebite.com/b1u2r1x6o0eeg, accessed 12 May 2009.

40 See Porphant Ouyyanont, “The Crown Property Bureau from Crisis to Opportunity,” in Pasuk Phongpaichit and Chris Baker, eds., *Thai Capital: After the 1997 Crisis* (Bangkok: Silkworm Books, 2008), pp. 155–86. Porphant’s article was one of the presentations at the 10th Thai Studies Conference held in Bangkok in early January 2008 which featured an unprecedented three panels dedicated to the monarchy and its role in society (and carefully watched by the police). See more at Chang Noi (pseud.), “Thai Studies and the Monarchy,” *Nation*, 22 Jan. 2008, available at: http://www.geocities.com/changnoi2/thaistudies10.htm , accessed 29 June 2008]. Also see Porphant Ouyyanont, “The Crown Property Bureau in Thailand and the Crisis of 1997,” *Journal of Contemporary Asia* 38(1) (Feb. 2008): 166–89.

41 Kongbannathikan warasan fah diew kan, “Rai-ngan: wa duai phramahakasat nai kanprachum thai suksa nana chat thi thammasat” [Editor Section, Fah Diew Kan Magazine, “Report: On the King in the International Thai Studies Conference at Thammasat], *Prachathai*, 21 Jan. 2551 [2008]; *Fah Diew Kan* 5(2) (Apr.–June 2549 [2006]): 111–12.

42 Somsak Jeamteerasakul, “Chaiya chana khong panyachon 17 tula (ton thi 2: kanplian plaeng praden khrang yai)” [Victory of the 17 Oct. Intellectuals (Part II: The Big Changing of Subject)], *Ratthaprahan 19 kanyayon* [The Coup of 19 September] (Krungthep: Fah Diew Kan, 2550 [2007]), pp. 382–430.

43 Samakhom nak khao nak nangsuphim haeng prathet thai [Thai Journalists Association], available at: http://www.tja.or.th/index.php?option = com_content &task = view&id = 491, accessed 29 Jan. 2008.

44 Thongchai Winichakul, “Toppling Democracy,” *Journal of Contemporary Asia* 38(1) (Feb. 2008): 19. The Thai government was very concerned over Paul Handley’s book, *The King Never Smiles*. Official documents leaked on 24 July 2006 show to what lengths the Thaksin government went to in trying to suppress the book, raising doubts as to accusations of Thaksin’s opposition to the monarchy. See http://www.reporter.co.th/content/view/5819/95/, accessed 5 Aug. 2006.

45 Kevin Hewison, “A Book, the King and the 2006 Coup,” *Journal of Contemporary Asia* 38(1) (Feb. 2008): 195. Probably the most daring examinations of the current role of the monarchy come from Duncan McCargo, “Network Monarchy and Legitimacy Crises,” *The Pacific Review* 18(4) (Dec. 2005): 499–519, and Handley, *The King Never Smiles*.

46 Michael Connors, *Democracy and National Identity in Thailand* (London: Routledge/Curzon, 2003), p. 134.

47 Kobkua Suwannatha-Pian, *King, Country and Constitutions* (London: Routledge-Curzon, 2003), p. 26.

48 The Thai Foreign Ministry was quick to question the figure of $35 billion, although it did not specify the king’s personal worth. See *Bangkok Post*, 24 Aug. 2008. See also *Asian Sentinel*, “How Thailand’s Royals Manage to Own All the Good Stuff,” 2 Mar. 2007.

49 Michael J. Montesano, “Contextualizing the Pattaya Summit Debacle: Four April Days, Four Thai Pathologies,” *Contemporary Southeast Asia* 31(2) (2009): 227–30.

50 *Nation*, 5 Dec. 2005.

51 "Khwamphit thana min phraboromdechanuphap [The Crime of *Lèse-majesté*], *Pajariyasan* 14(6) (Nov.–Dec. 1987): 21–23, 34.

52 "Democracy May End *Lèse-majeste* Law," *Nation*, 8 Oct. 1987.

53 *Nation*, Jan. 28, 2005, *Bangkok Post*, 7, 11 and 28 Feb., 9 Mar. 2005. The case was eventually dropped. See *Nation*, 28 Feb., 1 Mar. 2006.

54 Darren Schuettler "Academic Accused of Insulting Thai King in Exam Paper," Reuters News Wire, 2007; Telephone communication with Boonsoog Chaisingkananont, 2007. Numerous individuals who I contacted for this study, who had been accused or charged with *lèse-majesté*, reported that the police orally informed them that their cases had been dropped. In only one case had the suspect received a letter officially stating this. The statute of limitation for personal defamation is one year for civil suits and three months for criminal defamation. Sinfah, "Impact of Defamation Law on Freedom of Expression in Thailand," p. 4. As *lèse-majesté* is considered a serious crime, suspects could be charged for infractions committed up to a decade and a half earlier. Boonruam Thiamjan, comp., *The Criminal Code* (Krungthep: Sont Paisal Press, 2550 [2007]), p. 69. Such was the case of Harry Nicolaides, for whom an arrest warrant was issued as early as 2005. He had left the country numerous times before hearing of the warrant's existence; he was finally arrested as he was departing the country in mid-2008.

55 Jakrapob was charged on 24 March and stepped down from his ministerial post in late May (*Nation*, 25 Mar., 30, 31 May 2008). A major factor in the charge against Jakrapob might have been the possibly unprecedented accusation of *lèse-majesté* he made against Privy Councillor Prem Tinsulanonda and two judges in 2007 (*Bangkok Post*, 27 June 2007).

56 Anan Lao-lertworakul, "Decipher a Secret Code – A Dangerous Attitude of Jakrapob Penkair" photocopy, seven pages, in "additional evidence" provided to the police by Pol. Lt. Wattanasak Mungkandee, 30 June 2008. I thank Jonathan Head of the BBC for supplying copies of the documents on this case.

57 Ibid., p. 2.

58 Jakrapob's statement, "WE have to undo [the patronage system]. WE have to personalize [the] patron system by saying that, well, who keeps patronizing people. And I believe that the time is near to do that" [original emphasis]. Anan exclaims, "Who does he mean by 'we'? Does he mean himself as the speaker and also his listeners? Does he mean the Thai people at large? Or does he mean himself and Thaksin and all of Thaksin's hangers-on? When he says, 'the time is near' does he mean today or tomorrow?" [original emphasis, p. 5].

59 *The Nation* of 24 Apr. 2009.

60 *Nation*, 22 Apr. 2009. The Jakrapob case was a most fruitful one, producing a case against BBC correspondent Jonathan Head in 2008. In July 2009, Laksana Kornsilpa filed a complaint against the board of the Foreign Correspondents' Club of Thailand, saying it had committed *lèse-majesté* by distributing DVDs of Jakrapob's 2007 speech. She said the board "may be acting in an organised fashion and the goal may be to undermine the credibility of the high [*sic*] institution of Thailand." One person wrote on the ASTV Manager online web board that the board members should be jailed for 99 years; another person "asked the site to post a picture of Jonathan Head so the person could attack him if he or she ran into him," *Nation*, 2 July 2009; *Economist*, 2 July 2009.

61 *Nation*, 4 July 2008.

62 In 1978, a student was found guilty of *lèse-majesté* for not showing respect when the royal anthem was played (see note 22, p. 371). Later, the student did not turn the incident into a challenge. Thailand, Supreme Court, Supreme Court Decision 1294/2521 [1978] *PKSD 2521*, pp. 1581–82.

63 Thailand, Police Department, Pathumwan Police Station, Bangkok, "Banthuk kan jaeng khwam" [Accusation Report], 22 Apr. 2551 [2008].

64 *Prachathai*, 23 Apr. 2008. As an indication of the sensitivity of this case, this account, written by Pravit Rojanaphruk, was deemed unfit for print by *The Nation*; "a higher authority" at the paper felt that publication "carries certain risks." Available at: http://www.prachatai.com/english/news.php?id = 610, accessed 27 June 2008.

65 As of 15 Apr. 2009, Prachatai webmaster Chiranuch Premchaiporn faced up to 50 years in jail under the computer crimes act for web board comments that she did not remove promptly enough. See updates on her case at: http://thaipoliticalprisoners.wordpress.com/pendingcases/chiranuch-premchaiporn/, accessed 23 May 2009, and the "FACT – Freedom Against Censorship Thailand" website, http://facthai.wordpress.com.

66 Khon Kaen is in Thailand's Northeast, 450 kilometers from Bangkok.

67 *Prachatiai*, 29 Apr. 2008, available at: http://www.prachatai.com/english/news.php?id = 620, accessed 23 May 2009.

68 *Prachatiai*, 23 Apr. 2008 http://www.prachatai.com/english/news.php?id = 609, accessed 23 May 2009; http://www.managerradio.com/Radio/DetailRadio.asp?program_no = 1002&mmsID = 1002%2F1002%2D2870%2Ewma++&program_id = 13983, accessed 10 June 2009.

69 *Prachatai*, 25 Apr. 2008, available at: http://www.prachatai.com/english/news.php?id = 617, accessed 23 May 2009.

70 Despite assurances by Prime Minister Abhisit Vejjajiva in March, charges had not been dropped by mid-April 2009. Available at: http://thaipoliticalprisoners.wordpress.com/pendingcases/chotisak-onsoong/.

71 Bureau of Democracy, Human Rights, and Labor, US Department of State, "2008 Human Rights Report: Thailand," 25 Feb. 2009, available at: http://www.state.gov/g/drl/rls/hrrpt/2008/eap/119058.htm, accessed 24 May 2009.

72 Unnamed source.

73 Thailand, Central Labor Court (Samut Prakan) (san raeng-ngan klang), "Khadi mai lek dam thi s.p. 366/2551 / khadi mai lek daeng thi s.p. 639/2551" [Black Case No. s.p. 366/2008 / Red Case No. 639/2008], 27 Nov. 2008; personal communication with Jittra Khachadet, Seminar on the *lèse-majesté* law, Chulalongkorn University, 4 July 2008 and at Thammsat University, 22 Mar. 2009. Jittra appealed the decision, which is still pending.

74 Sulak Sivaraksa, "Kanmi sathaban kasat thuk kwa mi prathanathibodi" [Having a Monarchy Is Less Costly Than Having A President], interview in *Fah Diew Kan* 3:4 (Oct.–Dec. 2005), pp. 82–93. Interview conducted 8 Aug. 2005.

75 Interview with Sulak Sivaraksa, Bangkok, 5 July 2008. Sulak was subsequently arrested again in November 2008 for remarks he made at a human rights festival at Khon Kaen University the previous December (2007). *Bangkok Post*, 8 Nov. 2008, *Nation*, 3 May 2009.

76 For instance, the police were quick to describe the Jakrapob–Head incident above as part of a conspiracy. It is also commonly alluded to in some media, such as *Nation*, 1 Jun. 2007. Tej Bunnag, a veteran Thai diplomat and former advisor to the palace, admitted in early 2009 that the law "caused Thailand a lot of problems" and that prosecution "takes up a lot of people's time." He maintained that "There are always *lèse-majesté* cases before the Thai courts," and the law was not like defamation laws in other countries. However, he stressed the uniqueness of the Thai monarchy: "Certain institutions in certain countries are very sensitive. You cannot compare the members of the royal family of the United Kingdom with members of the royal family in Thailand," Leslie Koh, "Lese majeste laws 'a problem' for Thais," *Straits Times*, 22 Jan. 2009, available at: www.asianewsnet.net/news.php?id = 3548&sec = 1.

77 The speech is available on podcast at: http://www.mediafire.com/?x3cq0ymxwg9, accessed 22 Nov. 2008.

78 *Bangkok Post*, 23 Feb. 2009; "Da Torpedo Denied Bail Yet again," *Prachatai*, 8 June 2009, available at: http://www.prachatai.com/english/node/1017, accessed 10 June 2009. In June 2009, the judge ordered the media and other visitors out of the courtroom on grounds of national security. Daranee said, "The speech I am charged with was made at an open rally. I cannot accept that a closed trial will guarantee justice." The judge assured the exiting observers that she would get a fair trial. Available at: http://thaipoliticalprisoners.wordpress.com/2009/06/24/new-daranees-trial-closed-to-public-for-reasons-of-national-security/, accessed 26 June 2009.

79 We have to go back to 1912 to find a comparable case. Young officers, inspired by the overthrow of the emperor and establishment of a republic in China in 1911, held some preliminary meetings. They planned to depose the king and set up a republic, or at least a limited monarchy. After arrest, investigation, and trial, they were found guilty of planning to inflict harm on the king. The young officers in the case were ultimately punished more for their crime against the monarchy which at the time was roughly synonymous with the government and state. The sentencing of these Young Turks reflects the degree of malice each participant had against the king: those pushing for establishment of a republic and execution of the king were themselves executed; those who argued for a limited monarchy were given life sentences, and so on. See Thaemsook Numnonda, *Yang toek run raek kabot r.s. 130* [The First Generation of Young Turks, the 1912 Revolt] (Krungthep: Samnakphim ru'angsin, 2522 [1979]), particularly the military court's decision, pp. 236–80.

80 *Bangkok Post*, 28 Aug. 2009.

81 The English version is available on the Political Prisoners in Thailand website http://thaipoliticalprisoners.wordpress.com/pendingcases/ji-giles-ungpakorn/ accessed 10 June 2009; the Thai version is blocked with the following message: "This URL has been blocked by a Court order Or it could have an affect [*sic*] on or be against the security of the Kingdom, public order or good morals."

82 The writers unconsciously call into question Giles's neutrality as an academic, while at the same time proudly announcing their support for PAD (Chapter 12).

83 These statements implied that neither did the "red-shirts," who listened to him. Available at: http://www.manager.co.th/Daily/ViewNews.aspx?NewsID = 9520000017871, accessed 16 Feb. 2009.

84 http://www.manager.co.th/Politics/ViewNews.aspx?NewsID = 9520000016004, accessed 12 Feb. 2009.

85 Members of a group of low-ranking "Thai Islamic" officers in 1935 were tried in the newly established Special Court for planning to overthrow the government. Part of the charge was that they were trying to change the present governing system—"democracy with monarchy according to the constitution." Thai Noi, "Kabot nai sip pi 2478" [The Sergeants' Revolt, 1935] in *25 Khadi kabot* [25 Cases of Rebellion] (Krungthep: Rongphim ratthana kanphim, 2513 [1970]), pp. 164–67.

86 Personal communication with Dr. Sutthachai Yimprasert, 22 Mar. 2009.

87 Personal communication with Somchai Preechasilpakul, 21 Mar. 2009.

88 See, for instance, Jaran Cosananand, "Khwamrunraeng haeng thot thi mai pen tham lae kanpitkan "khwamjing" nai matra 112 haeng pramuan kotmai aya" [The Violence of Unjust Punishment and Keeping out of "the Truth" in Section 112 of the Criminal Code], in the panel, "sitthi manusayachon lae khwam klua nai sangkhom thai" [Human Rights and Fear in Thai Society], "Lak miti kotmai min phraboromratchanuphap" [Symposium on Legal Dimensions of the Lese Majesty Law], 21–22 Mar. 2009, Thammasat University.

89 Kobkua Suwannathat-Pian, "The Monarchy and Constitutional Change since 1972," in Duncan McCargo, ed., *Reforming Thai Politics* (Copenhagen: Nordic Institute of Asian Studies (NIAS), 2002), p. 69.

90 Connors has read the lack of royal intervention in early 2006 as a failure for royal liberalism. Was the coup the logical culmination of royal liberalism, or its continued defeat? See Michael K. Connors, "Article of Faith," pp. 143–65.

91 Note that these statistics do not include however many cases there have been for violations of the Computer Crimes Act. See note 54, p. 349. The government has made modest efforts to justify its stand on *lèse-majesté*. See the serious analysis in the document created by the Ministry of Interior: Legal Affairs Bureau, Office of the Permanent Secretary for Interior, "Kan ruapruam kho kotmai thi kiewkhong kap kan min praboromdechanuphap" [Compilation of Laws Relating to *lèse-majesté*], 2552 [2009]. Available at: www.law.moi.go.th/2552/ lese%20majesty-%20law%202.doc, accessed 6 Sept. 2009.

9 The people

1 It is not what "people believe" that is the standard, but more what people "should believe," as shown in the case of the defendant calling someone a ghost. It seems that most Thai have always believed in ghosts, feel a need to propitiate the spirits, and so on, and the court in the 1938 case had to admit as much and not deny that being called a ghost might cause a person to be disparaged and hated by others. Thailand, Supreme Court, Supreme Court Decision 590/2473 [1930], *PKSD 2473*, pp. 359–60.

2 In her 1991 article, Hamilton indicated just how little credence was given to the opinions of average Thai citizens: "Public opinion exists, if at all, only in the elite sector . . . the notion that the statistical quantity of opinion might have some special weight seems to be quite alien. The views of important and educated people are the only ones that count." See Hamilton, "Rumours, Foul Calumnies and the Safety of the State: Mass Media and National Identity in Thailand," in Craig J. Reynolds, ed., *National Identity and Its Defenders, Thailand, 1939–1989* (Clayton, Victoria: Centre of Southeast Asian Studies, Monash University, Monash Papers on Southeast Asia No. 25, 1991), p. 368. Although a number of institutions now carry out regular opinion polls, there is always a question about who makes up the sample. This issue became apparent in 2008 when Bangkok-based media continually reported on how Northeasterners supported Thaksin, with little or no actual news content derived from Northeastern interview. A few foreign news services did make the effort. See Marwaan Macan-Markar, "Town and Country Divide Runs Deep," 11 Jan. 2009, available at: http://ipsnews.net/news.asp?idnews = 45368 /accessed 16 Jan. 2009], and Seth Mydans, "In Thai Protests, a Divide Between Urban and Rural," *New York Times,* 12 Oct. 2008, available at: http://www.nytimes.com/2008/10/13/world/asia/13thai.html?_r = 1&ref = world&oref.

3 Michael Kelly Connors, *Democracy and National Identity in Thailand* (London and New York: Routledge/Curzon, 2003), pp. 25–26, 147. Connors defines democrasubjection or "people in democratic subjection," as "the potentially oppressive dimension of democracy, the never-succeeding project of subjecting people to new institutional and ideological forms of power in the construction of democratic subjects" (p. 22). The importance of Connors' work cannot be over-stressed for, without this longitudinal study, we cannot hope to understand the utter comprehensiveness of the state's and other political forces in constructing a system of utter and relentless subjection of Thai people. This chapter owes both much of its structure and content to this work.

4 Thongchai Winichakul, "Toppling Democracy," *Journal of Contemporary Asia* 38(1) (Feb. 2008), pp. 25–27; Chang Noi (pseud.), "The Facts About Vote-Buying and the Patronage System," *Nation*, 1 Sept. 2008, and "The Monarchy, Democracy, and the Politics of Polarization," *Nation*, 24 Nov. 2008.

5 Thailand, Government, "Phraratchakamnot laksana min pramat duai kanphut ru khian thoi kham thet ok khotsanakan rattanakosin sok 118" [Royal Edict on Defamation through False Spoken or Written Words Made Known of the Year 1900], p. 16.

6 Loos dates this to 1894, when other possible candidates to approximate "public"—*ratsadom* ("people," "multitude," "citizenry" but also "a king's subjects"), *prachumchon* ("the people"), *mahachon* ("the masses"), *khon thang lai* ("all the people") arose; the king chose *satharanachon* ("the public people"). Tamara Loos, "Gender Adjudicated: Translating Modern Legal Subjects in Siam," PhD dissertation, Cornell University, Ithaca, NY, 1999, p. 79. That the king should coin the word that, in its adjectival form, is used in the term, "public sphere," may seem odd. Jackson explains that the term has a very different thrust than the Western term *public*, and "can be understood to denote the collectivity of the populace as it had been mobilized to perform 'civilization' in the new domain of 'public space' "Peter A. Jackson, "The Performative State: Semi-coloniality and the Tyranny of Images in Modern Thailand," *Sojourn* 19(2) (2004): 248. Also, see McFarland, *Thai-English Dictionary*, p. 712.

7 Thailand, Government, "Phraratchakamnot laksana min pramat" [Royal Edict on Defamation], p. 140.

8 Thailand, Supreme Court, Supreme Court Decision 445/2462 [1919] 3 th. s. 272, *PKSD 2462*, pp. 272–77.

9 Thailand, Supreme Court, Supreme Court Decision 586/2462 [1919], *PKSD 2462*, pp. 368–72.

10 Thailand, Supreme Court, Supreme Court Decision 4/2477 [1934], *PKSD 2477*, pp. 20–26.

11 "People Overcrowd to Listen to Hearing in Trial of Rebellion Case, Prosecution Witness on the Contents of Kukrit Writing, Sounds as if Warning to Government to Stop Being Enemy of the People, To Not Have Protest Marches, To Beware of Communists," *Sayam Rat*, 19 May 2500 [1957].

12 "Cross-Examination of Prosecution Witness in Revolt Case in Afternoon," *Sayam Rat*, 21 May 2500 [1957].

13 Naeow ruam nak kotmai phua prachachon, klum naksuksa kotmai klum mai, *Rai la-iat khadi prawatisat min phraboromdetchanuphap "Thung chao fa jak kha chao din"* [Details of the Historic *Lèse-majesté* Case, "From the People of the Sky to the Slaves of the Land"] (Krungthep: Naeow ruam nak kotmai phua prachachon, 2518 [1975]), pp. 31–107.

14 Akiko Iijima, "The 'International Court' System," p. 46. I thank Justin McDaniel for bringing this article to my attention and providing me a copy of it.

15 Connors' entire book concerns this question of "the people." For an incomparable discussion of the pre- and early post-revolution period, see Chapter 3, pp. 34–59. Attachak also provides an excellent analysis of how the idea of "The Third Hand" is based on the idea that the common person is unable to initiate or sustain a movement; therefore a "third hand" has entered to manipulate the people. See Attachak, *Mu thi sam [The Third Hand]*, particularly on how the concept changed since 1958, pp. 237–88.

16 Thailand, Juridical Council, Newspaper clipping, "The Press Act Bill," n.d., in, "Press 1932–1934," Vol. 134/3.

17 Thailand, Juridical Council, Newspaper clipping, "The Assembly / The Press Act Discussed," n.d., in, in, "Press 1932–1934," Vol. 134/3.

18 Peter Vandergeest, "Constructing Thailand: Regulation, Everyday Resistance, and

Citizenship," *Comparative Studies of Society and History* 35(1) (1993): 136–37, 141.

19 Ibid., pp. 145–46. I have altered Vandergeest's transliteration system slightly in the selection.

20 "People Listen," *Sayam Rat*, 28 May 2500 [1957].

21 This case was eventually dismissed because the court did not feel that the witnesses testifying on behalf of the prosecution had proven that the offending words had caused them to feel rebelliousness toward the government.

22 Connors uses this to describe efforts by the Thai state to fashion a national identify based on Thainess, centered on the king, as a kind of nexus between the nation and "the Thai self." See Connors, *Democracy and National Identity in Thailand*, p. 167.

23 Chris Baker and Pasuk Phongpaichit, *A History of Thailand* (Cambridge: Cambridge University Press, 2005), p. 180. An unnamed Supreme Court judge interviewed for this book confirmed that, in the 1970s, the royal sash, once rarely given out, became common among the elite.

24 Thak Chaloemtiarana, *Thailand: The Politics of Despotic Paternalism* (Chiang Mai: Silkworm Books, 2007), pp. 111–34.

25 Bhumibol Adulyadej, King, *Collection of Royal Addresses and Speeches during the State and Official Visits of Their Majesties the King and Queen to Foreign Countries 1959–1967 (B.E. 2502–2510)* (Bangkok, 1974), p. 75, as quoted in, Kevin Hewison, "The Monarchy and Democratisation," in Kevin Hewison, ed. *Political Change in Thailand: democracy and participation* (London: Routledge, 1997), p. 64.

26 Katherine A. Bowie, *Rituals of National Loyalty: An Anthropology of the State and the Village Scout Movement in Thailand* (New York: Columbia University Press, 1997), pp. 282–83.

27 Paul Handley, *The King Never Smiles* (New Haven, CT: Yale University Press, 2006), p. 433. The term "dhammocracy" either originated with or was popularized by the prominent monk, Buddhadasa. See Peter A. Jackson, *Buddhadasa: Theravada Buddhism and Modernist Reform in Thailand* (Chiang Mai: Silkworm Books, 2003), p. 228. See also Koson Srisang "Dhammocracy in Thailand: a study in social ethics as a hermeneutic of Dhamma," 1973, PhD dissertation, University of Chicago. Kobkua suggests that the essence of this model was actually conceived and effectively implemented during the Sarit regime, under the urging of its ideological architect, Luang Wichit Watakan. She wrote,

> Sarit quickly introduced a new political system and ideology which he claimed was rooted in Thai culture, Thai social and traditional values, and the teachings of Buddhism. The new system was known as Thai Buddhist democracy; later given the more popular name, the *paw khun* style of government of despotic paternalism
>
> (ibid., p. 9)

See Suwannatha-Pian, *King, Country and Constitutions*, pp. 9–15, 20–22.

28 Connors, *Democracy and National Identity in Thailand*, p. 136.

29 Handley, *The King Never Smiles*, p. 269.

30 Ibid., p. 269.

31 Office of His Majesty's Principal Private Secretary, *A Memoir of His Majesty King Bhumibol Adulyadej* (Bangkok: Office of His Majesty's Principal Private Secretary, 1987), p. 52, quoted in, Hewison, "The Monarchy and Democratisation," p. 61.

32 Connors, *Democracy and National Identity in Thailand*, p. 133. A detailed description of the responsibilities of the Special Brach police as of the early 1980s is in

Anusaun 80 pi rong rian nai roi tamruat [80th Anniversary of the Royal Police Cadet Academy] (Krungthep: Rongphim Aksaun Samai, n.d.).

33 In this case, Wira Musikapong's alleged implication that the royalty did not work hard was in contrast to the official representation of the king and explained, in part, why the government so avidly pursued his case.

34 Handley, *The King Never Smiles*, p. 278.

35 Ibid., p. 289.

36 Hewison, "The Monarchy and Democratisation," p. 67.

37 Handley, *The King Never Smiles*, pp. 269–70.

38 Gray, "Hegemonic Images," p. 60.

39 Thailand, Supreme Court, Supreme Court Decision 607/2480 [1937], *PKSD 2480*, pp. 691–95. In this case, the defendant said to the mother of the plaintiff, "Be good and careful, Older Sister Ram. Your daughter's tummy's gonna [*sic*], provide Thai) get big." The court ruled that the words had an "inner meaning": that the defendant had lovers. Otherwise, the court asked itself, how else could she get a big tummy except through pregnancy? The court judged that with "words of this type, average individuals in general would well understand their meaning." It was not necessary to seek out some special meaning. In a note following the decision, a judge in the case opined that the principle used here was that, "if the words have an ordinary meaning" and there is no use of some "special slang or idiom," then the court is capable of interpreting the words for itself. Statements such as, "that lawyer cheats his clients" or "that woman has so many lovers she's going to get pregnant," the court "can interpret for itself like an ordinary person on whether the meaning is slanderous."

40 Although the present Thai law does not include the phrasing "to cause people to look down upon or hate such person," there is no reason to believe that it its principles deviate from those of other defamation-based laws. Scholars such as Jitti have emphasized the similarity of these laws.

41 The Criminal Procedure Code stipulates that expert testimony is admissible in court by

> Any person having, by profession or otherwise, expert knowledge on any subject such as science, art, work of skill, commerce, medicine or foreign law, and whose opinion may be of value for the adjudication of a case may . . . be a witness in matters such as the examination of the body or mind of the *injured person*, alleged offender or accused.
>
> (my emphasis)

An interesting question is who exactly is an expert in terms of *lèse-majesté*, especially when the identity of "the injured person" is not clearly defined. Is it the institution of the monarchy? The person of the king? The state? See, Boonruam Thiamjan, comp., *Pramuang kotmai withi phijarana khwam aya* [The Criminal Prcedure Code Up Date 2005–8] (Krungthep (?): Sutra Paisal Law Media, n.d.), p. 144.

42 Naeow ruam nak kotmai phua prachachon, *Rai la-iat khadi prawatisat min phraboromdetchanuphap*, pp. 35–36. See also David Streckfuss, "Kings in the Age of Nations—The Paradox of *Lèse-Majesté* as Political Crime in Thailand," *Comparative Studies in Society and History* 37(3) (July 1995), pp. 458 and 460.

43 Naeow ruam nak kotmai phua prachachon, *Rai la-iat khadi prawatisat min phraboromdetchanuphap*, pp. 31–107.

44 Thailand, Supreme Court, Supreme Court Decision 861/2521 [1978], *PKSD 2521*, pp. 1327–35.

45 Ibid., pp. 1329–30. His editor was sentenced to one year for *lèse-majesté* and two months for violation of the Printing Act.

46 For an in-depth analysis of Wira's case, see Streckfuss, "Kings in the Age of Nations," pp. 449–52, 454–57, 459.
47 *Bangkok Post*, 23 Aug. and 3 Sept. 1990; *Nation*, 24 Aug. 1990.
48 This class of person would figure as "Meritorious Persons" or "Persons of Virtue." See Chapter 6.
49 Thailand, Supreme Court, Supreme Court Decision 861/2521 [1978], *PKSD 2521*, p. 1335.
50 Somchai Jenchaijittarawanit, *Khadi prawatisat min phraboromdetchanuphap*, pp. 73–74, 128, 154, 187–91; Thailand, Supreme Court, Supreme Court Decision 2354/2531 [1988], *PKSD 2531*.
51 The same Veera who provided the probing and rational editorial on defamation cited at the beginning of this chapter now appears to applaud the *lèse-majesté* law. He claims that the *lèse-majesté* law "was crafted by our legal minds more than five decades ago" to protect the "monarchy." For Veera, the problem is in the uneven way police use the law. The police should have acted against Daranee immediately rather than waiting for a "push" from the army. Jakrapob's case would not have been acted upon had it not been for "the Democrats who got wind of this and cried foul against the police." He concludes that the police will not be able to do a better job until "a stop is put to political interference." *Bangkok Post*, July 25, 2008.
52 In his observations of the Thai political scene over the last number of decades, Klausner has noted that at various times the following entities make claim to being "the people's representatives": the military, university students, communist insurgents, members of parliament, and nongovernmental organizations (NGOs). See William J. Klausner, "The NGOs in Crisis: Danger and Opportunity," *Thai Culture in Transition* (Bangkok: The Siam Society, 2002), pp. 169–70.
53 Connors, *Democracy and National Identity in Thailand*, p. 147.

10 Culture and traitor

1 Thailand, Supreme Court, Supreme Court Decision 751–52/2478 [1935] 19 th. s. 1322, *PKSD 2478*, pp. 1322–27.
2 A more detailed description of the case can be found in David Streckfuss, "Culture and Murder," in *Santi Pracha Dhamma: Essays in Honour of the Late Puey Ungphakorn* (Bangkok: Santi Pracha Dhamma Institute, The Sathirakoses-Nagapradipa Foundation, and The Foundation for Children, 2001), pp. 205–19. Also Christine Gray, "Thailand: The Soteriological State in the 1970s," Ph.D. dissertation, the University of Chicago, 1986, pp. 406–10, and Maurizio Peleggi, *Thailand: The Worldly Kingdom* (London: Reaktion Books, 2007), pp. 112, 228.
3 Thailand, Supreme Court, Supreme Court Decision 445/2462 [1919] 3 th. s. 272, *PKSD 2462*, pp. 272–77; Thailand, Military Court of Bangkok (San thahan krungthep), "Khamphiphaksa, Khadi dam thi 277 k./2507, Khadi daeng thi 192 k./2509, 30 singhakhom 2509" [Decision, Black Case No. 277 k./1964, Red Case No. 192 k./1966, Military Court of Bangkok, 30 Aug. 1966], in Thai Noi, "Kabot phra phimontham pi 2509" [Phra Phimontham Revolt of 1966], in *25 Khadi kabot* [25 Cases of Rebellion] (Krungthep: Rongphim ratthana kanphim, 2513 [1970]), pp. 418–21.
4 *Phra* Phimontham (Asopmahathen), *Phajon man: banthuk chiwit 5 pi nai hong khang* [Confronting the Devil: Diary of Five Years of Incarceration] (Krungthep: Samnakngan klang kawng kan wipasanathura, Khana 5 Wat Mahathat, 2530), pp. 11–15; Thai Noi, *25 Khadi kabot*, pp. 442–43, 485–86.
5 George McFarland, *Thai-English Dictionary*, p. 993.
6 Thailand, Supreme Court, Supreme Court Decision 445/2462 [1919], 3 th. s. 272, *PKSD 2462*, pp. 272–77; Thai Noi, *25 Khadi kabot*, p. 486.

7 Once freed, *Phra* Phimontham re-ordained and, within a decade, recovered many of the titles due to him. However, he was nonetheless still deeply distrusted by the palace for his progressive views. See Paul Handley, *The King Never Smiles* (New Haven, CT: Yale University Press, 2006), pp. 286–87.

8 Michael Connors, *Democracy and National Identity in Thailand* (London and New York: RoutledgeCurzon, 2003), pp. 42–43.

9 Eric Hobsbawm, "Introduction: Inventing Traditions," in Eric Hobsbawm and Terence Ranger, eds., *The Invention of Tradition* (Cambridge: Cambridge University Press, 1986).

10 See Streckfuss, "Culture and Murder," for more details.

11 Thailand, Juridical Council, Letter from the Secretary-General of the Cabinet of Ministers to the Secretary-General of the Juridical Council, secret–very urgent [*lap – duan mak*], No. 802/2495 of 18 Jan. 2495 [1952], Subject: Anti-Communist Law, and "Note, Subject: Anti-Communist Law," n.d., in Thailand, Juridical Council, "Kotmai pongkan khommiewnit," in *Ruang set* [Finished Matters], Vol. 452.

12 Thailand, Juridical Council, "Draft Act on Control of Subversive Activities (Preliminary Draft)," 18 Jan. 2495 [1952], in "Kotmai pongkan khommiewnit," in *Ruang set* [Finished Matters], Vol. 452.

A 18 February 1952 draft shows a slight variation:

In this Act:

> "Activities endangering the nation" means any act, words, writings or printed matter by which any person or body of persons advocates or exhorts:
>
> a) to suppress forcibly the rights and liberties of the subject as provided in the Constitution; or
> b) to impose the dictatorship of a party which has forcibly conquered power and to deprive all the other parties of political rights and of the constitutional exercise of the democratic and parliamentary institutions; or
> c) to bring about transformations of the economic institutions of the country, by which private ownership and means of production shall be transferred to the State by way of confiscation or other process devoid of just compensation; or
> d) to compel by terrorism, fear, sabotage, or any means whatever, people to adhere to, help or support in any manner activities purporting to realize or to maintain the objects here above specified in a, b, and c.
> e) to make propaganda in order to encourage people to adhere to, help or support in any manner activities purporting to realize or to maintain the object specified in a, b, and c.

13 Thailand, Juridical Council, Letter 11738/2495 *lap chapho* [confidential] from President of Cabinet of Ministers to the Secretary-General of the Juridical Council concerning letter n. 631/2495 of 13/03/95 proposing a draft of control of subversive acts act [ph.r.b. pongkan kankratham an pen phai to chat], 5 Sept. 2495 [1952], and "Draft submitted by Nai Yut," n.d., in Thailand, Juridical Council, "Kotmai pongkan khommiewnit," in *Ruang set* [Finished Matters], Vol. 452. From the order of the documents in this volume and from discussions at the Juridical Council, I estimate that this draft was submitted to the council sometime between 5 September and 9 October.

14 Thailand, Juridical Council, Juridical Council Committee, Meeting No. 61/2495, 14 Oct. 2495 [1952], "Agenda: Law preventing Communism," in "Kotmai pongkan khommiewnit," in *Ruang set* [Finished Matters], Vol. 452.

15 Thailand, Juridical Council, "P.B.," [Phichan Bunlayong], "Definition of Communism," 20 Oct. 2495 [1952], in "Kotmai paungkan khommiewnit," in *Ruang set* [Finished Matters], Vol. 452.

16 Thailand, Juridical Council, Handwritten copy of act, countersigned by Phibun Songkhram, n.d., in "Kotmai pongkan khommiewnit," in *Ruang set* [Finished Matters], Vol. 452.

17 Thailand, Office of the National Culture Commission, *Organizational Structure, Office of the National Culture Commission, Ministry of Education, Thailand* (Bangkok: United Production Press, n.d.), p. 2.

18 *International Translation Law Directory*, pp. 602–5.

19 Ibid., pp. 618–19.

20 Thailand, Government, "Phraratchabanyat pongkan kankratham," in *PKPS*, Vol. 65, pp. 365–67.

21 Thailand, Government, *Phraratchabanyat pongkan kankratham an pen khommiewnit ph.s. 2495* [Act on Prevention of Communist Activities of 1952] (Krungthep: Sut phaisan, 2533). Here I translate *khanop prapheni* as "traditions and customs," *chon chat thai* as "Thai race," and *latthi thi mi lakkan ru kanpatibat pen kan tham hai* as "doctrine which has principles and practices."

22 Of course, the law was not drafted to invite analysis. But if analysed, the framework collapses almost immediately. Under the law, could a doctor advocating modern medicines over traditional herbal ones conceivably be charged as a communist? Or, any competent philosophy instructor questioning the mythical beliefs of a religion? Would someone making the case that under "Thai traditons and customs," "collectively owned property" was probably the best way of describing the traditional system of land tenure of the Thai people be charged? Or the law itself?

23 Thailand, Government, *Phraratchabanyat pongkan kankratham an pen khommiewnit ph.s. 2495* [Act on Prevention of Communist Activities of 1952].

24 Thailand, Military Court of Bangkok prosecutors (aiyakan san thahan Krungthep), "*Fong*" [Charge Sheet], *Khadi prawattisat khadi 6 tula* [The Historic 6 October Case] (Krungthep: Baphit kanphim, 2521 [1978]), pp. 68–70.

25 Wichit was Secretary-General of the National Security Council from 1959 to 1961. Available at: http://www.nsc.go.th/index.php?option = com_content&task = view&id = 13&Itemid = 28, accessed 22 June 2009.

26 This point is clear in Thak Chaloemtiarana's excellent, enduring study of the Sarit, *Thailand: The Politics of Despotic Paternalism* (Chiang Mai: Silkworm Books, 2007). See especially Chapter 4, pp. 172–220.

27 The list goes on: national finances, the Ministry of Cooperatives, issues of land, the Ministry of Justice, the courts, the Ministry of Finance, foreign relations, the military, the police, youth, engineering, political parties, budget setting, water, munitions factories, society, crime, the digging of a canal across the Kra Isthmus, the student movement, land reform, royal projects, rural populations, drug addiction, the monarchy, popular values, education, the civil administration of Bangkok, research in technology, religion, order, social work, the United Nations, technological transfers, the role of universities, the king's mother's work, informal education, secondary education, public health in industrial factories, agricultural development, the political system, political development, economic wrongdoing, quality of life, commercial banks, and villages.

28 In fulfilling its task of defining Thai identity, the board declared Thai identity to be: (1) territory; (2) people; (3) independence and sovereignty; (4) religion; (5) monarchy; (6) government and administration; (7) culture; and (8) pride. However, the idea of Thai as a unique people began in the early twentieth century. In the 1920s, Prince Damrong Raanuphap—it is certainly no coincidence that he served as the kingdom's first minister of interior and minister of education—"had

already worked out the "characteristics of the Thai race [*uppanisai khong chonchat thai*] as, 'love of national independence, toleration, and power of assimilation.'" See, Craig J. Reynolds, "Introduction: National Identity and Its Defenders," in Craig J. Reynolds, ed., *National Identity and Its Defenders: Thailand, 1939–1989*, Monash Papers on Southeast Asia No. 25 (Clayton, Victoria: Centre of Southeast Asian Studies, Monash University, 1991), pp. 13–17. For an excellent treatment of the role of the National Identity Board, see Chapter 7, "With Compliments of the National Identity Office," in Niels Mulder, *Thai Images: The Culture of the Public World* (Chiang Mai: Silkworm Books, 1997), pp. 283–306.

29 Handley, *The King Never Smiles*, p. 269.

30 Connors, *Democracy and National Identity in Thailand*, pp. 18, 129.

31 The booklet is undated, but the commission was set up in 1979. Thailand, Office of the National Culture Commission, *Organizational Structure*, pp. 1–3.

32 "Phraratchabanyat samnakngan khana kammakan watthanatham haeng chat ph.s. 2522" [Office of the National Culture Commission Act of 1979], in *Phraratchabanyat watthanatham haeng chat ph.s. 2485* [National Culture Act of 1942] (Krungthep: Sut phaisan, 2532 [1989], p. 10.

33 Ibid., pp. 4, 12.

34 Ibid., pp. 15–16.

35 "Announcement of the Prime Minister's Office on National Culture Policy," 22 Nov. 1981, in ibid., pp. 32–33.

36 "Naew than nai kan raksa songsoem lae phatthana watthanatham ph.s. 2529 tam nayobai watthanatham haeng chat" [Guidelines in the Maintenance, Promotion, and Development of Culture of 1984 according to the National Culture Policies], in *Phraratchabanyat watthanatham*, pp. 54–60.

37 Prasong Soonsiri, "Phasa thai kap khwam mankhong haeng chat" [Thai language and national security], in Samnakngan soemsang ekkalak khong chat, samnak lekhathikan nayok ratthamontri [Office of National Identity Promotion, Secretariat of the Prime Minister], *Rai-ngan Phon Kan Sammana "Phasa thai kap sangkhom thai"* [Report of the Seminar, "Thai Language and Thai Society"], jat phim phoeiphrae ph.s. 2527 nuang nai kanchaloem 700 pi lai su thai [Published for Distribution in 1984 in the Celebration of 700 years of the Thai Script] (Krungthep[?]: Samnakphim prakaiphruk, 2527 [1984]), pp. 245–51.

38 Ekkawit na Thalang, "Ekkalak thai thi mi to kan raksa khwam mankhong haeng chat" [Thai Identity in Terms of Maintaining National Security], in Kamphon Klaewthanong, ed., Khana anukammakan udomkan khong chat nai khana kammakan ekkalak khong chat, samnak lekhathikan nayok ratthamontri [Subcommittee on National Ideology within the National Identity Board, Office of the Prime Minister], *Kan sammana ruang ekkalak khong chat kap kanphatthana chat thai* [Seminar on National Identity and Thai National Development] (Krungthep: Wiktoeri phaowoepoi, 2528 [1985]), pp. 120–31.

39 It should also be noted that in the competition over the Preah Vihear temple, the Thai government's initial approach in presenting its case to the judges of the World Court was to claim that the court did not have jurisdiction to hear the case, a sign of perceived exceptionalism, as will be discussed in the next chapter. Ronald Bruce St John, "Preah Vihear and the Cambodia-Thailand Borderland," available at: http://www.dur.ac.uk/resources/ibru/publications/full/bsb1–4_john.pdf, accessed 23 June 2009.

40 Thongchai Winichakul, *Siam Mapped: A History of the Geo-body of a Nation* (Chiang Mai: University of Hawaii Press/Silkworm Books, 1994), p. 167.

41 Anan Lao-lertworakul, "Decipher a Secret Code," p. 6.

11 Thai-ification and colonization

1 *Nation*, Dec. 29, 1997. This scoop was scored by *Thai Rath* newspaper, see 28 Dec. 1997.

2 Benedict R. O'G. Anderson, "Studies of the Thai State: The State of Thai Studies," in, Eliezer B. Ayal (ed.), *The Study of Thailand* (Athens, OH: Ohio Center for International Studies, Southeast Asia Program, 1978), particularly pp. 197–99; Thongchai Winichakul, "Siam's Colonial Conditions and the Birth of Thai History," paper presented at the conference, "Unraveling the Myths of Southeast Asian History," 24–26 Nov. 2006; Thongchai Winichakul, "The Others Within: Travel and Ethno-Spatial Differentiation of Siamese Subjects 1883–1910," in Andrew Turton, ed., *Civility and Savagery: Social Identity in Tai States* (Richmond, Surrey: Curzon, 2000), pp. 38–62.

3 An interesting variation of this schema is described by Article 301 of the Turkish penal code (Chapter 1). Turkish citizens are forbidden to express anything that "publicly denigrates Turkishness, the Republic or the Grand National Assembly of Turkey" (6 months to three years' imprisonment), or "the Government of the Republic of Turkey, the judicial institutions of the State, the military or security organizations" (6 months to 2 years' imprisonment). The law does not seem to cover non-Turkish citizens. Yet Noam Chomsky has been charged, as would any "Turkish citizen in another country" who denigrates Turkishness, with punishment (for some reason) increased by one third. Amnesty International Public Statement, "Turkey: Article 301 Is A Threat to Freedom of Expression and Must Be Repealed Now!," Dec. 1, 2005. Available at: http://www.amnestyusa.org/ document.php?lang = e&id = ENGEUR440352005, accessed 8 Mar. 2009.

4 See, for instance, when a newspaper reporter claimed the naming of a dinosaur discovered in present-day Thailand's Northeast "suggests the dinosaur's Thai heritage," *Nation*, 10 Nov. 2008.

5 Thak Chaloemtiarana, *Thailand: The Politics of Despotic Paternalism* (Chiang Mai: Silkworm Books, 2007), pp. 100–04. As Patrick Jory indicates, this "culturalist" conception had been floating around royalist circles since at least the mid-1940s. See Jory, "Historiography in Thailand from 1945 to the Present," forthcoming.

6 The king does not explicitly say that his favorite dog, Tongdaeng, is "Thai." In fact, he links Tongdaeng to an ancient race of African dogs. But he does highlight valued traits of "Thainess" found in Tongdaeng: loyalty, gratefulness, good manners, humility, and so on. See Bhumibol Adulyadej, King, *The Story of Thongdaeng* (Bangkok: Amarin Printing and Publishing, 2002).

7 Thongchai, "The Others Within," pp. 38–62.

8 Stanley Tambiah, *World Conqueror and World Renouncer* (Cambridge, MA: Cambridge University Press, 1976), pp. 208–18, 226–27, 236, 405–6.

9 Quoted in Kullada Kesboonchoo-Mead, *The Rise and Decline of Thai Absolutism* (London and New York: RoutledgeCurzon, 2004), p. 139.

10 Chris Baker and Pasuk Phongpaichit, *A History of Thailand* (Cambridge: Cambridge University Press, 2005), pp. 135–36.

11 Quoted in ibid, p. 177.

12 Ishii, *Sangha, State, and Society* (Honolulu: Hawaii University Press, 1986), pp. 136–42.

13 Duncan McCargo, "Buddhism, Democracy, and Identity in Thailand," *Democratization* 11(4) (Aug. 2004): 156, 160–61.

14 Tambiah, *World Conqueror and World Renouncer*, pp. 212–14.

15 See, for instance, Buddhadasa's description of psychology:

> Then there is Buddhism as Psychology . . . where the nature of the mind is described in remarkable detail. Buddhist psychology is a source of interest and astonishment to students of the mind even in the present day. It is far more detailed and profound than present day psychological knowledge.
>
> (Buddhadasa Bhikkhu, *Handbook for Mankind*, pp. 20–21)

16 Prayudh goes on to quote a former justice of the Supreme Court of Burma: "In the case of Buddhism . . . all the modern scientific concepts have been present from the beginning. There is no principle of science, from biological evolution to the General Theory of Relativity, that runs counter to any teaching of Gotama Buddha;" Donald Swearer of Swathmore College says:

> There are at least three principal ways in which the assertion of the scientific nature of Buddhism is presented: Buddhism is more scientific than other religions, . . . (viz., Christianity); there is a general agreement between the approach or method of Buddhism and science; and, science proves or validates particular Buddhist teachings such as the doctrines of rebirth (saṃsara) and impermanence (anicca).
>
> (Donald K. Swearer, *Buddhism in Transition* (Philadelphia: The Westminster Press, 1970), p. 70, as quoted in Phra Rajavaramuni (Prayudh Payutto), *Thai Buddhism in the Buddhist World: A Survey of the Buddhist Situation against a Historical Background* (Bangkok: Unity Progress Co., 1984), p. 136)

My intent here is not to debate the scientific nature of Buddhism. It is to examine the degree to which certain followers of Thai Buddhism make claims to "the truth" through highlighting the compatibility of Buddhism and science.

17 Dr. Chairong Brahmawong and his research team set out in 1998 "to present the findings proving that Buddhism [*sic*] was never originated in India." The banner of this group's website announces "BUDDHA BIRTHPLACE IN THAILAND; NOT IN INDIA OR NEPAL." Visitors can read the "Summary of Research Study / The Birthplace of the Lord Buddha Found to be in Thailand: Not in India or Nepal," and then vote on whether "Lord Buddha's birthplace should be in Thailand." Of the 1,600 who have voted, 62 percent are "highly convinced" or "convinced." Chairong and team admit some resistance to the idea among some Thai who have asked "Why don't you pay more attention to practice the teaching of Buddha rather than trying to prove Buddha was not born in India? Is it so significant to find out the truth on his authentic birthplace?" The response: "We, the research team, believe it is a very significant to reveal the truth on our Great Teacher. Nothing is wrong if you don't agree but it's our duties as Buddhists to find out the truth. Less than two hundred years ago, Lord Buddha and all his disciples had been the natives of this great land." Available at: http://www.life-alonguniversity.com/buddhabirthplace/pdf/budhasumeng.pdf, accessed 22 June 2009; Available at: http://www.life-alonguniversity.com/buddhabirthplace/eng/index.htm, accessed 22 June 2009.

18 *Nation*, 3, 4, 6, and 10 July 1993; *Bangkok Post*, 13 July 1993. I thank Douglas A. Bloch for providing the newspaper clippings on this story, mentioned in his "Constructing Conundrums: Pretenses of Sexuality in Contemporary Thai Society," unpublished manuscript, University of Washington, Oct. 1995.

19 *Bangkok Post*, 4 July 1993. Although I have not come to any secure conclusions, there seems enough evidence that the historical record will show that the Democrat Party in Thailand has been the primary advocate of defamation-based

accusations and the principal receiver of the benefits of such advocacy. While Thaksin is the undisputed leader in initiating personal defamation suits, the Democrats have often been behind the kind of defamation action in this example (the current Democrat leader, Abhisit Vejjajiva, "cut his political teeth" in the Longman incident), have showed little compunction in using personal defamation charges against citizens, and at the time of writing of this book have threatened to expand the penalty for *lese-majesté* to unprecedented heights (Chapters 1, 8, 13).

20 It is unclear from this statement exactly with whom Abhisit socialized, for it did not seem to include any of the hundreds of thousands of British males coming to Thailand annually, most of whom, it can be assumed, were aware of Bangkok's reputation.

21 *Nation*, 7 July 1993.

22 Ibid.

23 *Nation*, 7 July 1993; *Bangkok Post*, 4 and 7 July 1993.

24 Then Prime Minister Chuan Leekpai went on to say, off the point, that this "case should serve as a lesson to some local private organizations, and the media for the accuracy of information on Thailand they feed to foreigners," *Nation*, 7 July 1993. Chuan seemed to subscribe to the notion that the cause of so many commercial sex workers in Thailand was incorrect information getting to the outside world, rather than a legacy, often with government support, of a decades-long industry in Thailand.

25 From the flurry of articles, letters to the editor, and editorials, that the Longman incident might have actually stirred up some healthy public debate on the issues of sexuality, the causes of commercial sex, the rights of commercial sex workers, and so on. See, for instance, *Nation*, 1, 7, 8, 10, 15, 18, and 30 July 1993; *Bangkok Post*, 11 and 27 July 1993.

26 The editorial was written under the pseudonym, "Dr. M." See *Nation*, 25 July 1993.

27 *Matichon*, 8 Sept. 1978.

28 Thailand, Supreme Court, Supreme Court Decision 4/2477 [1934], *PKSD 2477*, pp. 20–26.

29 The first article, "In spite of our good will," made passing disparaging remarks about Thailand, but nothing specific. The harshest item might have been the observation by the writer while on a study tour in Thailand about the poor level of English in the host nation. She says her Thai hosts "remarked that [Thai did not speak English well] because our country had been a colony under the British. The remark was made more than once. Civilized people should pretend not to notice such weaknesses instead of making remarks." Ma Tin Win, "In Spite of Our Good Will," *The New Light of Myanmar*, 19 May 2001. Available at: http://www.myanmar.gov.mm/Article/Article2001/May/May19.html, accessed 10 June 2009.

30 Ma Tin Win, "How Did Opium Arrive at the Golden Triangle Region?," *The New Light of Myanmar*, 20 May 2001. Available at: http://www.myanmar.gov.mm/Article/Article2001/May/May20.html, accessed 10 June 2009.

31 Ma Tin Win, "Never Been Enslaved, but Real Slave," *The New Light of Myanmar*, 21 May 2001. Available at: http://www.myanmar.gov.mm/Article/Article2001/May/May21.html, accessed 10 June 2009.

32 Thailand, Ministry of Foreign Affairs, "Aide Memoire," 24 May 2001. Available at: http://www.mfa.go.th/web/200.php?id = 530, accessed 10 June 2009.

33 *Nation*, 25 May 2001. The "intolerable *lèse-majesté* elements" are hard to pinpoint. The law does not explicitly suggest that past kings are covered by the law. In this case, even if King Mongkut's legacy were protected, it might have been hard to prosecute, given that such sentiments are generally available in academic literature. However, the crux of the matter, what was truly intolerable, were suggestions

that the royalist-nationalist myth of concerning colonialism might not be true. See Chapter 13.

34 For a placement of the Anna story within the context of the monarchy in Thailand, see Patrick Jory, "The King and Us," *International Journal of Cultural Studies* 4:2 (2001), pp. 201–18.

35 Ibid., pp. 202–3.

36 One foreign historian of Thailand, John Bloefeld, described Mongkut as "one of the most talented and learned men Asia has ever produced and one of the most likeable characters in history," while describing Anna as "perfidious and mendacious." John Bloefeld, *Maha Mongkut of Siam* (Singapore: Asia Pacific Press, 1972), as quoted in Jory, "The King and Us," p. 205.

37 "Thai ban thwarts Chow Yun-Fat film plan," *South China Morning Post*, 24 Oct. 1998. Available at: http://www.geocities.com/Athens/8907/cn_oct98.html, accessed 18 Feb. 2009.

38 "Sanuk Dee," *Time*, 24 Mar. 1947, p. 33. Jory's explanation of the movie's banning in 1998 does not explain why the earlier version was shown. If King Mongkut were so popular and respected, then the 1946 version should not have passed, for many of the mannerisms objectionable in Yul Brenner's characterization were modelled on Rex Harrison's. See Jory, "The King and us," pp. 202–3.

39 NA 0701.9.10.15/1 Kammakan phitjarana phaphayon [2474–2503].

40 NA 0701.9.10.15/2 Kammakan phitjarana phaphayon [2503–6], and "The King and I," 27 July 2508 [1965], in NA 0701.9.10.15/3 Kamkan sapha phitjarana phaphayon [2506–7], also see mention of the issue in National Archives (NA) s.th. 0701.9.10.15/3 Kammakan sapha phitjarana phaphayon [2506–7].

41 The original book by Anna Leonowens was adapted by Margaret Landon to create another book on which the 1947 movie was then based. The musical, *The King and I*, was based then on that movie. The National Archives documents do not explain why the original movie was approved, other than to mention there was no royal opposition to it. But the timing is peculiar. King Rama VII died under mysterious circumstances in 1946 and doubts about who was involved destabilized the government. The coup group that overthrew the government in 1947 claimed the action was necessary to defend the throne. Thus, despite much controversy and anxiety about the monarchy at the time, the movie was still "good fun" and passed the movie board.

42 "The King and I," 27 July 2508 [1965], in Thailand, National Archives, s. th. 0701.9.10.15/3 Kammakan sapha phitjarana phaphayon (2506–7)" [Movie Censorship Council, 1963–64].

43 *Nation*, 29 Nov. 1998.

44 *Bangkok Post*, 7 Jan. 2000.

45 See Hong Lysa, "Does Popular History in Thailand Need Historians?" *Su wattanatham sanai mai rat vs prachachon-chat [Toward a modern culture state vs. the people-nation]* (Krungthep: Sathaban thai khadi suksa, 2547 [2003]) [*warasan thai khadi suksa* 1:2 (Apr.–Sept. 2547)], pp. 38–66; Chang Noi (pseud.), "Bad Neighbours, Woman Warriors, and Paddles," *Nation*, 9 July 2001.

46 The accusation is interesting because in the early 1960s the king *was* perceived as something of a hipster, meeting with Elvis Presley and jamming with Benny Goodman. A story from the *San Jose Mercury* was entitled, "King who's a real cool 'cat' visits IBM," in FCCT, *King of Thailand in World Focus*, p. 62. *San Jose Mercury*, 14 July 1960, p. 62.

47 Available at: http://www.onthemedia.org/yore/transcripts/transcripts_062802_thai.html, accessed 12 June 2008., "Hipster king' ad angers Thais" http://news.bbc.co.uk/2/hi/asia-pacific/2079232.stm, accessed 12 June 2008.; http://asianweek.com/2002_07_12/news_upfront.html, accessed 12 June 2008.; http://findarticles.com/p/articles/mi_m3190/is_29_36/ai_89817003, accessed 12 June 2008.

48 The general also offered the main cause of the coup: the Thaksin government had interfered with military appointments and the military budget. "Armed Forces Need Clear Role in Politics," *Bangkok Post*, 5 Aug. 2007.

49 Many foreign governments refused to recognize the military-installed government. The Ministry of Foreign Affairs was given a substantial budget to rectify the perception, by trying to convince those governments that Thailand was still a democracy.

50 In June 2009, the opposition in government called for the election commissioners to step down, as they had been illegitimately appointed by a coup government. *Bangkok Post*, 5 June 2009.

51 For criticism of the decision, see Pitch Pongsawat, "What Constitutes 'Legal' Changes with the Powers of the Day," *Nation*, 2 June 2007.

52 Pravit Rojanaphruk reported that the independent Poll Watch's chairman, General Saiyud Kerdphon, claimed, from the observations of 4,000 volunteers throughout the country, "that the referendum had the fingerprints of the junta and the military everywhere in trying to direct the vote to go in one direction." Pravit Rojanaphruk, "What Has the Junta Got to Hide?" *Nation*, 3 Sept. 2007

53 There was good reason for concern. The CNS had laid out a confidential plan to use the military to keep up surveillance and thwart efforts to defeat the constitution in the referendum. CNS chairman, Chalit Phukphasu, did admit that Sonthi did "write the confidential order," and the Election Commission found that "the CNS had failed to maintain its neutrality." Chalit said the plan had never been carried out. Rather than discuss the plan and whether it was carried out, military leaders' statements on the issue focused on how the confidential document had been obtained, whether it was authentic, and so on (*Bangkok Post*, 5 Dec. 2007). But more than a month before this issue became public, former CNS chairman Sonthi Boonyaratkalin told the Internal Security Operations Command (ISOC) "to put more efforts into ensuring voters understand democracy so the new lower house would have well qualified representatives" and instructed the Interior ministry to "teach voters to be careful in supporting candidates who would best serve the national interests." Sonthi reportedly "suggested the army and ISOC send troops to positions close to the people all across the country to boost its network of intelligence gathering" (*Bangkok Post*, 16 Oct. 2007). Also see, Chang Noi (pseud.), "A New Cold War Underway in Thailand," *Nation*, 26 Nov. 2007.

54 *Bangkok Post*, 25 Aug. 2007.

55 *Bangkok Post*, 4 Sept. 2007.

56 *Bangkok Post*, 7 Sept. 2007.

57 *Bangkok Post*, 4 Sept. 2007.

58 "European Union Election Monitoring Missions," 6 Sept. 2007. Available at: http://www.deltha.ec.europa.eu/news%202007/EOM%20Statement_6%20Sept_EN.htm, accessed 28 May 2009.

59 *Bangkok Post*, 4 Sept. 2007.

60 *Bangkok Post*, 30 Aug. 2007.

61 Ibid.

62 *Bangkok Post*, 4 Sept. 2007.

63 *Bangkok Post*, 7 Sept. 2007

64 In the end, the Election Commission (EC) voted unanimously not to sign the MoU with the EU, on the ostensible grounds that the EC had never signed a MoU with any foreign election observer body. The EC chairperson quickly added that the decision was "not a sign of resentment or of any intent to close off the country to the outside world." He added that "We're confident that our elections meet international standards. We're not afraid of being monitored. We're glad to welcome the observation by representatives of all countries, including the EU, but the observation must be under Thai law." *Bangkok Post*, 30 Aug. and 12 Sept. 2007.

65 Achara's fine piece points out that whenever the "Powers-that-be" "feel uneasy about a political situation, they play the nationalist card." She calls the response by the authorities over the EU offer "immature." Paraphrasing Gothom Arya, she writes: "Looked at from the outside in, the EU presence can be a positive move for recognition and understanding of the international community in Thailand's post-coup political development." See Achara Ashayagachat, "Quiet Diplomacy Would Have Sufficed," *Bangkok Post*, 4 Sept. 2007. Also see the rational position on the issue in Pravit Rojanaphruk, "What Has the Junta Got to Hide?" *Nation*, 3 Sept. 2007, and "EU monitors Would Boost Credibility of Poll: Anfrel" (Interview with executive director of the Asian Network for Free Elections (Anfrel) Somsri Hananuntasuk), *Nation*, 1 Sept. 2007.

66 *Bangkok Post*, 4 Sept. 2007.

67 *Bangkok Post*, 31 Aug. 2007.

68 *Bangkok Post*, 16 Sept. 2007.

69 Khien Theeravit, "Thailand's 'Coup de Grace' Is Not Lacking in Legitimacy," *Nation*, 18 Oct. 2006; Thitinan Pongsudhirak, "Thailand since the Coup," *Journal of Democracy* 19(4) (Oct. 2008): 140–53; Kasian Tejapira, "Toppling Thaksin," *New Left Review* (May–June 2006), pp. 5–37; Paul Handley, "What the Coup Was Really About," *Asian Sentinel*, 6 Nov. 2006. Available at: www.asiasentinel.com/index.php?option = com_content&task = view&id = 249&Itemid = 31, accessed 27 May 2009; Michael K. Connors and Kevin Hewison, "Introduction: Thailand and the 'Good Coup'," *Journal of Contemporary Asia* 38(1) (Feb. 2008): 1–10; Fah Diew Kan, *Rathaprahan 19 Kanya* [The Coup of 19 September] (Krungthepmahanakhorn: Fah Diew Kan, 2550 [2007]); and Giles Ji Ungpakorn, *A Coup for the Rich: Thailand's Political Crisis* (Bangkok: Workers Democracy Publishing, 2007); "Coup in Review: Year of Army Rule 'Has Failed on Most Fronts'," *Nation*, 17 Sept. 2007.

70 See, for instance, the peculiar way that Thanong juggles the role of the king, necessity, and force:

> The King did not approve of the 1992 coup launched by General Suchinda Kraprayoon, but since the Army had already toppled the government, the King could only go along with the coup because he had no power to stop the military. Without his endorsement, the country would be in anarchy . . . The King did not approve of or support the 2006 coup either. Again, since the Army had toppled the Thaksin government, he had no power to stop the military. He had to endorse the coup to keep the country moving. But this does not mean that the King supported the coup as some anti-monarchists have tried to defame him without any evidence.
>
> (Thanong Khanthong, editor of *Nation*, 6 Mar. 2009)

For my rebuttal, see David Streckfuss, "The Law is the Problem," *Seeds of Peace* 25:2 (May-Aug. 2552 (2009)), pp. 5–6.

Ivarson and Isager noted that, in 1981, King Juan Carlos I of Spain, also in the face of a military coup, chose to respond differently: he "acted swiftly to defend the constitution and denounce the coup. In that situation the king protected democracy," Søren Ivarsson and Lotte Isager, "Speaking the Unspeakable: Thailand's Monarchy and Style of Democracy," draft article, 2009, used with permission of the authors.

71 The 2008 Failed States list placed 177 countries into four categories: alert, warning, moderate, and sustainable. "Failed States list 2008," *Foreign Policy* Available at: http://www.foreignpolicy.com/story/cms.php?story_id = 3865, accessed 23 May 2009. Thailand has consistently been placed in the middle of the "warning" category since 2007.

72 Peter A. Jackson, "The Performative State," *Sojourn* 19(2) (2004): 247.
73 Ibid., pp. 248–49.

12 Defamation and truth

1 Thailand, Supreme Court, Supreme Court Decision 683/2479 [1936], *PKSD 2479*, pp. 840–53.
2 In the 1957 revised code, this privilege was extended to cover the expression of statements (presumably asserting something to be true). Jitti felt this change reflected a coming to understand that a constituent part of expressing an opinion is "citing the facts." As a result, courts were increasingly considering the question of facts in defamation cases. This change seems, at least in part, to separate the historical legal link in Thai law between honest opinion, good intentions, the truth of what was said, and the damage to the plaintiff's reputation. See Jitti Tingsaphat (1975), *Kham athibai kotmai aya* [Explanation of the Criminal Law Code], Section 1143, pp. 2176–80 and pp. 2216, 2227–28, and Jitti Tingsaphat (1989), *Kham athibai kotmai aya* [Explanation of the Criminal Law Code], pp. 2425–26.
3 We have already discussed Nidhi Eoseewong's perspectives on truth within the somewhat different context of historical truth and the shifting "think-world" of the late nineteenth and early twentieth centuries in Siam (Chapters 2 and 3).
4 Annette Hamilton, "Rumours, Foul Calumnies and the Safety of the State: Mass Media and National Identity in Thailand," in Craig J. Reynolds, ed., *National Identity and Its Defenders, Thailand, 1939–1989* (Clayton, Victoria: Centre of Southeast Asian Studies, Monash University, Monash Papers on Southeast Asia No. 25, 1991), p. 345.
5 Ibid., p. 358. McCargo argues that journalistic practices and Thai "objective" reporting have obscured the line between "comment" and "opinion." McCargo writes that newspapers make "a rigid distinction between news (presentation of facts and quotations) and comment (interpretation and discussion of facts and quotations)." "News," within this context, "is narrowly defined as literal descriptions of actual events, plus the statements of people involved." The "formula" for front page new stories is rather exact: It begins with quotes from Party A, followed by quotes, sometimes in response, from Party B, and then topped off with quotes from "academics or well-known public figures not directly involved in the party political fray." In seeming contrast, "comment," in the form of political columns, is made up "almost entirely of opinion, with very little factual material." Strictly forbidden is giving readers "any sort of explanation or background" that might illuminate the issue, the addition of which is considered "tantamount to putting [in] the personal opinions of the writers." Despite the apparent care given to the treatment of fact, the ironic result, McCargo concludes, is that "[a]lmost all political coverage in Thai newspapers" is "composed of opinions"—either a passive recording of opinions outside the newspaper or publishing of opinions inside it. This practice began in the late 1950s when newspapers quoted others making "controversial statements" to avoid being targeted for punishment by the government and of a skewed understanding of "objectivity" drawn from old Western news manuals. Duncan McCargo, *Politics and the Press in Thailand: Media Machinations* (London and New York: Routledge), pp. 33–37, 40–42, 139.
6 Interview, Lt. Col. Samphan Satthaphorn, Deputy-Superintendent of Sub-Division 3 of the Special Branch of the Police Department, Bangkok, 21 Aug. 1991. Samphan spoke authoritatively about the details of each case issued by the office, giving the impression that he had been the press officer for the entire period. The interview was in English and I have smoothed out some of phrasing for readability.
7 Warning order made to *Naew Na* for article appearing 7 Sept. 2527 [1984], as

quoted in, Buppha Changkaew, "Khamsang khana patirup kan pokkhrong phaendin chabap thi 42 kap kankhuapkhum nangsuphim doei ratthaban samai tang tang" [Order No. 42 of the National Administrative Reform Council and Control of the Press by Various Governments], unpublished thesis, Chulalongkorn University, 1991, pp. 180–81; Interview, Samphan Satthaphorn, 21 Aug. 1991. The incident concerned General Athit Kamlang-ek, at that time head of the army. When a coup was attempted in Bangkok while the army chief was in Europe, the newspaper reported that he was finally reached at a brothel.

8 Warning order made to *Naew Na* for article appearing 16 Dec. 2531 [1988], quoted in, Buppha Changkaew, "Khamsang khana patirup," pp. 192–93.

9 Interview, Lt. Col. Samphan Satthaphorn, 21 Aug. 1991.

10 Warning order made to *Phaya Khrut* newspaper for article appearing 21 Mar. 2533 [1990], quoted in Buppha Changkaew, "Khamsang khana patirup," pp. 198–99.

11 Warning order made to *Tawan Sayam* newspaper for article appearing on 1 Oct. 2520 [1977], quoted in Buppha Changkaew, "Khamsang khana patirup," p. 136.

12 "Kham sang khong khana patirup," *Phraratchabanyat kanphim ph.s. 2484*, pp. 48–50. The press officer did not have to specify which part of this clause a given newspaper had violated. It might have been the part about "prophecies." However, as we will see, it might just have well been seen as "false," or "tending to incite or arouse disorder," or all three at once.

13 Warning order made to *Tawan Ok Parithat* newspaper for article appearing 10 Oct. 2520 [1977], quoted in Buppha Changkaew, "Khamsang khana patirup," pp. 136–37.

14 Warning order made to *Khon Num* newspaper for article appearing on 6 Oct. 2521 [1978], quoted in Buppha Changkaew, "Khamsang khana patirup," p. 154.

15 Warning order made to *Naew Na* newspaper for article appearing 29 Nov. 2525 [1982], and to *Sayam Rat Sapda Wijan* for article appearing 14 Jan. 2526 [1983], quoted in Buppha Changkaew, "Khamsang khana patirup," p. 176.

16 I should mention that the story was actually describing something happening: in the 1980s Prem Tinsulanonda did work things out so he could stay on beyond retirement age. Paul Handley, *The King Never Smiles* (New Haven, CT: Yale University Press, 2006), p. 280.

17 Warning order to *Sayam Nikorn* newspaper for article appearing 29 Nov. 2523 [1980], to *Matichon* newspaper for article appearing 26 Apr. 2526 [1983], and to *Sayam Rat* newspaper for article appearing 26 Apr. 2531 [1988], quoted in, Buppha Changkaew, "Khamsang khana patirup," pp. 171, 178, 181–82.

18 Warning order made to *Dao Sayam* newspaper for article appearing 14 Dec. 2532 [1989], to *Naew Na* newspaper for article appearing 26 Sept. 2532 [1988], and to *Sayam Rat* newspaper for article appearing in July 2532 [1989], quoted in, Buppha Changkaew, "Khamsang khana patirup," pp. 197, 195, 195–97.

19 Interview, Samphan Satthaphorn, 21 Aug. 1991.

20 Warning order made to *Siang Puangchon* newspaper for article appearing 13 July 2520 [1977], quoted in, Buppha Changkaew, "Khamsang khana patirup," p. 138.

21 Interview, Samphan Satthaphorn, 21 Aug. 1991.

22 The political mover within the Santi Asoke movement was former military officer Chamlong Srimuang who was elected mayor of Bangkok twice in the 1980s. He was the key leader of the protest against the military government that ended in the May 1992 massacre and became one of the leaders of the People's Alliance for Democracy that supported the 2006 coup. For more on Chamlong's political career, see Duncan McCargo, *Chamlong Srimuang and the New Thai Politics* (New York: St. Martin's Press, 1997).

23 Warning order made to *Matichon* newspaper for article appearing 6 June 2532 [1989], quoted in, Buppha Changkaew, "Khamsang khana patirup," p. 194.

24 Interview, Samphan Satthaphorn, 21 Aug. 1991.

25 The name of this Japanese city became synonymous with mercury poisoning caused by industrial pollution.

26 Warning order made to *Matichon* newspaper for article appearing 31 Oct. 2532 [1989], quoted in, Buppha Changkaew, "Khamsang khana patirup," p. 196; Interview, Samphan Satthaphorn, 21 Aug. 1991.

27 Hamilton adds:

> There is a powerful expectation that all stories must end on a moral or uplifting note, providing hope for the future. Karmic consequences must be depicted in such a way as to reassure the audience that evil is punished while good understanding and reconciliation are always possible.
> [SRCE](Hamilton, "Rumours, Foul Calumnies and the Safety of the State," pp. 349)

For a more updated version of this effect, see Duncan McCargo, "Thai Politics as Reality TV," *The Journal of Asian Studies* 68(1) (2009): 7–19.

28 At least one published English-language monograph is dedicated to cinema in Thailand: Patsorn Sungsri, *Thai National Cinema* (Saarbrücken: VDM Verlag Dr. Müller Aktiengesellschaft & Co. KG, 2008). Shorter items are in *Nation*, 23 June 2007 and "A Harsh New Film Law," 29 Nov. 2007; and Kong Rithdee, "Beware the Watchdogs of Cinema," *Bangkok Post*, 23 June 2007, Article 19 and Forum-Asia, *Freedom of Expression and the Media in Thailand* (Dec. 2005), p. 22, and "Film Ratings to Protect Monarchy," 24 Feb. 2009. Available at: http://thaipoliticalprisoners.wordpress.com/page/25, accessed 24 May 2009.

29 Thailand, National Archives, "m.th. 0209/147 Naew nayobai kan truat phitjarana phaphayon khong krasuang mahat thai" [Ministry of Interior 0209/147 Guidelines for Checking Movies of the Ministry of Interior], 16 Jan. 2534 [1991], roneo copy. Apparently the original 1930 measure forbade the showing of any movie that was of the following nature:

1 the show of scorn and contempt of things of worship, or any action which would cause ill feelings toward any religion of the nation;
2 methods of a criminal persons;
3 biography of an infamous criminal;
4 a repulsive murder or execution;
5 acts of cruelty toward any person or animal, which show a lack of good morality; matters which are obscene, lewd, or sexually enticing;
6 expressions which are capable of causing disagreement between nations or between classes of people;
7 expressions which might cause insult toward the state or nation or the authorities of the government;
7 expressions concerned with politics which are capable of affecting the governance of the country, or incitement of disquietude in the land;
9 matters which are felt will instil undesirable traits in individuals which will lead them to commit evil;
10 mocking, scorn, or disdain of royalty [*ratchanuphap*].

In 1976, these violations were restructured, making insult to the royalty a crime against morals, culture, or tradition. The law also forbade any movie that would "cause deterioration to the noble culture and traditions of the nation, such as a child not showing respect to parents." See Thailand, Movie Censorship Board (Phanaek khuapkhum phaphayon), Kong kamkap kan 2 kong thabian, kong banchakan tamruat sopsuan klang, krom tamruat [Cinema Control Section, Directorship 2, Licensing Bureau, Central Investigation Division, Police

Department], *Sensoe* [Censor] (n.p., n.d.). Thongchai notes that a US State Department report on human rights in Thailand in 1994 listed that any movie touching on the events surrounding the massacre of 6 October 1976 was forbidden by the Thai authorities. See Thongchai Winichakul, "Remembering/Silencing the Traumatic Past: The Ambivalent Memories of the October 1976 Massacre in Bangkok," in, Shigeharu Tanabe and Charles F. Keyes, eds., *Cultural Crisis and Social Memory* (London: RoutledgeCurzon, 2002), pp. 243–83. For a discussion of movies and state control, see Hamilton, "Rumours, Foul Calumnies and the Safety of the State," pp. 354, 358, and more directly, Annette Hamilton, "Cinema and Nation: Dilemmas of Representation in Thailand." *East-West Film Journal* 7(1) (1993), pp. 81–105, and in, W. Dissanayake, ed., *Colonialism and Nationalism in Asian Cinema* (Bloomington, IN: Indiana University Press, 1993), pp. 141–61.

30 Thailand, Movie Censorship Board (Phanaek khuapkhum phaphayon), *Sensoe* [Censor] (n.p., n.d.).

31 Interview, Police Lt. Col. Nikhom Intasen, Assistant Director of the Movie Censorship Board, Bureau of Licensing, Central Investigation Department, Police Department, Bangkok, 15 July 1991.

32 However, Somchat Bangjaeng, Head of the National Film Archives, felt that the work of one Thai director, Prince Chatri Jaroenphon, was an exception; he had, indeed, depicted government officials negatively. Based on a novel by Suwanee Sukanya, he had made a movie of an idealistic doctor who graduated from the university and returned to his rural home to dedicate his knowledge to the people there. Along the way, the young doctor came up against corrupt officials and gambling policemen. However, Prince Chatri was able to get the Movie Censorship Board to pass his movie, largely because, Suchat felt, of the influence of the prince's father. Interview, Somchat Bangjaeng, Head of the National Film Archives, Bangkok, 17 May 1991.

33 Interview, Somchat Bangjaeng, Bangkok, 17 May 1991.

34 *Newsweek*'s David Ansen was put into "a state of euphoria" by the movie and recommended, "For those seeking a palette cleanser after a steady diet of Hollywood 'product,'" *Syndromes and a Century* is "as invigorating as a perfect sorbet." Available at: http://www.newsweek.com/id/35175, accessed 10 Dec. 2008.

35 Available at: http://www.imdb.com/title/tt0477731/news#ni0076671, accessed 16 Jan. 2009; http://www.imdb.com/title/tt0477731/news#ni0088530, accessed 16 Jan. 2009. This is reminiscent of one of the first acts of censorship in the nascent Siamese nation-state in 1885, in which the writer of a magazine article employed "realism" to depict monks sitting around talking normally. The abbot forbade future instalments of the conversation. See Benedict R.O'G. Anderson and Ruchira Mendiones, *In the Mirror: Literature and Politics in Siam in the American Era* (Bangkok: Editions Duang Kamol, 1985), p. 13.

36 Movies that came close, though, included *Khru ban nok* [The Rural Teacher] (1978), *Phu thaen nok sapha* [Representative Outside the Parliament (1983), and *Mu bun* [The Assassin/The Gunman]. Jon Ungpakorn's documentary, *Kamakorn Ying Hara* [The Factory Workers of Hara] (1976), also came out during this period. A number of other movies with strong political messages have been made but never shown. See Patsorn, *Thai National Media*, pp. 182–86.

37 Kong Rithdee, "A Critical History," 11 Oct. 2007. Available at: http://www.thaifilm.com/articleDetail_en.asp?id = 105, accessed 22 May 2009.

38 Interview, Somchat Bangjaeng, Bangkok, 17 May 1991.

39 Ibid.

40 *Nation*, 14 Mar. 2008. The proliferation of community radio stations and cable television allowed alternative views to be more accessible to many in Thai society. Such proliferation has made it nearly impossible for the government to control the content, and so when these new media become perceived as dangerous, recent Thai

governments have not hesitated to try (generally unsuccessfully) to ban broadcasting. See, for instance, "Red Media Thriving, Despite Govt Crackdown," *Nation*, 16 June 2009.

41 Thai Government, *Phraratchabanyat kanphim ph.s. 2484* (Krungthep: Samnakphim Sutphaisan, n.d.), pp. 33–38.

42 See, Kanchanaporn Chitsanga (Head Librarian, Faculty of Political Science, Thammasat University), "Banned in Bangkok: Banned Books in Thailand 2493–2542 [1950–99]," Freedom Against Censorship Thailand, Available at: http://facthai.wordpress.com. Also see: http://www.sarakadee.com/web/modules.php?name = Sections&op = viewarticle&artid = 610, accessed 8 Nov. 2008.

43 Thailand, Government, "Kham sang khong khana patirup kan pokkrong phaendin chabap thi 43 long wan thi 21 tulakhom 2519" [Order of National Administrative Reform Council No. 43, issued 21 Oct. 1976], and "Prakat krasuang mahat thai Ruang kamnot ekkasan lae sing phim thi ham mi hai phu dai mi wai nai khropkhrong" [Ministry of Interior Announcement Specifying Documents and Printed Materials Which are Forbidden to Have in One's Possession], in, Thailand, Government, *Phraratchabanyat kanphim ph.s. 2484*, pp. 51–79. The Ministry of Interior issued four separate lists of prohibited books under this announcement. The date, name of the Minister of Interior at the time, and the number of forbidden items are as follows: 3 Mar. 2520 [1977], Samak Sunthornawet, Minister of Interior (100 forbidden items); 6 Oct. 2520 [1977], Samak Sunthornawet, Minister of Interior (104 items); 6 June 2523 [1980], Prathuang Kiratibut, Minister of Interior (96 items); and 6 Nov. 2523 [1980], Prathuang Kiratibut, Minister of Interior (15 items).

44 The press officer censured a story that "revealed the identity of the burdens of the land [*nak phaendin*] [who planned] setting up a provisional Thai government in Laos, with a plan to divide Thailand into four states," in claiming that Khamsing Srinawk, noted author and government critic, had volunteered to be prime minister. See, Warning order made to *Dao Dara Yuk Sayam* newspaper for article appearing on 27 Jan. 2520 [1977], as quoted in, Buppha Changkaew, "Khamsang khana patirup," pp. 124–25.

45 Kavi Chongkittavorn, "Information Act Challenges Culture of Secrecy," *Nation*, 25 Jan. 1999, and Nakorm Serirak, "Two years of exercising the right to know in Thailand," *Nation*, 10 Mar. 2000. Sinfah Tunsarawuth, an researcher and writer on the issue of media freedom, reports that mechanisms under the Information Act work remarkably well. Personal communication, 21 Mar. 2009.

46 *Nation*, 30 May 2000.

47 *Nation*, 28 May and 22 June 1999. During this period, the Defense Ministry said it would black out the names of "individuals, organisations and political parties suspected of being implicated in inciting riots leading to the Black May bloodbath, citing them as private information." The official responsible said "withholding of some names was aimed at saving the ministry from possible libel suits." The chairperson of the Defense Information Committee said "his committee was keen to ensure that the public disclosure of military investigations should not infringe on individual privacy." He added that the committee "also recommended the withholding of names of military officers who were removed from their posts following the crackdown." *Nation*, 7 Mar. 1999 and "Black May Suspects' Names Erased," 3 July 1999. To make the report sound as if the military were protecting the privacy of those on the other side was a way of justifying blacking out everyone's name, thus rendering the report meaningless. For a short account of the efforts made in 1992 to investigate the tragedy, see David Murray, *Angels and Demons* (Bangkok: Orchid Press, 2000), pp. 175–81, 196–98.

48 *Nation*, 30 May 2000.

49 An instructive contrast can be made between the May 1992 Report and the

Widgery report issued by the British government on "Bloody Sunday" (30 Jan. 1972) in Northern Ireland, in which 13 protesters were killed. Fifteen names of lower ranking British soldiers were replaced with letters, and ellipses replace two of five "specific tasks" carried out by one military unit. (See, "Report of the Tribunal appointed to inquire into the events on Sunday, 30th January 1972 [Widgery Report]," Available at: http://cain.ulst.ac.uk/hmso/widgery.htm, accessed 15 Apr. 2009. The report was intelligible, though not thorough and was roundly condemned for excluding information, inconsistencies, and misinterpretation of evidence. A new inquiry was set up under Lord Seville in 1998. Available at: http://news.bbc.co.uk/1/hi/in_depth/northern_ireland/2000/bloody_sunday_inquiry/ 665100.stm, accessed 15 Apr. 2009. Although this report is not scheduled for release until late 2009, documents obtained through the Freedom of Information Act have revealed high-level British government involvement. Available at: http://www.timesonline.co.uk/tol/global/article1471409.ece, accessed 15 Apr. 2009.

50 Even more galling for public groups, the report not only failed to provide useful information about the military, it also placed the blame on the side gunned down. The report says,

> Propaganda was generated by the protest side, claiming huge losses of lives in a bid to inflame hatred toward the government. The propaganda was disseminated in a systematic and sophisticated way, indicating that some protest leaders intended to turn a normal rally situation into rioting, which is the real cause of the loss of lives and damage to public and private property.
>
> (*Nation*, 30 May 2000)

Thailand may not get the truth about the events in 1992, but it may get a monument. See, "Black May Monument Park to Be Built," *Bangkok Post*, 9 May 2009. Adul Khiewboriboon, who heads a committed of relatives of demonstrators killed in Black May, said "We're excited and happy about the project's progress as we have waited 16 years for it."

51 Thailand, Government, *Government Gazette*, Vol. 114, Part 46a, 10 Sept. 2540 [1997]. This is a common practice observed by many countries; governments comply with information access laws and still evade revealing too much. Thanks to Michael Connor on information on practices used by the Australian government.

52 The topic is discussed in, Antoon de Baets, "Defamation Cases against Historians," *History and Theory* 41(3) (Oct., 2002), pp. 346–66.

53 The decision of the Censorship Board may have also been made in consideration of Section 327 of the criminal code that forbids defamation of the dead, or the 1992 amended Provision 328 which includes "cinematograph film" as a possible medium of defamation. See Article 19 and Forum-Asia, *Freedom of Expression and the Media in Thailand* (Dec. 2005), p. 74.

54 Interview, Somchat Bangjaeng, Bangkok, 17 May 1991.

55 Interview, Police Lt. Col. Nikhom Intasen, Bangkok, 15 July 1991.

56 During mayoral campaigning, Samak sued Giles and a newspaper for an article entitled, "Do we want a Bangkok governor whose hands are blood-soaked from the October 6, 1976 incident?" As Samak was running for public office, Giles said, "I, like any other Bangkok resident, have the right to scrutinise Samak, who is a public figure, on his past and present activities." In the article, Giles said he did "not accuse Samak of being directly implicated in, or instigating, the crackdown on the Thammasat University students," but "questioned Samak on his stand relating to the Yan Kroh radio station. The station churned out hate propaganda against the students and Samak once praised it." After the bloody crackdown, Samak became Minister of Interior and "proceeded to close down several

newspapers. I want him to clarify his stand on democracy and press freedom." "Call for Samak to explain his actions, and drop lawsuit," *Nation*, 14 June 2000. A fact-finding committee set up to investigate the 6 October massacre produced two books made public in October 2001. Chulalongkorn University lecturers Giles Unphakorn and Suthachai Yimprasert wrote "State Crime in an Era of Change." Rangsit University Chonthira Sattyawattana wrote "Open the Wound in Search of the Truth" (both in Thai). "Daring books come out on Oct. 6 massacre," *Nation*, 4 Oct. 2001.

57 Whereas the report on the 1992 shootings is a matter of ascertaining facts, other kinds of history have experienced difficulty. There is now the famous case of Saiphin Kaewngamprasoet who, for her acts of deconstruction, had to flee for her life. In March of 1996, 50,000 demonstrators in Thailand's northeastern province of Nakhon Ratchasima met to protest the publication of an award-winning master's thesis by Saiphin, a history student at Thammasat University, entitled, "The Images of *Thao* Suranari in Thai History." The thesis and resulting book described how nationalist ideologues of the 1930s took a local heroine named *Thao* Suranari who had been involved in the suppression of the Lao "Jao Anu Rebellion" in the first half of the nineteenth century and made her into a national cult figure, a historical construct based on a local cult figure. Offended provincial residents, claiming that the publication "questioned the existence of the heroine," demanded that the author, who had since become a teacher in the province, be thrown out, copies of the book recalled and burned, her degree revoked, and her advisors investigated and punished with a cut in pay. They also demanded that the author and her advisors be forced to come and ask for forgiveness before the statue of *Thao* Suranari and for the author and the publisher to be charged with defamation and *lèse-majesté*. At the protest, effigies of the author, the rector of Thammasat University, and executives of the publishing house were burnt.

As we saw in Chapter 8, the road to *lèse-majesté* is often torturous. How did the book's contents commit *lèse-majesté*? *Thao* Suranarii had been awarded a royal title by a grateful King Rama III after her assistance in suppressing the rebellion some 170 years ago. To the angry residents of the province, the thesis implied that *Thao* Suranari was a myth. Only the craziest of kings would grant a myth a title. Therefore, to imply that she was a myth was both an insult to *Thao* Suranari and to King Rama III. To insult the latter was to insult the entire Chakri Dynasty, which in turn is an insult to the present king—the ninth of the Chakri Kings—who is covered by the *lèse-majesté* law. Therefore, to imply that *Thao* Suranarii is a historical myth is an insult to the present king. *Nation*, 5 March 1996; Saiphin Kaewngamprasoet, *Kanmuang nai anusawari thao suranari* [The Politics of the Monument of *Thao* Suranari] (*Silpa Watthanatham*, Special Issue, November) (Bangkok: Matichon Press, 1995). See the insightful account and analysis of the phenomenon in Charles F. Keyes, "National Heroine or Local Spirit? The Struggle over Memory in the Case of Thao Suranari of Nakhon Ratchasima," in, Shigeharu Tanabe and Charles F. Keyes, eds., *Cultural Crisis and Social Memory* (London: RoutledgeCurzon, 2002), pp. 113–36.

58 At several times during this speech, the king seems to invite criticism, with phrases like, "If I shall be open, criticise me that sometimes I may be wrong so that I know that I am wrong," and "If you say the King cannot be criticised, it means that the King is not human." At other points, though, the king qualifies the offer with phrases like, "If they criticise correctly, I have no problem." *Nation*, 5 Dec. 2005. The question, as always, is who will judge what correct criticism will be?

59 *Nation*, 30 Sept. 2008. Another variation of this thought came from Anand Panyarachun: "[The King's] remarks, whether made privately or publicly, are

circumspect and often couched in discreet and indirect terms. So while they are listened to with great attention, there is no guarantee that His Majesty's thinking is heard and properly understood." FCCT, *King of Thailand in World Focus*, p. 271.

60 Hamilton, "Rumours, Foul Calumnies and the Safety of the State," p. 359.

61 Ibid., pp. 361, 368–70.

62 McCargo addresses this in his discussion of columnists who, in an effort to show their "inside knowledge" of politics, use "allusions and cryptic references" that are "beyond the comprehension of many readers." However, the overall effect is to create greater "obfuscation" which requires greater dependence on those in the know. McCargo, *Politics and the Press in Thailand*, p. 139.

63 The recent and appalling exception to this principle was in the case of Harry Nicolaides who published a semi-autobiographical novel set in Thailand. Fifty copies were printed, seven were sold. One of those somehow fell into the hands of the police, who charged him with *lèse-majesté* due to a 103-word paragraph referring to certain proclivities of the crown prince. Despite being a novel (least realistic) and limited distribution (presumably six copies in the hands of the public), the words were so threatening to the state that he was refused bail numerous times, eventually found guilty and sentenced to three years' imprisonment, and a month later pardoned and allowed to return to Australia. See, "The Trouble with Harry," *The Economist*, 22 Jan. 2009; *Bangkok Post*, 23 Feb. 2009. Another rather obscure case is of Japanese national Koshi Takahashi whose book (in Japanese) about Northern Thailand included items deemed offensive to the queen and crown prince. He was found guilty but given a suspended sentence. See, "Japanese author convicted on lese majeste charges in Thailand," Agence France-Presse, 23 July 2003.

64 The leaders of the PAD and the leader of the Democrat Party use every angle of their partisan exceptionalism to explain why Somkiat's arrest was different and, so, deserved separate consideration from Jakrapop's. See *Bangkok Post*, 17, 20 July 2008. This should come as no surprise as the Democrat Party and PAD have risen to power under the auspices of a strengthened defamation regime.

13 Conclusion

1 Peter A. Jackson, "The Performative State," *Sojourn,* 19(2) (2004): 221.

2 Reviewing Nidhi's comment, *Chaophraya* Thiphakorawong (Kham Bunnag) seems more interested in resolving conflicts between traditional Buddhism and empirical science. Rather than Western science challenging the Thai view of human nature in the mid-nineteenth century, Thiphakorawong seemed intent on "purifying" Buddhist teachings, thus retaining a more traditional view of human nature. See Nidhi Eoseewong, *Pen and Sail* (Chiang Mai: Silkworm Books, 2006), pp. 25–53. Likewise, Reynolds notes that Thiphakorawong "separated the natural world from religion asserting that each had a set of laws that explained its own phenomena." Craig J. Reynolds, "A Thai-Buddhist Defense of Polygamy," *Seditious Histories Contesting Thai and Southeast Asian Pasts* (Seattle: University of Washington Press, 2006), p. 203.

3 Thongchai, *Siam Mapped*, pp. 56–61.

4 Christine Gray, "Thailand: The Soteriological State in the 1970s," Ph.D. dissertation, The University of Chicago, 1986, pp. 253–79.

5 Jackson, "The Performative State," p. 230.

6 Patrick Jory, "Problems in Contemporary Thai Nationalist Historiography," available at: http://kyotoreview.cseas.kyoto-u.ac.jp/issue/issue2/article_251.html, accessed 23 Jan. 2008.

7 Thongchai wrote:

> The defeat in the Franco-Siamese conflict was a serious agony, a trauma, for Thai rulers. They felt that the kingdom barely survived. King Chulalongkorn literally did so, not from any physical harm during the conflict but from psychological breakdown and demoralization in the wake of the crisis due to humiliation. The trauma must have led the Siamese elite to a serious and thorough rethinking of the world around them and the conditions that had brought them to such a cliff-hanging situation. Probably like many other countries that went through traumatic events, the Siamese rulers and intellectuals needed to come to terms with the new reality, to make sense of their place and roles in it, and to live on with confidence.

See Thongchai Winichakul, "Siam's Colonial Conditions and the Birth of Thai History," paper presented at the conference, "Unraveling the Myths of Southeast Asian History," 24–26 Nov. 2006, p. 13.

8 From 1986 to 2005, statistics calculated from the Annual Reports of the Office of the Attorney General show courts handed down decisions on 13,163 cases of defamation. Of those, only 391 were acquittals, a conviction rate of over 97 per cent. See Thailand, Attorney General's Office (Samnakngan Aiyakan Songsut), *Rai-ngan prajam pi 2527–2548* [Annual Report of the Attorney General's Office, 1984–2005] (Samnakngan aiyakan phiset fai sarasonthet, samnakngan wichakan).

9 Antoon de Baets, "Defamation Cases against Historians," *History and Theory* 41(3) (Oct. 2002): 348.

10 Carl Schmitt, *Political Theology*, trans. George Schwab (Chicago: University of Chicago Press, 1985), p. 8.

11 Ibid., p. 14.

12 According to Sinfah Tunsarawuth, who has conducted research on the issue of personal defamation in Thailand over the past number of years, the government has no experts reviewing or researching defamation. Personal communication, 21 Mar. 2009.

13 Thailand, Attorney General's Office (Samnakngan Aiyakan Songsut), *Rai-ngan prajam pi 2539–2548* [Annual Report of the Attorney General's Office, 1996–2005] (Samnakngan aiyakan phiset fai sarasonthet, samnakngan wichakan).and Thailand, Samnakngan San Yuttitham [Office of the Judiciary], *Rai-ngan sathiti khadi tua ratcha-anajak prajam pi (ph.s. 2549, 2550, 2551, 2552)* [English title provided is *Annual Judicial Statistics, Thailand 2006, 2007, 2008* and *2009*, respectively].

14 This point is excellently brought out in a report on media freedom in Thailand. See, Article 19 and Forum-Asia, *Freedom of Expression and the Media in Thailand* (Dec. 2005).

15 Thailand, Government, "Sangha Act Amendment (No.2) B.E. 2535 (A.D. 1992) to the 1962 Act," as quoted in Article 19 and Forum-Asia, *Freedom of Expression and the Media in Thailand*, p. 76.

16 Streckfuss, David and Mark Templeton, "Human Rights and Political Reform in Thailand," in Duncan McCargo, ed., *Reforming Thai Politics* (Copenhagen, Denmark: Nordic Institute of Asian Studies (NIAS), 2002), pp. 73–90.

17 A report on freedom of expression in Thailand suggested that the cause of the proposed legislation was,

> Senior Buddhist monks had at the time repeatedly been exposed for wrongdoing, there was infighting amongst groups of clerics, and the lawmakers' reaction was not to impose stricter controls and regulations on the monks-

hood, but to call for harsher censorship of the media to avoid such scandals being reported.

(Article 19 and Forum-Asia, *Freedom of Expression and the Media in Thailand*, p. 76)

18 *Bangkok Post*, 1 Nov. 2007; Thailand, Government, Parliament (Sapha Nitibanyat haeng Chat), "Raing Phrarachabanyat Upatham lae Khumkhrong Phraphutthasatsana ph.s. . . . ," 24 tulakhom 2550 [24 Oct. 2007].

19 *Nation*, 8 Oct. 2007.

20 Thailand, Government, Parliament, "Lek rap 115/2551 wan thi 29 t.kh. 2551, somnakngan kekhathikan sapha phuthaen ratsadorn; banthuk lakkan lae hetphon, prakop rang phraratchabanyat kaekhai phoemtoem pramuankotmai aya (chabap thi . . .), ph.s. . . . [Received no. 115/2008, 29 Oct. 2008, Office of the Secretary-General to the House of Representatives; "Notes on the principle and rationale, accompanying the Draft Act to revise and amend the criminal code (no. . . .), of. . . . .year]. I thank Thongchai Winichakul for help with translation.

21 Thailand, Government, "Computer Crime Act B.E. 2550[2007], *Government Gazette*, Vol. 124, Section 27 kor., 1, 18 June 2007. See Article 19's critique of the act in Article 19, "Thailand: Draft Computer Offences Act," London, Apr. 2007. See also, "Press Ignores Cyber Arrests," *Nation*, 24 Sept. 2007.

22 *Nation*, 19 Nov. 2008.

23 Marwaan Macan-Markar, "Blogger Gets 10 Years for Insulting Royalty," available at: http://ipsnews.net/text/news.asp?idnews = 46402, accessed 5 Apr. 2009; *Bangkok Post*, 4 Apr. 2009. Suvicha was given the maximum sentence for *lèse-majesté* and for computer crimes—15 plus given years.

24 With all the scurrying about with proposals to amend the laws protecting the monarchy and religion, Gen. Preecha Rojsen, chairman of the NLA committee on education, religion, and culture, moved to amend the National Flag Act of 1986, which would "stipulate that members of the public must stand at attention or be still and, in case they are driving or riding, stop their vehicles and face the direction from which they hear the anthem or see people raising or lowering the national flag." Preecha told the press that

> [H]e proposed the amendment because honouring the flag helped instil patriotism and emphasised people's awareness of national importance. If people were patriotic, society in general would be orderly and Thai culture would be promoted. Foreign visitors admire seeing Thais paying respect ot their flag and anthem.
> [SRCE](*Nation*, 23 Nov. 2007)

25 Duncan McCargo, "The Politics of Buddhist Identity in Thailand's Deep South: The Demise of Civil Religion?" *Journal of Southeast Asian Studies* 40(1) (2009): 12, 32. Accompanying the legislation in October 2007 on heresy and *lèse-majesté* legislation were other measures designed to maintain "Thainess," including thwarting efforts in the southernmost provinces to allow students to study in their own language, Yawi. Rectors of 26 universities confirmed the long-standing policy of making Thai classes compulsory, on the grounds that test scores of students in the south would improve if they were taught more Thai. See, "Rectors oppose plan to give Yawi priority," *Bangkok Post*, 15 Oct. 2007.

26 There do not appear to be many cases of contempt of court. In 2003, there was one new case and only 30 cases in all of "Offences against the Judicial Office," Sections 167 to 199 of the criminal code, tried throughout Thailand. Contempt is but one of such offence. Thailand, Attorney General's Office (Samnakngan

Aiyakan Songsut), *Rai-ngan prajam pi 2546* [Annual Report of the Attorney General's Office, 2003] (Samnakngan aiyakan phiset fai sarasonthet, samnakngan wichakan), p. 285.

27 Section 198 of the Thai criminal code punishes anyone "insulting the Court or the judge in the trial or deciding the cases, or obstructing the trial or adjudication of the Court . . . " Boonruam, *The Criminal Code*, p. 110. The Civil Procedure Code also provides punishment for contempt of the courts. Section 32 punishes authors, editors, and publishers may be punished with up to six-month's imprisonment and/or a 500-baht fine for publishing "any information or opinion disclosing any facts or circumstances of a case" the court has ordered not to disclose, or publication of any opinion or information "intended to influence the public sentiment or the Court or any party or witness in the case which appears likely to prejudice the fair trail . . . [through] (a) A misrepresentation of the facts of the case, or (b) A biased and inaccurate report, summary or comment of the proceedings of the case . . . " Boonruam Thiamjan, *The Civil Procedure Code* (Krungthep: Sont Paisal Press, 2551 [2008]), pp. 30–31.

28 The sentence and fine were both cut in half for her confession, and then further suspended for one year. Thailand, Lamphun Provincial Court (San Jangwat Lampun), "Rai-ngan Khadi" [Lamphun (Provincial) Court, Case Report], Khadi mailek dam 802/2546, Khadi mailek daeng thi 783/2526 [Black Case No. 802/2003, Red Case No. 783/2003], 14 May 2003. The offending article appeared in *Khao Sot*, 8 July 2545 [2002].

29 Somchai Preechasilpakul, Faculty of Law, Chiang Mai University, personal communication.

30 Unnamed source.

31 Klausner continues to say that Administrative Court judges take this oath, while those of the Constitutional Court do not, seemingly a recognition that the constitution is the highest law of the land. See William J. Klausner, "Thailand: A Social, Cultural and Political *Cul de* Sac," Institute of Security and International (ISIS), Chulalongkorn University, July 2008.

32 Notes 65 and 67 from Chapter 1 discuss the gap in academic work on Thai law, with English-language sources only from William J. Klausner, David M. Engel, and Frank Munger. Little scholarly work on the legal profession itself or the courts as a social and political agent has been done. We have little idea about what goes into training a judge, the debates within legal circles, and what informs such debates. Chang Noi (pseud.), "The Mysteries of the Law," *Nation*, 7 July 2008. Suchit Bunbongkarn, "A Reflection on the Role of a Justice of the Thai Constitutional Court," in Niyom Rathamarit, ed., *Focus on Thai Democracy National and Local Issues* (Bangkok: King Prajadhipok's Institute, 2006), pp. 41–48.

33 Chang Noi (pseud.), "Here Come the Judges," *Nation*, 29 Apr. 2006;

34 Thongchai Winichakul, "Toppling Democracy," *Journal of Contemporary Asia*, 38(1) (Feb. 2008): 32.

35 Ibid., p. 32. Thongchai remarks that it was Thirayuth Boonmi, former student leader of the 1970s, who coined the term *tulakanphiwat* [judicialization] in an article with the same title in *Matichon*, 1 June 2006. As a historian of law and the judiciary, I confess I was encouraged and optimistic to think of the courts playing a historical role. After the coup, my enthusiasm turned to puzzlement as, by late 2008, the courts seemed so partial as to defy belief. Nonetheless, I am on record as saying, "Until April 2006 there hadn't been much awareness that the courts should and could play such a decisive role in the country's politics. The king's speech directed the courts to be more active. And since then, the courts have been causing the government a lot of grief," in Marwaan Macan-Markar, "'Judicial Revolution' Changing Thailand's Political Landscape," 10 July 2008, *Irrawaddy*. In response to this partiality, I have since focused on impartiality. See David Streckfuss, "A

Call for Real National Heroes: Stand and Be Judged," *Bangkok Post*, 14 Apr. 2009.

36 Marwaan Macan-Markar, "Court Gains No Glory by Banning Ruling Party," 7 Dec. 2008, available at: http://ipsnews.net/news.asp?idnews = 45018, accessed 14 Dec. 2008; Simon Montlake, "Critics Slam Thailand's Activist Judges," *Christian Science Monitor*, 6 Oct. 2008. Available at: http://www.csmonitor.com/2008/1006/p07s03-woap.html, accessed 15 Oct. 2008., Thomas Fuller, "As Protesters Pause in Thailand, Their Grievances Against Elite Simmer," *New York Times*, 14 Apr. 2009. Available at: http://www.nytimes.com/2009/04/15/world/asia/15thai.html?_r = 1&ref = world, accessed 11 May 2009.

37 Chang Noi (pseud.), "From the People's Constitution to the Judges' Constitution," *Nation*, 30 Apr. 2007.

38 In a self-serving and telling manner, Aklarathorn "called on voters to be rational when deciding whether to vote for or against the draft constitution as he was afraid that many people might have fallen victim to ill-intentioned groups." *Bangkok Post*, 7 Aug. 2007.

39 Asian Human Right Commission, "THAILAND: Senate must delay vote on NHRC," 29 Apr. 2009. Available at: http://www.ahrchk.net/statements/mainfile.php/2009statements/1996/, accessed 3 June 2009.

40 Awzar Thi (pseud), "Thailand's Anti-Human Rights Commission," 14 May 2009. Available at: http://www.ahrc-thailand.net/index.php?option = com_content&task = view&id = 302&Itemid = 1, accessed 3 June 2009.

41 Human Rights Watch, "Thailand: Replace Flawed Rights Panel, Unqualified Candidates Were Selected by Secret and Illegal Process," 13 May 2009. Available at: http://www.hrw.org/en/news/2009/05/13/thailand-replace-flawed-rights-panel, accessed 3 June 2009.

42 Stroup made the case that Schmitt was more committed to political liberalism that it might first appear and that his work was more about addressing the conditions of the Weimar Republic than providing a framework for Nazism. However, Schmitt enthusiastically joined the Nazi Party when Hitler seized power. There is no indication that he would have quit the Nazi Party on his own; he was thrown out in 1938. Hence, it seems fair to call him a Nazi theorist. See John Stroup, "Political Theology and Secularization Theory in Germany, 1918–39: Emanuel Hirsch as a Phenomenon of His Time," *The Harvard Theological Review* 80(3) (July, 1987): 332.

43 Schmitt's translator defines the term further:

> a state of exception includes any kind of severe economic or political disturbance that requires the application of extraordinary measures. Whereas an exception presupposes a constitutional order that provides guidelines on how to confront crises in order to reestablish order and stability, a state of emergency need not have an existing order as a reference point.
>
> (Schmitt, *Political Theology*, p. 5)

44 Schmitt, *Political Theology*, p. 6.

45 Schmitt noted that seventeenth-century political philosophers examined "the exception" and "emergency law" with great enthusiasm, but the Enlightenment virtually banished the idea "when a relatively lasting order was established" in the eighteenth century. Ibid., pp. 13–14.

46 Schmitt wrote of the inherent "rightness" of absolute monarchy:

> In the struggle of opposing interests and coalitions, absolute monarchy made the decision and thereby created the unity of the state. The unity that a people represent does not possess this decisionist character; it is an organic unity,

and with national consciousness the ideas of the state originated as an organic whole.

(Ibid., pp. 48–49)

47 Ibid., p. 6.
48 Ibid., p. 6.
49 Thongchai, "Siam's Colonial Conditions and the Birth of Thai History," p. 13.
50 Schmitt, *Political Theology*, pp. 6–7.
51 Gong, Jackson, Fickle, *et al.* have made much about the imposition of extraterritoriality on Siam by Western powers. Jackson, drawing on Gong, writes, "in the second half of the nineteenth century the previously implicit standard of civilization espoused by the West took on an 'explicit juridical character'," and, "its imposition via the capitulations of extraterritorial legal regimes led to 'cultural humiliation, dislocation and accommodation'" (pp. 231–32). It is true that Siam's legal system, under these conditions, did develop "its distinctive characteristics" and was "one of the forms that imperial power took in the semi-colonial conditions of informal empire." Siam was "forced to conform to Western norms while political regimes, education systems, and cultural production remained in local hands" (p. 230). If Jackson's argument was to understand the roots of authoritarianism in Thailand, this interpretation went too far in making the Siamese elite the victim of colonialism and extended too much importance to extraterritoriality. Indeed, the presence of colonial powers might have been one of the principal factors that made the punishments in the 1900 edict on defamation relatively light. It was precisely when extraterritoriality ended in the 1920s that the Thai defamation regime really began to emerge, restrained no longer by external considerations. See Jackson, "The Performative State," pp. 230–34.
52 Ibid., p. 7.
53 Paraphrasing Bodin, Schmitt wrote that when "it becomes necessary to violate such commitments [of a constitution, etc.], or "to change laws or to suspend them entirely," it must be done "according to the requirements of a situation, a time, and a people." Here, Schmitt indicated that Bodin did not go far enough, for he failed to designate who is really sovereign. Schmitt, *Political Theology*, p. 9.
54 When the Supreme Court legitimized the coup action and what it established, it drew (probably unknowingly) on nineteenth-century counterrevolutionary literature. De Maistre, an advocate of this position, came to the same conclusion: "Any government is good once it is established," quoted in Schmitt, *Political Theology*, pp. 55–56.
55 Ibid., p. 12.
56 This state of affairs in Thailand's system of adjudication in the 1950s contrasted sharply with Schmitt's insistence that for the exceptional to occur, a normal situation and legal order needed to be in place first. The situation in the early 1920s in Germany was normal and so it was from this perspective that Schmitt could envision the decisive entrance of the one truly sovereign, one who could "definitely decides whether this normal situation actually exists." If so, then the state of the exception could be declared. But in Thailand, the legal norm had deteriorated and seemed to predict the advent of the sovereign (in the person of Sarit). Ibid., pp. 12–13.
57 Ibid., p. 12.
58 Ibid., pp. 12–13.
59 For one of the few Thai scholars to examine the impact of coups on laws, see Somchai Preechasilpakul, "Lak niti ratthaprahan" [Juridical Principles of Coups], in *Ratthaprahan 19 kanyayon* [The Coup of 19 September] (Krungthep: Fah Diew Kan, 2550 [2007]), pp. 190–202.
60 Schmitt, *Political Theology*, pp. 36–37.

61 Ibid., p. 66.

62 Schmitt focused on "the decision" to declare the state of the exception as laid out by De Maistre:

> a decision is inherent in the mere existence of a governmental authority, and the decision as such is in turn valuable precisely because as far as the most essential issues are concerned, making a decision is more important than how a decision is made. It is definitely not in our interest that a question be decided in one way or another but it be decided without delay and without appeal.
>
> (Ibid., pp. 55–56)

63 Quoted in Thak Chaloemtiarana, *Thailand: The Politics of Despotic Paternalism* (Chiang Mai: Silkworm Books, 2007), pp. 123–24.

64 Schmitt, *Political Theology*, p. 56.

65 Marwaan Macan-Markar, "'New Politics' to Disenfranchise the Poor," 15 Sept. 2008, available at: http://ipsnews.net/news.asp?idnews = 43874, accessed 29 Sept. 2008.

66 And its mouthpiece, *The Manager* newspaper/website and ASTV

67 Schmitt, *Political Theology*, p. 7.

68 I have constructed a social and political hierarchy that reflects the use of defamation-based laws, especially *lèse-majesté*. It is derived from a combination of sources, primarily Gray, "Thailand: The Soteriological State in the 1970s," Duncan McCargo, "Network Monarchy and Legitimacy Crises," *The Pacific Review,* 18(4) (Dec. 2005): 499–519, and to a lesser degree, Lucien Hanks, "Merit and Power in the Thai Social Order," *American Anthropologist,* 64 (1962): 1247–61. See, also, Gray, "Hegemonic Images," pp. 43–65.

69 Schmitt described in detail the evolution of political liberalism versus dictatorship in the West, linking the former with the Enlightenment and the French Revolution and a positive view of human nature and the latter with the Counter-revolution and a negative view of human nature which emphasized "traditionalism" as the only hope for humans, since "the intellect of the individual was considered too weak and wretched to be able to recognize truth by itself." Schmitt describes the thought of Donoso Cortés, a lead theoretician of dictatorship, who "retained the self-confident grandeur of a spiritual descendant of the Grand Inquisitors":

> the victory of evil is self-evident and natural, and only a miracle by God can avert it . . . Humanity reels blindly through a labyrinth that we call history, whose entrance, exit, and shape nobody knows; humanity is a boat aimlessly tossed about on the sea and manned by a mutinous, vulgar, forcibly recruited crew that howls and dances until God's rage pushes the rebellious rabble into the sea so that quiet can prevail once more.
>
> (Schmitt, *Political Theology*, pp. 54, 58–59)

70 Schmitt's description of the dilemma facing the middle class in Europe echoes that of the middle class in today's Thailand. On a more theological level, Schmitt recounted the "liberal bourgeoisie of the July Monarchy":

> Its liberal constitutionalism attempted to paralyze the king through parliament but permitted him to remain on the throne, an inconsistency committed by deism when it excluded God from the world but held onto his existence . . . Although the liberal bourgeoisie wanted a god, its god could not become active; it wanted a monarchy, but he had to be powerless; it demanded freedom and equality but limited voting rights to the propertied class in order to

> ensure the influence of education and property on legislation, as if education and property entitled that class to repress the poor.
>
> (Ibid., p. 59)

On a more political note:

> They wanted a monarch, in other words a supreme personal authority, with an independent will and independent action. Yet they made the king a mere executive organ with his every act dependent on the consent of the cabinet, thus removing once again the personal element They wanted a king who would be above parties, who would thus also have to be above the people's assembly; and simultaneously they insisted that the king could not do anything but execute the will of this people's assembly. They declared the person of the king to be inviolable but had him take an oath on the constitution, so that a violation of the constitution became possible but could not be pursued. . . . The hatred of monarchy and aristocracy drove the liberal bourgeois leftward; the fear of being dispossessed of his property, which was threatened by radical democracy and socialism, drove him in turn toward the right, to a powerful monarchy whose military could protect him. He thus oscillated between his two enemies and wanted to fool both.
>
> (Ibid., pp. 59–60)

71 Ibid., p. 63.

72 The definitive piece on this issue is Craig J. Reynolds, "National Identity and Cultural Nationalism," in *Seditious Histories Contrasting Thai and Southeast Asian Pasts* (Seattle: University of Washington Press, 2006), pp. 245–76.

73 Thongchai pointed out that this premise

> is the most fundamental framework that historians adhere to, while it is probably one of the most common items of knowledge of history that Thai people have, without having to pay much attention to any historical studies. Generations of historians in Thailand have produced a large number of studies that reinforce the master narrative until it becomes a reified history.
>
> (Thongchai, "Siam's Colonial Conditions and the Birth of Thai History," in Andrew Turton, ed., *Civility and Savagery: Social Identity in Tai States* (Richmond, Surrey: Curzon, 2000), pp. 3–5)

74 Michael Herzfeld, "The Absent Presence: Discourses of Crypto-Colonialism," *The South Atlantic Quarterly* 101(4) (Fall 2002): 902.

75 Ibid., pp. 902, 907.

76 Ibid., pp. 904–5.

77 Ibid., pp. 903, 907.

78 Ibid., p. 922.

79 Ibid., pp. 922–23.

80 I lift the phrase from Somsak, *Political Monsters*.

81 Jackson, "The Performative State," p. 223. The concept of "face" and its importance within Thai society might be an underlying factor within Thailand as a defamation regime. Accusations and adjudications of defamation might even be seen as a performative art. For the significance of "face" in Thai socio-psychology, Suntaree has observed,

> *Thai people have a very big ego . . . They cannot tolerate any violation of the 'ego' self. Despite the cool and calm front, they can be easily provoked to strong*

> *emotional reactions, if the "self" or anybody close to the "self" like one's father or mother, is insulted.*
>
> (original emphasis)

And

> As a result of the top concern for "ego", whenever there is any problem to be solved that would directly or indirectly involve persons, the first criterion to consider is saving the "face"—the "ego"—of the person involved . . . Most important is to avoid public confrontation, regardless of whether it involves an inferior, an equal, and worse still a superior. To make a person lose "face", regardless of ranks, is to be avoided at all costs.

An admission of innocence is the only way to respond to public accusations of wrongdoing. Charging the accuser with defamation grants the admission a certain level of seriousness. See Suntaree Komin, *Psychology of the Thai People* (Bangkok: Research Center, National Institute of Development Administration (NIDA), 1991), pp. 133, 135. Politics has been generally the realm of males, and so there may be a connection between politics, males, face, and defamation. See Niels Mulder, *Inside Thai Society: Interpretations of Everyday Life* (Amsterdam and Kuala Lumpur: The Pepin Press, 1996), p. 92.

82 Borwornsak Uwanno, "Lese Majeste: Abuse and Benevolence," *Bangkok Post*, 9 Apr. 2009.

83 Jory, drawing on Thongchai Winichakul, continued to say, "this stance has transformed them into the natural allies of their erstwhile enemies, the royalists and the king himself." See Jory, "Historiography in Thailand from 1945 to the Present," forthcoming.

84 FCCT, *King of Thailand in World Focus*, pp. 46–47.

85 I borrow much of this framework from Kevin Hewison, "The Monarchy and Democratisation," in Kevin Hewison, ed. *Political Change in Thailand: democracy and participation* (London: Routledge, 1997), pp. 63–73.

86 Ibid., p. 65.

87 N. O'Sullivan, *Conservatism* (London: Dent, 1976), pp. 14–15, as quoted in Hewison, "The Monarchy and Democratisation," p. 64.

88 King Bhumibol Adulyadej, *Collection of Royal Addresses and Speeches During the State and Official Visits of Their Majesties the King and Queen to Foreign Countries (1959–1967)* (Bangkok, n.p., 1974), p. 8, quoted in Hewison, "The Monarchy and Democratisation," p. 64.

89 Bhumibol Adulyadej, King, *Collection of Royal Addresses and Speeches*, p. 112, quoted in Hewison, "The Monarchy and Democratisation," p. 65.

90 Bhumibol Adulyadej, King, *Royal Advice by His Majesty the King 20 May 1992/2535 at 21.30* (Bangkok: Office of His Majesty's Principal Private Secretary, 1992), paragraph two, quoted in Hewison, "The Monarchy and Democratisation," p. 65.

91 Bhumibol Adulyadej, King, *Collection of Royal Addresses and Speeches*, p. 49, quoted in Hewison, "The Monarchy and Democratisation," p. 66.

92 Paul Handley, *The King Never Smiles* (New Haven, CT: Yale University Press, 2006), p. 170.

93 Tongnoi Tongyai, *Entering the Thai Heart* (Bangkok: Bangkok Post, 1983), p. 17, quoted in Hewison, "The Monarchy and Democratisation," p. 71.

94 Duncan McCargo, *Tearing Apart the Land*, p. 15.

95 Volker Grabowsky, "The Thai Census of 1904: Translation and Analysis," *Journal of the Siam Society* 84: Part I (1996), pp. 57.

96 Quoted in Grabowsky, "The Thai Census of 1904," pp. 57, 62. Grabowsky rightly called this a "silly argument."

97 These percentages are derived from Grabowsky's analysis, putting the number of Chinese in Siam in 1904 at 400,000. The figure excludes populations that eventually became parts of Cambodia and Malaysia, adds the populations in Monthons Udorn, Isan, and Phayap as "Lao," and splits half the population of Nakorn Ratchasima between Thai and Lao (without trying to figure in the percentage of Khmer speakers). See Grabowsky, "The Thai Census of 1904," pp. 52, 56–57, and 78.

98 Thailand, National Statistical Office and National Economic Development Board, *Thailand Population Census 1960 Whole Kingdom*, pp. 18–20. But even the figures are deceiving. Despite more than a three-quarters of a century of language policies designed to make Central Thai pre-eminent, even among "Tai" speakers in Thailand in the 1980s, only 33.2 percent spoke Central Thai as their first language/dialect (and 45.6 percent if including Southern Thai), while a majority (54.4 percent) spoke a Lao language/dialect. See Tony Diller, "What Makes Central Thai a National Language?" in Craig J. Reynolds, ed., *National Identity and Its Defenders, Thailand, 1939–1989* (Clayton, Victoria: Centre of Southeast Asian Studies, Monash University, Monash Papers on Southeast Asia No. 25, 1991), p. 95.

99 The exception is the deep South, where there was strong opposition to both Thaksin and resentment against Thai rule.

100 This has been hinted at in the work of Patrick Jory, "Political Decentralisation and the Resurgence of Regional Identities in Thailand," *Australian Journal of Social Issues* (Special Issue) 34(4) (Nov. 1999): 337–52, and Jory, "Historiography in Thailand from 1945 to the Present," forthcoming; Charles F. Keyes, "'Who are the Tai?' Reflections on the Invention of Identities," in Lola Romonucci-Ross and George De Vos, eds., *Ethnic Identity: Creation, Conflict and Accommodation* (Walnut Creek, CA: Sage, 1995), pp. 136–60; Charles F. Keyes, *Isan: Regionalism in Northeastern Thailand* (Ithaca, NY: Data Paper No. 65, Southeast Asia Program, Cornell University, 1967), and Duncan McCargo and Krisadawan Hongladarom, "Contesting Isan-ness: Discourses of Politics and Identity in Northeast Thailand," *Asian Ethnicity* 5(2) (June 2004): 219–34. In the context of the political turmoil since 2005, this thought has become more pronounced. See Marwaan Macan-Markar, "Violence Shakes Elite Myth of Thai Unity," *Inter Press Service*, 30 Nov. 2008. Available at: http://ipsnews.net/news.asp?idnews = 44913, accessed 13 Dec. 2008.

101 Michael Connors has shown just how contested the question of sovereignty was in the drafting of the 1997 constitution. The wording of Article 3 had at first read: "sovereignty comes from the people." But the phrasing was altered rather abruptly to "sovereignty belongs to the people." Connors attributed the change to fears by "conservatives and royal liberals" that the change, "along with the very expansive rights written into the new charter, were moving away from traditional concepts of political order, in which the monarchy figured greatly." Thai democracy was to be one where "the king is the mediator of democracy; it is through him that popular will is manifest. Sovereignty is seen as residing jointly in the king and the people." See Michael K. Connors, "Article of Faith," *Journal of Contemporary Asia* 38(1) (Feb. 2008): 150–51.

102 Unfortunately a long list of crimes have gone unpunished. The most recent was the court ruling that absolved all state security forces of responsibility in the Tak Bai incident of 25 Oct. 2004, in which 78 detainees died while in custody and another seven reportedly died due to injuries sustained from torture and beatings of security forces. A *Bangkok Post* editorial said,

> Last Friday's inquest ruled that security officials were carrying out their duty, and could not be blamed. One of the main points considered by the panel was an emergency law in effect at the time, which protected state officials from any civil, criminal or disciplinary liabilities while carrying out their official duties . . . such laws and martial declarations are out of tune with democracy and public expectation. The government or security forces cannot credibly absolve themselves to avoid responsibility.
>
> (*Bangkok Post*, 2 June 2009)

See, also, Marwaan Macan-Markar, "War on Drugs Reveals Culture of Impunity," *Irrawaddy*, 12 Mar. 2003. Available at: http://www.irrawaddy.org/article.php?art_id = 130&page = 1, accessed 15 May 2009., Kavi Chongkittavorn, "Time to End Culture of Impunity Around Disappearances," *Nation*, 1 Sept. 2008, and most directly, Karl Victor (pseud.), "CNS Can Cure Our Ailing Democracy," *Bangkok Post*, 17 Sept. 2007 and Streckfuss, "A Call For Real National Heroes," *Bangkok Post*, 14 Apr. 2009.

103 As Agamben pointed out, the tendency over the twentieth century was for states to make greater claim to the state of exception, as especially evident in "national-security states" such as the United States where, since the late 1940s, successive governments expanded the sphere of the state of exception and eroded civil rights. However, the combination of factors and principles employed in the construction of the US security state did not include defamation as a prominent feature. See Giorgio Agamben, *Homo Sacer: Sovereign Power and Bare Life* (Stanford, CA: Stanford University Press, 1998), pp. 171–72.

104 Patrick Jory, "Problems in Contemporary Thai Nationalist Historiography". Available at: http://kyotoreview.cseas.kyoto-u.ac.jp/issue/issue2/article_251.html, accessed 23 Jan. 2008.

105 Ibid., Benedict R.O'G. Anderson and Ruchira Mendiones, *In the Mirror: Literature and Politics in Siam in the American Era* (Bangkok: Editions Duang Kamol, 1985), pp. 12–40.

106 Gray, "Thailand: The Soteriological State in the 1970s."

107 In this vein, see Sulak "The Crisis of Siamese Identity," pp. 45–58 or Kasian Tejapira, "The Postmodernisation of Thainess," in Shigeharu Tanabe and Charles F. Keyes, eds., *Cultural Crisis and Social Memory* (London: RoutledgeCurzon, 2002), pp. 202–27.

108 Those who became politicized with the overthrow of dictatorship in 1973.

109 Rosana Tosirakul, "No 'People Power' Crusade, This," *Bangkok Post*, 14 Apr. 2009.

110 Kasian Tejapira said, "What seems to be remnants of the October spirit of fighting for democracy have become a divided force—one struggles against the resurgence of autocracy and military rule and another against the return of the capitalist power," Achara Ashayagachat, "October Generation 'Divided'," *Bangkok Post*, 15 Oct. 2007; "Politicians Avoid Oct 6 Memorial," *Bangkok Post*, 7 Oct. 2007; Somsak, "Chaiya chana khong panyachon 17 tula" [Victory of the 17 Oct. Intellectuals], pp. 382–430.

111 On a special note, the end of the NGO movement might be pegged to the death of Wanida Tantiwithayapitak in December 2007. Wanida was committed both to the Pak Mun villagers and to international standards of human rights; she was an active member of Amnesty International and a strong proponent of the United Nations' International Covenant on Economic, Social, and Cultural Rights. She was also sympathetic to the concept of community rights and its importance in the long-term struggle for social justice for the marginalized. With her passing, the NGO movement, such as it was, definitively broke. Much has been written about the failure of the left in Thailand: Ji Giles Ungpakorn, ed.,

Radicalising Thailand (Bangkok: Institute of Asian Studies, Chulalongkorn University, 2003), Michael K. Connors, "The Reforming State: Security, Development, and Culture in Democratic Times" (in Giles 2003, pp. 319–43); and others. Hewison wrote of the difficulties of basing a broad-based, effective movement on the concept of localism. Kevin Hewison, "Responding to Economic Crisis: Thailand's Localism," in Duncan McCargo, ed., *Reforming Thai Politics* (Copenhagen, Denmark: Nordic Institute of Asian Studies (NIAS), 2002), pp. 143–61. The World Social Forums have shown that, at least in other countries, it is possible to adopt localism and "anti-globalization" as part of a strategy capable of linking on national and international levels. The problem may come with the grassroots NGOs' tendency to reify "Thai village culture" since the 1980s; over time these sentiments came to resemble sentiments expressed by the king. Rather than take a principled stance, many NGOs allowed their work to be associated with the elite vision of Thai society. Although progressive elements within NGOs had been hesitant to join with Sondhi in late 2005 and early 2006, a significant number of NGOs did join up with PAD and a number of notable representatives became core members. Pravit Rojanaphruk and Subhatra Bhumiprabhas, "Activists Wary of Sondhi Bandwagon," *Nation*, 4 Dec. 2005. In the aftermath of the 2006 coup, especially with the reassembling of the PAD in May 2008, the entire grassroots movement faced collapse. NGO members sympathetic to the PAD who travelled abroad were mystified and angered at attitude of the international community about the coup and the human rights situation in Thailand. By not defining their political position clearly (supporting or condoning the coup, obfuscating about human rights), many NGOs have betrayed the grassroots communities that had depended on them. The deep-seated authoritarian nature viewed by the Thai as unique, coupled with a distrust of "outsiders," has probably lethally wounded the movement of supporters from the Left, progressives, and even normal liberals for the foreseeable future.

112 Thongchai Winichakul, "Toppling Democracy," particularly 30–33. I retain his choice of transliteration.

113 Thirayuth's vision is for a body comprising "incorruptible people, such as the privy councillors, military leaders, judges, the Elders, anti-globalisation activities and academics from well-known institutions"—essentially controlling any lower elected bodies. A remarkable convergence of scholarly and popular opinion about the broad composition of those now in power in Thailand has emerged. Thongchai calls them *apichon*, McCargo calls them leaders of "virtuous rule," Thaksin has called them *amartayathipatai* (rule by bureaucrats and judges), and I argue that they fit well within a Thai Theravada Buddhist moral hierarchy that places the Meritorious or *ayachon* on top (Chapter 6).

114 Thongchai, remarkimg that Anek's driving metaphor comes from the words King Chulalongkorn said a century ago, drew his summary from Anek Laothamatas, "Samphat phiset: rao tong du lae prachathipatai thi ngok jak din khong rao-eng" [Special Interview: We Must Care for Democracy that is Grown on Our Own Soil], *Nechan sutsapda* [*National Weekly*], 8 Dec. 2006; and "Kan plianplaeng rabop prachathipatai thai 2549" [Changes in Thai Democracy 2006], Speech at Thammasat University, 16 Nov. 2006. Available at: http://www.politic.tjanews.org, accessed 7 Mar. 2007.

115 Pravit Rojanaphruk, "Human Rights Defenders Split into Yellow and Red Camps," *Nation*, 28 Jan. 2009.

116 This construction combines the "official nationalism" or "royalist-nationalism" as it emerged around the turn of the nineteenth century with a more "folk" or *ethnicized* nationalism as picked up by the National Identity Board. Baker and Pasuk fittingly described the alteration of meaning: "The commoner nationalists shifted the meaning of a nation from the people enclosed within the national

territory and bound by loyalty to the sovereign, to a community defined by ethnic origins, a long and unique history, and a common language." But it should be noted here that commoner nationalism or what might called "local nationalisms" was never entirely severed from the royal-nationalist version. Chris Baker and Pasuk Phongpaichit, *A History of Thailand* (Cambridge: Cambridge University Press, 2005), p. 113.

117 Jackson, "The Performative State," p. 229.

118 *The Economist* fired the first volley with the publication of "A right royal mess" on 4 Dec. 2008. The police did not have to bother banning the issue, as *The Economist*'s distributor, Asia Books, agreed not to distribute it. After the Australian writer Harry Nicolaides was jailed and Giles Ungpakorn's *lèse-majesté* case progressed, *The Economist* continued its attacks, prompting royalists to rail against insensitive foreign reportage. See, for instance, Vasit Dejkunjorn's "Phaen kan lom rabob prachathipatai baep thi mi phramahakasat pen pramuk" [plan to overthrow the democratic system of government with the king as head of state], *Matichon*, 17 Mar. 2009.

119 James C. Scott, *et al*, "International Scholars Call for Reform of Thailand's Lese Majeste Law," *Seeds of Peace* 25(2) (May–Aug. 2552 (2009)): 7–9. Reporters Without Borders also made a similar call to the Thai government on 26 Apr. 2009: "Twenty-six IFEX members and other organisations urge government to amend lese majeste law". Available at: http://egypt.ifex.org/thailand/2009/04/28/twenty_six_ifex_members_and_other/index.html, accessed 8 June 2009. In response to increasing calls to revise the *lèse-majesté* law, a seminar at the National Institute of Development Administration was organized to defend the law's use. The resulting petition concluded:

> There have been a rather high number of lese majeste cases in the past few years. When considered on whole it can be seen that [these cases] are actions linked into a movement that aims for the abolishment of the institution of the monarchy, which would result in a change of the governing system of Thailand from a democratic governing system with the king as head of state to another form of governing. Therefore, the proposal to revise or abolish the lese majeste law which protects the king from being violated and from lese majeste is a matter of a political struggle of groups wanting to change the governing system of Thailand and not a honest call for rights and liberty of freedom of expression.

As seen throughout this work, it is inconceivable that any Thai wanting to change the present system could be seen as honest. See, "Thalaengkan nak-wichakan lae prachachon ruang kankhatkhan kho sanoe hai mi kanyokluk lae kaekhai kotmai thi kiew khong kap kanpokkhrong phramahakasat jak kan-lamoet," wan thi 13 minakhom 2552 na sathaban bandit phatthana borihansat ["Declaration of Academics and the People opposing the proposal to abolish or revise laws relating to a protecting the king from being violated," 13 Mar. 2009 at the National Institute of Development Administration (NIDA)] (original in Thai)

120 Khrongkan prakatsaniyabat kotmail mahachon, khana nitisat, mahawithayalai thammasat, et al., "Lak miti kotmai min phraboromratchanuphap" [Symposium on Legal Dimensions of the Lese Majesty Law], 21–22 Mar. 2009, Thammasat University

121 Somchai Preechasilpakul, on the panel entitled, "Kotmai min phraborom-detchanuphap kap khwam mankhong khong rat ["The lese majesty law and Security of the State," Symposium on Legal Dimensions of the Lese Majesty Law, ibid.

122 Borwornsak Uwanno, "The Law of Inviolability in Thailand," *Bangkok Post*, 7 Apr. 2009. Available at: http://www.bangkokpost.com/opinion/opinion/14660/the-law-of-inviolability-in-thailand, accessed 4 June 2009.

123 Borwornsak Uwanno, "Thai Culture and the Law on Lese Majeste," *Bangkok Post*, 8 Apr. 2009. Available at: http://www.bangkokpost.com/opinion/opinion/14766/lese-majeste-abuse-and-benevolence, accessed 4 June 2009. He counters the contention that there are no legal limits to the law, by stating that the courts can focus on the intent of a defendant in determining a suitable punishment, and the king has asked that the law not be applied "too liberally" as he "allows fair criticism." See the sharp response to Borwornsak's articles by Dutch ambassador to Thailand, Tjaco van den Hout, "Europe's Lese Majeste Laws and Freedom of Expression," *Bangkok Post*, 21 May 2009.

124 The one exception, where it could be argued that there was at least a semi-elected body representing that "societal consensus," was in the passing of the amended criminal code of 1957.

125 Borwornsak rather nonchalantly dismisses concerns over the draconian penalty of the law: "The severity of the lese majeste offence has significantly been reduced due to the benevolence of His Majesty the King. In most cases, if he learns of the matter or if there is a petition for a royal pardon for this offence, His Majesty will either express his wish that the case not proceed, or grant a pardon." Borwornsak Uwanno, "Lese majeste: Abuse and Benevolence," *Bangkok Post*, 9 Apr. 2009. The condition is, though, that the petitioner has to plead guilty and be suitably contrite. The king's deputy principal private secretary, Tongnoi Tongyai, pointed out in 1987 that former police major Anant Senakhan was never pardoned for his lese majeste convictions "because he has never admitted he committed lese majeste," *Nation*, 8 Oct. 1987. Harry Nicolaides felt he was innocent and at first considered fighting the case. But in the end he followed his lawyer's advice and was appropriately remorseful and affirmed Thai love of the king:

> On the King's 81st birthday I saw fireworks in the distance. Some prisoners had tears in their eyes, praising a man they regard not just as their king but their father. I may not be Thai, but I am a son, and I know what it means to love a father. I am applying for a royal pardon. I pray the King learns of my plight so I might enjoy his grace.

Nicolaides was released after a month of imprisonment, but Boonyuen Prasertying, a Thaksin backer, was not so lucky. She, too, confessed, but has been jailed without pardon since November 2008. (Her confession did get her sentence of 12 years cut in half). Available at: http://thaipoliticalprisoners.wordpress.com/decidedcases/boonyuen-prasertying/, accessed 3 June 2009.

The dynamics are peculiar. One way to read Borwornsak's argument might be that heavy punishment is maintained as a vehicle for the king's benevolence in pardoning the contrite. It is rather like going to a Buddhist temple and buying birds from a seller. One gains merit by the act of "freeing" the birds. But it could be argued that it would be best not to capture free birds in the first place.

126 *Nation*, 11 Oct. 2007.

127 In other constitutional monarchies, polls are regularly conducted to assess the royal institution and critical comment and expressions of republican sentiment are common, such as the following headline: "One third of Swedes want King to abdicate" (27 Feb. 2009). Available at: http://www.thelocal.se/17886/20090227/, accessed 3 Mar. 2009. When the Swedish king was cheered for his sixtieth birthday in a royal procession, the Republican Association passed out cakes. Its leader said that Sweden should be rid of "this old, undemocratic tradition [of the

monarchy]." When asked about the cheering crowds lining the procession, the association's leaders responded, "But at the same time, remember that this is a spectacle and a publicity stunt and a day off." 30 Apr. 2006. Expressions such as these are unheard of in Thailand. Available at: http://www.thelocal.se/3692/20060430/, accessed 3 Mar. 2009. Regular public polls are conducted on the work of the royal family. In 2007 for instance, 45 percent thought the Swedish monarchy was doing a good job, 19 percent felt it was doing a bad job, and more than a third were "neutral." See, "Confidence in monarchy rises," *The Local*, 20 Apr. 2007. Available at: http://www.thelocal.se/7061/20070420/, accessed 3 Mar. 2009.

128 In the same sense, one cannot judge from sentiments of a person threatened with a long sentence for *lèse-majesté*. See note 125 above.

129 The Communist Party of Thailand criticized the feudal classes and may have advocated a communist state which probably would not have had a monarchy. But even then nothing was said on the subject.

130 Thaksin made the accusation in late March 2009 (*Bangkok Post*, 27 Mar. 2009), and Prem's supporters demanded that the government charge Thaksin for defaming the king by claiming Prem had meddled in politics. The government did nothing. If it ordered Thaksin arrested for *lèse-majesté* for accusing Prem, the long-time misuse of the law would have been apparent (see *Bangkok Post*, 3 Apr. 2009). Considering Gray's comments in a 1991 piece, it does show a change in attitude. She said that persons such as privy councillors are virtually untouchable, due to their proximity to the king: "Since *barami* (virtue) rubs off on men who are close to royalty and who 'latch on to the royal virtue' (*phueng phrarachabarami*) by performing rituals or business in the king's name, no one dares publicly to criticize – or even 'say the names' of – some of his closest associates as well." See Gray, "Hegemonic Images," p. 49. But the names have been said. Connors suggested that the debate over the role of the Privy Council has "greatly affected" the monarchy's standing and threatens to "erode the ideological compact that has taken shape since the 1970s" and may herald "the emergence of a more widespread egalitarian sentiment to challenge the hierarchical and deferential sentiment that surrounds the monarchy." Connors, "Article of Faith," p. 161.

131 *Bangkok Post*, 3 Apr. 2009. Thaksin sued PAD's Sondhi Limthong for defamation and two billion baht in damages, saying that Sondhi had alleged that Thaksin had sought to overthrow the monarchy (*Bangkok Post*, 15 Sept. 2007). The suit was thrown out by the court in 2009. Thaksin brought a similar suit against Privy Councillor Pichitr Kullavanijaya in Apr. 2009 (*Nation*, 7 Apr. 2009). Thaksin won a libel case against the *Manager* daily in March 2009, for a series of articles that alleged that Thaksin had formulated the so-called Finland Plot that sought to overthrow the monarchy (*Bangkok Post*, 25 Mar. 2009). However, there is no evidence (yet) that Thaksin was involved or led a movement to overthrow the monarchy. It is likely that he and his associates contemplated redefining the role of the monarchy, perhaps even, as accused, of seeking to turn the king into "a symbolic head of state" (*Nation*, 25 May 2006). In the political chaos of April 2009, authorities claim that Thaksin in his broadcasts to Thailand and with foreign media broke the law 16 times, including *lèse-majesté* (*Bangkok Post*, 29 Apr. 2009). Thaksin affirmed his loyalty to the institution, saying that calling on the king to intervene, as PAD had done in 2006, did not constitute *lèse-majesté* (*Bangkok Post*, 15 May 2009).

132 "Thai lese-majeste trial shut "for national security," Reuters. Available at: http://thaipoliticalprisoners.wordpress.com/2009/06/24/new-daranees-trial-closed-to-public-for-reasons-of-national-security/ / accessed 27 June 2009.

133 Thailand, Government. *Constitution of the Kingdom of Thailand B.E. 2550*

(2007. Available at: http://www.isaanlawyers.com/constitution%20thailand%202007%20-%202550.pdf / accessed 23 May 2009.

134 See Chapter 8, note 65.

135 Michael Ignatieff, "Introduction," in Julian Edelstein, *Truth & Lies* (New York: The New Press, 2001), p. 15.

136 Ibid.

137 Chaiwat Satha-Anand, "The Silence of the Bullet Monument: Violence and 'Truth' Management, Dusun-nyor 1948, and Kru-Ze 2004," in Duncan McCargo, ed., *Rethinking Thailand's Southern Violence* (Singapore: Nus Press, 2007), pp. 13–14. Also see, Thongchai Winichakul, "Remembering/Silencing the Traumatic Past: The Ambivalent Memories of the October 1976 Massacre in Bangkok," in Shigeharu Tanabe and Charles F. Keyes, eds., *Cultural Crisis and Social Memory* (London: RoutledgeCurzon, 2002), pp. 243–83.

138 George Steiner, "The Hollow Miracle," in *George Steiner: A Reader* (New York: Oxford University Press, 1984), p. 208.

139 Ibid., pp. 210–11.

140 Benedict Anderson, "Withdrawal Symptoms: Social and Cultural Aspects of the October 6 Coup," *Bulletin of Concerned Asian Scholars* 9(3) (July–Sept. 1977): 20–21.

141 Kasian Tejapira. *Commodifying Marxism: The Formation of Modern Thai Radical Culture, 1927–1958* (Kyoto: Kyoto University Press, 2001), p. 18, as quoted in Jackson, "The Performative State," p. 246.

142 Ajahn Chah, Venerable, *Living Dhamma* (The Sangha, Bung Wai Forest Monastery, 1992), pp. 41–42.

143 Borwornsak Uwanno, "Lese majeste: Abuse and Benevolence," *Bangkok Post*, 9 April 2009. I thank Simon Montlake for pointing out the strange end to Borwornsak's piece.

144 Buddhadasa pointed out that the "Middle Way" was a key Buddhist tenet, saying "The expression 'Middle Way' can be applied generally in many situations. It can't lead you astray." Again, this may make sense for individuals, but does not provide much guidance in politics, perhaps because political configurations keep moving the middle, thus making the extreme ever more so. Buddhadasa Bhikkhu, *Buddha-Dhamma for Students* (Nonthaburi: The Dhamma Study & Practice Group, 1988), p. 3.

145 Jory, "Historiography in Thailand from 1945 to the Present," forthcoming.

146 Mukhon Wongthes, *Intellectual Might and National Myth: A Forensic Investigation of the Ram Khamhaeng Controversy in Thai Society* (Bangkok: Matichon Public Co. [Silapawattanatham Art & Culture chabap phiset], 2003); Charnvit Kasetsiri, *Sayam ru thai?* [Siam or Thailand?] (Bangkok: The Foundation for The Promotion of Social Science and Humanities Textbooks Project, n.d.). Also, Samnakphim Santitham, *Thai ru sayam jak banthoek khong pridi banomyong lae jak rai-ngan kanprachum sapha rang ratthathammanun ph.s. 2504* [Thai or Siam from the notes of Pridi Banomyong and from meeting reports of the constitution drafting council, 1961], (Nonthaburi: Samnakphim Santitham, n.d.). Available at: www.petitiononline.com/SIAM2008/petition.html, accessed 22 Jan. 2009; Charnvit Kasetsiri, "Siam to Thailand – A Historian's View," *Bangkok Post*, 23 June 2009.

Appendix I

Thai laws on defamation (slander and libel)

The Royal Edict of 1900

Exposing others to ridicule and causing loss of reputation through taking inappropriate words or things and making them known

Section 6.—Whosoever makes known . . . [something] in order to have the people . . . be informed in some way, or in any form of spoken words, or symbols that are written, or printed, or in any other visible way that can be understood, whether it is the truth or is not the truth, which that person intends to defame another, or ridicule another person [in a way] that makes others angry or resentful of him or her because of such contents or things mentioned above, which is reason for that person to be exposed and to receive hatred, ridicule, or insult from the masses, to the point of having to lose his good name and reputation, that person is guilty.

1908 criminal code

Section 282.—Whoever imputes anything to another person in a manner which might cause such person to lose his reputation, or cause people to look down upon or hate such person; if it is said to two or more persons, that person is said to commit defamation of others and is liable to three punishments. The first is imprisonment not exceeding six months; or the second punishment is a fine not exceeding one thousand baht, or a third punishment which is both imprisonment and a fine as stipulated above.

If the imputation to another person is committed by means of publication of a document or in a serial publication, or in a newspaper, or published in any form, or in any letter, the offender shall be liable to a heavier punishment, namely, imprisonment not exceeding one year, or a fine not exceeding two thousand baht, or both.

Section 283.—Whoever expresses their own honest opinion which is of the type of expression as detailed following in this section:

1 in an expression of one's own rectitude, or in one's own justifiable defense, or for the protection of any legitimate interest;
2 an official who makes a statement in a report within his position and duties;
3 politely praising or criticizing any person or thing which in the natural course of things the public is speaking about; or
4 the publication or speaking of any court proceedings or report of any meeting, if done politely.

The expression of these four types of opinions or views are not a violation of defamation.

Section 284.—It is forbidden for the court to allow the one accused to be charged with defamation in witness testimony on whether the truth has been told or not except in cases of the following nature:

1 when the court sees that in speaking there was an intention of being a benefit to the public;
2 when what was said accuses an official of acting illegally within his official position and duties;
3 when the plaintiff requests the court to consider the imputation and asks that the court judge whether such defamatory words are true or not.

If the court compels the accused in a defamation trial to prove the truth of what was said and it is not proven, then the offender shall be liable to imprisonment not exceeding two years or a fine not exceeding one thousand baht, or both.

1957 revised criminal code: slander

> ***Section 326.***—Whoever imputes anything to another person before a third person in a manner likely to impair the reputation of such another person or to expose such another person to hatred or contempt is said to commit defamation, and shall be liable to the punishment of imprisonment not exceeding six months or fine not exceeding one thousand baht, or both. [1957–76]

1976 amendment

> ***Section 326.***—Whoever, by communication made to a third person, imputes anything in a manner likely to injure the reputation of any other person or to expose such person to public hatred or contempt, is said to commit defamation, and shall be punished with imprisonment not exceeding one year or fine not exceeding two thousand baht, or both. [1976–92]

1992 amendment

> ***Section 326.***—Whoever imputes anything to another person before a third person in a manner likely to impair the reputation of such another person or to expose such another person to hatred or contempt is said to commit defamation, and shall be liable to the punishment of imprisonment not exceeding one year or fine not exceeding twenty thousand baht, or both.

1957 revised criminal code: libel

> ***Section 328.***—If the offence of defamation is committed by means of publication of a document, drawing, painting, cinematograph, picture, or letters made visible by any means, gramophone record or any other recording instrument, by broadcasting or by propagation by any other means, the offender shall be liable to the punishment of imprisonment not exceeding one year or fine not exceeding two thousand baht, or both. [1957–76]

1976 amendment

> ***Section 328.***—If the defamation be committed by means of publication of any document, drawing, painting, motion picture, or letters made visible by any means, record or recorder, or by broadcasting or propagation by any means, the offender shall be punished with imprisonment not exceeding two years or fine not exceeding four thousand baht, or both.

1992 amendment

> ***Section 328.***—If the offence of defamation is committed by means of publication of a document, drawing, painting, cinematograph, picture, or letters made visible by any means, gramophone record or any other recording instrument, by broadcasting or by propagation by any other means, the offender shall be liable to the punishment of imprisonment not exceeding two years and fine not exceeding two hundred thousand baht.

Section 329.—Whoever, in good faith, expresses any opinion or statement:

1 by way of justifiable self defence or for the protection of any legitimate interest;
2 in the status of being an official in the performance of his duties;
3 by way of fair comment on any person or thing, which is natural for the public to do; or
4 by way of fair report of open proceedings of any Court or meeting shall not be guilty of defamation.

Section 330.—In the case of defamation, if the alleged offender can prove that the statement alleged to be defamatory is true, he shall not be liable to punishment.

But, he should not be allowed to prove if the statement alleged to be defamatory is an imputation on a personal matter, and such proof will not be of benefit to the public.

Appendix II

Five versions of the Thai law on sedition

The Royal Edict of 1900

Inciting the subjects to be rebellious and oppose the power of the land

Section 5.—Whosoever speaks with the mouth among the meeting of people in general oneself, or makes an announcement oneself . . . in those spoken words or written words, or in any various symbols, or in any other way that it is clearly understood, or can be clearly seen, which has the contents or a thing becoming, with the desire of causing a bad event to occur, any of the three following clauses:

1 in order to incite or encourage the people to forsake their loyalty to the present King, the King's ministers, or the government, or the royal customs of governance which have been established by law, or Ministers of the Royal Council, or the considerations and legal judgments of the courts and laws of Siam overall to be defamed and looked down upon by the people in general;
2 in order to incite or promote the people to think of changing or altering the royal customs for the governance of Siam which have been established according to the law in any way except through a way that is in accordance with the law; and
3 in order to incite or promote the people to hate one another or create injury in any way, such a person is in violation. [Imprisonment of up to three years and fine of up to 1,500 baht.]

1908 criminal code

Section 104.—Whoever appears before the people in whatever fashion, with intention for whatever results, according to this section to:

1 create disloyalty or to insult the king, the government, or the country;
2 cause unrest and dissatisfaction among the people in a fashion that cause disturbances in the country; or
3 cause the people to transgress the royal laws.

[T]he one who commits such acts, with such motives, shall be punished with imprisonment of not more than three years and fined not more than one thousand baht, or both.

1927 amendment

Section 104.—(1) Whoever commits any act, or whoever by words or writings or printed documents or by any means whatever, advocates or teaches any political or economic doctrine or system, intended or calculated:

(a) to bring into hatred or contempt the Sovereign, the Government or the administration of the State; ... shall be punished with imprisonment not exceeding ten years and fine not exceeding five thousand baht.

1935 amendment

Section 104.—(1) Whoever commits any act, or whoever by words or writings or printed documents or by any means whatever, advocates or teaches any political or economic doctrine or system, intended or calculated:

(a) to bring into hatred or contempt the Sovereign, the Government or the administration of the State, by the people; . . . shall be punished with imprisonment not exceeding seven years and fine not exceeding two thousand baht.

[. . .]

Provided that there shall be no offence under this section when the said words or writing or printed documents or means whatsoever will merely be an expression of good faith or amount to a critical and unbiased comment on governmental or administrative acts within the spirit of the Constitution or for the public interest.

1957 revised criminal code

Section 116.—Whoever makes an appearance to the public by words, writings or any other means which is not an act within the purpose of the Constitution or for expressing an honest opinion or criticism in order:

(1) to bring about a change in the Laws of the Country or the Government by the use of force or violence;
(2) to raise unrest and disaffection amongst the people in a manner likely to cause disturbances in the Country; or
(3) to cause the people to transgress the Laws of the Country

. . . shall be punished with imprisonment not exceeding seven years.

Appendix III

Four versions of the Thai *lèse majesté* law and two proposed amendments

The Royal Edict of 1900

Defaming the King, the Major Concubine, Royal Progeny, . . .

Section 4.—Whosoever defames the reigning king of Siam or the major concubine, or the princes or princesses . . . with intemperate words which may clearly be seen as truly defamatory, this person has acted illegally." [Imprisonment up to three years/Fine of up to 1,500 baht.]

1908 criminal code

Section 98.—Whosoever displays malice toward or defames the King, the Queen Consort, the Heir-apparent, or Regent when he is carrying out his duties to the King, shall be liable to imprisonment not exceeding seven years or a fine of not more than five thousand baht, or both.

Section 100.—Whosoever displays malice toward or defames the princes or princesses from whichever reign, the punishment shall not exceed three years or a fine of not more than two thousand baht, or both.

1957 revised criminal code

Section 112.—Whosoever defames, insults or threatens the King, the Queen, the Heir-apparent, or the Regent shall be punished with imprisonment not exceeding seven years.

1976 amendment

Order of the National Administrative Reform Council No. 41.— Whereas the National Administration Reform Council considers that the penalties for insult or libel upon the King, the queen, the Crown Prince, the Regent, . . . are not proper for the present situation. These penalties should be aggravated. Therefore, the chief of the National Administration Reform Council has given the following orders: The provisions of Section 112 of the Penal Code [the Criminal Law Code] shall be repealed and replaced by the following: "Section 112. Whoever defames, insults or threatens the King, the Queen, the Heir apparent or the Regent shall be punished with imprisonment of three years to fifteen years.

***2007 proposed amendment*:**

"Section 112/1.—Whosoever defames, insults or threatens any Royal Prince or Princess shall be punished with imprisonment of one to seven years, or fined from 20,000 to 140,000 baht, or both."
"Section 112/2.—Whosoever defames, insults or threatens the President of the Privy Council, members of the Privy Council, or any Royal Representative appointed by the King shall be punished with imprisonment of six months to five years, or fined from 10,000 to 100,000 baht, or both."

[Those who defy court orders and report on current lese majesty cases shall be punished with imprisonment not exceeding three years, or fined up to 60,000 baht, or both.]

(2008) proposed amendment (key aspects):

- Extend protection to include relatives, descendants, and past kings of the dynasty
- Increase punishment to a minimum of 5, and a maximum 25 years in prison; increase to range from 500,000 to 1,000,000.
- Cases to be tried expeditiously.
- Defendant must prove innocence.

Appendix IV

Defamation-based coup decrees on defamation

Proclamation of the revolutionary group no. 17 (1958)

Order of the national administrative reform council no. 42 (1976)

The authorities were empowered to "give warnings or seize and destroy such paper, or order the revocation of the license of the printer, publisher, editor or owner of the paper," for publication of items of the following nature:

1 any matter infringing upon His Majesty the King, or defamatory, libellous, or contemptuous of the Queen, Royal Heir, or Regent;
2 any matter defamatory or contemptuous of the nation or Thai people as a whole, or any matter capable of causing the respect and confidence of foreign countries in regard to Thailand, the Thai Government, or Thai people in general, to diminish;
3 any matter ambiguously defamatory or contemptuous of the Thai Government, or any ministry, public body, or department of the government without stating clearly the fault and matter;
4 any matter ambiguously showing that the government or ministry, public body, or department of the government has deteriorated, is bad, or has committed a damaging offence without showing in what matter and particular;
5 any matter promoting approval of Communism, or apparently a Communist plot to disturb or undermine national security;
6 any false matter of a nature tending to panic, worry, or frighten the people or matter tending to incite, or arouse disorder, or conflict with public order or morality, or prophecies concerning the fate of the nation which might upset the people;
7 any matter using coarse language tending to lower national morals and culture;
8 any official secrets.

Appendix V

Thai constitutions, 1932–present

- 27 June 1932–10 Dec. 1932 (5 months, 12 days) (temporary, legally replaced)
- 10 Dec. 1932–9 May 1946 (13 years, 4 months, 29 days) (permanent, amended in 1939, and twice in 1940, legally replaced)
- 10 May 1946–8 Nov. 1947 (1 year, 5 months, 29 days) (permanent, deposed by coup)
- 9 Nov. 1947–23 March 1949 (1 year, 4 months, 14 days) (temporary coup constitution, amended in 1947 and twice in 1948, legally replaced)
- 23 March 1949–29 Nov. 1951 (2 years, 8 months, 6 days) (permanent, deposed by auto-coup)
- 8 March 1952–20 Oct. 1958 (6 years, 7 months, 12 days) (permanent, an amended version of the 1932 constitution, deposed by coup)
- 28 Jan. 1959–20 June 1968 (9 years, 4 months, 23 days) (coup constitution, legally replaced)
- 20 June 1968–17 Nov. 1971 (3 years, 4 months, 28 days) (permanent, deposed by auto-coup)
- 15 Dec. 1972–7 Oct. 1974 (1 year, 9 months, 22 days) (coup constitution)
- 7 Oct. 1974–9 Oct. 1976 (2 years) (permanent, deposed by coup)
- 22 Oct. 1976–20 Oct. 1977 (11 months, 28 days) (coup constitution, deposed by auto-coup)
- 9 Nov. 1977–22 Dec. 1978 (1 year, 1 month, 13 days) (interim, legally replaced)
- 22 Dec. 1978–23 Feb. 1991 (12 years, 2 months, 1 day) (permanent, deposed by coup)
- 1 March 1991–9 Dec. 1991 (9 months, 8 days) (coup constitution, legally replaced)
- 9 Dec. 1991–11 Oct. 1997 (5 years, 10 months, 2 days) (permanent, legally replaced)
- 11 Oct. 1997–19 Sept. 2006 (8 years, 11 months, 8 days) (permanent, deposed by coup)
- 1 Oct. 2006–24 Aug. 2007 (11 months, 5 days) ("temporary" coup constitution, legally replaced)

- 24 Aug. 2007–present

These are available at: http://phetchaburi.ect.go.th/e.htm.

Appendix VI

Court decisions

The Thai government publishes an abbreviated version of each year's Decisions of the Supreme Court. The bibliographical entry is: "Thailand, Supreme Court. *Pramuan khamphiphaksa san dika* [Collected Decisions of the Supreme Court], is shortened to *PKSD*, with the volume number, year, and page numbers, when possible. Decisions of the Appeals Court and Courts of First Instance are not published or generally available except to the litigants themselves. Decisions with no "*PSKD*" were obtained through the Supreme Court's search engine, available at: http://deka2007.supremecourt.or.th/deka/web/search.jsp or: http://www.thaijustice.com.

Decisions of the Supreme Court

1919

Decision 445/2462 [1919] 3 th. s. 272, *PKSD 2462*, pp. 272–77.
Decision 586/2462 [1919], *PKSD 2462*, pp. 368–72.

1930

Decision 363–64/2473 [1930], *PKSD 2473*, pp. 209–13.
Decision 590/2473 [1930], *PKSD 2473*, pp. 359–60.

1932

Decision 317/2475 [1932], *PKSD 2475*.
Decision 573/2475 [1932], *PKSD 2475*, pp. 539–41.
Decision 612/2475 16 [1932] th. s. 564, *PKSD 2475*, pp. 564–68.

1934

Decision 4/2477 [1934], *PKSD 2477*, pp. 20–26.

1935

Decision 456/2478 [1935] 19 th. s. 763, *PKSD 2478*, pp. 763–73.
Decision 751–52/2478 [1935] 19 th. s. 1322, *PKSD 2478*, pp. 1322–27.

1936

Decision 118/2479 [1936], *PKSD 2479*, pp. 149–54.
Decision 683/2479 [1936], *PKSD 2479*, pp. 840–53.

1937

Decision 607/2480 [1937], *PKSD 2480*, pp. 691–95.
Decision 1127/2480 [1937], *PKSD 2480* [1937], pp. 1183–87.

1938

Decision 1059/2481 [1938], *PKSD 2481*, pp. 1288–94.

1939

Decision 346/2482 [1939] 23 th. s. 440, *PKSD 2482*, pp. 440–43.
Decision 1081/2482 [1939], *PKSD 2482,* pp. 1650–53.

1941

Decision 97/2484 [1941] thau. sau. 119, *PKSD 2484*, pp. 119–26
Decision 143/2484 [1941] 25 th. s. 176, *PKSD 2484*, pp. 176–84.
Decision 209/2484 [1941] 25 th. s. 291, *PKSD 2484*, pp. 291–98.

1943

Decision 399/2486 [1947], *PKSD 2490.*

1947

Decision 56/2490 [1947], *PKSD 2490*, pp. 40–44.

1948

Decision 631/2491 [1948], *PKSD 2491*, pp. 759–65.

1952

Decision 1153–54/2495 [1952] d. 832, *PKSD 2495*, pp. 832–42.

1953

Decision 45/2496 [1953], *PKSD 2496*, pp. 55–67.

1954

Decision 1513–15/2497 [1954] d. 1319 m. 113, *PKSD 2497*, pp. 1319–50.
Decision 2097/2497 [1954], *PKSD 2497*, pp. 1853–55.

1955

Decision 1325/2498 [1955], *PKSD 2498*, pp. 1269–75.

1960

Decision 51/2503 [1960], *PKSD 2503*, dau. 73, pp. 73–78.
Decision 645/2503 [1960], *PKSD 2503*.

1962

Decision 1662/2505 [1962], *PKSD 2505*, pp. 1405–8.

1963

Decision 1559/2506 [1963]
Decision 1155/2506 [1963]

1964

Decision 321/2507 [1964]

1978

Decision 861/2521 [1978], *PKSD 2521*, pp. 1327–35.
Decision 1294/2521 [1978], *PKSD 2521*, pp. 1581–82.

1979

Decision 1978/2522 [1979]

1981

Decision 1959/2524 [1981]

1986

Decision 3243/2529 [1986], *PKSD 2529*, pp. 222–37

1988

Decision 2354/2531 [1988], *PKSD 2531*, pp. 888–923.

1993

Decision 913/2536 [1993] Available at: http://www.thaijustice.com/webboard.asp?sub = 0&id = 758216, accessed 2 Jul. 2009]

Decisions of other courts

- State of Illinois, Appellate court, "Docket No. 79712–Agenda 12–March 1996"; KIMBERLY BRYSON, Appellant, v. NEWS AMERICA PUBLICATIONS, INC., et al., Appellees; Opinion filed October 24, 1996.
- Thailand, Appeals Court (San Uthorn), "Khamphiphaksa," khadi mailek 3065/2541 [Judgment, Case No. 3065/1998, Appeals Court, 6 November, 1998].
- Thailand, Central Labour Court (Samut Prakan) (san raeng-ngan klang), "Khadi mai lek dam thi s.p. 366/2551 / khadi mai lek daeng thi s.p. 639/2551" [Black Case No. s.p. 366/2008 / Red Case No. 639/2008], 27 Nov. 2008.
- Thailand, Criminal Court, "Decision of the Court," Black Case No. 1901/36, 26 April 1995, in David Streckfuss, ed., *Modern Thai Monarchy and Cultural Politics: The Acquittal of Sulak Sivaraksa on the Charge of lèse-majesté in Siam 1995 and Its Consequences* (Bangkok: Santi Pracha Dhamma Institute, 1996), pp. 28–31.
- Thailand, Lamphun Provincial Court (San Jangwat Lampun), "Rai-ngan Khadi" [Lamphun (Provincial) Court, Case Report], Khadi mailek dam 802/2546, Khadi mailek daeng thi 783/2526 [Black Case No. 802/2003, Red Case No. 783/2003], 14 May 2003.
- Thailand, Military Court of Bangkok (San thahan krungthep), "Khamphiphaksa, Khadi dam thi 277 k./2507, Khadi daeng thi 192 k./2509, 30 singhakhom 2509" [Decision, Black Case No. 277 k./1964, Red Case No. 192 k./1966, Military Court of Bangkok, 30 Aug. 1966], in Thai Noi, "Kabot phra phimontham pi 2509" [Phra Phimontham Revolt of 1966], in *25 Khadi kabot* [25 Cases of Rebellion] (Krungthep: Rongphim ratthana kanphim, 2513 [1970]).

- Thailand, Special Court (San Phiset) (issued by Krom Khotsanakan, *Khamphiphaksa san phiset ph.s. 2482 ruang kabot* [Judgment of the Special Court of 1939 on the Case of Rebellion] (Krungthep: Krom khotsanakan, 2482 [1939]).

Documents from the Juridical Council

The library at the Juridical Council holds records of the Council's deliberations, and so serves as something of an archive. Sources from the Juridical Council used for this study include law drafts, meetings, and various notes. I have arranged cited documents chronologically and according to topic. In the endnotes, they are preceded with "Thailand, Juridical Council."

1. Anti-subversion and anti-communism laws (1932–34, 1950–52)

- "Draft Act on Control of Subversive Activities (Preliminary Draft)," 18 January 2495 [1952], in "Press 1932–34," Vol. 134.
- Pichan Bulayong [René Guyon], "Interpretation of the Constitution and the Declaration of Human Rights as far as Communism is concerned," 2 April 2494 [1951], in "Kotmai pongkan khommiewnit," *Ruang set* [Finished Matters], Vol. 452.
- "Kotmai pongkan khommiewnit," in *Ruang set* [Finished Matters], Vol. 452.
- Letter from the Secretary-General of the Cabinet of Ministers to the Secretary-General of the Juridical Council, secret-very urgent [*lap–duan mak*], No. 802/2495 of 18 January 2495 [1952], Subject: Anti-Communist Law, and "Note, Subject: Anti-Communist Law," n.d., *Ruang set* [Finished Matters], Vol. 452.
- Juridical Council Committee, Meeting No. 61/2495, 14 October 2495 [1952], "Agenda: Law preventing Communism," in "Kotmai pongkan khommiewnit," *Ruang set* [Finished Matters], Vol. 452.
- "P.B.," [Phichan Bunlayong], "Definition of Communism," 20 October 2495 [1952], in "Kotmai paungkan khommiewnit," *Ruang set* [Finished Matters], Vol. 452.
- "Kotmai pongkan khommiewnit," *Ruang set* [Finished Matters], Vol. 452.
- Handwritten copy of act, countersigned by Phibun Songkhram, n.d., in "Kotmai pongkan khommiewnit," *Ruang set* [Finished Matters], Vol. 452.

2. Criminal law code, amendments and revisions

- Report of the Committee on the Prevention of Communism, Bolshevism and Other Dangerous Propaganda," n.d., in "Rang phraratchabanyat kaekhai pramuan kotmai aya ph.s. 2470" [Draft of the Revision of the Criminal Code Act of 1927], *Ruang set* [Finished Matters], Vol. 19.

- "Penal Code Amendment Act B.E. 2470," *Ruang set* [Finished Matters], Vol. 19.
- "Penal Code Amendment Act B.E. 2470," in *Ruang set* [Finished Matters], Vol. 19.
- "Report of Meeting No. 7," 3 June 1939, Vol. 1, p. 13.
- "Rai-ngan kanprachum kammakan rang kotmai (anukammakan chut thi 3)" [Juridical Council Committee, Report of the Law-Drafting Committee (Sub-Committee No. 3)], Meeting No. 96/2485 [1942], 16 March 2485 [1942], Vol. 360, Part 9.
- "Rai-ngan kanprachum anukammakan truat phitjarana kaekhai pramuan kotmai aya," khrang thi 156, 28/1/82, lem 11 [Juridical Council Committee, Report of the Meeting of the Sub-committee on the Consideration and Revision of the Criminal Law Code, Meeting No. 156, 28 January 1939, Vol. 11].
- "Report of the Meeting of the Sub-committee on the Consideration and Revision of the Criminal Law Code," Meeting No. 298, 9 April 1942, in "Draft of Act," *Ruang set* [Finished Matters], Vol. 393.
- "Rai-ngan prachum kammakan rang kotmai (kammakan kong thi 1), khrang thi 367/2487" [Juridical Council Committee, Report of Meeting on Drafting of Law, Law Drafting Committee No. 1], Meeting No. 367/2487 [1944], 18 December 2487 [1944], in "Draft of Act," *Ruang set* [Finished Matters], Vol. 393.
- "Rai-ngan prachum kammakaan raang kotmai (kammakan kong thi 1), khrang thi 368/2487" [Juridical Council Committee, Report of Meeting on Drafting of Law, Law Drafting Committee No. 1], Meeting No. 368/2487 [1944], 19 December 2487 [1944], in "Draft of Act," *Ruang set* [Finished Matters], Vol. 393.

3. Constitutions

- Juridical Council. Juridical Council Library, Volume 218, "Constitutions," n.d., Vol. 218.
- Pichan Bulayong [René Guyon], "5th Meeting of the Assembly for drafting the Constitution," 21 July 2491 [1948]," in "Constitutions," "Part IV Rapports (personnels) of the Legislative Adviser as Observer on Behalf of the Government," Vol. 218.

4. "Government," on the use of the word

- Rule for using the word "Government," n.d., and "Rules for using the word, 'Government,' from The Secretary-General of the Council of Ministers to the President of the Council of Ministers, 30 April 2485 [1942], from the "Department of the Secretary-General of the Council of Ministers," in Juridical Council Archives, Vol. 360, Part 9; and

"Draft-Memorandum on word 'Government,'" 27 March 2485 [1942], Vol. 360, Part 9.

- "Letter," 5 March 2485 [1942], from the Secretary-General of the Council of Ministers to the Secretary-Gen. of the Juridical Council, Subject: On what occasion the word 'Government' should be used," and "Draft Note," n.d., Vol. 360, Part 9, "Ruang kan chai kham 'ratthaban'" [On the use of the word, "Government"].
- "Rang prakat samnak nayok ratthamontri Ruang kan chai kham wa 'ratthaban'" [Draft Announcement of the Office of the Prime Minister on the Use of the Word, 'Government'"], n.d., and "NOTE Concerning the interpretation of the word "Government," 20 March 2485 [1942], Vol. 360, Part 9
- "Report of Meeting No. 108," 25 March 2485 [1942], in Vol. 360, Part 9.

5. *Martial law/military courts/Special Court*

- "Rang phraratchabanyat jat tang san phiset ph.s. 2476 kaekhai phoemtoem ph.s. 2478" [Draft of the Special Court Establishment Act of 1933, as revised in 1935], *Ruang set* [Finished Matters], Vol. 158;
- "Rang phraratchabanyat jat tang san phiset ph.s. 2476 kaekhai phoemtoem ph.s. 2478" [Draft of the Special Court Establishment Act of 1933, as revised in 1935], *Ruang set* [Finished Matters], Vol. 158
- "Matra 7, Phraratchakamnot kaekhai phoemtoem phraratchabanyat kot ayakansuk ph.s. 2457 ph.s. 2488" [Section 7, Royal Edict amending the 1914 Martial Law Act of 1945], in "Tua baep bang matra kieowkap kot ayakansuk" [Some model provisions concerning martial law], n.d., in "Amnat san rawang chai kot aiyakansuk" [Power of the courts when martial law is in effect], *Ruang set*, [Finished Matter], Vol. 439/3.

6. *Persons dangerous to the nation (1944–45)*

- Letter from the Secretary of the Cabinet of Minister to the Secretary of the Juridical Council, Secret [*lap chapho*], Subject: Detaining persons who are a danger to the nation in times of emergency, 15 December 1943, in "Draft of Act," *Ruang set* [Finished Matters], Vol. 393.
- "Confidential-Urgent Letter," from Duan Bunnag, Secretary-General of the Juridical Council, to Secretary-General of the Council of Ministers, 23 January 2487 [1944], and "Rang, Ruang hai san thahan mi amnat phitjarana phiphaksa khadi aya bang praphet tam bot banyat haeng kot ayakansuk" [Draft, Giving the military court power to consider certain types of criminal cases as according to the legal provisions of martial law], in "Hai san phitjarana phiphaksa khadi tam phraratchabanyat kot aiyakansuk" [Courts trying cases according to the Martial Law Act], *Ruang set* [Finished Matters], Vol. 393/8.

- "Banthuk ruang kieowkap rongrian opprom jitjai" [Notes concerning the psychological training school], confidential [*lap*], from "Adul, Supreme Commander," 23 October 2487 [1944], in "Draft of Act for the Confinement of Persons Dangerous to Nation in Times of Emergency, ph.s. 2488 [1945]," *Ruang set* [Finished Matters], Vol. 393.
- "Rang phraratchakritsadika khuapkhum phu ja pen phai kae chat nai phawa khapkhan, ph.s. 24.," from the original draft of "Draft Edict for the Detention of persons who will be a danger to the nation in time of emergency," 30 October 2487 [1944], in "Draft of Act," *Ruang set* [Finished Matters], Vol. 393
- "Banthuk lakkan lae hetphon, prakob rang phraratchabanyat kakkhum phu pen phai kae chat nai phawa khapkhan ph.s. 24." [Notes on Principle and Reason, with draft of the Act for the Confinement of Persons Dangerous to the Nation in Times of Emergency of 19.], 20 December 2487 [1944], in "Draft of Act," *Ruang set* [Finished Matters], Vol. 393.

7. Press law

- Newspaper clipping, "The Assembly / The Press Act Discussed," n.d., in Juridical Council Archives, Press 1932–1934, vol. 134/3.
- Newspaper clipping, "The Press Act Bill," n.d., in "Press 1932–1934," Vol. 134/3.
- "Opinion of the Legislative Adviser re : the freedom of Press according to the Constitution," 22 April 2493 [1950], "Tentative Press Amendment Act in 2493–2496 (1950–53)," in "Tentative Amendment," *Ruang set* [Finished Matters], Vol. 331.
- "Letter," to the Secretary-General of the Juridical Council from the Secretary-General of the Council of Ministers, Re: Freedom of the Press according to the Constitution, 5 April 2493 [1950], "Tentative Press Amendment Act in 2493–2496 (1950–53)," in "Tentative Amendment Acts to the Press Act (1947–1952)," *Ruang set* [Finished Matters], Vol. 331.

8. Other

- "Letter" from the office of the Samakhom kammakan rang haeng sayam [Siam Drafting Committee], Juridical Council, "Nai Thawat Rittidet," 4 Oct. 2476 [1933], in relation to *Raingan kanprachum sapha phuthaen ratsadorn* [Report of Sessions of the House of Representatives], Session 121/2476 [1933], (saman) [general session], "Prathan sapha an nangsu nai thawat ritthidet ruang thuk ha wa minphraboromdetchaanuphaap" [House Speaker reads letter of Mr. Thawat Ritthidet on being accused of lese majeste], pp. 580–90.

9. Archival materials

- *k/p7/p3/2517/3* Momratchawong Kukrit Pramot thuk klaoha chai thoikham minphraboromdetchanuph*a*p [Kukrit Pramoj accused of using words [that are] *lèse-majesté*] (30/10/17–5/11/17)
- *m.r.* 5 *y.*/1 *bet set k. yuttitham*, (farang wiwat kap khon thai) Ruang nai roemti Mr. lilii kae khaog nangsuuphim) [Miscellaneous, Ministry of Justice, (Westerner disputes with Thai people) The matter of punishing Mr. Lillie in rectifying newspaper].
- *m.th. 0209/147* Naew nayobai kan truat phitjarana phaphayon khong krasuang mahat thai" [Ministry of Interior 0209/147 Guidelines for Checking Movies of the Ministry of Interior], 16 January 2534 [1991], roneo copy.
- *m.th. 5.14/6 Ruang kae khao nangsuphim lae chi jaeng kho thetjing 2479* [Ministry of Interior 5.14/6 on Correcting News from Newspapers and Statement of the Facts, 1936].
- *m.th. 5.14/7 Ruang kae khao nangsuphim lae cii jaeng kho thetjing 2479* [Ministry of Interior 5.14/7 on Correcting News from Newspapers and Statement of the Facts, 1936].
- *p2/2515/3*, Karani Nai Uthai Phimjaichon Nai Anan Phakpraphai lae Nai Bunkoet Hirankham adit s.s. yun fong ho na khana patiwat [The Case of Mr. Uthai Phimjaichon, Mr. Anan Phakpraphai, and Mr. Bunkoet Hirankham, former MPs, taking the Revolutionary Council to court].
- *s.th.*0701.9.10.15/1 *Kammakan phitjarana phaphayon (2474–2503)* [Movie Censorship Board, 1931–60].
- *s.th.*0701.9.10.15/2 *Kammakan phitjarana phaphayon (2503–2506)* [Movie Censorship Board, 1960–63].
- *s.th.*0701.9.10.15/3 *Kammakan sapha phitjarana phaphayon (2506–07)* [Movie Censorship Council, 1963–64].

Bibliography and resources

Books, articles, and movies

14 October, the People's Fight (*Moonhunter*) (2001), Bhandit Rittakol, dir., Seksan Prasertkul, script writer.

Achara Ashayagachat, "Quiet diplomacy would have sufficed," *Bangkok Post*, 4 Sept. 2007.

Administrative Reform Group under the Democratic System with the King as the Head of State, "Initial Statement," 19 Sept. 2006. Available at: http://news.bbc.co.uk/2/hi/asia-pacific/5361756.stm, accessed 29 Nov. 2007.

Agamben, Giorgio, *Homo Sacer: Sovereign Power and Bare Life*, Stanford, CA: Stanford University Press, 1998.

Amicus Brief of Interights and Article 19, "Criminal Defamation Laws and the Right to Freedom of Expression," Joint Amicus Brief of Interights and Article 19 in Constitutional case N 16/98." Available at: http://74.125.153.132/search?q = cache. Available at: http://www.bghelsinki.org/fe/suggestions_en.html, accessed on 23 May 2009.

Ammattho Phra-inthapricha, *Kham athibai kotmai laksana aya phak 2 ton 1* [Explanation of Criminal Law, Part 2, Section 1. Krungthep: Rongphim Sokkanaphattanakorn, 2469 [1926].

Amnesty International, *Amnesty International Report 1984–85*, London: Amnesty International Publications, 1985.

——, *Amnesty International Report 1987–88*, London: Amnesty International Publications, 1988.

——, Public Statement, "Turkey: Article 301 is a threat to freedom of expression and must be repealed now!" December 1, 2005. Available at: http://www.amnestyusa.org/document.php?lang = e&id = ENGEUR440352005, accessed 8 March 2009.

Amnuai Khiewkham, "Minpramat thang aya: suksa chaphao het thi tham hai mai tong rap phit" [Criminal Defamation: A Study Specifically on Reasons for Exclusion from Guilt], thesis, Faculty of Law, Thammasat University, 2532 [1989].

Anan Lao-lertworakul, "Decipher A Secret Code – a Dangerous Attitude of Jakrapob Penkair," photocopy, seven pages, in "additional evidence" provided to the police by Pol. Lt. Wattanasak Mungkijandee, 30 June 2008.

Anderson, Benedict R. O'G., "Withdrawal Symptoms: Social and Cultural Aspects of the October 6 Coup," *Bulletin of Concerned Asian Scholars*, 9(3) (July–September 1977); 13–31.

——, "Studies of the Thai State: The State of Thai Studies," in Eliezer B. Ayal (ed.), *The Study of Thailand*, Athens, OH: Ohio Center for International Studies, Southeast Asia Program, 1978, pp. 193–247.

——, *Imagined Communities: Reflections on the Origin and Spread of Nationalism*, London: Verso, 1991.

——, "The Idea of Power in Javanese Culture," in *Language and Power: Exploring Political Culture in Indonesia*, Jakarta: Equinox Publishing, 2006a, pp. 17–77.

——, *Language and Power: Exploring Political Culture in Indonesia*, Jakarta: Equinox Publishing, 2006b.

Anderson, Benedict R. O'G., and Mendiones, Ruchira, eds., *In the Mirror: Literature and Politics in Siam in the American Era*, Bangkok: Editions Duang Kamol, 1985.

Anderson, Frank G., "Thai Traditions: Lese majeste in Thailand," *Khorat Post*, 2 May 2008.

Anek Laothamatas, "Kan plianplaeng rabop prachathipatai thai 2549" [Changes in Thai Democracy 2006], speech at Thammasat University, 16 Nov. 2006. Available at: http://www.politic.tjanews.org, accessed 7 March 2007.

——, "Samphat phiset: rao tong du lae prachathipatai thi ngok jak din khong rao-eng" [Special Interview: We Must Care for Democracy that is Grown on Our Own Soil], *Nechan sutsapda* [*National Weekly*], 8 Dec. 2006.

Arendt, Hannah, *Between Past and Future: Eight Exercises in Political Thought*, New York: Penguin Books, 1967.

Article 19, "Handbook." Available at: http://www.article19.org/publications/law/the-handbook.html, accessed on 14 Nov. 2008.

——, "Thailand: Draft Computer Offences Act," London, April 2007.

Article 19 and Forum-Asia, *Freedom of Expression and the Media in Thailand* (Dec. 2005). Available at: http://www.article19.org/pdfs/publications/thailand-baseline-study.pdf, accessed 19 May 2009.

Article 19 and the National Press Council of Thailand, "Impact of Defamation Law on Freedom of Expression in Thailand" (compiled by Sinfah Tunsarawuth), Mar. 2009 [draft copy].

Asian Human Right Commission, "THAILAND: Senate Must Delay Vote on NHRC," 29 April 2009. Available at: http://www.ahrchk.net/statements/mainfile.php/2009statements/1996/, accessed 3 June 2009.

Asian Sentinel, "How Thailand's Royals Manage to Own All the Good Stuff," 2 March 2007. Available at: http://pages.citebite.com/b1u2r1x6o0eeg, accessed 12 May 2009.

Askew, Marc, "Landscapes of Fear, Horizons of Trust: Villagers Dealing with Danger in Thailand's Insurgent South," *Journal of Southeast Asian Studies*, 40(1) (Feb. 2009): 59–86.

Attachak Satayanurak, *Kanplianplaeng lokkathat khong chan phunam thai tangtae ratchakan thi 4 – ph.s. 2475* [Change in the Worldview of the Thai Governing Elite from the Fourth Reign to 1932], Krungthep: Samnakphim julalongkorn mahawitthayalai, 2538 [1995].

——, "*Mu thi sam" nai prawattisat kanmuang thai* ["The Third Hand" in Thai Political History; author's title: "Truths" and Dealing with "Truths" in the Context of the "Third-Party Culture" (1957–the Present Time)," Krungthep: Khrongkan jatphim khop fai, 2549 [2006]).

Atthakaiwanlathi, Luang, and Suk Frunawin "Rabop aiyakan lae san thahan" [System of Prosecution and the Military Court], n.d.

Awzar Thi (pseud), "Thailand's Anti-Human Rights Commission," 14 May 2009. Available at: http://www.ahrc-thailand.net/index.php?option = com_content&task = view&id = 302&Itemid = 1, accessed 3 June 2009.

Ayşe Gül Altinay, *The Myth of the Military-Nation*, New York, Palgrave Macmillan, 2004.

Baker, Chris and Pasuk Phongpaichit, *A History of Thailand*, Cambridge: Cambridge University Press, 2005.

——, *Khun Chang Khun Phaen*, forthcoming.

Baker, Keith Michael, "Defining the Public Sphere in Eighteenth-Century France: Variations on a Theme by Habermas," in Craig Calhoun, ed., *Habermas and the Public Sphere*, Cambridge, MA: The MIT Press, 1992), pp. 181–211.

Banyat Suchiwa, "Min pramat" [Defamation], *Bot Bandit*, 27(1) (2513): 149–53.

Barmé, Scott, *Luang Wichit Wathakan and the Creation of a Thai Identity*, Singapore: Institute of Southeast Asian Studies, 1993), pp. 163–71.

BBC, "Author's Trial Set to Test Turkey" 14 Dec. 2005. Available at: http://news.bbc.co.uk/2/hi/europe/4527318.stm, accessed 3 May 2008.

Benhabib, Seyla, "Models of Public Space: Hannah Arendt, the Liberal Tradition, and Jürgen Habermas," in Craig Calhoun, ed., *Habermas and the Public Sphere*, Cambridge, MA: The MIT Press, 1992, pp. 73–98.

Bhumibol Adulyadej, King, *Collection of Royal Addresses and Speeches during the State and Official Visits of Their Majesties the King and Queen to Foreign Countries 1959–1967 (B.E. 2502–2510)*, Bangkok, n.p., 1974.

——, *Royal Advice by His Majesty the King 20 May 1992/2535 at 21.30*, Bangkok: Office of His Majesty's Principal Private Secretary, 1992.

——, *The Story of Thongdaeng*, Bangkok: Amarin Printing and Publishing, 2002.

Bloch, Douglas A. "Constructing Conundrums: Pretenses of Sexuality in Contemporary Thai Society," unpublished manuscript, University of Washington, October 1995.

Bloefeld, John, *Maha Mongkut of Siam*, Singapore: Asia Pacific Press, 1972.

Boonruam Thiamjan, comp., *Pramuang kotmai withi phijarana khwam aya* [The Criminal Prcedure Code Update, 2005–8], Krungthep: Sutra Paisal Law Media, n.d.

——, comp., *The Criminal Code*, Krungthep: Sont Paisal Press, 2550 [2007].

Boowa Hyanasampanno, Phra Acharn Maha, *The Venerable Phra Acharn Mun Bhurudatto Thera, Meditation Master* (trans. Siri Buddhasukh), Bangkok: Mahamakut Rajawidyalaya Press, 1976.

Boonruam Thiamjan, *The Civil Procedure Code*, Krungthep: Sont Paisal Press, 2551 [2008].

Borwornsak Uwanno, *Kotmai mahachon 2: kanbaeng yaek kotmai mahachon – ekachon lae phatthanakan kotmai mahachon nai prathet thai* [Public Law 2: Dividing Public/Private Law and Development of Public Law in Thailand], Krungthep: Nittitham, 2537 [1994].

——, "The Law of Inviolability in Thailand," *Bangkok Post*, 7 Apr. 2009.

——, "Lese Majeste: Abuse and Benevolence," *Bangkok Post*, 9 Apr. 2009.

——, "Thai Culture and the law on lese majeste," *Bangkok Post*, 8 Apr. 2009.

Bowie, Katherine A., *Rituals of National Loyalty: An Anthropology of the State and the Village Scout Movement in Thailand*, New York: Columbia University Press, 1997.

Bromme, Jeffrey S., "Group Defamation: Five Guiding Factors," *Texas Law Review 64 Tex. L. Rev. 591*, Nov. 1985.

Buppha Changkaew. "Khamsang khana patirup kan pokkhrong phaendin chabap thi 42 kap kankhuapkhum nangsuphim doei ratthaban samai tang tang" [Order No. 42 of the National Administrative Reform Council and Control of the Press by Various Governments], unpublished thesis, Chulalongkorn University, 2534 [1991].

Buddhadas Bhikkhu, *Buddha-Dhamma for Students*, Nonthaburi: The Dhamma Study & Practice Group, 1988.

——, *Handbook for Mankind*, Bangkok: Mahachula Buddhist University Press, n.d.

Burrows, Simon, *Blackmail, Scandal, and Revolution: London's French Libellistes, 1758–92*, New York: Manchester University Press, 2006.

Cet. 1, ed., *Kebebasan pers dan pasal-pasal penghinan* [Defamation and Freedom of the Press in Indonesia] Jakarta: Dewan Pers: UNESCO, 2005.

Chaiwat Satha-Anand, "Sangkhomsat kap kapkaenjatkan 'khwam jing' nai sangkhom thai" [Social Science and "Truth" Management in Thai society], *Sangkohomsat Parithat* [Social Science Review], 19(2) (1998 [2541]): 44–55.

——, "The Silence of the Bullet Monument: Violence and 'Truth' Management, Dusun-nyor 1948, and Kru-Ze 2004," in Duncan McCargo, ed., *Rethinking Thailand's Southern Violence*, Singapore: NUS Press, 2007, pp. 11–34.

Chairong Brahmawong, "Summary of Research Study / The Birthplace of the Lord Buddha Found to be in Thailand: Not in India or Nepal." Available at: http://www.life-alonguniversity.com/buddhabirthplace/pdf/budhasumeng.pdf, accessed 22 June 2009.

Chalut Sawatdithat, "Mua phu tai thuk min pramat" [When the Deceased are Defamed], *Dunlapha*, 4(11) (Nov. 2500): 875–88.

Chang Noi (pseud.), "Bad Neighbours, Woman Warriors, and Paddles," *Nation*, 9 July 2001.

——, "Here Come the Judges," *Nation*, 29 Apr. 2006.

——, "What does the Sufficiency Economy Mean for This Government's Policy?" (1 and 2), *Nation*, 30 and 31 Oct. 2006.

——, "From the People's Constitution to the Judges' Constitution," *Nation*, 30 April 2007.

——, "A New Cold War Underway in Thailand," *Nation*, 26 Nov. 2007.

——,"Thai Studies and the Monarchy," *Nation*, 22 January 2008.

——, "The Mysteries of the Law," *Nation*, 7 July 2008.

——, "The Facts About Vote-Buying and the Patronage System," *Nation*, 1 Sept. 2008.

——, "The Monarchy, Democracy, and the Politics of Polarization," *Nation*, 24 Nov. 2008.

Chanida Chitbundid, *Khrongkan an nuangjak phraratchadamri: kan sathapana phraratcha-amnat nam nai phrabatsomedetphrajaoyuhua* [The Royally Initiated Project: The Making of King Bhumibol's Royal Hegemony], Krungthep: Munnithi khrongkan tamra sangkhomsat lae manutsat, 2550 [2007]

Charnvit Kasetsiri,"Siam to Thailand – A Historian's View," *Bangkok Post*, 23 June 2009.

——, *Sayam ru thai?* [Siam or Thailand?], Bangkok: The Foundation for the Promotion of Social Science and Humanities Textbooks Project, n.d.

Chartier, Roger, *The Cultural Origins of the French Revolution*, Durham, NC: Duke University Press, 1991

Chatthip Nartsupha, "Ideology of Holy Man Revolts," in Andrew Turton and Shigeharu Tanabe, eds., *History and Peasant Consciousness in South East Asia*, Senri

Ethnological Studies No. 13, Osaka: National Museum of Ethnology, 1984, pp. 111–34.

——, *The Thai Village Economy in the Past*, Chiang Mai: Silkworm Books, 1999.

Choke Jarujinda, "Du min jao phanak ngan" [Insulting Officials], *Bot Bandit*, 28(4) (2514 [1971]): 917–34.

Chomsky, Noam, "Afghanistan and South Vietnam," in James Peck, ed., *The Chomsky Reader*, New York: Pantheon Books, 1987, pp. 223–26.

Chuchoet Raktabut, "Amnat phitjarana phiphaksa khong san thahan" [The Power to Consider Cases of the Military Court], *Dunlapha*, 7(8) (Aug. 2503): 958–61.

Church, William F., *Richelieu and Reason of State*, Princeton, NJ: Princeton University Press, 1972.

Colic: dek hen phi [Colic: Baby Sees a Ghost], 2006, Patchanon Thammajira, dir.

Connors, Michael K., *Democracy and National Identity in Thailand*, London: RoutledgeCurzon, 2003.

——, "The Reforming State: Security, Development, and Culture in Democratic Times," in Giles Ji Ungpakorn, ed., *Radicalising Thailand*, Bangkok: Institute of Asian Studies, Chulalongkorn University, 2003, pp. 319–43.

————, "Article of Faith: The Failure of Royal Liberalism in Thailand," *Journal of Contemporary Asia*, 38(1): (February 2008): 143–65.

Connors, Michael K. and Hewison, Kevin, "Introduction: Thailand and the 'Good Coup'," *Journal of Contemporary Asia*, 38(1) (Feb. 2008): 1–10.

Copeland, Matthew, "Contested Nationalism and the 1932 Overthrow of the Absolute Monarchy in Siam," unpublished Ph.D. dissertation, Australia National University, 1993.

Coronel, Antonio P., *Libel and the Journalist*, Quezon City: AFA Publications, 1991.

Cottrell, Jill, *Law of Defamation in Commonwealth Africa*, Hants, England: Ashgates Publishing Company, 1998.

Daranee Charnchoengsilpakul (alias, Da Torpedo), "Speech." Available at: http://www.mediafire.com/?x3cq0ymxwg9, accessed 22 Nov. 2008.

Darling, Frank C., "The Evolution of Law in Thailand," *The Review of Politics*, 33(3) (April 1970): 197–202.

Davis, Lennard J., *Resisting Novels: Ideology and Fiction*, New Yourk and London: Methuen, 1987.

De Baets, Antoon, "Defamation Cases against Historians," *History and Theory*, 41(3) (Oct., 2002a): 346–66.

——, *Censorship of Historical Thought: A World Guide 1945–2000*, Westport, CT and London: Greenwood, 2002b.

Diller, Tony, "What Makes Central Thai a National Language?" in Craig Reynolds, ed., *National Identity and Its Defenders, Thailand, 1939–1989*, Clayton, Victoria: Centre of Southeast Asian Studies, Monash University, Monash Papers on Southeast Asia No. 25, 1991, pp. 86–132.

Douglas, Mary, *Purity and Danger*, London and New York: Routledge, 2005.

Duan Jitrakorn, "Minpramat nai thang aya" [Criminal Defamation], thesis, Faculty of Law, Thammasat University, n.d.

Dunlayasatpathiwet, Luang, *Pramuan kotmai aya phrom duai khamplae phasa angkrit* [The Criminal Code accompanied with English translation, as compiled by Suchat Jiwachat], Krungthep mahanakhorn: Samnakphim nitibannakan, 2516 [1973]), and its 1985 edition Krungthep mahanakhorn: Rongphim jaratsanitthawong, 2528.

Ekkawit na Thalang, "Ekkalak thai thi mi to kan raksa khwam mankhong haeng chat" [Thai identity in terms of maintaining national security], in Kamphon Klaewthanong, ed., Khana anukammakan udomkan khong chat nai khana kammakan ekkalak khong chat, samnak lekhathikan nayok ratthamontri [Subcommittee on National Ideology within the National Identity Board, Office of the Prime Minister], *Kan sammana ruang ekkalak khong chat kap kanphatthana chat thai* [Seminar on National Identity and Thai National Development], Krungthep: Wiktoeri phaowoepoi, 2528 [1985]), pp. 120–31.

Engel, David M., *Law and Kingship in Thailand during the Reign of King Chulalongkorn*, Ann Arbor: University of Michigan Center for South and Southeast Asian Studies, 1975.

——, *Culture and Power in Traditional Siamese Government*, Southeast Asian Program Publications, Ithaca, NY: Cornell University Press, 2001.

——, "Globalization and the Decline of Legal Consciousness: Torts, Ghosts, and Karma in Thailand," *Law & Social Inquiry*, 30 (2005): 469–514.

——, "Landscape of the Law: Injury, Remedy, and Social Change in Thailand," *Law and Society Review*, 43(March 2009): 61–94.

Englehart, Neil A., *Culture and Power in Traditional Siamese Government*, Ithaca, NY: Southeast Asia Program Publications, 2001.

EU, "European Union Election Monitoring Missions," 6 Sept. 2007. Available at: http://www.deltha.ec.europa.eu/news%202007/EOM%20Statement_6%20Sept_EN.htm, accessed 28 May 2009.

Evans, Grant, "Modern Monarchy and Inviolability," *Bangkok Post*, 13 Feb. 2009.

Evans, Keith R., *The Law of Defamation in Singapore and Malaysia* (2nd edn.), Singapore: Butterworths Asia, 1993.

Fah Diew Kan, *Rathaprahan 19 Kanya* [The Coup of 19 September], Krungthepmahanakhorn: Fah Diew Kan, 2550 [2007].

Ferrari, Robert, "Political Crime," *Columbia Law Review*, 20(3) (March 1920).

Foreign Correspondents' Club of Thailand (FCCT), *King of Thailand in World Focus*, Singapore: Didier Millet, 2008.

Foreign Policy, "Failed States List 2008." Available at: http://www.foreignpolicy.com/story/cms.php?story_id = 3865, accessed 23 May 2009.

Foucault, Michael, "Truth and Juridical Forms," in James D. Faubion, ed., *Power*, New York: The New Press, 2000a, pp. 1–89.

——, "Truth and Power," in James D. Faubion, ed., *Power*, New York: The New Press, 2000b, pp. 111–33.

Fraser, Nancy, "Rethinking the Public Sphere: A Contribution to the Critique of Actually Existing Democracies," in Craig Calhoun, ed., *Habermas and the Public Sphere*, Cambridge, MA: The MIT Press, 1992, pp. 109–42.

Fuang Ratchataphan, "Khadi thi san phonlaruan tong yok fong tae san thahan long thot dai" [Cases that civilian courts must dismiss but which the military court can rule], *Bot Bandit*, 21(2) (Apr. 2506): 265–68.

Fuller, Thomas, "As Protesters Pause in Thailand, Their Grievances Against Elite Simmer," *New York Times*, 14 April 2009. Available at: http://www.nytimes.com/2009/04/15/world/asia/15thai.html?_r = 1&ref = world, accessed 11 May 2009.

Geertz, Clifford, "Centers, Kings, and Charisma: Reflections on the Symbolics of Power," in Joseph Ben-David and Terry Nicchols Clark, eds., *Culture and Its Creators Essays in Honor of Edward Shils*, Chicago: The University of Chicago Press, 1977, pp. 150–71.

Giles Ji Ungpakorn, ed., *Radicalising Thailand*, Bangkok: Institute of Asian Studies, Chulalongkorn University, 2003.

——, *Negara: The Theater State in Nineteenth-Century Bali*, Princeton, NJ: Princeton University Press, 1980.

——, *A Coup for the Rich: Thailand's Political Crisis*, Bangkok: Workers Democracy Publishing, 2007.

Goldstein, Norm, ed., *The Associated Press Stylebook and Briefing on Media Law*, New York: Basic Books, 2004.

Grabowsky, Volker, "The Thai Census of 1904: Translation and Analysis," *The Journal of the Siam Societ,y* 84: Part I (1996): 49–86

Gray, Christine E., "Thailand: The Soteriological State in the 1970s," Ph.D. dissertation, The University of Chicago, 1986.

—— "Hegemonic Images: Language and Silence in the Royal Thai Polity," *Man*, 26 March 1991, pp. 43–65.

Habermas, Jürgen, *The Structural Transformation of the Public Sphere: An Inquiry into a Category of Bourgeois Society*, Cambridge, MA: The MIT Press, 1991.

Hamilton, Annette, "Rumours, Foul Calumnies and the Safety of the State: Mass Media and National Identity in Thailand," in Craig Reynolds, ed., *National Identity and Its Defenders, Thailand, 1939–1989*, Clayton, Victoria: Centre of Southeast Asian Studies, Monash University, Monash Papers on Southeast Asia No. 25, 1991, pp. 341–79.

——, "Cinema and Nation: Dilemmas of Representation in Thailand," *East-West Film Journal*, 7(1) (1993): 81–105, and in W. Dissanayake, ed., *Colonialism and Nationalism in Asian Cinema*, Bloomington, IN: Indiana University Press, 1993, pp. 141–61.

Handley, Paul, "What the Coup Was Really About," *Asian Sentinel*, 6 Nov. 2006a, available at: www.asiasentinel.com/index.php?option = com_content&task = view&id = 249&Itemid = 31, accessed 27 May 2009.

——, *The King Never Smiles*, New Haven, CT: Yale University Press, 2006b.

Hanrahan, Michael, "Defamation as Political Contest During the Reign of Richard II," *Medium Aevum*, 72 2003, pp. 259–76.

Hansen, Anne Ruth, *How to Behave: Buddhism and Modernity in Colonial Cambodia, 1860–1930*, Honolulu: University of Hawaii Press, 2007.

Herman, Edward S. and Chomsky, Noam, *Manufacturing Consent: The Political Economy of the Mass Media*, New York: Pantheon Books, 1988.

Herzfeld, Michael, "The Absent Presence: Discourses of Crypto-Colonialism," *The South Atlantic Quarterly*, 101(4) (Fall 2002): 899–926.

Hewison, Kevin, "The Monarchy and Democratisation," in Kevin Hewison, ed. *Political Change in Thailand: Democracy and Participation*, London: Routledge, 1997, pp. 58–74.

——, "Responding to Economic Crisis: Thailand's Localism," in Duncan McCargo, ed., *Reforming Thai Politics* Copenhagen, Denmark: Nordic Institute of Asian Studies (NIAS), 2002, pp. 143–61.

——, "A Book, the King and the 2006 Coup," *Journal of Contemporary Asia*, 38(1) (February 2008): 190–211.

Hinke, CJ, "Thai Means Free: FACT Coordinator CJ Hinke Comments on Lese Majeste," 29 April 2008. Available at: http://www.prachatai.com/english/news.php?id = 619, accessed 12 July 2008.

Hobsbawm, Eric, "Introduction: Inventing Traditions," in Eric Hobsbawm and

Terence Ranger, eds., *The Invention of Tradition*, Cambridge: Cambridge University Press, 1986.

Hong Lysa, "Does Popular History in Thailand Need Historians?" *Su wattanatham sanai mai rat vs prachachon-chat* [Toward a Modern Culture State vs. the People-nation], Krungthep: Sathaban thai khadi suksa, 2547 [2003] [*warasan thai khadi suksa* 1:2 (Apr.–Sept. 2547)], pp. 38–66.

Human Rights Watch, "Thailand: Replace Flawed Rights Panel, Unqualified Candidates Were Selected by Secret and Illegal Process," 13 May 2009. Available at: http://www.hrw.org/en/news/2009/05/13/thailand-replace-flawed-rights-panel, accessed 3 June 2009.

Ignatieff, Michael, "Introduction," in Jillian Edelstein, *Truth & Lies*, New York: The New Press, 2001, pp. 15–21.

Iijima, Akiko, "The 'International Court' System in the Colonial History of Siam," *Taiwan Journal of Southeast Asian Studies*, 5(1) (2008): 31–64.

Ishii, Yoneo, *Sangha, State, and Society: Thai Buddhism in History*, Honolulu: Hawaii University Press, 1986.

Jackson, Peter A., *Buddhadasa: A Buddhist Thinker for the Modern World*, Bangkok: The Siam Society, 1989.

——, "Thai-Buddhist Identity," in Craig Reynolds, ed., *National Identity and Its Defenders, Thailand, 1939–1989*, Clayton, Victoria: Centre of Southeast Asian Studies, Monash University, Monash Papers on Southeast Asia No. 25, 1991, pp. 191–232.

——, "Re-Interpreting the Traiphum Phra Ruang: Political Factions of Buddhist Symbolism in Contemporary Thailand," in Trevor Ling, ed., *Buddhist Trends in Southeast Asia*, Singapore: Institute of Southeast Asian Studies, 1993, pp. 64–100.

——, *Buddhadasa: Theravada Buddhism and Modernist Reform in Thailand*, Chiang Mai: Silkworm Books, 2003.

——, "The Performative State: Semi-coloniality and the Tyranny of Images in Modern Thailand," *Sojourn*, 19(2) (2004): 219–53.

Jaran Cosananand, "Khwamrunraeng haeng thot thi mai pen tham lae kanpitkan "khwamjing" nai matra 112 haeng pramuan kotmai aya" [The Violence of Unjust Punishment and keeping out of "the truth" in Section 112 of the Criminal Code], on the panel, "sitthi manusayachon lae khwam klua nai sangkhom thai" [Human Rights and Fear in Thai Society], "Lak miti kotmai min phraboromratchanuphap" [Symposium on Legal Dimensions of the Lese Majesty Law], 21–22 March 2009, Thammasat University.

Jarunee Thanarataphorn, "Kot aiyakan suk lae khet amnat san yuthitham mua mi kanprakat kot aiyakan suk" [Martial Law and Jurisdiction of the [regular] Courts When Martial Law has been Declared], *Dunlapha*, 28(6) (Nov.–Dec. 2524): 81–110.

Jerryson, Michael, "Appropriating a Space for Violence: State Buddhism in Southern Thailand," *Journal of Southeast Asian Studies* 40: 1 Feb. 2009, pp. 33–57.

Jiti Jaroencham, "Yang mai thung khanat du min" [Not Quite Yet an Insult], 16: 189 (2536) [1993a], pp. 127–30.

——, "Klao doei sujarit phua khwam chop tham" [Speaking in Good Faith for Fairness], *Warasan Aiyakan* 16:179 (2536) [1993b], pp. 68–73.

Jitti Tingsaphat, *Kham athibai pramuan kotmai aya (phak 2 tonn thi 1)* [Explanation of the Criminal Law Code], Phranakhorn: Rongphim thai phitthaya, 2510 [1967].

——, *Kham athibai pramuan kotmai aya (phak 2 ton thi 2)* [Explanation of the

Criminal Law Code], Krungthep: Samnakngan opphrom suksa kotmai haeng nettibandittaya sapha, 2518 [1975].

——, *Kham athibai pramuan kotmai aya phak 2 ton thi 1* [Explanation of the Criminal Law Code] Krungthep: Samnak opromsuksa kotmai haeng netibandittayasapha, 2531 [1988].

——, *Kham athibai pramuan kotmai aya (phak 2 ton 2 lae phak 3)* [Explanation of the Criminal Law Code], Krungthep: Samnakngan opphrom suksa kotmai haeng nettibandittaya sapha, 2532 [1989].

Jon Ungpakorn, "Another Nail in the Coffin of Thai Democracy," *Bangkok Post*, 10 Oct. 2007.

Jones, Derek, ed., *Censorship: A World Encyclopedi,a* London and Chicago: Fitzroy Dearborn, 2001.

Jones, Thomas D., "Group Defamation under British, Canadian, Indian and Nigerian Law," *International Journal on Minority and Group Rights*, 5 (1998): 281–335.

Jory, Patrick, "Political Decentralisation and the Resurgence of Regional Identities in Thailand," *Australian Journal of Social Issues* (Special Issue), 34(4) (1999): 337–52.

——, "The King and Us: Representations of Monarchy in Thailand and the Case of *Anna and the King*," *International Journal of Cultural Studies*, 4(2) (2001): 201–18.

——, "Thai and Western Buddhist Scholarship in the Age of Colonialism: King Chulalongkorn Redefines the Jatakas," *The Journal of Asian Studies*, 61(3) (2002): 1–28.

——, "The *Vessantara Jataka*, *Barami*, and the *Bodhisatta*-Kings: The Origins and Spread of a Premodern Thai Concept of Power," *Crossroads: An Interdisciplinary Journal of Southeast Asian Studies*, 16(1) (2002), pp. 152–94.

——, "Problems in Contemporary Thai Nationalist Historiography." Available at: http://kyotoreview.cseas.kyoto-u.ac.jp/issue/issue2/article_251.html, accessed 23 Jan. 2008.

——, "Historiography in Thailand from 1945 to the Present," in Axel Schneider and Daniel Woolf, eds., *The Oxford History of Historical Writing, Volume 5, 1945–Present*, Oxford: Oxford University Press, forthcoming.

Kamakorn Ying Hara [The Factory Workers of Hara] (1976), Jon Ungpakorn, dir.

Kanchanaporn Chitsanga, "Banned in Bangkok: Banned Books in Thailand 2493–2542 [1950–99],"

Kaplan, M. Lindsay, *The Culture of Slander in Early Modern England*, New York: Cambridge University Press, 1997.

Kasian Tejapira. *Commodifying Marxism: The Formation of Modern Thai Radical Culture, 1927–1958* Kyoto: Kyoto University Press, 2001.

——, "The Postmodernisation of Thainess," in Shigeharu Tanabe and Charles F. Keyes, eds., *Cultural Crisis and Social Memory*, London: RoutledgeCurzon, 2002, pp. 202–27.

——, "Toppling Thaksin," *New Left Review* (May–June 2006), pp. 5–37.

Kavi Chongkittavorn, "Information Act Challenges Culture of Secrecy," *Nation*, 25 Jan. 1999; "Time to End Culture of Impunity Around Disappearances," *Nation*, 1 Sept. 2008; "Our Country's Media Freedom: Myth and Reality," *Nation*, 9 March 2009.

Kershaw, Roger, *Monarchy in South-East Asia*, London: Routledge, 2001.

Keyes, Charles F., *Isan: Reionalism in Northeastern Thailand*, Data Paper No. 65, Southeast Asia Program, Ithaca, NY: Cornell University Press, 1967.

——, *Thailand: Buddhist Kingdom as Modern Nation-State*, Boulder, CO: Westview Press, 1987.

——, "'Who Are the Tai?' Reflections on the Invention of Identities," in Lola Romonucci-Ross and George De Vos, eds., *Ethnic Identity: Creation, Conflict and Accommodation*, Walnut Creek, CA: Sage, 1995, pp. 136–60.

——, "National Heroine or Local Spirit? The Struggle over Memory in the Case of Thao Suranari of Nakhon Ratchasima," in Shigeharu Tanabe and Charles F. Keyes, eds., *Cultural Crisis and Social Memory*, London: RoutledgeCurzon, 2002, pp. 113–36.

Khana Nitisat, Mahawitthayalai Thammasat, *Pramuan kotmai ratchakan thi nung julasakarat 1166, phim tam chabap luang tra sam duang*, lem 2 [The Three Seals Law, vol. 2], Krungthep: Rongphim ruankaew kanphim, 2529 [1986].

Khanit na Nakhorn, *Kotmai aya phak khwamphit* [Criminal Law Criminal Offence Section], 3rd edn. (Samnakphim mahawitthayalai thammasat, 2532 [1989]), and 9th edn., Krungthep: Winyuchon Publication House, 2549 [2006].

Khien Theeravit, "Thailand's 'Coup De Grace' Is Not Lacking in Legitimacy," *Nation*, 18 Oct. 2006.

Khrongkan prakatsaniyabat kotmail mahachon, khana nitisat, mahawithayalai thammasat, et al., "Lak miti kotmai min phraboromratchanuphap" [Symposium on Legal Dimensions of the Lese Majesty Law], 21–22 March 2009, Thammasat University.

Khru ban nok [The Rural Teacher] (1978), Surasee Pahtham, dir.

Kiatkhajorn Wajanasawat, *Kham athibai kotmai phak 1 (chabap phim khrang thi 10)* [Explanation of the Criminal Code, 10th edn.], Krungthep: Samnakphim phon-(la)sayam printing, 2551 [2008].

King Rama VI, Phrabatsomdetphra Mongkutklao jaoyuhua, *Bot lakhorn ruang minpramat san tobta chuai amnat lae nam yok ao nam bong*, Krungthep: Khurusapha, 2506.

Klausner, William J., "Law and Society." Available at: http://www.thailawforum.com/articles/lawwilliam5.html, accessed 28 June 2008.

——, "The NGOs in Crisis: Danger and Opportunity," *Thai Culture in Transition*, Bangkok: The Siam Society, 2002, pp. 169–70.

——, "Thailand: A Social, Cultural and Political *Cul de Sac*," Institute of Security and International Studies (ISIS), Chulalongkorn University, July 2008.

Kobkua Suwannatha-Pian, King, "The Monarchy and Constitutional Change since 1972," in Duncan McCargo, ed., Reforming Thai Politics, Copenhagen, Denmark: Nordic Institute of Asian Studies (NIAS), 2002, pp. 57–71.

——, *Country and Constitutions: Thailand's Political Development 1932–2000*, London and New York: RoutledgeCurzon, 2003.

Koh, Leslie, "Lese majeste Laws 'a Problem' for Thais," *Straits Times*, 22 Jan. 2009 www.asianewsnet.net/news.php?id = 3548&sec = 1.

Kong Rithdee, "Beware the Watchdogs of Cinema," *Bangkok Post*, 23 June 2007.

Kongbannathikan warasan fah diew kan, "Rai-ngan: wa duai phramahakasat nai kanprachum thai suksa nana chat thi thammasat" [Editor Section, Fah Diew Kan Magazine, "Report: On the King in the International Thai Studies Conference at Thammasat], *Prachathai*, 21 Jan. 2551 [2008]; *Fah Diew Kan* 5:2 Apr.–June 2549 [2006], pp. 111–12.

Koret, Peter, "The Gestation Period for Miracles: The True Story of a Siamese Man's

Attempts to Create World Peace and Million-Ton Bread Ovens," unpublished manuscript.

Kullada Kesboonchoo-Mead, *The Rise and Decline of Thai Absolutism*, London and New York: RoutledgeCurzon, 2004.

Law Faculty, Thammasat University, Chamlae kotmai khruangmu khong kanmuang banthuk kansammana Ruang "ja kae panha kanchai kotmai pen khruangmu thang kanmuang dai yang rai" [Cutting Out Laws (Used as) Tools of Politics: Proceedings of the Seminar, "How to Solve the Problem of Laws Being Used as Tools of Politics"]. Bangkok, 22 December 1992. Krungthep: Asornmuangnit, 2536 [1993].

Le Bret, Cardin, *De Souveraineté du Roy*, Paris, 1632

Lev, Daniel S., "Introduction," in *Legal Evolution and Political Authority in Indonesia: Selected Essays*, The Hague; Boston: Kluwer Law International, 2000.

Leyland, Peter, "The Emergence of Administrative Justice in Thailand under the 1997 Constitution," in Tom Ginsberg and Albert H. Y. Chen, eds., *Administrative Law and Governance in Asia*, London and New York: Routledge, 2009, pp. 230–56.

Ling, Trevor, *Buddhism and the Mythology of Evil: A Study of Theravada Buddhism*, Oxford: Oneworld Publications, 1997.

Loos, Tamara, "Issaraphap: Limits of Individual Liberty in Thai Jurisprudence," *Crossroads: An Interdisciplinary Journal of Southeast Asian Studies*, 12(1) (1998): 35–75.

——, "Gender Adjudicated: Translating Modern Legal Subjects in Siam," Ph.D. dissertation, Cornell University, Ithaca, NY, 1999.

——, *Subject Siam: Family, Law, and Colonial Modernity in Thailand*, Bangkok: Silkworm Books, 2002.

Luang Pho III [Venerable Father (monk), Part III]] 1991.

Ma Tin Win, "In Spite of our Good Will," *The New Light of Myanmar*, 19 May 2001. Available at: http://www.myanmar.gov.mm/Article/Article2001/May/May19.html, accessed 10 June 2009.

——, "How Did Opium Arrive at the Goldren Triangle Region?," *The New Light of Myanmar*, 20 May 2001. Available at: http://www.myanmar.gov.mm/Article/Article2001/May/May20.html, accessed 10 June 2009.

——, "Never Been Enslaved, But Real Slave," *The New Light of Myanmar*, 21 May 2001. Available at: http://www.myanmar.gov.mm/Article/Article2001/May/May21.html, accessed 10 June 2009.

Macan-Markar, Marwaan, "War on Drugs Reveals Culture of Impunity," 12 March 2003. Available at: http://www.irrawaddy.org/article.php?art_id = 130&page = 1, accessed 15 May 2009.

——, "'Judicial Revolution' Changing Thailand's Political Landscape," 10 July 2008. Available at http://www.irrawaddy.org/article.php?art_id=13245.

——, "'New Politics' to Disenfranchise the Poor," 15 Sept. 2008. Available at: http://ipsnews.net/news.asp?idnews = 43874, accessed 29 Sept. 2008.

——, "Violence Shakes Elite Myth of Thai Unity," 30 Nov. 2008. Available at: http://ipsnews.net/news.asp?idnews = 44913, accessed 13 Dec. 2008.

——, "Court Gains No Glory by Banning Ruling Party," 7 Dec. 2008. Available at: http://ipsnews.net/news.asp?idnews = 45018, accessed 14 Dec. 2008.

——, "Town and country divide runs deep," 11 Jan. 2009. Available at: http://ipsnews.net/news.asp?idnews = 45368, accessed 16 Jan. 2009.

——, "Don Challenges Lese-Majeste Law – Risks Jail Term," 27 Jan. 2009. Available at: http://ipsnews.net/print.asp?idnews = 45566, accessed 29 Jan. 2009.

——, "Blogger Gets 10 Years for Insulting Royalty." Available at: http://ipsnews.net/text/news.asp?idnews = 46402, accessed 5 April 2009.

Mahawitthayalai wicha Thammasat lae kanmuang, *Kotmai tra 3 duang chabap phim* lem 1 (kae khai mai) [Three Seals Law, Vol. 1, newly revised] Krungthep mahanakorn: Sathaban pridi panomyong, 2548 2005].

Malinowski, Bronislaw, *Sex and Repression in Savage Society*, London and New York: Routledge, 2001.

Marcus, Ellyn Tracy, "Group Defamation and Individual Actions: A New Look at an Old Rule," *California Law Review 71 Calif. L. Rev. 1532*, Sept. 1983.

McCargo, Duncan, *Chamlong Srimuang and the New Thai Politics*, New York: St. Martin's Press, 1997.

——, *Politics and the Press in Thailand: Media Machinations*, London and New York: Routledge, 2002.

——, "Buddhism, Democracy, and Identity in Thailand," *Democratization*, 11(4) (August 2004): 155–70.

——, "Network Monarchy and Legitimacy Crises," *Pacific Review*, 18(4) (December 2005): 499–519.

——, "Thai Buddhism, Thai Buddhists and the Southern Conflict," *Journal of Southeast Asian Studies*, 40(1) (Feb. 2009): 1–10.

——, "Thai Politics as Reality TV," *Journal of Asian Studies*, 68(1) (February 2009): 7–19.

——, "The Politics of Buddhist Identity in Thailand's Deep South: The Demise of Civil Religion?" *Journal of Southeast Asian Studies*, 40(1) (2009): 11–32.

——, *Tearing Apart the Land: Islam and Legitimacy in Southern Thailand*, Singapore: NUS Press, 2009.

McCargo, Duncan and Krisadawan Hongladarom, "Contesting Isan-ness: Discourses of Politics and Identity in Northeast Thailand," *Asian Ethnicity*, 5(2) (June 2004): 219–34.

McDonald, N. A., *A Missionary in Siam (1860–1870)*, Bangkok: White Lotus Books, 1999.

McEwen, Robert and Lewis, Philip, *Gatley on Libel and Slander*, 17th edn. London: Sweet & Maxwell Limited, 1974.

McFarland, George, *Thai-English Dictionary*, Stanford, CA: Stanford University Press, 1944.

Meechai Ruchuphan, "Meechai's Liberal Thoughts: Are We Still Thais?," in Niyom Rathamarit, ed., *Focus on Thai Democracy National and Local Issues*, Bangkok: King Prajadhipok's Institute, 2006, pp. 584–87.

Merrick, Jeffrey, *The Desacralization of the French Monarchy in the Eighteenth Century*, Baton Rouge: Louisiana State University Press, 1990.

Montesano, Michael J., "Contextualizing the Pattaya Summit Debacle: Four April Days, Four Thai Pathologies," *Contemporary Southeast Asia*, 31(2) (2009): 217–48.

Montlake, Simon, "Critics Slam Thailand's Activist Judges," *Christian Science Monitor*, 6 October 2008. Available at: http://www.csmonitor.com/2008/1006/p07s03-woap.html, accessed 15 Oct. 2008.

Morakot Jewachinda, *The Images of Pridi Banomyong and Thai Politics, 1932–1983* (1987)

Mu bun [The Assassin/The Gunman] 1983.

Mukhon Wongthes, *Intellectual Might and National Myth: A Forensic Investigation of the Ram Khamhaeng Controversy in Thai Society* Bangkok: Matichon Public Co. [Silapawattanatham Art & Culture chabap phiset], 2003.

Mulder, Niels, *Inside Thai Society: Interpretations of Everyday Life*, Amsterdam and Kuala Lumpur: The Pepin Press, 1996.

——, *Thai Images: The Culture of the Public World*, Chiang Mai: Silkworm Books, 1997.

Munger, Frank, "Constitutional Reform, Legal Consciousness, and Citizen Participation in Thailand," *Cornell International Law Journal*, 40 (2007): 455–75.

——, "Culture, Power, and Law: Thinking About the Anthropology of Rights in Thailand in an Era of Globalization." Available at: http://www.thailawforum.com/articles/Culture.html., accessed 28 June 2008.

——, "Environmental Rights in Thailand: A Role for 'Cause' Lawyers?" paper prepared for the 4th International Conference on "Law in a Changing World," Thammasat University, 9 Dec. 2008.

——, "Globalization, Investing in Law, and the Careers of Lawyers for Social Causes: Taking on Rights in Thailand," *New York Law Review*, 45 (2009): 745–802.

Murray, David, *Angels and Demons*, Bangkok: Orchid Press, 2000.

Mydans, Seth, "In Thai Protests, a Divide Between Urban and Rural," *New York Times*, 12 Oct. 2008. Available at: http://www.nytimes.com/2008/10/13/world/asia/13thai.html?_r = 1&ref = world&oref.

Naeow ruam nak kotmai phua prachachon, klum naksuksa kotmai klum mai, *Rai la-iat khadi prawatisat min phraboromdetchanuphap "Thung chao fa jak kha chao din"* [Details of the Historic Case, "From the People of the Sky to the Slaves of the Land"] Krungthep: Naeow ruam nak kotmai phua prachachon, 2518 [1975].

Nakorm Serirak, "Two Years of Exercising the Right To Know in Thailand," *Nation*, 10 March 2000.

Narong Jaihan, "Thot lae kha sia hai nai karani min pramat" [Punishment and compensation in the case of defamation], *Warasan Nitisat* 2:3 (2534 [1991]), pp. 450–52.

Nattapoll Chaiching, "The Monarch and the Royalist Movement in Modern Thai Politics, 1932–57," unpublished manuscript.

Nidhi Aeusriwong [Eoseewong], "Hitler's Moustache and Protection of the Institution," in Niyom Rathamarit, ed., *Focus on Thai Democracy National and Local Issues*, Bangkok: King Prajadhipok's Institute, 2006a, pp. 578–81.

——. *Pen and Sail*, Chiang Mai: Silkworm Books, 2006b.

——, on the panel entitled, "Kotmai min phraboromdetchanuphap kap khwam mankhong khong rat" [The Lese majesty Law and Security of the State], Khrongkan prakatsaniyabat kotmail mahachon, khana nitisat, mahawithayalai thammasat, *et al.*, "Lak miti kotmai min phraboromratchanuphap" [Symposium on Legal Dimensions of the Lese Majesty Law], 21–22 March 2009, Thammasat University.

——. *Pak kai lae bai rua* [Pen and Sail], Krungthep: Amarin kanphim, 2527 [1984].

Niphon Jaemduang, comp., *Phiphaksa sangkhom thai phiphaksa s. siwarak: khumu suksa kandamnoen khadi aya laksana khwam phit thana min phraboromdechanuphap lae min pramat* (sathaban santiprachatham, 2539) [A Judgment on Thai society, a judgment on S. Sivaraksa: A Handbook For Defence On The Criminal Charge Of Lèse-Majesté And Defamation] Pracha Santi Pracha Dhamma Institute, 1996.

Nom Sisanphang, "San thahan nai wela mai pokkati" [Military Courts in Abnormal Times], *Dunlapha*, 5 (12 Dec 2501): 807–9.

Norway, Government, Statistics Norway. Available at: http://www.ssb.no/straffkjede_en/tab-2002{hy}06{hy}18{hy}03-en.html, accessed 15 Aug. 2009.

Office of His Majesty's Principal Private Secretary, *A Memoir of His Majesty King Bhumibol Adulyadej*, Bangkok: Office of His Majesty's Principal Private Secretary, 1987.

O'Sullivan, Noel, *Conservatism*, London: Dent, 1976.

Oxford English Dictionary, Online.

Pajariyasan, *"Khwamphit thana min phraboromdetchanuphap kap kan pokkhrong rabop prachathipatai thi mi phra maha kasat pen pramuk"* [The Crime of lèse-majesté and the Democratic Governance System with the King as Head of State], *Pajariyasan*, 14(6) (November–December 1987): 12–45.

Pallegoix, Jean-Baptiste, *Description of the Thai Kingdom or Siam*, Bangkok: White Lotus, 2000.

Patsorn Sungsri, *Thai National Cinema*, Saarbrücken: VDM Verlag Dr. Müller Aktiengesellschaft & Co. KG, 2008.

Payutto, P. A. (also goes by Prayudh Payutto, Phra Rajavaramuni, Pha Thammpidok), *Good, Evil and Beyond: Kamma in the Buddha's Teachings* (Bhikkhu Puriso, trans.), Bangkok: Buddhadhasa Foundation, 1993.

——, (under Phra Rajavaramuni), *Thai Buddhism in the Buddhist World: A Survey of the Buddhist Situation against a Historical Background*, Bangkok: Unity Progress Co., 1984, p. 136.

——, (under Phra Thammpidok), *Photjananukrom phutthasat chabap pramuan sap* [Buddhist Dictionary], Krungthep: Mahawitthayalai mahajulalongkoranaratchawitthayalai, 2543 [2000].

Peleggi, Maurizio, *Thailand: The Worldly Kingdom*, London: Reaktion Books, 2007.

Phaibun Phianrujop, "Minpramat phu tai" [Defamation of the Dead], pp. 311–16. Available at: http://www.library.coj.go.th/Article/data/d5_5_5.pdf, accessed 4 July 2009.

Phattana Chaiyaset, "Kotmai nirathotsakam kap phu tham kan patiwat ru rattha prahan" [The Amnesty Law and those who carry out a revolution or coup d'état," *Warasan Aiyakan* 4:45 (k.y. 2524), pp. 9–13.

Phimontham (Asopmahathen) (*Phra*), *Phajon man: banthuk chiwit 5 pi nai hong khang* [Confronting the Devil: Diary of Five Years of Incarceration] Krungthep: Samnakngan klang kawng kan wipasanathura, Khana 5 Wat Mahathat, 2530 [1987].

Phrakraisi (Thiam), Khunluang, *Lak kotmai aya* [Principles of Criminal Law], Krungthep: Rongphim kong lahuthot, r.s. 122 [1904].

Phu thaen nok sapha [Representative Outside the Parliament] (movie) (1983)

Pitch Pongsawat, "What Constitutes 'Legal' Changes with the Powers of the Day," *Nation*, 2 June 2007.

Porphant Ouyyanont, "The Crown Property Bureau from Crisis to Opportunity," in Pasuk Phongpaichit and Chris Baker, eds., *Thai Capital: After the 1997 Crisis*, Bangkok: Silkworm Books, 2008a, pp. 155–86.

——, "The Crown Property Bureau in Thailand and the Crisis of 1997," *Journal of Contemporary Asia*, 38(1) (February 2008b): 166–89.

Postman, Neil, *Technopoly: The Surrender of Culture to Technolog,y* New York: Vintage Books, 1993.

——, *Building a Bridge to the Eighteenth Centur,y* New York: Vintage Books, 1999.

Pramun Suwanasorn, "Min pramat" [Defamation], *Dunlapha*, 6(1) (2502): 2–18.

——, "Min pramat" [Defamation], in *Anusorn nai ngan phraratchathan phloeng sop nai pramun suwannasorn* [Commemoration of the royally-sponored cremation of Mr. Pramun Suwannason] Krungthep: Hanghun suan jamkat Siwaphorn, 2524 [1981].

Prasong Soonsiri, "Phasa thai kap khwam mankhong haeng chat" [Thai language and national security], in Samnakngan soemsang ekkalak khong chat, samnak lekhathikan nayok ratthamontri [Office of National Identity Promotion, Secretariat of the Prime Minister], *Rai-ngan Phon Kan Sammana "Phasa thai kap sangkhom thai"* [Report of the Seminar, "Thai Language and Thai Society"], jat phim phoeiphrae ph.s. 2527 nuang nai kanchaloem 700 pi lai su thai [published for distribution in 1984 on the celebration of 700 years of the Thai script] Krungthep: Samnakphim prakaiphruk, 2527 [1984], pp. 245–51.

Prathin Phattanatham, *Kantamnoen khadi aya nai santhahan* [Prosecution of Criminal Cases in the Military Court] Krungthep: Baphitthakanphim, 2525.

Pravit Rojanaphruk and Subhatra Bhumiprabhas, "Activists Wary of Sondhi Bandwagon," *Nation*, 4 Dec. 2005.

Pravit Rojanaphruk, "EU monitors would boost credibility of poll: Anfrel" (Interview with executive director of the Asian Network for Free Elections (Anfrel) Somsri.

——, "What Has Junta Got to Hide?" *Nation*, 3 Sept. 2007.

——, "Kotmai min phraboromdechanuphap lae kan sensor tua eng" [The *lèse-majesté* law and self-censorship], *Fah Diew Kan* 6:1 Jan.–March 2008, pp. 158–70.

——, "Human Rights Defenders Split into Yellow and Red Camps," *Nation*, 28 Jan. 2009.

Prinya Jittrakaranathikit, *Khwam phit thana min pramat-du min sung na* [The crime of defamation and slander], (3rd ed.), Krungthep: Samnakphim nititham, 2538 [1995].

Prosser, William Lloyd, Keeton, W. Page, Owen, David G., et al., eds., *Proser and Keeton on the Law of Torts* (5th edn.) St. Paul, MN: West Group, 1984.

Raktham Rakthai [pseudonym of Saman Kongsuphon], *Kao Ratchakan* [Nine Reigns], "2nd edition," (n.p., n.d.).

Ramamoorthy, R., *Law of Malicious Prosecution and Defamation*, Bombay: N. M. Tripathi, 1976.

Ratchabanditayasathan, *Photjananukrom*, Krungthep: Aksornjaroenthat, 2539.

——, *Photjananukrom chabap ratchabandittayasathan ph.s. 2542*, Krungthep: Nanmi Book Publishing, 2546.

"Report of the Tribunal Appointed to Inquire into the Events on Sunday, 30th January 1972" [Widgery Report]." Available at: http://cain.ulst.ac.uk/hmso/widgery.htm, accessed 15 April 2009.

Reporters sans frontières, "Annual Worldwide Press Freedom Index," 2002 to 2007. Available at: http://www.rsf.org/en-classement298–2002.html. through http://www.rsf.org/en-classement794–2008.html, accessed last 9 June 2009.

——, "Twenty-six IFEX Members and Other Organisations Urge Government to Amend Lese Majeste Law," 26 April 2009. Available at: http://egypt.ifex.org/thailand/2009/04/28/twenty_six_ifex_members_and_other/index.html, accessed 8 June 2009.

Reporters without Borders, "Defining Defamation: Principles on Freedom of

Expression and Protection of Reputation." Available at: http://www.article19.org/pdfs/standards/definingdefamation.pdf, accessed on 14 Nov. 2008.

Reynolds, Craig J., "National identity and its defenders," in Craig J. Reynolds, ed., *National Identity and Its Defenders: Thailand, 1939–1989*, Monash Papers on Southeast Asia No. 25, Clayton, Victoria: Centre of Southeast Asian Studies, Monash University, 1991a, pp. 1–40.

——, "Sedition in Thai history: A Nineteenth-Century Poem and Its Critics," in Manas Chitakasem and Andrew Turton, eds., *Thai Constructions of Knowledge*, Southampton: School of Oriental and African Studies, University of London, 1991b, pp. 15–36.

——, "A Seditious Poem and Its History," *Seditious Histories Contesting Thai and Southeast Asian Pasts*, Seattle: University of Washington Press, 2006a, pp. 80–101.

——, "A Thai-Buddhist Defense of Polygamy," *Seditious Histories Contesting Thai and Southeast Asian Pasts*, Seattle: University of Washington Press, 2006b, pp. 185–213.

——, "Buddhist Cosmography in Thai Intellectual History," in Craig Reynolds, *Seditious Histories Contesting Thai and Southeast Asian Pasts*, Seattle: University of Washington Press, 2006c, pp. 161–84.

——, "National Identity and Cultural Nationalism," *Seditious Histories Contesting Thai and Southeast Asian Pasts*, Seattle: University of Washington Press, 2006d, pp. 245–76.

——, "Paradigms of the Premodern State," in *Seditious Histories Contesting Thai and Southeast Asian Pasts*, Seattle: University of Washington Press, 2006e, pp. 31–52.

——, "Thai Manual Knowledge: Theory and Practice," in *Seditious Histories Contesting Thai and Southeast Asian Pasts*, Seattle: University of Washington Press, 2006f, pp. 214–42.

Reynolds, Frank E., "Dhamma in Dispute: The Interactions of Religion and Law in Thailand," *Law and Society Review*, 28 (1994): 433–55.

Reynolds, Frank E. and Mani B. Reynolds (trans.), *Three Worlds According to King Ruang: A Thai Buddhist Cosmology*, Berkeley, CA: Regents of the University of California, 1982.

Rhys Davids, T.W., trans., *The Questions of King Milinda*, vol. 1, Delhi: Motital Banarsidass, 1975 [originally published in 1890].

Rosana Tosirakul, "No 'People Power' Crusade, This," *Bangkok Post*, 14 April 2009.

Saiphin Kaewngamprasoet, *Kanmuang nai anusawari thao suranari* [The Politics of the Monument of *Thao Suranari*] (*Silpa Watthanatham*, Special Issue, November), Bangkok: Matichon Press, 1995.

Samakhom nak khao nak nangsuphim haeng prathet thai [Thai Journalists Association]. Available at: http://www.tja.or.th/index.php?option = com_content&task = view&id = 491, accessed 29 Jan. 2008.

Samran Kanphrapha, "Military Judicial System of Thailand," *Military Law Review*, 14 (Oct 1961): 171–81.

——, "Arai nai san dika thahan" [What's in the High Military Court?] *Dulapha*, 25(6) (Nov.–Dec. 2521 [1978]): 20–37.

Sanchai Satjawanit, "Min pramat – du min" [Defamation—Insult], *Bot Bandit* 29:2 and 29:3(2515), pp. 366–89 and 541–73, respectively.

——, "San thahan tam prakat khong khana patiwat" [The Military Court According to the Decree of the Revolutionary Council] *Botbandit*, 28(4) (2514 [1978]): 876–79.

Sanitsuda Ekachai, *Keeping the Faith: Thai Buddhism at the Crossroads*, Bangkok: Post Books, 2001.

Schmitt, Carl, *Political Theology* [trans. George Schwab], Chicago: University of Chicago Press, 1985.

Schuettler, Darren, "Academic Accused of Insulting Thai King in Exam Paper," Reuters News Wire, 2007.

Schuster, Ernest J., "Lèse-majesté in Germany," *Journal of the Society of Comparative Legislation*, 3(1) (1901): 41–45.

Scott, James C., *Seeing Like a State*, New Haven, CT: Yale University Press, 1998.

Scott, James C., *et al*, "International Scholars Call for Reform of Thailand's Lese Majeste Law," *Seeds of Peace*, 25(2) (May–Aug. 2552 (2009)): 7–9.

Sinfah Tunsarawuth for Article 19 and National Press Council of Thailand, entitled "Impact of Defamation Law on Freedom of Expression in Thailand," March 2009 [draft copy].

Sming Tailangka, "Military judicial system of Thailand," *Military Law Review*, 64 (Spring 1974): 151–58.

Somchai Jenchaijittarawanit, *Khadi prawatisat min phraborom detchanuphap: Wira Musikaphong tit khuk phro kanmuang!* [A Historic *lèse-majesté* Case: Wira Musikaphong Jailed Because of Politics!] Krungthep: Samnakngan phua sawaengha khwamyuttitham nai sangkhom, 2531 [1988].

Somchai Preechasilpakul, "Lak niti ratthaprahan" [Juridical Principles of Coups], in *Ratthaprahan 19 kanyayon* [The Coup of 19 September], Krungthep: Fah Diew Kan, 2550 [2007], pp. 190–202.

——, "Min phraboromdechanuphap" [*Lèse-majesté*], *Fah Diew Kan* 6:1 (Jan.–March 2008), pp. 148–57.

——, on the panel entitled, "Kotmai min phraboromdetchanuphap kap khwam mankhong khong rat ["The lese majesty law and Security of the State," Symposium on Legal Dimensions of the Lese Majesty Law, 21–22 March 2009, Thammasat University.

Somchai Preechasilpakul and David Streckfuss, "Ramification and Re-Sacralization of the Lese Majesty Law in Thailand," paper presented at the 10th International Conference on Thai Studies Bangkok: The Thai Khadi Research Institute/ Thammasat University, January 9–11, 2008.

Somdet Phra Maha Samana Chao Krom Phraya Vajirananavarorasa, *Navakovda*: *Instructions for Newly-Ordained Bhikkus and Samaneras* Bangkok: Mahanakut Rajavidya Press, 1993

Somkhit Loetphaiboon, "Kanprapprung prakat khong khana patiwat" [Addressing Coup Decrees," *Raphisan* vol. 1, (April–June 2536 [1993].

Somsak Jeamteerasakul, "Chaiya chana khong panyachon 17 tula (ton thi 2: kanplian plaeng praden khrang yai)" [Victory of the 17 Oct. Intellectuals (Part II: The Big Changing of Subject)], *Ratthaprahan 19 kanyayon* [The Coup of 19 September] Krungthep: Fah Diew Kan, 2550 [2007], pp. 382–430.

Somsak Raksuwan, *Political Monsters* (published on the occasion of the exhibit, "Political Monsters" by Somsak Raksuwan at Jamjuri Art Gallery, Bangkok: Amarin Printing, 2007.

Sopon Onkgara, "The Urban-Rural Divide Grows Dangerous," *Nation*, 30 July 2000 and 6 Aug. 2000.

Spain, Government, Instituto Nacional Estadistica. Available at: http:*//www.ine.es/jaxi/tabla.do*, accessed 15 Aug. 2009.

St. John, Ronald Bruce, "Preah Vihear and the Cambodia-Thailand Borderland." Available at: http://www.dur.ac.uk/resources/ibru/publications/full/bsb1–4_john.pdf, accessed 23 Jun. 2009.

Steiner, George, "The Hollow Miracle," in *George Steiner: A Reader*, New York: Oxford University Press, 1984, pp. 207–22.

Stephens, Mark, "The Ban on Legal Aid for Defendants in Libel Cases Needs to Be Overturned after *McLibel*," *The Lawyer*, (Feb. 2005), available at http://www.thelawyer.com/legal-widow/114212.article.

Streckfuss, David [interview], *Fah Diew Kan*, "Kotmai minphraboromdechanuphap khu setsak udom kanmuang khong phadetkan" [The Lese Majeste Law Is an Ideological Remnant of Dictatorship], *Fah Diew Kan*, 4(2) (April–June 2549 [2006]): 52–65.

Streckfuss, David, "The Mixed Colonial Legacy in Siam: Origins of Thai Racialist Thought, 1890–1910," in Laurie Sears, ed., *Autonomous Histories, Particular Truths: Essays in the Honor of John R. W. Smail*, Madison, WI: Center for Southeast Asian Studies, 1993, pp. 123–53.

——, "Kings in the Age of Nations—The Paradox of *Lèse-Majesté* as Political Crime in Thailand," *Comparative Studies in Society and History*, 37(3) (July 1995): 445–75.

——, ed., *Modern Thai Monarchy and Cultural Politics: The Acquittal of Sulak Sivaraksa on the Charge of lèse-majesté in Siam 1995 and Its Consequences*, Bangkok: Santi Pracha Dhamma Institute, 1996.

——, "The Poetics of Subversion: Civil Liberty and Lesè-Majesté in the Modern Thai State," Ph.D. dissertation, University of Wisconsin, 1998.

——, "Culture and Murder," in *Santi Pracha Dhamma: Essays in Honour of the Late Puey Ungphakorn*, Bangkok: Santi Pracha Dhamma Institute, The Sathirakoses-Nagapradipa Foundation, and The Foundation for Children, 2001, pp. 205–19.

——, "Truth Is Jailed Under a Defamation Regime," *Nation*, 30 May 2005.

——, "A Call for Real National Heroes: Stand and Be Judged," *Bangkok Post*, 14 April 2009.

——, "Thailand's Tough Law," *Dateline Bangkok* [Foreign Correspondents' Club of Thailand Magazine] (Second Quarter 2008), pp. 20–23.

——, "The Law is the Problem," *Seeds of Peace*, 25:2 (May–Aug. 2552 (2009)), pp. 5–6.

Streckfuss, David and Templeton, Mark, "Human Rights and Political Reform in Thailand," in Duncan McCargo, ed., *Reforming Thai Politics*, Copenhagen, Denmark: Nordic Institute of Asian Studies (NIAS), 2002, pp. 73–90.

Streckfuss, Richard, "News before Newspapers," *Journalism and Mass Communication Quarterly*, 75(1) (Spring 1998): 84–97.

Stroup, John, "Political Theology and Secularization Theory in Germany, 1918–39: Emanuel Hirsch as a Phenomenon of His Time," *The Harvard Theological Review*, 80(3) (July, 1987): 321–68.

Suchit Bunbongkarn, "A Reflection on the Role of a Justice of the Thai Constitutional Court," in Niyom Rathamarit, ed., *Focus on Thai Democracy National and Local Issues*, Bangkok: King Prajadhipok's Institute, 2006, pp. 41–48.

Sulak Sivaraksa, "Kanmi sathaban kasat thuk kwa mi prathanathibodi" [Habing a Monarchy is less costly than having a president], interview in *Fah Diew Kan* 3:4 (Oct.–Dec. 2005), pp. 82–93 (Interview was conducted on 8 August 2005).

——, *Siamese Resurgence*, Bangkok: Asian Cultural Forum on Development, 1985.

——, "The Crisis of Siamese Identity," in Craig Reynolds, ed., *National Identity and Its Defenders, Thailand, 1939–1989*, Clayton, Victoria: Centre of Southeast Asian Studies, Monash University, Monash Papers on Southeast Asia No. 25, 1991, pp. 41–58.

Suntaree Komin, *Psychology of the Thai People*, Bangkok: Research Center, National Institute of Development Administration (NIDA), 1991.

Suphon Issarasena, *Kandamnoen khadi minpramat* [Carrying out Defamation Cases] Krungthep: Nitibanyakan, 2546 [2003].

Surapol Nitikraiphot, *Thai Post* [Thai-language newspaper], 15 Oct. 2549 [2006]

Surat Rattana-udom, "San thahan nai wela mai pokkati" [Military Courts in Abnormal Times], *Dunlapha* 6(3) (Mar 2502 [1959]): 192–95.

Suthin Loetwirut, "Phu sia hai nai khwam phit thana min pramat" [The Damaged Party in Defamation Cases], *Dunlapha*, 5 (2501 [1959]): 3–19.

Sutthachai Yimprasert, *Phaen ching chat thai* [Contest for the Thai Nation], Krungthep: Samnakphim 6 tula ramluk, 2550 [2007].

Swearer, Donald K., *Buddhism in Transition*, Philadelphia: The Westminster Press, 1970.

——, "Center and Periphery: Buddhism and Politics in Modern Thailand," in Ian Harris, ed., *Buddhism and Politics in Twentieth-century Asia*, London: Continuum, 2001, pp. 194–228.

Syndromes and a Century 2007, Apichatpong Weerasetthakul, dir.

Tambiah, Stanley J., *World Conqueror and World Renouncer*, Cambridge, MA: Cambridge University Press, 1976.

——, *The Buddhist Saints of the Forest and the Cult of Amulets*, Cambridge: Cambridge University Press, 1984.

——, *Buddhism Betrayed? Religion, Politics, and Violence in Sri Lanka*, Chicago: University of Chicago Press, 2002.

Tanabe, Shigeharu and Keyes, Charles F., eds., *Cultural Crisis and Social Memory*, London: RoutledgeCurzon, 2002.

Tavernise, Sabrina and Arsu, Sebnem, "An identity forged from a painful past," *Bangkok Post*, 13 Oct. 2007.

Terwiel, B. J., "Thai National Identity: Popular Themes of the 1930s," in Craig Reynolds, ed., *National Identity and Its Defenders, Thailand, 1939–1989*, Clayton, Victoria: Centre of Southeast Asian Studies, Monash University, Monash Papers on Southeast Asia No. 25, 1991, pp. 133–56.

Thai Noi, *25 Khadi kabot* [25 Cases of Rebellion], Krungthep: Rongphim ratthana kanphim, 2513 [1970].

Thailand. Attorney General's Office (Samnakngan Aiyakan Songsut), *Rai-ngan prajam pi* [Annual Report of the Attorney General's Office] (Samnakngan aiyakan phiset fai sarasonthet, samnakngan wichakan) [each year individually from 1984 to 2005; year 1996 and 1997 are combined into a single volume].

Thailand, Government. *Constitution of the Kingdom of Thailand B.E. 2550 (2007)*. Available at: http://www.isaanlawyers.com/constitution%20thailand%202007%20-%202550.pdf]

——, *Pramuan khamphiphaksa san dika* [Collected Decisions of the Supreme Court]

Thailand, Military Court of Bangkok Prosecutors (aiyakan san thahan Krungthep), "*Fong*" [Charge Sheet], *Khadi prawattisat khadi 6 tula* [The Historic 6 October Case], Krungthep: Baphit kanphim, 2521 [1978], pp. 67–75.

Thailand, Ministry of Foreign Affairs, "Aide Memoire," 24 May 2001. Available at: http://www.mfa.go.th/web/200.php?id = 530, accessed 10 June 2009]

Thailand, Ministry of Interior, Legal Affairs Bureau, Office of the Permanent Secretary for Interior, "Kan ruapruam kho kotmai thi kiewkhong kap kan min praboromdechanuphap" [Compilation of laws relating to *lèse-majesté*], 2552 [2009]. Available at: www.law.moi.go.th/2552/lese%20majesty%20law%202.doc, accessed 6 Sept. 2009.

Thailand, Ministry of Justice, *Rai-ngan krasuang yuttitham prajam pi ph.s. 2504–2509* [Annual Report of the Ministry of Justice, 1961–66] (Ronghim sahakorn khai song haeng pratehet thai, k.t.m., n.d.).

——, *Rai-ngan krasuang yuthitham prajam pi* [Annual Report of the Ministry of Justice], 2504–27 [1961–84]

——, *Rai-ngan krasuang yuttitham prajam pi ph.s. 2510–2516* [Annual Report of the Ministry of Justice, 1967–73] (n.p., n.d.).

——, *Rai-ngan krasuang yuttitham prajam pi ph.s. 2517–2519* [Annual Report of the Ministry of Justice, 1974–76] (Rongphim ruangtham, k.t.m. 2523 [1980]).

——, *Rai-ngan krasuang yuttitham prajam pi ph.s. 2520* [Annual Report of the Ministry of Justice, 1977] (n.p, n.d.).

——, *Rai-ngan krasuang yuttitham prajam pi ph.s. 2521* [Annual Report of the Ministry of Justice, 1978] (n.p, n.d.).

——, *Rai-ngan krasuang yuttitham prajam pi ph.s. 2522* [Annual Report of the Ministry of Justice, 1979].

——, Samnakngan Aiyakan Songsut, *Rai-ngan prajam pi 2529 – 2548* [Annual Reports of the Attorny-General's Office, 1986–2005] (Samnakngan aiyakan phiset fai sarasonthet, samnakngan wichakan) [issued separately each year].

Thailand, Movie Censorship Board (Phanaek khuapkhum phaphayon), Kong kamkap kan 2 kong thabian, kong banchakan tamruat sopsuan klang, krom tamruat [Cinema Control Section, Directorship 2, Licensing Bureau, Central Investigation Division, Police Department], *Sensoe* [Censor] (n.p., n.d.).

Thailand, National Statistical Office and National Economic Development Board, *Thailand Population Census 1960 Whole Kingdom.*

Thailand, Office of the National Culture Commission, *Organizational Structure, Office of the National Culture Commission, Ministry of Education, Thailand,* Bangkok: United Production Press, n.d.

Thailand, Police Department, Pathumwan Police Station, Bangkok, "Banthuk kan jaeng khwam" [Accusation Report], 22 Apr. 2551 [2008].

——, *Anusaun 80 pi rong rian nai roi tamruat* [80th Anniversary of the Royal Police Cadet Academy] Krungthep: Rongphim Aksaun Samai, n.d.

——, (Krom Tamruat), *Rai-ngan prajam pi* [Annual Report of the Police Department] [each year with individual set of statistics, from 1947 to 1989] [issued separately each year].

Thailand, Samnakngan San Yuttitham [Office of the Judiciary], *Rai-ngan sathiti khadi thua ratcha-anajak prajam pi (ph.s. 2549, 2550, 2551, 2552)* [Annual Judicial Statistics, years 2006, 2007, 2008, 2009] [issued separately each year].

Thak Chaloemtiarana, ed., *Thai Politics: Extracts and Documents 1932–1957*, Bangkok: The Social Science Association of Thailand, 1978.

——, *Thailand: The Politics of Despotic Paternalism*, Chiang Mai: Silkworm Books, 2007.

"Thalaengkan nakwichakan lae prachachon ruang kankhatkhan kho sanoe hai mi kanyokluk lae kaekhai kotmai thi kiew khong kap kanpokkhrong phramahakasat jak kanlamoet," wan thi 13 minakhom 2552 na sathaban bandit phatthana borihansat ["Declaration of Academics and the People opposing the proposal to abolish or revise laws relating to a protecting the king from being violated," 13 March 2009 at the National Institute of Development Administration (NIDA).

Thaemsook Numnonda, *Yang toek run raek kabot r.s. 130* [The First Generation of Young Turks, the 1912 Revolt] Krungthep: Samnakphim ru'angsin, 2522 [1979].

Thanapol Eawsakul, "Min phraboromdechanuphap nai sangkhom thai" [Lese Majesty in Thai Society], *Fah Diew Kan* (April-June 2006), pp. 67–81.

Thanet Aphornsuwan, "Slavery and Modernity: Freedom in the Making of Modern Siam," in David Kelly and Anthony Reid, eds., *Asian Freedoms: Journeys of an Idea in the Context of East and Southeast Asia*, London: Cambridge University Press, 1998, pp. 161–86.

Thanong Khanthong, "Lese Majeste Law Allows Criticism but Not Abuse," 6 March 2009.

Thawee Kasiyaphong, "Kabot" [Rebellion], *Warasan Kotmai*, 3(1) (Jan.–June 2520 [1977]): 105–16.

Thiphakonwong (Chaophraya), *The Dynastic Chronicles, Bangkok Era, The First Reign, Volume One: Text* (translated and edited by Thadeus and Chadin Flood), Tokyo: The Centre for East Asian Cultural Studies, 1978a.

——, *The Dynastic Chronicles, Bangkok Era, The First Reign, Volume Two: Text* (translated and edited by Thadeus and Chadin Flood),Tokyo: Centre for East Asian Cultural Studies, 1978b.

——, *The Dynastic Chronicles, Bangkok Era, The Fourth Reign, Volume Two: Text* (translated and edited by Thadeus and Chadin Flood), Tokyo: Centre for East Asian Cultural Studies, 1978c.

Thirayuth Boonmi, "Tulakanphiwat" [Judicialisation], *Matichon*, 1 June 2006.

Thitinan Pongsudhirak, Thailand's Media: Whose Watchdog?" in Kevin Hewison, ed. *Political Change in Thailand: Democracy and Participation*, London: Routledge, 1997, pp. 217–32.

——, "Thailand since the Coup," *Journal of Democracy*, 19(4) (October 2008): 140–53.

Thongchai Winichakul, *Siam Mapped: A History of the Geo-body of a Nation*, Chiang Mai: University of Hawaii Press/Silkworm Books, 1994.

——, "Remembering/Silencing the Traumatic Past: The Ambivalent Memories of the October 1976 Massacre in Bangkok," in Shigeharu Tanabe and Charles F. Keyes, eds., *Cultural Crisis and Social Memory*, London: RoutledgeCurzon, 2002, pp. 243–83.

——, "The Others Within: Travel and Ethno-Spatial Differentiation of Siamese Subjects 1883–1910," in Andrew Turton, ed., *Civility and Savagery: Social Identity in Tai States*, Richmond, Surrey: Curzon, 2000, pp. 38–62.

——, "Lese majeste law still problematic," *Nation*, 11 Oct. 2007.

——, "Kan khui ruang sathaban kasat to satharanachon pen sing thi pen pai dai" [Talking about the institution of the monarchy to the public is something possible], *Fah Diew Kan* 6:1 (Jan.-March 2008), pp. 94–103.

——, "Toppling Democracy," *Journal of Contemporary Asia*, 38:1 (February 2008), pp 11–37.

——, "Siam's Colonial Conditions and the Birth of Thai History," paper presented at the conference, "Unraveling the Myths of Southeast Asian History," 24–26 Nov. 2006, forthcoming.

Tongnoi Tongyai, *Entering the Thai Hear,t* Bangkok: Bangkok Post, 1983.

Turton, Andrew, "Thai Institutions of Slavery," in James L. Watson, ed., *Asian and African Systems of Slavery*, Oxford: Basil Blackwell, 1980, pp. 251–92.

——, "State poetics and civic rhetoric: an introduction to 'Thai constructions of knowledge'," in Manas Chitakasem and Andrew Turton, eds., *Thai Constructions of Knowledge*, London: School of Oriental and African Studies, University of London, 1991, 1–14.

Twekiat Menakanist. *Pramuan kotmai aya chabap ang ing* [The Criminal Law Code, reference edition] Krungthep: Winyuchon Publication House, 1997.

Uan Monthianthong, phontho, "San thahan sung phrae saphap jak san phonlaruan" [The Military Court when changed into a Civilian Court], *Bot bandit*, 23:4 (Oct. 2508), pp. 821–43.

Ukrist Pathmanand, "A Different *Coup d'État*?" *Journal of Contemporary Asia*, 38(1) (February 2008): 124–42.

Ukrit Mongkhonnawin, "Khwam sa-ngop riap-roi lae sinlatham an di khong prachachon" [Peace and Order and the Public Morality], *Bot Bandit*, 32(1) (Jan 2518): 11–32.

Uthai Suphanit, comp., *Sap kotmai thai nai adit lae patjuban* [Thai Legal Terms in the Past and Present] (Krungthep: Samnakphim prakaiphruk, 2526 [1983]).

United States, Department of State, "1994 Human Rights Report: THAILAND." Available at: http://stockholm.usembassy.gov/human/human95/Thailand.htm, accessed 12 Nov. 2008.

United States, Bureau of Democracy, Human Rights, and Labor, US Department of State, "2008 Human Rights Report: Thailand," February 25, 2009. Available at: http://www.state.gov/g/drl/rls/hrrpt/2008/eap/119058.htm, accessed 24 May 2009.

Ura Wangomklang, "San thahan nai wela mai pokkati" [The Military Court in Abnormal Times], mimeographed, Rongrian nai roi Phrajulajomklao, n.d.

Uthai Suphanit, comp., *Sap kotmai thai nai adit lae patjuban* [Thai Legal Terms in the Past and Present] (Krungthep: Samnakphim prakaiphruk, 2526 [1983]).

van den Hout, Tjaco "Europe's Lese Majeste Laws And Freedom Of Expression," *Bangkok Post*, 21 May 2009.

Van Kley, Dale K., *The Daniens Affair and the Unravelling of the Ancient Régime, 1750–1770*, Princeton, NJ: Princeton University Press, 1984.

Vandergeest, Peter, "Constructing Thailand: Regulation, Everyday Resistance, and Citizenship," *Comparative Studies of Society and History*, 35(1) (1993): 133–58.

Vasit Dejkunjorn's "Phaen kan lom rabob prachathipatai baep thi mi phramahakasat pen pramuk" [Plan to Overthrow the Democratic System of Government with the King as Head of State], *Matichon*, 17 March 2009.

Vickery, Michael, "The Constitution of Ayutthaya: An Investigation into the Three Seals Code," in Andrew Huxley, ed., *Thai Law: Buddhist Law*, Bangkok: White Orchid Press, 1996, pp. 133–210.

Victor, Karl (pseud.), "CNS Can Cure Our Ailing Democracy," *Bangkok Post*, 17 Sept. 2007.

Vidal, Georges, *Cours de droit criminel et de science penitentiare*, 5th edn, Paris: Arthur Rousseau, 1916.

Visanu Khrua-ngam, "Serriphap nai kansadaeng khwam khit hen" [Freedom of Expression of Opinions], *Warasan Kotmai* 11:4 (2524 [1981]), pp. 570–76.

——, *Kotmai ratthathammanun, phim khrang thi 3* [Constitutional Law, 3rd edition] (Krungtheip: Samnakphim Nitiban, 2530 [1987]).

Wassana Nanuam, "Taskforce 6080 tracks down those who would impugn," *Bangkok Post*, 2 and 29 October 2008.

Weber, Max, *Sociology of Religion*, Boston: Beacon Press, 1963.

Wijit Wijan, "Min pramat phu tai" Defamation of the Deceased], pp. 92–94. Available at: http://www.library.coj.go.th/Article/data/d5_2_6.pdf, accessed 4 July 2009.

Wilson, David A., *Politics in Thailand*, Ithaca, NY: Cornell University Press, 1962.

Wyatt, David K., *Thailand: A Short History*, New Haven: Yale University Press, 1982.

Yi-Ling Teo, *Media Law in Singapore*, Singapore: Sweet & Maxwell Asia, 2003.

Yilmaz, Metin, Available at: http://my.telegraph.co.uk/metin_yilmaz/blog/2008/04/15/article_301_turkish_penal_code_and_democratic_and_free_penal_codes_in_the_eu_countries_, accessed Nov. 3, 2008.

Yut Saeng-uthai, *Kham athibai kotmai laksana aya r.s. 123* [Explanation of Criminal Law [Code] 1908], Krungtheip: Winyuchon Publication House, 2005.

——, *Kotmai aya phak 2–3* [Criminal Law, Books/Sections I–II] (Twekiat Menakanist, ed.), Krungthep: Somnakphim Mahawitthayalai Thammasat, 2540 [1997].

Laws and law drafts

Thailand, Government, "Prakat kan khap lai ok" [Announcement of Deportation], *Prachum kotmai prajam sok* [Annual Collected Laws], Vol. 16, r.s. 116–17 [1898–1900], pp. 157–58. Dated "11 March r.s. 116, the 10,713th day of this reign."

Thailand, Government, "Phraratchakamnot laksana min pramat duai kanphut ru khian thoi kham thet ok khotsanakan rattanakosin sok 118" [Royal Edict on Defamation through False Spoken or Written Words Made Known of the Year 1900], *Prachum kotmai prajam sok* [Annual Collected Laws], Vol. 17, r.s 118–19 [1898–1900].

Thailand, Government. "Kot aiyakansuk rattanakosin sok 126" [Martial Law of 1907], *PKPS*, Vol. 21, pp. 314–16.

Thailand, Government, "Phraratchabanyat jat tang san phiset ph.s. 2477" [Special Court Establishment Act of 1933], in *PKPS* Vol. 46, pp. 410–11

Thailand, Government, "Phraratchabanyat kaekhai phoemtoem kotmai laksana aya ph.s. 2478 (chabap thi 3)" [Amendment to the Criminal Law Code of 1935], in *PKPS*, Vol. 49, 2479 [1936] (20 August 2478 [1935]), pp. 46–76.

Thailand, Govrnment, *Ratchakitjanubeksa* [Royal Gazette], Vol. 61, Part 6 (19 April 2479 [1936]).

Thailand, Government, *Ratchakitjanubeksa* [Royal Gazette], Vol. 55 (22 August 2481 [1938]), p. 288.

Thailand, Government, "Phraratcha kamnot jat tang san phiset phua phitjarana phiphaksa khadi khwam phit thana khabot phai nok phraratcha-anajak ph.s. 2483" [Royal Decree establishing a Special Court to judge cases of violating the law of external rebellion of the kingdom of 1940], in *PKPS*, Vol. 54, pp. 142–44.

Thailand, Government, *Phraratchabanyat kanphim ph.s. 2484,* Krungthep: Samnakphim Sutphaisan, n.d., pp. 33–38.

Thailand. Government, *Phraratchabanyat watthanatham haeng chat ph.s. 2485* [National Culture Act of 1942], Krungthep: Sut phaisan, 2532 [1989].

Thailand, Government, "Phraratchabanyat kot ayakansuk (chabap thi 3) ph.s. 2487" [Martial Law Act (No. 3) of 1944], in *PKPS* Vol. 57, pp. 860–65.

Thailand, Government, "Phraratchabanyat kak khum phu pen phai kae chat nai phawa khapkhan ph.s. 2488" [Act for the Confinement of Persons Dangerous to the nation in Times of Emergency of 1944], 12 January 2488 [1945], in *PKPS*, Vol. 58, pp. 74–78.

Thailand, Government. "Amnesty Act B.E. 2494 [1951], Granted to Persons in the Course of Reviving the Constitution of B.E. 2475 [1932]," issued on 31 December 1951, *International Translation Law Directory* (n.p., 1958).

Thailand, Government, "Emergency Administration Act B.E. 2495" [1952], *International Translation Law Directory* (n.p., 1958), pp. 81–83.

Thailand, Government, *Phraratchabanyat pongkan kankratham an pen khommiewnit ph.s. 2495* [Act on Prevention of Communist Activities of 1952] Krungthep: Sut phaisan, 2533.

Thailand, Government. "Ph.r.b. thammanun san thahan ph.s. 2498" [Act on Organization of Military Courts of 1955]. Available at: http://www.kodmhai.com/m4/m4–7/H7/H-7.html, accessed 10 June 2009].

Thailand, Government, "Proclamation of the Revolutionary Group No. 12," issued 22 October 1958, in *International Translation Law Directory* (n.p., 1958), p. 609.

Thailand, Government, *Ratchakitjanubeksa, (chabap phiset)*, lem 75, Section 85, 27 Oct. 2501 [1958]; [Coup Decree No. 16], pp. 5–6, and [Coup Decree No. 17], pp. 7–10.

Thailand, Government, "Proclamation of the Revolutionary Group No. 17," *International Translation Law Directory* (n.p., 1958), pp. 612–13.

Thailand, Government, "Kham sang khong khana patirup kan pokkrong phaendin chabap thi 43 long want thi 21 tulakhom ph.s. 2519" [Order of National Administrative Reform Council No. 43, issued 21 Oct. 1976], in Thailand, Government, *Phraratchabanyat kanphim ph.s. 2484* [The Press Act of 1941], Krungthep: Sut phaisan, 2531 [1988].

Thailand, Government, "Prakat krasuang mahat thai Ruang kamnot ekkasan lae sing phim thi ham mi hai phu dai mi wai nai khropkhrong" [Ministry of Interior Announcement Specifying Documents and Printed Materials Which are Forbidden to Have in One's Possession], in Thailand, Government, *Phraratchabanyat kanphim ph.s. 2484* [The Press Act of 1941], Krungthep: Sut phaisan, 2531 [1988].

Thailand, Government, "Kham sang khong khana patirup kanpokkrong phaendin chabap thi 42 long want thi 21 tulakhom ph.s. 2519" [Order of the National Administrative Reform Council No. 42, issued 21 Oct. 1976], in *Phraratchabanyat kanphim ph.s. 2484* [The Press Act of 1941], Krungthep: Sut phaisan, 2531 [1988], pp. 48–50.

Thailand, Government, "Khamsang khana patirup pokkhrong phaendin chabap thi 41 long want thi 21 tulakhom ph.s. 2519" [Order of the National Administrative Council No. 41, issued 21 Oct. 1976], *Ratchakitjanubeksa* [Royal Gazette] Special Issue, Vol. 93, Part 134.

Thailand, Government, Parliament, "Ekasan prakop kan phijarana rang phraratchabanyat kae khai phoem doem pramuan kotmai aya, (chabap thi . .) ph.s . . . ," Sapha nitibanyat haeng chat, a.ph.[92] / 2531 [1988].

Thailand, Government. "Criminal Code Amendment, (No. 11), B.E. 2535." *Ratchakitjanubeksa* [Royal Gazette] Vol. 109, Part 13, 25 February 2535 [1992], pp. 1–2.

Thailand, Government, "Sangha Act Amendment (No.2) B.E. 2535 (A.D. 1992) to the 1962 Act," as quoted in Article 19 and Forum-Asia, *Freedom of Expression and the Media in Thailand*, p. 76.

Thailand, Governent, *Government Gazette*, Vol. 114, Part 46a, 10 September 2540 [1997].

Thailand, Government, National Security Council. Available at: http://www.nsc.go.th/index.php?option = com_content&task = view&id = 13&Itemid = 28, accessed 22 June 2009]

Thailand, Government, Parliament (Sapha Nitibanyat haeng Chat), "Raing Phrarachabanyat Upatham lae Khumkhrong Phraphutthasatsana ph.s . . . ," 24 tulakhom 2550 [24 Oct. 2007].

Thailand, Government, "Computer Crime Act B.E. 2550 [2007], *Government Gazette*, Vol. 124, Section 27 kor., 1, 18 June 2007.

Thailand, Government, Parliament, "Lek rap 115/2551 wan thi 29 t.kh. 2551, somnakngan kekhathikan sapha phuthaen ratsadorn; banthuk lakkan lae hetphon, prakop rang phraratchabanyat kaekhai phoemtoem pramuankotmai aya (chabap thi . . .), ph.s. . . . [Received no. 115/2008, 29 Oct. 2008, Office of the Secretary-General to the House of Representatives; "Notes on the Principle and Rationale, Accompanying the Draft Act to Revise and Amend The Criminal Code (no. . . .), of . . . year].

International and Thai English-language newspapers

Bangkok Post: **1967**: 7, 9 Nov.; **1977**: 11 Feb.; **1983**: 20 Aug.; 30 Dec.; **1990**: 23 Aug.; 3 Sept.; **1993**: 4, 7, 11, 13, 27 July; **1996**: 5 Mar.; 4, 5, 6 Aug.; **2000**: 7 Jan.; 20 July; **2002**: 3 Mar.; **2004**: 6 Sept.; **2005**: 7, 11, 28 Feb.; 9 Mar.; 1 May; **2007**: 27 June; 17, 20 July; 5, 7, 25, 30, 31 Aug.; 4, 7, 12, 15, 16 Sept.; 7, 15, 16 Oct.; 1 Nov.; 5 Dec.; **2008**: 14 Mar.; 10, 12 June; 25 Jul.; 24 Aug.; 28, 30 Oct.; 1, 3, 4, 8, 11, 12 Nov.; 9, 13 Dec.; **2009**: 10, 23, 25 Feb.; 25, 27, 29 Mar.; 3, 9, 29 Apr.; 9, 15, 21 May; 2, 5, 16 June; 28 Aug.

Economist: 4 Dec. 2008; 2009: 22 Jan.; 2 July.

Financial Times: 9 Dec. 2005.

Hürriyet: 21, 25 Jan. 2007

The Local (Sweden): 20 Apr. 2007. Available at: http://www.thelocal.se/7061/20070420/, accessed 3 March 2009]; 27 Feb. 2009. Available at: http://www.thelocal.se/17886/20090227/, accessed 3 March 2009]

Nation / Nation Review: **1976:** 10 Dec.; **1983:** 12, 19, July; **1987:** 8 Oct.; **1990:** 24 Aug.; **1993:** 1, 3, 4, 6, 7, 8, 10, 15, 18, 25, 30 July; 3 Aug.; **1996:** 8, 9 June; 4, 6 Aug.; 29 Dec.; **1997:** 8, 9, 16 June; **1998:** 21 Mar.; 29 Nov.; **1999:** 7 Mar.; 28 May; 22, 23 June; 3 July; **2000:** 20 Jan.; 30 May; 14, 16, 20, 22, 26 June; 17, 18, 21, 23, 27 July; 7 Aug.; 17 Sept.; **2001:** 22 Feb.; 25 May; 4 Oct.; **2003:** 10 May; **2004:** 14 May; 8, 15, 16, 17 Oct.; 3 Dec.; **2005:** 28 Jan.; 31 May; 5 Dec.; **2006**: 28 Feb.; 1, 16, 17 Mar.; 29 Apr.; 25 May; 11 Sept.; **2007**: 28 Feb.; 1, 23 June; 24 Sept.; 8, 11, 18 Oct.; 23, 29 Nov.; **2008**: 25 Mar.; 29, 30, 31 May; 4, 22, 24 July; 10, 30 Sept.; 28 Oct.; 10, 19 Nov.; **2009**: 6 Feb.; 7, 22, 24 Apr.; 3 May; 2 July.

New York Times: **1894**: 22 Nov.; **1897**: 23 Jan., 14 May, 16 Oct., 6 Nov., 13 Nov., 18 Dec.; **1898**: 23 Jan., 6 Nov., 21 Dec.; **1899**: 3 and 22; 5 Feb., 26 Feb. **1900**: 10 and 28 Oct.; **1902**: 5 Oct., 12 Dec.; **1903**: 18 Oct.; **1904**: 11 Nov.; **1906**: 10 June, 26 Aug.; **1907**: 21 Nov.

San Francisco Chronicle: 15 May 2009. Available at: http://sfgate.com/cgi-bin/article.cgi?f = /c/a/2009/05/15/MN7I17KKT6.DTL, accessed 2 June 2009.

San Jose Mercury: 14 July 1960.

South China Morning Post: 24 Oct. 1998. Available at: http://www.geocities.com/Athens/8907/cn_oct98.html, accessed 18 Feb. 2009.
Time (news magazine): 24 Mar. 1947.
Today's Zaman: 30 April 2008.
Washington Post: 23 Jan. 1982.

Thai-language newspapers

Chao Thai: 11, 12, 14, 16, 24 Feb. 2499 [1956]; 29 June 2515 [1972]; (or *Phim Thai*), 30 Oct. 2517[1974].
Dao Sayam: 14 Dec. 2532 [1989].
Deli Niew: 26 Nov. 2510 [1967]; 14, 15 Dec. 2519 [1976].
Khao Phanit: 11 Feb. 2499 [1956].
Khao Sot: 18, 23 July 2543 [2000]; 8 July 2545 [2002].
Khon Num: 6 Oct. 2521 [1978].
Kiattisak: 8 Nov. 2510 [1967].
Matichon: 8 Sept. 2521 [1978]; 26 Apr. 2526 [1983]; 6 June 2532 [1989]; 31 Oct. 2532 [1989]; 1 June 2549 [2006].
Naew Na: 29 Nov. 2525 [1982]; 26 Sept. 2532 [1988]; 16 Dec. 2531 [1988].
Phaya Khrut: 21 March 2533 [1990].
Prachathipatai: 12 Feb. 2499 [1956].
Prachatai (online): 23 Apr. 2008. Available at: http://www.prachatai.com/english/news.php?id = 610, accessed 27 June 2008; 23 Apr. 2008. Available at: http://www.prachatai.com/english/news.php?id = 609, accessed 23 May 2009; 25 Apr. 2008. Available at: http://www.prachatai.com/english/news.php?id = 617, accessed 23 May 2009; 29 Apr. 2008. Available at: http://www.prachatai.com/english/news.php?id = 620, accessed 23 May 2009; 8 June 2009. Available at: http://www.prachatai.com/english/node/1017, accessed 10 June 2009.
San Seri: 23, 26 May 2507 [1964].
Sayam Nikorn: 11 Feb. 2499 [1956]; 20 Aug. 2502[1959]; 9 Nov. 2510 [1967]; 29 Nov. 2523 [1980].
Sayam Rat: 21 Feb. 2465 [1922]
Sayam Rat: 12 Feb. 2499 [1956]; 19 May 2500 [1957]; 21 May 2500 [1957]; 28 May 2500 [1957]; 20 Nov. 2516[1973]; 26 Apr. 2531 [1988]; July 2532 [1989].
Sayam Rat Sapda Wijan: 14 Jan. 2526 [1983].
Sayam Ratsadorn: 29 Jan. 2465 [1922].
Siang Puangchon: 13 July 2520 [1977].
Tawan Ok Parithat: 10 Oct. 2520 [1977].
Tawan Sayam: 1 Oct. 2520 [1977].

Interviews and communications

Boonsoog Chaisingkananont, telephone communication, 2007.
Frost, Stephen, interview, Bangkok, 21 May 2007.
Jittra Khachadet, personal communication, Bangkok, 4 July 2008 and 22 Mar. 2009.
Kavi Chongkittavorn, *The Nation*, interview, Bangkok, 15 Feb. 2001.
Kiatichai Pongpanich, *Khao Sot*, interview, Bangkok, 22 Feb. 2001.

Nikhom Intasen (Police Lt. Col.), Assistant Director of the Movie Censorship Board, Bureau of Licensing, Central Investigation Department, Police Department, interview, Bangkok, 15 July 1991.

Samphan Satthaphorn (Lt. Col.), Deputy-Superintendent of Sub-Division 3 of the Special Branch of the Police Department, interview, Bangkok, 21 August 1991.

Somchai Krusuansombat, *Thai Post*, interview, 20 Oct. 2002.

Somchai Preechasilpakul, personal communication, 21 March 2009.

Somchat Bangjaeng, Head of the National Film Archives, interview, Bangkok, 17 May 1991.

Suchart Srisuwan, *Matichon*, interview, Bangkok, 23 Feb. 2001.

Sulak Sivaraksa, interviews, various locales, 20 Sept. 1993, 21 Feb. 2001 and 5 July 2008.

Surasee Kosolnavin, National Human Rights Commissioner, interview, Bangkok, 5 July 2006 and 9 May 2007.

Suthiphong (Police Superintendent), Press Officer of Bangkok of the Police Special Force, interview, Bangkok, 23 Feb. 2001

Sutthachai Yimprasert, personal communication, 22 March 2009.

Thakul Boonparn, *Khao Sot*, interview, Bangkok, 22 Feb. 2001.

Wattanasak Mungkandee (Police Lt. Col.), interview, Bangkok, 28 October 2008.

Blogs and regular commentary

Bangkok Punit, available at: http://bangkokpundit.blogspot.com/.

FACT—Freedom Against Censorship Thailand, available at: http://facthai.wordpress.com.

Fah Diew Kan, available at: www.sameskybooks.org/.

LM watch, available at: http://lmwatch.blogspot.com.

Marwaan Macan-Markar, "Letter from South-East Asia," available at: http://www.ipsnews.net/new_focus/marwaan/.

Michael K. Connors, "Sovereign Myths," available at: http://sovereignmyth.blogspot.com/2008/02/democrats-did-not-win-majority-in-party.html.

Midnight University, available at: www.midnightuniv.org/.

New Mandala, available at: http://rspas.anu.edu.au/rmap/newmandala.

Political Prisoners in Thailand, available at: http://thaipoliticalprisoners.wordpress.com/.

Prachatai, available at: www.prachatai.com.

Thitinan Pongsudhirak's regular column in *The Bangkok Post*. Available at: http://bangkokpost.com/.

Websites cited

http://en.wikipedia.org/wiki/Censorship_in_Thailand#cite_ref-57, accessed last 10 June 2009.

http://en.wikipedia.org/wiki/Lese_majeste#cite_note-9, accessed 2 June 2009

http://lexrex.com/enlightened/laws/alien_sedition.html, accessed 7 May 2009.

http://news.bbc.co.uk/1/hi/in_depth/northern_ireland/2000/bloody_sunday_inquiry/665100.stm, accessed 15 April 2009.

http://news.bbc.co.uk/2/hi/asia-pacific/2079232.stm, accessed 12 June 2008.
http://asianweek.com/2002_07_12/news_upfront.html, accessed 12 June 2008.
http://findarticles.com/p/articles/mi_m3190/is_29_36/ai_89817003, accessed 12 June 2008.
http://sanpaworn.vissaventure.com/log/243/the-kings-speech-can-do-no-wrong, accessed 10 Nov. 2008.
http://thaipoliticalprisoners.wordpress.com/decidedcases/boonyuen-prasertying/, accessed 3 June 2009.
http://thaipoliticalprisoners.wordpress.com/pendingcases/bundith-arniya/, accessed 2 June 2009.
http://thaipoliticalprisoners.wordpress.com/pendingcases/chiranuch-premchaiporn/, accessed 23 May 2009.
http://thaipoliticalprisoners.wordpress.com/pendingcases/chotisak-onsoong/.
http://thaipoliticalprisoners.wordpress.com/pendingcases/ji-giles-ungpakorn/, accessed 10 June 2009.
http://www.article19.org/advocacy/defamationmap/map/, accessed 14 Nov. 2008.
http://www.atour.com/~aahgn/news/20001003f.html, accessed 3 Feb. 2009. http://turkofile.wordpress.com/2008/07/12/turkey-the-eu-and-the-armenian-genocide/, accessed 8 Feb. 2009.
http://www.hrw.org/en/news/2004/08/31/thailand-libel-suit-deepens-assault-press, accessed last 12 June 2009.
http://www.imdb.com/title/tt0477731/news#ni0076671, accessed 16 Jan. 2009.
http://www.imdb.com/title/tt0477731/news#ni0088530, accessed 16 Jan. 2009.
http://www.law.umkc.edu/faculty/projects/ftrials/zenger/zengeraccount.html, accessed 21 August, 2008.
http://www.manager.co.th/Daily/ViewNews.aspx?NewsID = 9520000017871, accessed 16 Feb. 2009.
http://www.manager.co.th/Politics/ViewNews.aspx?NewsID = 9510000138489.,
http://www.manager.co.th/Politics/ViewNews.aspx?NewsID = 9510000138509, accessed 15 March 2009.
http://www.manager.co.th/Politics/ViewNews.aspx?NewsID = 9520000016004, accessed 12 Feb. 2009.
http://www.managerradio.com/Radio/DetailRadio.asp?program_no = 1002&mms ID = 1002%2F1002%2D2870%2Ewma++&program_id = 13983, accessed 10 June 2009.
http://www.onthemedia.org/yore/transcripts/transcripts_062802_thai.html, accessed 12 June 2008.
www.petitiononline.com/SIAM2008/petition.html.
http://www.prachatai.com/english/news.php?id = 617, accessed 15 June 2008.
http://www.reporter.co.th/content/view/5819/95/, accessed 5 Aug. 2006.
http://www.rsf.org/article.php3?id_article = 19388, accessed 14 Nov. 2008.
http://www.sarakadee.com/web/modules.php?name = Sections&op = viewarticle &artid = 610, accessed 22 Feb. 2009.
http://www.sarakadee.com/web/modules.php?name = Sections&op = viewarticle &artid = 610.
http://www.seapabkk.org/news/2004/12/20041203.html, accessed on 14 Dec. 2008.
http://www.thecheers.org/news/Europe/news_17756_A-man-has-been-jailed-for-four-months-for-insulting-Queen-Beatrix.html, accessed 3 Jan. 2009.
http://www.thelocal.se/3692/20060430, accessed 3 March 2009.

http://www.timesonline.co.uk/tol/global/article1471409.ece, accessed 15 April 2009.
http://www.tja.or.th/modules.php?name = News&file = article&sid = 398, accessed 29 June 2008.

Index